POLITICAL ECONOMY

A HISTORICAL PERSPECTIVE

Edited by

HORST CLAUS RECKTENWALD

COLLIER-MACMILLAN PUBLISHERS
A division of Crowell Collier and Macmillan Publishers Limited
LONDON

Collier-Macmillan Publishers

A Division of Crowell Collier and Macmillan Publishers Limited
Blue Star House
Highgate Hill
London N19 5NY

First Printing 1973

ISBN 0 02 978030 6 (paper)
0 02 978040 3 (cased)

Printed in Great Britain by
The Camelot Press Ltd, London and Southampton

POLITICAL ECONOMY

A historical perspective

Professor T. W. Hutchison

ein bescheidener Ausdruck meines
Dankes für die positive, zustimmende
und faire Aufnahme meines Smith-Buches
(EJ, 1977)

mit freundlichem Gruß aus
Laufamholz

Horst Claus Recktenwald

Friedrich-Alexander-Universität
Erlangen-Nürnberg
im Juli 1977

CONTENTS

To Robert Phillip Nöll von der
Nahmer and in memory of the
Wealth of Nations whose bicentenary
we commemorate
1776 to 1976

Es gibt kein gewagteres Unternehmen als den Versuch, ein Individuum darzustellen.
H. V. HOFMANNSTHAL

A person is not likely to be a good economist who is nothing else.
J. S. MILL

Fórmulas sencillas para resolver problemas complejos, no las conozco.
M. J. DE LARRA

A study of the history of opinion is a necessary preliminary to the emancipation of the mind.

The ideas of economists and political philosophers, both when they are right and when they are wrong, are more powerful than is commonly understood. . . . I am sure that the power of vested interests is vastly exaggerated compared with the gradual encroachment of ideas.
J. M. KEYNES

Ce n'est pas l'erreur qui s'oppose aux progrès de la vérité. Ce sont la mollesse, l'entêtement, l'esprit de routine, tout ce qui porte à l'inaction.
A. R. J. TURGOT

A student whose only acquaintance is with mediocre books and with mediocre minds has lost something of the sense of potentiality of the human organism, even though we may only dimly perceive what that potentiality can be.
K. E. BOULDING

Important Scholars in the History of Economic Science

AN APPRECIATION

Every branch of science can be illuminated by an examination of the lives of those who have made a creative contribution to the study of their subject; thus a genuine tradition of scholarship is both founded and developed. This is true of the older as well as the newer disciplines, such as physics or political economy. The purpose of this work is, however, far more modest. Although it seeks to illustrate the continuity in the development of economic ideas as reflected in the thoughts and works of eminent scholars, it nevertheless deliberately avoids any exclusively problem-orientated arrangement or classification. Nor does it aim at any comprehensiveness, whatever notion may be attached to this term. Yet, though not intended as a complete history of economics, it can nevertheless provide an introduction to the history of political economy by describing, with the aid of biographical studies of great scholars, the long and often painful process of thought from which modern knowledge has resulted.

In this way the anthology seeks to respond to a threefold concern of our time. First of all, its aim is to help in making economic and social science more accessible to interested and educated people, by paying tribute to and evaluating the important achievements of this branch of science as reflected in the lives and works of its representatives. Generals and statesmen, poets and artists, and occasionally scientists too, more easily command public attention (let alone achieve historical greatness) than do political economists, sociologists, lawyers, physicists, or technologists. There may be many reasons for this. Undoubtedly, one of them is often an underlying suspicion that a desire for profit and material gain, or at least utilitarian considerations, might be at the root of their creative thought and activity. The very quest of these researchers for cause, order, and principles inherent in man's desire for prosperity is occasionally equated, by primitive simplification, with personal aspiration for material profit. Although everyone knows how important it is, particularly in our technical age, to understand the economic and social structure of our complex society if we are to fulfil the vital tasks of central importance to mankind,the attitude of educated people towards economic science is still as reserved and sceptical as it was before. Nevertheless, an interest in its aims seems to be growing, and a change in attitude is emerging which cannot only be explained by the fact that a modern (Anglo-Saxon tinted) positivism is gaining ground in science.

The Englishman Lord Keynes, one of the great economists of our time, once said: "The ideas of political economists and political philosophers, both when they are right and when they are wrong, are more powerful than is commonly understood. In truth the world is ruled by little else." Though one may not entirely share this view, it is particularly the European who will admit that the opposite notion, i.e. that in reality solely tangible interests or privileges prevail, is at least no less one-sided.

Secondly, it is hoped that the anthology will promote an interest in the history of this specialized branch of knowledge by describing, in chronological order, the lives, personalities, and works of outstanding thinkers, listing the characteristic ideas and achievements of each one without neglecting to emphasize the extent to which they were grounded in and conditioned by their time and their influence on our generation. Thus a chronological and "personal" sequence, in its historical context, gives a vivid picture of the development of economic science, without attempting or, indeed, being able, to compete with a history of ideas in the strict sense of the word, or with a history of theories such as Schumpeter's *History of Economic Analysis* or Spengler-Allen's *Essays in Economic Thought*. Such an approach should interest even the non-economist since it reveals how many years of intellectual effort frequently preceded not only many an epochal conception but a good deal of relatively small progress as well, and since it throws light on the genius involved in the individual's achievements. "Many a physicist has gained immortality by achieving less", said Schumpeter about a single achievement of the tireless Alfred Marshall.

Such a presentation confronts scientific progress with what is at the present time considered as substantiated truth and thus illustrates the tensions between tradition and novelty, and between past, present, and future within the personality of the thinker concerned. It is hoped that this presentation may help to stimulate an interest in history, both general and specialized, which is lacking in the present generation. If a scientific discipline consists primarily of what its representatives know and constantly work over in their minds and not of what lies unused in dusty volumes, then it is these men that best reflect the flow of theoretical development.

Those who take the trouble to think a little about the causes for that phenomenon of our age which is sometimes exaggeratedly called boredom with history or even hostility towards history, will discover two major reasons for the educated younger generation's bias.

First, there is the extreme reaction of the older generation to the exaggerated emphasis on history, especially in political economy, which, in spite of its over-asserted "realistic nature" was quite helpless and failed completely when confronted with the phenomenon of the Great Depression at the beginning of the thirties. Erwin von Beckerath described this surely excessive reaction in these vivid terms: "Modern theory has so completely killed the emphasis on history (*Historismus*) that even historical thinking has died of it, too."

The second reason may be the weakness of some writings and lectures in which particular theories or ideas of the past are seldom related to the questions of our age. They are presented in isolation, detached even from their own time and space; they almost lead a life of their own. This is by no means to say that every great thought and every original system must be measured by what it can contribute to the understanding of the academic and practical problems of our age. This would undoubtedly be an extremely one-sided and unfair yardstick. A history of ideas, however, which is a mere collection and a more or less *formal* orderly arrangement of historical facts and dogma will not help us very much in the pursuit of truth and in understanding and shaping our rapidly changing environment. Theoreticians and researchers should at least be able to learn from the study of history 1. how the particular circumstances of an era have misled its thinkers into ascribing *general* validity to their own hypotheses or theories (Keynes' *General Theory* could be mentioned as an example); 2. how to define clearly in their minds the limits of their own horizons or of the subjectively chosen object of their investigation by comparing the inquiries, methods, and results of other researchers, and finally 3. how fruitful is the "endless give and take between theory and reality". With this understanding they will always be on guard against seeing and interpreting history according to their *a priori* conception of the moment. An understanding of this sort also sharpens appreciation for true greatness and academic progress, the arch-enemy of which is admirably defined by A. R. J. Turgot: "Ce n'est pas l'erreur qui s'oppose au progrès de la vérité. Ce sont la mollesse, l'entêtement, l'esprit de routine, tout ce qui porte a l'inaction."

The third aim of this book pertains to a renewed concern with and consciousness of unity in the *Universitas litterarum*, the practical results of which are beginning to reveal themselves in the tentative plans for the reorganization of universities. Like every other branch of knowledge, political economy is subject to the positive as well as to the negative consequences of the principle of specialization, a principle which is, moreover, chiefly to be explained by this very science. In the intellectual world, too, specialization can only be meaningful and lead to real scientific progress when the exchange of ideas and experiences is many-sided, "multilateral", beyond the limits of a single faculty. Therefore, it would seem advisable for many research workers, especially for younger ones who emphasize progress in specialized fields, to learn to see their results in wider contexts, so that they always bear in mind the relative nature and limitations of their own knowledge and can counteract an overweening evaluation of it which may sometimes turn into hubris.

From whom but the great thinkers of all periods educated in the humanities and scientifically active do we find the stimulus to see and evaluate limited and specialized knowledge in the light of other disciplines and as part of a larger pattern? It is sometimes held that encompassing summaries of the entire learning of an age, such as were regularly made by scholars in the past, are simply no longer possible today because of the tremendous specialization in individual areas. This is by no means always an easy pretext or excuse. This development towards the highest degree of specialization should not release us from the obligation to try to examine the institutionalized sciences in a more comparative light, even though this may be beyond an individual's capabilities. Is not the most lasting progress achieved in those very fields which constitute an intellectual borderland, or no-man's land—for instance, at the boundary between physics and chemistry, or between financial and economic theory? Moreover, the great figures of our own age, like J. M. Keynes or J. A. Schumpeter, or, in the sciences, M. Planck or A. Einstein, undoubtedly possess the intellectual power and vision not only to synthesize, in a meaningful way, the different aspects and methods of their own branch of learning, but simultaneously to place them in a wider and thus higher context which thereby makes for a greater unity of the sciences and prevents myopia in the specialists.

In any case, the study of thinkers' lives and academic work can be stimulating and fruitful for students as well as scholars. Perhaps we should recall in this context that no lesser man than J. W. von Goethe himself always used the *personality* of a scholar and thinker as his starting point when he was dealing with the man's knowledge and ideas.

What were the criteria for the selection of the "heroes" and their biographers represented in this work? If we first consider what really accounts for the greatness of a scholar, we may come up with two answers: his achievement in his own particular field and his significance for wider spheres of knowledge.

To begin with, it is easy to see that, depending on the viewer's standpoint, the answers may be highly divergent and, indeed, they are hardly ever identical. Let us consider the latter criterion first. Jacob Burckhardt, in his *Weltgeschichtliche Betrachtungen,* and Theodor Heuss, in his reflections on *Maßstäbe geschichtlicher Würdigung*, have both attempted to explore the prerequisites for a historical personality to achieve greatness or fame. They establish an "abundance of contributing factors" but do not catalogue them according to their importance. As for non-economic factors, or, in simpler terms, from the point of view of the general historian, one of the objective criteria would certainly be the influence exerted by the scholar on the total intellectual development of his age. Even influence on a branch of learning akin to political economy, be it ethics or history, mathematics or sociology, which has the effect of stimulating progress beyond the narrow limits of the special field, can be a criterion for our choice.

But the creative content of an idea should not be the only standard by which to measure historic greatness. Why not include also the effects, direct and indirect, of a doctrine and the success of a formative power in practical application, e.g. in the struggle for safeguarding or for effectively improving the living conditions of mankind? Finally, a lasting influence on the intellectual and material development of later generations is also an outstanding, unique merit which deserves consideration when making selection for an anthology of this kind.

Let us return now to our first standard, the most important one for our purposes, namely that of achievement within the field of political economy: here the essential criteria certainly include a creative imagination coupled with realism, scholarliness and strength in logic, intellectual depth and breadth, and above all, originality and a positive contribution to scientific progress. Even though the content of the last two varies with time and place, and though the degree of originality may be judged differently (as George Joseph Stigler recently tried to prove in his interesting article published in *Economica*, *Originality and Scientific Progress*, which uses John Stuart Mill as an example), the person making the selection nevertheless has a considerably easier task in the area of technical achievement, since in many cases the "greatness" of the individual in question appears to have been more or less acknowledged for some decades or even for some centuries, and since he can make critical reference to the carefully considered judgements of experienced economists.

And yet the formative power of each era can occasionally change the professional image of the political economist to a considerable extent. It is sufficient for our generation to name John Stuart Mill, Léon Walras and Gustav Cassel, and to compare their evaluation or mere mention in a current history of dogma and in Schumpeter's *History*.

Fortunately the historical aim of this work releases its author from the thankless and insoluble task of drawing up a list of illustrious figures arranged according to rank and importance. Even by the narrow standard of purely theoretical achievement coupled with that of "vision", an ordering of this kind would be extremely problematical. Why? While we can see whether a political economist has changed the views, horizon or interests of the majority of economists and thereby the political economy of his age (A. Smith, J. M. Keynes) or of a later generation

(A. A. Cournot, L. Walras) with new perspectives arising from an old conception or—in a visionary way—with new ideas, how can we rate precisely the importance of this influence? Must the preparatory work leading up to the ultimate discovery of new knowledge be rated as a lesser achievement than a new generalization itself? And should the latter be graded higher than the analytic improvement of a generally accepted theory? How is the confirmation of a hypothesis, or the conclusive proof that it is false, to be assessed with regard to the outlined progress of a science? Obviously, a great deal of courage is required, in addition to really profound and comprehensive knowledge and great experience, to measure the degree of originality and the importance of a contribution to the progress of one or several branches of knowledge, with the purpose of establishing a ranking order. Joseph Schumpeter dared to do it. Bearing in mind the two considerations discussed above—i.e. contribution to theory and visionary insight or intuition—he put Léon Walras at the top of his list as by far the greatest political economist of all times. He is followed in the hierarchy by Adam Smith, Augustin Cournot, and François Quesnay and in turn, still under the aspect of pure theory, by the *dii minores*. In this succession, which place is fitting for Schumpeter himself or for Keynes, for instance? It is well known that Schumpeter in his monumental work, the *History*, does not mention a single one of his own outstanding and original achievements, let alone evaluate them.

If, however, the scholar's personality is of importance, then, according to Schumpeter, Knut Wicksell, who is his ideal in this respect, would be the next in line. But when we extend the criteria as we have done in this work, a ranking list is simply no longer meaningful. Moreover, we should not forget that a certain ambivalence in Schumpeter's judgement of political economists is at least partly due to the fact that his standards vary from case to case. In his admiration for formal theory he tended towards the end of his life to overestimate the pure analyst who had previously been somewhat neglected, and to underestimate a little the economic substance of a theory or a concept, after having striven for and demanded, throughout his life, unity between theory (mathematics) and reality (history)! Simon Kuznets expressed this omnipresent and eternal antinomy and the temptations to which particularly the modern economist is exposed in his striving for progress in the economic sciences in the following words: "It is important to recognize how strong today is the temptation to withdraw into the security of imaginary models, only distantly relevant to historical reality—regardless of how mathematically elaborate such models may be. It is important to see how ever present is the opposite temptation—to elaborate and check details without concern for their place in the broader framework. And while these two lines of intellectual pursuit are moderately useful in the development of science, the third direction, equally tempting—to give up hope of finding any intellectual order and to resolve the problem by withdrawal into esthetic fancy or intellectual cynicism—can be of negative value alone. . . ." And, referring to W. C. Mitchell's life as a scholar he says optimistically that it was "an inspiring demonstration of how effectively such temptations can be combated, and how the spirit of objective inquiry can yield rich results in the study of human society."

Independently of the "re-evaluations" which are constantly made on the basis of changing environment and knowledge, in short, of modern viewpoints, a long catalogue of criteria such as ours ensures that the number of borderline cases is not exactly small. Most of the famous economists who have not been dealt with here are likely to have been considered, often having equal "claims", but they then became victims of lack of space, if they had not already been excluded as mere commentators or imitators. Whoever fails to find *his* economist in this portrait gallery may be consoled a little by the fact that the historical background and related ideas, in the context of the evaluation of other scholars, are somewhat more comprehensive than usual. As an example I mention the "socialists" and the theoreticians of the communist economy and draw attention to the comprehensive essays on Karl Marx.

And now a word about the sequence, which as I have tried to demonstrate cannot be a ranking order. With a view to minimizing such speculations on "rank", however attractive, I have proceeded in a simple chronological way. I have deliberately omitted to make even a problem-oriented grouping since the individuals discussed have been selected predominantly for their impact on economic theory, and their contribution to economics is often so many-sided that classification is difficult, always a little arbitrary and at least questionable. Moreover, an appended chronological table will make historical orientation and perspective easier for the reader because it lists the most significant dates in the lives of the authors and their most important works and the year of publication.

It only remains to explain the principles used in selecting the biographical essays. The work seeks to be an anthology, a "hand-picked bouquet" of comprehensive portraits of the life and work of great political economists, covering their intellectual and political achievements. Their thoughts and activities are considered as conditioned by their talents and their family, by local, social, and national environment; their original power and the lasting influence of their work as a whole on their own and on our age is evaluated. Thus the emphasis is on the life of the creative personality as portrayed against its historical background. When an essay did not entirely fulfil this basic aim, it was completed by the insertion of an additional one, either in its entirety or in parts. Any overlapping was avoided in order not to impede the flow of the narrative.

In many cases, the authors of the essays are of the same rank as those about whom they write. This makes for particularly fascinating reading since famous political economists are, so to speak, writing about and judging other famous political economists. The biographies have been completed and updated in keeping with the present state of research. They reflect, of course, the spirit of their author, some exhibiting craftsmanship, perhaps simplicity at times, while others are more essay-like in their form; in most of them one senses some restrained tension. No essay suffers from pathos, none is overdone, none is hollow in style, even though this is where the "tendency of the period" manifests itself most obviously. National characteristics, too, are seldom stressed overly. Where it is a question of a relationship between pupil and teacher or where the allegiance to a school or philosophy is the basis of observation and judgment, the emotional values range from personal respect and esteem to affection and even reverence. Although, here again, there is no lack of perspective or of scientific scepticism or criticism without which objectivity and progress are impossible, the attitudes never turn into cynicism. Yet one can sense in every biography a certain human warmth and understanding for the weaknesses which are always so close to human greatness. In this context one may refer to the two essays on Karl Marx, and especially to that of the Oxford scholar Isaiah Berlin, as well as to John Maynard Keynes' essay on Alfred Marshall, his teacher who had a propensity to hypochondria. In any case, I feel one should join with Hugo von Hofmannsthal in remembering that there is "no more daring enterprise than to attempt to portray an individual".

One more thing. The biographers and essayists were deliberately chosen so as not to belong to any one generation or era. The danger inherent in drawing on authors from the same generation, for example, the biographer who is a contemporary, friend, or pupil, is that their criticism may lack historical and human perspective. For the correct balance to be struck in an evaluation of this kind, a certain distance is necessary which cannot be replaced by critical stringency, however well-meant, or by an uncompromising determination to be objective. Exaggeration, or at least distortion, is often the case. On the other hand, whenever a contemporary critic evaluates in retrospect basic ideas and achievements in the light of present-day experience, environment, and theory, he is undoubtedly susceptible to the temptation of interpreting and explaining the fundamental methods and ideas of his hero in too modern a way. This has lately been true of those evaluations which, following the example set by Schumpeter, tend to give a little too much weight to mathematical and quantitative analysis when judging the greatness of a political economist.

Whatever the aspects may be to which we give priority when evaluating an intellectual achievement, when we are assessing economic theories, ideas, and systems we should not overlook Max Weber's most valuable experience which H. von Hofmannsthal expresses thus: "The fact that the dignity of norms is only discovered in their living application is the decisive knowledge gained when he had reached the summit of his life and which continued thereafter to be the leading thought of this truly great personality."

Finally a word about the illustrations and the short characterizations which precede every biographical essay. They are intended for the hurried reader (who, however, must be something of an expert in the field) for whom they outline, with almost aphoristic brevity, something essential about the life, personality, and work of the economist under discussion. As a rule, I selected the statements and judgments of authors who are in some sense authorities but whose contribution could not, for some reason, be included in the work. The "mottos" are intentionally left untranslated since a lot depends here on allusions and on what cannot be translated; the same applies to Condorcet's appreciation in Old French of the personality of A. R. J. Turgot.

The likenesses and signatures are intended to round off the essays and to complete the portrait of the personality contained in the biography. Not only do they have a documentary value in conjunction with the other illustrations—such as the famous *Tableau économique* or Quesnay's letter to Mirabeau, or the preface of David Ricardo's *Principles*—their chief aim is, above all, to facilitate access to the man, as well as to arouse interest in his intellectual achievement.

There are considerable changes in the English edition as compared with the first German edition (*Lebensbilder großer Nationalökonomen, Einführung in die Geschichte der Politischen Ökonomie*) which was soon out of print, and also the second German edition (*Geschichte der Politischen Ökonomie, Eine Einführung in Lebensbildern*). Some essays on political economists whose teachings influenced chiefly the English-speaking countries were added, and others were deleted. Recent results of historical research, e.g. on Adam Smith's life and work, have been taken into account. The articles at the end of the book are new, too, in which Kenneth Ewart Boulding and I have summarized the present state of political economy, and where we have reviewed the future development of economic science. Readers with some knowledge in economics may start by reading that survey first and then proceed to the study of individuals.

The criticism and approval of a number of experienced colleagues were of great benefit to my project. Although our views were occasionally highly divergent, it was precisely the differences of opinion which stimulated me to analyse the respective achievements even more thoroughly than before. I wish to emphasize the great interest shown by Erwin von Beckerath, Joseph Dorfman, Gottfried Haberler, Friedrich August von Hayek and Edgar Salin in the growth of this project. For checking the rough draft of the manuscript and for critical annotations as regards specialized questions I am particularly grateful to Professors Erwin von Beckerath, Kenneth Ewart Boulding, Joseph Dorfman, Luigi Einaudi, Milton Friedman, Herbert Giersch, Gottfried Haberler, Heinz Haller, Friedrich August von Hayek, Wassily Leontief, Gunnar Myrdal, Anton Felix Napp-Zinn, Fausto Nicolini, Jürg Niehans, Lord Robbins, Austin Robinson, Edgar Salin, Paul Anthony Samuelson, Alfred Sauvy, Joseph Spengler, George Joseph Stigler and Jacob Viner.

All contributions, abridged or unabridged, portraits, signatures, and the other illustrations, were printed and translated with the express consent of the author, publisher, editor, galleries, libraries, and archives. I wish to express once again my best thanks to them. Finally, my gratitude is due to Konrad Roessler for his diligent and painstaking co-operation and to his successor Bernd Hügle. Gisela Grohmann, Wilfried Hake, and Klaus Norbert Münch assisted me in preparing the English edition. Juliane Bauer helped in typing the new manuscripts.

My acknowledgments would be incomplete if I failed to mention how grateful I am to my wife who so patiently assisted me particularly in doing one or the other translation. Anyone who has ever translated texts from foreign languages and from different periods knows the many difficulties involved in rendering them stylistically satisfactory without distorting the true meaning of the original.

Horst Claus Recktenwald

FRANÇOIS QUESNAY

1694–1774

He was pedantic and doctrinaire to a degree and must have been an awful bore. But he had all the force of character that often goes with pedantry. It is pleasant to add that he was also thoroughly upright and honest.

The fact that he was the only creative force in his circle is somewhat obscured by his inability or unwillingness to work out his ideas fully and systematically.

J. A. SCHUMPETER

Ex natura jus, ordo et leges. Ex homine arbitrium, regimen et coercitio.

Motto of the physiocrats, from F. Quesnay, *Maximes générales*

Depuis le commencement du monde, il y a eu trois découvertes qui ont donné aux sociétés politiques leur principale solidité. La première est l'invention de l'écriture, qui seule donne au genre humain la faculté de transmettre sans l'altération ses lois, ses conventions, ses annales et ses découvertes. La seconde est l'invention de la monnaie, ce lien commun qui unit toutes les nations civilisées. La troisième qui est le résultat des deux autres, mais qui les complète, puisqu'elle porte leur objet à sa perfection, est le Tableau économique, la grande découverte qui fait la gloire de notre siècle et dont la postérité recueillera les fruits.

V. R. MARQUIS DE MIRABEAU

I
THE LIFE OF FRANÇOIS QUESNAY

Quesnay's family came from Méré, in Seine-et-Oise near Montfort-l'Amaury, and not from Ecqueville as has sometimes been claimed. The surname Quesnay makes it possible to trace their true regional origin. *Quesnay* is the form of the word *chênaie* in Normandy and Picardy. It is a local or provincial name. His ancestors would therefore have been Norman peasants who, at some time, came to settle in Beauce.[1]

A legend circulated for a long time about Quesnay's father. He was said to be an advocate at the tribunal or the Parliament of Montfort, more inclined to bring two parties to agreement than to stir up quarrels. It was Hévin, François Quesnay's son-in-law, who was behind this legend. At his father-in-law's death, attempting to disguise his modest origins, he hoped to turn the simple working man, which Nicolas Quesnay was, into a gentleman of the legal profession, carefree, cultivated and munificent. In fact, Nicolas was never anything but a working man, a merchant, and for some years, 1689–95, an almsman of the monastery of Saint-Magloire. François Quesnay was certainly "born on a farm", "a son of the soil", and any ancestry in the legal profession is pure fiction.

At the age of twenty-seven, Nicolas married Louise Giroux, aged seventeen, whose ancestors were likewise only peasants. Nicolas and his wife were blessed with a very large family: thirteen children were born to them from 1683 onwards, nine girls and four boys of whom only six were alive in 1710; the eighth child, François, who was to make the name of Quesnay famous, came into the world on Thursday, 4 June 1694.

An affable and easygoing man, but one of the most dilatory, Nicolas was little disposed to see to the education of his children or to manage the resources of his family. He had divested himself of household cares and turned them over to his wife, who did not attend too much to the intellectual development of her brood. The result was that, at eleven years of age, young François did not know how to read.

The one and only educational precept which his father bequeathed him was: "My son, the temple of virtue rests on four pillars, honour, reward, shame and punishment; consider well which pillar you will use for your support, for one must choose success by means of emulation, interest, modesty or fear." A fine paternal sentiment that Fréron later spitefully described as gibberish betraying the village lawyer.

François therefore looked for other teachers than his parents. The daily gardener is said to have taught him to read in the famous *Agriculture et maison rustique* by the doctors Charles Estienne and Jean Liébaut. This

[1] We cannot therefore attribute the same origin to Quesnay's name and that of Keynes, however tempting this coincidence may be. The biographer of Keynes, R. F. Harrod, traced him back to his earliest ancestor: William de Keynes, companion to William the Conqueror, who took his name from the village of Cahagnes in Calvados. The spelling Keynes appeared in Great Britain from the year 1300 onwards. So the similarity between the names of Quesnay and of Keynes is only apparent; the two economists have nothing in common but a distant Norman origin, an origin they share, moreover, with another great forerunner, Boisguillebert, and maybe also with Cantillon.

picturesque work was really the book that decided Quesnay's destiny, for, not only did it increase his knowledge of the countryside, but it also implanted in him his medical vocation. His appetite once whetted by this simple reading, Quesnay decided to take up Latin and Greek. And so he no doubt turned to the curate of Méré or perhaps to Bertrand Giroux, the priest at Montfort, who buried his father and who may have been one of the family. What is certainly more doubtful is that he ever obtained his parents' permission to attend the courses of the grammar school at Montfort. At all events it was during this period that Quesnay became familiar with Plato, Aristotle and Cicero.

His father's death on 19 June 1707, when Quesnay was only thirteen years old, made his education still more difficult, his mother now having an additional reason for keeping him with her. Towards 1711, being perhaps influenced by a family relation, Masselin, a surgeon in Montfort, Quesnay made up his mind to devote his life to surgery. His mother allowed him to learn the first rudiments of blood-letting from a surgeon in the neighbourhood, Jean de la Vigne, who practised in Ecquevilly. Quesnay no doubt became aware of the limited competence of his teacher, for he asked his mother to allow him to continue his studies in Paris. Louise Giroux finally consented, on condition that her son found an occupation which later allowed him to earn a living. By mutual agreement they decided on engraving, which was then a fashionable profession.

On 1 October 1711, Quesnay started his five years' apprenticeship with Pierre de Rochefort, regular engraver to the King for the Academy of Sciences.

Living in the heart of the Quartier Latin, Quesnay hastened to enrol for the medical courses of the Faculty and for the courses in surgery at Saint-Côme. He was permitted to attend when the "chiefs" came to the Hôtel-Dieu, not so much as a student but rather in the capacity of draughtsman to the engraver of the Academy. He set about studying botany, pharmacy, chemistry, anatomy, mathematics and even philosophy, and "reading the works of Descartes and Père Malebranche, especially the latter's book *Recherche de la vérité*, was his favourite intellectual pursuit". It was certainly during this period that he obtained the Master of Arts degree, giving him the right to teach the humanities and philosophy.

Towards the end of 1716, Quesnay, having completed his term as an engraver's apprentice, went for a time to practise as a surgeon in Orgerus, near Montfort, where he also devoted himself to the study of botany, before finally returning to Paris where he married. His betrothed, Jeanne-Catherine Dauphin, was the daughter of Catherine Champion and Antoine Dauphin, a grocer in the Rue des Fossés-Saint-Sulpice. Again, Quesnay's son-in-law later tried to hide the origins of his mother-in-law and presented her as the daughter of "an important middle-class tradesman of Paris". All biographers discreetly followed him in saying that she was the daughter of a well-to-do merchant.[2]

As soon as he was married, Quesnay tried to open a practice in the vicinity of Paris. Mantes appeared to him to be a favourable place, and so he sought admission to the guild of master surgeons of that town. But they refused, being little inclined to admit another rival into their midst. The only recourse open to Quesnay was to take the Master's degree at Paris, in spite of the higher fees, for the title of master surgeon of the capital ensured professional admission to all the societies of the kingdom.

Quesnay took his Master's degree on 9 August 1718. Malaval, the Provost of the College of Surgery, was later to recall with satisfaction "the mark of distinction which his colleagues and he had accorded this candidate, who mastered all the examinations with superior ability". The surgeons of Mantes were now obliged to admit their new colleague, whether they liked it or not.

Quesnay established himself with his wife in the Rue du Vieux-Pilori. Four children were born to them, but only two survived: Jeanne-Catherine died after ten years of married life, and the last ties binding the young surgeon to Méré were broken one by one. Quesnay, who at thirty-four was left a widower with two children, did not remarry, nor did any other woman enter his life.

In September 1723, the title of Royal Surgeon was bestowed on him by letters patent.

Quesnay thus began with a peasant practice and only later managed to gain middle-class patients. He soon penetrated into the most aristocratic circles of the district and gained the patronage of powerful men like Mgr D'Abos or the Marshal de Noailles. Quesnay had made the acquaintance of the Duc de Retz, later to become Duc de Villeroy, in the salons of the Marshal de Noailles at Saint-Germain. The Duke was captivated by his qualities and, together with La Peyronie, offered to take him to Paris in his personal service. After long hesitation Quesnay finally accepted and left Mantes between April and December 1734.

The Duc de Villeroy, who treated Quesnay more as a friend than his physician, gave him ample proof of his favour. After his entry into his household, he had him elected a member of the Academy at Lyons, of which he was patron. In 1739 the Duc de Villeroy accorded Quesnay the

[2] The marriage contract was signed on 8 January 1717. The Dauphins gave their daughter a dowry of 3000 livres and Louise Giroux gave the same sum to her son, of which 1000 livres were to be paid out in cash on the eve of his wedding, and 2000 livres were in estates and inheritance. The dowry was given on 29 and the wedding celebrated on 30 January.

favour of making him a Commissary of War to the town of Lyons, which appointment was worth 900 livres a year. Quesnay received this until his death.

Thanks to the patronage of La Peyronie, first surgeon to the king, Quesnay obtained several important posts.

On 9 September 1744, the degree of Doctor of Medicine was conferred on him by the Faculty of Pont-à-Mousson, "after careful examination and rigorous questioning following upon open discussion", and after the Faculty had been assured of his Catholic faith. His thesis *De Affectibus Saporosis in Genere* was printed and preserved by Hévin.

As Marquise de Pompadour's physician, Quesnay came to live at Versailles in the spring of 1749.[3]

All the evidence agrees in representing Quesnay as leading a scholarly life at Versailles, far removed from the intrigues and tumult of the world.

He was on excellent terms with the King, who called him his thinker; but the thought that his sovereign had the power to have him beheaded sometimes disturbed him.

Quesnay was neither striking in stature nor in figure, but "as mischievous as a monkey" he knew how to charm the ladies by his conversation to the end of his life. He has often been compared to Socrates whose mode of inquiry he would doubtless have adopted. Harsh towards himself but sensitive to suffering humanity, he knew how to use the confidence placed in him fairly and discreetly.

The King accorded Quesnay and his descendants the rank of esquire, permitting them to obtain fiefs or seigneuries and to bear a coat of arms. His patent of nobility gave Quesnay the right to acquire a nobleman's lands. His choice fell on an estate in Nivernais (Beauvoir).

It was on account of his election to the Academy of Sciences in 1751 that Quesnay was nominated a member of the Royal Society of London a year later. During the eighteenth century, the relations between the two learned societies of London and Paris had become very close.

From the time of his employment by Madame de Pompadour, Quesnay had turned to fresh studies, first in philosophy and then in economics. In his youth he had been much concerned with Descartes and Malebranche and, since he came to Court, he had consorted with a philosophical circle

[3] He was "completely provided for", and his salary was fixed at 3000 livres. The Marquise also wished to attach him to the King and she obtained for him the post of medical consultant without salary, as a replacement for Sidobre on 30 March 1749. Before drawing his salary, which had meanwhile risen to 9000 livres, he had to wait until the death of the medical consultant Terray on 30 March 1759. On 3 April 1752, Quesnay also purchased, for the sum of 40 000 livres, the right to succeed the first physician in ordinary of the king, who was at that time Marcot.

made up of bold thinkers and men of great ideas. D'Alembert and Buffon, his associates at the Academy of Sciences, Diderot who had supported him in his dispute with the physicians, Duclos, Helvétius and Condillac, were all frequent visitors to his entresol in Versailles. All encouraged Quesnay to take part in the great intellectual and philosophical revival of the age.

When d'Alembert and Diderot asked Quesnay to collaborate in the *Encylopédie*, the doctor quite naturally wrote them two first-class philosophical articles on *Évidence* and *Fonction de lâme*.[4] But the *Encylopédie* had already been condemned in 1752, and Quesnay was obliged to be prudent in view of the situation at Court and insisted on remaining anonymous. He included in the first article the very foundations of his future philosophical, economic and even geometric system and showed his great indebtedness to Malebranche. The article enjoyed the fate of almost all such works, of being little read, still less understood, and strongly criticized.

How did the doctor come to take an interest in political economy? "Anyone who is astonished that a doctor should occupy himself with this subject," Dr Clerc, author of *Yule-Grand*, once said, "forgets that a doctor is born a friend to mankind, and that moral vice produces graver illness than physical causes."

On the other hand, agriculture, which he had practised in his childhood, had become the fashionable subject. From the year 1750 onwards, as Voltaire remarked, the capricious French nation, satiated with operas, comedies and novels, set itself to thinking about corn.

So Quesnay followed his own private inclinations, at the same time as the general movement, when he started to collect material in some specialist publications: those of Vauban, Boisguillebert, Melon, Cantillon, Naveau, Herbert, Plumart de Dangeul, Egon de Beaumont, Dupré de Saint-Maur, and Forbonnais.

Having written his first article on economics, Quesnay felt the need to create a following and form a school of economics. He looked round for authors whom he might convert and charge with the dissemination of ideas which his position at the Court prevented him expressing freely.

Towards the middle of 1757, the Marquis de Mirabeau, who according to his own testimony was "no more an economist than his cat", had published a work strongly influenced by Cantillon, *L'Ami des hommes,* which had a tremendous success. The reading of it greatly interested Quesnay, who wrote on his own copy: "The Infant has been suckled with bad milk; his powerful temperament often redeems his conclusions, but he knows nothing of the principles." He later invited the author to pay him a visit. The meeting took place at the entresol at Versailles on 27 July 1757. The discussion was heated. Quesnay tried to show the Marquis that he had put

[4] This article was never published; nobody knows why.

the cart before the horse by placing the population at the source of wealth, and that the authors by whom he had been inspired were nothing but blockheads. Mirabeau first took the doctor for a madman, but in the evening, during a second talk together, he was forced to admit his mistake: "That was the moment when Goliath's skull was split." And from this moment, the proud aristocrat surrendered body and soul to the doctor and "became a pupil, who loudly and tenaciously renounced his error".

In 1757–8 the first elements of what was to become the physiocratic school gathered round Quesnay and Mirabeau. Gournay, Turgot and Mercier de la Rivière made Quesnay's acquaintance at more or less the same time as Mirabeau. According to Mirabeau, Gournay "had known our master and regarded him as his own" since before the publication of *L'Ami des hommes*. Neither Turgot nor Gournay were, properly speaking, followers of Quesnay. One of them was the leader of a separate school, the other never wished to be considered an economist, let alone an encyclopaedist. As for Mercier de la Rivière, he was considered by Quesnay to be a man of the greatest genius and the best suited to administering finances. As Counsellor at Parliament he doubtless owed to Quesnay's recommendation to Madame de Pompadour his nomination as Governor of Martinique in 1759.

By the end of 1758 Quesnay had formulated the principles of the new science. He attempted to express them in a clear, schematic form which would readily engage and convince the King by showing him where his true interests lay. Since 1757, Marmontel had seen Quesnay busy tracing the "graph" of the net product. The graph turned out well, for Quesnay easily managed to convince Madame de Pompadour that some handicraft would be an excellent distraction for the King. A start was made by getting Louis XV to turn out snuff-boxes for the whole Court; then a small printing press was installed in the palace, a luxurious toy indeed, with formes of polished tin, golden composing-sticks, a mahogany press and rosewood cases. And when a text was looked for to enhance all this luxury, Quesnay thought it the right moment for him to present his *Tableau économique*. "Sire," he said to the King, "in hunting you have seen much of the land, of farms and labourers, you have seen all that is of interest to your kingdom and your Majesty. You shall print how these people create your wealth and how they are divided in society." Louis XV printed almost half of the manuscript, read through the proofs several times and willingly admitted: "it is a pity the doctor is not an expert in the field, he knows more about it than all the others."

The first edition of the *Tableau* dates from November or December, 1758. It was magnificent, it seems, but not a single copy has come down to us. According to the three-page manuscript copy preserved in the Archives

Nationales, Quesnay based his calculations on a revenue of 400 livres. Brief notes framed the graph on either side and this was followed by 22 *Remarques sur les variations de la distribution des revenus annuels d'une nation.*

Quesnay sent Mirabeau a copy of this first edition. But the Marquis found some difficulty in following the continuity of the *Tableau* and Quesnay had to explain to him how the graph, which was well conceived, curtailed the details. At the same time he told him that he would send him a second enlarged and revised edition, of which he would have three copies printed and for which he would base his calculation on a revenue of 600 livres, "In order to make the share somewhat larger for everyone". In this second edition, which dates from the spring of 1759, the marginal notes were augmented by a paragraph on either side. The *Remarques,* which later became known as *Extrait des Economies royales de M. de Sully,* reached a total of 23 and filled six pages in all.

Towards the middle or end of 1759, Quesnay had a third edition printed, which was destined to have a wider circulation. The *Tableau,* calculated on its basis of 600 livres, was followed by an *Explication du Tableau économique* of 12 pages and by an *Extrait des économies royales de M. de Sully* of 22 pages. The maxims numbered 24 and the very copious notes were almost comparable to those of the *Physiocratie.*

Quesnay spent the year 1760 principally in writing the *Théorie de l'Impôt,* in conjunction with Mirabeau and with the help of Butré, Morin and Le Grand in the arithmetical calculations. The *Théorie de l'Impôt* appeared towards the end of 1760, carrying with it Mirabeau's hopes of being nominated prime minister. But his attacks on the tax officials had no other effect than to cause his arrest. Quesnay was completely thunderstruck and tried to convince Madame de Pompadour and the lieutenant of police of his friends' good intentions. But the King had been deeply hurt by being told that he could only gain the loyalty of his subjects by means of money and that it was precisely his coffers which were empty.

It was in DuPont de Nemours that Mirabeau and Quesnay found one of their best recruits. DuPont had prepared a treatise, *Traité sur l'exportation et l'importation des grains,* which Quesnay considered good enough to be dedicated to Madame de Pompadour. He presented DuPont to the Marquise, who took a fancy to him and had him nominated secretary of the parliamentary commission charged with inspecting finances. Shortly afterwards the Marquise fell ill. Quesnay came to treat her, mainly letting nature do its work. However, she had a sudden relapse. She died on 15 April 1764, without the King showing any sign of real emotion. In her will, dated 1757, she left Quesnay a pension of 4000 livres.

Quesnay and his followers now began to feel the need of popularizing their doctrine among the public. Mirabeau had thought of creating a chair of Economics at a provincial university. But Quesnay saw a better means of propaganda in the press. In July 1765, a supplement to the *Gazette du commerce* was created. This supplement, which was to deal with doctrinal controversies, appeared under the title *Journal de l'agriculture, du commerce et des finances*. The economists now had a public platform at their disposal. Quesnay was one of the most active contributors to the journal. Few editions appeared that did not bear his signature under an article, as M.H., M.N., M. de l'Isle or M. Nisaque.

In order further to increase the circle of adherents, Quesnay and Mirabeau decided to open a course on economics, or economic "arithmetic" as Quesnay preferred to call it, beginning on 15 September 1767, at the house of the Abbé Choquart, Rue Saint-Dominique.

The following month saw the publication by DuPont of a collection of works selected by Quesnay, entitled *Physiocratie*. This neologism had no doubt been coined by Quesnay himself, great lover of Greek and Latin that he was. The work appeared in two volumes, with continuous pagination, in Leyden and Paris, from the press of Merlin. The first volume was entitled: *Physiocratie, ou Constitution naturelle du gouvernement le plus avantageux au genre humain* ("Physiocracy, or the natural constitution of the government of the greatest benefit to the human race"); and the second *Discussions et développements sur quelques-unes des notions de l'économie politique, pour servir de seconde partie au receuil intitulé*: *Physiocratie* ("Deliberations and developments on some ideas on political economy, constituting the second part of the collection entitled: Physiocracy").

The two volumes, introduced by DuPont, contained Quesnay's most orthodox articles, all "revised with care" and considerably supplemented. He had placed the articles in the most logical order, publishing in the first volume "Droit naturel", "L'analyse de la formule arithmétique du tableau économique" and the "Maximes générales du gouvernement économique d'un royaume agricole"(now retitled "Économies royales"), of which there were now thirty. The second volume contained the "Problème économique", the "Dialogues sur la commerce et les travaux des artisans" and a new article especially written by Quesnay for *Physiocratie*, the "Seconde problème économique".

New voices were raised everywhere against the physiocrats and their works. Voltaire, Mably, Linguet and Grimm attacked them. But it was Galiani, well known in the salons where everybody was fond of his intellect, who was to strike the school its hardest blow. For him, "Quesnay is the Antichrist and his physiognomy is the Apocalypse". Even the people, troubled by the persistent high price of grain and stirred up by the behaviour of the bankers and provision-dealers, rioted and laid the blame for all their misfortunes on the "*Économistes*".

Towards the end of his life, Quesnay, disconcerted by mishaps to his physiocracy and perhaps by the partial incomprehension on the part of his followers, became more and more disinterested in his work on economics and turned towards mathematics. He had always been attracted by "arithmetical hieroglyphs" and had constantly stressed the need for calculation in economics. But it was above all geometry on which he concentrated his studies, for, according to Quesnay of Saint-Germain, he regarded algebra with its "sublime calculations" as mere "brilliant futility".

In 1770 when Sénac died, Quesnay very nearly became the King's first physician. But being too old and too lame, he was not chosen. He fell from grace and had to leave the palace.

Quesnay moved into the Grand-Commun, of which he was the physician.

In December 1774, Quesnay reached his eightieth birthday. He had grown old with dignified resignation and saw in old age no more than nature's slow work which cleared away the ruins. But for several months his gout, from which he had been suffering since his youth, had not given him a moment's peace. He bore his suffering with stoicism, replying to those who pitied him: "One must have a few complaints at my age; others have gall-stones, suffer from paralysis, are blind, deaf or senile; well, I've got my gout! I am no more to be pitied than they." And he would turn the conversation to more cheerful matters. In spite of all his goodwill, however, it became increasingly difficult for him to apply himself to abstract studies.

On Tuesday, 13 December, when his condition deteriorated, the news immediately spread through Paris. The Abbé Baudeau hastened to his master's bedside, who for some days past had received nobody and had hardly spoken at all. Quesnay rallied at the sight of his follower, and asked him for news of the "school" and the journal. After Baudeau's departure, according to Mirabeau, he sank back in exhaustion. According to Hévin, he learned with marked joy, on the evening of Wednesday, 14th, or Thursday, 15th, that the King had laid the foundation stone of the new College of Surgery (now the Faculty of Medicine). The details of the ceremony may have been told him by his two grandsons, Beauvoir and Saint-Germain, both of them gendarmes in the royal guard. At the end of his life, Quesnay thus saw the triumph of physiocracy as well as of surgery.

He was still able to address some words of comfort to his faithful manservant, Guyot, who was in tears: "Do not grieve, I was not born never to die. Look at that portrait in front of me, read the year of my birth at the bottom, judge for yourself whether I have lived long enough." Then on Friday, 16 December, having received the sacraments, he passed away peacefully in his room in the Grand-Commun towards six in the evening, in the presence of Hévin, Guyot and Quesnay of Saint-Germain. On the following day he was buried in the old church of Saint Julien in the parish of Notre-Dame.

Jacqueline Hecht

II
QUESNAY: PHILOSOPHER, EMPIRICIST, ECONOMIST

Outstanding among the very small number of figures who established economics as a science is François Quesnay. Indeed, Quesnay and his disciples were described by Karl Marx as "the true source of modern economics" on the basis of their analysis of capital, a contribution also justly praised by Schumpeter.

In his writings Quesnay interested himself, like all economists of note, in a wide range of economic questions, some of which continue to command our interest today. While many of his prejudices were adopted by the physiocratic school, his followers did not wholly share in his philosophy, interpretation, methods or implicit comprehension of the scope of economics. They preferred to give their works a more deductive and rationalistic character.

How the economist interprets the world of economic objects and events depends in part upon his general conception of the world. One cannot interpret an Aeschylean universe, in which infringement of the moral law inevitably leads to judgment, in the same way as a universe subject to accidents of uncertainty as well as to reward and punishment. Quesnay was aware of this. He shared with his contemporaries that "sense of order" which, as Whitehead has observed, the Middle Ages bestowed on following eras. Whether he was influenced by R. Cumberland or by N. Malebranche or by others, he presumed that Nature, behind which stood an orderly supreme being, could readily be made to subserve man's ends and contribute to his happiness; that man is quite capable of learning to make use of Nature; and that man's propensities, except when dormant (for example, in poor peasants) lead him to act in his own interest, at least on the economic level. While it was largely by appealing to Locke's theory of knowledge that Quesnay backed up his own theory of "*évidence*", he seems to owe some inspiration to Malebranche in thinking that the laws of the natural order are discoverable, thanks especially to the direct effect of God's action on the soul. Because these laws can be discovered and accordingly communicated, Quesnay emphasized the need to teach men to respect them.

Quesnay was a modern man. He favoured the establishment of institutions which, while taking account of man's inherent failings, could contribute to the reign of justice. That was why he attached so much importance to the rules and institutions which allow satisfactory economic behaviour. He relied on his disciples to develop more completely the political principles implicit in his economic philosophy. Being aware of the difficulties in the way of introducing a "*droit positif*" compatible with the "*lois de l'ordre naturel*", Quesnay foresaw the need for entrusting to a supreme judicial system, for example, the responsibility for seeing that appropriate "*lois positives*" are passed and kept. It was from this idea that his followers worked out a complete doctrine of judicial control.

Provided that a body keeps the application of this doctrine under control, the incompatibilities between "positive laws" and "natural order" would progressively be toned down and the system of "*droit positif*" would finish up by representing very faithfully the underlying natural order.

Quesnay could not state precisely the conditions which permit an optimum division of productive agents between various economic sectors, for he did not have a suitable productivity theory at his disposal. He supposed, however, that, as long as conditions making for economic liberty obtained and competition remained the rule, a satisfactory price structure would be maintained and the factors of production would be properly divided between sectors and appropriately rewarded. Here one finds the state of mind of the French entrepreneurs of the period who had become strong supporters of commercial and industrial freedom. One discovers, too, the influence of the new psychological school which emphasized the decisive power of man's passions, and appetites. Quesnay actually believed that most men let themselves be guided by their own self-interest and the prospect of obtaining profit or advantage. As he also realized that men are quick to cull the tempting fruits of privilege, Quesnay insisted on protecting competition from attack by those who stood to gain from its curtailment. He specifically said, moreover, that the salutary role of competition would be most effective if the policy pursued in tax and fiscal matters were correct. He took it for granted that, because of inter-individual differences in effort, aptitude and so on, inequality was unavoidable and permanent.

Quesnay did not attempt any precise definition of the modern competitive system, possibly because he feared getting too far from reality. He was content to write of "*libre concurrence du commerce extérieur*", "*la plus grande liberté*" of internal and external commerce, "*la plus grande concurrence possible*", and so on. He remarked that "*la police naturelle du commerce est donc la concurrence libre et immense*" which assures to every nation "*le prix le plus avantageux dans ses ventes et dans ses achats*".

The aspect of Quesnay's system which attracted most attention in his day was his conception of circular flow as represented in both his abbreviated and his unabbreviated tables. By a kind of irony this scheme fell into oblivion (though Say's "Law" was apparently a replica) until the moment when Marx borrowed from it. Interest was renewed, in 1894, with the reprinting of the 1758 edition, and again, in 1941, when W. W. Leontief described the *Tableau* as a forerunner of his input–output model.

Quesnay's tables aim at showing, on the one hand, the regrettable effects of ill-advised diversions of expenditure from agriculture and, on the other hand, the manner in which goods and money circulated between the three classes of French society.

Quesnay's theory of distribution was primitive. He did not make use of the "imputation" process of late-nineteenth-century economists, nor was it given to him to foresee the Walras–Pareto concept which reduced the so-called distribution problem into one of simultaneous pricing of productive elements and finished goods. For Quesnay, gross production is distributed between three classes, each with its own function to perform in French society; but he did not generally correlate the magnitude of an agent's reward (except for net rent, the amount of which, he noted incidentally, is a "natural sequel" to administration) with the importance of his role or function (see below).

Quesnay showed a lively interest in economic development; this was, indeed, his principal concern. He set himself the basic objective of transforming France's agrarian economy, not into an industrial economy, but into one in which capital—intense and technologically progressive *grande culture* took the place of backward, unproductive *petite culture*. This objective was to be achieved, according to him, not through the extension of monopolistic and related privileges to farmers and landowners, but principally through the setting up of a competitive regime. Realization of this objective had been checked in the past by unwise forms of interventionism, and above all by the special privileges granted to manufacturers and distributors in the hope that the beneficiaries would accelerate the development of the non-agrarian sector of the French economy and thereby that of agriculture itself. This policy, for Quesnay as for Adam Smith, was putting the cart before the horse. Economic development proceeded naturally and at a relatively fast pace only when expansion in the non-agrarian sector took place in response to prior expansion in the agrarian sector, "unique source des richesses" and of the net product whence flowed capital. "*La classe stérile s'étendra toujours à proportion des richesses du pays.*" World demand for agricultural products would grow simultaneously with the growth of population and net product; while the possibility of satisfying this demand would increase in proportion both as manpower grew by natural demographic evolution and as the *grande culture* spread, for this last would enable relatively more of the world population to be occupied in non-agrarian professions. Similarly, the growth of the *classe des propriétaires* was conditioned by the growth of the net product and hence of the amount of revenue passing to this class. So long, therefore, as agriculture was free to make the maximum progress, other parts of the economy could take advantage of it and expand.

Quesnay apparently did not suppose, as Hobbes did, that hypothetical simple primitive societies would be a prey to internal struggles. Neither, for that matter, did he think that man's self-centredness would always tally with his social affections, nor that human interests would naturally correspond with one another or with the general interest. An effective defence, a good use of resources, etc., presupposed the fixing of appropriate rules, the setting up of institutions, and the laying down of other limits to man's exercise of "droit naturel". Like Hume, however, Quesnay reckoned that a suitable authority could reconcile egoism and interests. It could do so by enforcing positive laws consistent with the natural order and conceived in such a way as to create a situation in which individuals would find it advantageous to pursue activities compatible with those of others and the general interest.

Quesnay gave various examples of disharmony, notably in Chapter 8 of his *Despotisme de la Chine*. The members of each principal social group, the great landowners, the nobility, the common people and, above all, people not engaged in agriculture, have a tendency to misinterpret their true interests and so to damage the true interests of other groups. For want of a good government, monopolies and other favoured groups come into being at the expense of the rest of the population; various suppliers and middlemen, not belonging to the agrarian class, escape the limits competition sets on them and overcharge their customers; and people situated in key posts (financiers, money-lenders, tax-farmers, beneficiaries of domestic and colonial trading privileges) can be in a position to exploit the people they are dealing with.

As has been indicated, harmony between the classes was not automatic, nor was social welfare, by whatever definition, necessarily at its highest level. These objectives were more likely to be realized through intervention of the public powers, provided that it was in keeping with the natural order. Quesnay thus assigned a larger role to the state than Adam Smith; and yet, the main objectives of these two economists were not so very different.

Quesnay's conception of the natural order and the role of the state, may be summarized as follows:

Les lois constitutives des sociétés sont les lois de l'ordre naturel les plus avantageux au genre humain. Ces lois sont ou physiques ou morales.

On entend par loi physique constitutive du gouvernement, *la marche réglée de tout événement physique de l'ordre naturel évidemment le plus avantageux au genre humain*. On entend par une loi morale constitutive du gouvernement, *la marche réglée toute action morale de l'ordre naturel évidemment le plus avantageux au genre humain*. Ces lois forment ensemble ce qu'on appelle la loi naturelle.

While these laws had a more divine than human origin, their observance was effected through the medium of a "tutelary authority" which deduced just, positive laws by inspiration from the fundamental, primitive laws, which made these laws known to the population and which ratified their violation, thereby preventing disorder and enabling men to maximize their welfare. It was not difficult to see to the observance of these positive laws: considering that, in fact, these positive laws conformed to the laws of the natural order, their transgressors automatically suffered whereas people who observed them would be "certain of reward". When, on the other hand, the positive laws were out of keeping with the natural order, then compliance with them could be bad for the economy, and so it would be necessary to amend them. As an example of these bad laws which especially concerned him, Quesnay specified protectionist legislation, which, though meant to stimulate industry, actually injured agriculture and so checked industrial progress (see the *Analyse du tableau économique* and *Maximes générales*). It was for the purpose of ensuring correspondence between positive laws and natural right that Quesnay's followers especially were to recommend judicial control; for men in general, except for evil-doers, realizing where their real interests lie, can only have respect for positive right, in line with natural right, because it brings them every advantage; they could then enjoy their natural rights and, at the same time, their legitimate rights, as recognized by positive laws.

Quesnay's recommendations in the fiscal sphere are simple. He proposed that tax be levied only on rent-yielding land, because the weight of taxation would eventually fall on net rent anyway. It was not, then, merely a desire to simplify collection, as has long been thought, that made him recommend a single tax. No income except rent, at any rate in conditions of free competition, could produce a taxable surplus, in relation to production costs. So, taxes levied on wages, payments in kind and so on would have to be shifted onto the only existing surplus, namely net rent. It was, therefore, simpler and more economical for the sovereign, considered as a co-proprietor with the landowners, to impose a tax directly on this surplus. Nevertheless, it was essential at the same time to restrict the proportion of this surplus taken by the state, since only a fraction of it was truly available; in taking more of it, the state would run the risk of limiting consumption of produce and investment in agriculture and, in the long run, cutting down the basis of taxation. Quesnay, therefore, recommended fixing the proprietor's share at 58 per cent or thereabouts; the sovereign's share would stand at between one-third and one-half of the net product. This amount, in his view, would allow the sovereign to fulfil his role. A higher level of appropriation would reduce investment in agriculture, and the consequential diminution of net product would leave too little money for financing other functions.

Joseph John Spengler

III
THE TABLEAU ÉCONOMIQUE AS A SIMPLE LEONTIEF MODEL

Quesnay presented his *Tableau* in two forms. The more familiar one is from the 1759 edition discovered by Dr Bauer. This table is not, however, an analysis of the whole of an economy but rather a diagrammatic representation of the regeneration of income due to the expenditure of a member of the proprietor class. It illustrates how 600 livres received by one landowner as rent are spent, half on agricultural products and half on the products of artisans. Then, in their turn, farmers buy industrial products, artisans buy food and raw materials, and so on back and forth down the table in ever lessening subdivisions of the original 600 livres spent. According to Quesnay's interpretation, with a given amount of permanent land improvements and fixed capital (*avances foncières* and *avances primitives*), the value of production in agriculture exceeds the cost of labour, seed, other recurring annual costs, interest and depreciation (*avances annuelles*) and, with the re-spending of the original 600 livres going on indefinitely, this surplus over cost will result in a total of 600 livres being repaid to the proprietor. In fact, of course, the 600 livres go to the proprietor class, not necessarily to the proprietor who initiated the expenditure stream.

This "zigzag" table is difficult to interpret. Later editions of the *Tableau* simplify the illustration by changing the figures to those of proprietors, farmers and artisans, each as a whole class, and by giving only their total annual receipts and expenditures. Figure 1 is reproduced from Quesnay's "Analyse du Tableau Économique" which was published in the *Journal d'agriculture, du commerce et des finances,* June 1766. In this version, proprietors spent two milliards (two thousand million livres): one milliard on agricultural products and one milliard for the goods of artisans. These are shown in Table 1 by the two dotted lines from the proprietors' two milliards of revenue down to the farmers (*la classe productive*) and artisans (*la classe stérile*) respectively. Artisans spend two milliards also, but all of this is for agricultural products—food and raw materials. The table shows two dotted lines from them to farmers to represent these purchases. Farmers purchase only one milliard of goods, this from the artisans, but they retain two milliards of their own production. Quesnay's total reproduction of five milliards is the sum of agricultural production and is composed of the one milliard purchased by proprietors, the two milliards purchased by artisans and the two milliards retained by farmers. This is the clearest diagram of the *Tableau* that Quesnay provided. In the next section [see below] the same data will be presented as an input–output model and the nature of the Quesnay analysis becomes more clear:

A three-industry closed Leontief model is of the form,

$$\begin{aligned} +(1-a_{11})X_1 \quad & -a_{12}X_2 & -a_{13}X_3 &= 0 \\ -a_{21}X_1 \quad & +(1-a_{22})X_2 & -a_{23}X_3 &= 0 \\ -a_{31}X_1 \quad & -a_{32}X_2 & +(1-a_{33})X_3 &= 0 \end{aligned} \qquad (1)$$

where X_1, X_2 and X_3 are the rates of output of each of the three industries and the a_{ij} coefficients represent the requirements of the jth industry for the ith industry's product per unit output of the jth industry. That is, for example,

$$a_{12} = \frac{x_{12}}{X_2}$$

where the x_{12} is the amount of the first industry's product which the second industry purchases. These equations describe the truistic condition that, if the three industries comprise the total economy, the total output of an industry is equal to the amount retained by that industry plus the amount sold to the other industries. More formally, the equations state that the amount of the product of an industry which it does not retain, $(1-a_{ii})X_i$, less the amounts purchased from it by other industries is equal to zero.

From the *Tableau*, let farmers be industry 1, proprietors be industry 2, and artisans be industry 3. We may then prepare a transactions table from which to compute the required coefficients from the information which Quesnay provided (see Table 2). Farmers produce a total of five milliards, two of which they keep. One milliard is sold to proprietors and another two milliards is sold to artisans. Farmers purchase the two retained milliards of their own goods, two milliards of rental services from proprietors and one milliard of goods from artisans. Proprietors "produce" two milliards of rental services, all of which is sold to farmers. Artisans produce two milliards of goods, half of which is purchased by proprietors and half by farmers. The whole *Tableau* is thus simply presented by this two-way transactions diagram.

TABLE 2

TRANSACTIONS TABLE FOR THE TABLEAU ÉCONOMIQUE

(Value of real goods in milliards)

Producing Industry	Purchasing Industry: 1 Farmers	2 Proprietors	3 Artisans	Total Production
1 Farmers	2	1	2	5
2 Proprietors	2	0	0	2
3 Artisans	1	1	0	2
Total Purchases	5	2	2	9

Using the values of Table 2, the input–output coefficients of the *Tableau* appear as follows:

$$\begin{array}{lll} a_{11} = 0{\cdot}4 & a_{12} = 0{\cdot}5 & a_{13} = 1{\cdot}0 \\ a_{21} = 0{\cdot}4 & a_{22} = 0 & a_{23} = 0 \\ a_{31} = 0{\cdot}2 & a_{32} = 0{\cdot}5 & a_{33} = 0 \end{array} \qquad (2)$$

Substituting these values into the closed Leontief system of equation set (1), we have,

$$\begin{array}{l} +\,0{\cdot}6\,(5) - 0{\cdot}5\,(2) - 1{\cdot}0\,(2) = 0 \\ -\,0{\cdot}4\,(5) + 1{\cdot}0\,(2) - 0\,(2) = 0 \\ -\,0{\cdot}2\,(5) - 0{\cdot}5\,(2) + 1{\cdot}0\,(2) = 0 \end{array}$$

The actual values for X_1, X_2 and X_3 which Quesnay gave are only one of an infinite number of values for them which would satisfy the Leontief equations. Being a closed system of linear and homogeneous equations and with no part of the demand for products given autonomously, the equations are met by any set of values for X_1, X_2 and X_3 which are in the same proportions as 5, 2 and 2 respectively. It is impossible, given only the coefficients, to solve for anything other than the proportion which the output of one "industry" is to the output of one of the others. On the other hand, given the coefficients and the rate of output for any one industry, all the other rates of output are determined.

The presentation of the *Tableau* in input–output form makes it possible to clarify some of the more obscure parts of Quesnay's analysis. Quesnay was apparently troubled by the problem of explaining where the money came from to get his process started. To solve this he used a sort of period analysis not completely unlike that used in the Robertsonian method for analysing national income. The two milliards which proprietors spend are described by Quesnay as being those received from the previous year's rent. That is, spending in one income period is the result of income received during the previous period. Similarly, of the two milliards received by artisans, half is retained for initial expenditures in the following year.

There is surely no error in putting such leads and lags into the *Tableau*, but they do make it more difficult to understand. Table 2 indicates that Quesnay's economy could more easily be pictured as a circular flow, since each of the industries has total receipts (production) equal to total expenditures (purchases). No leads and lags are necessary, each sector simply spending in each income period the receipts of the same period.

Presenting the *Tableau* as an input–output system also clarifies the frequently mystifying nature of the *avances annuelles* and the *avances primitives*. In the edition of the *Tableau* from which the figures for Table 2 are taken, Quesnay assumed that fixed capital in agriculture, excluding land and permanent improvements to land (*avances foncières*), amounted to ten milliards. He called this *avances primitives* and there is some confusion regarding its maintenance. At one point Quesnay speaks of an interest payment amounting to 10 per cent of the ten milliards, but this is not shown in the *Tableau*. At another point, speaking of the same milliard of expenditures by farmers, Quesnay describes them as purchases from the artisan class, which are shown in the *Tableau*. It seems preferable to regard the 10 per cent rate as one of depreciation rather than interest. Then 10 per cent of the fixed capital wears out each year but is replaced by purchases from the artisans. In this way fixed capital is assumed to remain constant and the stationary, circular equilibrium is maintained. Such an interpretation seems to capture Quesnay's real meaning.

The *avances annuelles* are most simply described as the non-capital, non-rent costs of production and are assumed by Quesnay to amount to milliards per year. In the *Tableau* these are represented by the two milliards of their own production which farmers retain. These are the costs for seed, fertilizer, agricultural wages (subsistence) and other recurring annual expenses other than depreciation.

The total of the *avances annuelles* and the *avances primitives* Quesnay calls *les reprises*, all production costs other than rent. They amount, of course, to three milliards. In Table 2, *les reprises* are shown as the two milliards which farmers purchase from themselves and the one milliard which they purchase from artisans.

The physiocratic "net product" is equivalent to agricultural rent payments. And these bear a striking resemblance to the then unknown Ricardian differential surplus, the difference between the value of the product of the land and the cost of non-land productive factors. Only agriculture appears to produce a net product since, by assumption, only farmers pay rent. Perhaps the typically small-scale craft shops of artisans, principally owner-operated, concealed from the physiocrats the payment of rents to nonproductive property owners in other than agricultural production. Certainly it would have been illogical for the physiocratic doctrine to accept the agricultural net product theory had rent payments been assumed for the other industries.

Quesnay's *Tableau Économique* may be viewed as a static, closed Leontief system. Presented in this way, the circularity of the economy becomes more apparent and some interpretive difficulties are lessened. More important, Quesnay's brilliance in formulating a system of general interdependence becomes clear by such analysis. It leads one to consider his contribution to economic thought much as did Marx: "Never before had thinking in political economy reached such heights of genius." The *Tableau Économique* marks the beginning of general equilibrium economic theories and well deserves mention in preface to Walras, Pareto, Cassel and Leontief.

Almarin Phillips

SOURCES

Essay I

Jacqueline Hecht, "La vie de François Quesnay", in *François Quesnay et la Physiocratie* (Institut national d'études démographiques, Paris, 1958). Abridged.

Essay II

Joseph John Spengler, "Quesnay, philosophe, émpiriste, économiste", in *François Quesnay et la Physiocratie* (Institut national d'études démographiques, Paris, 1958). Abridged.

Essay III

Almarin Phillips, "The *Tableau économique* as a simple Leontief model", *Quarterly Journal of Economics*, 69 (1955). Abridged.

Signature

Bibliothèque nationale, Paris.

Portrait

Engraving by J. G. Will from a portrait by J. Chevalier, 1747 (archives nationales; Paris).

BIBLIOGRAPHY

E. Daire, "Notice sur la vie et les travaux de François Quesnay", in *Les Physiocrates* (Paris, 1846).

J. R. MacCulloch, "François Quesnay", in *Treatises and Essays on Subjects Connected with Economical Policy; with Biographical Sketches of Quesnay, A. Smith and Ricardo* (Edinburgh, 1853).

L. Lavergne, *Les Économistes français du XVIIIe siècle* (Paris, 1870).

J. Benzacar, "Le créateur d'une science nouvelle au XVIIIe siècle: François Quesnay", *Revue économique de Bordeaux* (1896).

A. Oncken, "Zur Biographie des Stifters der Physiokratie François Quesnay", *Zeitschrift für Literatur und Geschichte der Staatswissenschaften*, 2–4, Leipzig (1894–5).

G. Schelle, *François Quesnay* (Paris, 1902).

H. Waentig, "François Quesnay" in *Physiokratische Schriften*, vol. 2 (Jena, 1921).

M. Beer, *An Inquiry into Physiocracy* (London, 1939).

I. Hishiyama, "The *Tableau économique* of Quesnay: its analysis, reconstruction, and application", *Kyoto University Economic Review*, 30 (1960).

B. F. Hoselitz, François Quesnay, in *International Encyclopaedia of the Social Sciences*, Vol. 13 (New York, 1968).

M. Kuczynski (ed.), *François Quesnay: Ökonomische Schriften*, several vols. (Berlin, 1971).

DAVID HUME

1711–1776

Aquinas and Hume expressed ideas which when further developed brought about the disintegration of the whole body of ideas which each, respectively, was presenting. Both of these great thinkers combined synthesis with innovation. In Hume's case the innovation was so striking that synthetic aspects of his economic thought have been neglected.

To the extent that Hume incorporated earlier ideas into his economic thought, he fused these ideas into a tentative system. In doing so, he demonstrated, better than any other writer, the contradictions which were contained in the economic thought of his age and prepared the way for a new set of doctrines consciously designed to replace the traditional teaching of Adam Smith's predecessors.

E. A. J. JOHNSON

While it is not difficult to appreciate the sheer intellectual brilliance of Hume's work—he was, indeed, the first distinguished man of letters to make a fortune from literature alone and still preserve his independence—the modern significance of his economic thought, particularly, goes very much further than that. Because of their fundamental attempt to incorporate economics into a broader study of human experience, Hume's essays can still be re-read today with great profit.

The day may well come when teachers and students instinctively set back their time-charts from 1776 to 1742 and divide the history of economic thought into two main periods—before and after the work of David Hume. M. ARKIN

Hume has an eminent place among economists, and for one for whom the study of such phenomena was but a casual inquiry, it is marvellous how much he saw.

H. J. LASKI

I
MY OWN LIFE

18 of April 1776

It is difficult for a man to speak long of himself without Vanity: Therefore I shall be short. It may be thought an Instance of Vanity, that I pretend at all to write my Life: But indeed, almost all my Life has been spent in literary Pursuits and Occupations. The first Success of most of my writings was not such as to be an Object of Vanity.

I was born the 26 of April 1711, O.S. at Edinburgh. I was of a good Family both by Father and Mother. My Father's Family is a Branch of the Earl of Home's or Hume's; and my Ancestors had been Proprietors of the Estate, which my Brother possesses, for several Generations. My Mother was Daughter of Sir David Falconar, President of the College of Justice: The Title of Lord Halkerton came by Succession to her Brother.

My Family, however, was not rich. My Father, who passed for a man of Parts, dyed, when I was an Infant; leaving me, with an elder Brother and a Sister under the care of our Mother, a woman of singular Merit, who, though young and handsome, devoted herself entirely to the rearing and educating of her Children. I passed through the ordinary Course of Education with Success; and was seized very early with a passion for Literature which has been the ruling Passion of my Life, and the great Source of my Enjoyments. My studious Disposition, my Sobriety, and my Industry gave my Family a Notion that the Law was a proper Profession for me: But I found an unsurmountable Aversion to everything but the pursuits of Philosophy and general Learning; and while they fancyed I was poring over Voet and Vinnius, Cicero and Virgil were the Authors which I was secretly devouring.

My very slender Fortune, however, being unsuitable to this plan of Life, and my Health being a little broken by my ardent Application, I was tempted or rather forced to make a very feeble Trial for entering into a more active Scene of Life. In 1734, I went to Bristol with some Recommendations to eminent Merchants; but in a few Months found that Scene totally unsuitable to me. I went over to France, with a View of prosecuting my Studies in a Country Retreat; and I there [?then] laid that Plan of Life, which I have steddily and successfully pursued: I resolved to make a very rigid Frugality supply my Deficiency of Fortune, to maintain unimpaired my Independency, and to regard every object as contemptible, except the Improvement of my Talents in Literature.

During my Retreat in France, I composed my *Treatise of Human Nature*. After passing three Years very agreeably in that Countrey, I came over to London in 1737. In the End of 1738, I published my Treatise; and immediatly went down to my Mother and my Brother.

Never literary Attempt was more unfortunate than my Treatise of human Nature. It fell *dead-born from the Press*; without reaching such distinction as even to excite a Murmur among the Zealots. But being naturally of a cheerful and sanguine Temper, I very soon recovered the Blow, and prosecuted with great Ardour my Studies in the Country. In 1742, I printed at Edinburgh the first part of my Essays: The work was favourably received, and soon made me entirely forget my former Disappointment.

In 1745, I received a Letter from the Marquess of Annandale, inviting me to come and live with him in England: I found also, that the Friends and Family of that young Nobleman, were desirous of putting him under my Care and Direction: For the State of his Mind and Health required it. I lived with him a Twelvemonth: My Appointments during that time made a considerable Accession to my small Fortune. I then received an Invitation from General S^{t}clair to attend him as Secretary to his Expedition, which was at first meant against Canada, but ended in an Incursion on the Coast of France: Next Year, to wit 1747, I received an Invitation from the General to attend him in the same Station in his military Embassy to the Courts of Vienna and Turin. I there wore the Uniform of an Officer; and was introduced at these courts as Aide-de-camp to the General, along with Sir Harry Erskine and Capt Grant, now General Grant. These two Years were almost the only Interruptions which my Studies have received in the Course of my Life: I passed them agreeably and in good Company: And my Appointments, with my Frugality, had made me reach a Fortune, which I called independent, though most of my Friends were inclined to smile when I said so: In short I was now Master of near a thousand Pound.

I had always entertained a Notion, that my want of Success, in publishing the *Treatise of Human Nature*, had proceeded more from the manner than the matter; and that I had been guilty of a very usual Indiscretion, in going to the Press too early. I therefore cast the first part of that work anew in the *Enquiry concerning human Understanding*, which was published while I was at Turin. But this piece was at first but little more successful than the *Treatise of Human Nature*. On my return from Italy, I had the Mortification to find all England in a Ferment on account of Dr. Middletons Free Enquiry; while my Performance was entirely overlooked and neglected. A new Edition, which had been published at London of my Essays, moral and political, met not with a much better reception.

Such is the force of natural Temper, that these disappointments made little or no Impression on me. I went down in 1749 and lived two Years with my Brother at his Country house: For my Mother was now dead. I there composed the second Part of my Essays, which I called *Political Discourses*: and also my Enquiry concerning the *Principles of Morals*, which is another part of my Treatise, that I cast anew. Mean-while, my Bookseller, A. Millar, informed me, that my former Publications (all but the unfortunate Treatise) were beginning to be the Subject of Conversation, that the Sale of them was gradually encreasing, and that new Editions were demanded. These Symptoms of a rising Reputation gave me Encouragement as I was ever more disposed to see the favourable than unfavourable Side of things; a turn of Mind, which it is more happy to possess than be born to an Estate of ten thousand a Year.

In 1751, I removed from the Countrey to the Town; the true Scene for a man of Letters. In 1752, were published at Edinburgh, where I then lived, my *Political Discourses*, the only work of mine, that was successful on the first Publication: It was well received abroad and at home. In the same Year was published at London my Enquiry concerning the *Principles of Morals*, which, in my own opinion (who ought not to judge on that subject) is of all my writings, historical, philosopical, or literary, incomparably the best: It came unnoticed and unobserved into the World.

In 1752, the Faculty of Advocates chose me their Librarian, an Office from which I received little or no Emolument, but which gave me the Command of a large Library. I then formed the Plan of writing the History of England; but being frightened with the Notion of continuing a Narrative, through a Period of 1700 years, I commenced with the Accession of the House of Stuart. I was, I own, sanguine in my Expectations of the Success of this work. I thought, that, I was the only Historian, that had at once neglected present Power, Interest, and Authority, and the Cry of popular Prejudices; and as the Subject was suited to every Capacity, I expected proportional Applause: But miserable was my Disappointment: I was assailed by one Cry of Reproach, Disapprobation, and even Detestation. And after the first Ebullitions of this Fury were over, what was still more mortifying, the Book seemed to sink into Oblivion. Mr Millar told me, that in a twelvemonth he sold only forty five Copies of it.

I was, I confess, discouraged; and had not the War been at that time breaking out between France and England, I had certainly retired to some provincial Town of the former Kingdom, have changed my Name, and never more have returned to my native Country. But as this Scheme was not now practicable, and the subsequent Volume was considerably advanced, I resolved to pick up Courage and to persevere.

In this Interval I published at London, my *Natural History of Religion* along with some other small Pieces: Its public Entry was rather obscure.

In 1756, two Years after the fall of the first Volume, was published the second Volume of my History, containing the Period from the Death of Charles I, till the Revolution. This Performance happened to give less Displeasure to the Whigs, and was better received. It not only rose itself; but helped to buoy up its unfortunate Brother.

But though I had been taught by Experience, that the Whig Party were in possession of bestowing all places, both in the State and in Literature, I was so little inclined to yield to their senseless Clamour, that in above a hundred Alterations, which farther Study, Reading, or Reflection engaged me to make in the Reigns of the two first Stuarts, I have made all of them invariably to the Tory Side. It is ridiculous to consider the English Constitution before that Period as a regular Plan of Liberty.

In 1759 I published my *History of the House of Tudor*. The Clamour against this Performance was almost equal to that against the History of the two first Stuarts. But I was now callous against the Impressions of public Folly; and continued very peacably and contentedly in my Retreat at Edinburgh, to finish in two Volumes the more early part of the English History; which I gave to the public in 1761 with tolerable, and but tolerable Success.

But notwithstanding this Variety of Winds and Seasons, to which my Writings had been exposed, they had still been making such Advances, that Copy Money, given me by the Booksellers, much exceeded any thing formerly known in England: I was become not only independant, but opulent. I retired to my native Country of Scotland, determined never more to set my Foot out of it; and retaining the Satisfaction of never having preferred a Request to one great Man or even making Advances of Friendship to any of them. As I was now turned of fifty, I thought of passing all the rest of my Life in this philosophical manner; when I received in 1763 an Invitation from Lord Hertford, with whom I was not in the least acquainted, to attend him on his Embassy to Paris, with a near Prospect of being appointed Secretary to the Embassy, and in the mean while, of performing the functions of that office. This Offer, however inviting, I at first declined; both because I was reluctant to begin Connexions with the Great, and because I was afraid that the Civilities and gay Company of Paris would prove disagreeable to a Person of my Age and Humour: But on his Lordship's repeating the Invitation, I accepted of it.

Those who have not seen the strange Effect of Modes will never imagine the Reception I met with at Paris, from Men and Women of all Ranks and Stations. The more I recoiled from their excessive Civilities, the more I was loaded with them. There is, however, a real Satisfaction in living at Paris from the great Number of sensible, knowing, and polite Company with which the City abounds above all places in the Universe. I thought once of settling there for Life.

I was appointed Secretary to the Embassy, and in Summer 1765, Lord Hertford left me being appointed Lord Lieutenant of Ireland. I was *chargé d'affaires*, till the Arrival of the Duke of Richmond towards the End of the Year. In the beginning of 1766, I left Paris and next summer, went to Edinburgh, with the same view as formerly of burying myself in a philosophical Retreat. I returned to that place, not richer, but with much more money and a much larger Income by means of Lord Hertford's Friendship, than I left it; and I was desirous of trying what Superfluity coud produce, as I had formerly made an Experiment of a Competency. But in 1767, I received from Mr Conway an invitation to be Under-Secretary; and this Invitation both the Character of the Person, and my Connexions with Lord Hertford, prevented me from declining. I returned to

Edinburgh in 1769, very opulent (for I possessed a Revenue of 1000 pounds a year) healthy, and though somewhat stricken in Years, with the Prospect of enjoying long my Ease and of seeing the Encrease of my Reputation.

In spring 1775, I was struck with a Disorder in my Bowels, which at first gave me no Alarm, but has since, as I apprehend it, become mortal and incurable. I now reckon upon a speedy Dissolution. I have suffered very little pain from my Disorder. I possess the same Ardor as ever in Study, and the same Gaiety in Company. I consider besides, that a Man of sixty five, by dying, cuts off only a few Years of Infirmities: And though I see many Symptoms of my literary Reputation's breaking out at last with additional Lustre, I know, that I had but few Years to enjoy it. It is difficult to be more detached from Life than I am at present.

To conclude historically with my own Character—I am, or rather was (for that is the Style, I must now use in speaking of myself; which emboldens me the more to speak my Sentiments) I was, I say, a man of mild Dispositions, of Command of Temper, of an open, social, and cheerful Humour, capable of Attachment, but little susceptible of Enmity, and of great Moderation in all my Passions. Even my Love of literary Fame, my ruling Passion, never soured my humour, notwithstanding my frequent Disappointments. My Company was not unacceptable to the young and careless, as well as to the Studious and literary: And as I took a particular Pleasure in the Company of modest women, I had no Reason to be displeased with the Reception I met with from them. In a word, though most men any wise eminent, have found reason to complain of Calumny, I never was touched, or even attacked by her baleful Tooth: And though I wantonly exposed myself to the Rage of both civil and religious Factions, they seemed to be disarmed in my behalf of their wonted Fury: My Friends never had occasion to vindicate any one Circumstance of my Character and Conduct: Not but that the Zealots, we may well suppose, wou'd have been glad to invent and propagate any Story to my Disadvantage, but they coud never find any which, they thought, would wear the Face of Probability. I cannot say, there is no Vanity in making this funeral Oration of myself; but I hope it is not a misplac'd one; and this is a Matter of Fact which is easily cleard and ascertained.

David Hume

II
ADAM SMITH TO WILLIAM STRAHAN, A LETTER ABOUT HUME'S DEATH, 1776

Kirkaldy, Fifeshire, Nov. 9, 1776.

Dear Sir,

It is with a real, though a very melancholy pleasure, that I sit down to give you some account of the behaviour of our late excellent friend, Mr Hume, during his last illness.

Though in his own judgment his disease was mortal and incurable, yet he allowed himself to be prevailed upon, by the entreaty of his friends, to try what might be the effects of a long journey. . . . Upon his return to Edinburgh, though he found himself much weaker, yet his cheerfulness never abated, and he continued to divert himself, as usual, with correcting his own works for a new edition, with reading books of amusement, with the conversation of his friends; and sometimes in the evening with a party at his favourite game of whist. His cheerfulness was so great, and his conversation and amusements ran so much in their usual strain, that notwithstanding all bad symptoms, many people could not believe he was dying. "I shall tell your friend Colonel Edmonstoune," said Dr Dundas to him one day, "that I left you much better, and in a fair way of recovery." "Doctor, said he, "as I believe you would not choose to tell any thing but the truth, you had better tell him I am dying as fast as my enemies, if I have any, could wish, and as easily and cheerfully as my best friends could desire." Colonel Edmonstoune soon afterwards came to see him, and take leave of him; and on his way home he could not forbear writing him a letter, bidding him once more an eternal adieu, and applying to him, as to a dying man, the beautiful French verses in which the Abbé Chaulieu, in expectation of his own death, laments his approaching separation from his friend, the Marquise de la Fare. Mr Hume's magnanimity and firmness were such, that his most affectionate friends knew that they hazarded nothing in talking and writing to him as to a dying man; and that so far from being hurt by this frankness, he was rather pleased and flattered by it. I happened to come into his room while he was reading this letter, which he had just received, and which he immediately showed me. I told him, that although I was sensible how very much he was weakened, and that appearances were in many respects very bad, yet his cheerfulness was still so great, the spirit of life seemed still to be so very strong in him, that I could not help entertaining some faint hopes. He answered, "Your hopes are groundless. An habitual diarrhoea of more than a year's standing would be a very bad disease at any age; at my age it is a mortal one. When I lie down in the evening I feel myself weaker than when I rose in the morning; and when I rise in the morning weaker than when I lay down in the evening. I am sensible, besides, that some of my vital parts are affected, so that I must soon die." "Well," said I, "if it must be so, you have at least the satisfaction of leaving all your friends, your brother's family in particular, in great prosperity." He said that he felt that satisfaction so sensibly, that when he was reading, a few days before, Lucian's *Dialogues of the Dead*, among all the excuses which are alleged to Charon for not entering readily into his boat, he could not find one that fitted him: he had no house to finish, he had no daughter to provide for, he had no enemies upon whom he wished to revenge himself. "I could not well imagine," said he, "what excuse I could make to Charon, in order to obtain a little delay. I have done every thing of consequence which I ever meant to do, and I could at no time expect to leave my relations and friends in a better situation than that in which I am now likely to leave them: I therefore have all reason to die contented." He then diverted himself with inventing several jocular excuses, which he supposed he might make to Charon, and with imagining the very surly answers which it might suit the character of Charon to return to them. "Upon further consideration," said he, "I thought I might say to him, 'Good Charon, I have been correcting my works for a new edition. Allow me a little time that I may see how the public receives the alterations.' But Charon would answer, 'When you have seen the effect of these, you will be for making other alterations. There will be no end of such excuses; so, honest friend, please step into the boat.' But I might still urge, 'Have a little patience, good Charon, I have been endeavouring to open the eyes of the public. If I live a few years longer, I may have the satisfaction of seeing the downfall of some of the prevailing systems of superstition.' But Charon would then lose all temper and decency. 'You loitering rogue, that will not happen these many hundred years. Do you fancy I will grant you a lease for so long a term? Get into the boat this instant, you lazy loitering rogue.' "

But though Mr Hume always talked of his approaching dissolution with great cheerfulness, he never affected to make any parade of his great magnanimity. He never mentioned the subject but when the conversation naturally led to it, and never dwelt longer upon it than the course of the conversation happened to require; it was a subject indeed which occurred pretty frequently, in consequence of the inquiries which his friends, who came to see him, naturally made concerning the state of his health.

Thus died our most excellent, and never-to-be-forgotten friend; concerning whose philosophical opinions men will no doubt judge variously, every one approving or condemning them according as they happen to coincide, or disagree with his own; but concerning whose character and conduct there can scarce be a difference of opinion. His temper, indeed, seemed to be more happily balanced, if I may be allowed such an expression, than that perhaps of any other man I have ever known. Even in the lowest state of his fortune, his great and necessary frugality never hindered him from exercising, upon proper occasions, acts both of charity and generosity. It was a frugality founded not upon avarice, but upon the love of independency. The extreme gentleness of his nature never weakened either the firmness of his mind, or the steadiness of his resolutions. His constant pleasantry was the genuine effusion of good nature and good humour, tempered with delicacy and modesty, and without even the slightest tincture of malignity, so frequently the disagreeable source of what is called wit in other men. It never was the meaning of his raillery to mortify; and therefore, far from offending, it seldom failed to please and delight even those who were the objects of it. To his friends, who were frequently the objects of it, there was not perhaps any one of all his great and amiable qualities which contributed more to endear his conversation. And that gaiety of temper, so agreeable in society, but which is so often accompanied with frivolous and superficial qualities, was in him certainly attended with the most severe application, the most extensive learning, the greatest depth of thought, and a capacity in every respect the most comprehensive. Upon the whole, I have always considered him, both in his lifetime, and since his death, as approaching as nearly to the idea of a perfectly wise and virtuous man, as perhaps the nature of human frailty will admit.

I am ever, Dear Sir,
Most affectionately yours,
ADAM SMITH

III
DAVID HUME AS AN ECONOMIST

David Hume's writings span many disiplines. Though his major work lay in philosophy, he was a political theorist, an æsthete, a sociologist and a historian, as well as an economist. Since the analysis of his economic thought requires specialized training, it has generally been treated in a compartmentalized fashion and, in consequence, it has appeared that Hume's economic writings bore little or no relationship to his philosophy.

Hume, however, framed his philosophy with the expectation that it would perform an integral function in his treatment of economics. This is evident in his *Treatise of Human Nature*, where he points out that he intends his philosophy to serve as the "capital or centre" of all the "moral (that is, psychological) sciences" and makes it clear, moreover, that he later hoped to add a treatment of these "moral sciences" (including "politics", which was meant to cover economics) to the *Treatise* itself. Owing probably to the poor reception accorded his *Treatise*, Hume left most of the treatment of these "sciences" to the many essays he was to write later. But the elements of continuity between these essays and the *Treatise* are often basic. And this is strikingly true of the economic essays. Hume, indeed, deserves recognition as the outstanding "philosopher-economist" of the eighteenth century.

What, more precisely, is the nature of the relationship between Hume's philosophy and his economic thought? The "capital or centre" of his general system of thought consisted of "principles of human nature"—the core of his philosophical analysis—or elements and relations which Hume believed to be irreducible and common to all mankind. Treated in Books 1 and 2 of the *Treatise* these comprise the analytical phase of Hume's thought. The second and synthetic phase consists of laws of human behaviour in which Hume is concerned to show how different aspects of man's behaviour are results of the impact of environmental influences on "human nature". It is these laws which make up the various "moral sciences". An emphasis on psychology is thus characteristic of Hume's treatment of economics (as for the moral sciences generally).

The role of history is similarly of fundamental importance in Hume's thought. Hume early developed an interest in history, and his last work was his pioneering *History of England*. Of special relevance here, however, is that—as a moral scientist—Hume sought to develop scientific history or, as he called it, "natural history" (the term "natural" denoting the recurrent or the probable). Here he attempted, by employing his principles of human nature, to frame historical laws, or laws which explained basic transformations in human behaviour. Such laws are to be found in many portions of his work and they are of major significance in his economic writings.

The importance of the perspective of "natural history" may be seen if Hume's economic thought is considered at three different levels of analysis.

The first is Hume's economic psychology, which links his economic thought to its "capital or centre" in the *Treatise*. Here the treatment takes the form of a natural history of "the rise and progress of commerce", in which Hume seeks to explain the economic development of his own general period in terms of the impact of changing environmental influences on specific human passions (which in the context of his economic analysis are termed "causes of labour"). Because it is based on a more general analysis of human nature, Hume's treatment is strikingly multi-dimensional. It appears so even when compared with much of the economic psychology of later periods. In addition to noting the role of the desire for consumption as an economic incentive, Hume thus stresses the importance of the desire for action itself: that is, economic activity is gratifying because it is, along with pursuits like "gaming and hunting", an interesting form of action. Action and consumption pleasures are desired, moreover, because they satisfy the desire for "liveliness", which, most generally construed, includes a desire to have and pursue wants.

Beyond this, Hume relates the desire for gain to economic activity *qua* action and treats it mainly as a desire to accumulate symbols of success in the "economic game". All these motives are integral to the expansion of economic activity. The initial stimulus which touches off the expansion process is found in the opening of international trade. In Hume's view this plays a strategic role in the growth of home industry, both because of the stimulating effects on the spirit of industry of the new and exotic items of consumption, and because of the unusual profits which, at least at the inception, can be made in international trade.

The second level of Hume's economic thought is his political economy, or his analysis of specific aspects of market relations. Here he considers several major problems of his time: monetary theory, interest theory, the issue of free trade, the shifting and incidence of taxes, and fiscal policy. In this context the perspective of natural history is seen in the nature of Hume's appraisal of the doctrines of his own time.

1. In his treatment of the quantity theory specie flow mechanism (in the famous essay, "Of the Balance of Trade") Hume's major purpose is to show that there is no basis for the mercantilist fear that, without trade restrictions, a nation would lose its money supply. Such fears are unfounded, he argues, because it is historical conditions, as reflected in a nation's level of economic development (or in its "people and industry", "skill and ingenuity" and the like), that determine the national output and hence (through the quantity theory effects) the amount of money that a nation can attract and retain.

2. The "natural history" plays an especially important role in Hume's interest theory (in the essay "Of Interest"). Here, arguing that interest is not a monetary phenomenon, Hume anticipates the later classical emphasis on the importance of real capital. But, more than this, he is concerned to show that, through its effects on the "causes of labour", it is economic development that determines the availability of real capital and hence the interest rate. In this context, all the major laws of behaviour of his natural history are introduced. In an agrarian economy, as he argues, interest rates are high because the peasants are unable to accumulate capital, while the landowners (seeking to compensate through consumption pleasures for the absence of the liveliness provided by interesting action) are typically

borrowers. An industrially expanding economy, however, provides opportunities for action in the form of "lucrative employment". This offers an alternative to consumption pleasures as a means of gratifying the desire for "liveliness" and also intensifies the desire for gain—as a symbol of success in economic pursuits. On both scores there is a growth of frugality and, as the industrial class produces and acquires more income, there is thus an increase in the supply of capital which brings down the interest rate.

3. There are some important elements of contradiction in Hume's monetary and interest theory but these inconsistencies themselves spring from Hume's attempt to stress the significance of historical considerations. Thus Hume generally uses the quantity theory to show that it is not money but economic growth that is of importance to a nation. But in the essay "Of Money" he contends that a long-run expansion of the money supply (as distinct from a larger absolute quantity of money as such) is very beneficial because, by enhancing the spirit of industry through its stimulating effects on employment, it promotes economic growth. Likewise, in his interest theory he concedes that, where the expansion of the money supply stimulates economic growth, it will reduce interest rates.

4. In his analysis of the free-trade issue, Hume anticipates the classical position—the view that free trade brings about a more effective allocation of resources and so increases real income at any given level of economic development. But again, as compared with the view of the later classical economists, his argument (specifically as contained in "Of the Jealousy of Trade") gives notably more weight to historical considerations. Meeting the mercantilist argument for trade restrictions on its own terms, he attempts to show that economic growth among nations does not involve a conflict of interest, but is essentially a harmonious and self-sustaining process. A growth of foreign industry, he argues, commonly affords new technology, which the home country can adopt, and, as it increases foreign income, it likewise increases the market for home exports. Even where the foreign expansion involves some competition with home industry, Hume argues, the stimulating effect of such competition on the home "spirit of industry" facilitates the adjustment: the home country, in virtue of its greater industriousness, can more readily divert unemployed resources to new uses. Moreover, as the nation diversifies its use of resources generally, this will reduce the employment effects of any fluctuations of demand in specific markets. It is to be noted that while, in earlier essays, Hume anticipates portions of his position in "Of the Jealousy of Trade" (which appeared six years after the other *Political Discourses*), this position is not entirely consistent with the remainder of his doctrine. Earlier, Hume had, in fact, argued that the longer-run interests of nations were fundamentally opposed —a view which probably explains his one explicit concession to the case

for tariffs. In "Of the Jealousy of Trade" itself, there is also evidence of the persistence of some of the old doubts—in particular, in Hume's awareness that industriousness alone might not be sufficient to make resource diversion easy when, because of foreign competition, a nation has lost important markets. It thus seems probable that, even in his final statement, Hume remained aware of the short and intermediate period costs of free trade but that he repudiated protectionism because he was persuaded that these costs were well outweighed by the long-run benefits to be gained from the contribution of free trade to the rate of economic growth.

5. Hume's analysis of the shifting and incidence of taxes (in the essay "Of Taxes") is concerned with the view that excises affecting labour's living costs would not be shifted because they would evoke more labour effort. The two aspects of his position here clearly reveal the relationship of his analysis to his treatment of economic growth. On the one hand, in accordance with his emphasis on the importance of the desire for action, he grants that, by creating additional difficulty (which in his "natural history" he had treated as "challenge"), taxes may evoke additional effort. On the other hand, calling attention to the importance of the desire for consumption pleasures, he argues that very high taxes (which he believed to be common in Europe) will induce despair and so reduce the labour supply.

Hume's treatment of fiscal policy (in his essay "Of Public Credit") is too lengthy to be considered in detail here. It is important to note, however, that the bulk of it takes the form of a natural history of "the rise and fall of public credit" and that Hume's analysis reveals in striking degree the breadth of his perspective as a moral scientist. In addition to a broad range of economic considerations, he discusses the effect of public debt on population movements, the level of cultural refinement and the political life of society.

The third level of Hume's economic thought is his economic philosophy, where he presents an ethical justification of a commercial and industrial society. Contained in one of the opening essays, "Of Refinement in the Arts", his treatment of this question occupies a key position in his economic thought. In view of Hume's interest in moral issues, this is not surprising. In his appraisal, Hume draws upon the utilitarian ethic, which he had earlier stated and defended in Book 3 of the *Treatise* and in his *Enquiry Concerning the Principles of Morals*, and throughout the analysis clearly exhibits the perspective of "natural history".

His discussion is concerned with the impact of economic growth both on individual happiness and on society at large. With respect to the former, the "causes of labour" (consumption pleasures, action, and liveliness) are now treated as "ends" whose attainment is promoted by the growth of economic activity; and the analysis, both in its detail and its pluralistic position on human happiness, bears a direct relation to an earlier series of essays on the "good life" entitled "The Epicurean", "The Stoic", "The Platonist", and "The Sceptic". Among all "ends", Hume accords highest priority to action (in the sense of striving in response to challenge); and when considering this in the broadest sense, as he does in "The Stoic", it is clear that he was referring to the value now commonly emphasized in justifying a free society: the striving for self-realization.

In dealing with the general social impact of economic development, Hume considers the effects on the intellectual, cultural, moral and political life of society. He contends, for example, that increases in "industry, knowledge and humanity, are linked together by an indissoluble chain", that, in economically advanced nations, political relations will be less faction-ridden, government will be more efficient and political liberty will be more fully developed. With respect to the last he argues that the economic decentralization and individualism represented in the growth of the merchant class was primarily responsible for the development of parliamentary government (a point which Adam Smith, crediting Hume, later treated as "by far the most important of all" the effects of commerce).

There is evidence that in his defence of luxury, Hume was over-indulging his distaste for the excesses of puritanism (though he calls attention to "vicious luxury"). Also, in particular respects, his knowledge of the societies of the Middle Ages (with which he compares an economically advanced society) was limited. Despite these shortcomings, Hume's economic philosophy will withstand scrutiny as an extraordinarily insightful analysis of the moral foundations of a free society.

During Hume's time, others had given attention to the psychological and historical aspects of economic activity; and it may be presumed that Hume drew upon these portions of the literature—as he doubtless drew upon the more general and largely philosophical writings of the period—in developing his own position. However, Hume's treatment is distinguished by the scope and penetration of his economic psychology, his perception of the relationships between various aspects of economic development and, perhaps most important, by the extensive and systematic use which he made of psychology and history as the basis for the analysis of the major issues of his period. If, as has been said, the "natural history" of the eighteenth century (which in various ways is found in other writings of the period) constituted a serious effort to establish the foundations for a scientific study of man, then Hume's economic thought represents an unusually striking example of this approach.

The distinctiveness of Hume's treatment is apparent in a comparison of his economic thought with the work of Adam Smith, his close friend, who also came to economics from philosophy. Though there is much historical and psychological material in Smith's *Wealth of Nations*, most of it is particularistic rather than of a general theoretical nature. Moreover, general behaviour patterns, which in Hume's treatment appear as historical variables, are regarded as universal by Smith. Also important in a comparison of the two men is the greater emphasis Hume accords to historical conditions in his treatment of the free-trade issue. Of the two, Hume's approach was generally the more genetic and evolutionary. This would hold *a fortiori* when Hume is compared with the later classical economists who, far more than Smith, stressed the static aspects of economics involved in the questions of value and distribution (to which Hume gives relatively little attention).

Since the eighteenth century, many economists have given a prominent place to the psychological and historical aspects of economic activity. The "historical" and "institutional" schools of the nineteenth and twentieth centuries are illustrative cases. Other parallels are to be found in the contemporary literature, which, after intensive elaboration of the "orthodox" phases of the field, has increasingly reflected an interest in broadening the scope of economic inquiry. This is apparent in the revived interest in economic development (a product of the concern with under-developed economies), in the more intensive analysis of the psychology underlying aggregative behaviour (an offshoot of the interest in the problem of full employment), in the greater attention given the psychology of individual units and collective entities (including business organizations and trade unions) and in the interest in alternative economic systems, which has been prompted by the relative rapidity of institutional change in recent years and which has required more explicit consideration of questions of a normative and historical character.

Eugène Rotwein

SOURCES

Essay I

David Hume, *My Own Life*, ed. Adam Smith (London, 1777). Reproduced from *The Letters of David Hume*, I, ed. J. Y. T. Greig (Clarendon Press, Oxford, 1932).

Essay II

Adam Smith to William Strahan, a Letter about Hume's Death, 1776: reproduced from *The Letters of David Hume*, II, ed. J. Y. T. Greig (Clarendon Press, Oxford, 1932).

Essay III

Eugène Rotwein, "David Hume as an Economist", previously unpublished paper.

Signature

National Library of Scotland, Edinburgh.

Portrait

Portrait painted by Allan Ramsay, 1766, engraved in mezzotint by David Martin, 1767. (Scottish National Portrait Gallery, Edinburgh.)

BIBLIOGRAPHY

J. H. Burton, *Life and Correspondence of David Hume* (Edinburgh, 1846).
A. Schatz, *L'oeuvre économique de David Hume* (Paris, 1902).
T. H. Huxley, *Hume* (London, 1879).
R. Metz, *David Hume, Leben und Philosophie* (Stuttgart, 1929).
J. Y. T. Greig, *David Hume* (London, 1931).
T. E. Jessop, *A Bibliography of David Hume and of Scottish Philosophy from Francis Hutcheson to Lord Balfour* (London and Hull, 1938).
M. dal Pra, *David Hume* (Milan, 1949).
N. K. Smith, *The Philosophy of David Hume: A Critical Study of its Origins and Central Doctrines* (London, 1949).
E. C. Mossner, *The Life of David Hume* (Austin, 1954).
J. B. Stewart, *The Moral and Political Philosophy of David Hume* (New York, 1963).
E. Rotwein, "David Hume" in *International Encyclopedia of the Social Sciences*, Vol. 6 (New York, 1968).

ADAM SMITH

1723–1790

In almost every relation of life Adam Smith was fortunate. He had the gift of inspiring friendship in those whose affection was most worth having. As far as it counted with him, his connections amongst influential people were both numerous and important. There was a particularly close and tender tie between him and his mother, and he was blessed in that she was spared to be with him till very near to the end of his life. In one direction he failed. None of the ladies he sought in marriage (for there appear to have been more than one) accepted him.

W. R. SCOTT

To be sure, the amateur never appreciates the nuances of Smith's position: his scepticism about the businessman's passion for tough competition; his definite role for limited government; his general pragmatism rather than dogmatism.

P. A. SAMUELSON

The student who learns to love his quiet wit and keen but gentle observation of humanity will never degenerate into a narrow-minded specialist.

K. E. BOULDING

The Treatise on the Law of War and Peace, the Essay on the Human Understanding, the Spirit of Laws, and the Inquiry into the Causes of the Wealth of Nations, are the works which have most directly influenced the general opinion of Europe during the two last centuries. They are also the most conspicuous land-marks in the progress of the sciences of which they relate. It is remarkable that the defects of all these great works are very similar. The leading notions of none of them can, in the strictest sense, be said to be original, though Locke and Smith in that respect surpass their illustrious rivals. . . . None of them are happy in the choice, or constant in the use of technical terms; and in none do we find much of that rigorous precision which is the first beauty of philosophical language. . . . Locke and Smith chose an easy, clear, and free but somewhat loose and verbose, style—more concise in Locke, more elegant in Smith—in both exempt from pedantry, but not void of ambiguity and repetition. Perhaps all these apparent defects contributed in some degree to the specific usefulness of these great works; and, by rendering their contents more accessible to the majority of readers, have more completely blended their principles with the common opinions of mankind.

SIR JAMES MACKINTOSH *on the works of Grotius, Locke, Montesquieu and Smith*

I
LIFE OF ADAM SMITH

Adam Smith was born at Kirkcaldy, in the county of Fife, Scotland, on 5 June 1723.[1] He was the son of Adam Smith, Writer to the Signet, Judge Advocate for Scotland and Comptroller of the Customs in the Kirkcaldy district, by Margaret, daughter of John Douglas of Strathendry, a considerable landed proprietor in the same county.[2]

Smith's father died in the spring of 1723, a few months before his famous son was born.

His mother[3] was from first to last the heart of Smith's life. He being an only child, and she an only parent, they had been everything to one another during his infancy and boyhood, and after he was full of years and honours her presence was the same shelter to him as it was when a boy. His friends often spoke of the beautiful affection and worship with which he cherished her. He was a delicate child, and afflicted even in childhood with those fits of absence and that habit of speaking to himself which he carried all through life.[4]

As he grew up in boyhood his health became stronger, and he was in due time sent to the Burgh School of Kirkcaldy, one of the best secondary

[1] This is the date of the baptism; we do not know the actual date of Smith's birth.

[2] Of his father little is known. He was a native of Aberdeen, and his people must have been in a position to make interest in influential quarters, for we find him immediately after his admission to the Society of Writers to the Signet in 1707, appointed to the newly established office of Judge-Advocate for Scotland, and in the following year to the post of Private Secretary to the Secretary of State for Scotland, the Earl of Loudoun. When he lost this post in consequence of Lord Loudoun's retirement from office in 1713, he was provided for with the Comptrollership of Customs at Kirkcaldy, which he continued to hold, along with the Judge-Advocateship, till his premature death in 1723.

[3] On the mother's side his kindred were much connected with the army. His uncle, Robert Douglas of Strathendry, and three of his uncle's sons were military officers, and so was his cousin, Captain Skene, the laird of the neighbouring estate of Pitlour.

[4] Scott interprets Smith's habit of absence of mind and of speaking to himself as an early sign of intense powers of concentration.

schools of Scotland at that period. Its principal master, Mr David Millar, had the name of being one of the best schoolmasters of his day. When Smith first went to school we cannot say, but it seems probable that he began Latin in 1733, for *Eutropius* is the text-book of a beginner in Latin, and the *Eutropius* which Smith used as a text-book still exists, and contains his signature with the date of that year. As he left school in 1737, he thus had at least four years' training in the classics before he proceeded to university.

A small town like Kirkcaldy—it had then only 1,500 inhabitants—is a not unfavourable observatory for beginning one's knowledge of the world. It has more sorts and conditions of men to exhibit than a rural district can furnish, and it exhibits each more completely in all their ways, pursuits, troubles, characters, than can possibly be done in a city. Smith, who despite his absence of mind was always an excellent observer, would grow up in the knowledge of all about everybody in that little place.

At school Smith was marked for his studious disposition, his love of reading, and his power of memory; and by the age of fourteen he had advanced sufficiently in classics and mathematics to be sent to Glasgow College, with a view to obtaining a Snell exhibition[5] to Oxford.

Smith entered Glasgow College in 1737, no doubt in October, when the session began, and he remained there till the spring of 1740. The arts curriculum at that time extended over five sessions, so that Smith did not complete the course required for a degree.[6] In the three sessions he attended he would go through the classes of Latin, Greek, mathematics, and moral philosophy, and have thus listened to the lectures of the three eminent teachers who were then drawing students to this little western college from the most distant quarters, and keeping its courts alive with a remarkable intellectual activity. These three were Alexander Dunlop, professor of Greek, a man of fine scholarship and taste, and an unusually engaging method of instruction; Robert Simson, the professor of Mathematics, an original if eccentric genius, who enjoyed a European reputation as the restorer of the geometry of the ancients; and above all, Francis Hutcheson, a thinker of great original power, and an unrivalled academic lecturer.

The most powerful and enduring influence he came under at Glasgow was undoubtedly that of Hutcheson—"the never-to-be-forgotten Hutcheson". No other man, indeed, whether teacher or writer, did so much to awaken Smith's mind or give a bent to his ideas. He is sometimes considered a disciple of Hume and sometimes considered a disciple of Quesnay; if he

[5] This was a very valuable scholarship, being four or five times as much as most others of the time.

[6] Scott corrects Rae's statement. According to new information, Smith completed his course for the MA degree with great distinction and graduated.

was any man's disciple, he was Hutcheson's, who was one of the most impressive lecturers that ever spoke from an academic chair. Smith left Scotland for Oxford in June 1740, riding the whole way on horseback.

He matriculated at the University on 7 July as *Adamus Smith e Coll. Ball, Gen. Fil. Jul. 7mo 1740*. He himself said that literary composition never grew easier to him with experience; neither apparently did handwriting. His letters are all written in the same big round characters, connected together manifestly by a slow, difficult, deliberate process.

He remained at Oxford till 15 August 1746; but up till that day he resided at Oxford continuously from the time of his matriculation. He did not leave between terms, and was thus six years on end away from home.

His studies took a new turn at Oxford; he laid aside the mathematics for which he showed a liking at Glasgow, and gave his strength to the ancient Latin and Greek classics, possibly for no better reason than he could get nobody at Oxford to take the trouble of teaching him the former and that the Balliol library furnished him with the means of cultivating the latter by himself. He did so, moreover, to some purpose, for all through life he showed a knowledge of Greek and Latin literature not only uncommonly extensive but uncommonly exact.

There was only one fruit in the garden of which he might not freely eat, and that was the produce of modern rationalism. A story has come down that he was one day detected reading Hume's *Treatise of Human Nature*—probably the very copy presented him by the author at the apparent suggestion of Hutcheson—and was punished by a severe reprimand and the confiscation of the evil book. It is at least entirely consistent with all we know of the spirit of darkness then ruling in Oxford that it should be considered an offence of peculiar aggravation for a student to read a great work of modern thought which had been actually placed in his hands by his professor at Glasgow.

In returning to Scotland Smith's ideas were probably fixed from the first on a Scotch university chair as an eventual acquisition, but he decided in the meantime to obtain a travelling tutorship with a young man of rank and wealth, then a much-desired and, according to the standard of the times, a highly remunerated occupation; later he gave up his chair to take such employment with the Duke of Buccleugh.[7] While casting about for a place of that kind he stayed at home with his mother in Kirkcaldy, and he had to remain there without any regular employment for two full years, from the autumn of 1746 till the autumn of 1748.

The appointment never came; because from his absent manner and bad

[7] Such a tutorship of a young nobleman was at that time a recognized avenue to a University professorship or to other positions suitable to a person with some considerable scholarship.

address, we are told, he seemed to the ordinary parental mind a most unsuitable person to be entrusted with the care of spirited and perhaps thoughtless young gentlemen. But the visits he paid to Edinburgh in pursuit of this work bore fruit by giving him quite as good a start in life, and a much shorter cut to the professorial position for which he was best fitted.

During the winter of 1748–9 he made a most successful beginning as a public lecturer by delivering a course on the then comparatively untried subject of English literature. Smith seems at this early period of his life to have had dreams of some day figuring as a poet himself.

Besides his lectures on English literature, which he delivered for three successive winters, he delivered at least one winter a course on economics; and in this course, written in the year 1749, and delivered in 1750–1, Smith advocated the doctrines of commercial liberty on which he was nurtured by Hutcheson, and which he was afterwards to do so much to advance. He states this fact himself in a paper read before a learned society in Glasgow in 1755, which afterwards fell into the hands of Dugald Stewart, and from which Stewart extracts a passage or two. They certainly contain a plain enough statement of the doctrine of natural liberty.

The Edinburgh lectures soon bore fruit. On the death of Mr Loudon, Professor of Logic in Glasgow College, in 1750, Smith was appointed to the vacant chair, and so began that period of thirteen years of active academic work which he always looked back upon, he tells us, "as by far the most useful and therefore by far the happiest and most honourable period" of his life.

Smith was appointed Craigie's successor on 27 November 1751 and took up the post on 29 April 1752.

His characteristics as a lecturer are thus described by Millar (Smith's pupil and, later, colleague, when he held the chair of jurisprudence): "There was no situation in which the abilities of Mr. Smith appeared to greater advantage than as a professor. In delivering his lectures he trusted almost entirely to extemporary elocution. His manner, though not graceful, was plain and unaffected, and as he seemed to be always interested in the subject, he never failed to interest his hearers. Each discourse consisted commonly of several distinct propositions, which he successively endeavoured to prove and illustrate. These propositions when announced in general terms had, from their extent, not unfrequently something of the air of a paradox. In his attempts to explain them, he often appeared at first not to be sufficiently possessed of the subject, and spoke with some hesitation. As he advanced, however, his manner became warm and animated, and his expression easy and fluent. On points susceptible of controversy you could easily discern that he secretly conceived an opposition to his opinions, and that he was led upon this account to support them with greater energy and vehemence. By the fulness and variety of his illustrations the subject gradually swelled in his hands and acquired a dimension which, without a tedious repetition of the same views, was calculated to seize the attention of his audience, and to afford them pleasure as well as instruction in following the same subject through all the diversity of shades and aspects in which it was presented, and afterwards in tracing it backwards to that original proposition or general truth from which this beautiful train of speculation had proceeded."

Smith's popularity as a lecturer grew year by year. His opinions became the subject of general discussion, the topics he lectured on became fashionable in the town, the sons of the wealthier citizens used to go to the College to take his class though they had no intention of completing a university course, stucco busts of him appeared in booksellers' windows, and the very peculiarities of his voice and pronunciation received the homage of imitation. Long before the publication of the *Wealth of Nations*, therefore, the new light was shining clearly from Smith's chair in Glasgow College, and winning its first converts in the practical world. One can accordingly well understand the emotion with which J. B. Say sat in this chair when he visited Glasgow in 1815. Dugald Stewart states, on the authority of students in the moral philosophy class at Glasgow in 1752 or 1753 that Smith delivered as early as that lectures containing the fundamental principles of the *Wealth of Nations*; and in 1755—the year Cantillon's *Essai* first saw the light and the year before Quesnay published his first writings on economics—Smith was not only expounding his system of natural liberty to his students, but publicly asserting his claim to the authorship of that system in a Glasgow economics society—perhaps the first such society established anywhere.

During his residence in Glasgow Smith continued to maintain intimate relations with his old friends in Edinburgh.

His chief friend in Edinburgh was David Hume. Though their first relations were begun apparently in 1739, they could not have met much personally before Smith's settlement in Glasgow. Before Smith was a year in Glasgow he had already entered on that correspondence with the elder philosopher which, beginning with the respectful "Dear sir", grew shortly into the warmer style of "My dearest friend" as their memorable and Roman friendship ripened. Hume never paid Smith a visit in Glasgow, though he had often promised to do so, but Smith on his trips to Edinburgh spent more and more of his time with Hume, and latterly at any rate made Hume's house his regular Edinburgh home.

Smith enjoyed a very high Scots reputation long before his name was known to the great public by any contribution to literature. But in 1759 he gave his *Theory of Moral Sentiments* to the press, and took his place, by almost immediate and universal recognition, in the first rank of contemporary writers. The book is an essay supporting and illustrating the doctrine that moral approbation and disapprobation are in the last analysis expressions of sympathy with the feelings of an imaginary and impartial spectator, and its substance had already been given from year to year in his ordinary lectures to his students, though after its publication he thought it no longer necessary to dwell at the same length on this branch of his course, giving more time, no doubt, to jurisprudence and political economy.

Hume wrote to Smith from Edinburgh on 9 August 1763 intimating his appointment as Secretary to the English Embassy at Paris, and bidding him adieu. When Hume arrived in France the first letter he wrote to any of his friends at home was to Smith. Hume's hope of their "not impossible" meeting in Paris was destined to be gratified sooner than he could have conjectured. A few days before Smith received this letter from Hume he had received likewise a letter from Charles Townshend, intimating that the time had now come for the Duke of Buccleugh to go abroad and renewing to Smith the offer of the post of travelling tutor to his Grace.

Smith accepted the offer. The terms were a salary of £300 a year, with travelling expenses while abroad, and a pension of £300 a year for life afterwards. He was thus to have twice his Glasgow income, and to have it assured till death. The pension was no doubt a principal inducement to a Scotch professor in those days to take such a post, for a Scotch professor had then no resource in his old age except the price he happened to receive for his chair from his successor in the event of his resignation.

Smith joined his pupil in London in the end of January 1764, and they set out together for France in the beginning of February. They remained abroad two years and a half—ten days in Paris, eighteen months in Toulouse, two months travelling in the South of France, two months in Geneva, and ten months in Paris again. Smith kept no journal[8] and wrote as few letters as possible, but we are able from various sources to fill in some of the outlines of their course of travel. He probably could not as yet speak French, for even to the last he could only speak it very imperfectly.

Paris was merely a halting-place for the present; their immediate destination was Toulouse, at that time a favourite resort of the English.

At the end of August, Smith and his pupils left Toulouse and made what Stewart calls an extensive tour in the South of France. Smith told Rogers he had been in Voltaire's company on five or six different occasions, and he no doubt enjoyed, as most English visitors enjoyed, hospitable entertainment at Ferney, the beautiful little temporality of the great literary pontiff, overlooking the lake. There was no living name before which Smith bowed with profounder veneration than the name of Voltaire, and

[8] Scott denies this statement also made by Dugald Stewart.

his recollections of their intercourse on these occasions were always among those he cherished most warmly.

Smith left Geneva in December for Paris, where he arrived, according to Dugald Stewart, about Christmas 1765. Before leaving, Hume would have time to introduce his friend to the famous men of Paris itself, and to initiate him into those literary and fashionable circles in which he had moved like a demigod for the preceding two years. The *philosophe* was then king in Paris, and Hume was king of the *philosophes*, and everything that was great in court or salon fell down and did him obeisance.

Smith went more into society in the few months he resided in Paris than at any other period of his life. He was a regular guest in almost all the famous literary salons of that time—Baron d'Holbach's,[9] Helvetius', Madame de Geoffrin's, Comtesse de Boufflers', Mademoiselle l'Espinasse's,[10] and probably Madame Necker's. He was a constant visitor at Madame Riccoboni the novelist's. He attended the meetings of the new economist sect in the apartments of Dr Quesnay, and, though the economic dinners of the elder Mirabeau, the "Friend of Man", were not begun for a year after, he no doubt visited the Marquis, as we know he visited other members of the fraternity. He went to Compiègne when the Court removed to Compiègne, made frequent excursions to interesting places within reach, and was always seen with troops of friends about him.

He often met Turgot, as indeed he did everywhere he went, and of all the friends he met in France there was none in whose society he took more pleasure, or for whose mind and character he formed a profounder admiration, than that great thinker and statesman.

If his conversation with Morellet ran mainly on political and economic subjects, it would most probably run even more largely on such subjects with Turgot, for they were both at the moment busy writing their most important works on those subjects. He was in a position to meet Turgot on equal terms, and give full value for anything he might take, and if obligations must needs be assessed and the balance adjusted, who shall say whether Smith owes most to the conversation of Turgot or Turgot owes most to the conversation of Smith? Smith, with all his admiration for Turgot, thought him too simple-hearted for a practical statesman, too prone, as noble natures often are, to underrate the selfishness, stupidity and prejudice that prevail in the world and resist the course of just and rational

[9] The usual guests were the *philosophes* and encyclopaedists and men of letters—Diderot, Marmontel, Raynal, Galiani. The conversation ran largely towards metaphysics and theology, and, as Morellet, who was often there, states, the boldest theories were propounded, and things spoken which might well call down fire from heaven.

[10] Here Smith met with Turgot, D'Alembert, Grimm, Condillac and Gibbon.

reform. He described Turgot to Samuel Rogers as an excellent person, very honest and well-meaning, but so unacquainted with the world and human nature that it was a maxim with him, as he had himself told David Hume, that whatever is right may be done.

Madame Riccoboni was not the only Frenchwoman who was touched with Smith's personal charms; we hear of another, a marquise, "a woman too of talents and wit", who actually fell in love with him. She had just come (to Abbéville, where Smith's party was) from Paris, where she found all the world talking about Hume, and having heard that Smith was Hume's particular friend and almost as great a philosopher as he, she was bent on making so famous a conquest, but after many persistent efforts was obliged eventually to abandon the attempt. Her philosopher could not endure her, nor could he—and this greatly amused his own party—conceal his embarrassment; but it was not philosophy altogether that steeled his breast. The truth, according to Lloyd,[11] was that the philosopher was deeply in love with another, an English lady, who was also stopping in Abbéville at the time.

The Earl of Buchan says that Smith had no ear for music, but there are few things he seems to have nevertheless enjoyed better than the opera, both serious and comic.

Amid all this gaiety of salons and playhouses Smith found a graver retreat with the philanthropic sect of economists in the apartments of the King's physician, Dr Quesnay, in Paris and Versailles. Dupont de Nemours told J. B. Say that he had often met Smith at their little meetings, and that they looked on him as a judicious and simple man, and apparently nothing more, for, he adds, Smith had not at that time shown the stuff he was made of.

Arriving in London early in November 1766, Smith seems to have remained on in the capital for the next six months. Smith was publishing with Miller at this time a new edition of his *Theory of Moral Sentiments*—the third—which appeared in 1767, containing, like the second, the addition of the *Dissertation upon the Origin of Languages*. One of his reasons for staying so long in London this winter was no doubt to see the sheets through the press.

When Smith left Glasgow his mother and cousin went back again to Kirkcaldy, and he now joined them and remained with them there for the next eleven years.

Hume, who thought the country an unsuitable place for a man of letters, used every endeavour to persuade him to remove to Edinburgh, but without success. The gaiety and fullness of city life were evidently much less to him than they were to Hume, and he must have found what sufficed him

[11] Captain Lloyd, a retired officer and intimate friend of Smith's.

in the little town of his birth. He had his work, he had his mother, he had his books, he had his daily walks in the sea breeze, and he had Edinburgh always in the offing as a place of occasional resort. He is said to have taken much real pleasure, like Shakespeare at Stratford, in mingling again with the simple old folk who were about him in his youth, and he had a few neighbours whose pursuits corresponded more nearly with his own.

In the spring of 1773, Smith, having, as he thought, virtually completed the *Wealth of Nations*, set out with the manuscript for London, to give it perhaps some finishing touches and then place it in the hands of a publisher. But his labours had told so seriously on his health and spirits that he thought it not improbable he might die, and even die suddenly, before the work got through the press, and he wrote Hume a formal letter before he started on his journey, constituting him his literary executor, and giving him directions about the destination of the various unpublished manuscripts that lay in his depositories. Smith went to London shortly after writing this letter, and spent most of the next four years there. He was admitted to the Royal Society on 27 May 1773.

Much of the book as we know it must have been written in London. When he went up to London he had no idea that any fresh investigations he contemplated instituting there would detain him so long.[12]

The *Inquiry into the Nature and Causes of the Wealth of Nations* was at length published on 9 March 1776. Bishop Horne,[13] one of Smith's antagonists said the books which live longest are those which have been carried longest in the womb of the parent. The *Wealth of Nations* took

[12] Scott treats the problem of Smith's independence and the charge of plagiarism in the light of new information. On the first problem he writes: "Increasing knowledge of Adam Smith's life and surroundings has led to a revision of the views of his relation to the Physiocrats which have been held from Dugald Stewart to Thorold Rogers. Since 1895–6, when Professor Cannan identified, and accepted as authentic, the manuscript copy of a student's notes of the 'Lectures on Justice', opinion has moved in the opposite direction towards an increasing recognition of Adam Smith's independence. That movement should be reinforced almost as much by the discovery of what has been called 'an early draft of *The Wealth of Nations*' as by that of the *Glasgow Lectures*. For it is highly significant that the chief points which Cannan indicated as having been obtained by Adam Smith from intercourse with the Physiocrats are to be found, if in a partially developed form, in the recently discovered draft." Scott gives reasons "which show that it is most unlikely he was acquainted with any of the characteristic writings of the Physiocrats before he went to France". And he continues: "Now that the manuscript Catalogue of his library as it was in 1781, which is at Tokyo, can be collated with Dr Bonar's *Library of Adam Smith*, it is possible to speak with more confidence since we have the list of all his books at a period subsequent to the publication of *The Wealth of Nations*."

[13] Dr George Horne, President of Magdalen College, Oxford, Bishop of Norwich.

twelve years to write, and was in contemplation for probably twelve years before that. The book sold well. The first edition, of whose extent, however, we are ignorant, was exhausted in six months.

One of the first of these was, of course, sent to his old friend David Hume. He acknowledged receipt of it in a letter, which shows among other things that not even Hume had seen the manuscript of the book before publication.

Smith probably remained most of the year 1777 in London, for, as we have seen, one of his reasons for being there was to see the second edition of his work through the press, and the second edition of his work did not appear till 1778. But he was back in Kirkcaldy again before December, and while there he received from Lord North the appointment of Commissioner of Customs in Scotland. The offence he unexpectedly gave to the world's religious sensibilities by his account of Hume's[14] last days had not interfered, as he feared such an offence would, with his prospects of employment in the public service, nor, what is quite as remarkable, had his political opinions. For he was always a strong Whig, and the preferment was bestowed by a Tory ministry. It is usually attributed to the influence of the Duke of Buccleugh and Henry Dundas, then a member of the ministry as Lord Advocate for Scotland, and their word may no doubt have helped; but there is reason to believe that the appointment was really a direct reward to the author of the *Wealth of Nations* for the benefit Lord North, who was Chancellor of the Exchequer as well as Prime Minister, derived from that book in preparing the budgets for the years 1777 and 1778.

The appointment was worth £600 a year—£500 for the Commissionership of Customs and £100 for the Commissionership of the Salt Duties; and Smith still retained his pension of £300 from the House of Buccleugh. When he obtained this place he thought himself bound in honour to give up his Buccleugh pension, possibly because of the assistance he may have believed the Duke to have given in securing it; but he was informed that the pension was meant to be permanent and unconditional, and that if he were consulting his own honour in offering to give it up, he was not thinking of the honour of the Duke of Buccleugh.

On settling in Edinburgh Smith took a house in the Canongate—Panmure House. This house was his home for the rest of his days, and in it he died.

Smith brought over his mother and his cousin, Miss Douglas, from Kirkcaldy, and a few months later the youngest son of his cousin, Colonel Douglas of Strathendry, who was to attend school and college with a view to the bar, and whom he made his heir. Smith's house was noted for its

[14] His great work had not yet (1777) attracted much public notice. However, its merits were being fully recognized by the learned, and it was already leaving its mark on the budget of the year.

simple and unpretending hospitality. He liked to have his friends about him without the formality of an invitation, and few strangers of distinction visited Edinburgh without being entertained in Panmure House.[15]

His mother, his friends, his books—these were Smith's three great joys. He had a library of about 3000 volumes, as varied a collection in point of subject-matter as it would be possible to find.[16]

Smith attended his duties with uncommon diligence. His friends were perhaps right in lamenting that the duties of this office, light though they really were, used up his time and energy too completely to permit his application to the great work on government which he had projected. The principal materials of the works which he had announced had been long ago collected, as Dugald Stewart says, and little probably was wanting but a few years of health and retirement to bestow on them that systematical arrangement in which he delighted.

Besides, the work of composition seems to have grown really more arduous to him. He was always a slow writer, and had never acquired increased facility from increased practice.

Much of his time too was now given to the enjoyments of friendship. I have already mentioned his Sunday suppers, but besides these he founded, soon after settling in Edinburgh, in cooperation with the two friends who were his closest associates during the whole of this last period of his career—Black the chemist, and Hutton the geologist—a weekly dining club.[17] This friendship of Smith, Black and Hutton, if not so famous as the friendship between Smith and Hume, was not less really memorable. Each of them had founded—or done more than any other single person to found—a science; they may be called the fathers of modern chemistry, of modern geology, and of modern political economy; and for all their great achievements, they were yet men of the most unaffected simplicity of character. In other respects they were very different from one another, but their

[15] Smith was of medium height, well-built but not corpulent, with erect figure, well-set head, and large grey or light blue eyes, which are said to have beamed with "inexpressible benignity". He dressed well—so well that nobody seems to have remarked it; for while we hear, on the one hand, of Hume's black-spotted yellow coat and Gibbon's flowered velvet, and on the other, of Hulton's battered attire and Henry Erskine's grey hat with the torn rim, we meet with no allusion to Smith's dress either for fault or merit.

[16] Mr James Bonar has been able to collect a list of probably two-thirds of Smith's books—about 1000 titles, or 2200 volumes. Nearly a third of the whole are in French, another third in Latin, Greek, and Italian, and a little more than a third in English. According to Mr Bonar's analysis, a fifth of them were on literature and art; a fifth were Latin and Greek classics; a fifth on law, politics and biography; a fifth on political economy and history; and the remaining fifth on science and philosophy.

[17] Its name was the Oyster Club.

differences only knit them close together, and made them more interesting to their friends.

Smith's new duties did not pre-engage his pen from higher work altogether, for before the close of 1782 he had written some considerable additions to the *Wealth of Nations*, which he proposed to insert in the third edition, among them a history of the trading companies of Great Britain, including, no doubt, his history of the East India Company.

Burke had been elected Lord Rector of the University of Glasgow in November 1783 in succession to Dundas, and he came down to Scotland to be installed in the following April. He spent altogether eight or ten days in the country, and he spent them all in the company of Smith, who attended him wherever he went. Burke and Smith, always profound admirers of one another's writings, had grown warm friends during the recent lengthened residence of the latter in London.

After being brightened by the agreeable visit of Burke, Smith was presently cast into the deepest sadness by what seems to have been the first trouble of his singularly serene and smooth life—the death of his mother. She died on 23 May 1784 in her ninetieth year. They had lived together, off and on, for sixty years, and being most tenderly attached to her, he is said, after her death, never to have seemed the same again.

In April 1787 he had improved enough to undertake the journey to London to consult Hunter, but he was wasted to a skeleton. William Playfair—brother of his friend, the Professor of Mathematics, and afterwards one of the early editors of the *Wealth of Nations*—met him soon after his arrival in London, and says he was looking very ill, and was evidently going to decay.

No one in London was more interested to meet Smith than Pitt, the young minister who was carrying the economist's principles out so extensively in practical legislation. They met repeatedly, but they met on one occasion, of which recollection has been preserved, at Dundas's house on Wimbledon Green—Addington, Wilberforce and Grenville being also of the company; and it is said that when Smith, who was one of the last guests to arrive, entered the room, the whole company rose from their seats to receive him and remained standing. "Be seated, gentlemen," said Smith. "No", replied Pitt, "we will stand till you are first seated, for we are all your scholars."

Soon after his return to Edinburgh Smith received another, and to him a very touching, recognition of his merit in being chosen in November Lord Rector of his old *alma mater*, the University of Glasgow. The appointment lay with the whole University, professors and students together.[18]

[18] On receiving intimation of his appointment Smith wrote to Principal Davidson the following reply (abridged): Reverend and dear Sir, I have this

He was installed as Rector on 12 December 1787 with the usual ceremonies. He gave no inaugural address, nor apparently so much as a formal word of thanks. Smith, like Burke and Dundas, was re-elected for a second term, and was Rector therefore from November 1787 till November 1789.

Smith's health appears to have improved so much during the spring of 1788 that his friends, who had been seriously alarmed about his condition, were now again free from anxiety. He seemed to them to be "perfectly re-established". But in the autumn he suffered another great personal loss in the death of his cousin, Miss Jean Douglas, who had lived under his roof for so many years. His home was now desolate. Being a man for whom the domestic affections went for so much, there seemed, amid all the honour, love, obedience, troops of friends that enrich the close of an important career, to remain a void in his life that could not be filled.

A revision of the *Theory of Moral Sentiments* was a task Smith had long had in contemplation. The book had been thirty years before the world and had passed through five editions, but it had never undergone any revision or alteration whatever. This was the task of the last year of the author's life. He made considerable changes, especially by way of addition, and though he wrote the additions, as Stewart informs us, while he was suffering under severe illness, he has never written anything better in point of literary style.

Long and painful as his illness was, he bore it throughout not with patience merely but with a serene and even cheerful resignation.

When Smith felt his end to be approaching he evinced great anxiety to have all his papers destroyed except the few which he judged to be in a sufficiently finished state to deserve publication, and, being apparently too feeble to undertake the task himself, he repeatedly begged his friends Black and Hutton to destroy them for him. When the sixteen volumes of manuscript were burnt Smith's mind seemed to be greatly relieved. It appears to have been on a Sunday, and when his friends came, as they were accustomed

moment received the honour of your letter of the 15th instant. I accept with gratitude and pleasure the very great honour which the University of Glasgow have done me in electing me for the ensuing year to be the Rector of that illustrious Body. No preferment could have given me so much real satisfaction. No man can own greater obligations to a Society that I do to the University of Glasgow. They educated me, they sent me to Oxford, soon after my return to Scotland they elected me one of their own members, and afterwards preferred me to another office to which the abilities and virtues of the never-to-be-forgotten Dr Hutcheson had given a superior degree of illustration. The period of thirteen years which I spent as a member of that Society, I remember as by far the most useful and therefore as by far the happiest and most honourable period of my life; and now, after three-and-twenty years' absence, to be remembered in so very agreeable a manner by my old friends and protectors gives me a heart-felt joy which I cannot easily express to you.

to do, on the Sunday evening to supper—and they seem to have mustered strongly on this particular evening—he was able to receive them with something of his usual cheerfulness.

That was his last meeting with them in the earthly meeting-place. He had gone to the other world before the next Sunday came round, having died on Saturday, 17 July 1790. He was buried in the Canongate churchyard. The grave is marked by an unpretentious monument, stating that Adam Smith, the author of the *Wealth of Nations*, lies buried there.

By his will, dated 6 February 1790, he left his whole property to his cousin, David Douglas, afterwards Lord Reston, subject to the condition that the legatee should follow the instructions of Black and Hutton in disposing of the manuscripts and writings, and pay an annuity of £20 a year to Mrs Janet Douglas, and after her death, a sum of £400 to Professor Hugh Cleghorn of St Andrews and his wife. The property Smith left, however, was very moderate, and his friends could not at first help expressing some surprise that it should have been so little, because, though known to be very hospitable, he had never maintained anything more than a moderate establishment. But they had not then known, though many of them had long suspected, that he often gave large sums in secret to charity.

John Rae

II
CHARACTER AND HABITS OF ADAM SMITH

The more delicate and characteristical features of his mind it is perhaps impossible to trace. That there were many peculiarities, both in his manners and in his intellectual habits, was manifest to the most superficial observer; but although, to those who knew him, these peculiarities detracted nothing from the respect which his abilities commanded; and although, to his intimate friends, they added an inexpressible charm to his conversation, while they displayed, in the most interesting light, the artless simplicity of his heart; yet it would require a very skilful pencil to present them to the public eye. He was certainly not fitted for the general commerce of the world, or for the business of active life. The comprehensive speculations with which he had been occupied from his youth, and the variety of materials which his own invention continually supplied to his thoughts, rendered him habitually inattentive to familiar objects, and to common occurrences; and he frequently exhibited instances of absence, which had scarcely been surpassed by the fancy of La Bruyère. Even in company he was apt to be engrossed with his studies; and appeared at times, by the motion of his lips, as well as by his looks and gestures, to be in the fervour of composition. I have often, however, been struck, at the distance of years, with his accurate memory of the most trifling particulars; and am inclined to believe, from this and some other circumstances, that he possessed a power, not perhaps uncommon among absent men, of recollecting, in consequence of subsequent efforts of reflection, many occurrences which, at the time when they happened, did not seem to have sensibly attracted his notice.

To the defect now mentioned, it was probably owing, in part, that he did not fall in easily with the common dialogue of conversation, and that he was somewhat apt to convey his own ideas in the form of a lecture. When he did so, however, it never proceeded from a wish to engross the discourse, or to gratify his vanity. His own inclination disposed him so strongly to enjoy in silence the gaiety of those around him, that his friends were often led to concert little schemes, in order to engage him in the discussions most likely to interest him. Nor do I think I shall be accused of going too far when I say, that he was scarcely ever known to start a new topic himself, or to appear unprepared upon those topics that were introduced by others. Indeed, his conversation was never more amusing than when he gave a loose to his genius upon the very few branches of knowledge of which he only possessed the outlines.

The opinions he formed of men, upon a slight acquaintance, were frequently erroneous; but the tendency of his nature inclined him much more to blind partiality than to ill-founded prejudice. The enlarged views of human affairs, on which his mind habitually dwelt, left him neither time nor inclination to study, in detail, the uninteresting peculiarities of ordinary characters; and accordingly, though intimately acquainted with the capacities of the intellect, and the workings of the heart, and accustomed, in his theories, to mark, with the most delicate hand, the nicest shades, both of genius and of the passions; yet, in judging of individuals, it sometimes happened that his estimates were, in a surprising degree, wide of the truth.

The opinions, too, which, in the thoughtlessness and confidence of his social hours, he was accustomed to hazard on books, and on questions of speculation, were not uniformly such as might have been expected from the superiority of his understanding, and the singular consistency of his philosophical principles. They were liable to be influenced by accidental circumstances, and by the humour of the moment; and, when retailed by those who only saw him occasionally, suggested false and contradictory ideas of his real sentiments. On these, however, as on most other occasions, there was always much truth, as well as ingenuity, in his remarks; and if the different opinions which, at different times, he pronounced upon the same subject had been all combined together, so as to modify and limit each other, they would probably have afforded materials for a decision, equally comprehensive and just. But, in the society of his friends, he had no disposition to form those qualified conclusions that we admire in his writings; and he generally contented himself with a bold and masterly sketch of the object, from the first point of view in which his temper, or his fancy, presented it. Something of the same kind might be remarked, when he attempted, in the flow of his spirits, to delineate those characters which, from long intimacy, he might have been supposed to understand thoroughly. The picture was always lively and expressive, and commonly bore a strong and amusing resemblance to the original, when viewed under one particular aspect; but seldom, perhaps, conveyed a just and complete conception of it in all its dimensions and proportions. In a word, it was the fault of his unpremeditated judgement to be too systematical, and too much in extremes.

But, in whatever way these trifling peculiarities in his manners may be explained, there can be no doubt that they were intimately connected with the genuine artlessness of his mind. In this amiable quality, he often recalled to his friends the accounts that are given of good La Fontaine; a quality which in him derived a peculiar grace from the singularity of its combination with those powers of reason and of eloquence, which, in his political and moral writings, have long engaged the admiration of Europe.

In his external form and appearance there was nothing uncommon. When perfectly at ease, and when warmed with conversation, his gestures were animated, and not ungraceful: and, in the society of those he loved, his features were often brightened with a smile of inexpressible benignity. In the company of strangers, his tendency to absence, and perhaps still more his consciousness of this tendency, rendered his manner somewhat embarrassed;—an effect which was probably not a little heightened by those speculative ideas of propriety, which his recluse habits tended at once to perfect in his conception, and to diminish his power of realizing. He never sat for his picture; but the medallion of Tassie conveys an exact idea of his profile, and of the general expression of his countenance.

Dugald Stewart

III
ADAM SMITH AND LAISSEZ-FAIRE

An endeavour to make a just appraisal of Adam Smith's original contributions to economic doctrine would even today be a task of extraordinary difficulty. On the one hand, what was serviceable in his doctrines has become so thoroughly incorporated in our modern thinking that we discover it upon the slightest provocation in whatever we may read that was written before his day, and we are especially prone to make a virtue of obscurity in his predecessors by taking it for granted that it conceals premature insight rather than unduly prolonged lack of it. On the other hand, there is always great danger lest what we credit to a writer as priority of doctrine may not in reality be merely an indecent exposure of our own ignorance concerning his predecessors.

There is much weight of authority and of evidence, however, that Smith's major claim to originality, in English economic thought at least, was his detailed and elaborate application to the wilderness of economic phenomena of the unifying concept of a coordinated and mutually interdependent system of cause and effect relationships which philosophers and theologians had already applied to the world in general. Smith's doctrine that economic phenomena were manifestations of an underlying order in nature, governed by natural forces, gave to English economics for the first time a definite trend toward logically consistent synthesis of economic relationships, toward "system building". Smith's further doctrine that this underlying natural order required, for its most beneficent operation, a system of natural liberty, and that in the main public regulation and private monopoly were corruptions of that natural order, at once gave to economics a bond of union with the prevailing philosophy and theology, and to economists and statesmen a programme of practical reform.

Smith was *the* great eclectic. He drew upon all previous knowledge in developing his doctrine of a harmonious order in nature manifesting itself through the instincts of the individual man. The oldest source in which he expressly finds an approach to his own views is in the science of the classical philosophers: "In the first ages of the world, the idea of a universal mind, of a God of all, who originally formed the whole, and who governs the whole by general laws, directed to the conservation and prosperity of the whole, without regard to that of any private individual, was a notion to which [the Ancients] were utterly strangers . . . [but] as ignorance begot superstition, science gave birth to the first theism that arose among those nations, who were not enlightened by divine Revelation."

The Roman *jus naturale*, through Grotius and Pufendorf, strongly influenced Smith's thinking. The Renaissance emphasis on the individual, the naturalistic philosophy of Shaftesbury, Locke, Hume, Hutcheson, the optimistic theism of the Scotch philosophers, the empiricism of Montesquieu, were more immediate and more powerful influences. Science, philosophy, theology, psychology, history, contemporary observation of facts—all of them were made to produce, under Smith's capable management, an abundance of evidence of the existence of an order in nature in which beneficent intentions toward mankind could be discerned. If Smith at times showed more catholicity than scientific discrimination in what he accepted as supporting evidence, if some of this evidence appeared upon close scrutiny to be conjectural, contradictory, irrelevant or inconclusive, the richness of argument, the power of his exposition, the attractiveness of his conclusions served to overwhelm the captious critic and to postpone closer scrutiny to a later day.

Smith's major claim to fame, as I have said, seems to rest on his elaborate and detailed application to the economic world of the concept of a unified natural order, operating according to natural law, and if left to its own course producing results beneficial to mankind. On every detail, taken by itself, Smith appears to have had predecessors in plenty. On few details was Smith as penetrating as the best of his predecessors. There had been earlier pleas for freedom of internal trade, freedom of foreign trade, free trade in land, free choice of occupations, free choice of place of residence. Some philosophers, notably Shaftesbury and Smith's own teacher, Hutcheson, had already extended to economic phenomena, though sketchily, the concept of an underlying natural order manifesting itself through the operation of physical forces and individual psychology.

But Smith made an original forward step when he seriously applied himself to the task of analysing the whole range of economic process with the purpose of discovering the nature of the order which underlay its surface chaos. Claims have been made for the Physiocrats, but the evidence indicates that Smith had already formulated his central doctrine before he came into contact with them or their writings. As early as 1755 Smith had publicly asserted his claim to priority, as against some unnamed rival, in applying to the economic order the system of natural liberty. In doing so, he cited a lecture, delivered in 1749, which even in the fragment which has survived contains the essence of his fully developed doctrine, as expounded in the *Wealth of Nations*. It even uses an English equivalent of the very phrase "laissez-faire", which the Physiocrats were soon to make the war cry of the system of natural liberty:

"Projectors disturb nature in the course of her operations on human affairs, and it requires no more than to *leave her alone* and give her fair play in the pursuit of her ends that she may establish her own designs. Little else is required to carry a state to the highest degree of affluence from the lowest barbarism but peace, easy taxes, and a tolerable administration of justice; all the rest being brought about by the natural course of things. All governments which thwart this natural course, which force things into another channel, or which endeavour to arrest the progress of society at a particular point, are unnatural, and, to support themselves, are obliged to be oppressive and tyrannical."

In his *Theory of Moral Sentiments*, Smith develops his system of ethics on the basis of a doctrine of a harmonious order in nature guided by God, and in an incidental manner applies his general doctrine with strict consistency to the economic order. In his later work, the *Wealth of Nations*, Smith devotes himself to a specialized inquiry into the nature of the economic order.

I will endeavour to show that there are divergences between them which are impossible of reconciliation even by such heroic means as one writer has adopted of appeal to the existence in Smith's thought of a Kantian dualism. I will further endeavour to show that the *Wealth of Nations* was a better book because of its partial breach with the *Theory of Moral Sentiments*, and that it could not have remained, as it has, a living book were it not that in its methods of analysis, its basic assumptions, and its conclusions it abandoned the absolutism, the rigidity, the romanticism which characterize the earlier book. It can be convincingly demonstrated, I believe, that on the points at which they come into contact there is a substantial measure of irreconcilable divergence between the *Theory of Moral Sentiments* and the *Wealth of Nations*, with respect to the character of the natural order.

In the first case, the emphasis in the *Theory of Moral Sentiments* upon a benevolent deity as the author and guide of nature is almost, though not quite, completely absent in the *Wealth of Nations*. The significance for our purposes of this virtual disappearance is that it leaves Smith free to find defects in the order of nature without casting reflections on the workmanship of its Author.

Nowhere in the *Wealth of Nations* does Smith place any reliance for the proper working of the economic order upon the operation of benevolence and sympathy, the emphasis upon which was the novel feature in the account of human nature presented in the *Theory of Moral Sentiments*. In the *Wealth of Nations*, benevolence is not merely as a rule left out of the picture of the economic order; when mentioned, it is with the implication that it is a weak reed upon which to depend. "By pursuing his own interest he frequently promotes that of the society more effectually than when he really intends to promote it. I have never known much good done by those who affected to trade for the public good. It is an affectation, indeed, not very common among merchants, and very few words need be employed in dissuading them from it."

The consequences of the intervention of liberality apparently are not "natural", are not in accordance with the intent of nature! Smith shows little faith in the prevalence of benevolence in the economic sphere. Even the college professor cannot be expected to expend much energy in teaching effectively, cannot even be depended upon to teach at all, if it is not made to his interest to do so. In the case of the clergy, the situation seems even more desperate. If they are endowed, they become indolent, and their zeal and industry become impaired. If, on the other hand, they are dependent upon voluntary contributions for their support, they become too zealous.

Self-interest meant to Smith not only the desire for wealth, but self-love in all its possible manifestations. "It is the interest of every man to live as much at his ease as he can." "Avarice and ambition in the rich, in the poor the hatred of labour and the love of present ease and enjoyment," envy, malice and resentment, all of these are manifestations of self-interest, the agreeableness, the ease or hardship, the cleanliness or dirtiness, the honourableness or dishonourableness, of the different employments are all factors affecting the attractiveness to labour of different occupations, as well as the wages paid: "Honour makes a great part of the reward of all honourable professions."

Smith distinguishes also between what a man is interested in and what is to his interest. Man is sometimes ignorant of the latter. "But though the interest of the labourer is strictly connected with that of the society, he is incapable either of comprehending that interest, or of understanding its connection with his own." It is what a man regards as his interest, even though mistakenly, that controls his actions. But every possible impulse and motive to action is included under self-interest except a deliberate intention to promote the welfare of others than one's self.

From his examination of the operation of self-interest in specific phases of the economic order and of the consequences of government interference with the free operation of self-interest, Smith arrives at an extensive programme for the extension of the system of natural liberty through the abolition of existing systems of governmental regulation, though he nowhere brings the several items in that programme together.

The foregoing is familiar matter. What is not so familiar, however, is the extent to which Smith acknowledged exceptions to the doctrine of a natural harmony in the economic order even when left to take its natural course. Smith, himself, never brought these together; but if this is done, they make a surprisingly comprehensive list and they demonstrate beyond dispute the existence of a wide divergence between the perfectly harmonious, completely beneficent natural order of the *Theory of Moral Sentiments* and the partial and limited harmony in the economic order of the *Wealth of Nations*.

Masters and workmen have a conflict of interest with respect to wages, and the weakness in bargaining power of the latter ordinarily gives the advantage in any dispute to the former. Masters, traders and apprentices, on the one hand, and the public on the other, have divergent interests with respect to apprenticeship rules. The interest of merchants and manufacturers is in high profits, which are disadvantageous to the public. Merchants and manufacturers have interests opposed to those of the farmers and landlords, and of the general public. "People of the same trade seldom meet together, even for merriment and diversion, but the conversation ends in a conspiracy against the public, or in some contrivance to raise prices. It is impossible indeed to prevent such meetings, by any law which either could be executed, or would be consistent with liberty and justice." In old countries, "rent and profit eat up wages, and the two superior orders of people oppress the inferior one."

This is only a partial list of the defects in the natural order, even when left to take its own course, which Smith points out, though it would suffice to provide ammunition for several socialist orations. This is a far cry from the account given in the *Theory of Moral Sentiments* of a perfectly harmonious order of nature, operating under divine guidance, to promote its "great end, the order of the world, and the perfection and happiness of human nature".

Adam Smith, as has been shown, recognized that the economic order, when left to its natural course, was marked by serious conflicts between private interests and the interests of the general public. This would seem to suggest that there was an important sphere in which government interference with private interests might promote the general welfare.

In his one deliberate and comprehensive generalization dealing with the proper functions of the State, Smith made it clear, however, that he would narrowly restrict the activities of government. "According to the system of natural liberty, the sovereign has only three duties to attend to; . . . first, the duty of protecting the society from the violence and invasion of other independent societies; secondly, . . . the duty of establishing an exact administration of justice; and, thirdly, the duty of erecting and maintaining certain public works and certain public institutions." Even here, however, he grants to government a somewhat more extensive range of proper activities than in many scattered dicta throughout the remainder of the book, where he was primarily condemning some specific governmental activity and was not really giving serious consideration to the wider problem of the proper range of governmental activity.

Smith had himself undermined what is ordinarily regarded as his principal argument for laissez-faire, by demonstrating that the natural order, when left to take its own course, in many respects works against, instead of for, the general welfare. He nowhere gathered together in orderly fashion the exceptions which he would have made to his general restriction of government activity to protection, justice, and the maintenance of a few types of public works and public institutions. When considering in general terms the proper functions of government, he forgot all about these exceptions. If he had been brought face to face with a complete list of the modifications to the principle of laissez-faire to which he at one place or another had granted his approval, I have no doubt that he would have been astounded at his own moderation.

There is no possible room for doubt, however, that Smith in general believed that there was, to say the least, a strong presumption against government activity beyond its fundamental duties of protection against its foreign foes and maintenance of justice.

What were the considerations which brought Smith to his laissez-faire conclusions? His philosophical speculations about a harmonious order in nature undoubtedly made it easier for him to reach a laissez-faire policy, though I believe that the significance of the natural order in Smith's economic doctrines has been grossly exaggerated. But was not government itself a part of the order of nature, and its activities as "natural" as those of the individuals whom it governed? Smith is obscure on this point, and an adequate answer to this question, if possible at all, would require a detailed examination of Smith's position in the evolution of political theory, especially with respect to the origin of government and the character of the state of nature in the absence of government. It is clear, however, that to Smith the activities of government in the maintenance of justice are an essential part of the order of nature in its full development, and that such activities are not interferences with the system of natural liberty.

In the *Wealth of Nations* Smith draws a definite line between those activities of government which are, and those which are not, in accord with the natural order, on the basis of empirical data. Government activity is natural and therefore good where it promotes the general welfare, and is an interference with nature and therefore bad when it injures the general interests of society. Whether in particular circumstances it works well or ill is to be determined only by examination of the character of those circumstances, though in most cases such examination may be expected *a priori* to reveal that it works badly.

Smith had encountered few instances in which government was rendering intelligent and efficient service to the public welfare outside of the fields of protection and justice. The English government of his day was in the hands of an aristocratic clique, the place-jobbing, corrupt, cynical and class-biased flower of the British gentry, who clung to the traditional mercantilism not so much because of a strong faith that it met the problems of a growing trade struggling to burst its fetters, but because they did not know anything else to do.

Even when Smith was prepared to admit that the system of natural liberty would not serve the public welfare with optimum effectiveness, he did not feel driven necessarily to the conclusion that government intervention was preferable to laissez-faire. The evils of unrestrained selfishness might be better than the evils of incompetent and corrupt govern-

TABLEAU ÉCONOMIQUE.

Objets à considérer, 1°. Trois sortes de dépenses; 2°. leur source; 3°. leurs avances; 4°. leur distribution; 5°. leurs effets; 6°. leur reproduction; 7°. leurs rapports entr'elles; 8°. leurs rapports avec la population; 9° avec l'Agriculture; 10°. avec l'industrie; 11°. avec le commerce; 12°. avec la masse des richesses d'une Nation.

DÉPENSES PRODUCTIVES relatives à l'Agriculture, &c.	DÉPENSES DU REVENU, l'Impôt prélevé, se partagent aux Dépenses productives et aux Dépenses stériles.	DÉPENSES STÉRILES relatives à l'industrie, &c.
Avances annuelles pour produire un revenu de 600lt sont 600lt	Revenu annuel de	Avances annuelles pour les Ouvrages des Dépenses Stériles, sont
600lt produisent net	600lt	300lt
Productions	moitié passe icy	Ouvrages, &c.
300lt reproduisent net	300lt	300lt
150 reproduisent net	150.	150.
75 reproduisent net	75.	75.
37..10 reproduisent net	37..10.	37..10
18..15 reproduisent net	18..15.	18..15
9...7...6d reproduisent net	9...7...6d	9..7..6d
4..13...9 reproduisent net	4..13...9.	4..13...9
2..6..10 reproduisent net	2...6..10.	2..6..10
1...3...5 reproduisent net	1...3...5.	1..3..5
0..11...8 reproduisent net	0...11...8.	0..11....8
0...5..10 reproduisent net	0...5..10.	0...5...10
0...2..11 reproduisent net	0...2..11.	0...2..11
0...1...5 reproduisent net	0...1...5.	0....1....5

&c.

REPRODUIT TOTAL ....600lt de revenu; de plus, les frais annuels de 600lt et les intérêts des avances primitives du Laboureur, de 300lt que la terre restitue. Ainsi la réproduction est de 1500lt compris le revenu de 600lt qui est la base du calcul, abstraction faite de l'impôt prélevé, et des avances qu'exige sa reproduction annuelle, &c. Voyez l'Explication à la page suivante.

François Quesnay's *Tableau Économique*

François Quesnay (1694–1774)

M 784 no 70!

Jay taché de faire un tableau fondamental
de l'ordre oeconomique pour y representer les
depenses et les produits sous un aspect facile a
saisir, et pour juger clairement des arrangemens
et des derangemens que le gouvernement peut y
causer, vous verrez si je suis parvenu a mon but.
Vous avez vu d'autres tableaux ces jours ci
il y a dequoi mediter sur le present et sur l'avenir
Je suis de la derniere surprise de ce que le parlement
ne presente de resources pour la reparation
de l'etat que dans l'oeconomie, il n'en scait pas
si long que l'intendant d'un seigneur qui depensoit
plus qu'il n'avoit de revenu, et qui le pressoit de
lui trouver des resources, celui la ne lui dit
pas epargnez, mais il lui representa qu'il ne falloit
pas mettre les chevaux de labour au carrosse
et de ne pas retenir les chevaux de carosse a
l'ecurie, et que tout etant a sa place, il pourroit
depenser encore davantage sans se
ruiner. Il paroit donc que nos remontrans ne
sont que des citadins bien peu instruits sur les
matieres dont ils parlent et sont par la
d'un foible secours pour le public. Votre derniere
lettre remarque bien que les efforts des particuliers
sont fort steriles mais il ne faut pas se decourager
car la crise est effrayante viendra et il faudra
avoir recours aux lumieres de Medecine.

Vale

A letter concerning the *Tableau Économique*

David Hume (1711–1776)

Adam Smith (1723–1790)

Anne Robert Jacques Turgot (1727–1781)

Thomas Robert Malthus (1766–1834)

Jean-Baptiste Say (1767–1832)

ment. In this connection, Smith has, indeed, a lesson to teach the "new economics" of the present day, which is peddling antique nostrums under new trademarks, and which has substituted for the answer to all economic problems of the classically trained parrot, "demand and supply", the equally magical phrase, "social control". If the standards of public administration are low, progress from a life regulated by the law of demand and supply to a life under the realm of social control may be progress from the discomforts of the frying-pan to the agonies of the fire.

Where, by exception, good government made its appearance, Smith was ready to grant it a wider range of activities.

Adam Smith was not a doctrinaire advocate of laissez-faire. He saw a wide and elastic range of activity for government, and he was prepared to extend it even farther if government, by improving its standards of competence, honesty, and public spirit, showed itself entitled to wider responsibilities. He attributed great capacity to serve the general welfare to individual initiative applied in competitive ways to promote individual ends. He devoted more effort to the presentation of his case for individual freedom than to exploring the possibilities of service through government. He helped greatly to free England from the bonds of a set of regulatory measures which had always been ill advised and based on fallacious economic notions, but he did not foresee that England would soon need a new set of regulations to protect her labouring masses against new, and to them dangerous, methods of industrial organization and industrial technique.

Smith was endowed with more than the ordinary allotment of common sense, but he was not a prophet. But even in his own day, when it was not so easy to see, Smith saw that self-interest and competition were sometimes treacherous to the public interest they were supposed to serve, and he was prepared to have government exercise some measure of control over them where the need could be shown and the competence of government for the task demonstrated. His sympathy with the humble and the lowly, with the farmer and the labourer, was made plain for all to see. He had not succeeded in completely freeing himself from mercantilistic delusions, and he had his own peculiar doctrinal and class prejudices. But his prejudices, such as they were, were against the powerful and the grasping, and it was the interests of the general masses that he wished above all to promote, in an age when even philosophers rarely condescended to deal sympathetically with their needs.

He had little trust in the competence or good faith of government. He knew who controlled it, and whose purposes they tried to serve, though against the local magistrate his indictment was probably unduly harsh. He saw, nevertheless, that it was necessary, in the absence of a better instrument, to rely upon government for the performance of many tasks which individuals as such would not do, or could not do, or could do only badly. He did not believe that laissez-faire was always good, or always bad. It depended on circumstances; and as best he could, Adam Smith took into account all of the circumstances he could find.

In these days of contending schools, each of them with the deep, though momentary, conviction that it, and it alone, knows the one and only path to economic truth, how refreshing it is to return to the *Wealth of Nations* with its eclecticism, its good temper, its common sense, and its willingness to grant that those who saw things differently from itself were only partly wrong.

Jacob Viner

SOURCES

Essay I

John Rae, *Life of Adam Smith* (Macmillan and Co, London, 1895). Abridged. With supplementary notes of William Robert Scott, *Adam Smith as Student and Professor* (Jackson, Son & Co, Glasgow, 1937). Scott collected and interpreted new information and material but it appeared to him that the time was not yet ripe for writing a definite biography of Adam Smith.

John Rae's *Life of Adam Smith* is as complete as materials then available permitted. The chief concern of Scott's book—Bonar read and improved the manuscript—is the period before Smith went to France because "The secret of his genius is to be found in that part of his life before he became celebrated". Scott supposes that our knowledge of this period of his life would be immensely increased if a diary, which it is reported that he kept while he was abroad, could be traced. According to the account of an Edinburgh bookseller, the original manuscript was in his possession a number of years ago, but he lacks particulars of the person to whom he sold it.

Essay II

Dugald Stewart, *Account of the Life and Writings of Adam Smith, LL.D.* (Edinburgh, 1811). Extract from the chapter "Character and habits of Adam Smith".

Essay III

Jacob Viner, "Adam Smith and laissez-faire", *Journal of Political Economy*, 35 (1927). Abridged.

Signature

University Library, Glasgow.

Portrait

Medallion by J. Tassie, 1787 (National Portrait Gallery, London).

BIBLIOGRAPHY

W. Playfair, "The Life of Dr Adam Smith" in A. Smith, *Inquiry into the Nature and Causes of the Wealth of Nations*, Vol. I (London, 1805).

J. R. MacCulloch, "Adam Smith" in: *Treatises and Essays on Subjects Connected with Economical Policy; with Biographical Sketches of Quesnay, Smith and Ricardo* (Edinburgh, 1853).

A. Oncken, *Adam Smith in der Culturgeschichte* (Vienna, 1874).

E. Leser, *Untersuchungen zur Geschichte der Nationalökonomie*, Vol. I, *Aus der Lebensgeschichte des Adam Smith* (Jena, 1881).

R. B. Haldane, *The Life of Adam Smith* (London, 1887).

K. Walcker, *Adam Smith, der Begründer der modernen Nationalökonomie* (Berlin, 1890).

K. Jentsch, *Adam Smith* (Berlin, 1905).

A. Amonn, "Adam Smith, der Begründer der Nationalökonomie", *Zeitschrift für die gesamte Staatswissenschaft*" (1925–6).

H. Hollander, "Adam Smith", Journal of Political Economy, 35 (1927).

J. M. Keynes, "Adam Smith as student and professor", *Economic Journal* 48 (1938) (Supplement "Economic History", Feb. 1938).

J. Bittermann, "Adam Smith's empiricism and the law of nature", *Journal of Political Economy*, 48 (1940).

A. Gray, *Adam Smith* (London, 1948).

A. L. Macfie "Adam Smith's moral sentiments as foundation for his Wealth of Nations", *Oxford Economic Papers*, New Series, II (1959).

J. Spengler, "Adam Smith's theory of economic growth", *Southern Economic Journal*, 25–6 (1959).

N. Rosenberg, "Adam Smith on the division of labour. Two views or one?" *Economica*, New Series, 32 (1965).

ANNE ROBERT JACQUES TURGOT

1727–1781

Résolu de partager sa vie entre les lettres, les sciences et les devoirs de la magistrature, Turgot ne s'était pas borné à des études théologiques. Il s'était livré avec beaucoup d'application à celle du droit et surtout à celle de la morale et de la justice, aux mathématiques, à la physique, à l'astronomie. Il connaissait parfaitement le ciel.

Turgot s'exprimait en latin aussi parfaitement, qu'il est possible aux modernes de le faire. Il savait le grec, il étudia l'hébreu, il apprit l'allemand, l'italien, l'anglais, un peu d'espagnol. P. S. DU PONT DE NEMOURS

Turgot était l'esclave de ses idées. L. SAY

Well-timed reform to avert revolution! This was the keynote of his public life. W. W. STEPHENS

As concerns his theory of entrepreneurship, he is clearly superior to Smith, and yet this fact seems not to have been noted heretofore. B. F. HOSELITZ

. . . analytic economics took a century to get where it could have got in twenty years after the publication of Turgot's treatise had its content been properly understood and absorbed by an alert profession. As it was, even J.-B. Say—the most important link between Turgot and Walras—did not know how to exploit it fully. J. A. SCHUMPETER

THE LIFE AND WRITINGS OF TURGOT

Anne Robert Jacques Turgot, third son of Michel Étienne Turgot and Madeleine Françoise Martineau, was born in Paris on 10 May 1727. His ancestors for many generations had occupied high positions in several departments of the State.

The home education of young Turgot was not fortunate. His father, probably, was too deeply involved in his laborious public duties to afford much time to his son's upbringing. Between the mother and the son there was some want of sympathy. Probably she disliked his fondness for books and for serious studies. With her, as with most French women, a graceful carriage and refined manners in a youth were almost everything. Unfortunately these were wanting in her son, and he made no effort to acquire them. Every hour, every minute spent otherwise than in thinking, in reading, in noting his studies, in self-culture was for him lost time. A boy with these tendencies overindulged could not fail to make himself often disagreeable to those about him, and especially to a mother whose theory of life was very different from his. This awkwardness, for which she was continually blaming him, was, long afterwards, in public life, often imputed to him by his enemies, and was sometimes apologized for by his friends. His manner to strangers, and to those with whom he did not much sympathize, was felt to be stiff and reserved. It is possible that the seeds of this constrained manner were sown by the unnatural seclusion and the excessive devotion to study of his boyhood, and that, instead of being then gently eradicated by parental care, they were subjected to a treatment which gave them only firmer root.

He had a tutor who, it appears, was not very efficient. But the Collège Louis-Le-Grand, the one selected for him, was at that time under the ablest direction, and here he soon made a very decided advance. Afterwards, for the higher classes, he attended the Collège du Plessis. Here he was fortunate in having most distinguished masters. One of these was the Abbé Sigorgne, who was the first professor in France to substitute for the fanciful theories of Descartes the sublime and mathematically demonstrable physics of Newton. Turgot enthusiastically embraced the new doctrine.

As customary for the youngest son of the family, Turgot, being intended for the Church, left the Collège du Plessis for the seminary of Saint-Sulpice. There he gained the distinction of being admitted to the degree of Bachelor of Theology (1747), before the usual period, by special sanction of the Faculty. His next step was to enter (1749) the House of the Sorbonne in order to study for his licence.

In the Society of the Sorbonne he was fortunate to have, as fellow students, several highly cultivated young men, with many of whom he contracted a warm and lifelong friendship. Among these were Morellet, afterwards the distinguished *littérateur* and economist, and Loménie de Brienne, afterwards Archbishop of Toulouse and Cardinal. Turgot's two years in the House of the Sorbonne were the seed-time of his life. It was in accordance with his high aims, and with the serious spirit in which he pursued his studies, that the earliest literary work to which he gave a deliberate treament, at a considerable length, was a treatise "On the Existence of God". Only three fragments of it remain.

In December, 1749, Turgot was unanimously elected Prior of the Society of the Sorbonne for the following year. This office was mostly an honorary one, conferred generally on the most promising young student, who had not already held it. In this capacity it was his duty to deliver two Latin discourses, one at the summer, the other at the winter session.

In the second discourse he gave expression to his ideas on what has since been called the "philosophy of history" in these words, which have often been quoted: "All the ages are linked together by a sequence of causes and effects, which connects the existing state of the world with all that has preceded it. The multiform signs of language and of writing, by giving to men the means of insuring the possession of their ideas, and of communicating them to others, have made of all the individual funds of knowledge a common treasure, which one generation transmits to the next, along with an inheritance always increased by the discoveries of each age. Thus the human race, seen from its origin, appears to the eye of a philosopher as one vast whole, which itself, like each individual composing it, has had its infancy and its development."

Meanwhile he was earnestly strengthening his intellect, and extending his knowledge, by the help of the excellent library of the Sorbonne. He gave much of his time to making at considerable length translations into French of the masterpieces in other languages. DuPont de Nemours gives us particulars of these, which introduce us to Turgot's favourite authors at this period. The translations include Homer, Seneca, Caesar, Ovid, Tacitus, Horace, Tibullus, Virgil, Tasso, Klopstock, Gessner. His knowledge of languages is seen to have been considerable. His two discourses before the Sorbonne were delivered in Latin; his translations include works in that language, in Greek, Hebrew, German, Italian and English. Later on in life, if not then, he wrote in English with ease and correctness. To these acquirements he added a remarkable facility of writing in verse, and this with some epigrammatic point. He did not limit himself to the study of literature and of political economy. His knowledge of chemistry and physical science generally, and especially of astronomy, was far beyond that possessed by the majority of educated men. The ambitious student claimed the whole world of thought as his domain. Among his papers was found a list, in his own handwriting, drawn up at the Sorbonne period, of the literary projects he had then in view, which comprised a grand course of treatises on language, history, sciences, metaphysical philosophy, theology, morals, laws, politics and principles of administration. It is pleasant to know that this scheme was never really shelved, that he kept working at it, more or less, all his life, even while involved in pressing public duties.

Turgot's earliest literary work, remaining to us in an entire state, is his letter to Buffon, the celebrated naturalist. He had been reading the *Theory of the Earth*, and some parts of the speculation appeared to him to be inconsistent with strictly scientific and Newtonian principles. His next essay that we know of was his first work in the field of political economy—a science whose birth dates from scarcely a generation before Turgot, and of which, in its larger and modern acceptation, he became one of the founders. It was a short treatise on paper money in the form of a letter dated 7 April 1749.

During 1750 he set himself to refute the metaphysical doctrines of Berkeley in two short essays which are published in his collected works, and which he threw into a more succinct form for the *Encylopédie* in the article "Existence". In the same year he attacked another metaphysician of note, Maupertius, mostly with reference to the philosophy of language.

He was now over three-and-twenty. Some of his comrades in the Society already suspected his growing repugnance to the Church and his growing preference of the State for a career. Turgot had laid before his father the reasons he had for renouncing the profession of the Church, and had requested permission for adopting, instead, that of the law. The father's consent had been obtained, and his influence was about to be exerted to gain for his son a favourable introduction, when in February 1751 he died. This event brought to a close Turgot's residence at the Sorbonne.

At no period of his life, probably, did he see more of what is called "society" than at the one we have reached. In a short time he found himself launched upon a world almost new to him, consisting of those select assemblies of cultured and brilliant men and women for which Paris has always been famous. Among his associates were Montesquieu, D'Alembert, Helvetius, Morellet, Galiani, Raynal and Marmontel. But now, as well as during all the rest of his life, he instinctively recoiled from surrendering himself entirely to any literary or other coterie. His dislike for the spirit of party or of sect was always ready to be expressed.

Turgot decided to accept (5 January 1752) the position of "Deputy Councillor" of the Procurator-General. On 30 December of the same year he was admitted as Councillor in the Parliament of Paris, and shortly afterwards he was appointed Master of Requests (28 March 1753), which position he held until he was promoted to be Intendant of Limoges in 1761.

These nine years and a half, as far as spent in the magistracy, are necessarily uneventful for us. During the period of his judicial office he found time to make some valuable contributions to the discussion of public questions. The first of these, in order of time and of importance, was his *Letters on Toleration*, suggested by the commotion which had been caused throughout France by the controversy between the Church and the

Parliament of Paris upon their respective spheres of jurisdiction. This was followed (1 May 1754) by the publication of a short tract entitled *Le Conciliateur*.

During his leisure from magisterial duties he translated, annotated and published an essay by one of our own political writers of that time—Dr Josiah Tucker—on *Questions on the Naturalisation of Foreign Protestants*. He contributed five articles to the *Encyclopédie*: "Etymologie", "Existence", "Expansibilité", "Foires" and "Fondations". They were all lengthy articles, and would together make up a good-sized volume. "The appearance of the article 'Existence'," says M. Léon Say, "was a real literary and philosophical event. The world of the literati and the encyclopaedists was struck by the precision and clearness of the style, the originality and depth of the ideas."

In 1755, or earlier, Turgot had attached himself, as nearly as his independent spirit would permit, to the party of the "economists", then rising into importance, which was eventually to influence so profoundly the intellectual and political movements in France and Great Britain. He had for his friends the two great founders of the school—Quesnay, the author of several works in propagation of its doctrines, and Gournay, Intendant of Commerce, the author of the celebrated formula of *laissez-faire et laissez-passer*. With Gournay he formed a very deep and tender friendship. It was one of the official duties of the Intendant of Commerce to inspect different provinces of the kingdom. When Gournay died the loss was felt by Turgot as irreparable. He raised a lasting memorial to him by composing his *Éloge*. Marmontel had been officially charged with the duty, and Turgot's paper was modestly offered as furnishing some materials for the academician's use, but there remained little, if anything, to be added to it.

Gournay had had a friend of longer standing than Turgot, and also greatly valued, M. Trudaine, one of the Intendants of Finance and Director of Roads and Bridges. Turgot became Trudaine's guest for some time at his country seat of Montigny. He left Montigny for a tour in Switzerland and the east of France. It was when passing through Geneva on this tour that he made the acquaintance of Voltaire.

There were essential differences between the mental character of Voltaire and that of Turgot, but these did not prevent Turgot from recognizing Voltaire's brilliant, versatile, and altogether astonishing genius, and his signal services to civil and religious freedom, in spite of his frequent bitterness, his intemperance in controversy, and occasional malice with which Turgot had no sympathy. Turgot, with a tithe of Voltaire's genius, had a much better balanced moral character, and looked at things in a serious, never in a mocking spirit. It is possible that Voltaire appreciated the presence in Turgot of qualities in which he was himself deficient. At all events, throughout Turgot's whole career, Voltaire paid him constant enthusiastic homage. It was to Turgot, on his retiring from public life, that Voltaire addressed the epistle in verse bearing the title—itself one of the noblest of tributes—"To a Man".

He had not long returned to his judicial duties when he received, 8 August 1761, the appointment to a high office of State, his intendancy of the provinces of Limousin, Angoumois, and Basse-Marche (shortly called the "intendancy of Limoges").

The condition of the people over whom Turgot was placed as governor, differed only for the worse from that of the agricultural and industrial classes in France generally. Like other provinces, owing to the miserable appliances in the art of agriculture, and the grievous oppression of a system of taxation, which left the cultivator no saving to form capital, and bereft him of all hope of improvement, Limousin was subject to a chronic state of agricultural distress, varied periodically by acute outbreaks of famine. And of all the provinces of France, Limousin was perhaps the most unfortunate, for its soil was naturally about the poorest.

It is, of course, impossible to review adequately even the most important acts of an administration which lasted for thirteen years, and had its every day full of work. The most we can do is to endeavour to form some idea of the spirit in which Turgot accepted his mission, and of some of the means he used to prosecute it.

Bound always, by the necessity of his mind, to possess himself with a clear knowledge of the facts with which he had to deal, one of his first acts was, with that view, to address a circular to his "sub-delegates" (the officials under his control), specifying the points on which he required information, while he anxiously endeavoured to inspire them with his own earnestness. Not content with using, for the amelioration of his province, all the machinery belonging to his own administrative office, he sought to enlist the influence of every volunteer agency procurable for the same end, particularly the influence of the district clergy.

The oppression suffered by the people of France under the operation of the *taille* and *corvées* formed one of the most important factors in the production of the French Revolution.

The *taille*, a personal tax of feudal origin of variable amount, had in the changed conditions of France, under a succession of expensive governments, become grievously arbitrary and burdensome.[1] This hateful tax it was now

[1] The amount of *taille* paid on the average by the small peasant proprietor was about a sixth of his income, after allowing for his mere necessaries of life, and it was only a part of the burden of taxation that pressed upon him. But the ugliest feature of the *taille* remains to be named. While it bore, with such aggravated severity, upon the poor, hardworking peasantry, it was a tax from which

Turgot's duty to raise from his poor province. He never ceased to condemn its iniquity. But it was beyond the power of an intendant to abolish or reform a law of State; the utmost he could do was to administer it with as much fairness and as little injustice as possible.

The most glaring abuse that existed in the agricultural districts of France was the institution of the *corvée*, the forced employment of the peasantry, and without payment, upon the making and repairing of the roads. Each province having the management of its own roads, Turgot was able here to achieve for Limousin a reform which, had it been followed by the other intendants over the kingdom, would have saved France from incalculable turmoil.

He had been intendant about eight years when a crisis occurred which put to the severest trial his capacity as a ruler, his prudence and his moral strength. The crisis involved questions of greater magnitude than the *taille* or the *corvée*, or even free trade, for it was a matter literally of life or death—in 1770 and 1771 a famine devastated the province. To mitigate the sufferings induced by this dreadful calamity, his whole energy was called forth.

No question had more interest for him as an economist, and none more occupied his mind and heart when intendant and minister, than that of agricultural improvement. He inaugurated the improvement in his own province by instituting the Royal Society of Agriculture of Limoges, of which he was naturally elected the president. The Society offered each year a prize on some subject related to the practical utility of rural economy, and Turgot added to that a prize, from himself, on some subject of political economy or on some function of the administration with which the success of agriculture was concerned.

One of his chief aims was to remedy, by the introduction of clover, lucern and sainfoin, the natural deficiencies of Limousin in good pasture land; he procured considerable quantities of the seeds of these plants, distributed them to the three Bureaux of Agriculture, and through them to the most intelligent cultivators, with most excellent effect.

He earned the distinction of making known to the peasantry the potato, and of establishing its culture in the province.

Although during the thirteen years of his intendancy he remained almost constantly at his post, it was necessary that he should visit Paris from time to time, if only to receive instructions from the Government. On one of his visits he made the acquaintance of Adam Smith, and this soon ripened into a real friendship.

their superiors in rank and wealth were exempted. It was levied on "all *roturiers* not privileged". It is estimated there were 270 000 in the privileged classes: 140 000 nobles and 130 000 clergy.

The intercourse of Turgot with Adam Smith, and at the date mentioned, is of great historical importance, taken in connection with the fact that it was in 1766 that Turgot published his *Réflexions sur la formation et la distribution des richesses.*

During his early years at Limoges, and before the publication of the *Réflexions* he had written the following minor works on taxation: *Plan d'un mémoire sur les impositions en général*, *Comparaison de l'impôt sur le revenu des propriétaires et de l'impôt sur les consommations* and *Observations sur un projet d'édit sur les vingtièmes*, besides several papers in connection with the prize essays of the agricultural society already mentioned. Throughout all these works it was his main design to enforce the advantages of direct over indirect taxation.

In 1769 he published his *Mémoire sur les prêts d'argent*, and it had reached a second editon before DuPont included it in the collected works. His "mémoir" is, in fact, a treatise, developing the principle that interest being the price of money in commerce, this price ought to be left to the course of events, and to the bargaining of commerce to adjust itself.

During a tour of his province, towards the end of 1770, he wrote a series of letters to the Comptroller-General, M. Terray, on the interminable question, *La Liberté du commerce des grains*. The letters were seven in number, each written from a different place on his journey. The letters were written with astonishing ability, and for completeness in the collection and statement of facts, for application of right dealing with these, and for the exhaustive anticipation of every possible argument on the opposite side, they form quite a model of controversial debate.

His last work of importance while intendant was his letter to the Comptroller-General: *Sur la marque des fers*. It is dated 24 December 1773. The *Marque des fers* was the brand distinguishing the native iron of France from the foreign article. Since 1608, each Finance Minister in turn had proposed scheme after scheme of duties and regulations, with a view to encouraging the production of French iron and discouraging the use of foreign metal and metalwork. He recapitulates his argument in this terse dictum: "The truth is, that in aiming at injuring others, we injure only ourselves." It is astonishing in how deep an ignorance of moral and economical principles nations calling themselves the most enlightened still remain on these "native industry" questions.

The *marque des fers* was the last treatise of an economic kind which he had the opportunity of composing. Within a few months after it was written, Louis XV died. A new king and a new prime minister invited Turgot to a seat in the Cabinet. Turgot was nominated to the Ministry of Marine on 20 July 1774. Turgot's brief tenure of the Ministry of Marine was barely sufficient for him even to take measure of the disorganized state of the naval administration. But he was soon called upon to serve France in the most important work which at that time lay before her, and the prosecution of which has, much more than any other event in his career, made his name illustrious.

On 24 August 1774, he was appointed Comptroller-General of the Finances. Turgot had now attained to really the most responsible position in France.

The King was deeply impressed by Turgot's earnest nature, and by the prospects raised before him of a reign devoted only to the public welfare and to be recompensed by his people's love. With a full heart, he assured Turgot that, as Minister, he might count with confidence on the King's as well as the man's full sympathy and steadfast support. Turgot was so elated by this favourable interview, that he asked the King's permission to make a memorandum of it, and, on this being granted, he addressed a letter to the King, which, when read in the light of after events, became one of the documents of French history.

Within twenty days from his accession to the comptrollership Turgot had to decide now for the whole kingdom the question that occupied him so much, on a smaller scale, during his intendancy of Limoges—the free commerce in corn. By the new decree, Article I he declares that "all persons shall be free to carry on, as it may seem best to them, their trade in corn and flour, to sell and to buy it, in whatever places they choose throughout the kingdom", and by Article II the King reserves the right to enact the freedom of export when circumstances shall have become more favourable. On 28 September, he issued a cirular letter to the intendants of the provinces, on the *octrois municipaux* (town dues). He had, for many years, been painfully impressed by the abuses in the assessment and the collection of the *octrois*, particularly in the country towns.

The year 1775 had just begun, when, amidst the efforts he was making so earnestly, so laboriously and so unflinchingly, to fulfil the duties that lay before him, he was struck down by a serious illness. Gout had been for long hereditary in his family. In ordinary circumstances, the present attack might have been overcome, but most unfortunately at this very time there occurred in the southern provinces of France a cattle plague, demanding his immediate and unceasing vigilance, and the anxiety thus produced so aggravated his illness as to bring the gout into his chest. For nearly four months he was unable to leave his room. The calamity was an outbreak of cattle plague (*épizootie*) early in January 1775, which soon spread to a most alarming extent.

The gout had just somewhat abated when he forced himself, in spite of medical advice, to return to active superintendence of his bureau, which had now a new difficulty to encounter. This was the series of corn riots that were taking place in different parts of the kingdom. The origin and progress of these riots were a puzzle to historians of their own time, and remain still a puzzle to this day. It is possible that the law passed by Turgot for the free circulation of corn may have had something to do with them. A district with natural agricultural advantages over others would have in its principal town an exceptionally large stock of corn, and generally the price in the adjacent country places would be low. The inhabitants would feel a claim to these natural advantages, and would grudge to see the stock in the local granaries being reduced to supply other parts of the kingdom. A rise in price would be taking place, and as the stock became further reduced popular anxiety and discontent would be excited. The spirit of discontent might easily spread to quarters where the conditions were different. It might then become an instrument in the hands of a political faction to be used for political purposes.

During this period of the corn riots a name of some eminence came into conflict with Turgot's. Shortly before the riots had broken out appeared M. Necker's work *Sur la législation et le commerce des grains*, which was little else than an apology for the popular prejudices against the free circulation of corn, and was evidently intended to check the rising influence of Turgot in the Government. It was within Turgot's power to suppress the work, and he was strongly advised by some to do so, but he was too true a friend of free discussion to listen to such advice. The unpractical, superficial, and almost puerile character of Necker's ideas may be seen from the leading proposal made in his work.

In 1775, Turgot (assisted by his devoted friend and secretary, DuPont de Nemours), during the intervals of more urgent affairs, had laid down the lines of a scheme of "municipalities". Circumstances did not permit of the scheme being ever submitted to the King and the Council. It deserves our notice, however, as indicating the direction in which his policy would have advanced, had he retained power. The memorandum on municipalities is admirable if for nothing else than the prominence given in it to "the first and most important of all the institutions necessary, and the one most fit to immortalize your Majesty's reign", the organization by the state of a system of national education, an organization not attempted by the French Government (nor even, adequately, by any other) for nearly another hundred years. From the earnestness of his language when dwelling upon this topic, we may reasonably conclude that, had he been allowed to remain in power a plan of national education would have formed his principal work.

In January 1776, Turgot addressed his memorandum to the King on the fatal "six projects of edicts". These were: 1, for the suppression of the *corvée*; 2, 3, 5 and 6, for the suppression of several regulations, duties and offices interfering with the provisioning of Paris; and 4, for the suppression of the *jurandes* (the government of privileged corporations). As it was upon numbers 1 and 4 of the edicts, the suppression of the *corvée* and of the *jurandes*, that the battle, the last battle between Turgot and his enemies, was mainly fought, we confine ourselves to the consideration of these two. They were certainly the most important reforms he had yet attempted. It is possible, nay, probable, that fearing it would be beyond his power to carry them into effect, he had advisedly confined his first efforts to the framing of measures that could provoke least controversy, that he might at all events accomplish some of the needed financial improvements. But it was not possible for him to shirk the more perilous duties that lay before him. Until the *corvées* and the *jurandes* were abolished, neither the peasants in the provinces nor the artisans in the towns were free to make the best of their labour, and thus a spirit of discontent was nourished, in town and country, that must some day explode.

After passing the Council, the six edicts, in order to acquire legal force, had to be registered by the Parliament. By the exercise of the King's prerogative, all the edicts were duly registered by the unwilling Parliament. Turgot had gained a victory, but by the victory he lost his ministry. The Parliament was exasperated by its defeat. His enemies drew reinforcements, from all sides, in order to crush the man who, because he suppressed some flagrant abuses, was accused, as usual in such circumstances, of "unsettling everything".

Against Turgot intrigue followed upon intrigue. His reputation even as a minister of finance, which a year ago was so undisputed, was now to be assailed, in order that the King's confidence in this also should be shaken. There is reason to believe that Maurepas lent himself to this plot. Turgot, soon, could not but feel conscious, in his interviews with the King, that there was less of the old frank cordiality between them, and he saw what was coming. He wrote a series of four private letters to the King, in the passionate earnestness of his desire to enlighten him upon the serious crisis, for himself and for France, in which he was now called upon to act. A crisis it certainly was. These four private letters were expressed in the most unreserved language. The King sent no reply.

"Turgot carried to his retreat," said a close friend, "a mind of undisturbed serenity. Although his health was shattered, that bore no influence on his temper; never had he been more amiable or dearer to those who had the advantage to live in his society. Literature and science, and the care to relieve the unfortunate, filled all the time which his malady left him to enjoy. He applied himself to advanced geometry with the Abbé Bossut, chemistry with Lavoisier, optics and astronomy with the Abbé Rochon—the latest of his friends but not the least dear."

He attended as often as was possible to him at the Académie des Inscriptions, of which he had been elected honorary member (March 1776), and of which he was Vice-Director in 1777. He returned with renewed zest to the favourite literary work of his youth, that of assimilating to his mind the classic masterpieces, by the process of translating them into verse. He kept up a studied correspondence with many distinguished men of the time, notably with Adam Smith on economic questions, with Dr Richard Price on the Constitution of the United States, and with Benjamin Franklin, his esteemed friend, to whom he addressed a treatise on the "true principles of taxation". His more frequent, more general, and more spontaneous correspondence was with Condorcet.

Towards the end of 1780 he had an attack of gout, more prolonged and and more painful than he had previously experienced. In January 1781, he applied himself to literary composition for the last time by translating into verse Horace's Ode "Aequam memento", into which he felt might be read much of himself and his situation. In little more than two months, on 18 March 1781, he died, in his fifty-fourth year. He had never expected to survive the period of middle life. "You blame me for attempting too much," he said to his friends, "but you know in my family we die of gout at fifty."

William Walker Stephens

II
TURGOT AND THE SIX EDICTS

To the economist, interest in Turgot centres in him as a factor in the economic interpretation of history, and in his contributions to the literature and facts of economic science. So much of his work had to do with permanent principles rather than with changeful social forms that the interpretation of his doctrines becomes most timely and helpful to the practical economist of the present.

Hitherto the interpretation of Turgot's economic doctrines has been based largely on his *Réflexions sur la formation et la distribution des richesses*, the first known attempt to separate for study these related economic phenomena.[2] It is quite probable that no one would be more surprised than

[2] Schumpeter summarizes the contents of the *Réflexions*, as follows: "Roughly the first third of the treatise—the first 31 sections—presents the ground-work including the Cantillon-Quesnay schema of classes and an analysis of their relations in production and distribution that is splashed with physiocrat colors. Certain fundamental propositions, like the proposition that competition always reduces wages to the minimum-of-existence level, are insisted on from the first. Sections 32–50 contain a theory of barter, price, and money that, so far as it

the author at the conspicuous place accorded to this bit of writing. In a letter to Dr Tucker, written in September 1770, Turgot says: "That bit was written for the instruction of two Chinese who are in our country and to make them comprehend more clearly some questions which I addressed to them concerning the economic condition and constitution of their empire."

Early in his career he turned his attention to economic investigation, and his essay written to a fellow-student as an outgrowth of a conversation, on paper money, is of more than passing interest. At some time, probably during the period of his labours as a magistrate, he wrote a carefully reasoned essay on value and money. This essay demonstrates both his logical methods of reasoning and his conclusions at that time concerning that fundamental phase of economics. The Six Edicts, including the preambles and the defence of them against the criticisms of Keeper of the Seals, M. Hue Miroménil, are his last contributions of importance to the literature of the science. In the twenty-seven years intervening between his first attempts at economic discussion and his last, he found time to compose many comprehensive treatises on different subjects, but those on economic topics are by far the most important and of most permanent interest.

Turgot's place in the history of economics has been variously construed in later times, from Léon Say's verdict that "he is the founder of our present political economy, and, by the freedom of labour which he bequeathed us, he has stamped our century with its most distinctive mark", to Oncken's opposite opinion, wherein he assigns Turgot to a distinctively subordinate place. The final judgment is yet to be made.[3]

Robert Perry Shepherd

goes, is almost faultless, and barring explicit formulation of the marginal principle, within measurable distance of that of Böhm-Bawerk. The rest of the treatise is devoted mainly to a capital theory that anticipates most of the nineteenth-century work, and to the subjects of interest, saving and investment, and capital values. Originality in individual points is difficult to assert or to deny, the more so because Turgot does not quote—which is no reproach in the case of such a sketch. But comprehensive vision of all the essential facts and their interrelations plus excellence of formulation are in evidence to a degree that would make the whole of the work an original contribution even if no individual point had been Turgot's own. And there are practically no definite errors to be found in this first of all the treatises on value and distribution that were to become so popular in the later decades of the nineteenth century. It is not too much to say that analytic economics took a century to get where it could have got in twenty years after the publication of Turgot's treatise had its content been properly understood and absorbed by an alert profession. As it was, even J. B. Say—the most important link between Turgot and Walras—did not know how to exploit it fully." (*History of Economic Analysis*, p. 249.)

[3] Schumpeter ranks Turgot in the following comparison: "If we now try to compare Turgot's scientific personality with those of Beccaria and A. Smith,

significant similarities strike us: all three were polyhistoric in learning and range of vision; all three stood outside the arena of business and political pursuits; all three displayed single-minded devotion to the duty in hand. Turgot was undoubtedly the most brilliant of the three, though his brilliance was somewhat tinged with superficiality, not in economics, but in his outlying intellectual domains. The main difference, from the standpoint of their scientific achievement, is that A. Smith expended very little of his energies on nonscientific work, Beccaria very much, and Turgot, from 1761 on, almost all he had. During the thirteen years at Limoges, Turgot can have had but scanty leisure; during his (nearly) two years of ministerial office, practically none: his creative work must have been done between the ages of 18 and 34. And this explains all there is to explain, not indeed about the comparative merits of the three works in question, but about the different degrees to which they were finished works at all.

"Turgot was much too able a man to write anything insignificant. Nevertheless, only the Turgot specialist needs to go beyond the *Réflexions*, and with one exception we shall confine ourselves to this. The slender work was evidently written in hot haste and never thoroughly revised. It looks as Marshall's *Principles* would look if text, notes, and appendices were destroyed and only the marginal summaries—and not all of those—were preserved. In fact, it is not much more than a very elaborate analytic table of contents written for a bulky but nonexistent treatise. Such as it is, however, Turgot's theoretical skeleton is, even irrespective of its priority, distinctly superior to the theoretical skeleton of the *Wealth of Nations*. In order to arrive at this opinion, it is not necessary to impute to Turgot anything he did not actually say or to credit him with any implications of what he did say that he may possibly not have seen himself. He actually delivered the goods. In calling the work unfinished or a skeleton, I do not mean to say that there is need for uncertain conjecture or generosity of interpretation in order to finish it. It presents a complete system of economic theory. What is lacking any competent economist could supply without adding (except criticism) from his own stock of knowledge. Of course, nobody admires the *Wealth of Nations* for its theoretical skeleton alone. It owes its position to its mature wisdom, its luxuriant illustrations, its effective advocacy of policies. And there is, also, something to be said for the ponderous creation of the academic professional: it was the product of patience, of meticulous care, of self-discipline—and we cannot be sure that Turgot would ever have produced something comparable to it, even if he had had all the leisure in the world. Still, a lesson does follow from the very different success of both works: in economics, at least, intellectual performance is not enough; finish counts; and so do elaboration, application, and illustration; even now the days are far off when it will be possible, as it is in physics, to shape international thought by an article that covers less than one page. Turgot's contribution fared as well as it did because of his eminence in another walk of life. Even so it never bore the fruits that it easily might have borne." (*History of Economic Analysis*, pp. 248–9.)

III
ON TURGOT'S PERSONALITY

From his early life, we can anticipate that here is a man who will never give in to anything or anyone, and that all his enterprises will be inspired by the same unchanging principles. As soon as one has a notion of these, nothing is less surprising than Turgot's political ideas. All that remains is to sit back and admire the precision of his intellectual workings, the complete absence of reaction in the face of unforeseen difficulties, and absolute scorn of impossibilities. "What ignorance of mankind!" the Marquis de Mirabeau said of him with a sort of wonder.

However, when reproached for being attached to a system, Turgot would vigorously defend himself. "The expression doctrinaire," he would retort, "has become a weapon wielded by those who are prejudiced in favour of maintaining certain abuses, or interested in keeping them, and against all those who propose changes of any kind." Let us rather say that he improvises nothing and will not accept ready-made ideas. "No system," said one of his biographers, "was ever completely admissible in all its parts—he never made a decision without having first scrupulously examined it and adopted nothing on trust." Thus, when he had adopted an opinion, he stuck stubbornly to it. "You have an abominable habit of never seeing anything but the thing itself," the Abbé de Veri said to him. "Without regard to people, never reconsidering your opinion due to ignorance of a thousand details concerning the subject, you dryly pronounce your judgment, as you never pronounce a single word which could justify the slightest hesitation."

Turgot did suffer from a shrinking timidity which he never shook off and a definite inaptitude for oral discussion. "His elocution," says Monthyon, "was laborious, diffuse and obscure . . . his conversation almost always resolved itself into a dissertation." But the main reason for his behaviour is that Turgot had in his own reasonings, his "judgment" as the Abbé de Veri put it, an unreserved confidence. As this was evident, people did not fail to accuse him of pride, his austere appearance and unsociability contributing to give this impression. However, this imperturbable intellectual assurance stemmed from a deeper source: Turgot's religion was the truth, and when he had made it his, he would have reproached himself for not following it through to the end. So far from all concession was he, that, judging others to be as himself, he was convinced that the truth always naturally imposed itself, and that his contemporaries were as disposed as himself to receive it. When he perceived that this was the contrary, he bore down upon the obstacle at the risk of accelerating his failure.

This is not without the danger implicit in the possible errors which such men can make in the choice of "their" truth. "Turgot", says Léon Say, "was the son of his meditations." This is precisely what could be disturbing. Turgot was a recluse who himself recognized his taste for retirement, and his foreignness to "the common way of life". During twenty-five years of studies, first in the very narrow milieu of college, of the Sorbonne, and even of the Parliament, from which he held aloof and which treated him in like fashion, he amassed a considerable amount of untested knowledge. It is remarkable that up to the time when he became acquainted with the Physiocrats, political economy was just about the only intellectual discipline which he had neglected in what he called his "intellectual libertinage". But it is true that at this time, as we can see by Rousseau's article in the *Encyclopédie*, economics was not dissociated from politics, which alone constituted a science, if not exact, at least certain. As many others had done, Turgot came to one through the other. He was to bring with him much philosophical knowledge, meant for something completely different than the government of economy, and such a great deal of solitary meditation that this inevitably determined his public activity.

On the other hand, Turgot has always been credited with an unquestionable honesty. Not only outspoken honesty, but a rarer and more strict intellectual honesty. "His integrity is absolute, he is motivated only by the good, as he sees it"; "Turgot is full of honesty"; an "incorruptible soul"; such are the remarks of Véri, Baudeau and the Marquis de Mirabeau amongst many others. Monsieur de Monthyon, who did not like him particularly, went so far as to say: "Turgot was ambitious for the important positions, but he sought power only as a means of doing good. His love of mankind and desire to contribute towards its happiness were his dominating, even only passions, of such great purity and of such a sublime nature that he wished only that success be realized, and he did not seek for himself as a necessary recompense the glory of having brought it about."

Thus Turgot was a superman, if the compliment of M. de Monthyon, chronicler without kindliness, was not voluntarily exaggerated. This also was disturbing, because a superman is very rarely a politician.

Turgot can be further explained by the boldly optimistic character of his political philosophy. He had conceived it thus from his studies at the Sorbonne but had not felt the need to think deeply about it, so much was it the philosophy of his century. It consists in saying that humanity can be compared to a man who has successively passed through a state of infancy, youth and virility. Today it has reached maturity. There is no reason why this maturity should not be vigorously maintained whilst adding to it new knowledge acquired from the cumulated results of preceding ages. Turgot believed mankind capable of indefinite progress, all error resulting from institutions and laws. No matter how solitary and confined he was within his meditations, Turgot had, as we have already seen, been subjected to the influence, not only of his time—which is inevitable—but of the more close circle in which he had lived since leaving the Sorbonne. For history, and already for his contemporaries, Turgot was an "economist"; when the term becomes known, he will be classed amongst the Physiocrats.

Against this categorizing, as indeed against all other categorizing, he protested in advance; he held aloof from all doctrinal adherence.

Nothing could catch him unprepared, because, equipped as a man of science, he was able to furnish an answer to any question. Let us say more exactly that for him there could exist no "case", no litigation nor any event which could not be attached to his system and treated according to his laws. Is this sufficient to further the good of mankind and the success of a policy, both of which enterprises demand intuition and sensitivity, as well as knowledge? There have always existed those who know all and have not the capacity to understand, and those who understand all and thus compensate for their lack of knowledge. Over and above these groups "profiting" equally, according to the expression of DuPont de Nemours, there are those who have luck and are gifted. Turgot had no doubt that he was gifted. It is not certain whether he really did say, as tradition would have it: "I firmly believe that I was born to regenerate France." If he did not say it, he thought it. The noble candour which, according to his contemporaries,[4] was witness of the sincerity of his faith, extended to his very pride.

Claude-Joseph Gignoux

[4] "Pour bien juger M. Turgot il falloit le connoître tout entier. On pouvoit le trouver froid, & sa raison seule l'avoit préservé d'être une homme très-passionné: on le jugeoit dédaigneux, & jamais homme ne sentit une estime plus profonde pour les talens & les vertus, & ne mit plus de prix aux efforts de la médiocrité modeste & utilement employé. Il paroissoit minucieux, & c'étoit parce qu'il avoit tout embrassé dans de vastes combinaisons, que tout étoit devenu important à ses yeux par des liaisons que lui seul souvent avoit su appercevoir. On le croyoit susceptivle de prévention, parce qu'il ne jugeoit que d'après lui-même & que l'opinion commune n'avoit sur lui aucun empire. On lui croyoit de l'orgeuill, parce qu'il ne cachoit ni le sentiment de sa force, ni la conviction ferme de ses opinions, & que sentant combien elles étoient liées entre elles, il ne vouloit ni les abandonner dans la conversation, ni en défendre séparément quelque partie isolée. Ces opinions elles-mêmes n'étoient pas connues, il n'existoit en Europe qu'un très-petit nombre d'hommes en état d'en saisir l'ensemble & de les juger; & comme il ne s'agissoit pas de découvertes isolées sur une seule science, d'ouvrages soumis au public, comment l'opinion entraînée par le préjugé auroit-elle pu le juger avec justice?" (J. A. C. Condorcet, *La Vie de Turgot.*)

SOURCES

Essay I

William Walker Stephens, *The Life and Writings of Turgot* (Longmans Green & Co, London, 1895). Biographical extracts.

Essay II

Robert Perry Shepherd, *Turgot and the Six Edicts* (Columbia University Press, New York, 1903). Brief extract. Supplemented by notes from J. A. Schumpeter, *History of Economic Analysis* (Allen & Unwin, London, 1955).

Essay III

Claude Joseph Gignoux, *Turgot* (Librairie Athène Fayard, Paris, 1945). Abridged. Supplemented by a note from J. A. C. Condorcet, *La Vie de Turgot* (Paris, 1786).

Signature

Bibliothèque nationale, Paris.

Portrait

Engraving by G. H. Watelet from a portrait by Ch. N. Cochin (Bibliothèque nationale, Paris).

BIBLIOGRAPHY

P. H. S. DuPont de Nemours, *Mémoires sur la vie et les ouvrages de M. Turgot* (Paris, 1782).

M. J. A. C. Marquis de Condorcet, *La vie de Turgot* (Paris, 1786).

M. Baudrillart, "Turgot," *Revue des deux mondes* (1846).

A. P. Batbie, *Turgot, philosophe, économiste et administrateur* (Paris, 1861).

A. Mastier, *Turgot, sa vie et sa doctrine* (Paris, 1862).

W. B. Hodgson, *Turgot, His Life, Times and Opinions* (London, 1870).

F. Cadet, *Turgot 1727–1781* (Paris, 1873).

A. Neymarck, *Turgot et ses doctrines* (Paris, 1885).

L. Say, *Turgot* (Paris 1887). Translated by M. B. Anderson: Chicago, 1888.

E. Dubois de l'Estang, *Turgot et la famille royale* (Paris, 1894).

F. Alengry, *Turgot (1727–1781), homme privé, homme d'état* (Paris, 1942).

W. Weddigen, *Anne Robert Jacques Turgot, Leben und Bedeutung des Finanzministers Ludwigs XVI* (Bamberg, 1950).

E. Faure, *La disgrâce de Turgot, 12 mai 1776* (Paris, 1961).

D. Datkin, *Turgot and the Ancien Régime in France* (New York, 1965).

W. Stark, "Anne Robert Jacques Turgot," in *International Encyclopedia of the Social Sciences*, Vol. 16 (New York, 1968).

THOMAS ROBERT MALTHUS

1766–1834

. . . the writer of this article, who has known him intimately for nearly fifty years, scarcely ever saw him ruffled, never angry, never above measure elated or depressed. BISHOP OTTER

A man who is born into a world already possessed, if he cannot get subsistence from his parents on whom he has a just demand, and if the society does not want his labour, has no claim of right *to the smallest portion of food, and, in fact, has no business to be where he is. At Nature's mighty feast there is no vacant cover for him. She tells him to be gone . . .* T. R. MALTHUS

Taking the whole earth, . . . and supposing the present population to be equal to a thousand millions, the human species would increase as the numbers 1, 2, 4, 8, 16, 32, 64, 128, 256, and subsistence as 1, 2, 3, 4, 5, 6, 7, 8, 9. In two centuries the population would be to the means of subsistence as 256 to 9; in three centuries as 4096 to 13 and in two thousand years the differences would be incalculable. T. R. MALTHUS

Der Weltkreis ruht von Ungeheuern trächtig
und der Geburten zahlenlose Plage
droht jeden Tag als mit dem Jüngsten Tage. J. W. GOETHE

In short, from being a caterpillar of a moral scientist and a chrysalis of an historician, he could at least spread the wings of his thought and survey the world as an economist.

I claim for Malthus a profound economic intuition and an unusual combination of keeping an open mind to the shifting picture of experience and of constantly applying to its interpretation the principles of formal thought. J. M. KEYNES

I
MALTHUS AND HIS WORK

The few facts that are known of the life of Malthus bring us nearer to him than we can come in his writings, and show us how well, on the whole, his antecedents and surroundings fitted him for his work.

The family of Malthus has been traced by John Orlebar Payne as far back as the fifteenth and sixteenth centuries. There were ancestors frequently at odds with the prevailing religion and government, a sign of strength of mind and conviction. One was an author. Daniel, his father, was born in 1730 and died in January 1800, his wife, Henrietta Graham (granddaughter of a king's apothecary), following him in April 1800.

Daniel matriculated at Oxford at Easter 1747, and entered Queen's College, a few months after Adam Smith had left Balliol for home. He got greater enjoyment there than Adam Smith, though he too had his reservations: "I used to think Oxford none the less pleasant and certainly not the less useful for being disburthened of some of its society; I imagine you will say the same of Cambridge," he wrote to Robert on 13 January 1786.

Like his father, Sydenham, Daniel was called to the Bar at Lincoln's Inn; married (1752) and settled down to a country life and the study of science, especially botany. He was acquainted with Rousseau.[1] They had in common the love of botany. Daniel is said to have corresponded with Voltaire, and to have been literary executor of Rousseau.

Daniel lived first at Hadstock, Essex. After some wanderings, he settled, in 1787, at Albury in Shaw's house, now pulled down. Sydenham, his eldest son, was born in 1754. The second son, Thomas Robert (both old family names), was born at the Rookery on 14 February 1766. They had six sisters. Besides his science, Thomas had studied Greek and Latin, and

[1] "Daniel Malthus was, in a sense, a disappointed man. In a letter to his son Robert, then in residence at Cambridge, he referred with regret to his own 'broken purposes and imperfect pursuits'. But he must have been a man of unusual qualities; for among his friends were two of the most celebrated men of his time—David Hume and Jean-Jacques Rousseau, who visited him together on 9 March 1766, when the future author of the *Essay on Population* was three weeks old. For many years Daniel Malthus had idolized Rousseau, had indeed in 1764 made bold to call upon him at Môtiers. He welcomed Hume's project of settling Rousseau near him in Surrey, and at the foot of Leith Hill found a cottage for him, which years later was pointed out to Fanny Burney as *L'asyle de Jean-Jacques*. But though Rousseau inspected the cottage he did not occupy it and, despite Daniel's entreaties to remain in Surrey, he left to begin his unfortunate sojourn at Wootton in Derbyshire. Daniel Malthus continued to correspond with Rousseau." (G. F. McCleary.)

(we may believe) German, or the translation of Werther would hardly have been set down to him. He held the *Allegro* to be the highest flight of poetry, a significant choice. The son like the father, though social, much enjoyed occasional solitude.

Of his mother, only a few touches are recorded. She appears from the private letters to have been the oracle of the household in practical matters. There is one letter of Robert to her written on 11 December 1783, in which familiarity and affection and respect are properly blended. From a letter of Daniel to Robert (21 April 1784), it appears that she did not want Robert to go to either of the two great Universities.

Neither of the boys was sent to a public school. Like Sydenham, Robert was sent to his father's old friend, Richard Graves, Rector of Claverton near Bath (1779).

From Graves he passed in 1782 into the hands of a stronger man, Gilbert Wakefield, whose sole pupil he was till he went to Cambridge. Robert admired Wakefield, and to have his sole attention was to Robert's advantage.

Wakefield, once (1776) Fellow of Jesus College, Cambridge, procured admission for Robert there as a pensioner or ordinary commoner in 1784, and he began residence in the winter term. He wrote on 14 November 1784, to his father: "I am now pretty well settled in my rooms. The lectures begin to-morrow; and, as I had time last week to look over my mathematics a little, I was, upon examination yesterday, found prepared to read with the year above me, though I believe I shall attend a few lectures at the same time with those of my own year. We begin with mechanics and Maclaurin, Newton, and Keill's *Physics*. We shall also have lectures on Mondays and Fridays in Duncan's *Logick*, and in Tacitus's *Life of Agricola* on Wednesdays and Saturdays. I have subscribed to a bookseller who has supplied me with all the books necessary. We have some clever men at college, and I think it seems rather the fashion to read. The chief study is mathematics, for all honour in taking a degree depends upon that science, and the great aim of most of the men is to take an honourable degree."

He did not narrowly confine himself to mathematics, nor did he show what his father conceived to be the Cambridge failing, the worship of pure theory and neglect of applications. He says he was "remarked in college for talking of what actually exists in nature or may be put to real practical use" rather than for abstract speculations. He took frequent refuge in literature, English and French. He took prizes for Latin, Greek and English declamations. We do not hear of Italian, which he certainly knew afterwards.

Long before Cambridge he had thought of taking orders. What he got when he left Cambridge was probably just what he wanted, not a living but a curacy, and time to think and study. He seems to have been of good physical health and strength. Once or twice we hear of rheumatism which his father reproaches him for misspelling: "Don't say *rhumatism*, but consider the derivation, and that no man should have a disorder which he can't spell, especially a man of Jesus."

Malthus was fortunate in his father. He was also fortunate in his tutor, William Frend.[2] Frend was afterwards to be removed from his fellowship because of his *Thoughts on Subscription to Religious Tests* (1789) and from the University because of his book on *Peace and Union* (1793).

Malthus finished his course with credit, as ninth Wrangler, 1788. He had thought himself lucky if he became a Wrangler at all, but he had "kept on act" (defended a thesis) in the schools with some credit, and probably no one else was surprised at his place. He writes on 17 April 1788, after the event: "I have laid aside my chemistry for a while and am at present endeavouring to get some knowledge of general history and geography. I have been lately reading Gibbon's *Decline of the Roman Empire*."

Malthus seems to have taken orders immediately after the Wranglership. He became MA in 1791. About 1796 he ceased residence and was curate at Albury, Surrey, to which address his father wrote from Bath when Robert had written his first pamphlet, *The Crisis*, and had in vain tried to get Debrett to print it.

The private letters do not help us in the interval between *The Crisis* and the *Essay*. It is clear from the Preface to the *Essay* of 1798 that he had been forming his opinions on political economy: "The most important argument that I shall adduce is certainly not new. The principles on which it depends have been explained in part by Hume and more at large by Dr Adam Smith." He feels his judgment sufficiently mature to warrant him in criticizing the latter drastically enough.

His sense of humour helped to lengthen his days and made him by general vote a pleasant companion and host. The signs of it departed from his writings, with the early lightness of touch, after 1798 or at least after 1800. He had found the work of his life, to set one neglected truth before the world, and he devoted himself to this task, pushing his inquiries in all ways possible to him, study, conversation, travel among the chief. In 1806 he was in Wales with Francis Horner, a warm admirer; in 1817 in Kerry and Westmeath; in 1825 in France "for the sake of Mrs Malthus" on the death of his daughter; in 1826 with Henry Cockburn in the Highlands. He was visited by Dr Thomas Chalmers in 1822, and of course by Ricardo frequently till Ricardo's death in 1823. A. H. Everett, an American critic, was

[2] Frend is said to have been friend and teacher of David Ricardo, a speculative statement, which according to Sraffa cannot be proved.

charmed with his personality. Dismalness and he were many miles asunder.[3]

In his view of life and the prospects of humanity he passed from pessimism to a moderate optimism, and was never too old in spirit to confess a fault. The composition is bald and sometimes diffuse. But the meaning of each sentence is always clear, and, when we are learning a single truth in its full bearing, the repetition of the same phrases in different connections is unavoidable, in proportion to the thoroughness of the discussion. The abundant metaphors of the first *Essay* had led to many misunderstandings. It may be said, however, that his own command of metaphor and consciousness of its drawbacks made him quick to turn the edge of an opponent's metaphor. His first published writing after the *Essay* was still anonymous, though the authorship was generally known.

Pitt was at Cambridge on a sort of canvassing visit in December 1800. It was after the dissolution that preceded the first united Parliament of Great Britain and Ireland. He went to "a supper at Jesus Lodge, where, in the company of some young travellers, particularly Mr Malthus, he was induced to unbend in a very easy conversation respecting Sir Sidney Smith, the massacre at Jaffa, the Pacha of Acre, Clarke, Carlisle." He thought some of Carlisle's translations from the Arabic beautiful, and seemed to know them by heart. Being still a man of influence, he may have contributed to the appointment of Malthus as Professor of History and Political Economy (perhaps the first professorship of the latter) in the newly founded East India College at Haileybury in 1805.[4]

In view of this post Malthus married, on 13 March 1804. Mrs Malthus was his junior by eleven years and survived him thirty. She is said to have sided with Owen in the fireside discussions, perhaps from politeness to her guest. A compliment paid (by Otter) to Malthus, that his servants stayed long with him, justly belongs to his wife. They had three children, of whom the two eldest survived him. Lucy, the youngest (born 1808), died in

[3] "He was not a laughing philosopher like his friend Sidney Smith; but dismal he was not any more than his subject. To be *dismal* is to be afflicted with an extreme form of pessimism, more familiar to Carlyle than to Malthus. If he showed signs of the complaint in 1798 at thirty-two years of age, he recovered from the mild attack. He was personally a normal Englishman more given to merriment than sadness. So his friend Daniel Clarke tells us—and we all know about that time of life, thirty-two, a man is just beginning to overcome a certain 'oscillation' between melancholy and merriment, such as led Milton to his immortal contrast of them. Malthus was passing out of that stage of our diversified human life and becoming able to see the possibility of a good time coming for his own country and even for Europe and the world after all." (Bonar.)

[4] "It was not an inspiring place for any professor who could hope now and then to have an inspiration from his pupils. But it allowed him leisure to write books and pamphlets and letters to like-minded friends, and leisure enough to pursue his own thoughts." (Bonar.)

1825. The Rev. Henry Malthus lived till 1882, and Emily (Mrs Pringle) till 1885.

Malthus held this professorship for the rest of his life. There were drawbacks, but on the whole it was thoroughly congenial. *Hoc erat in votis.* The rest of his life's story is mainly a record of his writings and his friends.

The *Essay* reached several editions in his lifetime; Johnson published the first three, Murray the remainder. His other substantial book was the *Political Economy*, 1820, of which the second edition appeared posthumously in 1836.

From 1810, the date when Ricardo's letters to Malthus begin, we may be certain that the debates by word of mouth and by letter with so strong a critic had great influence on his friend, were it only by way of opposition. We have comparatively few of his own letters.[5] The fundamental difference of opinion appears clearly in the Ricardo–Malthus letters. Ricardo thought the depression after the war was due to a scarcity of capital; Malthus, that it was due to a glut of commodities.

Malthus even in his own lifetime was more often "refuted" than any other economist. He still retains the distinction, and (to parody a well-known saying) "there is a great deal of refutation in Malthus". His illustrations may have gone; but his arguments remain.[6] They are, however, two-edged weapons of which wise controversialists make cautious and sparing use.

His contemporaries gave him a fair measure of recognition. Otter says that he became a Fellow of the Royal Society in 1819 and was made a Member of the French Institute and of the Berlin Royal Academy. He was

[5] Some letters are reprinted in Volumes 6–9 of Sraffa's edition of *The Works and Correspondence of David Ricardo.*

[6] "As Adam Smith was of excellence the economist of policy and Ricardo the path-breaker in monetary thought, so the distinctive contribution of Malthus lay in the field of social economy. He launched the interest and in part the method which travelled through Nassau Senior and Stuart Mill to the social investigations of a later day, where the statistician not less than the theorist is in the line of descent from him. And statisticians can never forget that Malthus's *Essay* of 1798 was among the influences which provoked the taking of the first census of the people three years later in 1801. By his ratios of increase, arithmetical for Nature and geometrical for Man (for, as our University Calendar reminds us, he was ninth Wrangler of 1788, four places below Gunning of Christ's), he framed a startling disharmony between population with its capacity for cumulative increase and natural resources which are limited and exhaustible. Although the middle link of his doctrine has been broken by the triumphs of technology in transport and agriculture in conjunction with the practice of birth control, yet it remains formidable at either end—in the New World, where resources have been recklessly exploited, and in the old world of Asia, where population teems upon areas so recently reclaimed from flood or desert by the capital and engineering skill of Europe." (Fay.)

certainly made Associate of the Académie des Sciences Morales et Politiques on its reconstitution in 1833. He was a member of the Royal Society of Literature.

He helped to found the Political Economy Club in 1821 and the Statistical Society in 1834. He seems to have belonged to the Geological Society, and perhaps, like Ricardo, to their dining club. The private letters show his liking for such studies. He was present with his son Henry at the Cambridge meeting of the British Association in 1833.

His post was honourable though not lucrative. There is no sign that he desired more money or wanted to be more in the sun. He had perfect health, says Mackintosh. Some of his friends indeed wanted more for him.

The college at Haileybury was an educational experiment due to the suggestions of Governor-General Wellesley, brother of the great Duke. The course was to be of about two years, and the general education was to be on the lines of Oxford and Cambridge.

For posterity the work of Malthus was not in the East India College, but in his writings. But his connection with the college was perhaps the most important of the external facts of his life, and it has helped to preserve a record of scenes and incidents revealing fine shades of character more clearly than the laudations of friends with their broad generalities and occasional misjudgments.[7] Samuel Rogers, the poet, thought Mackintosh, Malthus, and Bobus Smith to be "the three acutest men" he had ever known; they all agreed in a theological tenet (the limitation of attributes). It was the tenet also of J. S. Mill.

It is not inconsistent with the cosmology of the first *Essay*. But Rogers is hardly a good authority. There is a sounder and saner word from Mackintosh. "I have known Adam Smith slightly, Ricardo well, Malthus intimately. Is it not something to say for a science that its three great masters were about the three best men I ever knew?"

Sinclair's *Correspondence* gives the handwriting of all three. All are legible. Adam Smith's is a large, bold, schoolboy hand; the writing of Malthus is regular without being clerkly; Ricardo's the same with even more character and firmness. The portrait of Malthus in old age painted by John Linnell, shows him erect and cheerful. It bears out the description in the *Gentleman's Magazine*: in person "he was tall and elegantly formed". Mrs Malthus was short.

Malthus died suddenly of heart disease on Monday 29 December 1834,

[7] "Paradoxically, Malthus, who was all his life never more rabid than a mild Whig, became a hero of the Philosophical Radicals. John Stuart Mill, once one of them, tells us that Malthus was recognized by them for what he had really done; he had not closed the door to progress, he had for the first time opened it." (Bonar.)

when on a visit to his wife's old home at Claverton. He is buried in Bath Abbey in the north aisle of the nave.

James Bonar

II
PRINCIPLES OF POLITICAL ECONOMY CONSIDERED WITH A VIEW TO THEIR PRACTICAL APPLICATION

Mr Ricardo and Mr Malthus lived together on the most friendly terms. Although, whenever they met or wrote, they appeared to meet and write only to discuss their differences, yet their friendship never suffered the slightest diminution on that account. It may be of use to coarser natures to see a specimen or two of the manner in which great minds can differ and communicate their differences.

It is not often that criticism is invited with the ingenuous sincerity contained in the following challenge:

"With regard to any remarks on my opinions, you must be governed by your own discretion. If those opinions are wrong, I should like to see them refuted, but, thinking as I do, that they are, in all essential points, founded on correct principles, I ask for no mercy. I do not care how severely they are attacked; there is nothing you could say of them which would hurt me, if what you said did not express contempt, and that I know you do not feel for me. Act, therefore, towards me as if I were a perfect stranger, and notice me or not as you think best." (March 1815.) "When I say mine is the true faith, I mean to express only my strong conviction that I am right. I hope you do not attach any thing like arrogance to the expression. I am in the habit of asserting my opinion strongly to you, and I am sure you would not wish me to do otherwise. I am satisfied that you should do the same by yours, and I dare say you will agree with me that you are not more inclined to mere authority without being convinced than I am." (October 1820.)

Ricardo acknowledges a compliment, which Mr Malthus had paid him in the first edition of his *Political Economy*.

"The compliment you pay me in one of your notes is most flattering. I am pleased at knowing that you entertain a favourable opinion of me, but I fear that the world will think as I think, that your kind partiality has blinded you in this instance." (4 May 1820.)

The last sentence in what we believe was the last letter which Mr Ricardo wrote to Mr Malthus before his death, is a fit conclusion to this remarkable correspondence.

"And now, my dear Malthus, I have done. Like other disputants, after much discussion, we each retain our own opinions. These discussions, however, never influence our friendship; I should not like you more than I do if you agreed in opinion with me." (31 August 1823.)

Mr Malthus was not, what we sometimes see, a philosopher on paper only: able to legislate for society—unable to judge wisely, to will resolutely, and to act consistently at home. He knew himself and the degrees according to which different things were either suitable to or desirable for him. If he had judged of mankind by his own standard, he must have admitted as a truth that which he was constantly reproving as an error—the supposition, that all people were endowed with the requisite sagacity for discovering their true interest, and with the requisite strength of character to steadily abide by it. This power seemed in his own case to be so thoroughly innate, that we have often wondered whether it always was so, or what were the sort of difficulties which he had to overcome. While he had no fear of the masters of the earth getting in the way of his sunshine, he was sensible of the advantages of money and station up to a certain point. On the other hand, he saw that the point was reached, and that the turn at which the disadvantages begin to preponderate, takes place much sooner than many, who are yet neither misers nor spendthrifts, are in the least aware.

With him, "Goodness and greatness were not means but ends." Impassive to abuse, almost unconscious of neglect, he was nevertheless peculiarly susceptible to praise. He often spoke of it as the thing which more than any other affected him to tears. Few things could have touched him more sensibly than any mark of public gratitude and private sympathy from the members of a government in whose political creed he perfectly agreed. The faculties and qualities of Mr Malthus appeared not simply to be in harmony with, but to be supported by each other. The keeping was so complete, that you could not imagine them apart. Instead of the waste of intellectual power, or the wear and tear of moral struggles, in which so much of ordinary existence is consumed, he had always the clear mastery and possession of himself.

Mr Malthus combined and reconciled opposite natures in his own. He was upright without severity, blameless without insipidity, amiable without weakness. There was no counterbalancing of great virtues by great faults. But more than this. The endowments of head and heart which were most characteristic of Mr Malthus were precisely those which are more captivating than striking. They did not break out in sparkles, or come up in bubbles on the surface at a moment's notice; but were in their nature so calm and deep, that a superficial looker-on might pass them over altogether. We can easily understand that persons may have been thrown into his company, at a dinner party, or even at the Political Economy

Club, and have gone away with a certain feeling of disappointment.

Mr Malthus was a perfect gentleman, at all times and under all circumstances. But it was by degrees—seeing him day after day—that the extent and beauty of his nature unfolded itself to your view.

Mr Malthus had also this great advantage—whatever was his understanding, he always gave himself the full use of it. Its light was dry light, there was nothing of temper to discolour it, or of obliquity to turn it. The rectitude of his judgment was not simply left undisturbed; it was invariably aided by the rectitude of his purpose. In estimating the relative importance of different subjects he had no criterion but their tendency to promote or to retard the happiness of mankind. In investigating the particular subject on which he might happen at any time to be engaged, he seemed to have no conception of the possibility of any other object than the discovery of truth. The combination of these two characteristics made him in all private relations, however serious or however trifling, always the same, strictly equitable and considerately indulgent. We have seen his sense of equity severely tried. As soon as he saw his way, there was not a moment's pause. The ease with which he rose, as it were, upon the wing and bore away into a purer region, was morally sublime.

He was far from being indifferent to fame. But his devotion to truth was so intense that he seemed physically incapable of arguing for victory. He was by no means unconscious of the value of his philosophical services. But there was an utter absence of all personal consideration in the main satisfaction which he derived from the survey of them; and he cared little in comparison who it was that had been right, provided only that the right prevailed.

William Empson

III
MALTHUS IN THE TWENTIETH CENTURY

The first proposition of the theory is that the level of population in a given society tends to gravitate to that which just permits subsistence standards of living for the great majority of its inhabitants. If for any reason the standard of living rises above the subsistence level, then better living conditions will promote earlier marriages and a fall in mortality rates, so that the growth in population cancels out any increase in the means of subsistence. If this contrary movement proceeds so far that the general standard of living falls below the subsistence minimum, then marriages are discouraged, higher mortality rates are experienced, so that eventually the pressure of human numbers falls and the subsistence minimum is again established. This "sort of oscillation", as Malthus called it, tends to perpetuate itself.

It is true that this "sort of oscillation" occurs only if the conception of a subsistence minimum is a purely physiological one. The check on population growth is then starvation and disease. But, as Malthus argued in the *Summary View*, the preventive check of moral restraint is a possible alternative—that is to say, the conception of the subsistence level may be a psychological one. But Malthus could not have regarded moral restraint as an automatic and universal check, otherwise what would have been the point of writing the *Essay* at all?

Now, this proposition regarding the connection between the level of subsistence and population growth can be true only if we accept another one. The second proposition holds that with the application of successive units of labour to a fixed quantity of land and capital, a stage is reached when the output per head of the population begins to diminish. Thus a necessary condition for the first proposition to be true is that the particular type of economy we are considering is characterized by what is popularly known as "diminishing returns". Only in such a situation would an increase in population, and thus in the supply of labour, result in a fall in output per head; conversely, a decrease in population will lead to a rise in output per head.

The first objection to the theory is based on the empirical evidence available of the economic development of Western economies. Where substantial improvements have taken place in general living standards, while the absolute level of population has risen, the rate of population increases has diminished remarkably. Thus, in Great Britain, the birth-rate has fallen from 34·1 per 1000 of population in 1851 to 15·1 per 1000 in 1938. Although there has been a pronounced fall in mortality rates, the annual rate of increase in population has fallen from 12·3 to 3·5 per 1000. I think we must note very briefly the causes of this decline in fertility. One is explicable in Malthusian terms. The subsistence minimum is determined by social habit and custom as much as by physiological factors, and the desire to have children may be weakened by a revision in the general conception of that minimum. Children are expensive, and an expansion of other opportunities for expenditure means that they compete with other needs. But the possibility of family limitation as distinct from the desire to have fewer children was extended only with the spread of knowledge of birth control. This is a development which Malthus could not very well have anticipated, and of which he most certainly would have disapproved.

The protagonist of the Malthusian theory might interject at this stage: "I grant you that the decline in fertility has been caused by a change in social habit and custom, and is therefore independent of economic conditions, and that some of the symmetry of the theory is lost. I grant you that the standard of living in countries such as Great Britain and other European countries rose considerably in the nineteenth century. However, the absolute level of population did rise after all, and could it not be argued that, if it had risen less rapidly, the average standard of living might have risen to an even higher level if the rate of population increase had been smaller?"

This rejoinder is usually answered by a second and more important objection. The law of diminishing returns assumes that labour is applied to a fixed quantity of land and capital. Now the adjustment of population to a rise in the standard of living must take time, and we have no reason to suppose that cultivable land and capital will in fact remain fixed throughout this period. Throughout the nineteenth century this was certainly not the case. This part of the objection seems obvious enough; but not so obvious is the part which labour itself may play in modifying the operation of the law.

Labour itself may become more efficient for at least two reasons. Alfred Marshall provides the first one. The second reason associated with the change in the efficiency of labour is the fact that an expanding population is likely to be associated with a young labour force, which is likely to be extremely adaptable to quickly changing economic conditions.

Now all the objections we have listed so far were current in the nineteenth century as well as today. However, there is one argument which is characteristic of the economics of the twentieth century, and it has virtually silenced theoretical discussion of the Malthusian position, at least in Western economic literature. This argument concerns the influence of the consumption on the level of output and employment, and is particularly associated with the name of Keynes.

In Malthus's own day it had been argued that an expanding population, through its effect on the demand for labour's product, facilitated specialization and division of labour, and thus brought improvement in the methods of production. But quite apart from the effect of an expanding population on the efficiency of particular industries, there is its effect on the general level of output and employment. Thus the argument of Malthus's contemporaries gains further support from the famous Keynesian analysis of the causes of unemployment. The utilization of the resources of any given community depends not only on the potential productive power, but also on the effective demand for the goods and services produced.

So far as the demand for investment goods is concerned, it has been argued by Keynes and some of his American followers that demand for many forms of investment, particularly housing and public utilities, depends on an expanding population. Conversely, a declining and ageing population is likely to be associated with a fall in demand, particularly for investment goods, and thus with under-employment of resources.

The surprising thing about Keynes's view is that he claimed the authority of Malthus in support of it. Although Malthus did point out that economic crises may be caused by lack of effective demand, he did not relate his conclusion to his theory of population. But let me quote Keynes on the subject:

"We have now learned that we have another devil at our elbow at least as fierce as the Malthusian—namely the devil of unemployment escaping through the breakdown of effective demand. Perhaps we could call this devil too a Malthusian devil, since it was Malthus himself who first told us about him. For just as the young Malthus was disturbed by the facts of population as he saw them round him and sought to rationalize the problem, so the older Malthus was no less disturbed by the facts of unemployment and sought to rationalize that problem too. Now when Malthusian devil P is chained up, Malthusian devil U is liable to break loose. When devil P of Population is chained up, we are free of one menace; but we are more exposed to the other devil U of Unemployed Resources than we were before."

Are we to conclude from these objections that, as Schumpeter has put it, "the only valuable things about Malthus's law of population are its qualifications"? I think not. It is to be noticed that the quarrel with the theory is not with the logic, but with the assumptions about the relation between the standard of living and population on the one hand and the ubiquity of diminishing returns on the other. Like any other theory, the theory of population must be regarded as a conditional hypothesis. Before we can state that it is an unrealistic hypothesis, we have to assume that the current and future development of less mature economies will follow a similar pattern to that of Western economies and will experience similar changes in their social and political institutions; for, as I have pointed out, the objections to the Malthusian theory are largely based on what has happened in the West since Malthus's day. But the Neo-Malthusians argue that the assumptions do no violence to reality. They *are* prepared to argue that population is a function of the standard of living and that the law of diminishing returns operates; and they hold that their argument is valid for economies which support some 60 per cent of the human race as at present distributed. Let me state their case for them.

Let us consider the population factor first. The size of the populations of such economies as India, Malaya, and China depends, as in other economies, upon birth and mortality rates and migration. Their birth-rates are still much higher than those of industrial economies. But more important still for population growth in these economies is the very considerable reduction in mortality rates in recent years over a very short period of time. Relatively speaking, migration is not an important factor in determining the absolute level of population, and it is unlikely, given the present world political situation, that emigration of Asiatic peoples to other areas would be at all practicable, quite apart from any economic incentives which might promote population movement. The percentage rate of growth in population in the Middle and Far East, in Latin America and Africa is still well over 1 per cent per year. For the Indian continent alone this means an annual addition to the population which exceeds the present total population of Scotland! Thus the Neo-Malthusians would hold that any measure which causes a rise in the standard of living will also bring about an increase in population, not necessarily through increasing birth-rates, but certainly through declining mortality rates.

Let us turn now to the problem of the law of diminishing returns. The real income per capita in any country depends on the total disposable national product, and in any given period this is equal to what is produced in that country by way of goods and services plus imports of goods and services from abroad and minus exports to foreigners in payment for imports. In turn, the disposable national product depends on the productivity of the factors of production—that is to say, on its capital resources, human and material. Now, the general characteristic of these areas, so far as resources are concerned, is abundant labour but relatively meagre resources in land (on account of population density), and in capital equipment. Even then a prerequisite of the efficient use of the plentiful factor, labour, is literacy and good health. This is certainly not a marked feature of the countries we have mentioned. In one sense, also, the Keynesian argument is relevant in the determination of the level of disposable national product. Many so-called under-developed areas are exporters of primary products. Thus what is available for distribution depends on the terms of exchange between exports of these products and imports, say, of manufactured products and capital equipment. The demand for their exports depends mainly on the effective demand, and thus the level of income and employment, of developed economies. Quite apart from the amplitude of the fluctuations in demand for primary products in past periods, on account of alternating booms and depressions, some economists claim to have discovered a secular decline in the terms of trade of countries exporting primary products in exchange for manufactured products. Roughly speaking, this means that an increasing volume of exports will be required in future, in order to obtain a given fixed volume of imports. Accepting these arguments, it does not appear to be likely that much can be done to raise the level of per capita income quick enough to offset increases in population.

The *pièce de résistance* of the Neo-Malthusian argument is the parallel drawn between the Malthusian conception of social policy in the nineteenth century and the implications of the Colombo Plan, which has as its aim the promotion of international investment in under-developed territories. The practical implication of the nineteenth-century view was that redistribution of wealth from richer to poorer classes would defeat its own ends, for the rise in living standards would stimulate population growth, and this would merely swallow up the increase in the disposable national product. Similarly, it might be argued that the redistribution of wealth from richer to poorer countries (which seems the obvious implication of argument in the last two paragraphs), while it may aid technological progress, will also accentuate the population problem, not perhaps through increases in the birth-rate, but through a pronounced decline in mortality rates. More specifically, if this redistribution takes the form of better health and sanitary conditions, the decline may very well be most marked in the case of infant mortality, thus causing an increase in the number of consumers rather than in the number of actual or potential producers. This is a disturbing conclusion reminiscent of Mr Fax's "fearful pre-eminence" of men over corn. I think that I can best employ the space left to me in considering it in more detail.

I am inclined to accept the Neo-Malthusian argument as an explanation of what will happen in the short run—that is to say, it is a theory which explains a crucial phase of economic development, but which is not valid as a general theory of economic development. I go further, and contend that this crucial phase is now about to be experienced in Asian countries and may well be a formidable barrier to improvements in living conditions, even if foreign aid to these countries is forthcoming; for the gap between the birth-rate and the mortality rate is likely to be considerable for some time to come.

However, even in the short run the position is not quite so bad as Neo-Malthusians make out. Even without extensive foreign aid there are some capital projects which are largely labour-using—irrigation schemes and roads—and labour is the most plentiful factor of production. Moreover, the argument that the terms of trade have a long-run tendency to turn against primary-producing areas is not a well-established thesis, and the evidence is contradictory. Again, if the recommendations of the United Nations regarding economic stability are to have any force at all, then primary producers will be saved from the scourge of large fluctuations in the prices paid for their exports. Indeed, it is a moot point whether this is not a practical alternative in some degree to the import of foreign capital. It presupposes, however, that under-developed areas can find some means of encouraging primary producers to save and to lend their savings for the finance of capital projects. Alternatively it means that some means will have to be found to tax the profits of prosperous primary producers in order to finance government capital projects without at the same time reducing their incentive to export.

If extensive foreign aid is forthcoming, what projects are most likely to increase productivity rapidly? At first sight it seems necessary to finance the purchase of fixed capital and equipment of all kinds, agricultural machinery, power plants, and so on. On the other hand, the operation of technical instruments of production presupposes at least some rudiments of education not only in order to operate these instruments, but in order to appreciate the benefits they may provide. Scientists, technicians, administrators, and a skilled labour force are as scarce factors as material capital. Accordingly, despite the short-run effects of better health conditions on the increase in human numbers, investment in specialized types of public health is necessary. In education also we should find an echo of Marshall's support for redistribution—namely, that better education will increase the earning power of future generations. But here again the choice is difficult. Political aspirations may demand the development of universal education, while purely economic considerations suggest a concentration of effort in technical education for a limited number. Foreign aid is not unlimited. The economic problem of the allocation of scarce means between different competing uses eventually dominates the technical problem of the use of these resources for any particular project. In commercial projects, the use of these resources can be judged in terms of the return on capital invested, but the return on education and health is difficult to measure, and inevitably the choice between investment in human beings and material investment is a hard one to make if the means provided are limited.

Assuming that, in the long run, either through foreign aid or the development of home resources, under-developed areas can increase real output at a more rapid rate—and this appears reasonable enough—what of the population factor?

Now, it is extremely difficult to forecast what may happen in the more distant future. If increases in the standard of living are sufficient in the short run to diversify the content of the goods and services available, it seems reasonable to suppose that the desire to have children may be weakened. But what matters so far as population growth is concerned is the sexual instinct rather than the procreative instinct. Here we must assume that the spread of knowledge of birth control, already apparent in India, will be a major factor in the years to come, and that the practices implied will not be opposed by the sanction of moral and religious codes. But this is an assumption, and it does not behove the economist to decide whether it is a reasonable one or not. However, I feel that the economist has as much right as anyone to pose certain questions to those who are more intrepid than he may be in forecasting economic progress over the next centuries.

To sum up, I think it can be said with some force that the Malthusian theory of population does at least give prominence to the relevant factors which influence economic development in the broad sense, even in the present century. Consequently, it is churlish to dismiss him as a second-rate economist and a sort of amateur anthropologist. It is true that it may not be possible to accept that there is any automatic link between the level of subsistence and the birth-rate and that what is left of the theory may amount to a truism. Nevertheless, in the next decades, in view of the imminent decline in mortality rates in under-developed countries, "Malthusian Devil of Population" may be a constant danger. It is a moot point whether Malthus's *Essay* was a warning rather than a prophecy. We can accept the warning, perhaps, even if we do not accept the Malthusian remedies. If what I have said is true, then, with Mr Fax,[8] we shall agree that "there are degrees and modes of well-grounded reliance on futurity, sufficient to justify the enterprises of prudence".

Alan T. Peacock

[8] The pleasant literary embodiment of Malthus found in Thomas Love Peacock's novel, *Melincourt*.

SOURCES

Essay I

James Bonar, *Malthus and his Work*, 2nd ed. (Macmillan, London, 1924). Abridged. Supplemented by notes from G. F. McCleary, *The Malthusian Population Theory* (Faber & Faber, London, 1953) and C. R. Fay and James Bonar, "Addresses delivered on the occasion of the centenary of Malthus's death, at the University of Cambridge", *Economic Journal*, 45 (1935).

Essay II

William Empson, Review of "*Principles of Political Economy Considered with a View to their Practical Application.* By the Rev. T. R. Malthus, F.R.S., Second Edition, to which is prefixed a Memoir of the Author's Life, 8 vol., London, 1836", *Edinburgh Review*, 64 (1837), excerpts.

Essay III

From Alan T. Peacock, "Malthus in the Twentieth Century", in *Introduction to Malthus*, ed. D. V. Glass (Watts & Co, London; Wiley, New York, 1953). Abridged.

Signature

British Museum, London.

Portrait

Painted and engraved by John Linnell (National Portrait Gallery, London).

BIBLIOGRAPHY

Ch. Comte, *La vie et les travaux de Malthus* (Académie des Sciences morales et politiques, Paris, 1836).

J. M. Keynes, *Thomas Robert Malthus, Essays in Biography* (London, 1933).

J. Bonar, C. R. Fay, J. M. Keynes, "Commemoration of Th. R. Malthus", *Economic Journal*, 45 (1935).

D. V. Glass, *Introduction to Malthus* (London, 1953).

G. F. McCleary, *The Malthusian Population Theory* (London 1953); chapter, "Malthus as professor".

B. Semmel (ed.), *Occasional Papers of* T. R. *Malthus* (New York, 1963).

M. Blaug, "Thomas Robert Malthus", in *International Encyclopedia of the Social Sciences*, Vol. 9 (New York 1968).

S. Hollander, "Malthus and the Post-Napoleonic Depression", *History of Political Economy* (1969).

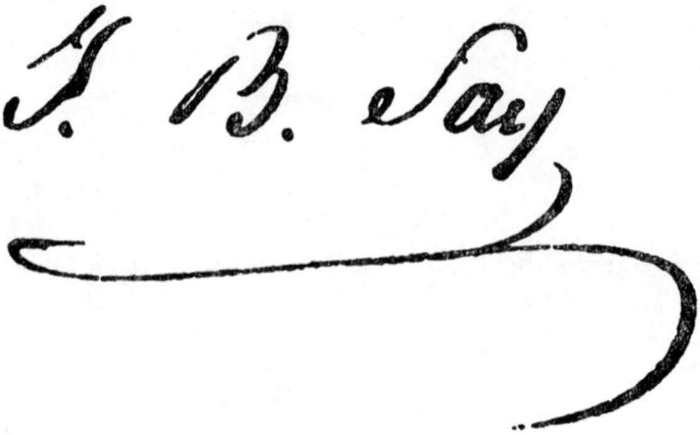

JEAN-BAPTISTE SAY

1767–1832

Il est mort comme il avait vécu, fidèle à ses doctrines économiques, philosophiques, politiques; quelque peu susceptible et fier, comme un homme sûr de lui-même et qui n'a jamais baissé le front devant aucun pouvoir, peuple ou roi; mais toujours sincèrement préoccupé des intérêts de l'humanité. A. BLANQUI

Sein persönlicher Anschluß an die Smithsche Lehre ließ seine eigene Leistung so weit zurücktreten, daß er weithin nur als der Popularisator Smithens erschien, zumal nachdem ihn Lorenz v. Stein in einem seiner mehr glanzals gehaltvollen Urteile so abgestempelt hatte. E. SALIN

His really great contribution to analytic economics is his conception of economic equilibrium, hazy and unperfectly formulated though it was: Say's work is the most important of the links in the chain that leads from Cantillon and Turgot to Walras. J. A. SCHUMPETER

I
LIFE AND PERSONALITY OF JEAN-BAPTISTE SAY

The family of Jean-Baptiste Say originally came from Nîmes, from whence it was exiled towards the end of the seventeenth century when the Edict of Nantes was suddenly repealed. One piece of evidence of this event has come down to the present generation, namely the basket in which the fugitive grandmother carried off the remnants of a hard-earned fortune. Geneva opened its gates to the outlaws and it was there that Jean-Étienne Say, father of Jean-Baptiste, was born in 1739. When times took a turn for the better, Jean-Étienne, still very young, was able to move to Lyons for a business apprenticeship with Monsieur Castanet, a Protestant like the Says and, like them, a native of Nîmes. These links between employee and employer soon became more intimate and Jean-Étienne Say succeeded Monsieur Castanet, after marrying one of his daughters. From this marriage

Jean-Baptiste Say was born at Lyons on 5 January 1767. His childhood was spent in this small industrial town which he always loved to revisit, and to which he was bound by vivid and profound memories.

His father, a man of good sense, took upon himself the task of instilling into him sound and positive ideas from an early age. An Oratorian, Father Lefèvre, provided a very well-attended course of experimental physics at Lyons. The child Jean-Baptiste became one of his most attentive pupils and, having some elementary knowledge, drew from his lessons an acquaintance with method and a manner of thinking uncommon for this age. In later years Jean-Baptiste Say was happy to recall the help that this initial instruction had been to him and this precocious excursion into the field of natural phenomena. At the age of nine the time had come for him to enter a boarding-school. Two Italian scholars called Giro and Gorati had come to found an institution, in the village of Ecully near Lyons, which was trying out new methods and above all striving to resist the pressure of current prejudices. It was here that the young Say was brought up, under the influence of names and ideas that did honour to that century, amid the noise of intellectual conquests, and amid the whispering of passions which inspired succeeding generations. Such impressions were to become indelibly imprinted in a well-tempered character like Say's. He grew up with the ideas of his time, made a kind of cult of them and associated them with the discoveries which were to make his name famous.

A number of changes in his father's fortune led to the sudden interruption of his education; the young Say had to follow his family to Paris and to leave the boarding-school for the shop-counter. However, as soon as things took a more favourable turn again, he succeeded in getting to England with his brother Horace, to complete his business studies. The two men crossed the Channel and took lodgings in the village of Croydon a few miles from London. It was a decisive turn in Jean-Baptiste Say's life. For, if he had not been initiated into the secrets of the English language on the very spot and through hard practice, the economist's vocation might, perhaps, have never been aroused in him, for want of being able to read Adam Smith in the original. The sight of the industrial revolution in England also left a deep impression in his memory. Jean-Baptiste Say saw this system at its finest hour, in the intoxication of its first success, when, served by a mechanical revolution, England's island industry was springing forth to conquer the world's markets. Asked for his opinion later, he admitted his enthusiastic memories, and the crises which ensued, while not escaping his notice, could not change his view nor shake his confidence.[1]

[1] At this stage of his life a little incident occurred of which he loved to tell as one of the things which put him on the path of political economy. He occupied a room in Croydon lit by two small casement-windows, which was no great

Following a second brief commercial apprenticeship in London, Jean-Baptiste Say accompanied his new employer on a journey, which was taken, as a last resort, on medical advice. He saw him die in Bordeaux; and so, finding himself back in France, he once more sought the bosom of his family, after gathering experience of men and circumstances which his strength of mind would duly render profitable. During this period of his life he had the doubts and ups and downs which normally beset a young man at the time of choosing a career. While family traditions and his father's wishes pushed him towards industry or commerce, Jean-Baptiste's own inclination tended towards letters. He resigned himself and, full of zeal, took up employment in a life insurance company, where Clavière, who later became a minister, was managing director; but, instead of allowing himself to become absorbed in a purely mechanical task, it was here, in these very offices, that he embraced the science which he would adorn as one of its most celebrated students. Clavière possessed a copy of Adam Smith's *Wealth of Nations*, which had not yet been translated into French. On his advice, Jean-Baptiste Say read the book, which was a complete revelation to him: he was an economist. He promptly ordered a copy from London, studied it, made notes and, from that moment, never again did without it.

Science, however, was still too grave a matter for his age and it was to give way for the time being to literary tastes, above all to theatre, and the young economist himself loved to take part in plays. Soon he could not fail getting caught up by the gravity of the events in store and by the movement of social regeneration which electrified all minds. His first literary effort was a brochure published in 1789, in favour of freedom of the press.

When the invasion of national territory by coalition troops of foreign armies called young Frenchmen to arms, Jean-Baptiste Say served as a volunteer in the campaign of 1792 in Champagne. He had joined a number of artists and writers who had formed a *compagnie des arts*.

Shortly after his return from active service on 25 May 1793, he married Mlle Deloche, daughter of a former barrister; this marriage was to become for him a constant source of happiness and to provide him with that peace

luxury under a sky with all too little light to spare. One day two masons, armed with bricks and mortar, entered his abode and silently set to work. Their business was to brick up one of the two apertures; the door and window tax had just been passed by Parliament, and the owner of the house, a wary man, considered it advisable to reduce his taxable substance by a half. The young Say had to give in, but his common sense rebelled. His lodgings were made gloomier, less agreeable and that to no one's advantage—"I have lost a window", he said to himself, "and the Treasury has gained nothing. Obviously, there are only dupes in all this." When, long afterwards, he wrote a curious chapter about taxes which produce no revenue for the Exchequer, our economist, by then a famous man, was doubtless taking his revenge for his experience in Croydon.

of mind without which it could often have been hard for him to have endured the trials of life.

The young couple settled in the country; plans were drawn up for the founding of a school where young boys, in restricted numbers, might be taught with special care and receive a liberal and varied education. The project might have succeeded but was soon abandoned after a visit paid one day by a certain group of literary men. They came to offer Jean-Baptiste Say the editorship of a periodical that was destined to revive the cult of good taste and a healthy philosophy in France. The offer thus made by Guinguené and Andrieux, of dear and gracious memory, was accepted, and the first number of the *Décade philosophique, littéraire et politique, par un société de républicains* appeared in the month of Floréal, the year II (29 April 1794).

His brother, Horace Say, the military engineer, died of wounds received at Saint-Jean-d'Acre in Syria. This loss was a cruel blow for Jean-Baptiste Say; he had lost his closest friend, the confidant of all his thoughts, with whom he had delighted to engage in dreams about the future. Youth's illusions fell, and the reality, the difficulties and the serious work of middle age began. He still had a younger brother whom he had invited to be near him, but who was to leave him soon to follow a commercial career. Louis Say became a sugar-refiner at Nantes and, drawing inspirations from his brother's works, he also published several pamphlets on similar subjects.

In November 1799, Jean-Baptiste Say was appointed a member of the Tribunal and from then on gave up editing the *Décade philosophique*. He was attached to the finance committee. The tribunes' task was to discuss, before a dumb legislative body, legal projects that had been prepared by the Council of State and put forward in the name of the First Consul. Jean-Baptiste Say's independent spirit could not settle for the role they tried to thrust upon him, and it was to cast him into this courageous opposition which resisted for as long as possible the injuries inflicted upon liberty, on which his warnings—it was later on regretted—went unheard. Not being able to convince him or seduce him in his opposition, they decided to get rid of him from the Tribunal.

Study and literary activity offered consolation for political disappointment. For the previous three years, the faculty of moral and political sciences in the Institut de France had set the following question for a competition: "By what methods, and then, by what institutions, should morality be established in a nation?" Jean-Baptiste Say tardily decided to compete, but was not able to submit to the prescribed regulations; but, in sketching out some precepts, he considered it his duty to apply them and produce them to the light of day. His *Mémoire*, published in the year 8, was entitled: *Olbie, ou Essai sur les moyens d'améliorer les moeurs d'une nation*. The author imagines a nation of people, whom he calls the Olbiens, who, having freed themselves of the yoke that had weighed heavily on them for centuries, have adopted the most suitable means of reforming their vices and making virtue reign victorious.

The *Mémoire* for the Institut was the forerunner of the *Traité d'économie politique* which was published four years later. It appeared for the first time in 1803, when the author was thirty-six. This fine production, even before the improvements it received in its six subsequent editions, was already a gigantic task. The truths half-glimpsed by the economists of the eighteenth century, which Adam Smith had vigorously demonstrated, were at last coordinated in a logical arrangement.

From the moment it appeared, the *Traité d'économie politique* had an unqualified success and brought its author to the notice of the Head of State. The man who was so adept at acquiring for his own ends all that was most glorious and talented, resolved to make some further efforts at seduction. After dinner at Malmaison, the First Consul took Jean-Baptiste Say aside along the park walks and enthusiastically expounded his proposals for improving the financial situation, trying to persuade him that their practical success essentially depended on his offering his services, because from then on books would be of the greatest use in justifying in the eyes of the public any measures that might turn out to be necessary. So, a new edition of the *Traité* should be made, and made into a book to suit the hour. The master did not fail to press his point, but it is unlikely to have kept a happy memory of the discussion. The disciple lacked a suppleness of mind, which was an all too common feature of this age; his convictions had been formed by serious study and his conscience was uncompromising.

It was not long before he was expelled from the Tribunal; but, by one of those contradictions typical of those who hold power, which sufficiently explains the desire to silence any recrimination on his part, he was simultaneously able to read in the *Moniteur* of his appointment to the office of director of *droits réunis*.[2] As a father of four children, without any fortune, it looked like being necessary for him to accept the post: however, he refused, because his conscience forbade him to comply with the application of a system that he deemed would prove fatal for France.

When the second edition of the *Traité* was ready, it was no longer possible to print it; the publisher had been summoned by the *direction de la librairie* to be told that he must refrain from publishing such a work. The First Consul was to become an all-powerful emperor; his inquisitorial police presented a distinct threat to all conscientious men with independent minds.

[2] *Droits réunis*: indirect taxation, united in a single administration at the time of the First Empire, which was most unpopular.

As Say had voluntarily forgone a career in public service there was no other way to provide for his family than by turning towards trade or industry. He made a journey to Sédan to try to interest himself in a cloth factory and then pressed on to Geneva.

On this occasion he was invited by Monsieur Necker to Coppet. Madame de Staël was charming, as she always was in society. The reverence she felt towards her father spread out, in his presence, over the sallies of her wit, a kind of transparent veil which softened, without masking, any tones that were too brusque and gave them a new attraction. Benjamin Constant was also present and his keen mind shared the same delights, which made the conversation constantly alive and varied.

On his return to Paris, Jean-Baptiste Say settled for the cotton mill. He had been a witness to the revolution brought about by Arkwright's great invention in this industry in England; similar advances would be taking place in France; in order to participate, however, and to know how to control the workers, one had first to master every aspect of a difficult art and to begin by working with one's own hands. Whole production-lines were moved from England and installed in the *Conservatoire*,[3] where Monsieur Say became a worker and his ten-year-old son Horace served as his assistant. Neither of them took long to become proficient in their trade.

Jean-Baptiste Say's mill, first situated in the Abbey building of Maubisson, was later moved to Auchy near Hesdin in the Province of Pas-de-Calais where it still stands. Under such good management the business prospered, and on all sides poverty was seen to be replaced by easy circumstances.

This long stay in active withdrawal was not, by any means, unfavourable to study. Placed outside the political movement, the economist observed, as an impartial although not indifferent spectator, the mistakes of the Empire, the continental system, licensed trade and all those numerous measures that more often sprang from anger than from reason. Early rising was the rule at Auchy, yet the daylight hours were always too short. Literature and the arts were cultivated for the sake of relaxation and there was no lack of company.

The customs duty on cotton had been raised to a ridiculously high level and the problem of communications further increased the price of this staple commodity. Jean-Baptiste Say foresaw the imminent collapse of a system that was also contrary to the true interests of the people. Following some disagreements with his partner on this subject he decided to retire, which brought him in a modest capital. He returned to Paris with his

[3] Conservatoire des arts et métiers is a public institution founded in Paris in 1794, for the instruction of applied arts and sciences.

family in 1813, when events were only too soon and too severely to justify the philosopher's predictions for France.

Thanks to the partial liberty that could not be refused a country which had been worn out by too much war, the *Traité d'économie politique* was reprinted, and this edition was soon to be followed by several others.

Peace restored communications that had been broken off for a quarter of a century. It was interesting, above all for the French, to seek to reckon up the progress that the English had been able to achieve, whose industry, favoured by supremacy at sea, had made such rapid development. Say got the government to send him on a mission to England to study its economy and to return with all the relevant information for practical application in France. This task of exploration was made easy for him by his knowledge of the English tongue, his own experience as a manufacturer and the esteem his reputation earned him. He was warmly received by the economists, particularly by Ricardo, by Bentham and by the professors of the English and Scottish universities. He embarked on an extremely instructive journey which provided him with happy memories. At Glasgow he was asked to sit in the professorial chair of Adam Smith and it was with considerable emotion that he told his audience one day at the *Conservatoire des arts et métiers* about this episode on his journey.

Political economy had always frightened the Government in France and had, accordingly, been thrust upon the Opposition. So, it was a great attraction for the public when Jean-Baptiste Say began a course of lectures in that science at the Athenaeum in 1815; it was attended by crowds and was a complete success. Encouraged by the homage paid him, the professor redoubled his efforts to propagate the doctrines he considered so vital to the future of nations. In *Le catéchisme d'économie politique*, he used the familiar form of dialogue, which enables the author rapidly to state those difficulties he considers it essential to resolve, whilst leaving out the less important issues which could only be discussed with lengthy dissertation. *Le catéchisme d'économie politique*, first published in 1817, has had numerous editions and has, like the *Traité*, been translated into almost all the European languages.

Political economy, however, did not take up all of Jean-Baptiste Say's time; in order to assess its proper sphere and to define its limits, he had also been obliged to make a complete study of the whole of moral and political sciences. He left numerous fragments, indicating that, if he had had the time, he meant to write a treatise on ethics and another on practical politics. The observations he had seen fit to write down were methodically classified and those which were not destined for purely scientific works would have been included in writings of a more familiar nature. *La Correspondance d'un docteur* and his own *Mémoires* seemed to him to furnish an appropriate outline; but the task of propagating useful truths enabled him to overlook no aspect of the art of eloquence, and his preparatory notes for *Lettres à une dame sur le talent d'écrire* give us cause for regret that this work was never finished. Being ever aware that time was lacking for him to bring all his projects to an end and to complete all his sketches, he collected some of his ideas, selected those which came to him readily and rapidly, submitted them for publication and allowed them to appear under the title: *Petit Volume, contenant quelques aperçus des hommes et la société.* This book introduces the author and depicts him better than his other writings.

Not long after the publication of the *Petit Volume* appeared the brochure, *De l'Importance du port de la villette.*

The third edition of the *Traité d'économie politique* had, like the second, run to a great number of copies, but it was almost entirely sold out in the same year. In 1819 it appeared in a fourth edition with corrections and considerable additions. The author used new arguments in the chapters dealing with the balance of trade, the grain trade and the use of capital; he almost completely revised the first five chapters of Book 2 and made some important additions to some chapters of Book 3.

The financial and commercial crises in England furnished him with useful information on these matters. Jean-Baptiste Say kept himself up to date on all the relevant publications and maintained an active correspondence with all those who were engaged upon the subject and could lay claim to authority. While Say willingly acknowledged the important services to science rendered by Ricardo's works on money, he was not afraid to challenge him in some respects on the analysis to which he had recourse in dealing with ground rent, which Say considered to be far too subtle.

The appearance of *Nouveaux principes d'économie politique* by Malthus led to a polemic which was duly sent to press. Six *Lettres à Malthus* contain excellent dissertations on the causes of commercial crises, on the theory of marketing and on those of immaterial goods.

The replies to Malthus also served, in many cases, to refute some of Sismondi's objections regarding the disadvantages of the freedom of labour and competition. A special article, *Balance des productions et des consommations*, completed the defence of principles without in any way altering the excellent accounts that united two men equally devoted to goodness and truth.

There was good cause for surprise that a science so important to mankind, so useful to consult for the successful management of national affairs, was still left out of all French public education. So, the first thing was to try to get a chair of political economy set up in one of the *écoles supérieures.* The chair in the Law School was decided on in principle, without making this a permanent institution, and the chair at the Conservatoire itself was only founded after altering the title of the course of study. As the word "political" proved too alarming for over-sensitive authority, one had to be content to teach "industrial" economy. These restrictions and the place chosen for instruction deprived the course of much of its attraction, and it was only after 1830 that, already weakened by age, Jean-Baptiste Say was to be nominated as Professor of political economy proper at the Collège de France.

Everywhere he spoke, his lectures were followed with a lively interest and his teaching always given with lucidity, with elegance and, above all, with a warm conviction that inspired confidence. The professor might, perhaps, be criticized for asking of his audience a too prolonged attention in delivering lectures that contained too many facts. This was partly due to a desire to make an effort to include the whole of economics in the framework of the course, and partly to the fact that his lectures were written. Those who knew him and had heard his conversation, always rich in fact and varied in expression, bitterly regretted that he never brought himself to take the risk of improvising during his professorship. The only explanation for this reticence on his part can be found in his extreme self-criticism, in his fear of wasting audiences' time by useless repetition, and in his desire for always stating well-established truths as clearly and concisely as he could. "I have hardly ever been satisfied with my conversation," he wrote one day. "My second thought is generally better than the first, and unfortunately it is always the latter which is produced in conversation. I feel tempted to say with Madame Riccoboni, who was reproached with not speaking as well as she wrote, and who replied: 'It's because I speak as I revise'." Jean-Baptiste Say did, in fact, revise as he wrote, and if chance often brought him a happy turn of phrase, one might say that he well deserved the benefits of chance.

The lectures, which he wrote before delivering them, were generally extracts from a piece of work prepared in longhand for the printer, which were subsequently published in 1828 and 1829 in six volumes under the title *Cours complet d'économie politique pratique*.

While his reputation grew abroad the author shut himself up in a modest way of life; he rarely showed himself in the noisy world but lived apart, surrounded by his family and a small circle of friends. Here, once a week, he would receive a few distinguished men and foreign economists, of whom none failed to pay him homage. The high level of his mind revealed itself in these intimate conversations which he would enliven by his brilliantly original sallies and an inexhaustible variety of knowledge. He loved to mock the men of power and never missed an opportunity of censuring bad books and bad measures in political economy. The Continental System of the Empire, and the customs legislation of the Restoration that imposed such fatal dues on iron, wool and cattle, never had a more outspoken critic. No one worked with more persistence to discredit war, its hindrances and prohibitions, so as, on the contrary, to make men value the importance of public works, of roads, canals and free communication between all men.

Furthermore, his health had long been undermined. His powerful and nervous temperament appeared to suffer from the sedentary work of a study to which he was enslaved, and in his last years he fell victim to attacks of nervous apoplexy, which progressively enfeebled him, foreshadowing his early death. A cruel loss was to deal him a fatal blow, which he bore with courage but could not long survive: Madame Say died on 10 January 1830; only those people who had known her realized the inexpressible charm she had succeeded in bestowing on her husband's life.

Indeed, from then on, Jean-Baptiste Say's health went steadily downhill. There was an effort to distract him with a journey; he was visiting his brother at Nantes when the July Revolution broke out. Nominated shortly afterwards to membership of the *conseil général* in the department of Seine, he found that, as the end of a few months, he was obliged through tiredness to resign his duties; it required great efforts and great willpower to continue with his course at the Collège de France. On 15 November 1832, he suffered another attack which was to be the last. Not feeling capable of working that day, he had gone out to pay a few visits. He called in at his aunt's, his mother's sister, suddenly lost consciousness and after fourteen hours of agony he breathed his last in his own children's arms. He was then sixty-six years old.

The observation has been made that men whose lives have been devoted to profound and conscientious study of political economy have generally been excellent citizens, sincere and enlightened friends of liberty. Perhaps this science shows better than others the effects of faulty measures of government; perhaps it allows of no illusions as to the nature and value of services to the public; or perhaps it guards one against mistaking the true source of wealth. Jean-Baptiste Say, who from 1789 declared himself in favour of the cause of freedom, and who served this cause by all means in his power, remained true to his principles until the end of his career. Nothing in the world would have made him associate his name with any measure that his conscience disapproved.

The greater part of the academies of Europe numbered him among their members. Only the belated reorganization of the faculty of moral and political sciences prevented the Institut de France from making good, in his respect, a great injustice.

Charles Comte, Eugène Daire, Horace Say

II
THE WORK OF JEAN-BAPTISTE SAY

The law of markets has done more for the fame of Say than all the rest of his work put together. This would not have surprised its author, who wrote: "The theory of heat, the theory of the lever, and the theory of the inclined plane have put all Nature at mankind's disposal. But it is the theory of exchange and outlet that will change world politics." He did not doubt that he had found the argument that was to realize the benefits of economic liberalism.

What, then, did this discovery consist of? Say approaches the question in chapter 15, Book 1, of the *Traité*, dealing with the "incidental circumstances favourable or contrary to the production of wealth", and he approaches the same problem in a more developed way in chapter 2, Part 3, of the *Cours*, devoted to exchange and currency, which shows that the importance of the problem became more apparent to him later, and that he connected it more closely with the question of liberalism.

A few very simple statements indicate the author's chain of reasoning:

1. If products cost nothing, the demand for them would be infinite, and their outlets enormous, always supposing there were men born to consume them.

2. So, it is not the will to acquire possessions which is lacking, but the means, that is, the money.

3. But money comes into our hands, either because we have products to sell, or because we receive a share of those which have been sold.

4. What can we conclude from this? If it is with products that we purchase products, then each product will find all the more purchasers as other products multiply.

Four fundamental consequences can be deduced from this formula:

1. If our production reaches as high a level as possible, and this is necessary, the outlets will open of their own accord. The result is productivity, reinforced by this view of economic activity; but a still more important result, for Say at least, is liberalism, for, in order to produce, it is essential not to shackle the initiative of the producers—(Say is also thinking of the corporations).

2. The amount of currency in circulation is of little importance for the opening of outlets; it is wrong that business interests should always have their eyes fixed on this factor. As the total value of currency varies with the total value of of the volume of goods, there is always enough money for

circulation purposes. Since currency does its own job by itself, what is the use of forcing the very nature of things by an artificial monetary policy?

3. In the last analysis, every individual is interested in the wealth of every other individual; every enterprise and every nation is concerned with all the rest; which points to a great lesson in the field of human relations, where one can denounce the use of custom duties, quota systems, bans, and all like measures as injurious to the very people who decide upon them and believe that they will profit by them. It was ignorance of this basic law of political economy that led to Bonaparte's downfall.

4. And lastly, in more general terms, the law of outlets shows that economic balance is spontaneous; how could general crises possibly happen, since excessive production is not possible? Since each act of production opens its own outlet? Say's conception of balance is an appeal for total liberty in every sphere of the economy.

This theory, one imagines, seemed as grandiose as it was simple, bringing the economy and man together at the very moment when the pessimism of a Ricardo would have opened up a breach, which Marx was later to enlarge still further.

As a matter of fact, comparing Say's ideas here with his predecessors' —the physiocrats and Adam Smith—one realizes that, at least at bottom, there was nothing absolutely novel in his contribution. Like Say, they had amply underlined the purely intermediary character of currency: but Say expresses it much better in a striking way, and his much more suggestive formula has managed to serve as a convenient point of departure for students of the theory of currency and exchange.

However, is it not possible that this simplicity and clarity are only achieved at the expense of fundamental meaning? For Say, in fact, only the goods whose value *is at least equal to their cost of production* are worthy of the name of "product". The product must be sufficiently *in demand* for the supplier to be able to recover his expenses. What is meant by this, except that the conception of a product necessarily comprises, by its very definition, that of a *débouché suffisant*? To state that products are always exchanged for other products is the same as saying that goods which find sufficient solvent consumers always find outlets.

On this point, all the author's arguments are purely verbal and confined to being tautological.

At the same time, they remain quite abstract: the law of outlets is introduced as a logical proposition before which the real facts ought to bow. Once having traced an ideal scheme in outline, without any other true examination of the issue, one asserts that it is borne out by the facts. Indeed, Say is not satisfied by merely stating that products are exchanged when there is nothing to disturb the normal course of events, but goes on to describe *what happens in reality*, and to show that after all, in spite of all the obstacles, products always do succeed in being exchanged for products.

He is right, of course, if we abide by his own definition of the word "product"; but his adversaries give production its contemporary and, what is more, its rightful meaning: they do not, in fact, say that an enterprise has produced nothing when its products are unsold. Say, moreover, benefits from this misunderstanding by proceeding from the narrow notion of production (when it is a question of showing, mainly, that there can be no over-production) to the wider notion (that, in fact, more generally adopted). Malthus has especially seen a surfeit of abstraction in Say's arguments and, in his *Principles*, reproaches our economist for his unrealistic attitude in treating goods as "algebraic formulae", by making an abstraction of the number of consumers and the nature of their needs.

We have now to put Say's work into its general background and to see to what extent it constitutes an original contribution.

First of all, it is necessary to adopt an attitude towards the tendencies to give Say either an exaggerated, or, on the contrary, too unobtrusive a role. It is by restoring our author to the place which was rightly his that we shall be able to understand his true value.

Certain commentators, as we have seen, have wanted to portray Say as a genius who formed the hub of nineteenth-century economic thought. It is essential not to confer on Say a kind of intellectual monopoly and to affirm that it is *his* naturalism and *his* rationalism which influence the writers of the subsequent decades.

We must distinguish carefully, as well, between the outline of a new idea (or even a simple suggestion) and the conscious and complete elaboration of a theory. Say has many good ideas. He approaches his subject from different angles, as his thought is sometimes far from unified, in spite of the impression to the contrary that can be given by the rigour of his style. Should this, then, lead us to conclude that modern economics has done no more than revive, on various points, the indications that he had already given?

In short, it does not seem possible for us to agree that it was Say who gave direction to, not only French liberalism, but also Saint-Simonism, Proudhon's doctrine, the American protectionism of a Carey, and the socialism of a Henry George. If this were so, Mr Aftalion (and his psychological method) would find himself on one of the numerous "spirals" Say initiated. The dialectic method (at least, Proudhon's), made up of a thesis, an antithesis and a synthesis, would thus have the same (Say's) origin. Indeed, there are partial influences, but they are sometimes very slight, and it seems to us that there is the risk, by reaction, of harming anything which is genuinely original and personal in Say's works, thus excessively extending the circuit of his intellectual action.

Other writers, as we have already noticed, seem to have misunderstood the role of our economist. Most often, they have thought of him as either a mere "translator" of Smith or as an author who would be content to juxtapose, without any originality, such diverse contributions as, apart from that of Smith, the ideas of Turgot, Condillac, or even Roederer.

The great problem which undoubtedly dominates all others here are the relations between Say and Adam Smith.

It is enough to read the *Traité* to realize the connecting links between them. On many occasions, Smith is quoted and approved by Say. In the abbreviated history of political economics which concludes his *Cours*, Say enthusiastically compares the author of the *Wealth of Nations* with the greatest men of genius and, in particular, with Newton. "I could never", he exclaims, "do justice to the progress Smith effected in political economy without writing a whole book about it."

But it would be incorrect to think of Say adopting slavishly the ideas of the man he recognizes as his master. The alphabetical table of contents, following the *Cours* and summarizing Say's ideas, leaves the impression, in the article on Smith, that the points in Smith's work criticized by the French economist are numerous.

What had determined Say's attitude to the *Wealth of Nations* were the political and economic upheavals of the years since its publication. Say's position, in relation to the physiocrats, for example, is much more categorical than Smith's: the picture is already quite transformed with land assuming more and more a secondary role after industrial progress.

Say, moreover, wrote in France, and was a French economist; we find in his works a more systematic, and above all clearer and more orderly, account of the general ideas. We find, especially, different influences, a more "psychological" conception of value and a less materialistic one of riches and production. Different economic customs in both countries allow Say to make a new distinction between the interest of the capitalist and the profit of the contractor; they also, to a certain extent, played a part in allowing the French author to attach less importance to the problem of income than his English colleagues, and to bring about the unification of the general mechanism of distribution.

But it is not especially these circumstances of time and place which give Say his originality, compared with Smith: to him his milieu by itself is insufficient to create a work of value. It is our economist's strong personality which has defined his new conceptions separately from the influence of the English school; this personality, completely centred on concrete realities, was different from Smith's. The Glasgow professor stayed a philosopher, and his very realism bore the imprint of a purely intellectual training; Say, descended from a line of merchants, stayed, in some ways, a practitioner. The far too uncritical nature of his scientific spirit shows a common tendency in men of action moving in the province of ideas where they retain a certain reverential fear.

His basic tendencies led our author in a very different direction from his master's: his industrialism, his productivity (not apparent in his theory of outlets), his admiration for technical progress and for men able to promote and apply it, might well have evoked in him an evolution very similar to that of Saint-Simon—towards an economy directed by an elite of suppliers. In this case, the practical tendencies of Say, his taste for reality and his sense of moderation, would no doubt have permitted him to avoid the excesses of Saint-Simon's *Illuminism*. He would, in fact, have been able to establish a balanced "social economy"; and it is this point which those who sing his praises extol openly.

Say has not gone as far as that; but the nature of his influence shows that the dual aspect of his work—the classical and liberal influence which it retained on the one hand, and the living and human influence it made apparent on the other—was not lost on either his contemporaries or his immediate successors.

So, we find a French liberal tradition which owes much to Say, because he has widened its horizons and defined its basic points of view.

Besides this first and most distinctive sphere of influence, we must point out Say's more limited work in various other fields.

1. It should first of all be realized that the French liberal school, and sometimes even that of other countries, of the first half of the nineteenth century, owes its most original elements to Say. To be sure, Bastiat was for a long time the best known by the general public, thanks to his talent for pamphleteering and his journalistic verve; but the author of *Harmonies économiques* (as today is generally admitted) is far from having Say's culture and level of thought. His basic ideas can, moreover, for the most part, be compared to either Say's or Carey's.

The optimism shown by Bastiat and the French liberal school, in contrast to the attitude of someone like Ricardo, only constitutes a synthesis of Say's more prudent thinking. The theory of free benefits revives the lead already given by the author of the *Traité*, as we saw, by his distinction between natural wealth (provided by nature) and social wealth, for which one has to pay. The arguments for free exchange, in spite of their original presentation, have already for the most part been supplied by Smith and his disciple. Say is here the real inspiration and grand master.

Say was also, to a large extent, the real inspiration and grand master in the liberal team of the *Censeur*, where he met Charles Comte, Dunoyer and

Augustin Thierry: it was his "industrialism", added to his love of freedom, that set the tone for the periodical.

The importance of the *Censeur* as the centre of Say's economic and political influence is great. This periodical defended the liberal opposition's policies, and recommended to the Parisian electorate Lafitte and Lafayette, for instance. At the same time, on the economic level, it underlined the difference between producers and non-producers. As we have already pointed out, the first kind—the industrialists, the tradespeople, the craftsmen and the workers—were often politically friendly to the liberals of that time, while the nonproducers—the office workers, and the clergy—were their enemies.

Whatever views historians have finally adopted, nearly all the liberal or semi-liberal French economists bear witness to Say's influence in varying degrees. His liberalism shows to best effect in Pellegrino Rossi's and Adolphe Blanqui's works, while Michel Chevalier and Baudrillart give the most industrialist and interventionist account.

2. But if the liberals of the first half of the century find inspiration in the thought of our economist, the consequences of this same influence are still apparent at the end of the century. In this connection, Rist is perfectly right in quoting an important comment made by Stanley Jevons: "The most obvious conclusion which I always reach is that the only way of attaining a true system of political economy is to reject, once and for all, the muddled and ludicrous hypotheses of the Ricardian school. The truth lies in the French school [and here he recognizes the importance of Say's influence] and the sooner we realize this, the better it will be."

Léon Walras equally, if only partly doing justice to Say, resumed in its broad outlines his conception of the association of productive services in production, and also used his notion of the contractor and his general scheme of equilibrium. He stated, however, rather paradoxically, that "Say has not altogether grasped the part played by the contractor: this character is missing from his theory." In taking up a position nearer Smith than Say, Walras was not being very fair to the latter. It is true that Say, in his turn, had treated Auguste Walras's theory on scarcity, as a basis for valuation, with contemptuous severity.

It would be possible to trace the influence of Say right up to the liberal or semi-liberal elements of our own time. The position of the French economist, as far as the law of outlets is concerned, is still, as we have seen, frequently commented upon. But two successive "revolutions", to mention only the most important, have destroyed belief in this law in such milieux. The first of these was the Wicksellian revolution, whose results were described in 1898 in Wicksell's own work *Geldzins und Güterpreise* where the author insists on the existence of *cumulative processes*, due to flux in currency or credit. With an "active" currency, Say's equivalence is no longer tenable.

The second is the Keynesian revolution, which dates from 1936 and the publication of Keynes's *General Theory*. From then on it was possible to recognize the plurality of possible balances, because a balance could exist at various levels of usage. The effect of "multiplying" upsets the old classical equivalence. Moreover, the conditions of formation for the rates of interest—a formation which becomes, in fact, a "prime factor" by comparison with the economy as a whole by acting on it without being acted on itself—completely destroy the equilibrium provided for between production and resultant buying power. There is a rift, also on the level of rates of interest, in the perfect "circulation of economic values", necessary for the maintenance of Say's equivalence.

3. It is noticeable that Say's ideas have played a large part, not only in influencing the liberals, but their opponents as well. We have seen the analogy between some of his ideas and those of Saint-Simon and the Saint-Simonists: at the beginning of the nineteenth century, the idea of the importance of producers, and the growth of economic in relation to political developments, stemmed from the economic revolution itself, and it is difficult to say to what extent Say shared in this expansion.

On the other hand, it seems that Proudhon, without actually owing Say as much as was imagined, did, however, borrow several important ideas from him. Starting from Say's basic equivalence, Proudhon denounces the "tolls" [*péages*] levied by the capitalists on buying power, who thus prevent the purchase of products with products. The possibility of "free credit" and an "exchange bank" is a consequence derived from the same principle: if currency and credit are to be normally passive intermediaries, always supplied in sufficient quantity, it is not apparent why the capitalist should receive an interest, unless it is because he robs those who borrow from him. By suppressing this unjust levy, economic balance is restored as well as justice.

Proudhon, like Say, allies rationalism and naturalism, and he is aware of the relationship between their attitudes of mind, because he does not spare his praises for the author of the *Traité*, whom he speaks of as a "man of genius".

The idea that it is necessary to re-establish equality between buying power and the value of supply, will haunt many other reformers who, while spurning Say's liberalism, accept his analysis of "equivalent" exchange, considered as an ideal. If the theorists of "under-consumption" have incessantly invoked Say and his theory of outlets, to oppose them, it is because they are in the position of "embattled brothers" with regard to Say. They never managed to escape from Say's scheme, which continued to remain the one that had to be. From the time of Sismondi until just before the Second World War, the partisans of under-consumption such as Major Douglas, Foster and Catchings, Ansiaux and Lederer, all try to show how a buying power, which should normally be in equilibrium with production, "escapes". The *practical* truth of the law of outlets is contested, but despite this, the law is taken as a theoretical basis of reference.

It appears that the most recent theory is in process of by-passing both the liberals and some of their opponents on the question of the law of outlets. Thorough research work shows that balance is *not* the rule, but that imbalances engendered by the movement of economic sizes constitute the norm; the "sequence models" method seeks to measure these imbalances and to forecast their results, and henceforward there is a tendency to break down reality in order to study it in more detail. This point of view in itself is much more analytical than Say's.

A more advanced analysis of the notion of "product" also shows the relativity of this idea; a "product", considered as such, is a flexible reality which varies with the fluctuations of *opinion*. Buying power is, therefore, not alone in undergoing eventual transformation; the product itself is economically unstable, even if materially durable. There is no "capital" for the product in the same way as there is a capital for a wage. Say's formula is only comprehensible if the production-exchange process is instantaneous.

Finally, all current studies on the psychology of the supplier as opposed to that of the consumer, show that the former is more dynamic, and has more "mental energy" than the latter. The supplier tires less quickly of launching new products on the market than the consumer of absorbing them. Sismondi, Malthus and Keynes have, by their own empirical observations, caught up with modern scientific viewpoints.

Must we then deduce from all that has been said that there is nothing for us to retain from Say's exertions in conceiving of the law of outlets? This would be a manifest injustice, as it would be equally unjust to fail to appreciate the efforts which he made in other spheres.

There are two great lessons Say has left us, and they are particularly valuable to the present-day development of economic science. First of all, the taste for harmony and synthesis: we must not, in the search for truth, lose sight of the fact that the general law is the object of economic research; other general schemes will no doubt replace Say's, but it will always be necessary to elaborate them in order to avoid the dissipation of research.

The second lesson to be learned from Say is his conception of science—calm, impartial in the face of prejudice and doctrine. In our age, when theory and doctrine are so easily confused, and when we speak not only of literature but of the "involved" sciences, one should meditate on such an example. Even if our author could not always keep to his original programme, it was a fine programme and its formulation was the more commendable because the era hardly lent itself to scientific detachment.

Pierre-Louis Reynaud

SOURCES

Essay I

Charles Comte, Eugène Daire, Horace Say, "Notice sur la vie et les ouvrages de J.-B. Say", in *Œuvres diverses de J.-B. Say* (Paris, 1848). Abridged.

Essay II

Pierre-Louis Reynaud, "Preface" to *Jean-Baptiste Say: Textes choisis* (Librairie Dalloz, Paris, 1953). Abridged.

Signature

Bayerische Staatsbibliothek, Munich.

Portrait

Engraving by H. Decaisne from *Œuvres diverses de J.-B. Say,* ed. C. Comte, E. Daire and H. Say (Paris, 1848).

BIBLIOGRAPHY

J. A. Blanqui, "Notice sur la vie et les ouvrages de J.-B. Say, lue à la séance annuelle des 5 academies, 3 mai 1841", *Recueil de l'Académie des Sciences Morales et Politiques,* 4 (Paris, 1841).

G. Michel, "Une dynastie d'économistes: Jean-Etienne, Jean-Baptiste et Horace Say", *Journal des Économistes* (Paris, 1898).

A. Liessse, "Un professeur d'économie politique sous la Restauration: J.-B. Say au Conservatoire des Arts et Métiers," *Journal des Economistes* (Paris, 1901).

E. Teilhac, *L'œuvre économique de Jean-Baptiste Say* (Paris, 1927).

G. Leduc, "Jean-Baptiste Say," in *International Encyclopedia of the Social Sciences,* Vol. 14 (New York, 1968).

DAVID RICARDO

1772–1823

A sweet man, Ricardo is certainly one of the luckiest that ever lived. And here I have not so much in mind his success in speculating; although he was no slouch in that department, as some facts from his biography illustrate.

Ricardo was lucky in being on the spot when Napoleonic Wars were causing the value of money to misbehave in the most interesting fashion. He was lucky to have James Mill as taskmaster and press agent. He was lucky in having been deprived of higher education, so that his resulting written expositions had the clumsiness necessary to give that ingredient of obscurity so conducive to a reputation for great profundity. Finally, and I hope it comes as no anticlimax, Ricardo was lucky in being profound.

In time Ricardo came to be the whipping boy for continental romantics and historicists. Yet there is not much evidence that they had to read him closely in order to find fault with his abstract methodology. I must confess that I find Ricardo hard to give semester-type grades to. He is par excellence an economist's economist.

P. A. SAMUELSON

I do not think Ricardo ever did much historical reading. But this is not what I mean. The trouble with him is akin to the trouble I have, in this respect, with my American students, who have plenty of historical material pushed down their throats. But it is to no purpose. They lack the historical sense *that no amount of factual study can give. This is why it is so much easier to make theorists of them than economists.*

J. A. SCHUMPETER

Could it be that an Englishman, and he not in academic bowers, but oppressed by mercantile and senatorial cares, had accomplished what all the universities of Europe, and a century of thought, had failed even to advance by one hair's breadth? All other writers had been crushed and overlaid by the enormous weight of facts and documents; Mr Ricardo alone had deduced, a priori, from the understanding itself, laws which first gave a ray of light into the unwieldy chaos of materials, and had constructed what had been but a collection of tentative discussions of regular proportions now first standing on an eternal basis.

THOMAS DE QUINCEY

I
A MEMOIR OF DAVID RICARDO

In the early history of Mr Ricardo's life there is nothing, the relation of which would be likely to excite either attention or interest. His father, a native of Holland, and of very respectable connections, came over on a visit to this country, when young, and preferring it to his own, became naturalized, and settled here. He entered the Stock Exchange; and being a man of good natural abilities, and of the strictest honour and integrity, made a corresponding progress; accquiring a respectable fortune, and possessing considerable influence within the circle in which he moved. He married, and was the father of a very numerous family, of which David, the subject of the present memoir, was the third.[1] He was born on 19 April 1772; and in point of education had the same advantages which are usually allotted to those who are destined for a mercantile line of life. When very young, he was sent to Holland. His father, who had designed him to follow the same business in which he was engaged, and whose transactions lay chiefly in that country, sent him thither not only with a view to his becoming acquainted with it, but also that he might be placed at a school of which he entertained a very high opinion.[2] After two years' absence he returned home, and continued the common school education till his father took him into business. At his intervals of leisure he was allowed any masters for private

[1] Abraham Israel Ricardo, David's father, was the youngest son of Joseph Israel Ricardo, "of the Portuguese Jewish Nation" (as he describes himself in his will), a stockbroker in Amsterdam, who died in 1762. The reports on the other ancestors of our economist are very unreliable. There is a legend that they were descended from a Spanish grandee of that name who lived in Andalusia in the sixteenth century. There is no evidence for this story but only for the relationship of the Dutch poet and theologian Isaac Da Costa (1798–1860) to the Ricardos.

Abraham Ricardo was married in 1769 to Abigail Delvalle, daughter of the tobacco- and snuff-merchant Abraham Delvalle and his wife Rebecca Henriques de Sequeira. These were the maternal grandparents of Ricardo. Abigail was only sixteen years of age and some twenty years his junior. Though David's father did not wish to have a large family, the marriage yet resulted in an astonishing number of children: no less than seventeen (and possibly as many as twenty-three), of whom fifteen grew up—nine sons and six daughters.

[2] He resided in the house of his father's relatives in Amsterdam from the age of eleven to thirteen and there can be little doubt that he attended the Talmud Tora, a school of great reputation, founded in 1616 and attached to the Portuguese Synagogue. The curriculum included, besides the Bible and the Talmud, Hebrew literature and rhetoric. Pupils of the seven-class school could continue their studies in the higher school, Ets Haim, at which Spinoza was a pupil. His two years in Holland left a deep impression on Ricardo.

instruction whom he chose to have: but he had not the benefit of what is called a classical education; and it is doubtful whether it would have been a benefit to him, or whether it might not have led his mind to a course of study, in early life, foreign to those habits of deep thinking, which in the end enabled him to develop the most abstruse and intricate subjects, and to be the author of important discoveries, instead of receiving passively the ideas of others.

It is not true, however, as has been more than insinuated, that Mr Ricardo was of very low origin, and that he had been wholly denied the advantages of education; a reflection upon his father which he by no means deserved.[3] The latter was always in affluent circumstances, most respectably connected, and both able and willing to afford his children all the advantages which the line of life for which they were destined appeared to require.

In the early years of Mr Ricardo but little appeared in his intellectual progress, which would have led even an acute observer to predict his future eminence. But after having seen him attain that station, they who have passed through life with him from his boyish days now bring to their recollection circumstances, which though overlooked as trivial at the time, serve to show that the plentiful harvest was the natural consequence of a genial spring.

In very early life he was remarkable for solidity and steadiness of character. At the age of fourteen his father began to employ him in the Stock Exchange, where he placed great confidence in him, and gave him such power as is rarely granted to persons considerably older than himself. At the age of sixteen he was entrusted with the care of two of his younger brothers, to convey them to Holland; and neither his father nor his mother felt the smallest anxiety for the charge which was confided to him. When young, Mr Ricardo showed a taste for abstract and general reasoning; and though he was without any inducement to its cultivation, or rather lay under positive discouragement, yet at the age of nineteen and twenty, works of that description which occasionally occupied his attention afforded him amusement and cause for reflection. Even at this time his mind disclosed a propensity to go to the bottom of the subjects by which it was attracted, and he showed the same manly and open adherence to the opinions which

[3] His father was a man of good intellect, but uncultivated. His prejudices were exceedingly strong; and they induced him to take the opinions of his forefathers in points of religion, politics, education etc., upon faith, and without investigation. Not only did he adopt this rule for himself, but he insisted on its being followed by his children; his son, however, never yielded his assent on any important subject, until after he had thoroughly investigated it. It was perhaps in opposing these strong prejudices, that he was first led to that freedom and independence of thought for which he was so remarkable, and which has indeed extended itself to the other branches of his family.

he had deliberately formed, and the same openness to conviction which distinguished his maturer years.

Soon after he had attained the age of twenty-one, Mr Ricardo married; and this threw him upon his own resources, as he quitted his father at the same time.[4] The general estimation in which he was held now manifested itself. All the most respectable members of the Stock Exchange came forward to testify the high opinion they entertained of him, with their eagerness to assist him in his undertakings.

His father's name stood as high as possible for honour and integrity, qualities of the first recommendation in a field where transactions of the utmost magnitude rest upon them as their only security. Sharing this character with his father, and possessing talents and other excellent qualities which had endeared him to all, he embarked with the fairest prospect of success. This success answered his most sanguine expectations; and in a very few years, certainly not wholly without some anxiety at first, he had secured to himself a handsome independence. During this time his mind was chiefly occupied by his business; but as his solicitude for its success lessened, he turned his attention to other subjects.

At this time, or about the age of twenty-five, by the example and instigation of a friend[5] with whom he was then very intimate, his leisure hours were devoted to some of the branches of mathematics, chemistry, geology

[4] The growing estrangement between the liberal son, the conservative father and the sternly religious mother, led eventually to an open breach with his family and the Jewish community when, against his parents' will, the twenty-one-year-old David married Priscilla Ann Wilkinson, a Christian, "a handsome, but very proud woman", on 20 December 1793. The breach between father and son was afterwards entirely healed, the earliest sign of reconciliation coming when the mother died in 1801. Edward Wilkinson (1728–1809), David's father-in-law, was a "very respectable surgeon and apothecary at Bow, in Middlesex"; he married Elizabeth Patteson, who bore him two sons and three daughters. Fanny married David Ricardo's brother Moses, who was almost certainly the author of this memoir, influenced by James Mill. David had three sons and four daughters, all of whom survived him.

[5] There is no positive evidence, whether William Frend or George (or Joshua) Basevi was the said companion. Frend, much senior to Ricardo, was a mathematician and the author of pamphlets on taxation and the quantity theory of money, who had been a tutor before being expelled from Cambridge for his radical opinions. Basevi, who was only one year senior to Ricardo, was a member of the Geological Society, appears to have been a member of the Political Economy Club, and shares with Mill and Malthus the distinction of being the only persons outside the family who are remembered in Ricardo's will. Whoever may have inspired these early mathematical and scientific studies, they must have influenced Ricardo's characteristic cast of mind more decisively than the teachings of his later mentors, James Mill and Bentham, whose approach was essentially that of jurisprudence and moral philosophy.

and mineralogy. He fitted up a laboratory, formed a collection of minerals, and was one of the original members of the Geological Society, but he never entered very warmly into the study of these subjects, and his interest in them totally vanished, when he became deeply involved in the investigation of his favourite topic.

The talent for obtaining wealth is not held in much estimation, but perhaps in nothing did Mr Ricardo more evince his extraordinary powers than he did in his business. His complete knowledge of all its intricacies; his surprising quickness at figures and calculation; his capability of getting through, without any apparent exertion, the immense transactions in which he was concerned; his coolness and judgment, combined certainly with (for him) a fortunate tissue of public events, enabled him to leave all his contemporaries at the Stock Exchange far behind,[6] and to raise himself infinitely higher not only in fortune, but in general character and estimation, than any man had ever done before in that house. Such was the impression which these qualities had made upon his competitors, that several of the most discerning among them, long before he had emerged into public notoriety, prognosticated, in their admiration, that he would live to fill some of the highest stations in the state.

It was not till Mr Ricardo was somewhat advanced in life that he turned his attention to the subject of political economy. While on a visit at Bath, where he was staying for the benefit of Mrs Ricardo's health, he took up, and read, the work of Adam Smith. It pleased him; and it is probable that the subject from that time occupied, with the other objects of his curiosity, a share of his thoughts, though it was not till some years after that he appeared to have fixed upon it much of his attention.

The immense transactions which he had with the Bank of England, in the course of business, tallying with the train of study on which he was then engaged, led Mr Ricardo to reflect upon the subject of the currency, to endeavour to account for the difference which existed between the value of the coin and the Bank notes, and to ascertain from what cause the depreciation of the latter arose. He was induced to put his thoughts upon paper, without the remotest view at the time to publication.

[6] Ricardo multiplied his property from £800 when he married to more than £700 000 at his death. In nearly twenty years he became a multimillionaire, if we evaluate his property at present prices. Sraffa estimates his annual income from the investments of which we know (estates, mortgages and French Stock) at about £28 000. In a letter of the year 1802 Ricardo describes himself as "one of Fortune's chief favourites". The largest single profit Ricardo ever made was with a war loan, the premium of which rose after the Battle of Waterloo from 2½ to 3¼ per cent to 13 to 16½. Malthus, at whose request Ricardo had reserved a share of £5000 in the loan, sold it too soon, when the premium was about 3 per cent.

The late Mr Perry, proprietor of the *Morning Chronicle*, was one of the few friends to whom Mr Ricardo showed his manuscript. Mr Perry urged him to allow it to be published in the *Morning Chronicle*; to which, not without some reluctance, Mr Ricardo consented; and it was inserted in the shape of letters under the signature of R., the first of which appeared on the 6th day of September, 1810. These letters produced various answers.

The interest which the subject excited was a motive with him for enlarging upon it, and publishing his views very shortly after, in the form of a pamphlet, entitled *On the Depreciation of the Currency*. Many were the publications which this elicited, some in defence of, and some in opposition to it. Some time after, the late Mr Horner brought the question before Parliament, and obtained a committee to investigate the subject; the result of the inquiry was a confirmation of Mr Ricardo's doctrines. The famous Bullion Report coincided mainly with his pamphlet; and the facts elicited from the evidence collected by the Committee afforded practical illustrations of the accuracy of his speculation.

By some, the credit of originating the bullion question is given to Mr Horner; but though much is due to him for his patient and persevering investigation of the subject, and the very able manner in which he drew up the report, yet to Mr Ricardo the credit of developing the doctrine of money, in its present perfect state, is mainly to be ascribed.

Among the other effects of this pamphlet, it is not surprising that it should have been the means of introducing Mr Ricardo to a number of first-rate literary characters. His society was courted by many, and his talents were duly appreciated by all who knew him. About this time, too, he became acquainted with Mr [James] Mill, the distinguished author of *The History of British India*, an acquaintance which ultimately grew into a warm and sincere attachment. With very few exceptions—perhaps with none—Mr Mill of all men possessed the greatest influence over him. Mr Ricardo always considered him as a man of the first intellectual capacity; and his judgment, his discrimination, and his opinion had greater weight with him than any other person's. This feeling appeared to be mutual; and the opinion which Mr Ricardo entertained of Mr Mill, it was easy to see, was equalled by the esteem in which he was held by his friend.

Mr Ricardo's next essay was on rent; and the suggestions of Mr Malthus, who had previously written upon the same subject, were followed up by him so ably, and the true nature of rent was so admirably expounded, that there was nothing further left for explanation upon that point.

It is well known that Mr Grenfell for some time had been engaged, as a Member of Parliament, in the investigation of the affairs of the Bank. Mr Ricardo took great interest in his proceedings. As his reputation was now high as a writer on the subject of money, he was urged to lend his aid to the work, which was so laudably begun. He expressed great reluctance, from that unfeigned distrust of himself with which he was habitually impressed; at last he yielded to persuasion, and his masterly exposition of the affairs of the Bank, together with his proposal for an economical currency, was the result. The high ascendancy which the Bank directors had acquired over the great mass of proprietors of Bank stock prevented those few who wished to have their transactions examined into from gaining their point. Many ineffectual attempts had been made: the majority of proprietors still supported the wish of the directors for secrecy; and they, shielding themselves behind that majority, withheld all account of their accumulated gains. Mr Ricardo took a view of their various transactions; showed what their annual savings ought to have been; and, following up the examination to the time at which he wrote, clearly pointed out to what, under proper management, their accumulation would have amounted.

In this pamphlet, Mr Ricardo suggested his plan for an economical currency. If there was any suggestion which emanated from him, upon which he seemed to pride himself more than any other, it was certainly this; and his wish to see it brought into effect at the time, induced him to step out of his usual course. He addressed a letter to Mr Perceval, then Chancellor of the Exchequer, upon the subject; but that gentleman expressed his dissent from Mr Ricardo's opinions, and on that account declined adopting his advice.

Mr Ricardo's next undertaking was his work on the *Principles of Political Economy and Taxation*—a work abounding with as strong marks of deep thought, and masterly comprehension of a difficult subject, as any that was ever published. The train of arguments is derived from a few luminous principles, and one is so consequent upon another, that the work cannot be examined in detail: it must be taken as a whole, and as such, its conclusions are demonstrated with almost mathematical precision. Mr Ricardo never courted notoriety: at first he shrunk from it, not so much because he undervalued it, as from a distrust, which not even success removed, of his powers. When he became sensible that he was held in some estimation, he seemed satisfied with what he had obtained, and was unwilling to risk it by a desire to accomplish more. These considerations made him very reluctant, first to write, and afterwards to publish this work; and it was only by the successive urgings of some of his most confidential friends, but particularly through the influence of Mr Mill, that he was at length prevailed upon to do so. The success which followed amply compensated him; and this book, upon a subject which had heretofore not been popular, in a very short time passed through three editions, and placed the author in the highest rank as a philosophical writer.

Mr Ricardo had now wholly retired from business, with an ample fortune, acquired without exciting any of those envious and unpleasant feelings which usually attend upon those who precede their competitors. In the year 1819 he became Member of Parliament for Portarlington; and perhaps few men, in so short a time, ever attained such influence, and, without eloquence, commanded such attention as he did in the House of Commons. He never spoke upon any subjects, but with a view to communicate ideas which he deemed important; and then he always spoke to the point. He was of no party; and at all times advocated such principles as he held to be sound and true, whether on the ministerial or the opposition side, or at variance with both. Attachment to party has generally made that neutral station a place of contempt, and those who have taken it have seldom obtained much consideration. Not so with Mr Ricardo: his independence was truly appreciated. Not courting popularity, not wanting or seeking any thing from either side of the House, he stood aloof, and claimed the respect and admiration of both. His influence and his self-confidence were gaining ground. During the session, Mr Ricardo's whole time was devoted to his duties as a Member of Parliament. His mornings were spent in study, in receiving visitors, in answering correspondents, or in attendance upon some committee; and in the evening he never missed going to the House. During the recess, he usually retired to his seat at Gatcomb Park, in Gloucestershire, where, in the bosom of his family, he spent his time in the enjoyment of contributing to the happiness of all around him.[7] In the recess of 1822 he went to the Continent; travelled with his family through Holland, Germany, Switzerland and Italy, and returned home, after an absence of five months, through France.[8]

Mr Ricardo never appeared more cheerful, or in better health, than he did during his last retirement in the country, just previous to his death. This premature event was occasioned by an affection of the ear, which ultimately extended itself to the internal part of the head. Mr Ricardo had

[7] Of Ricardo's physical appearance J. L. Mallet, a contemporary, writes: "His stature was somewhat under the common size, but well proportioned and active; his countenance open; and his features good, although with a light Jewish cast; his eye had a soft, beaming, intelligent and, at the same time, thoughtful expression, which is very successfully portrayed in Phillips's picture." "It is said that his voice, although sweet and pleasing, was pitched extremely high, and his distinct articulation gave him an advantage in the House of Commons by fixing attention, which is not the case with monotonous tones." "He was not a robust man, but of a sound constitution; and his habits were so temperate, that he would probably have lived to an advanced age if he had not been prematurely cut off by an inflammatory complaint in the head in his fifty-first year."

[8] As originally suggested by James Mill, Ricardo wrote a journal of his tour on the Continent in the form of letters. His account was privately printed in 1891 under the title, *Letters Written by David Ricardo during a Tour on the Continent*. P. Sraffa has fully reprinted the letters.

for many years not been entirely free from this complaint, of which he thought but slightly; for it had never before occasioned him any very serious inconvenience. He was attended through his last illness by one of his brothers, who had retired from the medical profession, and who was then on a visit to him. There were no symptoms that could excite the smallest anxiety about his recovery, till a very short time before his decease, when the transition was sudden, from perfect confidence to complete despair.

He died on Thursday, 11 September 1823, surrounded by his family, who had the misery of watching him throughout a whole day and night, expecting every moment to be his last. He was buried at Hardenhuish.

High as has been the testimony publicly borne to the merits of Mr R. since his death, it has not exceeded what he deserved. His private worth kept pace with those public qualities which earned him so great an estimation. To intellectual powers of the first order, he joined a candour, a modesty, a diffidence, which never allowed him to assume to himself a merit which he felt he did not deserve—a love of justice which never permitted him to be influenced by his feelings, or biased by any circumstances that might divert him from doing that which he thought strictly right; a disinterestedness which made him always regardless of his own personal benefit, in the maintenance of general principles. When a Bank proprietor, he argued strenuously and warmly against the inordinate gains of that body; he defended the cause of the fund-holders when he had ceased to be one; he was accused of an attempt to ruin the landed interest after he became a large landed proprietor; and while a Member of Parliament, he advocated the cause of reform, which, if adopted, would have deprived him of his seat. Superior to the misleading power of self-interest, his aim was the dissipation of erroneous, and the promulgation of true and correct principles, the adoption of which should tend to the amelioration of mankind, and the production of the greatest possible good. Such was Mr Ricardo: as a private character unexcelled; pre-eminent as a philosopher; and in his public capacity a model of what a legislator ought to be.

Moses Ricardo[9]

[9] Moses Ricardo, a surgeon by profession, became in effect Ricardo's family doctor. He was "doubtless" (Sraffa) the author of the Memoir.

II
SKETCH OF THE LIFE AND WRITINGS OF DAVID RICARDO

Mr Ricardo came, for the first time, before the public as an author in 1809. The rise in the market price of bullion, and the fall of the exchange that had taken place in the course of that year, had excited a good deal of attention. The tract entitled *The High Price of Bullion a Proof of the Depreciation of Bank Notes* led the way in the far-famed bullion controversy.

In this tract Mr Ricardo showed that redundancy and deficiency of currency are only *relative* terms; and that so long as the currency of any particular country consists exclusively of gold and silver coins, or of paper immediately convertible into such coins, its value can neither rise above nor fall below the value of the metallic currencies of other countries, by a greater sum than will suffice to defray the expense of importing foreign coin or bullion, if the currency be deficient; or of exporting a portion of the existing supply, if it be redundant. But when a country issues inconvertible paper notes (as was then the case in England), they cannot be exported to other countries in the event of their becoming redundant at home; and whenever, under such circumstances, the exchange with foreign states is depressed below, or the price of bullion rises above, its mint price, more than the cost of sending coin or bullion abroad, it shows conclusively that too much paper has been issued, and that its value is *depreciated from excess*. The principles which pervade the Report of the Bullion Committee, are substantially the same as those established by Mr Ricardo in this pamphlet. They were afterwards carried into full effect; and afford one of the most memorable examples in our history, of the triumph of principle over selfishness, sophistry and error.

The fourth edition of this tract is the most valuable. An appendix added to it has some acute observations on some difficult questions in the theory of exchange; and it also contains the first germ of the original idea of making bank notes exchangeable for bars of gold bullion.

His tract, entitled *Reply to Mr Bosanquet's Practical Observations on the Report of the Bullion Committee*, was published in 1811, and is one of the best essays that has appeared on any disputed question of political economy. In this pamphlet, Mr Ricardo met Mr Bosanquet on his own ground, and overthrew him with his own weapons. The victory of Mr Ricardo was perfect and complete; and the elaborate errors and mis-statements of Mr Bosanquet served only, to use the words of Dr Coppleston, "to illustrate the abilities of the writer who stepped forward to vindicate the truth".

This tract affords a striking example of the ascendancy which those who possess a knowledge both of principle and practice, have over those who are familiar only with the latter; and though the interest of the question which led to its publication has now subsided, it will always be read with delight by such as are not insensible of the high gratification which all ingenuous minds must feel in observing the ease with which a superior intellect clears away the irrelevant matter with which a question has been designedly embarrassed, reduces false facts to their just value, and traces and exhibits the constant operation of the same general principle through mazy intricacies of practical detail.

Mr Ricardo next appeared as an author in 1815, during the discussions on the bill, afterwards passed into a law, for raising the limit at which foreign corn might be imported for consumption, to £4. In his *Essay on the Influence of a Low Price of Corn on the Profits of Stock*, he showed the effect of an increase in the price of raw produce on wages and profits; and founded a strong argument in favour of the freedom of the corn trade, on the very grounds on which Mr Malthus had endeavoured to show the propriety of subjecting it to fresh restrictions.

In 1816, Mr Ricardo published his *Proposals for an Economical and Secure Currency, with Observations on the Profits of the Bank of England*. In this pamphlet he examined the circumstances which determine the value of money, when every individual has the power to supply it, and when that power is restricted or placed under a monopoly; and he showed that, in the former case, its value will depend, like that of all other freely supplied articles, on its cost; while in the latter, it will be unaffected by that circumstance, and will depend on the extent to which it may be issued compared with the demand. This is a principle of great importance; for it shows that intrinsic worth is not necessary to a currency and that, provided the supply of paper notes, declared to be legal tender, be sufficiently limited, their value may be maintained on a par with the value of gold, or raised to any higher level. If, therefore, it were practicable to devise a plan for preserving the value of paper on a level with that of gold, without making it convertible into coin at the pleasure of the holder, the heavy expense of a metallic currency would be saved. To effect this desirable object, Mr Ricardo proposed that, instead of being made exchangeable for gold coins, bank notes should be made exchangeable for *bars of gold bullion of the standard weight and purity*. Mr Ricardo's proposal was afterwards adopted in the bill [concerning the issue of notes by the Bank of England] introduced by Mr (later Sir Robert) Peel. In practice it was found completely to answer the object of checking over-issue.

At length, in 1817, Mr Ricardo published his great work on the *Principles of Political Economy and Taxation*. This was a step which he did not take without much hesitation. He was not, and did not affect to be, insensible of the value of literary and philosophical reputation. Its appearance forms a memorable era in the history of political science. Exclusive of many valuable subsidiary inquiries, Mr Ricardo has pointed out, in this work, the source and limiting principle of exchangeable value, and has traced the laws which determine the distribution of wealth among the various ranks and orders of society. The powers of mind displayed in these investigations, the dexterity with which the most abstruse questions are unravelled, the sagacity displayed in tracing the operation of general principles, in disentangling them from such as are of a secondary and accidental nature, and in perceiving and estimating their remote consequences, have never been surpassed; and will for ever secure the name of Ricardo a conspicuous place among those who have done most to unfold the mechanism of society, and to discover the circumstances on which the well-being of its various orders must always mainly depend.

What the researches of Locke and Smith did for the production of wealth, those of Ricardo have done for its value and distribution. The establishment of general principles being Mr Ricardo's great object, he has paid comparatively little attention to their practical application, and sometimes, indeed, he has in great measure overlooked the circumstances by which they are occasionally countervailed. But his is not a practical work; and it did not enter into his plan to exhibit the circumstances that give rise to the discrepancies in question. The *Principles of Political Economy and Taxation* is not even a systematic treatise, but is principally an inquiry respecting certain fundamental principles, most of which had previously been undiscovered.

That part of Mr Ricardo's work in which he applies his principles to discover the incidence of taxes on rent, profit, wages and raw produce is more practical than the others; and must always be a subject of careful study to those who wish to make themselves well acquainted with his department of political science.

In 1820, Mr Ricardo contributed an article on the funding system to the supplement to the *Encyclopaedia Britannica*. This tract, though somewhat confused in its arrangement, embraces many valuable discussions. He was a decided friend to the plan for raising the supplies for a war within the year, by an equivalent increase of taxation; and he also thought (in which opinion few probably will be disposed to concur), that it would be not only expedient but practicable to pay off the public debt by an assessment on capital.

In 1822, Mr Ricardo published, during the parliamentary discussions on the subject of the corn laws, his tract on *Protection to Agriculture*. This is the best of all his pamphlets, and is, indeed, a *chef d'oeuvre*. The important questions respecting remunerating price, the influence of a low and high value of corn over wages and profits, the influence of taxation over agriculture and manufactures, and many other topics of equal difficulty and interest, are all discussed in the short compass of eighty or ninety pages, with a precision and clearness that leaves nothing to be desired. Had Mr Ricardo never written anything else, this pamphlet would have placed him in the first rank of political economists.

Besides the publications previously enumerated, Mr Ricardo left one or two manuscripts. Among others, a *Plan for the Establishment of a National Bank* was found in a finished state, and was soon after published.

He also left *Notes* on Mr Malthus's *Principles of Political Economy*; containing a vindication of his own doctrines from the objections of Mr Malthus, and showing the mistakes into which he conceives Mr Malthus had fallen. But we doubt whether they have sufficient interest to warrant their publication.

Of the value of the services rendered by Mr Ricardo to political economy, there can be, among intelligent men, only one opinion. His works have made a very great addition to the mass of useful and universally interesting truths, and afford some of the finest examples to be met with of discriminating analysis, and of profound and refined discussion. The brevity with which he has stated some of his most important propositions; their intimate dependence on each other; the fewness of his illustrations; and the mathematical cast he has given to his reasoning, render it sometimes a little difficult for readers, unaccustomed to such investigations, readily to follow him. But we can venture to affirm, that those who will give to his works the attention of which they are so worthy, will find them to be as logical and conclusive as they are profound and important. It was the opinion of Quintilian, that the students of eloquence who were highly delighted with Cicero, had made no inconsiderable progress in their art: and the same may, without hesitation, be said of the students of political economy who find pleasure in the works of Mr Ricardo: *Ille se profecisse sciat, cui Ricardo valde placebit.*

John Ramsay McCulloch

III
THE RICARDIAN THEORY OF VALUE AND DISTRIBUTION

English economics was in a state of ferment at the beginning of the nineteenth century; Adam Smith had founded no cult. The period teemed with able economists; yet David Ricardo, within a decade of his debut, was the acknowledged leader of the young science of economics. Within this decade, indeed, his chief work was done; and it was sufficient to make him the most influential economist of his century. This was an extraordinary achievement of an extraordinary man.

In the theories of population and rent, Ricardo was chiefly a borrower, and he did not improve upon either theory in any basic respect. In the synthesis of these theories into a general theory of value and distribution, he struck out on his own. The peculiar combination of doctrines that makes up his system is truly original.

The outlines of his theory were beginning to emerge in his *Essay on the Influence of a Low Price of Corn on the Profits of Stock* (1815). We shall sketch the main elements of this theory before we turn to the *Principles*. The argument rested upon four propositions:

First, in the (domestic) production of corn, there is diminishing returns to composite dose of capital-and-labour.

Second, the return to this dose of capital (and labour) is equal to the marginal product—cost of production equals price.

Third, the return on capital in agriculture fixes the rate of return that must also be obtained in other industries.

Fourth, the rent of land will be equal to the total product minus the amount of agricultural capital times its profit rate.

This is not a complete system because, in the absence of more explicit theories of population and capital accumulation, the aggregate output of the economy is not determined. The system does determine the division of product between landlords and others, but not between capitalists and labourers. Ricardo avoided this latter problem (although the subsistence wage theory lurked in the background). He denied, in fact, that the division between wages and profits was determinate.

The *Essay* thus contained two main elements of the Ricardian system: the theory of rent and the dominant influence of diminishing returns in agriculture upon the rate of profits. The completed system required two further elements: the subsistence theory of wages and the measure of value. These were presented in the *Principles,* but neither the organization nor the exposition is very felicitous.

I shall not go further with the applications that Ricardo makes of his theory to taxation, currency, international trade, and in his polemics with other economists. These applications are not impeccable—for example, the celebrated chapter on machinery rests upon a logical error—but they were made with rare consistency. Much of the appeal of the Ricardian system must have come from these demonstrations of the certainty, almost the routine, with which it seemed to dispose of troublesome problems and opinions. The age of formulas had begun.

The legendary figure of Ricardo as a stern logician and a powerful debater is, I think, correct in essentials. I should prefer to say that his logic was severe in its simplifications rather than superlative in its rigour,[10] but the dominant characteristic of the man was undoubtedly his perseverance and consistency in dealing with a few basic ideas.

Economics is the body of substantive generalizations on the workings of economic systems. Ricardo did not enlarge much this body of knowledge: his one addition to Smith's work was the systematic, though only partial, recognition of diminishing returns. Perhaps no other economist has ever fully shared Smith's immense understanding of the forces that govern the structure and development of economies; certainly Ricardo was not distinguished for his ability to discover great inductive generalizations.

Economics is also an engine of analysis, and Ricardo, with his great powers of abstraction and synthesis, was a master analyst. Population, natural resources, capital accumulation, and the distribution of income—these were woven into a sweeping theoretical system. Measured by the significance of the variables and the manageability of the system, he fashioned what is probably the most impressive of all models in economic analysis.

It is here that Ricardo's service to economics lies. His naked logic and pseudologic helped to establish a professional frame of mind which did much to reduce promiscuous fact-gathering and *ad hoc* theorizing and to incite order and precision. This was the basic "Ricardo effect"; and, even with our modern knowledge of the painful extremes to which it can be carried, we must thank him for it.

George Joseph Stigler

SOURCES

Essay I

Moses Ricardo, "A Memoir of David Ricardo", published unsigned in *The Annual Biography and Obituary for the year 1824*, Vol. 8 (Longman, London 1824), reprinted in *The Works and Correspondence of David Ricardo*, 11 ed. Piero Sraffa with the collaboration of M. H. Dobb, University Press, Cambridge, 1955; enlarged by notes from the Sraffa edition.

[10] Paul A. Samuelson comes to a similar conclusion after examining Ricardo's theory in the light of modern knowledge (*Quarterly Journal of Economics*, 73 (1959), p. 230): "Ricardo's logical skills have been, I think, exaggerated. (If Ricardo has been overrated, Smith has in our days perhaps been underrated. I mean as a theorist.) He would have made a most excellent modern economist!"

Essay II

John Ramsay McCulloch, "Sketch of the Life and Writings of David Ricardo" in *Treatises and Essays on Subjects Connected with Economical Policy* (Adam and Charles Black, Edinburgh, 1853). Abridged.

Essay III

George Joseph Stigler, "The Ricardian Theory of Value and Distribution", *Journal of Political Economy*, 60, 1952. Abridged.

Signature

University Library, Glasgow.

Portrait

Engraving by Holl from a portrait by T. Philipps (Historiches Bildarchiv Handke, Bad Berneck).

BIBLIOGRAPHY

J. Mill, *David Ricardo*, letter, published in *Morning Chronicle*, September 1823, reprinted in A. Bain, *James Mill* (London, 1882).

J. R. McCulloch, *The Works of David Ricardo with a Notice of the Life and Writings of the Author*, 2nd ed. (London, 1852).

E. Cannan, "Ricardo in parliament", *Economic Journal*, 4 (1894).

L. Stephen, "David Ricardo", in *The English Utilitarians*, Vol. 2 (London, 1900).

J. H. Hollander, "David Ricardo: a centenary estimate", in *Studies in Historical and Political Science*", series 28, number 4 (Baltimore, 1910).

B. Földes, "Ricardo. Ein Gedenkblatt", *Jahrbücher fur Nationalökonomie und Statistik*, 59 (1920).

B. Franklin and G. Legman, *David Ricardo and Ricardian Theories: A Bibliographical Checklist* (New York, 1949).

O. St. Clair, *A Key to Ricardo* (London, 1957).

M. Blaug, "Ricardian Economics: A Historical Study", *Yale Studies in Economics* 8 (New Haven, 1958).

C. S. Shoup, *Ricardo on Taxation: An Analysis of the Chapters on Taxation in David Ricardo's Principles* (New York, 1960).

M. Blaug, "David Ricardo," in *International Encyclopedia of the Social Sciences*, Vol. 13 (New York, 1968).

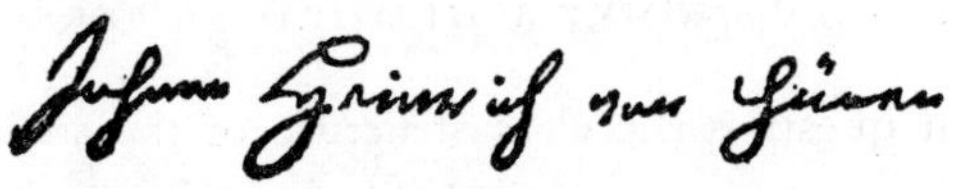

JOHANN HEINRICH VON THÜNEN

1783–1850

Von Thünen was a bona fide mathematician, but of less power: his blunder as to the natural wage is not of the same order as Cournot's little slips. But, to make up, he was a careful experimenter and student of facts, and with the mind at least as fully developed on the inductive as on the deductive side. Above all he was an ardent philanthropist. A. MARSHALL

Thünen teilt mit Gossen und Cournot das Schicksal aller großen Männer, die den eingetretenen Pfad traditionellen Denkens und Arbeitens verlassen und zum Pfadfinder für eine spätere Generation von Wissenschaftlern werden, indem sie ihrer eigenen Zeit weit vorauseilen. E. SCHNEIDER

If we judge both men exclusively by the amount of ability of the purely theoretical kind *that went into their work, then, I think, Thünen should be placed above* Ricardo *or indeed above any economist of the period, with the possible exception of Cournot.* J. A. SCHUMPETER

Sollte unsere Wissenschaft jemals sinken, so gehören die Werke von Thünens zu denjenigen, an welchen sie die Möglichkeit hat, sich wieder aufzurichten.

W. ROSCHER

I
JOHANN HEINRICH VON THÜNEN IN HIS AGE

The year of his birth, 1783, was six years before the French Revolution and seven years after the American War of Independence, events which over much of the earth heralded the end of that system of economy we economists call feudalism and which in the political sphere marked the irresistible rise of democracy. No echo of this twofold revolution was heard in the agrarian north—or in the years of Thünen's youth. He lived in a stable world of feudalism, grew up shaped by this world's educational methods, and accepted without question the class structure of the society in which he was to act.[1]

The feudal narrowness was matched by Thünen's education. He first attended the local school in Hooksiel and then went on to the High School in Jever. Although he was encouraged in arithmetic and mathematics, his powers of intellect were never really awakened nor those of his body ever strengthened. At sixteen the prospect of one day having to take over his father's estate induced him to serve an agricultural apprenticeship on the Gerietshausen estate near Hooksiel. The owner von Tungel is said to have been a good judge of horses and cattle, but he loathed anything to do with theory and science and had nothing but ridicule for those whom he called Latin farmers. The young apprentice later on told with much bitterness how miserably he "had spent this noble time" and how much more he could have learnt. This learning which he regretted having missed and which he advised his brother to start in good time is "scientific agriculture".

If Thünen's training had been different would he have played a greater part in the enormous upward surge of German culture which took place in his day? It is not possible to give a final answer to this question. In the châteaux of the eastern part of Germany I have found large numbers of books from the periods of enlightenment, classicism and romanticism. On the other hand we know little about the state of education and nothing at all about the composition of libraries in the châteaux and farmsteads of the Jeverland. Today we tend on the whole to overestimate the depth and extent of Weimar's influence. After *Werther* and *Götz*, Goethe never again had a wide public, and the only works of Goethe's which Thünen occasionally mentions are *Werther* and later on the correspondence with Schiller along with some passages from the posthumous writings. When, as in the case of his son, Heinrich, he himself had the opportunity of laying down the direction which education was to take, or at least of influencing it, it is quite clear that, for him, the right education was a pragmatic one. Contrary to the express wish of his father the son had begun Greek and had made considerable progress in it. Thünen would rather have seen his son confining his energy and attention to those subjects which "are so extremely important for one's effectiveness in future life".

Thünen's loose ties with the German educational system of his day are

[1] In 1822 he informed his wife with evident satisfaction that a count has treated him "always most generously and kindly". Ten years later he told her in a letter from Bad Sülz that he chanced to meet a lady-in-waiting before her room in the hotel and had the opportunity to "recommend to her protection" their daughter Helen. "Had it not been for this fortunate accident Nelly would have come to know life within prison."

most likely not due to the famous old High School of Jever having failed in its task, but are rather to be attributed to the bent of his interests and to his talent. His aptitudes could only have been satisfied by one of the new agricultural colleges of which at that time there were three in northern Germany: the Karstensche near Rostock, the Staudingersche near Hamburg, and the Thaersche in Celle. These were founded in the years 1793, 1798 and 1802—a clear sign that agricultural science made its debut in Germany during this decade. When in February 1802 the nineteen-year-old Thünen gave it his attention, he had the good fortune of being able to seek his teacher during the best, most hopeful opening stage. His step-father, von Buttel, sent him to Lukas Andreas Staudinger at the Agricultural College of Großflottbek. There he found the agricultural training and intellectual stimulus which he had missed. There he found in his teacher, who was a friend of Klopstock, a friend of his own. There he became acquainted with Baron von Voght, who had set up an English farm on his estate Klein-Flottbek, and this was a connection which influenced his entire future. There too he first struck upon the notion of the "isolated state".

The embryonic conception is found in "A Description of Farming in the Village of Großflottbek near Hamburg" written in 1803. "If it be supposed", we read there, "that in a region of 40 miles diameter there lies a large city, that this region can sell its products only in this city, and that the agriculture of this district is at the highest level of culture, then it may be assumed that the economic systems around this city would be divided into four classes . . ." Commenting on this, Schumacher remarks quite rightly that it was already clear to the youth that an economic ideal adapted to all conditions did not exist. "Just as a wanderer listens in the darkness of a forest to the mysterious murmur of water yet invisible to him," he writes, " so the youth hearkens in expectation beside the spring of eternal laws."

The process is in fact quite singular. We know that John Stuart Mill was a precocious child and that during boyhood he acquired from his father an interest in science. We know further that the life of many great artists and prophets produces remarkably ripe fruits between the ages of fourteen and twenty-one. Yet there is no further instance of a man having in his youth an inspiration which he never tires of elaborating his whole life long and which was and is really inexhaustible—a man who is never again to receive an inspiration of anywhere near the same profundity. Thünen was evidently aware of this himself. When, twenty-three years after this inspiration, the *Isolated State*, Part 1, was published, he wrote to his stepbrother, Christian von Buttel, of the "slowly conceived, slowly born isolated state": "Its diffusion through the public will now most likely be slow and so its entire life's span will be accorded the description *slow*." These often quoted words are characteristic of the author and the work.

But their sequel is even more revealing: "Perhaps it will yet fall into oblivion and then I shall remain in the quiet which suits me so well."

But before we attempt to learn, from such statements, about Thünen's method of work, let us return to the years of his youth whose inspiration and impressions became so decisive for his whole life. "My teacher in economics was Adam Smith, in scientific agriculture it was Thaer," says Thünen looking back in the year 1850. This order is systematic and accords with the later stage of Thünen's manner of working and thinking. Chronologically the order was reversed. Thaer was his first teacher, and my surmise is that the recognition of what Thaer was lacking first induced Thünen to take up his study of Adam Smith. Thünen remained only one short year with Staudinger and at the Easter of 1803 he went to Celle in order to hear Thaer, whose books had been diligently studied and discussed in Klein-Flottbek. There arose a relationship which was cultivated by both sides with great care and which lasted until Thaer's death. It would appear, however, that the personal acquaintances led at first to a great disappointment. "Unfortunately", Thünen writes to his brother Frederik, "Thaer has not by a long way given us the whole of economics; the most interesting half of it has been given us in only a few sentences." It was this disappointment, I suspect, which in the autumn induced Thünen to move on to Göttingen, and it is there no doubt that he concerned himself as *studiosus oeconomiae* with Adam Smith.

What was Thaer able to teach the young Thünen? Thaer was and is quite rightly regarded as the founder of rational agriculture and agricultural science, and Thünen always recognized these merits of his. But while Thaer never ceased to praise the costly system of crop rotation with stall-feeding on the English model as being the salvation of agriculture, Thünen found this thesis in particular to be unacceptable—it ran counter to his theoretical and historical views and he even hoped to demonstrate its limits mathematically.

The real difference probably lies even deeper. Thaer's scientific agriculture on the English pattern revolutionized an old agricultural tradition which in many places had been upheld through centuries or even through a millennium. In its rationality the new technique was linked to the prevailing spirit of enlightenment, and in its belief in progress it was related to the contemporary movement in the industrial field, which when accompanied by a social repercussion is termed an "industrial revolution". The rational element was kindred to Thünen's own disposition; the revolutionary one was not congenial to him. The *Isolated State* is anti-revolutionary and to this extent anti-Thaer since it proves the relative merit of all systems of cultivation. And this also holds good for the doctrine of "statics" (using the word in the sense it had at that time)—the doctrine of the maintenance of equilibrium between soil exhaustion and replacement through the use of dung—a doctrine which appeared to Thünen of such importance that he devoted years of his life to it. Rational, indeed rationalistic, with a keen eye for the achievements of the new techniques, on the one hand, and yet anti-revolutionary and full of respect for the products of historical evolution on the other hand—the very same traits are characteristic of Adam Smith. Hence it may have been this affinity which made Adam Smith *the* teacher of the twenty-year-old student in the subject of political economy, rather than say Justi or Beckmann or Büsch who at that time stood in high favour in Göttingen. Which of their works or which other works of political economy Thünen at that time read is unknown.

Adam Smith was Thünen's teacher. Yet Thünen did not become a Smithian. By combining Smith and Thaer he became aware of the limits of these two great thinkers and went on to formulate his own questions, a good many of which were asked on the other side of the Channel by Ricardo. This means that in this respect Thünen belongs, despite his originality in other respects, to the second generation of classic writers on econmics, as do Ricardo in England and Jean-Baptiste Say in France.

It is not possible here to give an account of the great differences in the theories of these writers. Ricardo's frame of reference is, of course, much wider; his attention to the basic laws of the distribution of the national product could have embraced the whole of Thünen's problems. But what appears to me more interesting is the fact that both of Smith's successors, Thünen and Ricardo, move independently on quite parallel lines. "What is the origin of land rent and what law determines its amount?"—this is one of the questions which Thünen found unanswered in Adam Smith and one which impelled him to undertake investigations of his own. Is it not the selfsame question that is put by Ricardo?

Even more interesting is the second coincidence. An opinion often held is that Ricardo's theory of the value of labour is to be considered a by-product of Smith's doctrine. I too would be inclined to believe that a polarity of values in Smith is here replaced by a monistic explanation. But is not the theory of the value of labour an almost necessary next step? The famous first words of Smith's book can support this contention. That it is correct becomes quite evident, however, when one realizes that Thünen's search for the natural wage and his well-known formula $\sqrt{a.p.}$ are founded in like manner on Smith's system, indeed even on his philosophy.

There is a third agreement. Thünen's ninth question runs: "What influence do important improvements in agriculture and the invention of new machines have for factories on their first appearance and what is their final effect?" If five of its words were deleted, this question of Thünen's could be placed above the chapter "On Machinery" which in 1821 Ricardo inserted into the third edition of his *Principles*. In this case, however, the agreement goes so far that one cannot really assume independence between the two great theoreticians. Thünen did not know Ricardo when he published the first edition of the *Isolated State*. Later, however, he read him and made excerpts.

It must be admitted, of course, that Thünen makes a notable advance beyond Ricardo by his inclusion of "important improvements in agriculture", and in fact many of the crisis theories of the ensuing period would have done well to follow Thünen's example by drawing attention to agriculture and industry—in the older terminology, to both branches of industry.

But we must again turn to that period of youth in which Thünen—already a self-willed thinker while still learning—laid the foundation of his entire practical and scientific career. Thünen's connection with Mecklenburg and subsequent move there were the outcome of a friendship formed in Göttingen with a young Mecklenburger, whose sister, Helene Berlin, he married at the beginning of 1806. In Mecklenburg, Thünen leased for a while an estate near Anklam and then purchased the Tellow estate the name of which will always be linked with his life and work. According to Schumacher the son's desire to move to Mecklenburg was the cause of great consternation to the parents in Jever.

The remainder of Thünen's life, interrupted on rare occasions by trips to watering places and visits to acquaintances and friends, was spent after 1810 in Tellow. It was passed in a very remarkable mixture of Jean Paul's eccentricity and Frisian practicality, of rationality in applied economics and fantasy in economic theory, of philosophical sobriety and natural mysticism. If space permitted one could examine Thünen's activities in the most diverse fields—as a practical and theoretical agriculturist, as a theoretical and practical economist, as educator and teacher, as adviser and politician. And it would then be necessary to show in detail how these various interests and activities, which changed from decade to decade, were able to assist and impede, fructify and disturb. And one would thus render explicable the astonishing fact that although Thünen's scientific work did not reach the degree of perfection which he wished to achieve, he did nevertheless achieve a perfection in the Goethian sense—a perfection of that work of art which his life represented.[2]

Since this great picture cannot be painted even in outline here, I shall pick out a few essential details. Thus I shall not deal with Thünen as the father of location theory or as the pioneer of marginal theory or as the

[2] Until his death in the year 1850 Thünen bore with detached, stoical calmness his eye trouble and the consequences of a protracted attack of pleurisy suffered at the age of twenty-five. His highly talented son died at the age of seventeen.

promoter of the natural wage, but will try instead to answer the question "How did Thünen actually work and what can we learn from this?"

Goethe once said that genius is industry. A person who has as many inspirations of genius as Goethe may indeed be allowed to take the necessary ingredient, energy, for the essence. We lesser beings cannot permit ourselves this kind of self-deception. The following could be said, however, of Thünen. After the idea of the *isolated state* dawned upon him in early youth, he possessed during the remainder of his life the genius of industry and was thus enabled to turn his estate into a model one and, in the closest connection with this, to shape his *isolated state* into a vessel of universal theory and theoretical politics. Nor should it be forgotten how difficult in every way this task was to him since the mental equipment and technical instruments were still very primitive compared with those available today. It is true, of course, that farm accounting had long been known, that since the physiocrats a kind of economic analysis, which we should nowadays call model analysis, had been in use, that the mathematical representation of economic problems had been utilized by Sir William Petty (whom Thünen had probably not read) and by the Italians (with whom he was certainly not acquainted). It was Thünen, however, who first combined the various methods. Thünen, moreover, rediscovered each method for himself, went through every step again on his own account. Ever since Quesnay and Smith, the science of economics owes its unifying continuity to the fact that—as in all other sciences—the questions and answers are handed on to the next generation, and that what appeared to be a solution is often called in question by disciples or by the disciples of disciples. Notwithstanding this continuity, however, there appear now and again superior intellects who, although they may often develop new doctrines in conflict with predecessors, have an inward drive towards economics so strong and original that one can but think they would have invented the science had it not already existed. Ricardo belongs to this type, and so do Karl Marx, Cournot, Vilfredo Pareto, and without any doubt Thünen also.

For ten years, from 24 June 1810 to 23 June 1820, Thünen's most important activity apart from managing his estate was the book-keeping at Tellow which he did in his own hand from beginning to end despite a severe eye complaint. This matter-of-fact, subordinate work Thünen considered to be too important to be left to the attention of helpers. Only figures he had himself checked for accuracy were able to serve his twofold purpose. In the first place he wished to support his statistical views with concrete data, his previous solution, which to him was a Columbus' egg, having been called in question by his brother Frederick because of its hypothetical character. Second, in this decade of violent fluctuations in the price of corn he wanted to obtain incontrovertible figures for the now particularly important question of the dependence of the economic system on corn prices. "Labour, corn and money accounts", Thünen states in a letter, "had to be equally comprehensive and equally accurate, and nearly all of this had to be carried out *by my own hand*, otherwise the whole would have been lacking in unity and intrinsic credibility." By doing so, we read in the same letter, he had imposed upon himself the hard law that requires one "to delay the advance of ideas and to apply all one's time and energy to the study of reality". This he did and so he is also of the opinion that the conclusions of the *Isolated State* are not the product of "mere ratiocination" but are deduced from a formula of the costs and yield of agriculture "the data of which have been drawn from reality". Thünen calls this his method. He says: "If the empirical observations are accurate and interpreted correctly and the conclusions based on them are valid, . . ." this method is able "to give mathematical certainty to a field in which as a result of mere rationcination there vie with one another the most conflicting views."

Every historian of whatever science knows full well that the actual method of scientists and of research is vastly different from, and often diametrically opposed to the method which the scientists imagine themselves to be using and which they regard as the only one possible. An exception to this rule is the economist Karl Marx, who, being as well versed in philosophy as in economics, clearly appreciated the difference between his method of research and mode of presentation. Further exceptions are John Stuart Mill and John Maynard Keynes. How does it stand with Thünen?

The sentences I quoted are from Thünen's later life. They were written after Thünen had studied Hegel and Feuerbach, and they attempt, if I am not mistaken, to express themselves in the philosophical terminology of the 1840s. It is in a different manner, more accurately, and in keeping with his actual procedure that Thünen expressed himself in earlier years when Kant's influence was stronger and when he spoke in general not of his "method" but of his "form of intuition", which in the preface to the second edition of the *Isolated State* he still regarded as "the most important thing in this entire book".

I am not alone, but am in agreement with such diverse scholars as Schumpeter and Spann when I perceive in the characterization "form of intuition" the feature in which Thünen differs say from Ricardo and by which every observable theory is distinguished from every purely rational theory. Where with Ricardo "simple cases" are investigated and where the modern theory of models constructs rational models as a tool for grasping reality, Thünen attempts by abstracting from reality to arrive at a picture which is reduced to main features and main problems. Using a pair of concepts coined by Ritschl, one could say that his picture is a constructive and not a reductive model. But I can set forth what is special about Thünen's method in its characteristic form only if I point out that the taking of data from reality is not the beginning, that—in distinction to Thünen's later formulation—we have at the beginning not measuring and calculating, nor even abstracting and reducing, but intuition. The latter gives rise to the vision of the isolated state or, as it was to be called originally, the ideal state. At the second stage this vision acquires data of reality. At the third stage all that has been derived from reality is subjected to testing and criticism and it is to this stage that the book-keeping at Tellow corresponds. Then follows the completion in the fourth stage, when the attempt is made to determine whatever conforms to law and to express this as far as possible in a mathematical form.

Thünen's manner of working can, I believe, be described in this way and it remained the same throughout his life. But this sameness is merely formal. In the contents there is a change in significance. It can be most appositely paraphrased as a change from Kant to Hegel. In the economic sense it would be best described—although Thünen was unaware of this—as a change from Ricardo back to Quesnay.

This is to be understood as follows. The young Thünen was concerned with the logical accuracy of his picture and with the mathematical accuracy of his data. History is of importance to him only in so far as he sees that the relative validity of historical economic systems is established by the isolated state. The old Thünen, however, like others at that time was under the influence of the concept of evolution. With Hegel he asked whether the existing is reasonable and with Quesnay he asked whether individual phenomena and their connections are "natural", whether they are in accordance with nature and in this sense in accordance with law. "In fact," he wrote later on, "it would be a wonderful accident if in reality where everything is in a process of becoming, if here the reasonable had become apparent at its highest peak. Had this miracle actually taken place, however, it would have to be demonstrated *that the existing is in accordance with reason and also why this is so*."

The young Thünen I have called antirevolutionary; it was an antirevolutionary that the old Thünen remained too. This is probably the reason why his admiration of Lorenz v. Stein's *Socialism and Communism in Present-day France* did not lead him to read the original socialist sources; and this may also be the reason why his genuine social feeling was converted but slowly and late in the day into social action. On the other hand, as Thünen's belief in the inevitability of social evolution became firmer, he became more convinced that his task was to contribute his utmost towards the better wages and the spiritual education of workers and of demonstrating scientifically "that both are compatible with the qualities and powers accorded to human nature".

In other words even when concerning himself with social policy the estate-owner Thünen remains true to science, even subservient to it, and in view of this it is all the more regrettable that he was prevented by illness from taking his seat in the Paulskirche. In the parliament of professors it might well have been that the practical and theoretical farmer would have consulted science and reason on a wider scale than all their official representatives. He did so at all events in working out a profit-sharing scheme for his workers, and it is evidence of the lack of discernment of his fellow farmers and of the shortsightedness of science that this scheme found no successor and for long attracted no attention.

Schumacher has given what is probably a very apt description of the old Thünen: "Characteristic of him was the way he held his head inclined somewhat towards the front and side in a reflective attitude, in keeping with the thoughtful lines which had formed themselves in his countenance—and furthermore a look which was in some measure directed inwards." That is not the appearance of a revolutionary. Evolution, not revolution is the motto of Thünen's political development. He was no hothead like List who, younger than Thünen by eight years, had been from 1819 until his suicide a champion of German unity, who conducted his fight from a variety of terrains and positions. Nor was he a passionate Hegelian like Marx who for the sake of the victory of the working class was ready and prepared to overthrow all hitherto existing order. But he too recognized that the institution of nation-states had outlived itself and he took pleasure in the deep movement felt throughout Germany in the forties. "There seems to be coming about", he wrote, "that which Hegel calls 'ruse of reason' and I 'providence'." What formerly appeared to him a Utopian dream, he now hopes is on the way to becoming reality. "A wonderful revolution has taken place", the otherwise so dispassionate Thünen cried enthusiastically after the March Revolution of 1848. "Rank, position, birth, riches, even knowledge—all have lost their significance, their predominance, and in their place *integrity and right thinking* have mounted the throne." And "in the mighty striving of the Germans towards national status and unity," he now saw, "the sole support and ray of hope". That Thünen, although elected to the Frankfurt parliament and made honorary freeman of the township of Teterow near Tellow, was not expressing the convictions of either the government of Mecklenburg or of the aristocracy is understandable; it is also not surprising that they consider the social-minded estate-owner of Tellow to be himself a revolutionary. "Tellow", Thünen wrote in a letter to Schumacher, the father of his pupil and later biographer, "is coming to be regarded by all property-owners as a dangerous source of the spreading weed."

Thünen's herb was of such a kind that only a very mild potion could have been brewed from it. For he remained conservative, social-conservative, being here akin to Rodbertus. Hence his ideal constitution contained four elective bodies, the first comprised of the scholars, the second of the larger landowners, the third and fourth of the two classes of taxpayers. If it were not a contradiction *in adjecto* the political-philosophical conviction from which this and similar notions stem would have to be designated *Mecklenburgian*—or perhaps even Jeverland—*Platonism*. The "Future of the Human Race", however, about which Thünen speculated and wrote, could not be directed into such peaceful bourgeois channels.

Thünen in his age—the picture as a whole must not be lost sight of if one wishes to keep the real greatness in view. If he is regarded merely as an economic theoretician, then the unanimous verdict will no doubt be that after Ricardo's death Thünen in the twenties and thirties was by far the most important one, not only in Germany but also in the West. But even in the forties his location theory did not provide an adequate basis. As an exponent of agricultural science, Thünen was, after Thaer's death, the great, world-renowned authority. But again—he had no eye for Liebig, nor therefore for the problems of the second half of the century. He was never a politician in the real sense of the word, for he shunned the public and believed that the will to power could be replaced by the power of knowledge. "What brought him the respect and love of all those who had close relationships with him", says his student and biographer, "was his goodwill towards his fellow men, the extreme justness and mildness of his judgment of others, even though he was not unaware of their weaknesses."

This highest sense of justice manifests itself in his work as intellectual honesty and integrity. Concepts which were raised by Max Weber to ethical demands were for Thünen the essence of his scientific work, indeed of his entire life. One cannot say of Thünen in Schiller's words that he satisfied the best of his time; for "the best" knew far less of him than he of them. And yet it was certainly a life in the Goethian sense that Thünen led. Since he limited himself to the fields of his talents and his inclinations and in these achieved perfection, the light of his image still reaches us, the influence of his work is still upon us, and he in his own age lived for many an age.

Edgar Salin

II
VON THÜNEN'S THEORY OF DISTRIBUTION AND THE ADVENT OF MARGINAL ANALYSIS

The pioneer contributions of the nineteenth-century German economist Johann Heinrich von Thünen to the development of the concept and technique of marginal analysis place him in a rank of first importance among economic thinkers. To the historian of economic thought his intricate theories and his distinctive approach to economic analysis hold peculiar interest. He is original in developing an explicit general application of the marginal productivity concept to the theory of distribution. His deductive reasoning is supplemented by inductive analysis based in part upon extensive facts and figures gathered from his own experimental estate in Mecklenburg, and he combines surprisingly advanced modern concepts with orthodox Ricardian doctrines. Yet Thünen's single published economic treatise, *Der isolierte Staat*, has not been widely read, owing perhaps to its voluminous proportions, to its formidable array of algebraic symbols, and, in the case of English-speaking students of economics, to the fact that it has never been translated into English. John Bates Clark and Alfred Marshall have recognized and praised Thünen's contribution to economic theory, but there is to the knowledge of the present writer no adequate English summary and discussion of his more important theories.

In the pages which follow an attempt is made to reproduce as clearly and completely as possible within the confines of a single article the principal theories of Thünen relating to marginal analysis and the theory of distribution. After two brief sections dealing with Thünen's explanations of land rent, interest, and entrepreneurs' profit there follows a condensed exposition of his theory of wage and interest rate determination. The paper ends with an evaluation of Thünen's theories in the light of modern economic doctrines. It should be noted at the outset that Thünen's work deserves study less for the conclusions at which he arrives, some of which are absurd, than for its highly significant contribution to the development of new and more fruitful methods of analysis.

To simplify and clarify his analysis, Thünen sets up a hypothetical model which he calls the "isolated state". He describes this model as a state composed of a single large city located in the centre of a broad plain which is all of equal fertility but void of navigable rivers and canals, the only means of transportation being the wagon. The inhabitants of the city supply the inhabitants of the surrounding country with manufactured articles in return for raw produce. Various kinds of agricultural products are grown in concentric circles around the city, the exact location at which each product is raised being determined by the cost of transporting it to the city. Cultivation is intensive because of the high price of land, and soil fertility is maintained by the application of fertilizer rather than by allowing a part of it to lie fallow each year. Surrounding the cultivated plain lies an impenetrable wilderness which separates the state from the rest of the world. The soil in the wilderness is as fertile as any other, and the limit of cultivation is determined only by transportation cost.

Thünen elaborates with minute and realistic detail upon the principles (including that of alternative cost) which govern the location of agricultural production and, with as much care, he points out that his simplifying assumptions, like those of a controlled laboratory experiment in physics, are in many ways unrealistic and acknowledges the danger of generalizing the conclusions derived from such assumptions. He is too much concerned with supporting his theory with realistic detail and actual statistics to confine himself rigidly to his hypothetical model, and he therefore changes his assumptions and compares his theory with observed fact at frequent intervals. Nevertheless, the concept of the isolated state forms the nucleus for most of his theoretical discussion.

Thünen's theory of land rent is based upon the same fundamental principles as that of Ricardo—differences in the value product of different units of labour and capital due to nonuniformity in land fertility or convenience of location and to the effects of intensive cultivation. He criticizes Adam Smith's definition of land rent as that part of the value of the products of the estate which remains after the tenant farmer has paid wages and the other expenses of the farm and has taken the usual interest on his capital, on the ground that such a definition fails to distinguish between the rent of the land itself and the interest on capital invested in buildings, fences, and other improvements. Acknowledging that Ricardo had rectified Adam Smith's error by confining the term "rent" to payment for the use of the "original and indestructible powers of the soil", Thünen points out that the estate revenue (*Gutsrente*) must be subdivided into its two component parts—ground rent or land rent (*Bodenrente* or *Landrente*) and interest on all capital invested in improvements. This distinction is based upon long-run mobility. Capital will not be invested in the development of a new estate unless the prospective estate revenue is at least sufficient to yield a return on the invested capital at the current rate of interest, yet the estate may be brought into cultivation if the revenue is no more than this amount (that is, if land rent proper is zero). If the revenue of an existing estate should fall, or if the current rate of interest should rise, the total estate revenue may fall short of the interest at the current rate on the capital invested in the estate. To the extent that estate revenue is less than interest on invested capital, the land rent is negative. In such circumstances the estate will continue under cultivation only until the capital invested in it can be withdrawn or disinvested through undermaintenance. In short, the concept of land rent as a residual can apply only to those qualities of the land itself which are strictly nontransferable, even in the long run.

In the isolated state, where all land is of equal fertility, estates located in the inner circles of cultivation yield a land rent by virtue of their relatively advantageous position with respect to the central city and the consequent lower cost of getting their produce to market. The price of wheat in the central city is determined by the production plus transportation cost of obtaining wheat from the most distant estates whose product is required to bring the city's supply of food to the necessary level. This cost depends upon the rates of wages and interest, which tend to maintain a uniform level throughout the state. Since the wheat produced on estates near the city and brought to market at low transportation costs sells at the same price in the city as does wheat brought in from distant estates at high transportation costs, the saving in transportation costs enjoyed by the more favourably situated estates constitutes their land rent. Land rent is zero in the most distant estates and increases steadily with decreasing distance from the market city. In the real world, differences in fertility as between estates gives rise to land rent in the same manner as do differences in location advantages. Thus, as a general rule, the land rent of an estate originates in the advantages enjoyed by that estate with respect to convenience of location or to soil quality as compared with other estates which must be cultivated to supply the demand.

Thünen recognizes a second origin of land rent in the phenomenon of diminishing returns which accompanies increasingly intensive cultivation of a given area of land. Rent arises from this source even though all land is equally well situated and of equal fertility, provided only that all such land is under cultivation. In illustration of this point, Thünen assumes a plain of uniform fertility with a large number of small cities distributed evenly over it and surrounded by a sandy desert. Under these circumstances, land rent from the first cause—the differential advantage of some estates over others with respect to fertility or location—would be negligible, but rent from the second cause—the influence of increasing intensity of cultivation—would arise provided only that all the arable land has been taken into cultivation.

Thünen's third component of land rent is the interest on capital invested in those improvements of the estate which once made can never be destroyed or separated from the soil. His inclusion of this element which appears at first to be in conflict with his earlier strict definition of land rent seems to be based upon the assumption that the improvements the interest of which is to be classed as land rent are, like land, wholly nontransferable, and that capital once invested in them can therefore command only a residual share of the product which may fall short of (but presumably could not exceed) the current interest rate.

Criticizing Adam Smith and most of the other English writers for lumping together as "profit" the interest on invested capital and the profit of the entrepreneur, Thünen makes a careful distinction between the two.

He defines capital as the product of past human labour used for the purpose of increasing the effectiveness of human labour, that is, used productively in such a way that it maintains itself permanently intact through replacement of consumed physical units and that it yields a revenue. It is distinct from natural or original forces, including land, and from commodities or "supplies" consumed without producing a substitute and without making labour more effective. His definition and explanation of interest must be inferred from various statements and passages scattered through his discussion. He treats interest as the price or the payment for the use of capital arising from the fact that capital increases the effectiveness or productiveness of labour and from the fact that no free individual will accumulate capital at the sacrifices involved in exerting labour and in forgoing the luxuries which might otherwise have been enjoyed unless he receives a compensation in the form of interest which is worthy of his sacrifice. In the rate of interest for loaned capital there are usually included two elements: 1. the compensation which the debtor pays for the temporary use of the capital under the condition that he will repay the sum loaned; and 2. an insurance premium against the possible loss of the capital, a risk which often accompanies long-period loans. He adds that what he calls interest in the present work includes only the first of these elements.

The entrepreneur's trade profit in the strict sense consists only of that part of his revenue which remains after the deduction of 1. the interest on his invested capital; 2. an insurance premium against fire, hail, shipwreck, and all other insurable risk; and 3. his salary of management and administration. This surplus or trade profit remains to the entrepreneur in spite of the competition of other entrepreneurs because there is no insurance against each and every danger which is connected with enterprise. A common example of such a noninsurable risk is the movement of prices. Although the chances of gain are often fully as great as the chances of loss, the former do not compensate wholly for the latter, since to the individual entrepreneur who risks his entire fortune and reputation in his enterprise, the pleasure of doubling his fortune is far less intense than the suffering which would result from the complete loss of his fortune.

Thünen's own attempt to develop a more satisfactory explanation of interest and wage rates occupies the major part of his second volume. In a seemingly tireless effort to make his theory airtight, he leads the reader through several long series of calculations, each begun from a different point of view and all arriving eventually at the same set of conclusions. He first approaches the problem of wage and interest rates by assuming 1. a community of persons having the technological knowledge of civilized European nations but no capital and living in a large tropical country rich in natural resources and favoured by climate. For further simplification, it is assumed 2. that the community is isolated from the rest of the world, 3. that it is large enough to take full advantage of the division of labour as soon as the requisite capital is present, 4. that the land is of equal fertility and of such vast expanse that everyone can take as much as he wants without cost, and 5. that all the inhabitants are workers, there being no employer–employee relationships.

Under these circumstances, one labouring family, working for one year without the aid of capital, can produce 110*c*, where *c* is a unit of the major subsistence commodity equal to a hundredth part of the quantity necessary to maintain one labouring family for one year. Since each family can produce in one year a surplus of 10*c* over and above the 100*c* necessary for its subsistence, it can, in the course of ten years, accumulate sufficient subsistence (abstracting from storage problems) either to live for one year without working or to spend that year in the production of useful tools such as bows and nets, that is, capital. Working with the capital it can produce in one year, a family can produce a net product (after maintaining capital) of 150*c*. With a yearly surplus of 50*c*, it need devote only two years labour to the production of subsistence before it is once more free to spend a year in capital production. But this particular family is already provided with sufficient bows, arrows and nets, and it therefore lends this newly created capital to another family which has not as yet acquired any capital. Since this second family can, with the aid of the borrowed capital, produce a yearly product of 150*c* after maintaining the capital and returning it intact, and since there is not as yet sufficient capital in the country to provide each working family with as much capital as can be produced by one year of labour, the lender can demand as payment for the use of his capital the full difference beween the 150*c* which the borrowing family can produce with the aid of the capital and the 110*c* which it could produce unassisted by capital, a payment which in this stage of development amounts to 40*c* and which will continue to accrue indefinitely to the capital-producing worker as interest on the capital he produced with one year of labour. The interest rate is calculated by dividing the yearly revenue (40*c*) by the wages of one year of labour (110*c*), and the result in this case is 36·4 per cent. Thus, for the surplus of one year of labour, the worker has the choice of receiving 10*c* in perishable consumables or a perpetual revenue of 3·64*c* per year. Here, says Thünen, we discover the origin and basis of interest and its relation to capital.

After every worker in the community has been supplied with as much capital as can be produced by the labour of one family working for one year, capital production will continue, though perhaps the new capital will take a different form, for example, spades and hatchets instead of bows and nets. Thus in the course of time, each worker will be supplied with capital amounting to the product of two, three, four, five and so on, years of labour. The product of each worker will rise with each increase in the quantity of capital with which he works. But the increase of revenue resulting from the use of increased quantities of capital does not keep pace with the increase of capital itself, so that each added unit of capital results in a smaller increment in revenue than had its predecessor. Different forms of capital enhance the efficiency of labour to different degrees. Capital-producing workers will at first produce those forms which are most effective in increasing the product of labour, but, when they have produced as many of such instruments as can be used to advantage, they must devote their efforts to the production of less efficient forms of capital. For this reason, therefore, the revenue of capital tends to decline as the quantity of capital increases.

Thünen next divides his workers into two classes, one group which specializes in capital production and another which works with capital borrowed from the first group; but he retains the simplifying assumption that all workers are their own masters, none being hired by others. Each member of the latter class retains as his wages his total product minus the interest on the capital which he borrows from the capital-producing labourers. Thus when each worker is supplied with as much capital as is produced by one year of labour, his total yearly product is 150*c*, the revenue of the capital which he uses is 40*c* as shown above, and his wages are 110*c*. When capital produced by two years of labour is used by each worker, however, the additional capital adds only 36*c* to the labourer's product, bringing it to a total of $110c + 40c + 36c = 186c$. When the quantity of capital in the community has reached this level, the capital-producing workers, because of the free competition among them, can obtain only 36*c* per year as revenue for *all* units of their capital, even though the first units used add as much as 40*c* to the product of labour. Under competitive conditions amounts of capital requiring equal quantities of labour for their production must receive equal revenue. Thus the revenue of all capital is determined by the revenue of the last added units of capital. Thünen stresses the importance of this law in the following words: "Die Rente, die das Kapital im Ganzen beim Ausleihen gewährt, wird bestimmt durch die Nutzung des zuletzt angelegten Kapitalteilchens. Dies ist einer der wichtigsten Sätze in der Lehre von den Zinsen".

The worker who, with the aid of two units of capital, can produce 186*c* must, therefore, pay to the capital-producing worker only 2 × 36*c* or 72*c* as interest on his borrowed capital and can retain 114*c* as his wages, which have thus risen by 4*c* as a result of his using the second unit of capital. Similarly, the revenue per unit of capital falls, and his wages rise as further additions are made to the capital with which he works.

Since the rate of interest in Thünen's analysis is calculated by dividing the revenue of a unit of capital by the wages of the labour required to produce a unit of capital, that rate must fall with the increase of capital even more abruptly than does the absolute revenue per unit of capital. Thus, when wages equal 110*c* and revenue per unit of capital equals 40*c*, the rate of interest equals 40*c*/110*c*, or 36·4 per cent; but, when two units of capital are used by each worker and wages rise to 114*c* while revenue falls to 36*c*, the interest rate falls to 36*c*/114*c*, or 31·6 per cent. This decline in the interest rate continues as the quantity of capital used by each worker increases to three, four, five, and so on, units.

Finally, Thünen presents an analysis of the equilibrium relationship between the quantity of labour and the quantity of capital employed by an entrepreneur, which is important because it strongly suggests the modern concept of the marginal rate of substitution and because it brings out quite clearly the principle that aggregate revenue is maximized when the marginal expenditure on each agent employed equals its marginal value productivity. He observes that capital and labour are mutual substitutes and presents a number of examples in support of this observation. Continuous labour may be replaced by the investment of capital. But not all investments are equally effective in replacing labour. In some cases the continuous labour of one man may be replaced by the investment of the labour of only ten men for one year, while in other cases as many as twenty, thirty or fifty man-years of labour would be necessary. It will be in the farmer's interest, says Thünen, to make all such investments in which the ratio of annual wages saved to cost of investment is greater than the rate of interest at which the capital can be borrowed. He then demonstrates by further detailed calculation that if z represents the interest rate and k represents the number of man-years of labour (units of capital) which must be invested to replace the continuous labour of one worker, then the ratio between the quantities of capital and labour employed is in equilibrium, and no increase in revenue can be obtained by the substitution of either for the other, when k equals $1/z$.

Thünen is guilty of several rather obvious technical errors in his analysis of wage and interest-rate determination. The first of these is his use of the yearly wage of a labouring family (in measures of wheat) to express the unit of capital upon which his calculations are based. This blunder involves not only the erroneous assumption that capital is produced wholly by labour and that the whole cost of producing a unit of capital is the wages of the labour employed in its production but also a serious internal inconsistency in his reasoning.

In addition to these technical blunders, Thünen falls into the error of oversimplification and overabstraction, notwithstanding his great respect for and ample use of facts and figures. After criticizing the subsistence theory of wages as it was expounded by his English contemporaries, Thünen proceeds to adopt a subsistence concept as one of the fundamental bases of his calculations and to use it as though it were subject to precise quantitative measurement and formulation. Thünen's error in this connection is an illustration of his general, though not wholly consistent, acceptance of the classical belief that labour produces all product value and is only "assisted" by capital. Finally, Thünen's model in which all capital is produced and owned either individually or in groups or societies by labourers who work for wages at the common rate appears to be too extreme an abstraction from the conditions even of nineteenth-century Germany to serve as a basis for analysing the "normal" rates of interest and wages supposed to prevail in the real world.

The errors and weaknesses strike at the very foundation of Thünen's theoretical structure, at least with respect to wage and interest-rate determination, and are sufficient to invalidate his formal conclusions regarding the equilibrium rates of wages and interest. It is therefore not at all upon these formal conclusions that his real importance as a contributor to the theory of distribution rests. That contribution is to be found rather in the methods which he used in arriving at his conclusions.

The most outstanding feature of Thünen's analysis of wage and interest-rate determination is his application to it of the principle of marginal productivity. He presents a far more precise and more refined statement of this theory than does any previous theorist known to the present writer. His insistence upon the infinitesimal increment, his use of the symbols of differential calculus to express marginal productivity, his clear statement of the principle of variable proportions and the mutual substitutability of labour and capital, and his rudimentary development of the concept of the marginal rate of substitution are cases in point. These contributions alone are sufficient to ensure him a place of first importance in any history of economic theory.

Thünen also deserves recognition for his broad application of the marginal productivity concept to wages as well as to the revenue of capital in all its forms. He was a pioneer in the use of marginal analysis to determine the proportions in which productive agents must be combined in a process to achieve maximum efficiency and maximum return; that is, to organize or to allocate scarce resources with a view to maximizing value product.

Another significant aspect of Thünen's discussion is his refined subdivision of the entrepreneur's gross revenue into true interest as the contribution of capital, a wage for the personal services of the entrepreneur himself, an insurance premium as compensation for risk, and pure "trade profit" as a final residual arising from the noninsurable uncertainty of the future. It represents an improvement over the English classical concept of "profit" as the entire revenue of the capitalist-entrepreneur which remains after the payment of rent and wages.

Also worthy of note is Thünen's extensive use of mathematical symbols in developing his theories at a time when such precise formulation was all too little used in economic literature. Many of his complex notions would be practically unintelligible were they not stated precisely and unmistakably in mathematical terms. Yet Thünen's work demonstrates not only that mathematics can be a very effective aid, in many cases an indispensable aid to analysis and exposition, but also that it can magnify the consequences of small errors if it is misused. In spite of his numerous mistakes, however, Thünen's high development of marginal analysis in conjunction with the mathematical formulation and exposition, which makes its application and use far easier and more effective, represents a contribution to economic theory of the first magnitude.

Arthur Hertel Leigh

SOURCES

Essay I

Edgar Salin, "Johann Heinrich von Thünen in seiner Zeit", *Zeitschrift für Agrargeschichte und Agrarsoziologie*: Sonderheft: *Johann Heinrich von Thünen,* 6 (1958). Abridged.

Essay II

Arthur Hertel Leigh, "Von Thünen's theory of distribution and the advent of marginal analysis", *Journal of Political Economy*, 54 (1946). Abridged.

Signature

Thünen-Archiv of the University, Rostock.

Portrait

Portrait by Ternite (Thünen-Archiv of the University, Rostock).

BIBLIOGRAPHY

H. Schumacher-Zarchlin, *Johann Heinrich von Thünen. Ein Forscherleben* (Rostock, 1868).

W. Seedorf and H. J. Seraphim, *Festschrift zum 150, Geburtstag von Johann Heinrich von Thünen* (Rostock, 1933).

E. Schneider, "Johann Heinrich von Thünen", *Econometrica*, 2 (1934).

W. Braeuer, "Der Mathematiker-Ökonom. Zur Erinnerung an Johann Heinrich von Thünen", *Kyklos*, 4 (1950).

F. Bülow, "Thünen als Raumdenker", *Weltwirtschaftliches Archiv*, 65 (1950).

G. Schröder-Lembke, "H. v. Thünen und seine mecklenburgischen Gutsnachbarn", *Zeitschrift für Agrargeschichte und Agrarsoziologie*, 2 (1954).

H. Niehaus, "Johann Heinrich von Thünen", in Die Großen Deutschen, Deutsche Biographie, ed. H. Heimpel, Th. Heuss and B. Reifenberg, Vol. 5 (Berlin, 1957).

F. Bülow, "Johann Heinrich von Thünen als forstwirtschaftlicher Denker", *Weltwirtschaftliches Archiv*, 80 (1958).

G. Franz (ed.), *Johann Heinrich von Thünen*, special edition of *Zeitschrift für Agrargeschichte und Agrarsoziologie* (1958).

A. H. Leigh, "Johann Heinrich von Thünen", in *International Encyclopedia of the Social Sciences*, Vol. 16 (New York, 1968).

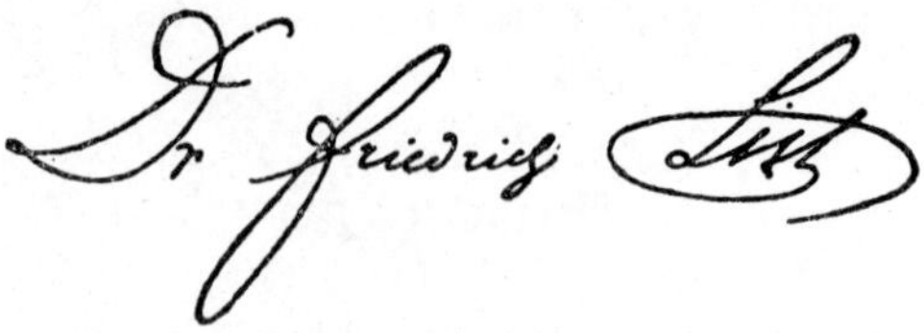

FRIEDRICH LIST

1789–1846

List war eine verkörperte Initiative. Darin lag seine Kraft. Er war ein organisierender Kopf unter allen den kritischen Größen unserer Tage, und darum überragte er sie. Er negierte, nivellierte, zerstörte nie, ohne neue Bauten aufzuführen—seine ganze geistige Tätigkeit war fortwährend eine schaffende, gestaltende. L. SCHÜCKING

Es ist nicht abzustreiten, daß das deutsche Volk in seiner verhängnisvollen Neigung, auch bei der Bewertung bedeutender Persönlichkeiten sich von wechselnden Extremen leiten zu lassen, versucht hat, was es dem lebenden List an Anerkennung versagte, dem toten List doppelt und dreifach zu geben. In einer bisweilen lächerlich wirkenden Art hat man gerade in den letzten Jahrzehnten es unternommen, List bald in literarischer, bald in politischer Exaltation zu einem Heros des deutschen Volkes zu machen. A. F. NAPP-ZINN

Thus to the array of important American economists I would add the name of Friedrich List. P. A. SAMUELSON

Denn List ist aktuell, noch immer oder sogar heute verstärkt aktuell. Außer Tocqueville und Marx hat kein Staatslehrer und kein Ökonom solch aufregende, hellsichtige "Blicke in die Zukunft", das heißt: in unsere Gegenwart getan. Und es sollte niemand über die Entwicklung unterentwickelter Länder schreiben, ohne bei dem großen Ahn der Wachstumstheorie und der Entwicklungspolitik in die Lehre zu gehen. E. SALIN, *aus einem Nachwort zur List-Ausgabe*

Et la patrie, et l'humanité! F. LIST

List's original contribution lay not in recognizing the dynamic nature of the transformation of the productive forces but in the role he assigned to the state in engineering that transformation. A. GERSCHENKRON

David Ricardo (1772–1823)

ON

THE PRINCIPLES

OF

POLITICAL ECONOMY,

AND

TAXATION.

BY DAVID RICARDO, ESQ.

LONDON:

JOHN MURRAY, ALBEMARLE-STREET.

1817.

The title page of Ricardo's
Principles of Political Economy and Taxation

Johann Heinrich von Thünen (1783–1850)

Friedrich List (1789–1846)

Antoine Augustin Cournot (1801–1877)

John Stuart Mill (1806–1873)

Entwickelung der Gesetze

des

menschlichen Verkehrs,

und der daraus fließenden

Regeln für menschliches Handeln

von

Hermann Heinrich Gossen,

Königlich preußischem Regierungs-Assessor außer Dienst.

Braunschweig,

Druck und Verlag von Friedrich Vieweg und Sohn.

1 8 5 4.

The title-page of the first edition of Gossen's *Entwicklung der Getsetze des menschlichen Verkehrs und der daraus fliessenden* Regeln *für menschliches Handeln*

Karl Marx (1818–1883)

I
FRIEDRICH LIST

When the name Friedrich List is mentioned German people get a bad conscience. They feel that the tragedy connected with him was of the sort that is possible only in Germany: it is a constant indictment. For a long time it seemed as if they even wanted to suppress any memory of him because of its persistent capacity to discomfort. But he could not be forgotten completely—there were always people who would bring up again the memory of his life and his works. But anyone wishing to follow this up and get in touch with List directly found himself in difficulties: only his main work and two or three smaller writings were reprinted. Otherwise one had to be lucky to get hold of Häusser's incomplete collection of the 1850s which occasionally appeared in second-hand bookshops. There was not lack of projects to publish List—one was intended as long ago as 1877 and it was attempted again in 1912—but only after the establishment of the Friedrich List Society in 1920 was the plan realized in an edition of ten imposing volumes, completed in the spring of 1933.

These introductory observations reflect a rather strange state of affairs and are not therefore just "bibliographical" but are in themselves a symptom of the long-lasting uncertainty about the man. Where should one place him? If within the history of the political sciences, as he surely must be placed, the question immediately arises: Was he a scientist? He had the right to the title of Professor but his academic career proved to be only a short and partly successful endeavour. This man's greatness, his undeniable albeit embarrassing greatness, lies in his agitation, in his political journalism and in his inclination to do practical work, rather than actual research. Are his teachings really his own and not just the thoughts of others, highly simplified and specially adapted for his time? But then if we accept that he should be considered a politican, he must have been a bad one if such men are to be judged according to their success. Everything, or almost everything, went wrong for him, and it is perhaps too cheap an excuse to blame only the conditions of his time or the malice of others for this. For the true politician reckons with these things in order to overcome them. List, however, when he committed suicide late on a grey November day in the year 1846, was himself overcome.

No, he does not belong to any one group: he falls between groups as between times—the notion of the untimely idea and the fate of such ideas can simply be read off from his case history, when one considers all the predictions of his that have "come true" in the light of a later period. Indeed, the incongruity that is apparent between the restless, spirited, imaginative man[1] and the comfortable provision and timid, or simply fractious, narrowness of the early Victorian period tempts one to extend his life-span and the period of his vigorous activity by a couple of decades. But indulgence in such thoughts becomes a game. For them, everything is open to question: how would List respond to the period, how would he solve the problems? There is the Paulskirche. It is not difficult for anyone to visualize this man in the German National Assembly, permeating it with his ideas and his policies. One may be sure that the citizens of Reutlingen who twice sent him as their representative to the provincial diet of Württemberg (and in doing so to the onset and cause of his misfortunes) almost thirty years before would be proud to repeat the choice of their fellow-citizens which by now would have become easier to make. But into what group should he be put? The evidence is collected, comparisons are drawn and scrutinized but the result does not add up. List remains bound to the reactionary period before the 1848 revolution.

Although developing in conflict with his time and being broken by it, he was nevertheless conditioned and affected by it. Those thirty-three years between 1815 and 1848, the Metternich era, condemned by the historical judgment of later times, witnessed the result: grey, exhausted and unhappy. These years contained private turmoil for him. Political expression in these years was only episodic, here and there, in conflicts over the constitution, in a few demonstrations, in some uproar in the press or lyrical confessions of faith. But meanwhile a new class was developing, with its own convictions and designs. It was constituted by that element of the middle class which had been forced out of the old orders and traditions by Napoleon's rearrangement of the boundaries of former German possessions, and which was obliged to get accustomed to the new order without being asked; and

[1] List's personality was very engaging. He was of medium size and heavy build; he had a large and extremely fine head with a high-domed forehead; large blue eyes which protruded somewhat; strong bushy eyebrows and an extraordinary way of blinking his eyes very slowly; his hair and his beard were white. Thick veins on his forehead and his temples were an indication of a strong and fiery character. His posture was that of a heavy-built man and his gait laborious, using short steps, especially in his final years after having suffered a broken leg. His conversation, brimming over with vivacity and flashes of wit, was very loud and frequently interrupted by hearty laughter. Since he was a sanguine person, delighting in his vital powers, and of a cheerful and light-hearted disposition, a more fortunate fate and better-rewarded endeavour would have developed in him also all the amiability which is inherent in characters of his type. But the vexations of his life, the endless losing battle, the thankless and unrewarded sacrifices—these things disturbed his inner balance, originally designed in fine harmony. He had much of the child in him. He loved children: he was able to devote himself to them for long periods, allowing his grey hair to be dishevelled by their little hands, with touching patience. Like a child, too, he clung to life.

now brought self-assurance and demands to bear upon the challenge. This holds true not only for Austria and the old Prussia, but also for the whole of Western and Southern Germany. There, for millions of German people there were new sovereigns and countries, for the "Reich" was dead. Was it worthwhile, or even reasonable, to let new sentimental ties develop, based on the mere chance of territorial division? What did the man from Speyer have to do with Munich; what did the one at Lake Constance have to do with Karlsruhe? He had not been consulted.

This tension is significant for the whole period and is given dramatic expression in List's own destiny. One should not forget this context. List came from a "Reichsstadt": as craftsmen his family did not belong to the upper class but nevertheless were firmly rooted in the traditions of Reutlingen, which was not lacking in legends directed against the Duchy of Württemberg. The year of his birth, 1789, was of almost symbolic importance for this rebel against convention—the news coming from the West may have excited him during his lively childhood years since the idea of a republic was in vogue. But it was not just a matter of reports, enthusiasm, alarms and disillusionment—far-reaching events affected the fate of his home-town; when the tanner's son was faced with a decision about his future career, having outgrown his initial apprenticeship as an artisan, Reutlingen had lost its independence and had become a mere provincial capital [Kreisstadt] in Württemberg. Since he meant to become a town clerk, his path as an intermediate administrative official led him out of his home-town. The situation to which he went was certainly not very important but, nevertheless, it soon offered an opportunity for exceptional promotion. The Stuttgart Council, noticing the talent that was making itself felt, consulted for advice and expert opinion the young civil servant who had gained experience as a petty official during his training. It even established a chair at the University of Tübingen for this twenty-eight-year-old who had never enjoyed a systematic education to prepare him for such a position. But it was an administration which was fighting a tough battle against the hard core of "old" Württemberg. Uhland's *Patriotic Poems* advocating the "good old order" were associated with this struggle: only in this part of Germany in the heart of the Swabian duchy, had the guild-order held its own up to the nineteenth century. It had become the pride of the country in the vigorous wrangling that had taken place, and the old guard were not willing to accept a change in it at the hands of the new sovereign rule. List, as a supporter of "New Württemberg", was passionately opposed to this and canvassed the reform of the constitution and administration in his paper *Volksfreund aus Schwaben* ("Swabian Patriot"). But when the minister, Wangenheim, had to resign, List lost his support. Intrigues and distrust set in—the consciousness that his work was coming under the shadow of suspicion was forced upon him. They wanted to get rid of him and the opportunity for that came in 1819. On behalf of a number of businessmen at the Frankfurt Exchange, List drafted a petition to the senate and, having carried it through and obtained permission to establish the *deutschen Handelsverein* ("German Trade Society"), he was ready to manage it. But when, because of this, new difficulties arose for him, he tendered his resignation from the civil service.

It was a historical moment. In 1818 the government of the City of Berlin had decided to abolish internal tariffs for the whole state, enlarged as it was after 1815. Trade and commerce which were recovering from times of depression, were to enjoy freedom of action, Prussia was becoming a unified economic area. But why should it just be Prussia—why not the whole of Germany? The senate in Frankfurt had set aside the petition—for what would become of it, if it began to concern itself with the requests of private individuals! It was, therefore, a matter of getting the support of governments and so List travelled throughout Germany, visiting royal courts and governments, and also saw Metternich in Vienna. The latter felt that something new was on its way. The interest of the nation had to be roused through periodicals and conferences. Many a thing gets off to a fine start: List came into contact with men who were unselfish and well-disposed to the idea and his feeling of serving a great and necessary purpose allowed him to ignore trivialities. At a later date, the function he performed at this time would be considered that of the legal representative of an association and naturally, there were some people who, at the time, saw him more or less in this light. (But such a type did not exist then, and certainly *he* was no type.) When he stood before monarchs and ministers, businessmen and factory owners, he did not consider himself as an advocate of special interests but as the ambassador of Germany's future.

But there was still a part of his past which acted as a constraint on the battle over the reorganization of Württemberg. At the very time when a general summons presented him with a great task to perform, his native town also remembered him. The constitution of Württemberg had been finished off in a compromise; Reutlingen elected List as its representative but the mandate was cancelled because he was not yet thirty years old, a few months being lacking. He was elected a second time and at the end of 1820 entered the Württemberg chamber of deputies. With great candour and a broad conception of his parliamentary duties, he then began to fight for the reforms which he had advocated in memoranda and political articles, a few years before. This was to cost him dear. Petitioning on behalf of his Reutlingen constituents, who recognized in List's strong statements their own way of thinking, he summarized what he considered base and rotten in public affairs: the inflated over-extended bureaucracy, which was feeble and harsh at the same time; he demanded that the districts be reorganized, that taxes be made fair, that court proceedings be conducted orally and in public; and that self-government be extended. There was nothing extraordinary in all of this—the comprehensive petition was, of course, unusual in being virtually a kind of government programme, or rather a counter-programme, expressed with great and powerful candour. The answer soon followed: the demand for a prosecution for agitating against the institutions of the state. In order to make this proceeding feasible, List had to be divested of his mandate. A wicked intrigue began. Even though a man like Uhland—who had been List's opponent in the earlier years of the struggle over the constitution—took his side, vengeful fervour and government pressure brought about the expulsion from the chamber of deputies of the Reutlingen representative. The court sentenced him to ten months' imprisonment. List, who in his optimistic way, had not reckoned on this, took to flight. Today, one may say that this was imprudent and strictly speaking put him in the wrong for the first time—but this is sophistry, which looks for the fault only in the outcome of an affair when there is so much that is blameworthy. His great sense of justice and freedom, sickened by more than a year of disputes, fled humiliation and absconded into the unknown. He went to Strasbourg, then to Switzerland—somehow or other he would be able to develop a new sphere of action. But the Stuttgart government was close on his heels—he was denied the possibility of settling down and had a hard time. Friends advised him to return home and beg for the mercy of the King. Had he not served with distinction as his first adviser? But Wilhelm I did not say a word. When he returned he was apprehended and brought to the Asperg, which had also been Schubart's miserable quarters. The prisoner spent his time sorting out pieces of uniform. After five months he was let off from the remaining term of his imprisonment in return for a promise to emigrate. His native country wanted to get rid of him. But was it really his native country and not rather the hatred of a bureaucracy which sensed enormous power in this man? It could not forgive him. How little it would forgive, the unwilling emigrant did not realize when he went abroad with his wife and his children. Just get out! In America there was Lafayette, the old general, with whom he had become acquainted during a visit to Paris. He wanted to help him and should have done so. But nothing came of either the intention or the hope. This was a young country where one did not yet live by means of recommendations and connections. One could make a venture. List took his chance farming on a small scale—he had to make a living. But he did not get on and in his thoughts he searched for some public activity. He took over the management of a German newspaper in Reading. The editor's office became a schoolroom in which he learned about America—

but in every sense List had always learned more outside the classroom. His work brought him into contact with tradespeople and businessmen, and there was then a recurrence of the events of the year 1819. For the newly-developing American industry, hesitating between free trade and protective tariffs, he mapped out a programme specially for its needs, which were to protect itself against British productive superiority. Ideas of this sort were not new over there. In contrast to the work he had tried to accomplish at home, which set out directly to effect negotiations, his efforts in America were carried into the realm of theoretical analysis: the fundamental principle of Adam Smith's theory on the general validity of the free play of economic forces came into question. This theme is heard, which was later to become the strongest in the development of his works—some remember only this motif. But really this is still just the beginning. Chance drew him into other business transactions: while on a hike, he discovered coal ready to be mined. Thus the farmer of the day before yesterday and the editor of yesterday suddenly became a mining entrepreneur. He was able to found a corporation; the enterprise got under way; he was relieved and it looked as though he could be rid of all his worries from now on. He was glad and almost thankful—this business also taught him what it might mean economically and otherwise if the newly invented railway became an integrated part of a nation's economy.

President Jackson thought highly of this useful and unselfish German, but he, in turn, experienced a strange unrest. Was this his mission, to teach the Americans how to gain wealth and independence? He did believe in his mission: during this time he wrote: "For me it is like being a mother with crippled children. . . . In the background of all my plans stands Germany." President Jackson appointed him consul of the Union in Hamburg and under its protection he believed he would be able to work. He left America on his own at the end of 1830 but in Le Havre he found out that the President's decision had not been approved by the senate. He stayed in Paris, working as a political correspondent. In 1832 the legal problems were overcome and he went to Leipzig as American Consul. The seeds which he had sown almost one and a half decades ago had begun to grow: tariffs between neighbouring states had been abolished in individual treaties and the German Customs Union—though excluding Austria and the Hanseatic towns—was close to becoming a reality and thereby establishing a unified economic region. But this could not be as far as it would go: the turnpikes on the borders were pulled out—which was good—but did this in itself portend a unified economy? Did it not require a direct link and connection? One may think that it was again a historical moment as in 1819; it was again List's job to give the signal of the day: the railway!

The years after 1832 were almost completely filled with propaganda for this idea. Saxony, especially Leipzig, was a well-chosen starting point because there one could perceive how trade and rising commerce could benefit from speed and safety in the transport of goods. A group of distinguished men supported List, when he tried to make use of theoretical knowledge in the realization of the plans. The government, though well-disposed to this experiment, did not, as yet, recognize that a special new task was in store for it and while List's main occupation concerned national economic objectives, he had however to stimulate private business interests at the same time. There were profits to be made in railways—bring your money to found a joint-stock company and you will earn magnificent dividends! Thus was the company which later built the railway from Dresden to Leipzig established—but indeed List got little joy from it. Intrigues robbed him of his share of the success; his expectations were disappointed and when the proceeds from his American property melted away, he again left to go abroad. In 1837 he went to Paris.

His support for the cause of the railway was not without effect. The pamphlet in which he had outlined, costed and substantiated the plan for a Saxon railway system as the nucleus of an all-German network impressed his contemporaries. In later times people tried to see, in this plan especially, the prophetic quality of the man. But more impressive and really shattering was the power of his imagination in forming a picture of the future world, as set forth in the two articles published in 1834 and 1836 by the *Allgemeine Militärzeitung* ("German Military News"). In these, the experiences of later wars seem to be anticipated in the description of the sort of defensive power a country would attain from an extensive railway network. War on two fronts is envisioned, strategic massing using unexpected movements of entire armies; times and costs are calculated; and even the benefit of hospital-trains are described. Admittedly, the conclusion of this thrilling essay has been refuted by history. List, who even wanted to convince the investor that capital invested in the building of railroads would not be too much endangered in war, consoles him by saying that the more complete the railway network, the stronger its power to prevent the venture of an aggressive war: for "victories cannot be followed up into the interior". Therefore, railways will help "to do away with war itself". That is the pithy conclusion of the essay—it is no sentimentality but rather a technical and strategic case. Of course, history did not obey—and yet, while reading it we remember the great military operations of the First World War and the role of the railroads: is this not a commentary on the strategic massing in the autumn of 1914, written eighty years before the event? However, it is more than that: it is the wonderfully plastic expression of a talent which saw the technical-economic hundred-kilometres experiment, the ideology of which involved interest-rates and rents, in the magnifying glass of world politics and thus in a completely new way.

He went to Paris. The French really treated him much better than his fellow-countrymen; they listened to his economic advice. He made a living as a journalist but, in addition, found time now to systematize his economic ideas. A problem, open to competition, stimulated him and, although his solution did not come up to expectations, this forced him to collect his most important ideas. For the Americans, he wrote a handbook for their future in English and, for the French, he wrote one in French. It was also in Paris that he produced the great outline of his work, in which he expounded for the German people, but not for them alone, the coming order of the world: *The National System of Political Economy*, with the appropriate motto on the title page: "*et la patrie et l'humanité*". It was published in the autumn of 1840 and, in the spring, he returned to Germany probably hoping that the situation would have changed for him there. But it was a false hope. Certainly, his work made an impression; it met with agreement in business circles, but opposition in the universities. But List looked in vain for a practical proposition that was suitable for him and seemed appropriate. No German state wanted to employ his services. What was left for him to do? With a new journalistic weapon, the "Customs Union Paper", he fought an open battle for his ideas—it was a splendid journalistic achievement, but the proceeds from it were not enough to free him from need. The most shameful moment of his life befell him when somebody denounced him as a paid writer and he published his yearly income, defending his honour by demonstrating his poverty. Yet, in his misery and disappointment he developed great productivity, travelling to Belgium, to Hungary where they honoured him with gratitude, and to London—the camp of the "enemy"—for the whole battle during these years had been directed against the "English School" and the method of British politics. He liked it there with the "enemy"—he was respected and he breathed, deeply and freely, the air enriched by the sea, which seemed to him free from the constriction and unpleasantness of the particularist endeavours of the early Victorian period. He dreamed of a plan that when Germany had realized her strength, she would enter into a political alliance with England despite English economic policy. For the day might come when France and Russia were found together—he thought of this in the summer of 1846. But the autumn put to flight these vivid pictures of future hopes; life frightened him: how was he to make a living, would he have his health for long now? He expected to find rest in the South but during this trip, hastily decided upon, he took his own life in Kufstein.

His personality is partly obscured by legends but it remains discernible in letters and documents and conclusively, more than anywhere else, in his very powerful, individual style of writing. His death makes him appear a tragic figure but his natural predispositions contained few such elements. For he had a highly optimistic disposition, he was really the sort of person, who later came to be called—in a slightly derogatory way—a "believer in progress". In his encounters with other people he showed ingenuous candour, energy and readiness to help; he was also known as a person of quiet humour. He was witty and versatile, and hasty in argument—flaring up when he encountered someone raw or second rate. As a young civil servant a lively sense of justice and a great capacity for sympathy were already among his characteristics. But this alert sensitivity to others turned into restrained pride and a gradual groping distrust, when he was forced to fight for his work and later for his honour. Some of the critical reports from people with whom he dealt make much of his self-conceit and impetuosity. But it is easy to understand how the traits of a stout person, which usually are even temper, good humour and kindness, could change into positive tension and obstinacy, which "got on the other's nerves" and seemed like unsociability and disputatiousness but really were only self-defence. Well, did they want to rob him of his good name, to declare him a paid agent, plagiarist, adventurer, and whiner? At that, his anger was inclined to break out or pride in his own fine valour tended to rise up suddenly, menacingly and insultingly. Knowledge of his own worth sustained him, and it was not petty vanity openly to defend his independence and individuality. But it must have been terrible to be waiting for the nation to react and to get no response. Fear overcame him: how much longer like this, in financial difficulties, with precarious ability to work? He had been an incomparably hard worker. Was it all to be in vain? The year 1846 had seen him travelling, writing and talking with inspired creativity. Thus he was tired and a peaceful rest in Italy was to relieve him of the pressure. Hastily, with little luggage, he left the November gloom and set out southwards. In Kufstein he interrupted his trip for a rest. A barely audible shot fades away among the mountains. Under a light cover of snow the body of the dead man is found.

List's journalistic power was characterized by rhythm, polish, stimulus and a high degree of perspicuity. It is not uniform, for in order to prove his theoretical powers, he forced himself, at times, to use somewhat intricate concepts, which seem old-fashioned to us. But then again his eloquence flows colourfully and evocatively, in lively and natural imagery. No one before him had talked to the German people on "dry" subjects, in such a way. And he educated them, having a never-tiring need for discussion and education and a journalistic zeal, not paralysed by disappointment, to read politics and think economics.

Theodor Heuss

II
POLITICAL ECONOMY

Various factors combined to deprive List's achievement in the nineteenth century of its possible impact on the economic sciences. It is not only the total lack of understanding for the theoretical content of his doctrine amongst the "professionals" (with the sole exception of Eugen Dühring) and even in the case of his biographer and the editor of some of his writings, the historian Ludwig Häusser, but also the unfinished state of his work which prevented anything more than superficial success. *Das natürliche System der politischen Ökonomie,* the theoretically well-reasoned Paris prize-essay, did not become known until 1927; *Das nationale System der politischen Ökonomie*, though called Volume I (*Der internationale Handel, die Handelspolitik und der deutsche Zollverein*), was so well-rounded and so complete in itself that the misconception that List had only one theory of trade policy could easily arise. That the *Nationale System* was planned on a large scale and envisaged as consisting of nine parts was no more taken into account than is the fact that Marx's *Kapital* represents only the first part of what was to be a comprehensive system including volumes about landed property, wage policy, the state, foreign trade, and the world market. Consequently List's agricultural policy was overlooked, as was his theory of the correspondence between agriculture and industry in every nation and also his theory of the importance of the domestic market. Furthermore, List's concepts are not always precise and his evidence is not always sound—the rational element in his illustrative theory (*anschauliche Theorie*) is not equal to the magnitude of the task which he set himself. Finally, in the conflict about protective duties and free trade, which List himself helped to kindle, it was more important to some that he had advocated the *educational tariff* as a means of industrial education which was to develop the productive powers of the nation, whereas to others it was more important that he had declared free trade to be his ultimate goal. Both factions, however, failed to realize that neither of these positions was in itself important for the future. What did prove significant was his insight into the fundamental indivisibility and organic growth of the national economy and its consequent periodic need for protection, so that the whole theory of trade was divested of its absolute character and every decision concerning trade policy required a direct reference to the total state of the economy at the specific time. Both factions also failed to see that List's concept of "free trade" is of an entirely different nature from the classic one, that it has nothing in common with the ideal of optimum welfare cherished by those of independent means in England, but that it signifies something active and "energetic", that it is *educational free trade*, which is designed to "guard farmers, manufacturers and merchants against indolence" and to "encourage them to maintain the superiority that has been achieved".

This general ignorance of the theoretical content and the sociological framework of List's doctrines meant that interested parties and nationalists could misuse his name and that some of the excesses of high capitalism were supported by reference to List. Biased industrialists saw in him the "first syndic". In all those agricultural countries which were gradually developing their industries he became a "kind of patron saint" (Röpke). Even Bismarck's change to solidarity protectionism—that is, to *protective* tariffs for industrial *and* agricultural products—was misunderstood as the realization of List's demands, and what is more, in matters of foreign policy his name was used to support every anti-English measure and demand. Against this it must be remembered that the *Natürliche System* and the *Nationale System* are headed by the liberal motto taken from the Freemasons: "*Et la patrie, et l'humanité*", and furthermore, it should be noted that List's *theory of successive stages* (*Stufenlehre*), which determines the dynamic character of both his theory and his politics, is related in rhythm and aim to the eighteenth-century concept of harmony. For it is the harmonious development of all economic forces which List sees realized in the *Normalnation*; for him the economic development of the state takes place in three successive stages: 1. that of agriculture; 2. that of agriculture and manufacturing; and 3. that of agriculture, manufacturing and commerce. This progression contains not only a stimulus to those agricultural countries whose industry is still underdeveloped, but also, properly understood and consequentially extended, a warning against over-industrialization and any decline in agriculture.

List's picture of the political future is also free of all those excesses which mark the nihilistic nationalism of the twentieth century. For the harmonious development and preservation of the legal code seemed to this liberal Swabian, who had suffered enough from despotism himself, to be the cultural precondition, ethical norm and political goal for the life of individuals as of nations. The pioneer of the German Customs Union (*Zollverein*), the herald of the "political and economic national unity of the Germans", he also had sufficient sense of proportion—and especially in questions of foreign policy—to perceive and define the limits of a possible rise of Germany. More far-sighted than all the politicians of his time, List foresaw in his *Vermächtnis* ("Last Will and Testament") the inescapable division of the world into a few great empires. He correctly discerned the magnitude of the upheavals which Russia's culture, constitution, judiciary and administration still needed to go through in order to secure "its existence as one of the foremost world powers". And without commission, title or post he devoted his last energies to the fight for an Anglo-German alliance which was to guarantee "world hegemony" for England through union with a united Germany.

In these political writings of his last years, List gradually assumes the role of the only German counterweight to Karl Marx. Decidedly inferior to Marx in clarity of logical thought, little interested in the internal antagonisms of capitalist economy, and consequently with no eye for the violence of social convulsions or for economic and social reform, List surpasses him in his knowledge of the sources of energy available to a people and a nation and in his grasp of the significance and demonic character of power. Just as Marx becomes the founder of socialism, he becomes the seer and admonisher of national and supranational imperialism.

Edgar Salin

III
THE WORK OF FRIEDRICH LIST

Friedrich List holds a great place both in the opinion and in the affections of his countrymen. This is owing to his successful championship of the customs union of the German States (*Zollverein*), the embryo of German national unity. What this association means to Germans cannot be understood by members of those fortunate nations for which the right to national existence and national ambitions is a matter of course. It means that List, like all those whose names are associated with that long and painful struggle, is a national hero. Far be it for me to criticize this attitude or to withhold admiration from List in any other respect except the one that unfortunately happens to be the only one that counts in this book.[2] Even as a scientific economist, however, List had one of the elements of greatness, namely, the grand vision of a national situation, which, though not in itself a scientific achievement, is a prerequisite for a certain type of scientific achievement—that type of which, in our own day, Keynes is an outstanding example. Nor was List deficient in the specifically scientific requisites that must come in to implement vision if it is to bear scientific fruits; his analytic apparatus was in fact ideally adequate for his practical purpose. But the individual pieces of this analytic apparatus were not particularly novel.

List saw a nation that struggled in the fetters imposed by a miserable immediate past, but he also saw all its economic potentialities. The national future, therefore, was the real object of his thought, the present was

[2] Schumpeter's concern in his *History* is economic analysis or theory in a more or less narrow sense. "Theories and not persons are the heroes of this volume."

nothing but a state of transition. He realized that, in an essentially transitional state of this kind, policies lose their meaning when they are geared to the task of administering an existing set of conditions that is visualized as substantially permanent. This he expressed by his doctrine of "stages"—a felicitous device, so far as his educational purpose was concerned, but in itself not more than an old eighteenth-century idea. Furthermore, he realized (like Soden) that emphasis upon the national future modifies welfare considerations *ex visu* of the present. This he expressed by his doctrine of "productive forces" (*Produktionskräfte*) that in his system hold place of honour as compared with the consumers' goods that can be made available at a given level of the productive forces—not unfelicitous, this, as an educational device but not much more than a label for an unsolved problem. Finally, as regards his bet-known contribution to the education of German public opinion on economic policy, the infant-industry argument, this is clearly Hamiltonian and part of the economic wisdom that List imbibed during his stay in the United States. So fully Americanized had List become then that he actually advocated financing railroad construction by the issue of banknotes, for which practice there were only—and hardly wholly creditable—American precedents. It should be remarked, in passing, that List's argument about protection issues into the free-trade argument: if this is not obvious, we can convince ourselves of it by noticing the fact that J. S. Mill accepted the infant-industry theory, evidently realizing that it ran within the free-trade logic.[3]

This, I think, does justice to, and at the same time reduces to its proper proportions, List's analytic gifts and performance. Those who insist on making their hero the possessor of merits of all conceivable types have put his thought into spurious relations of the kind that create spurious history. He was an heir to eighteenth-century thought. He was an offshoot of romanticism. He was a forerunner of the historical school of economics. There is not more in all this than that everyone is heir to everything that went before him and a forerunner of everything that comes after him. He was a great patriot, a brilliant journalist with definite purpose, and an able economist who coordinated well whatever seemed useful for implementing his vision. Is this not enough? Of all his writings the *Outlines of American Political Economy* (1827) is the most interesting for us because it displays his system in its earliest stage of development. His mature work that grew out of this, *Das nationale System der politischen Ökonomie* (1841; English trans. 1885), remains a classic in the eulogistic sense of the word, all the comments above notwithstanding.

Joseph Alois Schumpeter

[3] Incidentally, it may be remarked that to call List's plans "nationalist" or "imperialist" is to play upon double meanings in both cases.

SOURCES

Essay I

Theodor Heuss, "Friedrich List", in *Die grossen Deutschen: Deutsche Biographie*, ed. H. Heimpel, T. Heuss and B. Reifenberg, 3 (Propyläen-Verlag bei Ullstein, Berlin, 1956).

Essay II

Edgar Salin, *Politische Ökonomie*, 5th ed. (J. C. B. Mohr Paul Siebeck, Tübingen, 1967) pp. 124–6.

Essay III

Joseph Alois Schumpeter, *History of Economic Analysis*, ed. E. B. Schumpeter (George Allen & Unwin Ltd, London, 1955), pp. 504–5.

Signature

Württembergische Landesbibliothek, Stuttgart.

Portrait

Engraving by J. Kriehuber, 1845, Vienna (Württembergische Landesbibliothek, Stuttgart).

BIBLIOGRAPHY

L. Häusser, preface, in *Friedrich List, Gesammelte Schriften,* 3 parts, ed. L. Häusser (Stuttgart and Tübingen, 1850).

G. Goldschmidt, *Friedrich List, Deutschlands größter Volkswirt* (Berlin, 1878).

E. Leser, *Friedrich List, Allgemeine Deutsche Biographie*, Vol. 18 (Leipzig, 1883).

K. Jentsch, *Friedrich List* (Berlin, 1901).

M. E. Hirst, *The Life of Friedrich List and Selections from his Writings* (London and New York, 1909).

K. Goeser, *Der junge Friedrich List. Ein schwäbischer Politiker. Biographischer Versuch* (Stuttgart, 1914).

W. Notz, "Friedrich List in Amerika". *Weltwirtschaftliches Archiv,* 21 and 22 (1925).

A. Meusel, *List und Marx: Eine vergleichende Betrachtung* (Jena, 1928).

E. Salin (ed.) *Friedrich List, Schriften, Reden, Briefe* (Berlin 1927–35); reprinted 1962.

F. Lenz, *Friedrich List, der Mann und das Werk* (München and Berlin, 1936).

H. Ritschl, *Friedrich Lists Leben und Lehre* (Tübingen and Stuttgart, 1947).

C. Brinkmann, *Friedrich List* (Berlin and München, 1949).

F. Bülow, *Friedrich List* (Göttingen, Berlin and Frankfurt, 1959).

E. Salin, "Friedrich Lists Lehre von den Wirtschaftsstufen und die Bedeutung der Typik". *Schmollers Jahrbuch*, 45 (1921), reprinted in E. Salin, *Lynkeus: Gestalten und Probleme aus Wirtschaft und Politik* (Tübingen, 1963).

E. Salin and R. L. Frey, "Friedrich List", in *International Encyclopedia of the Social Sciences*, Vol. 9 (New York, 1968).

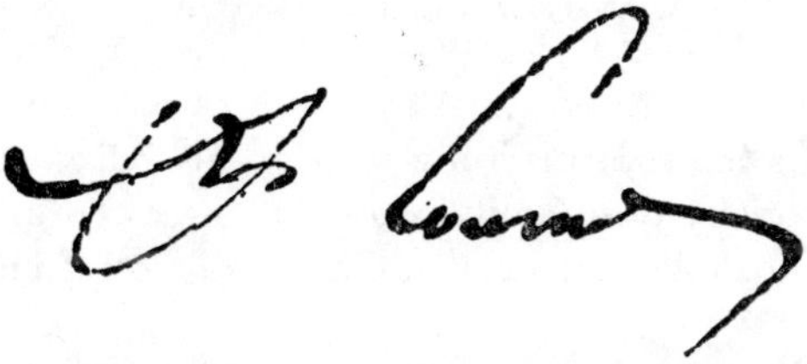

ANTOINE AUGUSTIN COURNOT

1801–1877

Pendant plus de quarante ans, il a mis au service de la philosophie une science profonde de géomètre, des connaissances encyclopédiques, une pénétration peu commune d'analyse d'éminentes qualités d'invention, et une rare indépendance de pensée. L. LIARD

To feel Cournot's power and stimulus, the reader must actually "pass through his hands". He will scarcely fail to come away with a "new mental activity".

I. FISHER

L'œuvre de Cournot est située à un grand carrefour du développement de l'esprit humain: elle ne saurait être vaine, ou il faudrait désespérer des efforts séculaires de l'intelligence humaine. F. MENTRÉ

[*Die* Recherches] *stellen einen Wurf von solcher Geschlossenheit und Originalität dar, daß sie ihren Verfasser trotz zahlreicher Vorläufer und einer fast ein halbes Jahrhundert währenden Ignorierung zum klassichen Meister und eigentlichen* Begründer der mathematischen Schule *der Nationalökonomie machten.—*

Gradmesser für die Wissenschaftlichkeit einer Disziplin sei [*nach Cournot*] *stets der ihr zukommende Umfang an Gewißheit, und das methodische Prinzip sei eben die Bestimmung dieses Umfanges mit dem Werkzeug der* Wahrscheinlichkeitsanalyse. H. REICHARDT

I
THE PERSONALITY OF ANTOINE AUGUSTIN COURNOT

The Cournot family, a family of agriculturists, lived from time immemorial in the Franche-Comté, near the town of Dôle. The family records may be traced to the middle of the sixteenth century, the date that family registration began in the province. In fact, a relative had traced the Cournot genealogy through three centuries, when Augustin Cournot began to write his *Souvenirs*, and this led him playfully to urge his relatives to preserve the papers for the novelty of a family record of three centuries of *roturiers*.

He was born on 28 August 1801, at Gray, and received the name Antoine Augustin.

No further reference of interest is made to his parents, but in the annals of his childhood he speaks at length of the oldest of his uncles, to whom he was affectionately devoted, and to whom, he says, too generously, he owed all of good in himself.[1] This uncle was educated by Jesuits, and remained loyal to them throughout the terrible days of the Revolution and the anxious period that followed. He had a varied reading, a great capacity for work, a still greater capacity for self-sacrifice.

Two maiden aunts, together with the favourite uncle, lived with Cournot's aged grandmother; and the young Antoine was adopted into this family. The home influences of these early years were particularly favourable to the development of his independent judgment. The elder of the aunts was closely connected with the constitutional coterie of the town, holding, in this respect, views diametrically opposed to those of her brother and the other members of the little family, and producing thereby a painful breach in the unity of the family attitude towards political principles and religious faith.

In 1809 Antoine entered the preparatory class of the Collège de Gray. His instructor, an admirer of Napoleon, vented his political enthusiasm upon his pupils. In his Latin course, for example, he substituted in place of the ancient illustrations *Deus santus, amo Deum,* the form *Napoleo magnus debellavit Austriacos!* Cournot remained at school in Gray until he was fifteen years of age. The following four years he directed his own reading and employment. He spent a short while in reading law, but the greater part of the time he pursued privately the study of his favourite subjects. There is a story in the family to the effect that, when he was seventeen years of age, he successfully defended a lawsuit in which his father had considerable property involved.

In later life, Cournot referred to this period of four years as having been nearly wasted, but the testimony of his *Souvenirs* would seem to indicate

[1] Only incidental references are made in the *Souvenirs* to Cournot's parents. The circumstances of his birth are given as follows: "*Pour mon propre comte, je suis redevable de mon apparition dans ce monde à la révolution de 18 brumaire. Quelque temps après ce grand événement, mon père, parvenu à la quarantine, crut les choses assez rassises et la liberté de conscience assez assurée pour songer à prendre charge de femme et d'enfants. Cependant, comme je suis né en 1801, six mois avant le Concordat, j'ai encore été, à la manière des temps primitifs, baptisé en chambre par un prêtre qui se cachait ou qui était censé se cacher, car, dans la réalité, on ne craignait plus l'application des lois révolutionnaires.*"

that they were not only criticial years, so far as concerned the choice of his life's work, but were also unusually fruitful in the preparation for that work. His habit of independent thinking, which had developed much earlier, was strengthened and directed through the finding of a method and the choice of a subject. No one has made more clear than Cournot, in his various essays, that the pursuits of early life are likely to affect all the subsequent thinking of a philosopher so that the student is particularly curious to know the early scientific interests of the master himself. Fontenelle and Laplace gave him the desire to learn to use the mathematical instrument which alone made possible the mastery of the sciences they developed,[2] and the genius of Leibnitz determined the direction of his philosophic thinking.

Having once determined that the mastery of mathematics was essential to the highest development of science, he began to make plans for his further education. In his nineteenth year, MM. Poinsot and Andrezel, general inspectors of the University, came, in the course of their tour, to Besançon. Cournot had heard vague reports of the École Normale at Paris, and had determined to take this opportunity to find out from the inspectors the conditions of admission to the scientific department of the famous school. He hurried off to Besançon, but upon his arrival he was ashamed to approach the inspectors, to whom he was an entire stranger, and, instead of addressing them, he obtained the necessary information from friends in the town. He found that in order to enter the desired department at the École Normale it was necessary to complete a special course of higher mathematics, whereas he had not had so much as an adequate elementary course.

But this deficiency did not deter him from following his plan. He at once entered upon the elementary course at the Collège Royal of Besançon.[3]

In the month of August 1821, Cournot passed the entrance examination of the École Normale.

[2] Condorcet's pamphlet *Essai sur l'application de l'analyse à la probabilité des décisions rendues à la pluralité des voix* and that of Laplace: *Essai philosophique sur les probabilités* inspired the circle of his friends to study *Mathématique sociale*; and here we find the deepest roots of the *Théorie des richesses*, as G. Waffenschmidt rightly points out.

[3] His reflections upon his reception at Besançon gives an interesting but too modest estimate of his sources of strength and weakness: "*Les chefs de l'académie et du collège, prévenus favorablement, voulurent bien voir en moi mieux qu'une recrue ordinaire et me traiter comme quelqu'un qui devait faire un jour honneur ou terroir. Grâce à une certaine aptitude générale des choses qui sont du domaine de la raison, j'ai toujours été prisé trop haut à tous mes débuts, tandis que j'avais tres-nettement conscience de ce qui me manquait, à savoir du don special d'invention qui procure à bon droit la renommé et les honneurs académiques, ou la puissance du travail qui, dans un champ circonscrit, y supplie quelquefois et qui m'a toujours été refusée par suite de l'infirmité de ma vue.*"

The student days in Paris were rich in friendships, experiences, and instruction.

While the courses at the École Normale were, during the first year, a partial repetition of the courses at Besançon. and in that respect a disappointment, the time was nevertheless well spent because of the stimulating spirit of the place. M. Geréneau de Mussy, a royalist and sympathizer with Jansenist principles and traditions, was the director; the *maîtres de conférences*, with one exception, did not share the Jansenist views of the director; the student body, as was to be expected, was filled with the spirit of ardent liberalism; Cournot says of himself that he was almost alone in pleading for a *juste-milieu*.

In 1822 the École Normale was suppressed by public order. The students were divided into two classes, and the members of one class placed in positions of instruction, while the others were left without places, but received assistance at the rate of fifty francs a month for twenty months. The latter class was more or less under the surveillance of political police, who seem to have rendered periodic accounts of the individual students. Cournot expressed surprise that, notwithstanding his conservative opinions, he found himself in this latter group. The report of the *surveillants* during these months bore the comment, "*Bonnes opinions politiques, mais il n'a pas une piété tendre*," which doubtless meant no more than that he avoided cant and snubbed the police; for there are reasons for believing that at this time his religious opinions were as essentially conservative as were his opinions in politics.

The period at the Sorbonne was the happiest of his life. "*Je n'avais rien à lire, rien à composer, rien à trouver, rien à projeter; je n'avais qu'à écouter et à réfléchir: ce temps a été le plus heureux de ma vie.*" In addition to the opportunities of seeing and knowing the leaders of French scientific thought through his connection at the Sorbonne, Cournot was brought into friendly relations with another group of scholars and men of affairs as a consequence of the friendship of M. Droz, the Academician. Among the notables who were met in the salon of M. Droz was Proudhon, *le terrible*. In later years, after the appearance of Cournot's first economic essay, he and Proudhon met by chance at M. Droz'. An economic discussion was precipitated, but no progress was made; for apparently neither one was able to understand the theories of the other.

In 1823 Cournot entered upon an engagement that lasted for the next ten years. In the summer of that year, Marshal Gouvion Saint-Cyr, who was writing his military memoirs, was in search of someone who would be capable of acting as adviser and critic in his own task, and be willing to assume the direction of the education of his young son. His attention was called to the group of students who had been recently set adrift by the suppression of the École Normale as being most likely to furnish the scholar for whom he was in search. The grounds of the Marshal's choice of Cournot are not given, but the latter's reasons for acceptance were the prospect of leisure with the consequent opportunity to pursue his own work, a continued residence in or near Paris, and the possibility of knowing the ways and thoughts of soldiers, statesmen, and the nobility of the time.

He entered upon the new occupation towards the end of October of 1823.

While in the employment of Marshal Saint-Cyr, Cournot had occasion, of course, to see the leading representatives of the highest life in France.

During the ten years spent with the family of Gouvion Saint-Cyr, Cournot continued his scientific investigations. In fact, the expected leisure, together with the opportunity of remaining in Paris and pursuing his own studies in his own way, had been the chief reason for his accepting the appointment. During this period he acquired the degree of *docteur ès sciences*, and published a series of articles, some of which came under the notice of Poisson, who since the death of Laplace was the authority in mathematics in the University.[4]

Poisson was anxious to place the author of the articles in a position worthy of his ability. Friends repeated the favourable criticisms to Cournot, and urged him, particularly after the death of Marshal Saint-Cyr, to offer his services to the University. He had not, at this time, made the acquaintance of Poisson, and suspected that nothing but a minor position in some provincial college would be offered. This was exactly what he was unwilling to accept: "*Si j'abdiquais pour dix ans mon indépendance, ce n'était pas dans l'intention de faire toute ma vie le métier de pédagogue.*" In the summer of 1833, however, the engagement with the family of Gouvion Saint-Cyr came to a close, and Cournot notified Poisson that he held himself at the disposition of the University. He was received as the lost sheep returned to the fold. Immediately a temporary appointment was made, until a more satisfactory one could be provided. While awaiting for his permanent appointment, he translated, in the year 1833–4, Sir John Herschel's *Astronomy* and Lardner's *Mechanics*. From the point of view of what is frequently called success, this was the most successful literary work he ever did; for it secured him reputation and profit, even though the profit was only the price of a translation.

An acceptable post was found before the year was out. He was appointed

[4] The impression made upon Poisson by Cournot's studies is characteristically told by the latter: "*Il y trouva de la pénétration philosophique, en quoi je pense bonnement qu'il n'avait pas tout à fait torte; et de plus, il en augura que je ferais un grand chemin dans le champ de la pure spéculation mathématique, ce qui fut (je l'ai toujours pensé et n'ai jamais hésité à le dire) une de ses erreurs.*"

to the chair of analysis and mechanics in the newly installed faculty of science at Lyons. This professorship was attractive because of the nature of the work, and the location of Lyons in the country of Cournot's birth.

The chair at Lyons was held only one year. While Cournot was on his vacation in Switzerland, Poisson, without consulting him, procured for him the rectorship of the Academy of Grenoble. He hesitated to accept the position because, as he said, he knew too well the responsibilities, without knowing the duties, of a rector. He was made to see the wisdom of the choice, however, and went to Paris to receive his commission. Guizot, the minister of public instruction, whose acquaintance he had made at the home of Marshal Saint-Cyr, wrote a laudatory letter to the prefect of the Isère instead of sending the usual formal notice; and this led to Cournot's being received at Grenoble in a way befitting one whose rare merits and friendships had secured him the promotion to a rectorship at the age of thirty-four.

His administration of the Academy of Grenoble was in all respects successful: "*Je m'aperçus bien vite que ce que l'on nomme administration ne se compose que deux choses, de mécanisme et de bon sens; de mécanisme pour la forme et de bon sens pour le fond des affaires.*" There is reason to believe that in all of the many public offices held by Cournot in the course of his career he was an unusually acceptable administrator; for, besides learning very early the essentials of good administration, he brought to the task the necessary qualities of rapid and sound judgment, freedom from prejudice, scrupulous patience, and a rare respect for the dignity of the character of others.

The Grenoble success raised still higher his reputation at Paris, and secured still further promotion. In 1836, while Ampère, the great physicist, and M. Matter were making their regular tour, as general inspectors of the university, Ampère died at Marseilles. Cournot was temporarily appointed the colleague of M. Matter for the next two years, at the same time retaining his rectorate at Grenoble.

A further promotion was made in 1838. While he was visiting in his native town of Gray, his friends, among whom was the ever helpful and faithful Poisson, secured him the appointment of *inspecteur-général en titre*. The new honour was a surprise and at the same time a disappointment; for Cournot loved the Rhône country in which he was born, and, besides, he had made plans for the development of the Academy of Grenoble which were only partially executed, and which he had hoped to complete. It was therefore with sorrow that he went to Paris to take up the duties of the new appointment.

During the following year he received still further proof of confidence and esteem. As a consequence of multitudinous as well as intense labours, Poisson's health began to fail, making necessary the relinquishment of some part of his official work. He chose Cournot to preside in his stead at the *concours d'agrégation de mathématiques*. This position, which he held for fourteen years, secured him, in the eyes of his associates, almost the prestige of a member of the Royal Council.

Cournot's second treatise, *Traité élémentaire de la théorie des fonctions et de calcul infinitésimal*, was published in 1841 with this dedication: "*A la mémoire de M. Poisson, pair de France, membre de L'Académie des sciences et du conseil royal de l'instruction publique: Témoinage de reconnaissance et de pieux attachement.*" This treatise on the infinitesimal calculus was the outcome of his lectures on the same subject when he was professor at Lyons. The time intervening between the conception of this work and its publication is typical of his painstaking care and thoroughness. He was always slow to publish his books.

In the autumn of 1844 Cournot made a journey to Italy in the hope that rest and diversion would bring some relief to his weak eyes, which had recently given him more trouble than usual. During his stay in Rome he was persuaded to make a visit to the Pope. At the appointed time he sought the very best fiacre he could find, and presented himself at St Peter's. He was admitted, in company with a French banker, to an audience with Gregory XVI, who, to his great surprise, was full of joviality and even of banter.

When the *Commission des hautes études* was constituted after the Revolution of 1848, Cournot was made a member. He was not a revolutionist nor even a republican either of the old or of the new type, and his appointment can be accounted for only on the ground of efficiency.

The reorganization of public instruction during the Second Empire brought changes in his status. He was at first member of the *Conseil Impérial de l'instruction publique*. In 1854 the minister of public instruction, Fortoul, offered him the rectorate of Toulouse, which he declined for characteristic reasons. M. Fortoul, who had himself been professor at Toulouse, was especially anxious to preserve his influence in that place, and Cournot foresaw that, if he accepted this particular appointment at the hands of M. Fortoul, it meant that he would go to Toulouse *comme son système incarné*! In refusing to go to Toulouse, however, he stated that for personal reasons, among which was the wish to return to his native country, he would be glad to accept the corresponding post at Dijon. As this was officially considered a less desirable appointment, his suggestion was at once appropriated, and he was made rector of the Academy of Dijon.

"*De mon côté, je n'eus pas de regret de m'être un peu précipitamment avancé. L'homme, sur son déclin, revient volontiers près de son berceau; après avoir porté longtemps le titre d'inspecteur général des études, comme l'avaient porté les Ampère et les Letronne, il me tardait de quitter des fonctions singulièrement rapetissées, quoique plus largement rétribuées, et c'était une manière d'en finir.*"

The words just quoted indicate the mood in which the *Souvenirs* were written. He was utterly tired of his function as *inspecteur général*, was disappointed with the policy of his department at the beginning of the Second Empire, and believed, besides, that his own work was near an end. In fact, in 1859, the year in which the *Souvenirs* close, he was already preparing to give up the rectorate at Dijon, and planning the publication of what he expected would be his last work. He retired from public service in 1862, and went to Paris, where he remained, for the most part, until his death.

In stature, Cournot was above the average. He was square-shouldered, and, in later years, a little stooped. His forehead was broad and high. His eyes, owing to his lifelong affliction, were habitually drawn, as if in effort to reduce the amount of light. His nose was straight with expanded nostrils, his mouth large and his lips full.

Throughout his life his habits were regular, as was necessary to achieve the amount of work that was done. But during the last period in Paris, ill-health, together with a desire to make the most of his strength and remaining years, led him to follow the most methodical routine. He arose regularly at the same hour, and retired at the same hour.

He seems to have known but one luxury—his snuffbox. The affection of his eyes grew worse with increasing age, compelling him more and more to do his thinking with the minimum assistance of writing and reading. It was consequently a frequent occurrence, when he was absorbed in thought, for him to sit for hours with his snuffbox in hand, his legs crossed, nervously swinging his foot.

In his general personal relations he was discriminating and inexpansive. His speech in official matters was direct and clear, never coloured to produce an effect or to please a friend. His friendships were few, but of unusual richness and strength, as would have been expected from his personal qualities. In these intimate relations his sternness disappeared, giving place to *bonhomie* and kindly humour.

Cournot's excessive modesty and reticence make it impossible to give a satisfactorily definite account of his political and religious principles, although as regards the former, at least, an evolution may be traced. Politics peculiarly interested him from the earliest years. The opposing sentiments of his uncle and aunt led him at an extraordinarily early age to weigh the respective claims of their respective principles. Before he was fifteen years old, he had read a large part of the work of Voltaire, and knew Boileau de Brossette by heart. Besides, his aunt had given him in secret the *Lettres provinciales* of Pascale. There was no danger, therefore, of his accepting blindly the Jesuit cause of his uncle.

In 1815 he was a member of a royalist club, reading with avidity the political journals of the day.

The economic and political Utopias of Saint-Simon and Fourier had no attraction whatever for Cournot, no more than the pretended "French Catholic Church" of Abbé Châtel, which shared public interest about 1830. The next change in his political opinions occurred towards 1840, when, owing to the excesses of the press, the continuous intrigues at court, the deplorable effects of the campaign against Molé by the coalition at the head of which was Guizot, and the ineffectual Guizot ministry itself, he lost faith in parliamentary royalty.

In the election of 1848 Cournot voted for General Cavaignac as against Louis Napoleon. He suspected, as every one should have suspected, the ultimate purposes of the nephew of the Emperor. He believed that the president of a republic should be a republican, and at this particular time there was needed to save the republic a vigorous and honest president. General Cavaignac, he believed, fulfilled these requirements.

This same year, 1848, the electoral committee of his department of Haute-Saône had made overtures to Cournot relative to his becoming a candidate for the office of representative of the department. The ground of his refusal is noteworthy. At the time there was no legal objection to his being both representative of his province and a general inspector in the department of public instruction, but he was unwilling to hold a representative office when it might seem that his authority and independence would be weakened in consequence of his being a public functionary.

Three years later, however, his dissatisfaction with the administration of public instruction, together with an impatient desire to contribute something towards a much-needed stability of government, led him to announce his candidacy for the future elections of the Haute-Saône. But the *coup d'état* of 1851, which resulted in a reduction of the deputation of the Haute-Saône, put an end to his plans for active political life.

Intimate friends had repeatedly urged Cournot to become a candidate for admission to the Institute. His modesty and unwillingness to become a solicitor, even in so important an interest, invariably defeated their well-meant plans. When, however, his health was almost completely broken, and through sheer physical exhaustion he was no longer master of his own purposes, his intimates, among whom the Academician Vacherot was most urgent, brought him to a partial consent to undergo the preliminary formalities. This deviation from his lifelong course, which undiscerning friends in their affectionate kindness sought to achieve, was made impossible by his sudden death in Paris on 30 March 1877. His remains are buried in the Paris cemetery of Montparnasse together with those of his wife and son.

The question has sometimes been asked why Cournot's reputation has not been equal to the merit of his work, and why with friends, opportunities and ability, theoretical and practical, of the first order, he did not rise to a higher rank in French scientific and political history. The complete answer to this question would require an analysis of his many-sided publications, which is not contemplated here. But, so far as purely personal causes are concerned, a partial answer may be given: it was his masterful independence and absolute truthfulness, together with an invincible repugnance to self-advertisement and the exploitation of friends.

Henry Ludwell Moore

II
COURNOT AND MATHEMATICAL ECONOMICS

Cournot wrote only two economic works: *Recherches sur les principes mathématiques de la théorie des richesses*, published in 1838; and *Principes de la théorie des richesses*, published in 1863. In fact the second of these contains no mathematics, but returns to the ideas expounded in the first, perfecting them in the process. This means that the first book contains the gist of all the various factors of the problems dealt with by Cournot.

In order to appreciate the importance of his contribution to economics, we have only to remember the opinion stated by Léon Walras, founder of the Lausanne School. When reading his paper on barter to the Academy of Moral and Political Science in Paris in 1873, he stated that Cournot was the first writer to make a bold and serious attempt to apply mathematics to political economy. Indeed Walras declared quite openly that the *Recherches* had made a strong impression on him, by orienting him towards studies which were eventually to lead him to formulate the principles of economic equilibrium.

So the value of Cournot's work is not disputed, though he was not in fact the first person to try his hand at presenting economic phenomena by means of mathematics. Among his predecessors only two appear to be worthy of note: Isnard, a government civil engineer, who published a *Traité des richesses* in 1781; and von Thünen, whose first work, published in 1826, can also be considered as a milestone in the history of mathematical economics.

But Cournot's work is not limited to the sphere of economics. In order to appreciate fully the importance of his contribution in this field, it is essential to give a list, however brief, of the books that he published at the various stages of his life. He had an acute mind and thought deeply on many subjects, developing his thinking simultaneously in a variety of disciplines: pure mathematics, philosophy, history and sociology.

As well as his doctoral thesis, he also published two works on pure mathematics: the *Traité élémentaire de la théorie des fonctions et du calcul infinitesimal* (1841), and the *Exposition de la théorie des chances et des probabilités* (1843). But he was attracted by historical and social questions early in his career. He even studied law, and achieved recognition in philosophy with the publication of his *Essai sur le fondement de nos connaissances et sur le caractère de la critique philosophique*, which appeared in 1851, and above all with his *Traité de l'enchaînement des idées fondamentales dans les sciences et dans l'histoire* (1861).

In the field of science, Cournot makes a distinction between what he calls the "quantitative" sciences, such as physics, and the "sciences of combination", which include the social sciences. The first group require little empirical verification, while for the second it is essential to maintain a permanent check on the facts in order to ascertain whether they conform to one's theories. In Cournot's view, scientific laws are essentially contingent. In the economic field in particular, the relationships that are established within societies have the effect of gradually eliminating the influence of chance phenomena; they thus, in a sufficiently advanced phase of development, reveal only relationships that conform strictly to the terms of the laws governing these social phenomena. Cournot thus considered that one day it would be possible to calculate the precise influence of a variation in the price of an article on the demand for it.

Moreover, this prospect of indefinite progress in the "sciences of combination" is dependent on observations of a very large number of individuals, to whom the law of statistical regularity can be applied. Cournot was on friendly terms with Poisson, and was not unaware of the way that Laplace had made use of the concept of probability; he had no doubt that similar principles could be envisaged as a basis for economic studies. But for him the concept of probability lay in the very nature of things, outside any philosophic concept, while for Laplace it merely showed that our knowledge is imperfect. At any rate, Cournot was fortunately able to have recourse to the law of the majority in order to make use, in the social sphere, of mathematical variables which are indeterminate but continuous and therefore capable of being analysed. When we study his theory of elasticity, we shall see the extent to which he took advantage of this method.

According to Cournot, the laws of nature must be capable of being reduced to very simple expressions. This view is once again in keeping with contemporary attempts at synthesis in the physical sciences. Moreover, the importance of the concept of statistical regularity in the economic sphere led Cournot to advocate the use of statistics in order to eliminate the influence of chance events. The only causes of variation to subsist are those that are in the nature of permanent and fixed causes.

Like other governing principles, Cournot frequently has recourse to the laws that arise from the physical world, such as the principle of least action; this is expressed in the world of economics as the hedonistic principle, by which individuals endeavour to obtain the maximum satisfaction by means of the minimum effort. Similarly, he has the happy idea of applying to economic problems the concept of stable equilibrium, with all its consequences, as well as the concept of momentum, from which he deduces his theoretical market. Yet he is far from likening human communities to the intangible wholes with which the physicist is concerned. And although the concept of force is for him a very powerful stimulus, he takes fully into account the specific element in human societies, by appealing to the "vital force" which cannot be reduced to purely mechanistic elements. In this respect, our ideas have scarcely developed since then, and the contemporary "vitalist" doctrine is very close to the theories put forward by Cournot concerning the evolution of human societies.

To sum up, Cournot's guiding theory is basically made up of the concepts of statistical regularity and probability, whose success in contemporary physics, and even in biology, is well known.

As for the use of mathematics in political economy, Cournot recommends this procedure because of his faith in the strength of this analysis and of the evolving nature of the social sciences. The arguments put forward in support of similar methods can be summarized as follows:

1. Only the use of mathematics can result in clear and precise definitions and simple statements.
2. The use of mathematics also allows one to use functions and, consequently, to solve the problems of maxima and minima that frequently occur in political economy.
3. The functional relationships to which the mathematician has recourse establish relationships of mutual dependence between the various economic parameters which totally exclude the causality link.

Here we come to one of the most delicate areas of economics, which, like all the sciences of observation, is not open to experimentation, and lends itself exclusively to the study of phenomena which vary simultaneously in time. On the other hand, formal logic, which has recourse to syllogism, cannot eliminate causality links and cannot embrace a collection of facts that modify themselves by reacting on each other. Cournot, like Auguste Comte, never loses sight of the unified nature of the systems under discussion, both in the social sphere and in the physical sphere.

These complex considerations, which are so familiar to us today and even appear as mere commonplaces, were, in fact, highly revolutionary when they were first developed. This probably accounts for the coldness with which they were received.

We must also note that, despite his faith in the fertile nature of mathematics, Cournot lays down as a basic principle that it is always essential to bring the results of any piece of scientific analysis face to face with reality, either in order to correct the premises on which it was based or to restrict the field in which the conclusions can be applied. But it must be admitted that Cournot very often departed from this principle, and that certain of his conclusions were subsequently found wanting when they were put to the test of the facts.

Having postulated these general principles, we can now study the broad outlines of the economic problems which Cournot dealt with, and particularly those which his critics of almost a hundred years ago were unable to tackle.

Before examining in detail the economic questions that Cournot dealt with, it is essential to clarify the spirit in which he approached them. In his view, the science of wealth must be cultivated, like the other scientific disciplines, for its own sake and solely in the interests of truth, with no consideration of its concrete applications.

In taking up this position Cournot made a clear break with the economists who went before him, all of whom were concerned with solving political problems as much as specifically economic ones. Whether they were "profiteers", physiocrats or liberals, they always reasoned as statesmen, and it would not have occurred to them to cultivate economics for anything but practical ends. Cournot's high ideal, on the other hand, allowed him to bestow impartiality on economic studies and grant them, so to speak, the right to belong in the realm of pure science. Those who sincerely believe in theoretical speculation owe it to themselves to feel a certain gratitude to Cournot, in view of the new direction he gave to the analysis of such phenomena.

The most curious thing of all is to realize that, as often happens in similar circumstances, some of the theories elaborated by him have had immediate practical applications, as is shown, for instance, by the most widely adopted method for the commercial exploitation of monopolies.

The scientific nature of economics compelled Cournot to resort to certain abstractions, but he was quick to recognize that they are not indispensable and are more arbitrary than in the realm of the sciences that have reached a more advanced stage of development.

Among the subjects which Cournot studied the most important will be dealt with here, namely the theory of demand, monopoly and foreign trade.

1. *The Theory of Demand*

Cournot's theory of elasticity (or "law of demand") represents the way in which the real demand for a commodity varies as a function of its price.

In this respect it is essential to note Cournot's attitude, which involves considering that in the phenomena of barter, supply and demand are not generally symmetrical: demand represents the essential factor, because it expresses, for the individual, the necessity of consuming certain commodities in order to satisfy his various needs, whereas supply merely represents the obligatory "other party" and is thus the subordinate factor. Walras was to adopt the same attitude, whereas other economists such as Marshall were to consider that supply, conditioned by the phenomena of production, constitutes in the last analysis the incentive for all economic activity. Although I do not aim to settle the debate here, I am inclined to believe, with Cournot, that demand represents the essential phenomenon of the two aspects of economic activity, since in this field everything comes down in the last analysis to consumer transactions that are subject to the law of demand.

It is also essential, when presenting Cournot's ideas, to specify the conditions under which the demand for an article varies, as a function of its price. Although Cournot considered that the economic world constitutes a whole, made up of various different elements that inevitably react one on the other, in his theory of demand he elaborated an abstract concept: the idea that the demand for a commodity is dependent on one variable only—its price. Moreover, this way of looking at the question is for Cournot only an approximation, by virtue of which the variations affecting the demand for and the price of all other articles must be considered as of secondary importance, and therefore negligible compared with those that affect the commodity under discussion. This statement goes against those put forward by Walras and Pareto, who introduce into their equations of economic equilibrium functions of demand with several variables. But Walras realizes that in a market which brings together a very large number of free traders dealing in a very large number of commodities, it is possible to consider demand functions that are exclusively dependent upon the price of the commodity in question.

With the proviso that substitution phenomena must be taken into account and the range of variation in the price of each article must therefore be restricted, the theory of elasticity outlined by Cournot renders the greatest possible service to economics and leads to the solution of specific problems such as the theory of monopoly.

In the second place, Cournot uses the concept of statistical regularity and assumes that demand is a continuous function of price. He also postulates, as a general rule, that this function is a decreasing one. This principle, which is still accepted today, though with certain reservations, is the point of departure for all Cournot's conclusions concerning monopoly, competition, national income and foreign trade.

Moreover, Cournot was already making distinctions between various commodities according to the variation in demand for them as a function of their price. He would certainly have subscribed to the definition of the coefficient of elasticity given by Marshall, which can be used to advantage in all detailed studies of demand.

Taking his theory of demand as his starting-point, Cournot also considers the variations in the value of a stock of a good caused by changes in demand for it. He even classifies the various types of commodity according to the direction in which this quantity varies in terms of their price. Taking matters to extremes, he bases his estimate of national income on the total amount of the stock values of all goods and, although he later draws a distinction between this "nominal income" and the "real income", in this respect he resembles certain seventeenth-century economists from whom profiteers drew their inspiration.

In spite of everything, it seems very much as if recent research into demand has revived the questions relating to stock value; the direction in which the latter varies is, as is well-known, closely related to the coefficient of elasticity.

Finally, let us note, regarding the theory of demand and the problem of price determination, that the theoretical market envisaged by Cournot reflects his mechanistic views, in the sense that he disregards all forms of passive resistance. The perfect market still remains today one of the finest titles to fame of the man who founded the mathematical school.

2. *Monopoly*

The theory of monopoly occupies an important place in Cournot's economic writings since he takes it as his point of departure for a gradual advance, which leads him by degrees to perfect competition.

We aim simply to bring out Cournot's conclusions, which are still valid and without which the exploitation of monopolies would probably not have progressed as much as it has since then.

Using his theory of demand, Cournot was the first person to demonstrate the existence of a monopoly price, i.e. the price which procures the maximum gross proceeds (in cases where we can assume that working expenses are nil), or the maximum net proceeds (when we accept that there are working expenses). Moreover, Cournot's main preoccupation is with the tapping of natural resources, which are subject to the law of diminishing returns. On this particular point it is quite clear that our ideas have progressed, since at the present time monopoly is practised in a large number of industries manufacturing products at a decreasing cost price.

The interesting point to be remembered here is that this method is simple, sound and accurate and virtually nothing in it needs to be adjusted today. The theory of monopoly is closely related to the concept of stock value and Cournot shrewdly noted that competition must usually be preferred to monopoly, because with a monopoly the hedonistic principle encourages producers to increase the nominal income but not the real national income.

It should also be noted that, in the conclusions that he draws with regard to tapping natural resources, Cournot formulates very precisely the law of the costs of marginal production as we know it today. Marshall was only too willing to recognize his influence in this respect.

Finally, thanks to the theory of monopoly, Cournot was the first person to envisage the possibility of expansion of income, which he considered as due to the existence of a considerable disparity between the sale price and the cost price. He was particularly aware of phenomena such as that of income raised by taking advantage of a patent.

He was no doubt less successful when he formulated his theory of offsetting demand, which in his view was nothing more than an application of the theory of errors and thus an approximation which disregarded variations of a subsidiary nature, but which, by contradicting the unity of the economic system and the interdependence of the various elements at stake, was to lead him in the course of his studies of the variations of national income to conclusions that are clearly questionable.

Let us at any rate remember the way in which he was able to turn to good account the use of indeterminate functions, tackling with great success the theory of monopoly with which his name will always be associated.

3. *Foreign Trade*

For questions relating to international trade, Cournot always employs the same methods. He examines what happens in the case of a single commodity, disregarding the effects of other commodities and studying the variations in both nominal and real income.

The conclusions he draws tend on the whole to recommend that each nation should increase its imports of products extracted from the soil and its exports of manufactured goods.

These conclusions fit in perfectly with Cournot's views on the part played by the State in the life of societies, for both in home trade and in international trade he proves to be a resolute interventionist. It was only at the end of his life, notably in 1877 in his *Revue sommaire des doctrines économiques* that, fearful of socialism, he preached a doctrine of economic liberalism, feeling that the uninterrupted progress of interventionism requires increasingly complex control which would clearly be in direct opposition to the simplicity of the laws of nature.

Apart from the theory of international exchange, in which Cournot very judiciously defines the role of arbitration and postulates the relationship between the exchange rates of the various countries, his work on international trade does not have the same solidity as his studies of the theories of demand and monopoly. It seems in fact that he applied mathematical analysis too early to problems that will no doubt lend themselves to it one day, but which the state of scientific knowledge at that time did not permit to be so treated.

When we read the preface to the *Théorie des richesses* we cannot fail to notice a certain bitterness about the relative failure of this work, published in 1838. It is tempting to wonder about the reason for this failure. Moreover, it was not only Cournot's economic work that was judged unfavourably by his contemporaries—and particularly his compatriots. In fact both his historical work and his philosophical or social ideas were received with almost total indifference.

Ever since his work regained the position it deserved, we have had good reason to think that the attitude of his contemporaries was due merely to the nature of the ideas that prevailed in the middle of the nineteenth century.

Cournot was clearly isolated by his intellectual training, by the profundity of his ideas and by the geometric structure of his statements in an age when philosophy was inspired by dialectism and was not anxious to resort to genuinely scientific methods such as positivism, which was soon to win general acclaim.

Cournot was certainly ahead of his time, both in the novelty of his ideas and in their sheer audacity—and for this he had to suffer the disfavour which greets all innovators.

In the preface to which we referred above he expressed the modest hope that his research would be properly appreciated in the future. It is gratifying to see this wish granted today. Apart from the economists we have already mentioned, the entire intellectual world now recognizes Cournot's influence in the many spheres in which he exercised his shrewd intellect.

Thanks to his extraordinarily powerful intellect, which was well suited to grapple with the most varied branches of knowledge, Cournot's economic work bears the stamp of great originality in its cohesion, i.e. in his desire to link his thesis to a small number of very general principles. There is no question that he sometimes overestimated his strength and tried to solve problems which were not yet suitable for mathematical analysis. His errors should help us to limit our studies to solving problems which are clearly defined, until such time as progress in economics enables us to undertake wider studies.

Cournot has emerged from all the controversies to which his work has given rise with his fame enhanced. Despite his austere pessimism, he remains one of the most attractive figures of his day and in his lofty intellectual integrity he was one of the best servants ever known to science (in the highest sense of the word).

We can, therefore, as Cournot hoped, state with absolute conviction that posterity has quashed the verdict passed on him by his contemporaries, to the benefit of scientific truth. We should recognize him as one of the most eminent precursors of the movement which is emerging in every country today and which aims to ground economic studies on solid and truly scientific foundations.

René Roy

SOURCES

Essay I

Henry Ludwell Moore, "The Personality of Antoine Augustin Cournot", *Quarterly Journal of Economics* 19 (1905). Abridged.

Essay II

René Roy, "Cournot et l'école mathématique" *Econometrica,* 1 (1933). Abridged.

Signature

From marriage certificate of A. A. Cournot and Colombe Antoinette Petitguyot, Mairie de Gray (Haute-Saône).

Portrait

Reproduced from *Revue de métaphysique et de morale*, 13 (1905).

BIBLIOGRAPHY

L. Liard, "Cournot", *Revue des Mondes* (1877).

F. Y. Edgeworth, "Antoine Augustin Cournot", in R. H. J. Palgrave, *Palgrave's Dictionary of Political Economy*, Vol. 1 (New York 1894, reprint 1963).

I. Fisher, "Cournot and Mathematical Economics", *Quarterly Journal of Economics*, 12 (1898).

H. L. Moore, "Antoine Augustin Cournot", *Revue de métaphysique et de morale*, 13 (1905).

F. Mentré, *Cournot et la renaissance du probabilisme au XIXe siècle* (Paris, 1908).

J. Segond, *Cournot et la psychologie vitaliste* (Paris, 1911).

E. P. Bottinelli, *A. Cournot: Métaphysicien de la connaissance* (Paris, 1913).

A. A. Cournot, *Souvenirs* (Paris, 1913).

G. Loiseau, *Les doctrines économiques de Cournot* (Paris, 1913).

F. Mentré, *Pour qu'on lise Cournot* (Paris, 1927).

G. Milhaud, *Études sur Cournot* (Paris, 1927).

F. Bompaire, *Du principe de liberté économique dans l'œuvre de Cournot et dans celle de l'école de Lausanne* (Paris, 1931).

E. Antonelli (ed.), "Léon Walras et sa correspondance avec Augustin Cournot et Stanley Jevons", *Econometrica*, 3 (1935).

E. Liefmann-Keil, "Die wissenschaftliche Methode und das Gesamtwerk Cournots", *Archiv fur mathematische Wirtschafts- und Sozialforschung*, 3 (1937).

I. Fisher, "Cournot forty years ago", *Econometrica*, 6 (1938).

A. Nichol, "Tragedies in the life of Cournot", *Econometrica*, 6 (1938).

H. Guitton, "Antoine Augustin Cournot", in *International Encyclopedia of the Social Sciences*, Vol. 3 (New York, 1968).

JOHN STUART MILL

1806–1873

I never was a boy. *From a letter of* J. S. MILL

One who knew Mill only through his writings knew but half of him, and that not the best half. F. STEPHEN

. . . he will again be recognized as one of the really great figures of his period, one in whom even his purely intellectual achievements are mainly due to his profound conviction of the supreme moral value of unrelenting intellectual effort. Not by temperament but out of a deeply ingrained sense that this was his duty did Mill grow to be the "Saint of Rationalism", as Gladstone once so justly described him.
F. A. VON HAYEK

But even in his most arid reflections on woman's similarity with man and on the nature of Logic, Mill is in reality a romantic. K. HAGBERG

Not so original nor so well equilibrated as Hume, not so sure in judgement or literary skill as Smith, and lacking the profound analytical vision and genial personality of Ricardo, Mill yet stands out as one of the great figures of the Classical tradition, not unworthy to be mentioned in the same breath as these giants: a man of massive powers of intellectual synthesis and of burning idealism and integrity, willing to follow thought wherever it led him, somewhat oversolemn and not a very good judge of men but courageous, generous and sensitive, a rare spirit, conspicuous even in his own great age, with a message of candour and humanity which . . . has still much relevance for ours. LORD ROBBINS

I
AUTOBIOGRAPHY

I was born in London, on 20 May 1806, and was the eldest son of James Mill, the author of the *History of British India*. My father, the son of a petty tradesman and (I believe) small farmer, at Northwater Bridge, in the county of Angus, was, when a boy, recommended by his abilities to the notice of Sir John Stuart of Fettercairn, one of the Barons of the Exchequer in Scotland, and was, in consequence, sent to the University of Edinburgh at the expense of a fund established by Lady Jane Stuart (the wife of Sir John Stuart) and some other ladies for educating young men for the Scottish Church. He there went through the usual course of study, and was licensed as a preacher, but never followed the profession; having satisfied himself that he could not believe the doctrines of that or any other Church. For a few years he was a private tutor in various families in Scotland, among others that of the Marquis of Tweeddale; but ended by taking up his residence in London, and devoting himself to authorship. Nor had he any other means of support until 1819, when he obtained an appointment in the India House.

In this period of my father's life there are two things which it is impossible not to be struck with. The first is, that in his position, with no resource but the precarious one of writing in periodicals, he married and had a large family: conduct than which nothing could be more opposed, both as a matter of good sense and of duty, to the opinions which, at least at a later period of life, he strenuously upheld. The other circumstance is the extraordinary energy which was required to lead the life he led, with the disadvantages under which he laboured from the first, and with those which he brought upon himself by his marriage. It would have been no small thing, had he done no more than to support himself and his family during so many years by writing, without ever being in debt, or in any pecuniary difficulty; holding, as he did, opinions, both in politics and in religion, which were more odious to all persons of influence, and to the common run of prosperous Englishmen in that generation than either before or since; and being not only a man whom nothing would have induced to write against his convictions, but one who invariably threw into everything he wrote, as much of his convictions as he thought the circumstances would in any way permit: being, it must also be said, one who never did anything negligently. A considerable part of almost every day was employed in the instruction of his children; in the case of one of whom, myself, he exerted an amount of labour, care, and perseverance rarely, if ever, employed for a similar purpose, in endeavouring to give, according to his own conception, the highest order of intellectual education.

A man who, in his own practice, so vigorously acted up to the principle of losing no time, was likely to adhere to the same rule in the instruction of his pupil. I have no remembrance of the time when I began to learn Greek. I have been told that it was when I was three years old. My earliest recollection on the subject is that of committing to memory what my father termed vocables, being lists of common Greek words, with their signification in English, which he wrote out for me on cards. Of grammar, until some years later, I learnt no more than the inflections of the nouns and verbs, but, after a course of vocables, proceeded at once to translation; and I faintly remember going through Aesop's Fables, the first Greek book which I read.

The only thing besides Greek, that I learnt as a lesson in this part of my childhood, was arithmetic: this also my father taught me: it was the task of the evenings, and I well remember its disagreeableness. But the lessons were only a part of the daily instruction I received. Much of it consisted in the books I read by myself, and my father's discourses to me, chiefly during our walks. In these frequent talks about the books I read, he used, as opportunity offered, to give me explanations and ideas respecting civilization, government, morality, mental cultivation, which he required me afterwards to restate to him in my own words. He also made me read, and give him a verbal account of, many books which would not have interested me sufficiently to induce me to read them of myself.

In my eighth year I commenced learning Latin, in conjunction with a younger sister, to whom I taught it as I went on, and who afterwards repeated the lessons to my father. In the same year in which I began Latin, I made my first commencement in the Greek poets with the *Iliad*. From my eighth to my twelfth year I learnt elementary geometry and algebra thoroughly, the differential calculus, and other portions of the higher mathematics far from thoroughly: for my father, not having kept up this part of his early acquired knowledge, could not spare time to qualify himself for removing my difficulties, and left me to deal with them, with little other aid than that of books; while I was continually incurring his displeasure by my inability to solve difficult problems for which he did not see that I had not the necessary previous knowledge. As to my private reading, I can only speak of what I remember. History continued to be my strongest predilection, and most of all ancient history.

During this part of my childhood, one of my greatest amusements was experimental science; in the theoretical, however, not the practical sense of the word; not trying experiments—a kind of discipline which I have often regretted not having had—nor even seeing, but merely reading about them. I never remember being so wrapt up in any book, as I was in Joyce's *Scientific Dialogues*.

From about the age of twelve, I entered into another and more advanced stage in my course of instruction; in which the main object was no longer the aids and appliances of thought, but the thoughts themselves. This commenced with logic, in which I began at once with the Organon, and read it to the Analytics inclusive, but profited little by the Posterior Analytics, which belong to a branch of speculation I was not yet ripe for. My own consciousness and experience ultimately led me to appreciate quite as highly as he did, the value of an early practical familiarity with the school logic. I know nothing, in my education, to which I think myself more indebted for whatever capacity of thinking I have attained. I am persuaded that nothing, in modern education, tends so much, when properly used, to form exact thinkers, who attach a precise meaning to words and propositions, and are not imposed on by vague, loose or ambiguous terms. The boasted influence of mathematical studies is nothing to it; for in mathematical processes, none of the real difficulties of correct ratiocination occur. It is also a study peculiarly adapted to an early stage in the education of philosophical students, since it does not presuppose the slow process of acquiring, by experience and reflection, valuable thoughts of their own. They may become capable of disentangling the intricacies of confused and self-contradictory thought, before their own thinking faculties are much advanced; a power which, for want of some such discipline, many otherwise able men altogether lack.

Though Ricardo's great work was already in print, no didactic treatise embodying its doctrines, in a manner fit for learners, had yet appeared. My father, therefore, commenced instructing me in the science by a sort of lectures, which he delivered to me in our walks. After this I read Ricardo, giving an account daily of what I read, and discussing, in the best manner I could, the collateral points which offered themselves in our progress.

On money, as the most intricate part of the subject, he made me read in the same manner Ricardo's admirable pamphlets, written during what was called the bullion controversy; to these succeeded Adam Smith; and in this reading it was one of my father's main objects to make me apply to Smith's more superficial view of political economy, the superior lights of Ricardo, and detect what was fallacious in Smith's arguments, or erroneous in any of his conclusions. When I was about fourteen I left England for more than a year; and after my return, though my studies went on under my father's general direction, he was no longer my schoolmaster.

In 1820 Bentham invited me for a six months' visit to them in the South of France, which their kindness ultimately prolonged to nearly a twelvemonth. I accompanied them in an excursion to the Pyrenees. This first introduction to the highest order of mountain scenery made the deepest impression on me, and gave a colour to my tastes through life. But the greatest, perhaps, of the many advantages which I owed to this episode in my education, was that of having breathed for a whole year, the free and genial atmosphere of Continental life.

In my way through Paris, both going and returning, I passed some time in the house of M. Say, the eminent political economist, who was a friend and correspondent of my father, having become acquainted with him on a visit to England a year or two after the peace. He was a man of the later period of the French Revolution, a fine specimen of the best kind of French Republican, one of those who had never bent the knee to Bonaparte though courted by him to do so; a truly upright, brave and enlightened man. He lived a quiet and studious life, made happy by warm affections, public and private. He was acquainted with many of the chiefs of the Liberal party, and I saw various noteworthy persons while staying at his house; among whom I have pleasure in the recollection of having once seen Saint-Simon, not yet the founder either of a philosophy or a religion, and considered only as a clever *original*. The chief fruit which I carried away from the society I saw, was a strong and permanent interest in Continental liberalism, of which I ever afterwards kept myself *au courant*, as much as of English politics.

For the first year or two after my visit to France, I continued my old studies, with the addition of some new ones. My previous education had been, in a certain sense, already a course of Benthamism. The Benthamite standard of "the greatest happiness' was that which I had always been taught to apply. From this point I began to carry on my intellectual cultivation by writing still more than by reading. In the summer of 1822 I wrote my first argumentative essay. I had now also begun to converse, on general subjects, with the instructed men with whom I came into contact: and the opportunities of such contact naturally became more numerous.

In May, 1823, my professional occupation and status for the next thirty-five years of my life, were decided by my father's obtaining for me an appointment from the East India Company, in the office of the Examiner of India Correspondence, immediately under himself. The occupation of so much of my time by office work did not relax my attention to my own pursuits, which were never carried on more vigorously. It was about this time that I began to write in newspapers.

About the end of 1824, or beginning of 1825, Mr Bentham, having lately got back his papers on evidence from M. Dumont, resolved to have them printed in the original, and bethought himself of me as capable of preparing them for the press; I gladly undertook this task, and it occupied nearly all my leisure for about a year, exclusive of the time afterwards spent in seeing the five large volumes through the press. The time occupied in this editorial work was extremely well employed in respect to my own improvement.

While thus engaged in writing for the public, I did not neglect other modes of self-cultivation. It was at this time that I learnt German; begining it on the Hamiltonian method, for which purpose I and several of my companions formed a class. For several years from this period, our social studies assumed a shape which contributed very much to my mental progress. Our first subject was political economy. We chose some systematic treatise as our text-book; my father's *Elements* being our first choice. When we had enough of political economy, we took up the syllogistic logic in the same manner, Grote now joining us.

Our doings from 1825 to 1830 in the way of public speaking filled a considerable place in my life during those years, and they had important effects on my development. The Society,[1] and the preparation for it, together with the preparation for the morning conversations which were going on simultaneously, occupied the greater part of my leisure; and made me feel it a relief when, in the spring of 1828, I ceased to write for the *Westminster*. For some years after this I wrote very little, and nothing regularly, for publication.

But the time came when I awakened from this as from a dream. It was in the autumn of 1826. I was in a dull state of nerves, such as everybody is occasionally liable to; unsusceptible to enjoyment or pleasurable excitement; one of those moods when what is pleasure at other times, becomes insipid or indifferent. At first I hoped that the cloud would pass away of itself; but it did not. A night's sleep, the sovereign remedy for the smaller vexations of life, had no effect on it.

After 1829 I withdrew from attendance on the debating society. I had had enough of speech-making, and was glad to carry on my private studies and meditations without any immediate call for outward assertion of their results. I found the fabric of my old and taught opinions giving way in many fresh places, and I never allowed it to fall to pieces, but was incessantly occupied in weaving it anew. I never, in the course of my transition, was content to remain, for ever so short a time, confused and unsettled. When I had taken in any new idea, I could not rest till I had adjusted its relation to my old opinions, and ascertained exactly how far its effect ought to extend in modifying or superseding them.

The writers by whom, more than by any others, a new mode of political thinking was brought home to me, were those of the Saint-Simonian school in France. In 1829 and 1830 I became acquainted with some of their writings. Among their publications there was one which seemed to be far superior to

[1] A society of Owenites, called the Cooperation Society, which met for weekly public discussions in Chancery Lane.

the rest; in which the general idea was matured into something much more definite and instructive. This was an early work of Auguste Comte, who then called himself, and even announced himself on the title page as a pupil of Saint-Simon.

My father's tone of thought and feeling, I now felt myself at a great distance from: greater, indeed, than a full and calm explanation and reconsideration on both sides, might have shown to exist in reality. But my father was not one with whom calm and full explanations on fundamental points of doctrine could be expected, at least with one whom he might consider as, in some sort, a deserter from his standard.

It remains to speak of what I wrote during these years, which, independently of my contributions to newspapers, was considerable. In 1830 and 1831 I wrote the five Essays since published under the title of *Essays on some Unsettled Questions of Political Economy*. I offered them to a publisher, he declined them. They were only printed in 1844, after the success of the *System of Logic*.[2]

The only actual revolution which has ever taken place in my modes of thinking, was already complete. My new tendencies had to be confirmed in some respects, moderated in others: but the only substantial changes of opinion that were yet to come, related to politics, and consisted, on one hand, in a greater approximation, so far as regards the ultimate prospects of humanity, to a qualified Socialism, and on the other, a shifting of my political ideal from pure democracy, as commonly understood by its partisans, to the modified form of it, which is set forth in my *Considerations on Representative Government*.

During the whole of 1835 my father's health had been declining: his

[2] It was at the period of my mental progress which I have now reached that I formed the friendship which has been the honour and chief blessing of my existence as well as the source of a great part of all that I have attempted to do, or hope to effect hereafter, for human improvement. My first introduction to the lady who, after a friendship of twenty years, consented to become my wife, was in 1830, when I was in my twenty-fifth and she in her twenty-third year. With her husband's family it was the renewal of an old acquaintanceship.

At this period [Harriet Taylor] lived mostly with one young daughter, in a quiet part of the country, and only occasionally in town, with her first husband, Mr Taylor. I visited her equally in both places; and was greatly indebted to the strength of character which enabled her to disregard the false interpretations liable to be put on the frequency of my visits to her while living generally apart from Mr Taylor, and on our occasionally travelling together, though in all other respects our conduct during those years gave not the slightest ground for any other supposition than the true one, that our relation to each other at that time was one of strong affection and confidential intimacy only. For though we did not consider the ordinances of society binding on a subject so entirely personal, we did feel bound that our conduct should be such as in no degree to bring discredit on her husband, nor therefore on herself.

symptoms became unequivocally those of pulmonary consumption, and after lingering to the last stage of debility, he died on 23 June 1836. His place is an eminent one in the literary, and even in the political history of his country; and it is far from honourable to the generation which has benefited by his worth, that he is so seldom mentioned, and, compared with men far his inferiors, so little remembered.

From this time (1840), what is worth relating of my life will come into a very small compass; for I have no further mental changes to tell of, but only, as I hope, a continued mental progress; which does not admit of a consecutive history, and the results of which, if real, will be best found in my writings. The first use I made of the leisure which I gained by disconnecting myself from the *Review*, was to finish the *Logic*. At the end of 1841, the book being ready for the press, I offered it to Murray, who kept it until too late for publication that season, and then refused it, for reasons which could just as well have been given at first. It was published in the spring of 1843. My original expectations of success were extremely limited.

The *Principles of Political Economy* was far more rapidly executed than the *Logic*, or indeed than anything of importance which I had previously written. It was commenced in the autumn of 1845, and was ready for the press before the end of 1847. The rapid success of the *Political Economy* showed that the public wanted, and were prepared for such a book. It was, from the first, continually cited and referred to as an authority, because it was not a book merely of abstract science, but also of application, and treated political economy not as a thing by itself, but as a fragment of a greater whole; a branch of social philosophy, so interlinked with all the other branches, that its conclusions, even in its own peculiar province, are only true conditionally, subject to interference and counteraction from causes not directly within its scope: while to the character of a practical guide it has no pretension, apart from other classes of considerations. Political economy, in truth, has never pretended to give advice to mankind with no lights but its own; though people who knew nothing but political economy (and therefore knew that ill) have taken upon themselves to advise, and could only do so by such lights as they had.

Between the time of which I have now spoken, and the present, took place the most important events of my private life. The first of these was my marriage, in April 1851, to the lady whose incomparable worth had made her friendship the greatest source to me both of happiness and of improvement, during many years in which we never expected to be in any closer relation to one another.

During the years which intervened between the commencement of my married life and the catastrophe which closed it, the principal occurrences of my outward existence (unless I count as such a first attack of the family disease, and a consequent journey of more than six months for the recovery of health, in Italy, Sicily, and Greece) had reference to my position in the India House. In 1856 I was promoted to the rank of chief of the office in which I had served for upwards of thirty-three years.

During the two years which immediately preceded the cessation of my official life, my wife and I were working together at the *Liberty*. I had first planned and written it as a short essay in 1854. It was in mounting the steps to the Capitol, in January 1855, that the thought first arose of converting it into a volume. Its final revision was to have been a work of the winter of 1858–9, the first after my retirement, which we had arranged to pass in the South of Europe. That hope and every other were frustrated by the most unexpected and bitter calamity of her death—at Avignon, on our way to Montpellier, from a sudden attack of pulmonary congestion.

Since then I have sought for such alleviation as my state admitted of, by the mode of life which most enabled me to feel her still near me. I bought a cottage as close as possible to the place where she is buried, and there her daughter (my fellow-sufferer and now my chief comfort) and I, live constantly during a great portion of the year.[3] After my irreparable loss, one of my earliest cares was to print and publish the treatise, so much of which was the work of her whom I had lost, and consecrate it to her memory.

The political circumstances of the time induced me, shortly after, to complete and publish a pamphlet (*Thoughts on Parliamentary Reform*), part of which had been written some years previously, on the occasion of one of the abortive Reform Bills, and had at the time been approved and revised by her. The work of the years 1860 and 1861 consisted chiefly of two treatises, only one of which was intended for immediate publication. This was the *Considerations on Representative Government*; a connected exposition of what, by the thoughts of many years, I had come to regard as the best form of a popular constitution. The other treatise written at this time is the one which was published some years later (1869) under the title of *The Subjection of Women*. It was written at my daughter's suggestion. Soon after this time I took from their repository a portion of the unpublished papers which I had written during the last years of our married life, and shaped them, with some additional matter, into the little work entitled *Utilitarianism*.

These (and other) writings together with a small number of papers in periodicals which I have not deemed worth preserving, were the whole of the products of my activity as a writer during the years from 1859 to 1865. In the early part of the last-mentioned year, in compliance with a wish frequently expressed to me by working men, I published cheap people's

[3] Von Hayek has recently given an instructive picture of the relation between John Stuart Mill and Harriet Taylor in an excellent book (see "Bibliography").

editions of those of my writings which seemed the most likely to find readers among the working classes; namely, *Principles of Political Economy*, *Liberty* and *Representative Government*.

In this summary of my outward life I have now arrived at the period at which my tranquil and retired existence as a writer of books was to be exchanged for the less congenial occupation of a member of the House of Commons. I was a member of the House during the three sessions of the Parliament which passed the Reform Bill; during which time Parliament was necessarily my main occupation, except during the recess.

While I remained in Parliament my work as an author was unavoidably limited to the recess. During that time I wrote (besides the pamphlet on Ireland, already mentioned) the "Essay on Plato", published in the *Edinburgh Review*, and reprinted in the third volume of *Dissertations and Discussions*; and the Address which, conformably to custom, I delivered to the University of St Andrews, whose students had done me the honour of electing me to the office of Rector. During this period also I commenced (and completed soon after I had left Parliament) the performance of a duty to philosophy and to the memory of my father, by preparing and publishing an edition of the *Analysis of the Phenomena of the Human Mind*, with notes bringing up the doctrines of that admirable book to the latest improvements in science and in speculation.

Since that time (1868) little has occurred which there is need to commemorate in this place. I returned to my old pursuits and to the enjoyment of a country life in the South of Europe (near Avignon), alternating twice a year with a residence of some weeks or months in the neighbourhood of London.

John Stuart Mill

II
THE DEATH OF JOHN STUART MILL

As the shadows of his life began to lengthen, the mists of fame began to swirl up and obscure the man! The broad high forehead and the hatchet face; the grey and steadfast eyes; the thin, straight nose; the clean complexion and emphatic chin; the growth of curly light-brown hair running round the thinning cranium; the soft, incisive voice—all this is gone. In its place remains the legend left by Victorian misunderstanding, sedulously tinted by Carlyle, impressed by decades of schoolteachers and divines. A name, a black and shiny case left over from days of horse-drawn cabs and gaiters.

A name, indeed, to conjure with; a name at which, as one of Mill's modern adversaries has pointed out, we still instinctively take off our hats. But a name erudite and respectable; sober, censorious, and sad; prodigious, and at the same time somehow awful, a kind of moral Great Agrippa. Above all, as dry as dust.

On Saturday 3 May he duly made his expedition (near Avignon). After walking fifteen miles the hot day through, he went home tired and happy. But the evening air was chill. On the Monday he produced a fever. Towards evening, Helen called in Dr Chauffard. Mill died at seven o'clock on the morning of Wednesday 7 May 1873. His death was very sudden. Mill was carried down next day along the short road to the familiar grave. A light, warm rain was falling. No notice had been given and only five—Gurney and Chauffard, the two doctors, the Pastor and his wife, and Helen—followed him. But when they reached the cemetery gates, a large spontaneous crowd stood dumb and damp. And, although there was a rushed and tasteless effort to get his remains for Westminster Abbey; although a bronze statue later rose up on the Thames embankment, these were his real memorial. All his life he had fought for them, and for the millions they represented; fiercely, though never with unfair weapons. All his life they had looked to him, half-comprehending, full of trust.

M. St J. Packe

III
JOHN STUART MILL, A CRITICISM: WITH PERSONAL RECOLLECTIONS

Mill had, I believe, a very fine constitution physically. His father's brain was encased in an admirable framework. His muscle was good to the last; and his nutritive powers failed only in consequence of a strain that they should never have been subjected to. The nervous system was habitually kept at a high tension all through; this cannot be done for nothing.

The general cast of his mental powers was high in all the regions of mind. With a predominance of intellect, he had great power of will, and unusual depth of feeling. He had pre-eminently the sanguine temperament. Whenever the general system was in working order, enjoyment was with him the natural result. He was, I think, born for a happy life, if he had got only tolerably fair play. It was not the fault of nature that he was so often in the depths: his power of recovery attests the vital force of the system.

There can be little hesitation as to the specialities of his intellect. These were soon brought out by his early education, so far as books could do it.

Every species of literature was presented to his mind; and, while he imbibed something of all, it soon became evident that science was his forte. He had an intellect for the abstract and the logical, out of all proportion to his hold of the concrete and the poetical. His attempts at writing poetry could be little more than memory working upon the books that he had read, while their impression was fresh. He never attained to picturesqueness in the smallest degree; he could no doubt have succeeded by set purpose, but he had other matters to attend to. He was but moderately endowed with the faculty of language as such: the undoubted excellence of his mature style was arrived at by a series of efforts that may well be celebrated among triumphs of perseverance.

I think it perhaps a fortunate adjustment, to have possessed merely enough verbal power to give adequate expression to his thoughts, and not enough to make an artist to the extent occasionally realized even with great philosophers. That the thinking faculty, pure and simple, should have the predominating share of his intellectual force, was the condition of his peculiar subtlety as a thinker. Mill had not much memory for detail of any kind. He had read a vast quantity of history, of fiction, of travels and incidents; but you would not be aware of the fact from his conversation or from his writings. Neither in the illustration of doctrines, nor for figurative allusions, was he ready at reproducing facts in the concrete. He was, as a youth, well read in the Greek and Roman classics, but he scarcely ever made a happy original quotation. By express study, and frequent reference, he had amassed a store of facts bearing on political or sociological doctrines; and these he had at full command.

The enormous devotion of his early years to book study interfered with his activity as an observer of facts at first hand, whether in the physical, or in the mental world. He did, nevertheless, show a considerable wakefulness to what went on within his circle, yet with decided limitations. He could have imbibed physical facts with avidity, if his circumstances had been favourable; but his opportunities were very few. He was perhaps all the more disposed to notice mental and social facts; and it is wonderful how many of these he took hold of, in the remissions of book study. Of course, the larger mass of sociological details had to be gathered through books; yet a certain quantity of personal observation was needed as a basis for comprehending those that came by the other sources. His power of psychological observation was also good, and served him both as a theoretical psychologist, and as a practical philosopher, more especially in ethics, and in politics.

We come finally to the great distinguishing feature of such a mind as his: the rich storage of principles, doctrines, generalities of every degree, over several wide departments of knowledge. Principles had to be imbibed in copious draughts all through his education; the collision, combination, harmonizing, of these constitutes speculative insight, and conducts to original thinking. To read the productions of scientific men, to enter into the discussion of abstract themes with kindred minds, to excogitate and to reduce to writing new attempts at generalizing from the facts—such are the exercises of the discursive or scientific mind; and the natural avidity for those exercises is the test of the scientific endowment. Mill laid up in his capacious mind a variety of things; but, with all his getting, he got this special understanding—the understanding of principles. If you wanted, at any time, to commend yourself to his favourable regards, you had but to start a doctrinal discussion—to bring a new *logos* to his view.

With what success he plied his speculative faculty, what were the lines of his peculiar force, how far he rose above or fell below other speculators, his books alone will testify; and all of them have been freely and almost exhaustively criticized for those very questions. He is generally admitted to combine originality and clearness as only very few men have done. The attempts to undervalue his reputation on either head have met with little countenance. Tried by an absolute standard, he may be found defective at points; but who is entitled to cast the first stone? What other speculator from the beginning of philosophy has been equally original, and yet more uniformly precise, logical, and intelligible? He could split hairs with any scholastic. He could discern flaws in the closest dialectic; or turn the flank of the most circumspect disputant. Unless I am greatly deceived, time will not impair the fascination of that subtle intellect. The number of men that can handle such weapons can never be so great as to render his writings a superfluity; and, even when his doctrines shall have been more highly worked up, by other thinkers, his manner of putting them will be looked back upon with curious interest.

He himself speaks with not unbecoming pride of his being always open to new views. To the last, he continued (he says) to learn and to unlearn. Of no man can this be stated absolutely. Yet Mill stood very high on the point of receptiveness. He did not shut up his mind to new impressions at forty. This, however, was merely another form of his anxiety to know whatever could be said by any one upon any question. Wishing always to do his very best, he neglected no available means. Before beginning to produce, he took ample time to absorb; and, better than most men, hit the happy mean between haste and procrastination. He might have occasionally improved his work by a little more elaboration, but the loss in quantity would not have been compensated by the difference in quality.

I must still farther qualify Mill's claim to receptiveness, by adverting again to what I consider his greatest theoretical errors as a scientific thinker. The first is his doctrine of the natural equality of men. On this subject he was, in my opinion, blind to a whole region of facts. He inherited the mistake from his father, and could neither learn nor unlearn, in regard to it. The other error was perhaps less to be wondered at; I mean the disregard of the physical conditions of our mental life. He might have educated himself out of this error, but he never did. I do not mean to say that he made no allowances for the physical element of our being; my contention is, that he did not allow what every competent physiologist would now affirm to be the facts. I am afraid that, on both these errors, his feelings operated in giving his mind a bias. Whatever be the explanation, the effect was practically injurious.

It is now time to turn to the moral side of Mill's character. In what has been said on his intellect, moral and emotional elements have been assumed. The general impression made on the world by this part of his character has been highly favourable, on the whole. The generosity of his disposition manifested itself in many forms, and in high degrees; while it also had its limitations.

The entire total of the emotional aspect of human character comprehends the whole circle of sensibilities, tastes, likings, and the way that those are modified by sympathy and the sense of duty. These are the motives to action, and their relative strength and preponderance can be best judged by action or conduct. I said, with reference to James Mill, that intellect and will were dominant over feeling. Perhaps, of the son, we may say that there was a more nearly equal balance of all the three functions. The element of will, viewed apart from strength of motives—the pure spontaneous activity—was high in him too; without that he could not have been such a persistent worker. At the same time, I am disposed to believe that his superabundant energy and activity had its largest source in the strength of his feelings. I once made the remark to him, regarding the sources of energy of character, that these were either natural fulness of vigour, or else excitement through stimulation. He said, quickly, "There: stimulation is what people never sufficiently allow for." It is usually easy enough to determine which of the two sources is operative in any marked case. The extreme dependence on stimulation is shown by the tendency to total quiescence when motives are wanting. Mill no doubt had a good, but not excessive, spontaneity; and he had very large emotional susceptibilities that made him pre-eminently a worker. We are now to see what these were.

We need to dive into the depths of our emotional nature, to reach the main sources of his pleasures and the springs of his conduct. The tender feeling must in him have been very considerable. He was, throughout, affectionate, genial, kindly. After his first great physical crisis, when his activity and ambition no longer sufficed for his support, he had recourse to his tender susceptibilities, which had previously perhaps been cramped and confined, although not wholly dormant. He had not the sociable feeling in the form of large indiscrimate outpourings, and boundless capability of fellowship. A certain kindliness towards people in general, with a deep attachment to a few, was his peculiar mode; this, probably, took much less out of him—drew less upon his mental resources as a whole, than the other form of sociability. He formed few close friendships, and was absorbed very early by his one great attachment.

There is great difficulty in arriving at the precise degree of the fundamental or elementary emotions in almost any mind, still more in Mill, who, by training or culture, was a highly complex product. The remark is applicable to the tender feeling, viewed in its ultimate form; and even more to the other great source of human emotion—the malevolent or irascible feeling. Unless conspicuously present, or conspicuously absent, the amount of the feeling in the elementary shape can with difficulty be estimated in a character notable for growth, and for complication of impulses. In Mill, all the coarse, crude forms of angry passion were entirely wanting. He never got into a rage. His pleasures of malevolence, so far as existing, were of a very refined nature. Only in the punishment of offenders against his fellow-men, did he indulge revengeful sentiment. He could, on occasions, be very severe in his judgments and denunciations; but vulgar calumny, abuse, hatred for the mere sake of hatred, were completely crucified in him. He spent a large part of his life in polemics; and his treatment of opponents was a model of the ethics of controversy. The delight in victory was with him a genial, hearty chuckle, and no more.

Taking emotional and sensuous elements together, we may recount his chief tastes and diversions, irrespective of sympathy proper, which adds a new and all-important fact of character.

The love of scenery, in connection with touring excursions, was stimulated from an early date, and indulged in to the last. Whether he had a refined judgment of scenic effects, from an artist's point of view, I am unable to say. He did not become poetically inspired by nature, like Shelley or Wordsworth; perhpas he enjoyed it none the less. He made little use of his varied travels by allusions, or figures in his composition. His enjoyment of the concrete did not render his style much less abstract than it would have been although, like Kant, he had never left home.

His poetic tastes, as they revealed themselves after his great crisis, are beyond my powers to analyse or explain. Soon after I knew him, he endeavoured to make me interested in Wordsworth, and pointed out the poems that I should begin with; but his efforts were for the time unsuccessful. He seemed to look upon poetry as a religion, or rather as religion and philosophy in one. He took strongly to Tennyson, and was able to discern at once those beauties that the general world has since agreed upon; but his obtuseness to Shakespeare would suggest doubts as to his feeling for poetic effects of the kind that represent pure poetry, apart from either relgion or philosophy. I never could make sure whether the highest genius of style attracted him, without pointing some moral, or lending itself to a truth; yet, I found from one of his letters at a late period of his life, that he continued to read Carlyle with pleasure, after ceasing to care anything for his doctrinal views. His thorough mastery of the French language enabled him to enjoy the masterpieces of French prose.

He was absolutely without any feeling of rivalry, or jealousy of other men's success. His originality and fecundity of ideas would not have exempted him so completely from the dread of being anticipated in his discoveries, or baulked of his credit, had he not possessed a fund of generosity of character, for which sympathy is another name. He poured himself out in conversation, and his ideas were caught up and used, with or without acknowledgement; but he never disturbed himself one way or other. Of this part of his character, I can speak absolutely, and not by a figure of speech, under which we may turn a part into a whole. In other virtues, he had his limits, but in this he had none. Another point of conduct where his merits were absolute, had reference to fidelity in engagements, punctuality, and thorough reliableness, when he pledged his word. He never, to my knowledge, failed in any matter where people counted on him. I remember his having an important communication to make, by a given day, to the Women's Suffrage Committee. To obviate the possibility of miscarriage, he despatched a duplicate by a different channel. We must emphatically claim for him the merit of being, throughout his whole life a seeker for truth. To be found in error was no affront to his *amour propre*. He was not afraid to encounter an able opponent; simply because to change an opinion, under the force of new facts or reasonings, was not only not repugnant, it was welcome. His opinions were in marked opposition to his worldly interests, as his father's had been. He did not publicly avow his dissent from the orthodoxy of the country; but it was well enough known in a very wide private circle, and could be inferred from his published writings. He had long determined to throw off the mask entirely, when the time should be ripe for it. He intended, he said, to expend all the reputation he got by his books in upholding unpopular opinions; and was prevented from an earlier avowal of these, solely by the circumstance that the silent course of opinion was serving the interests of progress better than any violent shock, on his part would have done. Courage was a quality he was never deficient in; the reason being that he was ready to incur the sacrifice that it necessarily involves.

These aspects of his character properly connect themselves with the great central peculiarity of an ardent public spirit, contracted under his father's influence and fostered by his own natural dispositions. He is admitted on all hands to have had a pure and genuine love of his kind. It was the key to his life-long exertions; and had the very minimum of intermixture with purely personal ambition. He cordially sympathized with every form of improvement; and did whatever lay in him to aid the contrivers of new and beneficial schemes.

It is, then, to his zeal for the welfare of mankind, that we must refer the direction of his pursuits and the intensity of his labours. He knew what his own capabilities were, and placed them freely at the service of his fellow-beings, according to his best lights. Considering the high standard of excellence he had achieved, not simply in the invention, but also in the expression and elaboration, of his ideas, I am astonished at his avowals of sustained pleasure in writing. He used to say that the beginning of a work cost him a good deal of labour and pain; but when he was fairly launched, his enjoyment of the task predominated over the toil. His severe early training perhaps contributed to this rare and enviable endowment. He, more than once, to my recollection, after two or three months' touring in summer, retired to Avignon, to have a *holiday of work*; namely, to write a book.

I must now endeavour to point out what were the more conspicuous shortcomings of the generous or sympathetic side of Mill's nature. Had his judgment of the circumstances been perfect, the severity might have been right; but he at times assumed too readily his own infallibility, and condemned people accordingly. In the *Autobiography*, he recants the harshness of his judgment upon the radical leaders of the years following the Reform Bill; yet he does not apologize for his harsh language.

I think his habitual way of speaking of England, the English people, English society, as compared with other nations, was positively unjust, and served no good end. This remark occurs in the article on *The Claims of Labour*. "It is a just charge against the English nation, considered generally, that they do not know how to be kind, courteous, and considerate of the feelings of others. It is their character throughout Europe. They have much to learn from other nations in the arts not only of being serviceable and amiable with grace, but of being so at all."

The power of persuasion was with him not much a matter of mere style; it lay more in his command of thoughts, and in his tact in discerning what would suit the persons addressed. When he set himself to argue a point, his information and command of principles usually enabled him to exhaust his case. His political writing is enough to show this.

It was seldom that he was deficient in knowledge of his audience. If he ever failed here, it was in matters of religion, where he was necessarily little informed, and on the women question, where his feelings carried him too far. In the oratory of rhetoric, he was entirely wanting. He could appeal to men's feelings by suitable circumstances plainly and even forcibly stated; but that luxuriance of verbal display, whereby the emotions can be roused with a hurricane's might, was not a part of his equipment.

The powerful adjunct of wit was hardly within his reach, any more than rhetorical display in general. He had the sense of humour, but not a sufficient creative power to embody it in writing; and he was careful not to attempt what he could not do well.

I can account for his seeming hesitation of manner. Although he did not study grand and imposing talk, he always aimed at saying the right thing clearly and shortly. He was perfectly fluent, but yet would pause for an instant to get the best word, or the neatest collocation: and he also liked to finish with an epigrammatic turn.

His demeanour with reference to the other participants in the conversation was sufficiently marked. He never lectured or declaimed, or engrossed the talk. He paused at due intervals, to hear what the others had to say; and not merely heard, but took in, and embodied that in his reply. With him, talk was, what it ought to be, an exchange of information, thought, and argument, when it assumed the form of discussion; and an exchange of sympathies when the feelings were concerned.

It is mainly with reference to his conversation, that we are entitled to speak of him as possessing wit and humour. He had not sufficient originality of style to yield literary effects worthy of being printed; but, like many other people having the same limitations, he had more than enough to be entertaining and genial in society and in talk. For the same reason that wit fails to display itself in his books, he did not produce many quotable sayings; having so little love of display, he did not make any efforts in this direction.

Alexander Bain

IV
THE NATURE AND ROLE OF ORIGINALITY IN SCIENTIFIC PROGRESS

John Stuart Mill is now considered a mediocre economist of unusual literary power; a fluent, flabby echo of Ricardo. This judgment is well-nigh universal: I do not believe that Mill has had a fervent admirer in the twentieth century.

I attribute this low reputation to the fact that Mill had the perspective and balance, but not the full powers, of Smith and Marshall. He avoided all the tactics of easy success. He wrote with extraordinary balance, and his own ideas—considering their importance—received unbelievably little emphasis. The bland prose moved sedately over a corpus of knowledge organized with due regard to structure and significance, and hardly at all with regard to parentage.

One must search carefully in Mill's *Principles* to discover his own ideas. The only one of which he boasts—the immutability of the laws of production as against the social plasticity of the laws of distribution—is at least unhappy. The rest receive no fanfare: Mill devoted some seven pages to summarizing the work of John Rae on capital acccumulation and one paragraph to his own important idea of non-competing groups.

Yet however one judges Mill, it cannot be denied that he was original. In terms of identifiable theories, he was one of the most original economists in the history of the science. I shall list his major contributions, each of which was at least as original to him as any important theory is to the person with whom it is chiefly associated. The list is restricted to value theory—although we must remember that what shreds of originality Mill is commonly credited with were in international trade theory—because I can be more confident of the priorities.

1. *Non-competing groups.* "So complete, indeed, has hitherto been the separation, so strongly marked the line of demarcation, between the different grades of labourers, as to be almost equivalent to an hereditary distinction of caste; each employment being chiefly recruited from the children of those already employed in it, or in employments of the same rank with it in social estimation, or from the children of persons who, if originally on a lower rank, have succeeded in raising themselves by their exertions."

Smith's illustrious discussion of differences in wages was limited to differences consistent with full occupational mobility of the labour force in the long run. Mill made the first major advance beyond this theory by his recognition of the barriers to mobility erected by the costs of education.

2. *Joint products.* Mill clearly formulated the problem of joint production—that is, production of two or more products in fixed proportions. He gave the complete and correct solution: the sum of the prices of the products must equal their joint cost, and the price of each product is determined by the equality in equilibrium of quantity supplied and quantity demanded.

3. *Alternative costs.* "Land is used for other purposes than agriculture, especially for residence; and when so used, yields a rent, determined by principles similar to those already laid down. The ground rent of a building, and the rent of a garden or park attached to it, will not be less than the rent which the same land would afford in agriculture.

"But when land capable of yielding rent in agriculture is applied to some other purpose, the rent which it would have yielded is an element of the cost of production of the commodity which it is employed to produce."

This was a frank and clear recognition of the fact that rent is a cost of production even from the social viewpoint when land has alternative uses. Marshall was unwilling to depart thus far from Ricardian theory.

4. *The economics of the firm.* Mill's chapter (Book 1, chapter 9), "Of production on a large, and production on a small, scale", is the first systematic discussion of the economies of scale of the firm to be found in a general economic treatise. It would take us afield to analyse this chapter in detail, but we may point out that Mill was the first economist to notice that one can deduce information on the costs of firms of different sizes from their varying fortunes through time.

5. *Supply and demand.* Mill introduced into English economics the concept of demand as a schedule or function, and hence was able to state the "law of supply and demand" clearly and with substantial accuracy: "Demand and supply, the quantity demanded and the quantity supplied, will be made equal. If unequal at any moment, competition equalizes them, and the manner in which this is done is by an adjustment of the value. If the demand increases, the value rises; if the demand diminishes, the value falls: again, if the supply falls off, the value rises, and falls if the supply is increased. The value which a commodity will bring in any market is no other than the value which, in that market, gives a demand just sufficient to carry off the existing or expected supply."

This is, to be sure, very obvious once announced, but its explicit development was a highly useful addition to the Ricardian economics. Mill used the apparatus very competently in dealing with Thornton's absurd objections to the "law." (I do not assert that Mill's discussion was superior to all earlier discussion; Cournot in particular was more precise.)

6. *Say's Law.* Mill's discussion of the limitation to the proposition that there cannot be an overproduction of all commodities was penetrating as well as original:

"This argument is evidently founded on the supposition of a state of barter; and, on that supposition, it is perfectly incontestable.

"If, however, we suppose that money is used, these propositions cease to be exactly true.

"Interchange by means of money is therefore, as has been often observed, ultimately nothing but barter. But there is this difference—that in the case of barter, the selling and the buying are simultaneously confounded in one operation; you sell what you have and buy what you want, by one indivisible act, and you cannot do the one without doing the other. Now the effect of the employment of money, and even the utility of it, is, that it enables this one act of interchange to be divided into two separate acts or operations, one of which may be performed now, and the other a year hence, or whenever it shall be most convenient."

"It follows that at a given time people may wish to hasten sales and to postpone purchases, and this is then a period of 'general excess'.

"In order to render the argument for the impossibility of an excess of all commodities applicable to the case in which a circulating medium is employed, money must itself be considered as a commodity. It must, undoubtedly, be admitted that there cannot be an excess of all other commodities, and an excess of money at the same time."

Say's Law therefore is not inconsistent with the existence of periods of general excess and general deficiency, which arise out of the "unreasonable hopes and unreasonable fears [which] alternately rule with tyrannical sway over the minds of a majority of the mercantile public". Is this essay, written about 1830, the work of an unoriginal mind?

This is a very respectable list of contributions. But it is also a peculiar list: any one of the contributions could be made independently of all the others. Mill was not trying to build a new system but only to add improvements here and there to the Ricardian system. The fairest of economists, as Schumpeter has properly characterized Mill, unselfishly dedicated his abilities to the advancement of the science. And, yet, Mill's magisterial quality and conciliatory tone may have served less well than sharp and opinionated controversy in inciting his contemporaries to make advances.

George Joseph Stigler

SOURCES

Essays I and II

John Stuart Mill, *Autobiography*, 2nd ed. (O.U.P., London, 1924). Extracts. Supplemented with a passage on his death from M. St. J. Packe, *The Life of John Stuart Mill* (Secker and Warburg, London, 1954).

Essay III

Alexander Bain, *John Stuart Mill, a Criticism: with Personal Recollections* (Longmans, Green, and Co., London, 1882), chapter 5, "Character and influence". Abridged.

Essay IV

George Joseph Stigler, "The nature and role of originality in scientific progress", *Economica*, 22 (1955), Part 3, "The case of Mill".

Signature

British Museum.

Portrait

Portrait by G. F. Watts (National Portrait Gallery, London).

BIBLIOGRAPHY

M. D. Conway, *A Memorial Discourse in Honour of John Stuart Mill* (London, 1873).

H. Spencer *et al., John Stuart Mill, His Life and His Work, Twelve Sketches* (New York, 1873).

H. R. F. Bourne (ed.), *John Stuart Mill—Notices of His Life and His Works* (London, 1873).

W. L. Courtney, *The Life of John Stuart Mill* (New York, 1889).

Ch. Douglas, *John Stuart Mill* (Edinburgh and London, 1895).

L. Stephen, "John Stuart Mill", in *The English Utilitarians*, Vol. 3 (London, 1900).

S. Saenger, *John Stuart Mill, sein Leben und sein Werk* (Stuttgart, 1901).

E. Thouverez, *John Stuart Mill* (Paris, 1906).

L. P. Rey, *Le Roman de John Stuart Mill* (Paris, 1913).

J. West, *John Stuart Mill* (London, 1913).

H. Waentig, "John Stuart Mill", biographical preface to J. St. Mill, *Grundsätze der politischen Ökonomie,* 2nd ed. Vol. I (Jena, 1924).

M. A. Hamilton, *John Stuart Mill* (London, 1933).

F. A. von Hayek (ed.), *John Stuart Mill and Harriet Taylor. Their Friendship and Subsequent Marriage* (London and Chicago, 1951).

K. Britton, *John Stuart Mill* (London, 1953).

B. Russell, "John Stuart Mill", *Proceedings of the British Academy*, 41 (1955).

R. Borchard, *John Stuart Mill* (London, 1957).

M. Cranston, *John Stuart Mill* (London, New York and Toronto, 1958).

J. C. Rees, "John Stuart Mill, political contributions", in *International Encyclopedia of the Social Sciences*, Vol. 10 (New York, 1968).

V. W. Bladen, "John Stuart Mill, economic contributions", in *International Encyclopedia of the Social Sciences,* Vol. 10 (New York, 1968).

HERMANN HEINRICH GOSSEN

1810–1858

You yourself have realized how essential it is for the progress of the social sciences that the man should be known as well as his work and you have, consequently told the world what little it knows about Gossen.

From a letter of H. L. MOORE *to* L. WALRAS

He was a man of but one idea; but that was an immortal one. F. Y. EDGEWORTH

Was einem Kopernikus *zur Erklärung des Zusammenseins der Welten im Raum zu leisten gelang, das glaube ich für die Erklärung des Zusammenseins der Menschen auf der Erdoberfläche zu leisten. Ich glaube, daß es mir gelungen ist, die Kraft und in großen Umrissen das Gesetz ihrer Wirksamkeit zu entdecken, welche das Zusammensein der Menschen möglich macht und die Fortbildung des Menschengeschlechts unaufhaltsam bewirkt. Und wie die Entdeckungen jenes Mannes es möglich machten, die Bahnen der Weltkörper auf unbeschränkte Zeit zu bestimmen, so glaube ich mich durch meine Entdeckungen in den Stand gesetzt, dem Menschen mit untrüglicher Sicherheit die Bahn zu bezeichnen, die er zu wandeln hat, um seinen Lebenszweck in vollkommenster Weise zu erreichen.*

H. H. GOSSEN

Heinrich Gossen is one of the most tragic figures in the history of economics. He was a profound, original, and untrained thinker who did his thoughts behind painfully complex arithmetical and algebraic exercises. He displayed every trait of the crank, excepting only one: history has so far believed that he was right. Only a person who has laboured through the volume can savour the magnificent understatement of Edgeworth: "He may seem somewhat deficient in the quality of mathematical elegance."

G. J. STIGLER

I
HERMANN HEINRICH GOSSEN: AN UNKNOWN ECONOMIST

Gossen claimed the glory of Copernicus, which is due to him because of his concept of the mathematical equilibrium of the economic world. In my opinion he combines the glory of Copernicus with that of Newton because of his solution of the social question. Nothing else I could say would express my opinion of his merits.

I was much disturbed by the thought that a book such as his could pass unnoticed in a country such as Germany, where scientific work is claimed to be organized so efficiently that no ideas can get lost. I know that mankind, just as nature, progresses in a dreadfully wasteful manner. I have often said to myself that there are Copernicuses and Newtons who perish in their germinal stage or in their flower. But to see with my own eyes, and to hold in my hands, a great book, which had cost its author years of meditation and study and which had almost fallen into eternal oblivion—for this I was not prepared. I decided to obtain information concerning Gossen's life and to hold up his name for all the world to see. To obtain information on a man who had once been a Prussian official did not seem extremely difficult. But, nevertheless, three years had to pass from the moment when I heard of Gossen for the first time, before I was in the position to prepare this note.

Lausanne being a place where many foreigners reside, among them some of distinction, I did not have much trouble in finding someone in a position to make inquiries with the Prussian administration. In February 1879, when I had just prepared with the help of Mr Charles Secrétan the French translation of Gossen's book, I managed to find useful channels for the expression of my desire to obtain detailed information on the administrative and scientific career of the author by observing that a relative of Gossen's, if there was one anywhere, could doubtless furnish me with this. At the end of only one year I received a note letting me know that Gossen had died, at age 47, in Cologne on 13 February, 1858, and that he had left a sister, mother of Dr Hermann Kortum, Professor of Mathematics at the University of Bonn. In the possession of this name, I addressed myself to Professor Kortum on 21 February 1880. He immediately promised to fulfil my wishes; but not until 29 July 1881, when he had completed the necessary investigations among the papers of his uncle, did he send me the following information.

Hermann Heinrich Gossen was born on 7 September 1810 in the city of Düren, located halfway between Aix-la-Chapelle and Cologne, at that time under French rule and part of the Ruhr district. His father, of German nationality, was a tax collector in the service of the French government. After the fall of the French empire he was transferred, in the same position, to the Prussian government. In 1824 he gave up his job and went to Cologne, later to Muffendorf, near Bonn, and devoted himself to an agricultural enterprise. There Gossen obtained his early education, with his mathematical inclination soon becoming apparent. In the autumn of 1829, after having graduated, he entered the University of Bonn with the view of preparing himself, in accordance with the wishes of his father, for a career in public administration.

In February 1834, he underwent the first state examination. One of the reports written for this purpose had as subject "the comparative value of direct and indirect taxes from the point of view of the public credit". Gossen treated this question thoroughly, not historically but with the help of the theoretical method, which was to remain his characteristic. He was then appointed "referendary" at Cologne. Not only lacking the inclination for administrative duties but feeling aversion to such a career, he attempted, though in vain, to obtain from his father the permission and the means to spend two more years at the university in order to prepare himself for some other profession. He did not go through his second state examination until 1841, and in July 1844, was appointed "assessor" at Magdeburg, later at Erfurt. In 1847, after the death of his father, he quit the government service and went to Berlin. A liberal in politics, and already at that time occupied with social questions, he witnessed the revolution of 1848 with interest and sympathy but without taking any active part in it.

He then became acquainted with a Belgian who intended to found a general insurance company. Gossen associated himself with this project and took charge of hail and livestock insurance in Cologne in 1849. At that time he prepared with much care and effort the plan for a "General German Savings Bank" designed to do life-insurance business. But after the hail and livestock insurance failed to show good results, he withdrew from it in 1850 in order not to lose too much of his investment.

These various enterprises had supplied confirmation and precision to his economic ideas. He felt moved to present them in systematic form, and from 1850 to 1854 devoted himself entirely to this pursuit, living in Cologne in seclusion except for the company of his two sisters. He attached great importance to his work and placed high hopes on its publication. But the mathematical form—which was its original feature—prevented it from making any sort of impression, and even from being read by more than a few persons.

The lack of success, combined with poor health, darkened the last few years of Gossen's life. His health, which had been vigorous before, was ruined by a severe attack of typhoid fever in 1853. Soon there became apparent the first symptoms of tuberculosis of the lungs. The rapid aggravation of this disease prevented Gossen from establishing himself in a new position and confined him to seclusion. As he was a musician and violinist, he found some diversion in music and took up the serious study of its mathematical theory. Attended by his sisters with affectionate care, he died on 13 February 1858, a man of idealistic and optimistic tendencies, lacking in practical sense and with little concern about his personal interests, very kindhearted and amiable, full of frankness, sincerity, and probity, naïve in demeanour and childlike, as it were, of a nature which opened him all hearts.

For my part I will go farther than Jevons and state that, among the numerous examples of scientific injustice, there is none more grave than the ingratitude shown to Gossen. This man, in my opinion one of the most remarkable economists who have ever lived, made his way completely unnoticed. My aim here is not to say everything that should be said about his work and career, but only to make known what I know of him, to put those on their way who later on will do justice to this great, hidden talent in a manner worthy of him.

On 15 September 1878, Mr Jevons wrote to me: "The question[1] becomes more complicated because of the discovery of a work, published in Brunswick in 1854, which contains some of the principal points of our theory in a clearly elucidated form. It is by Hermann Heinrich Gossen, and its title reads about like this: *Entwickelung der Gesetze des menschlichen Verkehrs*. This work seems to be entirely unknown even in Germany; and since I don't read German, I was absolutely ignorant of its existence.

"Gossen evidently held the highest possible opinion of the importance of his own theory, for he commences by claiming honours in economic science equal to those of Copernicus in astronomy. He then at once insists that mathematical treatment, being the only sound one, must be applied throughout: but, out of consideration for the reader, the higher analysis will be explicitly introduced only when it is requisite to determine maxima and minima. The treatise then opens with the consideration of economics as the theory of pleasure and pain, that is as the theory of the procedure by which the individual and the aggregate of individuals constituting society, may realize the maximum of pleasure with the minimum of painful effort. The natural law of pleasure is then clearly stated, somewhat as follows: 'Increase of the same kind of consumption yields pleasure continuously diminishing up to the point of satiety.' This law he illustrates geometrically, and then proceeds to investigate the conditions under which the total pleasure from one or more objects may be raised to a maximum.

[1] The joint search for the forerunners of marginal utility theory.

"The term *Werth* is next introduced, which may, Professor Adamson thinks, be rendered with strict accuracy, as *utility*, and Gossen points out that the quantity of utility, material or immaterial, is measured by the quantity of pleasure which it affords. He classifies useful objects as, (1) those which possess pleasure-giving powers in themselves; (2) those which only possess such powers when in combination with other objects; (3) those which only serve as means toward the production of pleasure-giving objects. He is careful to point out that there is no such thing as absolute utility, utility being purely a relation between a thing and a person. He next proceeds to give the derivative laws of utility somewhat in the following manner: That separate portions of the same pleasure-giving object have very different degrees of utility, and that in general for each person only a limited number of such portions has utility; any addition beyond this limit is useless, but the point of uselessness is only reached after the utility has gone through all the stages or degrees of intensity. Hence he draws the practical conclusion that each person should so distribute his resources as to render the final increments of each pleasure-giving commodity of equal utility for him.

"In the next place Gossen deals with labour, starting from the proposition that the utility of any product must be estimated after deduction of the pains of labour required to produce it. He describes the variation of the pain of labour much as I have done, exhibiting it graphically, and inferring that we must carry on labour to the point at which the utility of the product equals the pain of production. In treating the theory of exchange he shows how barter gives rise to an immense increase of utility, and he infers that exchange will proceed up to the point at which the utilities of the portions next to be given and received are equal. A complicated geometrical representation of the theory of exchange is given. The theory of rent is investigated in a most general manner, and the work concludes with somewhat vague social speculations, which, in Professor Adamson's opinion, are of inferior merit compared with the earlier portions of the treatise."

This résumé probably does not tell much to those who are not acquainted with the problem. But to those who have read my first memoir and Mr Jevons's work, the preceding paragraphs will immediately indicate that Gossen has given mathematical expression to utility and has established a mathematical condition of maximum satisfaction before this was done by myself and Mr Jevons. Indeed, Mr Jevons, when yielding to Gossen, does so with no more hesitation and ado than shown by myself when I yielded to him. He censures Gossen for using straight lines in his diagrams instead of undetermined curves, and he states that Gossen has not reached the equations of exchange. But, taken all in all, he recognizes that his own theory, although its loses nothing of its importance, is by no means as completely novel as he had believed, and he restricts himself to protesting that, at the time of his writing, he did not know of Gossen nor of his work —an existence then so little known to the whole world that it was more difficult to uncover it than to uncover the theory of pleasure and pain.

"Almost nothing", he says in conclusion, "is known to me concerning Gossen; it is uncertain whether he is living or not. On the title-page he describes himself as *Königlich preussischer Regierungs-Assessor ausser Dienst*, which may be translated 'Royal Prussian Government Assessor, retired'; but the tone of his remarks here and there seems to indicate that he was a disappointed if not an injured man. The reception of his one work can have lent no relief to these feelings; rather it must have much deepened them. The book seems to have contained his one cherished theory; for I can find under the name of Gossen no trace of any other publication or scientific memoir whatever. The history of these forgotten works is, indeed, a strange and discouraging one; but the day must come when the eyes of those who cannot see will be opened. Then will due honour be given to all who like Cournot and Gossen have laboured in a thankless field of human knowledge, and have met with the neglect or ridicule they might well have expected. Not indeed that such men do really work for the sake of honour; they bring forth a theory as the tree brings forth its fruit."

Most certainly, the true scientist pursues truth only because of the pleasure of this pursuit, just as the genuine amateur of whist plays this noble game only because of the pleasure conveyed thereby. There is no need to emphasize that the search and discovery of theories such as those relating mathematics to various sciences exert an attraction incomparably greater than that exerted by any sort of game. But, just as it is legitimate to take a chance with small amounts of money while playing whist, so it is permitted, in the pursuit of scientific truth, to derive additional satisfaction from the thought that one is going to attach one's name to an important result. The very greatest men of science have not felt disdain for this feeling of satisfaction. Remember that those who were ingenious enough to invent the infinitesimal calculus were not free enough from self-love to share in propriety the honour of this invention. Nor was Gossen above this sentiment, and Mr Jevons confesses in all sincerity that he has felt it. I myself have no pretension at all of being above human weaknesses and ordinarily play whist for chips. So I will confess that on receiving Mr Jevons's letter of 15 September 1878, that is, a year before I was to read the preface to the second edition of his *Theory of Political Economy*, I was much disturbed and a bit worried about what would remain as my own after all the sucessively evolving priority claims had been satisfied.

The first thing to do was to search for a copy of Gossen's work, and I had much trouble obtaining one. Vieweg and Son, the publishers in Brunswick, informed me that Gossen had lived in Cologne around 1850, and that they had returned to him at that time, and on his request, all remaining copies of his work, "which was only an article of commission". While inquiring about the book with the publishers, I also addressed myself to various public libraries. Finally Mr Halm, librarian in Munich, sent it to Mr Charles Secrétan, his son-in-law and my colleague and friend. Together with him I read it with much attention during the first weeks of 1879, and made a complete translation.

It forms a volume of 277 pages of text, preceded by a preface of four pages, and is not divided into parts or chapters. A simple dash line, without heading, separates the various subjects treated successively by the author. Altogether this absence of divisions does no harm to the organization of the book, which in a natural manner falls into two parts of approximately equal length. The first part, devoted to pure theory, comprises the "laws of enjoyment and of work", with discussion and arithmetical tables, the "laws of exchange", and the "theory of rent". The other part, devoted to applied theory, comprises "rules of conduct pertaining to desires and pleasures", and the refutation of certain common errors concerning "education", "money", "credit", and "property". For each of his subjects the author provides a plan of organization. He is a strict utilitarian and liberal, that is, he is strongly opposed to government intervention, especially under conditions when individual initiative and free competition suffice as guiding principles of the economic order. The style is quite German, that is, somewhat diffuse and redundant. But the development of the ideas is always perfectly logical and clear.

Marie Esprit Léon Walras

II
THE WORK OF HERMANN HEINRICH GOSSEN AND ITS CONCEPT

The reader of the *Entwicklung* can see how summary and insufficient is our general conception of Gossen and his work. It has an importance, or rather, he believed it had an importance, going far beyond the abstract laws which carry his name. One must, I think, distinguish between at least four different Gossens:

1. *Gossen the prophet:* more or less inspired by God like so many others, with the mission, so it seems, of making known to humanity the important "truths": a strange religion this, however, made up of pure egoism.

2. *Gossen the Utopian:* seeking, again like so many others, happiness for mankind; an ultra-liberal, apparently not much in favour of inheritance of property, as contrary to individual egoism; but, from a realistic point of view, the projects he proposes are ridiculously out of proportion to the end he aims at, being badly thought out and impossible of application. If I remember rightly, it was on the subject of Fourier that Pareto, in his *Systèmes Socialistes*, writes: "He is like a man who harnesses a goat to a heavy goods-train". This could equally apply to Gossen.

3. *Gossen the economist:* here there are perhaps more things to bear in mind —von Hayek, for example, thinks his view on money interesting and modern; as a theoretical economist, however, he extracted little from the laws he laid down; what he says on prices is extremely insufficient and essentially debatable; nor had he any theory of capital or interest. The same man who believed that he was heralding a revolution bringing happiness to mankind, failed to understand the revolutionary consequences of the principles he formulated, in the realm of pure science, or at least to take an interest in them. Questions fundamentally affecting his own viewpoint, that is to say, concerning human well-being, are not even mentioned: that of population, for example, which is inadmissible. He also looks for economic welfare in objective satisfications, and deceives himself like others, in forgetting man's capacity to get accustomed to an increase in his standard of living.

For all these reasons, no comparison is possible between him, on the one hand, and his great successors, Jevons, Menger and Walras; we can only think of him as their forerunner.

4. *Gossen the psychologist of theoretical economics:* From this point of view, it was not only as the predecessor of these three illustrious economists that he appeared, but very much as their superior: Jevons recognized this in so far as it concerned him, while it is self-evident for Walras and Menger since they never envisaged disutility. It is undoubtedly possible to level certain technical criticism at him, but, for my part, I consider this to be of no particular importance. One can also make the point that Gossen's "first" law had already been foreshadowed—formulated even—more than once, before him. This "first" law, however, only derives its fame from association with the second law, for which he has no predecessor; at the most it could be said that Fr Ferrara had anticipated the existence of something of this kind. In Gossen the foundations of the modern theory of value are securely laid and more profoundly than in the above-named three economists. He left us forty-odd immortal pages on this theory, and it is a pity that, in dying, he had no idea, I fear, of the immense success which one part of his views was going to have, on being rediscovered later on by others.

True, it is doubtful whether this would have satisfied him, as his ambitions were so much greater. He would have liked the whole of his work to be of interest and, on this score, very little or, more precisely, nothing has been done for a century.

Gossen's thought is little known; amongst the works about him which I know of, none has covered all his work in its totality, as he wanted it to be presented to us. It has always been enough, in short, to study Gossen for his bearing on the history of economic science, in the strict sense of the term. The only way in which anyone wanted to see him was as the forerunner, albeit a remarkable forerunner, of the theories of marginal utility.

But, apart from that, there is the history of economic thought in a larger sense. I, for my part, find that much less interesting, but, when one thinks of the number of studies published by so many economists or sociologists on normative thought and on the general system, one can only conclude that Gossen has been too neglected. It is three-quarters of a century since Walras published his article entitled "Un économiste inconnu, H. H. Gossen"; and that title still holds good.

The reason is that Gossen's book is a forbidding one and basically unreadable. At the same time, it is not too early to advance the claim that Gossen's work, considered, as attempted here, from a synthetic point of view, is highly original and important; it deserves to be examined on its own account. I will not go so far as to say that Gossen was the greatest German economist of the nineteenth century—this title belongs to von Thünen—but Gossen seems to me to come immediately after him, that is to say, in the front rank, from the point of view of his originality.

Georges-Henri Bousquet

SOURCES

Essay I

Marie Esprit Léon Walras, "Un économiste inconnu, Hermann Heinrich Gossen", *Journal des économistes*, 4. série, 30 (1885). Abridged.

Essay II

Georges-Henri Bousquet, "Un Contenaire: l'oeuvre de Hermann Heinrich Gossen (1810–1858) et sa véritable structure", *Révue d'économie politique*, 68 (1958), section "Considérations finales".

Signature

Alexander von Humboldt--Universität, Berlin.

BIBLIOGRAPHY

F. Y. Edgeworth, "Hermann Heinrich Gossen", in R. H. Palgrave, *Dictionary of Political Economy*, Vol. 2 (London, 1896).

O. Kraus, "Hermann Heinrich Gossen", in *Allgemeine deutsche Biographie*, Vol. 55 (Leipzig, 1910).

G. Beyerhaus, "Hermann Heinrich Gossen und seine Zeit", *Zeitschrift für Volkswirtschaft und Sozialpolitik*, N.F., 5 (1926).

F. A. von Hayek (ed.), "Einführung", in Hermann Heinrich Gossen, *Die Entwicklung der Gesetze des menschlichen Verkehrs und der daraus fließenden Regeln für menschliches Handeln*, 3rd repr. (Braunschweig, 1927).

O. Weinberger, "Hermann Heinrich Gossen", *Schmollers Jahrbuch*, 51 (1927).

F. A. v. Hayek, "Hermann Heinrich Gossen", in *Encyclopaedia of the Social Sciences*, Vol. 7 (New York, 1932).

F. Behrens, *Hermann Heinrich Gossen* (Leipzig, 1949).

H. Riedle, *Hermann Heinrich Gossen 1810–1858: Ein Wegbereiter der modernen ökonomischen Theorie* (Winterthur, 1953).

T. Bagiotti, "Nel centennale del libro di Gossen", *Giornale degli economisti e annali di economia,* 14 (1955).

T. Bagiotti, "Reminiszensen anläßlich des hundertsten Jahrestages des Erscheinens des Buches von Gossen", *Zeitschrift für Nationalökonomie*, 12 (1957).

H. W. Spiegel, "Hermann Heinrich Gossen", in *International Encyclopaedia of the Social Sciences*, Vol. 6 (New York, 1968).

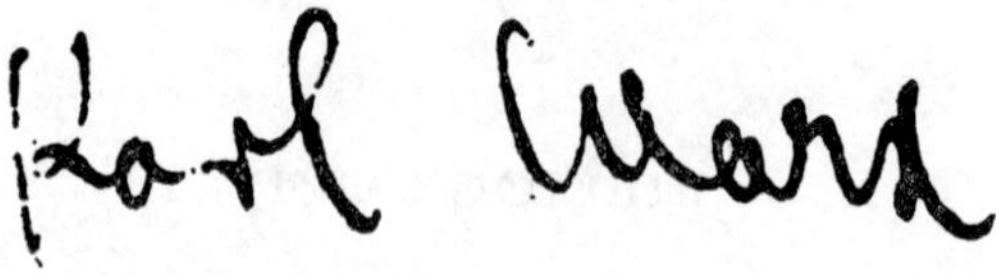

KARL MARX

1818–1883

Wir können nicht immer den Stand ergreifen, zu dem wir uns berufen glauben, unsere Verhältnisse in der Gesellschaft haben einigermaßen schon begonnen, ehe wir sie zu bestimmen imstande sind. K. MARX

He was by temperament a theorist and an intellectual, and instinctively avoided direct contact with the masses, to the studies of whose interests his entire life was devoted. To many of his followers he appeared in the role of a dogmatic and sententious German schoolmaster, prepared to repeat his theses indefinitely with rising sharpness, until their essence became irremovably lodged in his disciples' minds. I. BERLIN

Karl Marx ist als Schriftsteller ein beneidenswert glücklicher Mann gewesen. Niemand wird behaupten wollen, daß sein Werk zu den leicht lesbaren und leicht verständlichen Büchern gehört . . Marx ist trotzdem ein Apostel für weiteste Kreise und gerade für solche Kreise geworden, deren Sache sonst die Lektüre schwieriger Bücher nicht ist. Dabei waren seine dialektischen Argumentationen durchaus nicht etwa von einer fraglos bezwingenden Kraft und Klarheit . . . Es hätte dem Marxschen Werke somit leicht begegnen können, daß es bei keinem Teil des Publikums eine gute Stätte gefunden hätte: bei dem großen Publikum nicht, weil es sich auf seine schwierige Dialektik überhaupt nicht verstand, und bei den Fachleuten nicht, weil sie sich auf dieselbe und auf ihre Schwächen zu gut verstanden. Tatsächlich ist es anders gekommen. E. VON BÖHM-BAWERK

From the viewpoint of pure economic theory, Karl Marx can be regarded as a minor post-Ricardian . . . Political Economy in our sense of the word was the mere cap of Karl Marx's iceberg. Marx's bold economic or materialistic theory of history, his political theories of the class struggle, his transmutations of Hegelian philosophy have an importance for the historian of "ideas" that far transcends his façade of economics. P. A. SAMUELSON

I
KARL MARX: HIS LIFE AND ENVIRONMENT

No thinker in the nineteenth century has had so direct, deliberate and powerful an influence upon mankind as Karl Marx. Both during his lifetime and after it he exercised an intellectual and moral ascendancy over his followers, the strength of which was unique even in that golden age of democratic nationalism, an age which saw the rise of great popular heroes and martyrs, romantic, almost legendary figures, whose lives and words dominated the imagination of the masses and created a new revolutionary tradition in Europe. Yet Marx could not, at any time, be called a popular figure in the ordinary sense: certainly he was in no sense a popular writer or orator. He wrote extensively, but his works were not, during his lifetime, read widely; and when, in the late 'seventies, they began to reach the immense public which several among them afterwards obtained, the desire to read them was due not so much to a recognition of their intrinsic qualities as to the growth of the fame and notoriety of the movement with which he was identified.

Marx totally lacked the qualities of a great popular leader or agitator, was not a publicist of genius like the Russian democrat Alexander Herzen, nor did he possess Bakunin's marvellous eloquence; the greater part of his working life was spent in comparative obscurity in London, at his writing-desk and in the reading-room of the British Museum. He was little known to the general public, and while towards the end of his life he became the recognized, and admired, leader of a powerful international movement, nothing in his life or character stirred the imagination or evoked the boundless devotion, the intense, almost religious, worship, with which such men as Kossuth, Mazzini, and even Lassalle in his last years, were regarded by their followers.

His public appearances were neither frequent nor notably successful. On the few occasions on which he addressed banquets or public meetings, his speeches were overloaded with matter, and delivered with a combination of monotony and brusqueness, which commanded the respect but not the enthusiasm of his audience. He was by temperament a theorist and an intellectual, and instinctively avoided direct contact with the masses, to the study of whose interests his entire life was devoted. To many of his followers he appeared in the role of a dogmatic and sententious German schoolmaster, prepared to repeat his theses indefinitely, with rising sharpness, until their essence became irremovably lodged in his disciples' minds. The greater part of his economic teaching was given its first expression in lectures to working men: his exposition under these circumstances was by all accounts a model of lucidity and conciseness. But he wrote slowly and painfully, as sometimes happens with rapid and fertile thinkers, scarcely able to cope with the speed of their own ideas, impatient at once to communicate a new doctrine, and to forestall every possible objection; the published versions were generally turgid, clumsy and obscure in detail, although the central doctrine is never in serious doubt.

Karl Heinrich Marx, eldest son of Heinrich and Henrietta Marx, was born on 5 May 1818 in Trier, in the German Rhineland, where his father practised as a lawyer.

The elder Marx was a simple, serious, well-educated man, but he was neither conspicuously intelligent nor abnormally sensitive. A disciple of Leibniz and Voltaire, Lessing and Kant, he possessed in addition a gentle, timid and accommodating temper, and ultimately became a passionate Prussian patriot and monarchist, a position which he sought to justify by pointing to the figure of Frederick the Great—a tolerant and enlightened prince who compared favourably with Napoleon, with his notorious contempt for ideologists. After his baptism he adopted the Christian name of Heinrich, and educated his family as liberal protestants, faithful to the existing order and to the reigning King of Prussia.

His father had early become aware that while his other children were in no way remarkable, in Karl he had an unusual and difficult son; with a sharp and lucid intelligence he combined a stubborn and domineering temper, a truculent love of independence, exceptional emotional restraint, and over all a colossal, ungovernable intellectual appetite. In spite of growing uneasiness about his character and career, Heinrich Marx treated his son with an instinctive delicacy, and never attempted to oppose or bully him on any serious issue. Consequently their relations continued to be warm, intimate and grave until the death of the older Marx in 1838.

It seems certain that the father had a definite influence on his son's intellectual development. The elder Marx believed with Condorcet that man is by nature both good and rational, and that all that is needed to ensure the triumph of these qualities is the removal of unnatural obstacles from his path.

His own history seemed to him to corroborate this triumphantly. Born a Jew, a citizen of inferior legal and social status, he had attained to equality with his more enlightened neighbours, had earned their respect as a human being, and had become assimilated into what appeared to him as their more rational and dignified mode of life. He believed that a new day was dawning in the history of human emancipation, in the light of which his children would live their lives as free-born citizens in a just and liberal state. Elements of this belief are clearly apparent in his son's social doctrine.

Karl Marx did not, indeed, believe in the power of rational argument to influence action, but there is, nevertheless, a definite sense in which he remained both a rationalist and a perfectibilian to the end of his life. He believed in the complete intelligibility of the process of social evolution; he believed that society is inevitably progressive, that its movement from stage to stage is a forward movement, that each successive stage represents development, is nearer the rational ideal than its precursors. He detested, as passionately as any eighteenth-century thinker, emotionalism, belief in supernatural causes, visionary fantasy of every kind, and systematically under-estimated the influence of such non-rational forces as nationalism, and religious and racial solidarity. Although, therefore, it remains true that the Hegelian philosophy is the greatest single formative influence in his life, the principles of philosophical rationalism which were planted in him by his father and his father's friends, performed a definite work of inoculation, so that when later he encountered the romantic metaphysical systems developed by the romantic school, he was saved from that total surrender to their fascination which undid so many of his contemporaries.

Little is known of his childhood and early years in Trier. His mother played a singularly small part in his life; Henrietta Philips belonged to a family of Hungarian Jews settled in Holland, where her father was a Rabbi, and was a solid and uneducated woman entirely absorbed in the cares of her large household, who did not at any time show the slightest understanding of her son's gifts or inclinations, was shocked by his radicalism, and in later years appears to have lost all interest in his existence. Of the eight children of Heinrich and Henrietta Marx Karl was the second; apart from a mild affection as a child for his eldest sister Sophia, he showed little interest in his brothers and sisters either then or later. He was sent to the local High School where he obtained equal praise for his industry and the high-minded and earnest tone of his essays on moral and religious topics. He was moderately proficient in mathematics and theology, but his main interests were literary and artistic: a tendency due principally to the influence of two men from whom he learned most and of whom all his life he spoke with affection and respect. The first of these was his father; the other was their neighbour Freiherr Ludwig von Westphalen who was on friendly terms with the amiable lawyer and his family.

Westphalen was a distinguished Prussian government official, and belonged to that educated and liberal section of the German upper class whose representatives were to be found in the vanguard of every enlightened and progressive movement in their country in the first half of the nineteenth century. An open-minded attractive and cultivated man.

He was in later life fond of recalling his evenings with Westphalen, during what seemed to him to have been the happiest period of his life. He had been treated by a man much older than himself on terms of equality at a time when he was in particular need of sympathy and encouragement. His doctorate thesis contains a glowing dedication to Westphalen, full of gratitude and admiration. In 1837 Marx asked for the hand of his daughter Jenny in marriage and obtained his consent without difficulty; an act which, owing to the great difference in their social condition, is said to have dismayed her relations. Speaking of Westphalen in later life Marx, whose judgments of men are not noted for their generosity, grew almost sentimental.

He is one of the rare revolutionaries who were neither thwarted nor persecuted in their early life. Consequently, in spite of his abnormal sensitiveness, his *amour-propre*, his vanity, his aggressiveness and his arrogance, it is a singularly unbroken, positive and self-confident figure that faces us during forty years of illness, poverty and unceasing warfare.

He left the Trier school at the age of seventeen, and, following his father's advice, in the autumn of 1835 became a student in the faculty of law in the University of Bonn. Here he seems to have been entirely happy: he announced that he proposed to attend at least seven courses of weekly lectures, among them lectures on Homer by the celebrated Schlegel, lectures on mythology, on Latin poetry, on modern art. He lived the gay and dissipated life of the ordinary German student, played an active part in university societies, wrote Byronic poems, got into debt and on at least one occasion was arrested by the authorities for riotous behaviour. At the end of the summer term of 1836 he left Bonn and in the autumn was transferred to the University of Berlin.

This event marks a sharp crisis in his life. The conditions under which he had lived hitherto had been comparatively provincial: by comparison with Trier or Bonn, Berlin was an immensely large and populous city, modern, ugly, pretentious and intensely serious, at once the centre of the Prussian bureaucracy and the meeting-place of the discontented radical intellectuals who formed the nucleus of the growing opposition to it. Marx retained all his life a considerable capacity for enjoyment and a strong if rather ponderous sense of fun, but no one could even at that time describe him as superficial or frivolous. He was sobered by the tense and tragic atmosphere in which he suddenly felt himself, and with his accustomed energy began at once to explore and criticize his new environment.

Marx attended Savigny's lectures for two terms with great regularity, and the immense erudition and power of close historical argument for which the latter was notable was probably Marx's first contact with the new method of historical research, which demanded minute knowledge of facts as a basis for broad general theses. Savigny's chief professional opponent was the professor of criminal law, Eduard Gans, whose effect on

Marx was more considerable. Gans was one of Hegel's favourite disciples: he was by birth a Jew, a friend of Heine, and like him a humanitarian radical who did not share his teacher's low opinion of the French enlightenment. His free criticism of legal institutions and methods of legislation in the light of reason, with no trace of mysticism about the past, affected Marx profoundly, and inspired him with a conception of the proper purpose and method of theoretical criticism which he never completely lost.

Hegelianism at first repelled his naturally positivist intelligence. In a long and intimate letter to his father he described his efforts to construct a rival system; after sleepless nights and disordered days spent in wrestling with the adversary, he fell ill and left Berlin to recuperate. He returned with a sense of failure and frustration, equally unable to work or to rest.

He abandoned his legal studies, and became entirely absorbed in philosophy. No other subject seemed to him to possess sufficient contemporary significance: he planned to become a lecturer in philosophy in one of the universities. He frequented social and literary salons, met the celebrated Bettina von Arnim, the friend of Beethoven and Goethe, who was attracted by his audacity and wit; wrote a conventional philosophical dialogue, and composed a fragment of a Byronic tragedy and several volumes of bad verse, which he dedicated to Jenny von Westphalen, to whom he had in the meantime become secretly engaged.

He was now twenty-four years of age, an amateur philosopher of no fixed occupation, respected in advanced circles for his erudition and for his powers as an ironical and bitter controversialist.

His father, on whom he financially dependeded, died, leaving a barely sufficient competence to his widow and youngest children. At the same time, the Prussian Minister of Education finally decided to condemn the Hegelian Left officially, and expelled Bauer from his post. This effectually closed the possibility of an academic career to Marx who was heavily compromised in the Bauer affair, and forced him to look for another occupation. He did not have long to wait. Among his warmest admirers was a certain Moses Hess, a Jewish publicist from Cologne, a sincere and enthusiastic radical, who was even then far in advance of even the Hegelian Left. Hess managed to persuade a group of liberal industrialists in the Rhineland to finance the publication of a radical journal which was issued at Cologne and was called the *Rheinische Zeitung*.

Marx was invited, and eagerly consented, to contribute regular articles to this journal; ten months later he became its chief editor. It was his first experience of practical politics: he conducted his paper with immense vigour and intolerance: his dictatorial nature asserted itself early in the venture, and his subordinates were only too glad to let him do entirely as he pleased, and write as much of the paper as he wished. From a mildly liberal paper it rapidly became a vehemently radical one: one more violently hostile to the Government than any other German newspaper. The *Rheinische Zeitung* was suppressed without warning in April 1843, and Marx was free once more. Meanwhile he had been working with restless energy: he had taught himself French by reading the works of the Paris socialists, Fourier, Proudhon, Dézami, Cabet and Leroux. He read recent French and German history and Machiavelli's *Prince*.

In April 1843, he married Jenny von Westphalen, against the wishes of the greater part of her family. This hostility only served to increase the passionate loyalty of the serious and profoundly romantic young woman: her existence had been transformed by the revelation to her of a new world by her husband, and she dedicated her whole being to his life and his work. It was an entirely happy marriage. She loved, admired, and trusted him, and was, emotionally and intellectually, entirely dominated by him. He leaned on her unhesitatingly in all times of crisis and disaster, remained all his life proud of her beauty, her birth and her intelligence. The poet Heine, who knew them well in Paris, paid eloquent tribute to her charm and wit. In later years, when they were reduced to penury, she displayed great moral heroism in preserving intact the framework of a family and a household, which alone enabled her husband to continue his work.

Together they decided to emigrate to France. Marx left Prussian territory in November 1843, and two days later arrived in Paris. His reputation had to some extent preceded him: at that date he was principally thought of as a liberal journalist with a mordant pen, who was forced to leave Germany because he had too violently advocated democratic reform. Two years later he was known to the police of many lands as an uncompromising revolutionary communist, a sworn enemy of reformist liberalism, the notorious leader of a subversive movement with international ramifications. The years 1843–5 are the most decisive in his life: in Paris he underwent his final intellectual transformation. At the end of it he had arrived at a clear position personally and politically: the remainder of his life was devoted to its development and practical realization.

If what Marx required was a complete plan of action, based on the study of history and observation of the contemporary scene, he must have found himself singularly out of sympathy with the reformers and prophets who gathered in the salons and cafés of Paris at the time of his arrival. They were, indeed, more intelligent, more politically influential and more responsible than the café philosophers of Berlin, but to him they seemed either gifted visionaries like Robert Owen, reformist liberals like Ledru Rollin, or, like Mazzini, both at once, unprepared, in the last resort, to do anything for the working class: nevertheless he learnt much from them which he did not acknowledge, notably from Louis Blanc, whose book on the organization of labour influenced him in his view of the evolution and correct analysis of industrial society.

He was attracted far more strongly to the party, which, to distinguish itself from the moderates who came to be called socialists, adopted the name of communists. Neither was a party in the modern sense of the word: both consisted of loosely associated groups and individuals. Only one among the revolutionaries whom he met in Paris seemed to him to display a genuine understanding of the situation. This was a certain Friedrich Engels, well-to-do young German radical, son of a cotton manufacturer in Barmen. They met in Paris over the publication of economic articles by Engels in Marx's journal. The meeting proved decisive for both; it was the beginning of a remarkable career of friendship and collaboration which lasted during the remainder of their lives.

Engels began life as a radical poet and journalist and ended it, after the death of Marx, as the acknowledged leader of international socialism, which, in his own lifetime, had grown into a world movement. He was a man of solid and robust, but hardly creative mind; a man of exceptional integrity and strength of character, of many varied gifts, but in particular endowed with a remarkable capacity for the rapid assimilation of knowledge.

He possessed a shrewd and lucid intellect and a firm sense of reality which few, if any, among his radical contemporaries could claim. Himself little capable of original discovery, he had an exceptional talent for sifting, assessing and perceiving the practical applicability of the discoveries of others. His knack of writing rapidly and clearly, his unbounded loyalty and patience, made him an ideal ally and collaborator for the inhibited and difficult Marx, whose own writing was often clumsy, overcharged and obscure.

In his own lifetime Engels desired no better fate than to live in the light of Marx's teaching, perceiving in him a spring of original genius which gave life and scope to his own peculiar gifts; with him he identified himself and his work, to be rewarded by sharing in his master's immortality. Before they met he had independently arrived at a position not unlike that of Marx, and in later years understood his friend's new, only half-articulated, ideas sometimes better than he understood them himself, and clothed them in language more attractive and intelligible to the masses than Marx's often tortuous style. Most important of all, he possessed a quality essential for permanent intercourse with a man of Marx's temperament, a total uncompetitiveness in relation to him, absence of all desire to resist the impact of that powerful personality, to preserve and retain a protected position of his own; on the contrary, he was only too eager to receive his whole intellectual sustenance from Marx unquestioningly, like a devoted pupil, and repaid him by his sanity, his enthusiasm, his vitality, his gaiety and, finally, in the most literal sense, by supplying him with means of livelihood at moments of desperate poverty.

Marx, who like many dedicated intellectuals, was himself haunted by a perpetual feeling of insecurity, and was morbidly thin-skinned and jealously suspicious of the least sign of antagonism to his person or his doctrines, required at least one person who understood his outlook, in whom he could confide completely, on whom he could lean as heavily and as often as he wished. In Engels he found a devoted friend and intellectual ally, whose very pedestrianism restored his sense of perspective and his belief in himself and his purpose. Throughout the greater part of his life his actions were performed in the knowledge that this massive and dependable man was always at hand to support the burden in every contingency. For this he paid him with an affection, and a sense of pride in his qualities, which he gave to no one else beside his wife and children.

The two years which Marx passed in Paris were the first and last occasion in his life on which he met, and was on terms of friendly intercourse with, men who were his equals, if not in intelligence, at any rate in the originality of their personalities and their lives. The portrait of him which emerges from the memoirs of those who were his friends at this time, Ruge, Freiligrath, Heine, Annenkov, is that of a bold and energetic figure, a vehement, eager, contemptuous controversialist, applying to everything his cumbrous and heavy Hegelians weapons, but, in spite of the clumsiness of the mechanism, revealing an acute and powerful intellect, the quality of which even those who were most hostile to him—and there were few prominent radicals whom he had failed to wound and humiliate in some fashion—in later years acknowledged freely.

Bakunin recorded his view of Marx many years later in one of his political tracts. "M. Marx", he wrote, "is by origin a Jew. He unites in himself all the qualities and defects of that gifted race. Nervous, some say, to the point of cowardice, he is immensely malicious, vain, quarrelsome, as intolerant and autocratic as Jehovah, the God of his fathers, and like Him, insanely vindictive.

"There is no lie, no calumny, which he is not capable of using against anyone who has incurred his jealousy or his hatred; he will not stop at the basest intrigue if, in his opinion, it will serve to increase his position, his influence and his power.

"Such are his vices, but he also has many virtues. He is very clever, and widely learned. In about 1840 he was the life and soul of a very remarkable circle of radical Hegelians—Germans whose consistent cynicism left far behind even the most rabid Russian nihilists. Very few men have read so much and, it may be added, have read so intelligently, as M. Marx.

"Like M. Louis Blanc, he is a fanatical authoritarian—triply so, as a Jew, a German and a Hegelian—but where the former, in place of argument, uses declamatory rhetoric, the latter, as behoves a learned and ponderous German, has embellished this principle with all the tricks and fancies of the Hegelian dialectic, and with all the wealth of his many-sided learning."

Their mutual hatred became more and more evident as time went on: outwardly friendly relations continued uneasily for some years, saved from complete rupture by the reluctant and apprehensive respect which each had for the formidable qualities of the other.

When the conflict ultimately did break out it all but destroyed the work of both, and did incalculable damage to the cause of European socialism.

Marx was expelled from Paris in the beginning of 1845 by the Guizot Government, as a result of representations from Prussia, which had demanded the suppression of the socialist *Vorwärts* in which offensive comments had appeared concerning the character of the reigning Prussian king. The order of expulsion was originally intended to apply to the entire group, including Heine, Bakunin, Ruge and several other lesser foreign exiles. Bakunin went to Switzerland; Marx, with his wife and one-year-old daughter Jenny, to Brussels where shortly afterwards he was joined by Engels who had returned from England for this purpose. In Brussels he lost no time in establishing contact with the various German communist workers' organizations which contained members of the dissolved League of the Just, an international society of proletarian revolutionaries with a vague, but violent, programme, influenced by Weitling; it had branches in various European cities. He entered into relations with Belgian socialists and radicals, carried on an active correspondence with members of similar bodies in other countries, and established regular machinery for the exchange of political information, but the chief sphere of his activity lay among the German workmen in Brussels itself.

As soon as he concluded that the establishment of communism could only be achieved by an armed rising of the proletariat, his entire existence turned into an attempt to organize and discipline it for its task. His personal history which up to his point can be regarded as a series of episodes in the life of an individual, now becomes inseparable from the general history of socialism in Europe. The task of preparing the workers for the revolution was for him a scientific task, a routine occupation, something to be performed as solidly and efficiently as possible, and not a direct means of personal self-expression.

He set to work to create an international revolutionary organization. Under his guidance, the Communist League grew fast and began to embrace groups of radical workers, scattered for the most part in the industrial areas in Germany, with a sprinkling of army officers and professional men.

In 1847 the London centre of the Communist League showed its confidence in him by commissioning him to compose a document containing a definitive statement of its beliefs and aims. He eagerly embraced this opportunity for an explicit summary of the new doctrine which had lately assumed its final shape in his head. He delivered it into their hands early in 1848. It was published a few weeks before the outbreak of the Paris revolution under the title of *The Manifesto of the Communist Party.*

The result is the greatest of all socialist pamphlets. No other modern political movement or cause can claim to have produced anything comparable with it in eloquence or power. It is a document of prodigious dramatic force; in form it is an edifice of bold and arresting historical generalizations, mounting to a denunciation of the existing order in the name of the avenging forces of the future, much of it written in prose which has the lyrical quality of a great revolutionary hymn, whose effect overwhelming even now, was probably greater at the time. It opens with a menacing phrase which reveals its tone and its intention: "A spectre is wandering over Europe today—the spectre of communism. All the forces of Europe have united to exorcise it: the Pope and the Czar, Metternich and Guizot, French radicals and German policemen, it is recognized as a real force by all the European powers." It proceeds as a succession of interconnected theses which are developed and brilliantly embroidered, and ends with a famous and magnificent invocation addressed to the workers of the world.

The Belgian Government, which behaved with considerable tolerance to political exiles, could not overlook this formidable publication, and brusquely expelled him and his family from its territory. On the next day the long-expected revolution broke out in Paris. Flocon, a radical member of the new French Government, in a flattering letter, invited Marx to return to the revolutionary city. He set off immediately and arrived a day later.

Excitement among the Germans in Paris rose to fever pitch. To support the insurgent republicans a German Legion was formed, which the poet Georg Herwegh and a Prussian communist ex-soldier named Willich were to lead. It was to start at once. The French Government, not unwilling, perhaps, to see so many foreign agitators leave its soil, encouraged the project. Engels was greatly attracted by the scheme and would almost certainly have enlisted, but was dissuaded by Marx, who viewed the proceeding with the greatest mistrust and hostility. The elected popular congress which met in Frankfurt to decide the future government of Germany was a failure from the first, and the sudden appearance of a legion of untrained émigré intellectuals on German soil appeared to Marx a needless waste of revolutionary energy, likely to have a ludicrous or a pitiful end, and to be followed by a paralysing mood of shame and disillusionment. Consequently, Marx opposed the formation of the legion, took no interest in it and went to Cologne to see what could be done by propaganda in his native Rhineland. He was there largely instrumental in persuading a group of liberal industrialists and communist sympathizers to found a *Neue Rheinische Zeitung*, in succession to the journal of that name which had been suppressed five years before, and to appoint him its editor.

Presently the Prussian Government, by this time convinced it had nothing to fear from popular sentiment, ordered the dissolution of the democratic assembly. The latter replied by declaring all taxes imposed by the Government illegal. Marx vehemently supported this decision and called upon the people to resist attempts to collect the tax. This time the Government acted promptly and ordered the immediate suppression of the *Neue Rheinische Zeitung*. The last issue was printed in a red ink, contained an inflammatory article by Marx and a magnificent poem by Freiligrath, and was bought up as a collector's curiosity. Marx was arrested for incitement to sedition and tried before a Cologne jury. He turned the occasion into the opportunity of delivering a speech of great length and erudition in which he analysed in detail the social and political situation in Germany and abroad. The result was unexpected: the foreman of the jury in announcing the acquittal of the accused said that he wished to thank him in his own name and that of the jury for an unusually instructive and interesting lecture by which they had all greatly profited. The Prussian Government, which had annulled his Prussian citizenship four years previously, unable to reverse the verdict itself, in July 1849 expelled him from the Rhineland.

Marx arrived in Paris from the Rhineland in July; a month later a subscription among his friends, among whom Lassalle's name occurs for the first time, enabled him to pay his fare to England. He arrived in London on 24 August 1849; his family followed a month later, and Engels, after dallying in Switzerland, and making a long and agreeable sea voyage from Genoa, came in the beginning of November. He found Marx convinced that the revolution might at any moment break out once more, and engaged on a pamphlet against the conservative French republic.

Marx arrived in London in 1849 expecting to stay in England for a few weeks, perhaps months: and in the event lived there uninterruptedly until his death in 1883.

The isolation of England intellectually and socially from the main currents of Continental life had always been great, and the middle years of the nineteenth century offered no exception. The issues which shook the Continent took many years to cross the English Channel, and when they did, did so in some new and peculiar shape, transformed and anglicized in the process of transition. Foreign revolutionaries were on the whole left unmolested, provided they behaved themselves in an orderly and inconspicuous manner, but neither was any kind of contact established with them. Their hosts treated them with correctness and civility, mingled with a mild indifference to their affairs which at once irritated and amused them. Revolutionaries and men of letters, who for many years had spent their lives in a ferment of intellectual and political activity, found the London atmosphere inhumanly cold. The sense of total isolation and exile was brought home to them even more sharply by the benevolent, distant, often slightly patronizing manner in which they were treated by the few Englishmen with whom they came into contact; and while this tolerant and civilized attitude did indeed create a vacuum, in which it was possible to recover physically and morally after the nightmare of 1849, the very distance from events which created this feeling of tranquillity, the immense stability which the capitalist regime appeared to possess in England, the complete absence of any symptom of revolution, at times tended to induce a sense of hopeless stagnation, which demoralized and embittered all but very few of the men engaged in it.

In the case of Marx desperate poverty and squalor were added factors in desiccating his never unduly romantic or pliant character. While these years of enforced inactivity benefited him as a thinker and a revolutionary, they caused him to retire almost entirely into the narrow circle composed of his family, Engels, and a few intimate friends, such as Liebknecht, Wolff and Freiligrath. As a public personality his natural harshness, aggressiveness, and jealousy, his desire to crush all rivals, increased with years; his dislike of the society in which he lived became more and more acute and his personal contact with individual members of it more and more difficult: he quarrelled easily and disliked reconciliation. While he had Engels to lean on he required no other help; and towards the end of his life when the respect and admiration which he received were at their highest, no one else dared to approach him too closely for fear of some particularly humiliating rebuff. Like many great men he liked flattery, and even more, total submission: in his last years he obtained both in full measure, and died in greater honour and material comfort than he had enjoyed during any previous period of his life.

A lively description of the conditions in which he lived during the first seven years of exile survives in the report of a Prussian spy who somehow contrived to worm his way into the Dean Street establishment: "He lives in one of the worst and cheapest neighbourhoods in London. He occupies two rooms. There is not one clean or decent piece of furniture in either room, everything is broken, tattered, and torn, with thick dust over everything . . . manuscripts, books and newspapers lie beside the children's toys, bits and pieces from his wife's sewing basket, cups with broken rims, dirty spoons, knives, forks, lamps, an inkpot, tumblers, pipes, tobacco ash—all piled up on the same table. On entering the room smoke and tobacco fumes make your eyes water to such an extent that at first you seem to be groping about in a cavern—until you get used to it, and manage to make out certain objects in the haze. Sitting down is a dangerous business. Here is a chair with only three legs, there another which happens to be whole, on which the children are playing at cooking. That is the one that is offered to the visitor, but the children's cooking is not removed, and if you sit down you risk a pair of trousers. But all these things do not in the least embarrass Marx or his wife. You are received in the most friendly way and are cordially offered pipes, tobacco, and whatever else there may happen to be. Presently a clever and interesting conversation arises which repays for all the domestic deficiencies and this makes the discomfort bearable."

A man of genius forced to live in a garret, to go into hiding when his creditors grow importunate, or to lie in bed because his clothes are pawned, is a conventional subject of gay and sentimental comedy. Marx was not a bohemian, and his misfortunes affected him tragically. He was proud, excessively thin-skinned, and made great demands upon the world: the petty humiliations and insults to which his condition exposed him, the frustration of his desire for the commanding position to which he thought himself entitled, the repression of his colossal natural vitality, made him turn in upon himself in paroxysms of hatred and of rage. His bitter feeling often found outlet in his writings and in long and savage personal vendettas. He saw plots, persecution, and conspiracies everywhere; the more his victims protested their innocence, the more convinced he became of their duplicity and their guilt.

His mode of living consisted of daily visits to the British Museum reading-room, where he normally remained from nine in the morning until it closed at seven; this was followed by long hours of work at night, accompanied by ceaseless smoking, which from a luxury had become an indispensable anodyne; this affected his health permanently and he became liable to frequent attacks of a disease of the liver sometimes accompanied by boils and an inflammation of the eyes, which interfered with his work, exhausted and irritated him, and interrupted his never certain means of livelihood. "I am plagued like Job, though not so God-fearing," he wrote in 1858.

To this condition some slight relief was brought by the sudden invitation to write regular articles on affairs in Europe for the *New York Daily Tribune*. The offer was made by Charles Augustus Dana, its foreign editor, who had been introduced to Marx by Freiligrath in Cologne in 1849, and was greatly impressed by his political shrewdness. The *New York Tribune* was a radical newspaper, founded by a group of American followers of Fourier, which had at this period a circulation of over 200,000 copies, then probably the greatest of any newspaper in the world. For nearly ten years he wrote weekly dispatches for it roaming over a wide field of subjects, which are of some interest even now.

At the same time he was engaged in gathering material for the economic treatise which should serve as a weapon against the vague idealism of the loosely connected radical groups, which, in his view, led to confusion both of thought and of action, and paralysed the efforts of such few clear-headed leaders as the workers possessed. He applied himself to the task of establishing, in the place of this, a rigorous doctrine, unambiguous in theory and definite in practice, adherence to which would become at once the test, the reason and the guarantee of a united, and, above all, active body of social revolutionaries. Their strength would derive from their unity, and their unity from the coherence of the practical beliefs which they had in common.

The foundations of his doctrine were embodied in his previous writings, notably in the *Communist Manifesto.* In a letter written in 1852 he carefully stated what he regarded as original in it: "What I did that was new was to prove (1) that the *existence of classes* is only bound up with particular, historic phases in the development of production; (2) that the class struggle necessarily leads to the *dictatorship of the proletariat*; (3) that this dictatorship itself only constitutes the transition to the *abolition of all classes* and to a classless society." On these foundations the new movement was to be built.

In 1859 he finally published his *Critique of Political Economy*, but it was little read: its main theses were much more impressively stated eight years later, in the first volume of *Das Kapital.*

The first volume of *Das Kapital* was finally published in 1867. The appearance of this book was an epoch-making event in the history of international socialism and in Marx's own life. It was conceived as a comprehensive treatise on the laws and morphology of the economic organization of modern society, seeking to describe the processes of production, exchange and distribution as they actually occur, to explain their present state as a particular stage in the development constituted by the movement of the class struggle, in Marx's own words, "to discover the economic law of motion of modern society" by establishing the natural laws which govern the history of classes. The result was a curious amalgam of economic theory, history, sociology and propaganda which fits none of the accepted categories. Marx certainly regarded it as primarily a treatise on economic science. The earlier economists, according to Marx, misunderstood the nature of economic laws when they compared with the laws of physics and chemistry, and assumed that, although social conditions may change, the laws which govern them do not.

The publication of *Das Kapital* had at last provided a definite intellectual foundation for international socialism in the place of a scattered mass of vaguely defined and conflicting ideas. The interdependence of the historical, economic and political theses preached by Marx and Engels was revealed in this monumental compilation. It became the central objective of attack and defence. All subsequent forms of socialism hereafter defined themselves in terms of their attitude to the position taken in it, and were understood and classified by their resemblance to it. After a brief period of obscurity, its fame began to grow and reached an extraordinary height. It acquired a symbolic significance beyond anything written since the age of faith. It has been blindly worshipped, and blindly hated, by millions who have not read a line of it, or have read without understanding its obscure and tortuous prose.

In Marx's own life it marked a decisive moment. He intended it to be his greatest contribution to the emancipation of humanity, and had sacrificed to it fifteen years of his life and much of his public ambition. The labour which had gone towards it was truly prodigious. For its sake he endured poverty, illness and persecution both public and personal, suffering these not gladly indeed, but with a single-minded stoicism whose strength and harshness both moved and frightened those who came in contact with it. He offered to dedicate his book to Darwin, for whom he had a greater intellectual admiration than for any other of his contemporaries, regarding him as having, by his theory of evolution and natural selection, done for the morphology of the natural sciences what he himself was striving to do for human history. Darwin hastily declined the honour in a polite, cautiously phrased letter, saying that he was unhappily ignorant of economic science, but offered the author his good wishes in what he assumed to be their common end—the advancement of human knowledge. It was dedicated to the memory of Wilhelm Wolff, a Silesian communist, who had been his devoted follower since 1848, and had recently died in Manchester.

The second and third volumes of *Das Kapital*, edited by Engels, and the supplementary studies which formed the fourth volume, edited by Kautsky from posthumous material, are greatly inferior in mental power, lucidity and vigour to the first volume which has become a classic.

Physically he was declining fast. In 1881 Jenny Marx died of cancer after a long and painful illness. Each had come to conceive life impossible without the other. "With her the Moor has died too", Engels said to his daughter Eleanor. Marx lived for two more years, still carrying on an extensive correspondence with Italians, Spaniards, Russians, but his strength was virtually spent. In 1882, after a particularly severe winter, his doctor sent him to Algiers to recuperate. He arrived with acute pleurisy which he had caught on the journey. He spent a month in Northern Africa which was uncommonly cold and wet, and returned to Europe ill and exhausted. After some weeks of vain wandering from town to town on the French Riviera in search of the sun, he went to Paris, where he stayed for a time with his eldest daughter Jenny Longuet. Not long after his return to London, news came of her sudden death. He never recovered from this blow, and hardly wished to do so: he fell ill in the following year, developed an abscess in the lung, and on 14 March 1883 died in his sleep, seated in an armchair in his study. He was buried in Highgate cemetery and laid next to his wife.

Isaiah Berlin

II
CAPITALISM, SOCIALISM AND DEMOCRACY: MARX THE ECONOMIST

As an economic theorist Marx was first of all a very learned man. It may seem strange that I should think it necessary to give such prominence to this element in the case of an author whom I have called a genius and a prophet. Yet it is important to appreciate it. Geniuses and prophets do not usually excel in professional learning, and their originality, if any, is often due precisely to the fact that they do not. But nothing in Marx's economics can be accounted for by any want of scholarship or training in the technique of theoretical analysis. He was a voracious reader and an indefatigable worker. He missed very few contributions of significance. And whatever he read he digested, wrestling with every fact or argument with a passion for detail most unusual in one whose glance habitually encompassed entire civilizations and secular developments. Criticizing and rejecting or accepting and coordinating, he always went to the bottom of every matter. The outstanding proof of this is in his work, *Theories of Surplus Value*, which is a monument of theorectical ardour. This incessant endeavour to school himself and to master whatever there was to master went some way toward freeing him from prejudices and extra-scientific aims, though he certainly worked in order to verify a definite vision. To his powerful intellect, the interest in the problem as a problem was paramount in spite of himself; and however much he may have bent the import of his final *results*, while at work he was primarily concerned with sharpening the tools of analysis proffered by the science of his day, with straightening out logical difficulties, and with building on the foundation thus acquired a theory that in nature and intent was truly scientific whatever its shortcomings may have been.

It is easy to see why both friends and foes should have misunderstood the nature of his performance in the purely economic field. For the friends, he was so much more than a mere professional theorist that it would have seemed almost blasphemy to them to give too much prominence to this aspect of his work. The foes, who resented his attitudes and the setting of his theoretic argument, found it almost impossible to admit that in some parts of his work he did precisely the kind of thing which they valued so highly when presented by other hands. Moreover, the cold metal of economic theory is in Marx's pages immersed in such a wealth of steaming phrases as to acquire a temperature not naturally its own. Whoever shrugs his shoulders at Marx's claim to be considered an analyst in the scientific sense thinks of course of those phrases and not of the thought, of the impassioned language and of the glowing indictment of "exploitation" and "immiserization" (this is probably the best way to render the word *Verelendung*, which is no more good German than that English monster is good English. It is *immiserimento* in Italian). To be sure, all these things and many others, such as his spiteful innuendoes or his vulgar comment on Lady Orkney, are important parts of the show, were important to Marx himself, and are so both for the faithful and for the unbelievers. They explain in part why many people insist on seeing in Marx's theorems something more than, and even something fundamentally different from, the analogous propositions of his master. But they do not affect the nature of his analysis.

Marx had a master then? Yes. Real understanding of his economics begins with recognizing that, as a theorist, he was a pupil of Ricardo. He was his pupil not only in the sense that his own argument evidently starts from Ricardo's propositions but also in the much more significant sense that he had learned the art of theorizing from Ricardo. Ricardo is not the only influence which acted on Marx's economics, but no other than that of Quesnay, from whom Marx derived his fundamental conception of the economic process as a whole, need be mentioned in a sketch like this. The group of English writers who between 1800 and 1840 tried to develop the labour theory of value may have furnished many suggestions and details. but this is covered for our purpose by the reference to the Ricardian current of thought. Several authors, to some of whom Marx was unkind in inverse proportion to their distance from him and whose work ran in many points parallel to his (Sismondi, Rodbertus, John Stuart Mill), must be left out of account, as must everything not directly pertaining to the main argument —so, for instance, Marx's distinctly weak performance in the field of money, in which he did not succeed in coming up to the Ricardian standard.

Now for a desperately abbreviated outline of the Marxian argument, unavoidably unjust on many counts to the structure of *Das Kapital* which, partly unfinished, partly battered by successful attack, still stretches its mighty skyline before us!

Marx fell in with the ordinary run of the theorists of his own and also of a later epoch by making a theory of value the cornerstone of his theoretical structure. His theory of value is the Ricardian one. I believe that such an outstanding authority as Professor Taussig disagreed with this and always stressed the differences. There is plenty of difference in wording, method of deduction, and sociological implication, but there is none in the bare theorem, which alone matters to the theorist of today. Both Ricardo and Marx say that the value of every commodity is (in perfect equilibrium and perfect competition) proportional to the quantity of labour contained in the commodity, provided this labour is in accordance with the existing standard of efficiency of production (the "socially necessary quantity of labour"). Both measure this quantity in hours of work and use the same method in order to reduce different qualities of work to a single standard. Both encounter the threshold difficulties incident to this approach similarly (that is to say, Marx encounters them as he had learned to do from Ricardo). Neither has anything useful to say about monopoly or what we now call imperfect competition. Both answer critics by the same arguments. Marx's arguments are merely less polite, more prolix, and more "philosophical" in the worst sense of this word.

Everybody knows that this theory of value is unsatisfactory. To begin with, it does not work at all outside of the case of perfect competition. Second, even with perfect competition it never works *smoothly* unless labour is the only factor of production and, moreover, if labour is all of one kind. If either of these two conditions is not fulfilled, additional assumptions must be introduced and analytical difficulties increase to an extent that soon becomes unmanageable. Reasoning on the lines of the labour theory of value is hence reasoning on a very special case without practical importance, though something might be said for it if it be interpreted in the sense of a rough approximation to the historical tendencies of relative values. The theory which replaced it—in its earliest and now outmoded form, known as the theory of marginal utility—may claim superiority on many counts but the real argument for it is that it is much more general and applies equally well, on the one hand, to the cases of monopoly and imperfect competition and, on the other hand, to the presence of other factors and of labour of many different kinds and qualities.

Though neither Ricardo nor Marx seems to have been fully aware of all the weaknesses of the position in which they had placed themselves by adopting this starting point, they perceived some of them quite clearly. In particular, they both grappled with the problem of eliminating the element of "services of natural agents", which of course are deprived of their proper place in the process of production and distribution by a theory of value that rests upon quantity of labour alone. The familiar Ricardian theory of the rent of land is essentially an attempt to accomplish that elimination and the Marxian theory is another. As soon as we are in possession of an analytical apparatus which takes care of rent as naturally as it does of wages, the whole difficulty vanishes. Hence nothing more need be said about the intrinsic merits or demerits of Marx's doctrine of absolute as distinguished from differential rent, or about its relation to that of Rodbertus.

But even if we let that pass we are still left with the difficulty arising out of the presence of capital in the sense of a stock of means of production that are themselves produced. To Ricardo it presented itself very simply: in the famous section 4 of the first chapter of his *Principles* he introduces and accepts as a fact, without attempting to question it, that, where capital goods such as plant, machinery and raw materials are used in the production of a commodity, this commodity will sell at a price which will yield a net return to the owner of those capital goods. He realized that this fact has something to do with the period of time that elapses between the investment, and the emergence of saleable products and that it will enforce deviations of the actual values of these from proportionality to the man-hours "contained" in them—including the man-hours that went into the production of the capital goods themselves—whenever these periods are not the same in all industries. To this he points as coolly as if it followed from, instead of contradicting, his fundamental theorem about value, and beyond this he does not really go, confining himself to some secondary problems that arise in this connection and obviously believing that his theory still describes the basic determinant of value.

Marx also introduced, accepted and discussed that same fact and never questioned it as a fact. He also realized that it seems to give the lie to the labour theory of value. But he recognized the inadequacy of Ricardo's treatment of the problem and, while accepting the problem itself in the shape in which Ricardo presented it, set about to attack it in earnest, devoting to it about as many hundreds of pages as Ricardo devoted sentences.

In doing so he not only displayed much keener perception of the nature of the problem involved, but he also improved the conceptual apparatus he received. For instance, he replaced to good purpose Ricardo's distinction between fixed and circulating capital by the distinction between constant and variable (wage) capital and Ricardo's rudimentary notions about duration of the processes of production by the much more rigorous concept of "organic structure of capital", which turns on the relation between constant and variable capital. He also made many other contributions to the theory of capital. We will, however, confine ourselves now to his explanation of the net return to capital, his theory of exploitation.

The masses have not always felt themselves to be frustrated and exploited. But the intellectuals that formulated their views for them have always told them that they were, without necessarily meaning by it anything precise. Marx could not have done without the phrase even if he had wanted to. His merit and achievement were that he perceived the weakness of the various arguments by which the tutors of the mass mind before him had tried to show how exploitation came about and which even today supply the stock in trade of the ordinary radical. None of the usual slogans about bargaining power and cheating satisfied him. What he wanted to prove was that exploitation did not arise from individual situations occasionally and accidentally; but that it resulted from the very logic of the capitalist system, unavoidably and quite independently of any individual intention.

This is how he did it. The brain, muscles, and nerves of a labourer constitute, as it were, a fund or stock of potential labour (*Arbeitskraft*, usually translated not very satisfactorily by labour power). This fund or stock Marx looks upon as a sort of substance that exists in a definite quantity and in capitalist society is a commodity like any other.

Now since labour in that sense (not the labour *service* or the actual man-hour) is a commodity, the law of value must apply to it. That is to say, it must in equilibrium and perfect competition fetch a wage proportional to the number of labour *hours* that entered into its "production". But what number of labour *hours* enters into the "production" of the stock of potential labour that is stored up within a workman's skin? Well, the number of labour *hours* it took and takes to rear, feed, clothe, and house the labourer. This constitutes the value of that stock, and if he sells parts of it—expressed in days or weeks or years—he will receive wages that correspond to the labour value of these parts, just as a slave trader selling a slave would in equilibrium receive a price proportional to the total number of those labour *hours*.

But once the "capitalists" have acquired that stock of potential services they are in a position to make the labourer work more hours—render more actual services—than it takes to produce that stock or potential stock. They can exact, in this sense, more actual hours of labour than they have paid for. Since the resulting products also sell at a price proportional to the man-hours that enter into their production, there is a difference between the two values—arising from nothing but the *modus operandi* of the Marxian law of values—which necessarily and by virtue of the mechanism of capitalist markets goes to the capitalist. This is the surplus value (*Mehrwert*). By appropriating it the capitalist "exploits" labour, though he pays to the labourers not less than the full value of their labour potential and receives from consumers not more than the full value of the products he sells.

As regards the merits of this scientific argument we must carefully distinguish two aspects of it, one of which has been persistently neglected by critics. At the ordinary level of the theory of a stationary economic process it is easy to show that under Marx's own assumptions the doctrine of surplus value is untenable. The labour theory of value, even if we could grant it to be valid for every other commodity, can never be applied to the commodity labour, for this would imply that workmen, like machines, are being produced according to rational cost calculations. Since they are not, there is no warrant for assuming that the value of labour power will be proportional to the man-hours that enter into its "production". Logically Marx would have improved his position had he accepted Lassalle's iron law of wages or simply argued on Malthusian lines as Ricardo did. But since he very wisely refused to do that, his theory of exploitation loses one of its essential props from the start.

Moreover, it can be shown that perfectly competitive equilibrium cannot exist in a situation in which all capitalist-employers make exploitation gains. For in this case they would individually try to expand production, and the mass effect of this would unavoidably tend to increase wage rates and to reduce gains of that kind to zero.

But there is another aspect of the matter. We need only look at Marx's analytic aim in order to realize that he need not have accepted battle on the ground on which it is so easy to beat him. This is so easy only as long as we see in the theory of surplus value nothing but a proposition about stationary economic processes in perfect equilibrium. Since what he aimed at analysing was not a state of equilibrium which according to him capitalist society can never attain, but on the contrary a process of incessant change in the economic structure, criticism along the lines above is not completely decisive. Surplus values may be impossible in perfect equilibrium but can be ever present because that equilibrium is never allowed to establish itself. They may always *tend* to vanish and yet be always there because they are constantly re-created. This defence will not rescue the labour theory of value, particularly as applied to the commodity labour itself, or the argument about exploitation as it stands. But it will enable us to put a more favourable interpretation on the result, although a satisfactory theory of those surpluses will strip them of the specifically Marxian connotation. This aspect proves to be of considerable importance. It throws a new light also on other parts of Marx's apparatus of economic analysis and goes far towards explaining why that apparatus was not more fatally damaged by the successful criticisms directed against its very fundaments.

If, however, we go on at the level on which discussion of Marxian doctrines ordinarily moves, we get deeper and deeper into difficulties or rather we perceive that the faithful do when they try to follow the master on his way. To begin with, the doctrine of surplus value does not make it any easier to solve the problems, alluded to above, which are created by the discrepancy between the labour theory of value and the plain facts of economic reality. On the contrary it accentuates them because, according to it, constant capital—that is, non-wage capital—does not transmit to the product any more value than it loses in its production: only wage capital does that and the profits earned should in consequence vary, as between firms, according to the organic composition of their capitals. Marx relies on the competition between capitalists for bringing about a redistribution of the total "mass" of surplus value such that each firm should earn profits proportional to its total capital, or that individual rates of profits should be equalized. We readily see that the difficulty belongs to the class of spurious problems that always result from attempts to work an unsound theory, and the solution to the class of counsels of despair. Marx, however, believed not only that the latter availed to establish the emergence of uniform rates of profits and to explain how, because of it, relative prices of commodities will deviate from their values in terms of labour, but also that his theory offered an explanation of another "law" that held a great place in classical doctrine, namely, the statement that the rate of profit has an inherent tendency to fall. This follows in fact fairly plausibly from the increase in relative importance of the constant part of the total capital in the wage-good industries, if the relative importance of plant and equipment increases in those industries, as it does in the course of capitalist evolution, and if the rate of surplus value or the degree of exploitation remains the same, then the rate of return to total capital will in general decrease. This argument has elicited much admiration, and was presumably looked upon by Marx himself with all the satisfaction we are in the habit of feeling if a theory of ours explains an observation that did not enter into its construction.

The main part of the loot wrung from exploited labour (according to some of the disciples, practically all of it), capitalists turn into capital—means of production. In itself and barring the connotations called up by Marx's phraseology, this is of course no more than a statement of a very familiar fact ordinarily described in terms of saving and investment. For Marx however this mere fact was not enough: if the capitalist process was to unfold in inexorable logic, that fact had to be part of this logic which means, practically, that it had to be neccessary.

In setting forth the nature of that compulsion to save, I shall for the sake of convenience accept Marx's teaching on one point: that is to say, I shall assume as he does that saving by the capitalist class *ipso facto* implies a corresponding increase in real capital. This movement will in the first instance always occur in the variable part of total capital, the wage capital, even if the intention is to increase the constant part and in particular that part which Ricardo called fixed capital—mainly machinery.

When discussing Marx's theory of exploitation, I have pointed out that in a perfectly competitive economy exploitation gains would induce capitalists to expand production, or to attempt to expand it, because from the standpoint of every one of them that would mean more profit. In order to do so they would have to accumulate. Moreover the mass effect of this would tend to reduce surplus values through the ensuing rise in wage rates, if not also through an ensuing fall in the prices of products—a very nice instance of the contradictions inherent in capitalism that were so dear to Marx's heart. And that tendency itself would, also for the individual capitalist, constitute another reason why he should feel compelled to accumulate. Though again that would in the end make matters worse for the capitalist class as a whole. There would hence be a sort of compulsion to accumulate even in an otherwise stationary process which, as I mentioned before, could not reach stable equilibrium until accumulation had reduced surplus value to zero and thus destroyed capitalism itself.

Much more important and much more drastically compelling is something else, however. As a matter of fact, capitalist economy is not and cannot be stationary. Nor is it merely expanding in a steady manner. It is incessantly being revolutionized *from within* by new enterprise—that is, by the intrusion of new commodities or new methods of production or new commercial opportunities into the industrial structure as it exists at any moment. Any existing structures and all the conditions of doing business are always in a process of change. Every situation is being upset before it has had time to work itself out. Economic progress, in capitalist society, means turmoil. And, as we shall see in the next part, in this turmoil competition works in a manner completely different from the way it would work in a stationary process, however perfectly competitive. Possibilities of gains to be reaped by producing new things or by producing old things more cheaply are constantly materializing and calling for new investments. These new products and new methods compete with the old products and old methods not on equal terms but at a decisive advantage that may mean death to the latter. This is how "progress" comes about in capitalist society. In order to escape being undersold, *every* firm is in the end compelled to follow suit, to invest in its turn and, in order to be able to do so, to plough back part of its profits—that is, to accumulate. Thus, everyone else accumulates.

Taken as it stands, Marx's theory of surplus value is untenable. But since the capitalist process does produce recurrent waves of temporary surplus gains over cost which, though in a very un-Marxian way, other theories can account for all right, Marx's next step, inscribed to accumulation, is not completely vitiated by his previous slips. Similarly, Marx himself did not satisfactorily establish that compulsion to accumulate, which is so essential to his argument. But no great harm results from the shortcomings of his explanation because, we can readily supply a more satisfactory one ourselves, in which among other things the fall of profits drops into the right place by itself. The aggregate rate of profit on total industrial capital need not fall in the long run, either for the Marxian reason that the constant capital increases relatively to the variable capital or for any other.

Another example is afforded by the next link in Marx's chain, his theory of concentration, that is, his treatment of the tendency of the capitalist process to increase the size both of industrial plants and of units of control. All he has to offer in explanation, when stripped of his imagery, boils down to the unexciting statements that "the battle of competition is fought by cheapening commodities" which "depends, *ceteris paribus*, on the productiveness of labour"; that this again depends on the scale of production; and that "the larger capitals beat the smaller." This is much like what the current textbook says on the matter, and not very deep or admirable in itself. In particular it is inadequate because of the exclusive emphasis placed on the size of the individual "capitals" while in his description of effects Marx is much hampered by his technique which is unable to deal effectively with either monopoly or oligopoly.

Yet the admiration so many economists outside the fold profess to feel for this theory is not unjustified. For one thing, to predict the advent, of big business was, considering the conditions of Marx's day, an achievement in itself. But he did more than that. He neatly hitched concentration to the process of accumulation or rather he visualized the former as part of the latter, and not only as part of its factual pattern but also of its logic. He perceived some of the consequences correctly—for instance that "the increasing bulk of individual masses of capital becomes the material basis of an uninterrupted revolution in the mode of production itself"—and others at least in a one-sided or distorted manner.

Two more items will complete this sketch: Marx's theory of *Verelendung* or, to use the English equivalent I have ventured to adopt, of immiserization, and his (and Engels's) theory of the trade cycle. In the former, both analysis and vision fail beyond remedy: both show up to advantage in the latter.

Marx undoubtedly held that in the course of capitalist evolution real wage rates and the standard of life of the masses would fall in the better-paid, and fail to improve in the worst-paid, strata and that this would come about not through any accidental or environmental circumstances but by virtue of the very logic of the capitalist process. As a prediction, this was of course singularly infelicitous and Marxists of all types have been hard put to it to make the best of the clearly adverse evidence that confronted them.

There seems, however, to be a way out of the difficulty. A tendency may fail to show in our statistical time series—which may even show the opposite one as they do in this case—and yet it might be inherent in the system under investigation, for it might be suppressed by exceptional conditions. This is in fact the line that most modern Marxists take. The exceptional conditions are found in colonial expansion, or, more generally, in the opening up of new countries during the nineteenth century, which is held to have brought about a "closed season" for the victims of exploitation.

But the real trouble is that Marx's theoretical structure is anything but trustworthy in that sector: along with the vision, the analytic groundwork is there at fault. The basis of the theory of immiserization is the theory of the "industrial reserve army"—that is, of the unemployment created by the mechanization of the process of production. And the theory of the reserve army is in turn based upon the doctrine expounded in Ricardo's chapter on machinery. Nowhere else—excepting of course the theory of value—does Marx's argument so completely depend on that of Ricardo without adding anything essential. I am speaking of course of the pure theory of the phenomenon only. Marx did add, as always, many minor touches such as the felicitous generalization by which the replacement of skilled by unskilled workers is made to enter into the concept of unemployment; also he added an infinite wealth of illustration and phraseology; and, most important of all, he added the impressive setting, the wide backgrounds of his social process.

Ricardo had at first been inclined to share the view, very common at all times, that the introduction of machines into the productive process could hardly fail to benefit the masses. When he came to doubt that opinion or, at all events, its general validity, he with characteristic frankness revised his position. No less characteristically, he leaned backwards in doing so and, using his customary method of "imagining strong cases", produced a numerical example, well known to all economists, to show that things could also turn out the other way.

The example is correct as far as it goes. The somewhat more refined methods of today support its result to the extent that they admit the possibility it aimed at establishing as well as the opposite one; they go beyond it by stating the formal conditions which determine whether the one or the other consequence will ensue. That is of course all that pure theory can do. Further data are necessary in order to predict the actual effect. But for our purpose, Ricardo's example presents another interesting feature. He considers a firm owning a given amount of capital and employing a given number of workmen that decides to take a step in mechanization. Accordingly, it assigns a group of those workmen to the task of constructing a machine which when installed will enable the firm to dispense with part of that group. Profits may eventually remain the same (after the competitive adjustments which will do away with any temporary gain) but gross revenue will be destroyed to the exact amount of the wages previously paid to the workmen that have now been "set free". Marx's idea of the replacement of variable (wage) capital by constant capital is almost the exact replica of this way of putting it. Ricardo's emphasis upon the ensuing *redundancy* of population is likewise exactly paralleled by Marx's emphasis upon *surplus* population which term he uses as an alternative to the term "industrial reserve army". Ricardo's teaching is indeed being swallowed hook, line and sinker.

He had every reason for taking this course. For he badly needed a firm foundation for his theory of the reserve army which was to serve two fundamentally important purposes, besides some minor ones. First, we have seen that he deprived his doctrine of exploitation of what I have called an essential prop by his aversion, quite understandable in itself, to making use of the Malthusian theory of population. That prop was replaced by the ever-present, because ever-recreated reserve army. Second, the particularly narrow view of the process of mechanization he adopted was essential in order to motivate the resounding phrases in chapter 32 of the first volume of *Das Kapital* which in a sense are the crowning finale not only of that volume but of Marx's whole work.

Marx's performance in the field of business cycles is exceedingly difficult to appraise. The really valuable part of it consists of dozens of observations and comments, most of them of a casual nature, which are scattered over almost all his writings, many of his letters included. Attempts at reconstruction from such *membra disjecta* of a body that nowhere appears in the flesh and perhaps did not even exist in Marx's own mind except in an embryonic form, may easily yield different results in different hands and be vitiated by the understandable tendency of the admirer to credit Marx, by means of suitable interpretation, with practically all those results of later research of which the admirer himself approves.

We find practically all the elements that ever entered into any serious analysis of business cycles, and on the whole very little error. Moreover, it must not be forgotten that the mere perception of the existence of cyclical movements was a great achievement at the time. Many economists who went before him had an inkling of it. Marx was, I believe, the first economist to rise above that tradition and to anticipate—barring the statistical complement—the work of Clément Juglar. Though, as we have seen, he did not offer an adequate explanation of the business cycle, the phenomenon stood clearly before his eyes and he understood much of its mechanism. Also like Juglar, he unhesitatingly spoke of a decennial cycle "interrupted by minor fluctuations". He was intrigued by the question of what the cause of that period might be and considered the idea that it might have something to do with the life of machinery in the cotton industry. And there are many other signs of preoccupation with the problem of business cycles as distinguished from that of crises. This is enough to assure him high rank among the father of modern cycle research.

Finally, the idea that capitalist evolution will burst—or outgrow—the institutions of capitalist society (*Zusammenbruchstheorie*, or the theory of the inevitable catastrophe) affords a last example of the combination of a *non sequitur* with profound vision which helps to rescue the result.

Based as Marx's "dialectic deduction" is on the growth of misery and oppression that will goad the masses into revolt, it is invalidated by the *non sequitur* that vitiates the argument which was to establish that inevitable growth of misery. Moreover, otherwise orthodox Marxists have long ago begun to doubt the validity of the proposition that concentration of industrial control is necessarily incompatible with the "capitalist integument". The first of them to voice this doubt by means of a well-organized argument was Rudolf Hilferding, one of the leaders of the important group of Neo-Marxists, who actually inclined toward the opposite inference, namely, that through concentration capitalism might gain in stability.

However, even though Marx's facts and reasoning were still more at fault than they are, his result might nevertheless be true so far as it simply avers that capitalist evolution will destroy the foundations of capitalist society. I believe it is. And I do not think I am exaggerating if I call profound a vision in which that truth stood revealed beyond doubt in 1847. It is a commonplace now. The first to make it that was Gustav Schmoller. His Excellency, Professor von Schmoller, Prussian Privy Councillor and Member of the Prussian House of Lords, was not much of a revolutionary or much given to agitatorial gesticulations. But he quietly stated the same truth. The why and how of it he likewise left unsaid.

It is hardly necessary to sum up elaborately. However imperfect, our sketch should suffice to establish: first, that nobody who cares at all for purely economic analysis can speak of unqualified success; second, that nobody who cares at all for bold construction can speak of unqualified failure.

In the court that sits on theoretical technique, the verdict must be adverse. Adherence to an analytic apparatus that always had been inadequate and was in Marx's own day rapidly becoming obsolete; a long list of conclusions that do not follow or are downright wrong; mistakes which if corrected change essential inferences, sometimes into their opposites—all this can be rightfully charged against Marx, the theoretical technician.

Even in that court, however, qualification of the verdict will be necessary on two grounds.

First, though Marx was often—sometimes hopelessly—wrong, his critics were far from being always right. Since there were excellent economists among them, the fact should be recorded to his credit, particularly because most of them he was not able to meet himself.

Second, Marx's contributions, both critical and positive, to a great many individual problems, should be recognized.

But a court of appeal—even though still confined to theoretical matters—might feel inclined to reverse this verdict altogether. For there is one truly great achievement to be set against Marx's theoretical misdemeanours. Through all that is faulty or even unscientific in his analysis runs a fundamental idea that is neither—the idea of a theory, not merely of an indefinite number of disjointed individual patterns or of the logic of economic quantities in general, but of the actual sequence of those patterns or of the economic process as it goes on, under its own steam, in historic time, producing at every instant that state which will of itself determine the next one. Thus, the author of so many misconceptions was also the first to visualize what even at the present time is still the economic theory of the future for which we are slowly and laboriously accumulating stone and mortar, statistical facts and functional equations.

And he not only conceived that idea, but he tried to carry it out. All the shortcomings that disfigure his work must, because of the great purpose his argument attempted to serve, be judged differently even where they are not, as they are in some cases, fully redeemed thereby. There is however one thing of fundamental importance for the methodology of economics which he actually achieved. Economists always have either themselves done work in economic history or else used the historical work of others. But the facts of economic history were assigned to a separate compartment. They entered theory, if at all, merely in the role of illustrations, or possibly of verifications of results. They mixed with it only mechanically. Now Marx's mixture is a chemical one; that is to say, he introduced them into the very argument that produces the results. He was the first economist of top rank to see and to teach systematically how economic theory may be turned into historical analysis and how the historical narrative may be turned into *historic raisonée*. The analogous problem with respect to statistics he did not attempt to solve. But in a sense it is implied in the other. This also answers the question how far, in the way explained at the end of the preceding chapter, Marx's economic theory succeeds in implementing his sociological set-up. It does not succeed; but in failing, it establishes both a goal and a method.

Joseph Alois Schumpeter

SOURCES

Essay I

Isaiah Berlin, *Karl Marx: His Life and Environment*, 3rd ed. (O.U.P., London, 1963). Biographical extracts.

Essay II

Joseph Alois Schumpeter, *Capitalism, Socialism and Democracy* (Harper and Brothers New York, 1942), Chapter 3, "Marx the Economist". Abridged.

Signature

International Instituut voor Sociale Geschiedenis, Amsterdam.

Portrait

Photograph (International Instituut voor Sociale Geschiedenis, Amsterdam).

BIBLIOGRAPHY

W. Liebknecht, *Karl Marx zum Gedächtnis. Ein Lebensabriß und Erinnerungen* (Nuremberg, 1896).

W. Sombart, *Das Lebenswerk von Karl Marx* (Jena, 1909).

K. Zetkin, *Marx und sein Lebenswerk* (Elberfeld, 1913).

F. Mehring, *Karl Marx, Geschichte eines Lebens* (Leipzig, 1910. Reprint: Zürich, 1946. English translation: London, 1936).

D. Rjazanov, *Karl Marx and Friedrich Engels* (New York, 1927).

O. Rühle, *Karl Marx, Leben und Werk* (Hellerau, 1928).

E. Marx, P. Lafargue and F. Lessner, *Karl Marx als Denker, Mensch und Revolutionär. Ein Sammelbuch* (Wien and Berlin, 1928).

K. Vorländer, *Karl Marx. Sein Leben und sein Werk* (Leipzig, 1929).

B. Nicolajewsky and O. Mänchen-Helfen, *Karl und Jenny Marx* (Berlin, 1933).

K. Korsch, *Karl Marx* (London, 1938).

E. Wilson, *To the Finland Station* (New York, 1940).

L. Schwarzschild, *The Red Prussian. The Life and Legend of Karl Marx* (New York, 1947; London, 1948).

F. Marek, *Karl Marx* (Wien, 1951).

W. J. Lenin, *Karl Marx* (Berlin, 1931; last edition: Berlin, 1953).

M. Freund, "Karl Marx", in *Die Großen Deutschen, Deutsche Biographie*, ed. H. Heimpel, Th. Heuss, and B. Reifenberg, Vol. 3 (Berlin, 1956).

M. Rubel, *Karl Marx, Essai de biographie intellectuelle* (Paris, 1957).

F. Engels, "Marx, Biographie", in *Handwörterbuch der Sozialwissenschaften* Vol. 7 (1961).

W. Blumenberg, *Karl Marx* (Hamburg, 1962).

M. Rubel, "Karl Marx", in *International Encyclopedia of the Social Sciences*, Vol. 10 (New York, 1968).

M. Wolfson, "The Day Karl Marx Grew Up", *History of Political Economy*, 3 (1971).

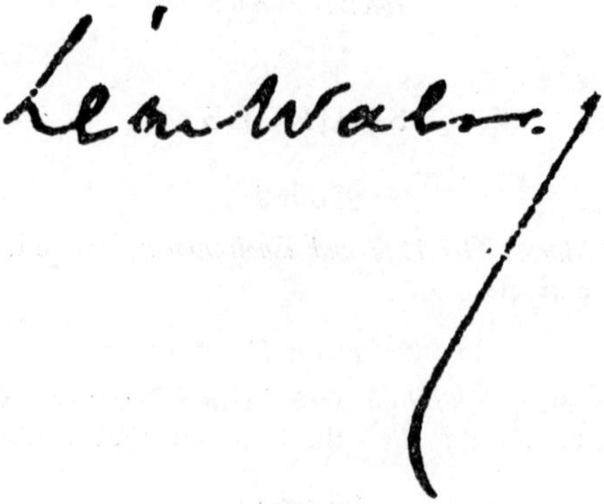

MARIE ESPRIT LÉON WALRAS

1834–1910

Ici le système du monde économique apparait déjà dans son étendue et sa complexité, et peut sembler aussi beau, c'est-à-dire aussi vaste et aussi simple à la fois, que le système du monde astronomique L. WALRAS

[Walras's] system of equations, defining (static) equilibrium in a system of interdependent quantities, is the Magna Carta of economic theory. J. A. SCHUMPETER

You are doing pure science; I am trying to apply this pure science. This is the main difference between our points of view. In other words: you are like the geometrician who writes a treatise on rational mechanics. I try to apply this science to machines after having learned it from your writings. I think that what you must now submit to the public in order to persuade it of the usefulness of the mathematical method is applications. V. PARETO

Walras has done more than perhaps any other economist to give us a framework for organizing our ideas, a way of looking at the economic system and describing it that facilitates the avoidance of mistakes in logic. It is no derogation of his contribution to emphasize that it is not by itself enough for a fruitful and meaningful economic theory. M. FRIEDMAN

Walras is the Laplace of economics. [He] transformed economics from a system in which each value was attached to its own particular cause to a system in which all values, whether of finished goods, intermediate products, or factors of production, are mutually determined by the interaction of the innumerable forces of desire upon the innumerable resistances of scarcity. K. E. BOULDING

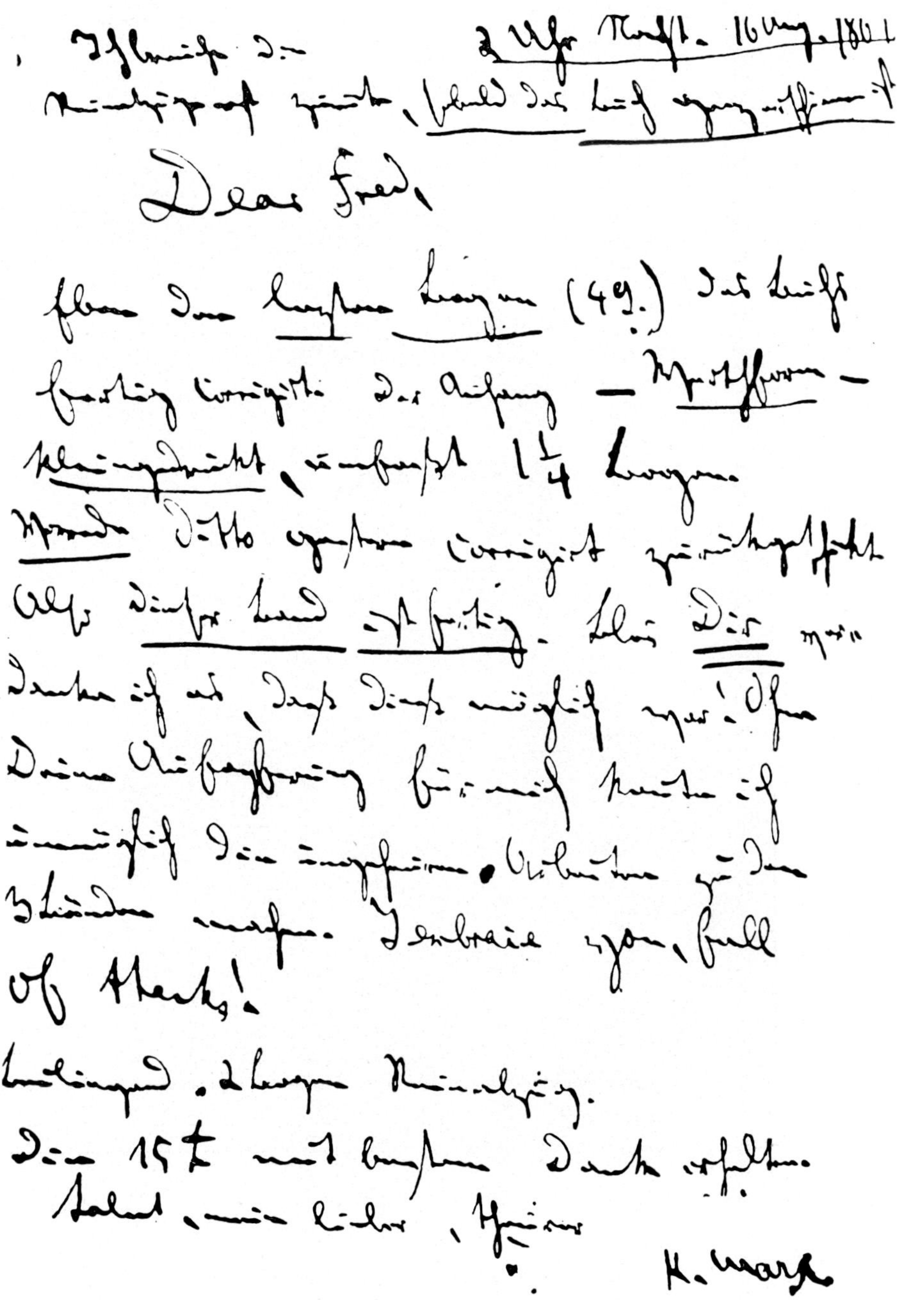

Ich brauche die 2 Uhr Nachts. 16 Aug. 1867
Reinabzüge zurück, sobald das Buch ganz erschienen ist

Dear Fred,

Eben den letzten Bogen (49.) des Buchs fertig corrigirt. Der Anhang – Werthform – kleingedruckt, umfasst 1 1/4 Bogen. Vorrede ditto gestern corrigirt zurückgeschickt. Also dieser Band ist fertig. Blos Dir verdanke ich es, dass dieß möglich war! Ohne Deine Aufopferung für mich konnte ich unmöglich die ungeheuren Arbeiten zu den 3 Bänden machen. I embrace you, full of thanks!

Beiliegend 2 Bogen Reinabzug.

Die 15 £ mit bestem Dank erhalten.

Salut, mein lieber, theurer Freund!

K. Marx

A letter of thanks from Marx to Engels on the completion of the proof reading of *Das Kapital*

Marie Esprit Léon Walras (1834–1910)

Gustav von Schmoller (1838–1917)

Alfred Marshall (1842–1924)

Vilfredo Pareto (1848–1923)

Johan Gustav Knut Wicksell (1851–1926)

Thorstein Bunde Veblen (1857–1929)

Max Weber (1864–1920)

I
LÉON WALRAS

Léon Walras (1834–1910), whose full name was Marie Esprit Léon Walras—the final *s* sounded—is celebrated among economists and econometricians as the first to have formulated a multi-equational general equilibrium model of economic relationships. He was born on 16 December 1834 in Evreux, a provincial town of Normandy, France. Though he spent more than half his adult life in Switzerland, he retained his French citizenship to the end. Léon's father, Auguste Walras, author of *De la nature de la richesse et de l'origine de la valeur* (1831), was an economist in his own right, though he failed to obtain a chair in economics and wasted his years as a minor administrator in the French educational system.

His mother, Louise Aline née Sainte Beuve (1811–93), the daughter of a notary of Evreux, came from a locally prominent family, which at times claimed the nobiliary particle *de*, but was not of the same line as that of the famous literary critic, Sainte Beuve. From his mother, Léon inherited the frugal, calculating temper of the Normans and eventually 100,000 francs.

Léon Walras's early education followed the usual course for youths of his station, culminating in two French baccalaureate degrees, one in letters (1851) and the other in science (1853). His curriculum included mathematics up to high-school algebra and analytical geometry but nothing much beyond. In fact, his mathematical attainments proved insufficient to enable him to gain entrance to the École Polytechnique. Finally, in 1854 he was admitted as a non-resident student of the École des Mines in Paris. With Bohemian insouciance he neglected his engineering studies, which he found distasteful, and turned to literature.

On realizing that he was not meant for a literary career, he promised his father in the summer of 1858 that he would devote his life to economics.

Professional openings for an economist in France of that epoch were extremely rare and remained all the more inaccessible to Léon Walras not only because he lacked the requisite formal university training but also because he stood outside the charmed circle of official French economists who formed a closed corporation dedicated to the existing order and to the dogma of unmitigated economic individualism. But Léon Walras's need to make a living was pressing particularly when he set up house around 1859 with an unmarried mother, Célestine Aline Ferbach (1835–79), and had twin daughters by her in 1863, one of them dying in infancy. It was not until 1869 that he married Mlle Ferbach. He tried his hand at journalism, but was soon discharged because of the independence of his opinions. He worked for a while at the secretariat of the Chemin de fer du Nord. Then in 1864 he became managing director of a bank for co-operatives in which Léon Say was interested, but the bank was compelled to liquidate in 1868. While he was directing the bank, he wrote and lectured on the organization of cooperatives which were looked upon in the 1860s as an antidote to the revolutionary threats of the working classes. For two years (1866–8), along with Léon Say, he edited a short-lived monthly cooperative organ, *Le Travail.* Finally, before receiving his call to the academy of Lausanne, he was corresponding secretary for a private banking establishment in Paris.

During the twelve years between his abandonment of the École des Mines and his entrance upon an academic career in Switzerland, Léon Walras was writing and cogitating on economic subjects. At an early stage, he formulated in broad outline the whole programme of his intellectual lifework: a trilogy made up of pure economics, applied economics and what he called "social economics" (*économie sociale*). Pure economics was conceived on the analogy of pure mechanics and was to consist in an explanatory model, mathematical in structure, depicting a comprehensive network of relationships rigorously derived from the assumption of supposedly perennial or "natural" economic forces independent of institutional arrangements. Applied economics was thought of in terms of the application of pure theory to problems of production, with a view to determining, in the classical tradition, the forms of industrial organization most conducive to the maximization of social output. While applied economics hovered between the positive and the prescriptive design, "social economics" was to be unreservedly normative, concerned with principles of "justice" (essentially Aristotelian and Thomistic) which should not only preside over the distribution of wealth, but also govern exchange.

Before going to Lausanne, Léon Walras made little or no progress in pure economics, publishing nothing on the subject. Nevertheless he made two fumbling attempts, which survive in manuscript, to apply the little mathematics he knew to economic analysis, and he arrived at only one concept of importance, his *équation d'échange*, a budget equation in all but the name. Nor did he make any advance in applied economics at this time. His attention was almost entirely absorbed in formulating the fundamental philosophical ideas of his "social economics". Of the books he published in this period, the first was *L'Économie politique et la justice*, 1860, which was essentially an ideological performance founded on his father's views. In 1860 he participated in an international congress on taxation held at Lausanne, where he first met a young Swiss lawyer and politician, Louis Ruchonnet, who ten years later aided him in obtaining his appointment to a newly established chair in political economy at Lausanne. In a series of public lectures delivered in Paris in 1867–8 and published under the title *Recherche de l'idéal social* (1868), he expounded his philosophy of social reform based on the metaphysical ideas of Étienne Vacherot and calling for a conciliation of interests. At the same time he resisted the efforts of his Saint-Simonian friends to enroll him among their number, because their socialism was "unscientific". He always thought of himself as a "scientific" socialist, with "scientific" reasons for advocating that the State take over (by purchase) whatever private property (land, natural monopolies, railways) could be shown analytically to be inconsistent with the attainment of the relative maximum welfare which free competition, when properly constrained by the inviolable rules of "justice", would bring about. The State, then, having its own income-producing property, would not, indeed should not, impose taxes, for taxation itself interferes with the beneficent operation of competitive forces. Neither in the *Recherche de l'idéal social* nor in any of the pre-Lausanne publications did Léon Walras display analytical acumen or give any inkling of what was to come.

On 16 December 1870, exactly his thirty-sixth birthday, Léon Walras delivered his first lecture as "professeur extraordinaire" in the Faculty of Law of the Academy (later the University) of Lausanne. Virtually up to the last moment, the path toward the realization of this long-cherished ambition had been beset with difficulties. With the Franco-Prussian War raging in France, it was hard enough for Walras to take up his post; but, before that, his appointment even for a trial period of one year had been opposed by three of the seven members of the Swiss *ad hoc* committee charged with the task of appraising candidates for the Lausanne chair of political economy. The minority report, while agreeing that Walras was superior to his competitors for the post, found his writings "communistic"! By 1871 all fears were allayed and Léon Walras was duly inaugurated as "professeur ordinaire"—with tenure. He now concentrated upon pure economics, which quickly became his dominant passion. In fact, when he later resumed writing on questions of policy, it was, as he confessed to a correspondent, mainly because he felt that his articles on current issues would eventually call attention to his analytical work.

Once at Lausanne, Walras began to teach himself the calculus so that he could apply the technique of binding maxima to the theory of utility. Thus Walras developed his mathematical theory of "*rareté*" (marginal utility), and presented the two-commodity case in simplified geometric form in a paper, "Principe d'une théorie mathématique de l'échange" (1873). After the publication of his first paper, he was dismayed to learn that W. Stanley Jevons had anticipated him in originating the theory of marginal utility. Walras honourably acknowledged Jevons's priority, consoling himself with the perfectly just reflection that he had done better than Jevons in establishing a correct relation between utility and demand. Nevertheless, his feelings of jealousy continued to rankle until he discovered that the German Gossen, now dead and consequently no longer a potential rival, had anticipated both Jevons and himself in 1854. To forestall further disappointments in his race for priority, Walras hastened his pace, publishing a series of three additional papers in pure economics, the substance of which was embodied in the first edition of his *Éléments d'économie politique pure* (1874–7).

Walras sought to make himself known to economists in France and elsewhere by sending them reprints of his articles and copies of his *Éléments*, accompanied by letters asking for criticism. From Italy, Germany, England, Holland and Denmark, he received encouraging responses. In France, however, to Walras's chagrin, his early work evoked either no comment at all or else outright antagonism, except from Cournot and the philosopher, Charles Renouvier.

As time went on Walras's economic correspondence assumed enormous proportions: literally thousands of letters passed between him and such of his contemporaries as Foxwell, Marshall, Edgeworth and Wicksteed in England; Menger, Böhm-Bawerk and Lieben in Austria; Pantaleoni, Pareto and Barone in Italy; Gide, Hermann Laurent, Henri Poincaré (on methodology) and Albert Aupetit in France; Bortkiewicz in Russia; Wicksell in Sweden; John Bates Clark, Irving Fisher and Henry Ludwell Moore in the United States. He thus became literally an economist's economist, for it was impossible for him to mould disciples among his law students at Lausanne, who regarded the course in economics as a tiresome excrescence. Outside of Lausanne, the novel mathematical character of his writing repelled the ordinary student with a purely literary training, and the marginal utility approach to value outraged the orthodox economists dedicated to the Ricardian cost of production approach. Only the elite of the profession took any interest at all in Walras's innovations, and with them he held a continuous seminar—by correspondence—exchanging criticisms that left their mark on the four successive editions of the *Éléments* which appeared during Walras's life-time.

While Walras had no economic colleagues at Lausanne with whom to take counsel, he had mathematical colleagues, not only Paul Piccard, but also Hermann Amstein, whom he pumped assiduously. When he asked Amstein to formulate the mathematical conditions of minimum cost of production, Amstein in 1877 presented him with an almost perfect marginal productivity model, even using the Lagrange multiplier method; but Walras knew too little mathematics to understand it, and Amstein too little economics to appreciate its significance. It was not until after Wicksteed's *Essay on the*

Coordination of the Laws of Distribution appeared in 1894, that Walras filled the empty niche in his theory of production by incorporating Barone's formulation of the marginal productivity theory into his *Éléments*, Amstein's still remaining beyond his ken.

For many years Walras thought that his chief claim to fame lay in his marginal utility theory which was certainly more rigorous and elegant than that of either Jevons or Carl Menger. He did not wake up to the full significance of his characteristic general equilibrium system until 1894 when Barone hailed it in the *Giornale degli Economisti* as "the most general, most comprehensive and most harmonious" that had yet appeared. Already in the 1870s, in the first edition of the *Éléments*, Walras had laid the groundwork for a unified model, comprising the theories of exchange, production, capital formation and money. In the subsequent revisions of the *Éléments*, he solidified the model by impregnating it throughout with the all-pervasive cement of utility maximization. Moreover, to link his model to the real world, he followed up each of his successive cumulative sub-models describing the static *determination* of equilibrium with a related quasi-dynamic theory of the emergence (or *establishment*) of equilibrium through the operation of the competitive market mechanism. He saw the process of automatic adjustments of the network of real markets to equilibrium as one of *tâtonnement*, that is, of groping without conscious direction. His argument that the process would culminate, under his assumptions, in a stable equilibrium was, nevertheless, intuitive, without any semblance of a rigorous demonstration. Despite this and other defects, lacunae and inconsistencies in detail, which were inevitable in so immense a pioneer work produced with primitive mathematical tools, Léon Walras's general equilibrium model earned for him the supreme encomium of Joseph Schumpeter, "As far as pure theory is concerned, Walras is in my opinion the greatest of all economists."

Walras was not the originator of the idea of general equilibrium. It had already been enunciated in 1690 by Nicholas Barbon, there were discernible adumbrations of the theory in Petty, Boisguilbert, Cantillon, and especially in Quesnay; and an implicit pattern of mutually interdependent relationships underlies the writings of the great classical founders of economics, Adam Smith, Ricardo and Jean-Baptiste Say. It is not, however, from these precursors that Walras could possibly have derived direct inspiration for his multi-equational model of interdependence. He liked to give the impression that his father and Cournot were the principal instigators of his economic theory, but Cournot mentioned the interconnection of all the parts of the economic system only to recoil from it as surpassing "the powers of mathematical analysis", and Auguste Walras furnished nothing but vague hints of general equilibrium.

The true *fons et origo* of Walras's multi-equational formulation of general equilibrium was Louis Poinsot's once famous textbook in pure mechanics, *Éléments de statique* (8th edition, 1842), which, as Walras confided to a friend in 1901, he first read at the age of nineteen and then kept by him as a companion book throughout his life. In Poinsot we find virtually the whole formal apparatus Walras later employed in his *Éléments d'économie politique pure*. Achille Nicholas Isnard's *Traité des richesses* (1781), which Walras rescued from oblivion by inserting it into Jevons's list of writings on mathematical economics (1879), also appears to have played a part in directly shaping Walras's formulation of his system. Walras praised Isnard for having correctly stated algebraically the inverse proportionality of values to quantities exchanged.

Though Walras was not really indebted to his father or to Cournot for his composite model, his pure theory still bears the sharp imprint of their influence. From his father, Léon Walras took over, for better or for worse, a good part of his terminology, his taxonomy and his conception of the object of economics. From Cournot, he first learned the meaning of functional relations between variables; and it was precisely his growing dissatisfaction with Cournot's particular demand function that first led him to seek a wider framework within which to express the quantity demanded of a commodity as a function, not of the price of that commodity alone, but of the entire constellation of prices. This was the "take-off" stage, from which he soared to his general equilibrium model.

Soon after the publication of the first edition of the *Élèments*, Walras's wife was stricken by a fatal illness, and his financial situation deteriorated. His academic salary, which had been raised in 1872 from the initial 3600 francs a year to 4000 francs still proved inadequate. To eke out the income he required for his family needs and his research and publication expenses, he had to give supplementary courses at Geneva and Neuchâtel, serve as a regular consulting actuary for a Swiss insurance company, write fortnightly feature articles (under the pseudonym "Paul") for the *Gazette de Lausanne*, contribute weighty articles to the *Bibliothèque Universelle*—and borrow. When, in 1879, his old friend, Jules Ferry, became Minister of Public Instruction in France, Walras thought he had a chance to obtain a university post in his native country and improve his situation. His efforts in this direction proved vain, notwithstanding his offer to help Jules Ferry modernize the whole French university system and, by the same token, pull the teaching of economics out of the law school rut and give it the status of a science. In 1881 the Academy of Lausanne increased his salary to 5000 francs. But it was only on his second marriage in 1884 that his financial condition took a substantial turn for the better. His second wife, Léonide Désirée Mailly (1826–1900), brought with her an annuity which more than doubled the income of the Walras household.

Relieved now of private financial worries, Walras returned to his work with a burst of renewed energy. He ventured upon a fundamental revision of his theories of money and capital; and took up the cudgels for monetary reform. In his monetary theory, he replaced his first conception of the demand for money as depending on the volume of transactions to be cleared ("*circulation à desservir*") by his later conception of a demand for cash balances ("*encaisse désirée*"). As Arthur Marget pointed out, this entailed the substitution of his earlier "Fisherian" equation of exchange by an equation essentially Keynesian in form. The change was made in the interests of symmetry and overall coherence in the general model, for now the same *primum mobile*, the maximization of utility, could operate in the theory of money as in the rest of his system. Walras's new monetary theory, first announced in his paper, "Equations de circulation", in 1899, was soon incorporated into the fourth edition (1900) of the *Éléments*. Into the same edition, he introduced his revised conception of the role of interest as an equilibrating factor between the aggregate demand for cash balances and the existing quantity of money.

Walras's revision and extension of his theory of capital formation was similarly motivated. In the fourth edition of the *Eléments*, in order to avoid the dilemma of either continuing to use his earlier empirical savings function unrelated to the utility maximization principle or of complicating his postulates with time preference functions, Walras chose to consider savings and investment, as he did consumption and production, exclusively at the moment of decision-making. He envisaged the decisions theoretically as bearing on a *fictive* commodity, "perpetual net income" (net of depreciation and insurance charges), each unit of which represents a perpetual yield of one unit of *numéraire* per year from whatever assets, human as well as marketable, an individual possesses. This commodity, having a utility function of its own, enters into the general equilibrium model on the same footing as any other commodity and renders the entire system homogenous.

In his writings on monetary reform Walras directed his attention to the questions, then current, of bimetallism and bank note issue. His article, "Théorie mathématique du bimétallisme" (1881), presented, in the form of an *ad hoc* model, a complete theory of the bimetallist standard with a fixed ratio. With this model as a basis, and on grounds of his utility theory and his conception of "justice", he advocated a symmetallist proposal in the shape of a gold standard with a regulatory silver token currency. The State was to regulate the quantity of a special silver token currency in such a way as to counteract the long-term fluctuations in the value of money. In the matter of banknote issue, Walrus maintained that any system that fell short of 100 per cent metallic coverage was dangerous.

These arduous labours exhausted Walras. By 1892 he felt he could no longer go on with his teaching. His mother's bequest of that year enabled him to purchase an annuity and repay his old debts, incurred mainly in the publication and free distribution of his books and economic papers. Thereupon, he retired from the University on a pension of 800 francs a year and was succeeded in his chair by his protégé, Vilfredo Pareto. He did not, however, lay down his pen. In the decade 1892-1902, as has been seen, he made some of his most important innovations in the theory of capital and money. He could not, however, find strength to write the systematic treatises he had in view on applied economics and "social economics", Instead, he published two volumes of collected papers on these subjects: *Études d'économie sociale* in 1896; and *Études d'économie politique appliquée* in 1898. From 1902 on, after completing his notations for the *édition définitive* of the *Éléments* (1926), he devoted himself to pottering and to propaganda in favour of his theory. Upon the death of his second wife in 1900, her annuity was extinguished; and Walras and his unmarried daughter, Aline, retreated, without regret, to the simple life, in a modest apartment at Clarens, near Montreux, Switzerland, where he died on 5 January 1910. Six months before his death, the University of Lausanne celebrated his jubilee as an economist, on which occasion he was acclaimed in messages from the four corners of the earth as the founder of the General Equilibrium School.

Though Walras had received occasional marks of recognition before his death, it was only posthumously that his reputation and influence grew to their present proportions. Walras's model has been the subject of continued emendations, controversy and fluctuating evaluations. His obscure notation has been streamlined; his crude mathematics polished, perfected and modernized; his utility theory superseded by a theory of ordinal preference unencumbered by assumptions of cardinal measurement and independence; his production theory freed from implications that had left the distinction between free and scarce goods in an empirical haze; his production functions generalized to admit more easily of variable coefficients of production; his investment theory disassociated from postulates of certainty of outcome; his unwarranted premise that equality between the number of unknowns and the number of independent equations is sufficient for a determinate solution supplanted by rigorous existence theorems. For all that, the main lines of the Walrasian model remain intact; and its authority is such that in 1949 Professor Milton Friedman was forced to admit, "We curtsy to Marshall, but we walk with Walras." Some critics, while conceding the aesthetic qualities of the general equilibrium model, hold it to be sterile, little realizing that pure economics is no more intended for direct application to practical problems than pure mechanics is intended for guidance to machinists. Besides, it is putting a strange construction upon the word "sterility" to apply it to a general theory that is the acknowledged forebear of input-output analysis and that directly begat the modern conception of exchange, production, saving, investment, interest and money, all neatly fitted into a single, coherent framework. This was the achievement of Léon Walras, a lonely, cantankerous savant, often in straitened circumstances, plagued with hypochondria and a paranoid temperament, plodding doggedly through hostile, uncharted territory to discover a fresh vantage point from which subsequent generations of economists could set out to make their own discoveries.

William Jaffé

II
WALRAS'S ECONOMIC SYSTEM

Like John Stuart Mill and John Maynard Keynes, Léon Walras was the son of an economist. His father, Auguste Walras, was one of those excellent people (they seem to have existed since very near the dawn of history) who taught the true but unhelpful doctrine that value depends on scarcity (*rareté*); the son followed the father's teaching, but added to it something which lifts it on to another plane of precision. He defined *rareté* as *l'intensité du dernier besoin satisfait par une quantité consommée de marchandise*; scarcity equals marginal utility.

His position with Jevons and Menger as one of the independent discoverers of the marginal utility principle is generally regarded as Léon Walras's chief title to fame; and this no doubt justly enough. But anyone who comes a little closer to these writers cannot help feeling a little resentment at the habit of classifying them together, even for the joint receipt of such an honourable title. For each of them made contribution to economics which are peculiarly his own, and it is for these special contributions that they are still worth reading today.

Indeed, the modern reader of Walras's *Éléments d'économie politique pure* is struck by its affinity, not with the work of Jevons or Menger, but with that of Marshall. For a quite considerable part of the way Walras and Marshall go together; and when they separate, it is a difference of interests, rather than of technique, that divides them. While Walras was seeking for the general principles which underlie the working of an exchange economy, Marshall forged an analytical instrument capable of easier application to particular problems of history or experience. Yet, since the followers of Walras cannot always afford to be pure philosophers, and

Marshallians have their moments of reflection, the two systems have inevitably tended to grow back into one another as the years pass by.

This affinity between two writers of different upbringing and obviously very different mental outlook—their simultaneous development of what was then a very new line of thought—looks at first sight surprising, and one feels almost obliged to explain it by the intrinsic excellence of the path they followed: "it seems no honest heart can stray." Yet in fact there is a clear historical reason for it, one decisive influence we know to have been felt by both. Each of them had read Cournot.

Now although each makes a specific acknowledgement to Cournot, it is in each case couched in very general terms. They each tell us that Cournot showed them how to use the differential calculus in economics, and this may mean much or little. But it is at least striking that certain very significant elements of Cournot's mathematical economics, going far beyond the mere idea of using mathematical methods, appear in Walras and appear in Marshall.

Walras's work on the theory of money, and his relatively uninteresting writings on applied economics, cannot detain us here. It was in pure economics that his real interest lay, and the discovery of the conditions of static equilibrium under perfect competition was his central achievement. Like many pioneers, he was a little vague about the exact meaning of some of his results, and was perhaps inclined to claim for them more than they are actually worth. Yet our consciousness of its limitations should not blind us to the greatness of his achievement. Static equilibrium is far from being the whole of economics, but it is an indispensable foundation; and the greater part of that foundation was laid by Cournot and Walras. There are very few economists who have contributed so much to the permanent body of established truth as Walras did.

Comment may be made in conclusion on two qualities of his work taken as a whole. One is the realization of the unity of economic life which emerges so forcefully from his pages. Other economists had had a sense of this unity, but none before had shown it so well. For the unity which Walras demonstrated is not a unity of resources being allotted among a single system of ends—the only unity which really appears in Menger—it is a unity of diverse individual ends reconciled through the mechanism of the market. Yet this unity is as real as the other. In a free economic system, under pefect competition,

> thou canst not stir a flower
> Without troubling of a star.

The other great quality of Walras's work to which we may here allude is its rigorous "methodological individualism". Far better than any earlier economist—better even than Marshall—he realized that the only economic explanation of a phenomenon is its reference back to individual acts of choice. Even he did not emancipate himself entirely from that sham utilitarianism which was the bane of his contemporaries, and which led them to suppose that the working of the free market "maximized utility" for the community as a whole. But this in his work is a mere excresence, and is easily disregarded. In his central doctrines he held firmly to the true significance of economic subjectivism, and therefore broke with the labour theory of value more drastically than Marshall, and quite as drastically as the Austrians. For him individual choice was all-important in its function as explanation; and it is our realization of this which has led us to understand that it is not, for the economist, necessarily anything more.

Walras's inspired achievement was his theory of *l'équilibre économique* of the total economy. He developed various models of a general balance, which are based both on subjective data (the behaviour and aims of the employer and the household) *and* on objective data (production factors, technical advances, the prevailing legal and social order), and range from a simple barter economy with only two commodities to a production economy, in which many commodities and services are exchanged under conditions of free competition on both the productive services and the product markets. Walras did not merely, as has long been erroneously maintained, devise a static and purely functional system of balance excluding time and causality; he also conceived a comparative-static and dynamic model, in which the economic data and the behaviour patterns of the employers and the consumers are the causes of the balance of prices and quantities.

Walras's systems are contained in four essays, which appeared in book form in 1876 with the title *Théorie mathématique de la richesse sociale.*

In order to give the reader some idea of the comprehensive theory of general balance we will now explain the basic relationships by means of a theoretical economy in which many commodities are exchanged.

In a given economy m partners exchange n commodities under conditions of free competition and a perfect market, and we assume (as does Pareto but not Walras) a given quantity and distribution of goods together with a certain sequence in their consumption. How is the general balance of prices and commodities exchanged, determined under these conditions?

Before the exchange m partners possess the following quantities of n commodities:

$$\begin{array}{l} x_{1a},\ x_{1b}, \ldots,\ x_{1n} \\ x_{2a},\ x_{2b}, \ldots,\ x_{2n} \\ \cdot \quad \cdot \quad \cdot \quad \cdot \quad \cdot \quad \cdot \quad \cdot \\ x_{ma},\ x_{mb}, \ldots,\ x_{mn} \end{array}$$

which may be represented as:

$$a_i,\ b_i,\ldots,\ n_i\ (i=1,\ldots,\ m).$$

After the exchange the partners have

$$\begin{array}{l} r_{1a}\ r_{1b},\ldots,\ r_{1n} \\ r_{2a},\ r_{2b},\ldots,\ r_{2n} \\ \cdot\quad\cdot\quad\cdot\quad\cdot\quad\cdot \\ r_{ma},\ r_{mb},\ldots,\ r_{mn} \end{array}$$

or, abbreviated:

$$a_i',\ b_i',\ldots,\ n_i'\ (i=1,\ldots,\ m).$$

Let the functions of the marginal profits on n commodities be

$$\frac{dN}{da},\ \frac{dN}{db},\ldots,\ \frac{dN}{dn},$$

Because, by virtue of H. H. Gossen's second law, the marginal profits on the commodities obtained with the aid of the prices must be the same at the end of the exchange, and we must use one commodity as a price commodity (in our example commodity a) the $m(n-1)$ equations express the balance in the budget with m exchange partners and $n-1$ prices:

$$\begin{array}{c} \frac{dN_1}{da_1'}=\frac{1}{p_b}\cdot\frac{dN_1}{db_1'}=\ldots=\frac{1}{p_n}\cdot\frac{dN_1}{dn_1'} \\ \cdot\quad\cdot\quad\cdot\quad\cdot\quad\cdot\quad\cdot\quad\cdot\quad\cdot \\ \frac{dN_m}{da_m'}=\frac{1}{p_b}\cdot\frac{dN_m}{db_m'}=\ldots=\frac{1}{p_n}\cdot\frac{dN_m}{dn_m'}. \end{array} \tag{1}$$

Since, moreover, the amount spent on the commodities obtained (quantity multiplied by the price) is equal to the amount gained from the commodities disposed of, the following set of equations is obtained:

$$\begin{array}{c} a_1+b_1p_b+\ldots+n_1p_n=a_1'+b_1'p_b+\ldots+n_1'p_n \\ \cdot\quad\cdot\quad\cdot\quad\cdot\quad\cdot\quad\cdot\quad\cdot\quad\cdot\quad\cdot\quad\cdot\quad\cdot\quad\cdot \\ a_m+b_mp_b+\ldots+n_mp_n=a_m'+b_m'p_b+\ldots+n_m'p_n \end{array} \tag{2}$$

Finally the market can only be in equilibrium when in the case of every commodity the demand equals the supply, in other words when the sum of all the available amounts of commodities is the same before and after the exchange:

$$\begin{array}{c} \Sigma a_i' - \Sigma a_i = 0 \\ \cdot\quad\cdot\quad\cdot\quad\cdot \\ \Sigma n_i' - \Sigma n_i = 0 \end{array} \tag{3}$$

While we now have n equations under (3), the number in (2) is reduced to $m-1$, since one is already contained in the result. If we combine (3) with (2) we then obtain the equation which may be eliminated.

Walras's system thus contains $nm + n-1$ equations with whose help the nm quantities exchanged and the $n-1$ prices can be calculated.

Walras then extended this model by introducing the private producer and replacing the quantities of commodities available for the exchange by the production functions as the expression of the appropriate combinations of production factors.

He was thus enabled to show not only the horizontal but also the vertical interdependence and at the same time to determine the conditions of balance.

John Richard Hicks and Horst Claus Recktenwald

SOURCES

Essay I

William Jaffé, "Léon Walras", *International Encyclopaedia of the Social Sciences,* Vol. 16 (New York, 1968), abridged.

Essay II

John Richard Hicks, "Léon Walras", *Econometrica,* (1934). Abridged. And Horst Claus Recktenwald, "Walras's Economic System," previously unpublished paper.

Signature

Université de Lausanne.

Portrait

Photograph (Université de Lausanne).

BIBLIOGRAPHY

G. H. Bousquet, "L'Autobibliographie inédite de Léon Walras (1906)", *Revue économique*, 15, (1964).

L. Walras, "Autobiografia", *Giornale degli economisti*, 37 (1908).

V. Pareto, "Léon Walras", *Economic Journal*, 20 (1910).

J. A. Schumpeter, "Léon Walras", *Zeitschrift für Volkswirtschaft, Socialpolitik und Verwaltung*, 19 (1910). Translated and reprinted in J. A. Schumpeter, *Ten Great Economists: From Marx to Keynes* (New York, 1951).

A. W. Marget, "Léon Walras and the 'cash balance approach' to the problem of the value of money", *Journal of Political Economy*, 39 (1931).

W. Jaffé, "Unpublished Papers and Letters of Léon Walras", *Journal of Political Economy*, 43 (1935).

J. Golay, G. Leduc and F. Dulés, "Léon Walras à Lausanne", *Revue économique et sociale*, 6 (1948).

M. Boson, *Léon Walras, fondateur de la politique économique scientifique* (Paris, 1951).

E. Beach, "Le souvenir de Léon Walras", *Economie appliquée*, 6 (1953).

D. Patinkin, "Walras' theory of tâtonnement; Walras' theory of money". in Don Patinkin, *Money, Interest and Prices: An Integration of Monetary and Value Theory*, 2nd ed. (New York, 1965).

W. Jaffé, "Walras' theory of tâtonnement: a critique of recent interpretations", *Journal of Political Economy*, 75 (1967).

GUSTAV VON SCHMOLLER

1838–1917

Schmollers Persönlichkeit ist nicht immer richtig verstanden worden. In erster Linie war nämlich aufs deutlichste erkennbar die unerhörte Geschäftsgewandtheit, die ihm innewohnte. Vereinsleitung, Fakultätsleitung, Leitung literarischer Unternehmungen, alles dies war großartig entwickelt und erregte bei manchen Betrachtern eine gewisse Unruhe; es hieß dann: er will immer etwas, und da er auch immer Erfolg hatte, so hielten ihn die ferner Stehenden für einen Mann der Geschäfte. Das war er nun allerdings, aber er war es nicht allein, er war es nur nebenher . . . Denn ihn trieb vor allem sein historischer Sinn und sein menschenfreundliches Herz. G. F. KNAPP

Schmoller undertakes to treat each one of the materials he takes up for discussion from four viewpoints. He likes, first, so far as it is possible, to discuss the historical evolution of any economic institution. . . . Second, so far as the materials are available, he likes to give a statistical picture of how matters stand with respect to the topic under discussion in recent times. In the third place, he regards it as part of his duty to give what would ordinarily be considered theoretical analysis of the problem in hand. And finally he is seldom content without telling what ought to be done about the matter in question. W. C. MITCHELL

Moderne Kritik hat den Historismus so gründlich totgeschlagen, daß auch das geschichtliche Denken daran gestorben ist. E. VON BECKERATH

Denn Historismus ohne zureichende Idee erwies sich als Holzweg. Aber "Theorie" ohne praktische Anschauung und geschichtliche Kenntnis wäre nicht nur ein Unglück, sondern müßte auf die Dauer jeden politischen Ökonomen, ja die gesamte ökonomische Wissenschaft um Sinn und Wirkung bringen. E. SALIN

I
THE LIFE OF GUSTAV VON SCHMOLLER

Gustav von Schmoller, Professor of Social Sciences at the University of Berlin and Privy Councillor, was born on 24 June 1838, in Heilbronn, and died on 27 June 1917, while on a trip in Harzburg.

Schmoller was the son of a public finance official in Württemberg whose great-grandfather had come to Swabia as the war commissioner of Bernhard von Weimar, during the Thirty Years War. On his mother's side, he was a descendant of the commercial aristocracy of Calw, the most important industrial centre of Old Württemberg. There, his grandfather and his great-grandfather Gärtner led a life of distinguished retirement as notable private scholars, scientists and botanists; the great-grandfather being a member of the Petersburg Academy under the Empress Catherine II, the grandfather having contact with Goethe and scientific correspondence with Darwin. He lost his mother very early in life. His father, a kindly man of earnest disposition but cheerful nature, educated him and his brothers and sisters virtually single-handed, and by precept and example kindled in him a desire to strive for a decent and fitting goal, by steady application to work. In his early years he was supposed to have been susceptible to tuberculosis, and because of this he was brought up to lead a healthy life with an orderly working timetable. The lessons at the grammar school of his home town did not especially appeal to him: nor did such philological studies and methods play an important role in his later life. He was interested more in everyday things, people and conditions in his home environment, as well as more general scientific ways of thinking. In keeping with the family tradition, his father had decided that he should become a civil servant and, taking into consideration his weak health, his father employed him for one year at his finance office, after he had left grammar school and before taking up his studies at the university.

There he had not only got to know the elements of financial and administrative law, but also gained vivid insight into the nature of the country and its inhabitants, and into social and economic conditions. He received his entire university education at the University of Tübingen near his home, in the four years between 1857 and 1861. The Professors of Economics, Schüz and Helferich, influenced him as little as the Professors of Law. He was more impressed by the history lectures of Max Duncker. Apart from history and philosophy, he devoted himself to physics, chemistry and mechanical engineering. At the end of his formal studies he set about the treatment of a problem, assigned by Schüz, which was open to competition, and concerned economic thought at the time of the Reformation. He won the competition, and on account of this study, which was published in the *Tübinger Zeitschrift*, the degree of Doctor of Social Sciences was conferred upon him.

At the same time, in 1861, he passed the first examination in public administration and was allowed to complete the first stage of his practical training as a junior administrator of financial affairs in his father's treasury at Heilbronn. Here he found leisure for his scientific reading. He began a thorough study of the philosophical systems which had influenced the development of economic theories between 1750 and 1850. Already at this time he favoured the historical approach which Hildebrand and Roscher had adopted and which was also followed by Knies. Since List's time, a leading argument against the general validity of the so-called classical system of English economic theory was that it was based upon conditions quite different from the reality of life in Germany; now Schmoller thought of proving that it also depended on philosophical concepts that were then considered outmoded in Germany. The book in which he wanted to prove this was never written, but the preparatory studies for it affected Schmoller's later works.

For Schmoller's further education, it became particularly important for him to be allowed to spend the second period of his practical training at the Statistical Bureau, whose management his brother-in-law, Gustav Rümelin, had taken over after resigning from the Department of Culture.[1] He entrusted to Schmoller the work on the trade-census in Württemberg which was being taken just at that time; and this statistical study, which was published in 1862 in the Württembergisches Jahrbuch later induced the curator of the University of Halle to propose the appointment of the author as a lecturer. Without hesitating, he accepted the appointment at Halle in the spring of 1864.

In that year he wrote an important article for the Preussisches Jahrbuch concerning the labour question. It can be considered the precursor of a new socio-political trend in German economic theory.

His transfer to Halle and particularly his succession in 1865 to the professorial chair of Eiselen, who had taught something like Prussian political science, meant that Schmoller had now to become as familiar with the territory of the Prussian state, its constitution, administration and economy as with his native state of Württemberg. In order to get first-hand knowledge of the administration of Halle, he became a town councillor, and

[1] This important man exerted a very strong influence upon the young Schmoller, on the one hand, setting the example of a scholar with broad, general knowledge, and, on the other, by instilling in him esteem for the Prussian governmental system, at that time an unusual attitude in Württemberg.

during his vacations worked in the Berlin archives, shrewdly selecting administrative history during the time of Friedrich Wilhelm I as the main subject of his studies. More and more, Prussia became his paradigm in his study of the relation between government and economic activity.

It was also in Halle that the young professor set up house by marrying Lucie Rathgen, the daughter of a privy councillor in the Weimar area and granddaughter of Niebuhr, a man whom he held in high esteem. From this very happy and harmonious marriage two children were born, a son and a daughter.

The main literary work of his years in Halle was *The History of Small Business in Nineteenth-century Germany*, published in 1870, which, in view of the principle of a free market just then gaining acceptance, pointed out the necessity of not leaving everything to the free play of competition. On the contrary it advised, in the interest of public welfare, an interventionist policy of control, encouragement and regulation as appropriate. This new slant caused a great stir and some displeasure among the then dominant extreme liberal supporters of the Congress of Economists. Attacking this book by Schmoller and, at the same time, the one by Brentano on English trade unions, Heinrich Bernard Oppenheim, one of the most influential journalists of that school, published an article in the *Nationalzeitung* which was to become famous. In it he publicly indicted as academic socialists (*Kathedersozialisten*) the new school of social politicians. Brentano, at that time a university lecturer in Berlin, accepted the challenge. Roused by him, Adolf Wagner, the professor in Berlin who had not been prominent in socio-political matters up till then, contacted Schmoller; and in the latter's house in Halle a small group, including Hildebrand and his disciple Conrad, agreed to meet in Eisenach. Here, on 5 and 6 October 1872, the Verein für Socialpolitik (Society for social Policy) was founded, with Schmoller giving the opening address. Erwin Nasse, the professor at Bonn, was made the first chairman and on his death in 1890, Schmoller succeeded to the position.

His appointment in 1872 to the newly established University of Strassburg led Schmoller to make thorough economic and socio-historical studies of Strassburg's past, specifically of the period between the thirteenth and fifteenth centuries. This eventually resulted in a book, published in 1879, about the clothmakers' and weavers' guild.

The political science seminar, which he directed together with Knapp and Lexis, induced Schmoller to establish a series of "political and social science studies" (*staats- und sozialwissenschaftliche Forschungen*), which—published by Duncker & Humblot from the year 1878—served to collate material for the realistic study of facts on which he strove to found his theory of economic life.

Thus when he moved to Berlin in 1882, where he had twice, in 1870 and 1879, been unsuccessfully proposed for a full professorship, but where the doubts of the ministry regarding his socio-political involvement were only now disappearing, Schmoller was a mature scholar of forceful character, distinct individuality and well-established reputation. This socio-political alignment was the permanent link between him and his colleague Adolph Wagner, whose theoretical method was in clear contrast to Schmoller's historical-realistic approach. But it was not with this eminent representative of the theoretical school, but with the Viennese economist, Carl Menger, that Schmoller found himself in a sensational methodological dispute during his first active years in Berlin.

In his *Outline* as well as in his lectures Schmoller was trying, above all, to provide well-defined concepts which could be used as substance and basis of further studies. But, on the other hand, he took care not to express matters in terms more simple and clear than they were in reality. He emphasized that his theoretical ideas were limited by the hypotheses on which they were based; the perplexities in the practical tasks of economic policy; the relative merits of opposed points of view; and the fact that economic policy measures are not independent of place and time. He was averse to all radical solutions and schematic simplifications. Though the result of more than thirty-five years of research and teaching, it was still only an *Outline*: concise, compendious and mild in tone.

From 1884 he was a member of the Prussian State Council and from 1899 he represented in the Upper House (Herrenhaus) the university of Berlin, whose Chancellor he had been shortly before that time (in 1897–8). He was himself something of a statesman even though he always remained a scholar and never wanted to be anything else. His ennoblement and the title of Excellency which he received in his later years, set the seal so to speak upon the eminent personal position which he had gained. But also a great number of other academies and scholastic societies elected him as a member: from 1899 he was a member of the civil list of the order "Pour le mérite".

Schmoller's prominent influence as head of the historical school of economics brought him many an enemy among those who thought he threatened their own importance.

For thirty-five years Schmoller was active in Berlin. He remained lively in his old age doing steady, untiring work. The cause of his death was an aneurysm which took him unawares during a vacation trip in Harzburg shortly after he had entered the eighth decade of his life. A kind fate spared him the experience of witnessing the failure of the ideas and principles he had believed in and for which he had worked. His life's work belongs to a past epoch. Today, science and politics have turned toward other paths than those he followed, and there is no lack of petty and malicious criticism of his work and character. But a more profound, unprejudiced view can well recognize, even today, the influence of his thoughts and works.

Otto Hintze

II
THE PERSONALITY OF GUSTAV VON SCHMOLLER

Gustav von Schmoller was one of those outstanding personalities of the University of Berlin who was just as great a scholar as a teacher. He valued highly the importance of the teaching profession and therefore devoted to it all the time it demands. He had sympathy for the troubles of young people and their needs and showed kindly understanding for them. For years Schmoller's lectures were among the most popular at the University of Berlin and for a long time he used the largest auditorium as a lecture-hall. He was able to captivate not only the interest of the limited circle of the economics students but also that of members of other faculties and of the great majority of law students. Many of his listeners he inspired with the sort of enthusiasm for the science and for himself that made study become for them the real substance of life and contact with the teacher a stimulating experience. He required of a professor the ability to capture the genuine interest of his listeners, and he could say nothing more unfavourable of a university professor than that he was boring. Even the outsider gains real insight into his lecturing when the remark in the preface of his *Outline* is recalled: "the greatest strain on the mental powers occurs while preparing a lecture and my best ideas come to me then".

The seminar was the climax of his university work. While still in Halle he was the first to introduce classes of the type the historians held and soon his seminar was an important centre for the teaching of our science. His influence was great and worked everywhere as a ferment, but all of those who worked under him have been able to preserve their individuality: his circle embraces all methodological alignments, all subjects, all political convictions. He was able to give something special to everyone; he encouraged everyone along his respective way. In his way of life, his *economics*, constitutes a classic foundation for the whole outlook; and in his *Outline* he laid out social policy within the broad framework of social history describing in detail its function in the economy and the state. Nowhere do the merits of his intellectual approach come into play better. Basic social problems are seldom appreciated with such depth of understanding or the necessity of social reform viewed in a wider context. The moral philosopher, sociologist, historian, economist and politician have contributed equally to this powerful and wise work.

Schmoller was never prominent as a politician or member of a political party, nor did he participate as a speaker in political agitation. He lacked demagogic passion as well as popular appeal. He had become a town-councillor in Halle because of his interest in problems of administration, and as representative of the University of Berlin in the Upper House he spoke mainly as a scholar and as a standard-bearer of social reform. But political questions in their narrower sense interested him greatly and he was always concerned with them; he expressed his opinion on all great political issues in journalism and his political views substantially influenced his socio-political standpoint. His attitude to the monarchy, officialdom and democracy had its roots in his own distinctive personal and scholarly character. He was no romanticist and ardour for the national dynasty was as foreign to him as enthusiasm for a government of the people and equality of all. As a historian with definite ideas about German peculiarities and needs, he arrived at his opinions using the methods of the psychologist and sociologist. He considered the growth of democracy an ineluctable but necessary and healthy development. To resist it forcefully he thought would be as harmful as it would be foolish and therefore he was as opposed to the law against socialists as he was to patriarchal social policy. But he was also conscious of the dangers of democracy.

Because he valued experience and a feeling for things imponderable and personal, Schmoller was something of a philosopher and sage with respect to scientific and political problems. His judgment was well weighed and he considered every aspect of a subject. Nothing was more unlike him than to try to find a complete explanation or to pass a final verdict after considering only one aspect of a problem. He was the opposite of doctrinaire while one could well say that his contemporaries tended to develop just one particular line in economics from a multitude of sources. Associated with his disposition for judicious reflection and conciliation was his mildness, his kindness and his wish to understand others and to treat them fairly. His unique intellectual and emotional qualities combined to moderate each other. And yet, he did not lack determination. Much as he liked to mediate, decisiveness and in certain circumstances even asperity were not out of character for him. The two sides of his personality did not clash, nor make him a complicated character. His strength and kindness, his eagerness for action and repudiation of absolute solutions combined to produce a strong and serene individual with an integrated life, which enabled him to concentrate and to fight and made a leader of him. This also explains why he radiated confidence and assurance.

The range of qualities which Schmoller put to use in his work would be incomplete if one forgot his role as a writer and speaker. His open-minded view of the world has a counterpart in his style of writing. His measured judgment is reflected in the smooth rhythm of his sentence structure. Many of his book reviews and much of his *Outline* had to be written down quickly. But his style of writing is, on the whole, a polished one. As a speaker, Schmoller could always be sure of great effect. He spoke slowly, simply and unaffectedly. Even at the beginning of the 1890s his Swabian dialect was sufficiently pronounced to make it hard for persons from the North of Germany to understand him immediately. But the rationality of his delivery captivated his listeners, his insight having a profound effect upon his style of speaking and an outward effect on the speaker himself.

The life-work of Schmoller was only made possible by his unusual working powers, passionate energy and ideal working conditions. For the mere spectator Schmoller's energy was breathtaking. Work was the passion of his life. Schmoller read and wrote all day long. He went for walks in the streets near his home, reading as he walked. He never read a book for pleasure: while he read he sat at his desk making numerous excerpts. Reading without a pen in the hand he considered mere dalliance. We know how highly he valued the teaching profession but despite the high income to be had from lecturing he never agreed to giving more than one main lecture. In the same way he forwent the deanship in Berlin in favour of his academic work. Because of this he probably alienated more and more all those who did not partake in his great tasks. In his youth he drew and painted, he derived simple enjoyment from music, and our great poets occupied him for a long time. In his last decades, however, he was completely absorbed in his professional interests. He hardly visited a theatre, a concert or a exhibition. Schmoller found mental distraction in the many facets of his work: a change of subject brought him relaxation and refreshment. Thus, his professional dedication did not make him indifferent or resistant to new ideas. Its many-sidedness kept his mind youthful and always enabled him to draw new subjects into his field.

Schmoller led a happy scholastic life and was able to work in unusually favourable working conditions. He was, on the whole, spared illnesses and other adverse circumstances. His greatest thanks he expressed to his wife in the dedication of his *Outline*, and everyone who knew this marriage knows that this was well-deserved. The ideal working conditions without which Schmoller's work would not have been possible were the result of her complete subordination of herself and of the whole household to the work of her husband: her suppression of all wish for a social life and entertainment despite her social graces; her assumptions of all the contingent duties which accompanied his position and her understanding and enjoyment of his creative work at first hand.

Arthur Spiethoff

III
THE WORK OF GUSTAV VON SCHMOLLER

Today when the memory of Schmoller is blurred, we should remember that his charismatic quality extended not only to those working in his own field, but also to eminent sociologists, philosophers and historians such as F. Tönnies, M. Weber, G. Simmel and O. Hintze. W. Dilthey's assessment can be found in his correspondence with York von Wartenburg; it is contained in the posthumous draft for a review of Schmoller's *Outline*. The *Methodenstreit* with the Viennese school of economics was a thing of the past when Joseph Schumpeter, who himself came from Vienna, analysed Schmoller's historical significance in a famous article (1926), comparing him with A. Marshall—both rose above "the economics of simple hypotheses and rough-edged results".

Nevertheless, Schmoller is today, strangely enough, still part of the intellectual scene. He lives on as a prototype of a movement which should strictly be condemned. He is praised little more than Klopstock in Lessing's famous epigram, more often he is criticized although very little read. By spokesmen of that school, which is directed as it should be towards pure theory, as well as by young scholars, who received their education after the Second World War, he is frequently seen as the destroyer of theoretical thinking, having done great harm to the science of economics in Germany. As if the authority of a single man could "destroy" a science if the new approach which he introduced and promoted were not sustained by strong intellectual foundations. Central to the controversy is the reproach about his basic "hostility towards theory". This accusation is, however, purely fictitious. At all times Schmoller considered it essential to think in simplified terms, in "thought-pictures"; to make use of abstraction and conceptual analysis, to make "deductions from accepted truths to well-established theses"—as was said at that time. Whether he himself had the ability to be a theorist of this type is another question. If one analyses the chapters of the *Outline* on value and price theory, especially "market value", "which in a way helped to establish the importance of all economic values", one can infer that he by no means exhausted the analytical possibilities as did the Viennese school, rather he aims at showing reality in its wealth of forms.

"The main line and clarity of pure theory are being obliterated" in this fight for reality (A. Spiethoff).

Any thinker who endeavours to find the essence of a science has the right to be understood not only in terms of his own mental individuality but also with reference to the influences that shaped him. Schmoller's way of thinking was a product of the classical-idealistic tradition of the first half of the nineteenth century. As was correctly pointed out by C. Brinkman in his book about Schmoller, this tradition was alien to the Austrian economists. Thus, Schmoller's ethical-historical philosophy stood in contrast to the natural law tradition of the rationalist Viennese school—a contrast which was the philosophical context for the above-mentioned *Methodenstreit* with Carl Menger. Superficially, its cause was the alleged "inductive-deductive" antithesis, which was for Schmoller a pseudo-problem that had been settled long ago, and which would not have caused such a great stir, had not underlying philosophical implications for the science been involved.

Today, it might be a matter of course to condemn the "historical-ethical" approach. Yet there are reasons to delay execution of the verdict. No reasonable person can deny that the subject matter of economics is changing continually in the course of time. The historical aspect attracted Schmoller so strongly that although he did not really fail to appreciate the possibility of arriving at an abstract solution hypothetically, he did not think very highly of it. Anyway, with regard to the older Schmoller it is not correct to claim that he mistook economic history, which conveys the wealth of forms of past economic life, for economic theory. He was well able to distinguish between the two. But he saw the essence and goal of his research to be an unbiased study of facts in order to clarify them through detailed work, and to understand them by "exact" causal analysis. Thereby he hoped to discover the basis path of development and to grasp the "fundamental principles of economic life" (Dilthey) by abstracting them from the multitude of real-life phenomena. Tracing everything back to the causes required taking into consideration psychological, ethical and cultural factors, and Schmoller always considered it essential to utilize the respective sciences for this purpose.

If one places Schmoller in the social setting of his time, he appears as an intellectual representative of the high bureaucracy and educated middle class. With the latter group he shared an optimistic philosophy of life. Even though economic "theories of stages of development", of which he contributed one himself, were only working hypotheses for him—valid only until revoked—he clearly expressed his belief in ethical progress in history which, however, is interrupted by "temporary epochs of physical, mental and moral decay". In this respect he was not using the dialectic position of Hegel but derived the idea of progress from an optimistic view of mankind, an idea which today is considered to belong to the last two hundred years. Schmoller believed social equalization to be the function of the State, whose sinews were the impartial officials, a work of art that, as he said, could only be accomplished in favourable circumstances. He had fewer doubts in the continued existence of the state than Bismarck himself, although Schmoller was by no means an unconditional admirer of Bismarck's art of government. His tendency toward "power politics" meant that he ignored his principles and argued in an apparently inconsistent way for pragmatic reasons, during a debate concerning protective tariffs and free trade.

Schmoller's scientific activity was very extensive. He was concerned about types of enterprise, the history of the city and government and especially about the political and economic development of Prussia. But his endeavours went further. W. Sombart praised him for his "vivid conception of the world and man", for his close attachment to philosophy and history. Today, this is more a criticism than a compliment. The progress of the science of economics, is a matter of self-limitation, should by no means be underrated: thinking in terms of models; the close connection of theory and statistics; and the macro-economic way of thinking contributed much to make economic science an essential basis of economic policy. But one must no less concede the right of existence to a science which goes beyond its limits in order to bring to light, together with other sciences, man's character and his skills. The true relevance of Schmoller's work lies in this, rather than in a dangerous narrowing of the horizon of the subject.

Erwin von Beckerath

SOURCES

Essay I

Otto Hintze, "Gustav von Schmoller", *Deutsches Biographisches Jahrbuch,* 2, 1917–20 (Deutsche Verlagsanstalt, Berlin and Leipzig, 1928).

Essay II

Arthur Spiethoff, "Gustav von Schmoller", *Schmollers Jahrbuch,* 42 (1918). Abridged.

Essay III

Erwin von Beckerath, "Gustav von Schmoller", *Staatslexikon,* 6 (Herder Verlag, Freiburg, 1961). Abridged.

Signature

University Library, Tübingen.

Portrait

Portrait by Schulte im Hofe, 1908, Berlin (University Library, Tübingen).

BIBLIOGRAPHY

O. Hintze, "Gustav Schmoller als Historiker", in O. Hintze, *Historische und politische Aufsätze,* Vol. 4 (Berlin, 1908).

H. Herkner, *Gedächtnisrede auf Gustav Schmoller.* Verhandlungen des Vereins für Sozialpolitik, 1919 (Munich and Leipzig, 1920).

C. Menger, "Gustav Schmoller", *Almanach der Akademie der Wissenschaften* (Vienna), 68 (1920).

G. v. Below, "Zur Stellung G. Schmollers in der Geschichte der Nationalökonomie, *Schmollers Jahrbuch*, 48 (1924).

H. Herkner, "Zur Stellung G. Schmollers in der Geschichte der Nationalökonomie", *Schmollers Jahrbuch*, 47 (1924).

E. Salin, "Zur Stellung G. Schmollers in der Geschichte der Nationalökonomie", *Schmollers Jahrbuch*, 48 (1924).

A. Spiethoff, "Zum Abschluß", *Schmollers Jahrbuch*, 48 (1924).

G. F. Knapp, "Gustav Schmoller", in *Einführung in einige Hauptgebiete der Nationalökonomie* (Munich and Leipzig, 1925).

C. Meitzel, "Gustav v. Schmoller", in *Handwörterbuch der Staatswissenschaften,* Vol. 7, 4th edition (Jena, 1925).

J. A. Schumpeter, "Gustav Schmoller und die Probleme von heute", *Schmollers Jahrbuch*, 50 (1926), reprinted in J. A. Schumpeter, *Dogmenhistorische und biographische Aufsätze* (Tübingen, 1954).

R. Michels, "Gustav Schmoller", in R. Michels, *Bedeutende Männer* (Leipzig, 1927).

F. Meinecke, "Drei Generationen deutscher Gelehrtenpolitik: Friedrich Theodor Visher—Gustav Schmoller—Max Weber", in F. Meinecke, *Staat und Persönlichkeit: Studien* (Berlin, 1933).

W. Mitscherlich, "Die ökonomischen Querschnitte Schmollers", in W. Mitscherlich, *Die Lehre von den beweglichen und starren Begriffen, erläutert an der Wirtschaftswissenschaft* (Stuttgart, 1936).

C. Brinkmann, *Gustav Schmoller und die Volkswirtschaftslehre* (Stuttgart, 1937).

A. Spiethoff (ed.), "Gustav Schmoller und die deutsche geschichtliche Volkswirtschaftslehre, Festgabe zur 100. Wiederkehr seines Geburtstages", *Schmollers Jahrbuch*, 62 (1938).

W. Eucken, "Wissenschaft im Stile Schmollers", *Weltwirtschaftliches Archiv,* 52 (1940).

Th. Heuss, *Gustav Schmoller, Deutsche Gestalten. Studien zum 19. Jahrhundert* (Stuttgart and Tübingen, 1947).

G. Ritzel, *Schmoller versus Menger: Eine Analyse des Methodenstreits im Hinblick auf den Historismus in der Nationalökonomie* (Frankfurt a.M., 1950).

C. Brinkmann, "Gustav Schmoller", in *Handwörterbuch der Sozialwissenschaften,* Vol. 9 (Stuttgart, 1953).

F. C. Lane, "Some Heirs of Gustav von Schmoller", in *Architects and Craftsmen in History: Festschrift for Abbott Payson Usher* (Tübingen, 1956).

W. Fischer, "Gustav v. Schmoller", in *International Encyclopedia of the Social Sciences,* Vol. 14 (New York, 1968).

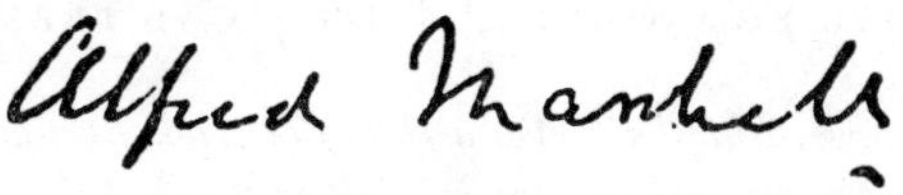

ALFRED MARSHALL

1842–1924

He had a strong feeling against half-baked work, pot-boilers, anything rapidly thrown off. For himself at all events, he felt that his strength was limited and that he must give all he had to perfected work of a kind that had promise of lasting significance. He was frail of body; and he believed himself frail of mind also, in the sense that he was sensitive to the strain of concentrated intellectual attention.

I mean only that by temperament he was a man of science, not a preacher. He explains, he rarely exhorts. F. W. TAUSSIG

I had a growing feeling in the later years of my work at the subject that a good mathematical theorem dealing with economic hypotheses was very unlikely to be good economics: and I went more and more on the rules—(1) Use mathematics as a shorthand language, rather than as an engine of inquiry. (2) Keep to them till you have done. (3) Translate into English. (4) Then illustrate by examples that are important in real life. (5) Burn the mathematics. (6) If you can't succeed in (4), burn (3). This last I did often. A. MARSHALL

The economics of group-action, of collective control, massive competition and mass bargaining have yet to be written. What we can say with confidence is that Marshall's Principles *contributed to the corpus of scientific ideas elements which were not only "architectonic" and "in some sense his own", but are still "an existing yeast working in the Cosmos" and far from dying. On the evidence so far available, its author abundantly deserves the title "classical" even on his own somewhat exacting standard.* G. F. SHOVE

He never forces an argument or a theory to a logical conclusion where it loses touch with reality.

The keynote of the Principles *is that it relates always to a dynamic world of change and movement and that all his tools are chosen with a view to throwing light on the working of economic forces in such a world.*

In just over one page, Marshall gives a theory of trade fluctuations which includes waves of optimism and pessimism, the shortage of effective demand, the multiplier, and the accelerator—it is all there. Professor Robertson holds that it is still the best short account of the trade cycle in the whole of economic literature.

C. W. GUILLEBAUD

I
ALFRED MARSHALL

Alfred Marshall was born at Clapham on 26 July 1842, the son of William Marshall, a cashier in the Bank of England, by his marriage with Rebecca Iliver. The Marshalls were a clerical family of the West, sprung from William Marshall, incumbent of Saltash, Cornwall, at the end of the seventeenth century.

His father, the cashier in the Bank of England, was a tough old character, of great resolution and perception, cast in the mould of the strictest Evangelicals, bony neck, bristly projecting chin, author of an Evangelical epic in a sort of Anglo-Saxon language of his own invention which found some favour in its appropriate circles, surviving despotically-minded into his ninety-second year. The nearest objects of his masterful instincts were his family, and their easiest victim his wife; but their empire extended in theory over the whole of womankind, the old gentleman writing a tract entitled *Man's Rights and Woman's Duties*. Heredity is mighty, and Alfred Marshall did not altogether escape the influence of the parental mould. An implanted masterfulness towards womankind warred in him with the deep affection and admiration which he bore to his own wife, and with an environment which threw him in closest touch with the education and liberation of women.

At nine years of age Alfred was sent to Merchant Taylors' School, for which his father, perceiving the child's ability, had begged a nomination from a Director of the Bank. He used to make the boy work with him for school, often at Hebrew, until eleven at night. Indeed Alfred was so much overworked by his father that, he used to say, his life was saved by his Aunt Louisa, with whom he spent long summer holidays near Dawlish. Rising to be Third Monitor, he became entitled in 1861, under old statutes, to a scholarship at St John's College, Oxford. It was the first step to ordination in the Evangelical ministry for which his father designed him. But this was not the main point for Alfred—it meant a continued servitude to the classics. He had painful recollections in later days of his tyrant father keeping him awake into the night for the better study of Hebrew, whilst at the same time forbidding him the fascinating paths of mathematics. His father hated the sight of a mathematical book, but Alfred would conceal Potts' Euclid in his pocket as he walked to and from school. He read a proposition and then worked it out in his mind as he walked along, standing still at intervals, with his toes turned in. The fact that the curriculum of the sixth form at Merchant Taylors' reached so far as the differential calculus, had excited native proclivities. Airy, the mathematical master, said that "he had a genius for mathematics". Mathematics represented for Alfred emancipation, and he used to rejoice greatly that his father could not understand it. No! he would not be buried at Oxford under dead languages; he would run away—to be a cabin-boy at Cambridge and climb the rigging of geometry and spy out the heavens.

At this point there comes on the scene a well-disposed uncle, willing to lend him a little money (for his father was too poor to help further, when the Oxford Scholarship was abandoned)—repaid by Alfred soon after taking his degree from what he earned by teaching—which, with a Parkin's Exhibition of £40 a year from St. John's College, Cambridge, opened to him the doors of mathematics and of Cambridge.

A power of intense concentration for brief periods, combined with a lack of power of continuous concentration, was characteristic of him all his life. He was seldom able to execute at white heat any considerable piece of work. He was also bothered by the lack of a retentive memory: even as an undergraduate his mathematical book-work troubled him as much as the problems did. As a boy he had a strong arithmetical faculty, which he afterwards lost.

Meanwhile at St John's College, Cambridge, Alfred Marshall fulfilled his ambitions. In 1865 he was Second Wrangler, the year when Lord Rayleigh was Senior, and he was immediately elected to a Fellowship. He proposed to devote himself to the study of molecular physics. Meanwhile he earned his living (and repaid Uncle Charles) by becoming for a brief period a mathematical master at Clifton, under Percival, for whom he had a great veneration. A little later he returned to Cambridge and took up coaching for the mathematical tripos for a short time. In this way "Mathematics", he said, "had paid my arrears. I was free for my own inclinations."

It was at this time and under these influences that there came the crisis in his mental development, of which in later years he often spoke. His design to study physics was (in his own words) "cut short by the sudden rise of a deep interest in the philosophical foundation of knowledge, especially in relation to theology".

In Marshall's undergraduate days at Cambridge a preference for mathematics over classics had not interfered with the integrity of his early religious beliefs. He still looked forward to ordination and his zeal directed itself at times towards the field of foreign missions. A missionary he remained all his life, but after a quick struggle religious beliefs dropped away, and he became, for the rest of his life, what used to be called an agnostic. Nevertheless Marshall, like Sidgwick, was as far as possible from adopting an "anti-religious" attitude. He sympathized with Christian morals and Christian ideals and Christian incentives. There is nothing in his writings depreciating religion in any form; few of his pupils could have spoken definitely about his religious opinions. At the end of his life he said, "Religion seems to me an attitude", and that, though he had given up theology, he believed more and more in religion.

From metaphysics, therefore, Marshall turned his mind to ethics. It would be true, I suppose, to say that Marshall never departed explicitly from the utilitarian ideas which dominated the generation of economists who preceded him. But it is remarkable with what caution—in which respect he goes far beyond Sidgwick and is at the opposite pole from Jevons—he handled all such matters. There is, I think, no passage in his works in which he links economic studies to any ethical doctrine in particular. The solution of economic problems was for Marshall, not an application of the hedonistic calculus, but a prior condition of the excess of man's higher faculties, irrespective, almost, of what we mean by "higher". The economist can claim, and this claim is sufficient for his purposes, that "the study of the causes of poverty is the study of the causes of the degradation of a large part of mankind". Correspondingly, the possibility of progress "depends in a great measure upon facts and inferences, which are within the province of economics; and this it is which gives to economic studies their chief and their highest interest". This remains true even though the question also "depends partly on the moral and political capabilities of human nature; and on these matters the economist has no special means of information; he must do as other do, and guess as best he can."

In 1868, when he was still in his metaphysical stage, a desire to read Kant in the original led him to Germany. "Kant my guide," he once said, "the only man I ever worshipped: but I could get no further: beyond seemed misty, and social problems came imperceptibly to the front. Are the opportunities of real life to be confined to a few?" He lived at Dresden with a German professor who had previously coached Henry Sidgwick. Hegel's *Philosophy of History* greatly influenced him. He also came in contact with the work of the German economists, particularly Roscher. Finally Dr Bateson, the Master of St. John's, was instrumental in giving him a career in life by persuading the College to establish for him a special lectureship in moral science. He soon settled down to economics, though for a time he gave short courses on other branches of moral science—on logic and on Bentham.

His dedication to economic study—for so he always considered it, not less ordained in spirit than if he had fulfilled his father's desire—was now effected. His two years of doubt and disturbance of mind left on his imagination a deep impression, to which in later years he would often recur with pupils whom he deemed worthy of the high calling—for so he reckoned it—of studying with scientific disinterestedness the modes and principles of the daily business of life, by which human happiness and the opportunities for good life are, in great measure, determined.

The study of economics does not seem to require any specialized gifts of an unusually high order. Is it not, intellectually regarded, a very easy subject compared with the higher branches of philosophy and pure science? Yet good, or even competent, economists are the rarest of birds. An easy subject, at which very few excel! The paradox finds its explanation, perhaps, in that the master-economist must possess a rare *combination* of gifts. He must reach a high standard in several different directions and must combine talents not often found together. He must be mathematician, historian, statesman, philosopher—in some degree. He must understand symbols and speak in words. He must contemplate the particular in terms of the general, and touch abstract and concrete in the same flight of thought. He must study the present in the light of the past for the purposes of the future. No part of man's nature or his institutions must lie entirely outside his regard. He must be purposeful and disinterested in a simultaneous mood; as aloof and incorruptible as an artist, yet sometimes as near the earth as a politician. Much, but not all, of this ideal many-sidedness Marshall possessed. But chiefly his mixed training and divided nature furnished him with the most essential and fundamental of the economist's necessary gifts—he was conspicuously historian and mathematician, a dealer in the particular and the general, the temporal and the eternal, at the same time.

The task of expounding the development of Marshall's economics is rendered difficult by the long intervals which generally separated the initial discovery and its oral communication to pupils from the final publication in a book to the world outside. Before attempting this, it will be convenient to trace briefly the outward course of his life from his appointment to a lectureship at St. John's College, Cambridge, in 1868 to his succession to the Chair of Political Economy in Cambridge in 1885.

For nine years Marshall remained Fellow and Lecturer of St. John's, laying the foundations of his subject but publishing nothing. At this time he used to go abroad almost every long vacation.

"These *Wanderjahre* gave him a love for the Alps which he always retained, and even in 1920 (for the last time) we went to the South Tyrol where he sat and worked in the high air." (Mrs Marshall.)

In 1875 Marshall visited the United States for four months. He toured the whole of the East, and travelled as far as San Francisco. At Harvard and Yale he had long talks with the academic economists, and he had many introductions everywhere to leading citizens. But his chief purpose was the "study of the problem of protection in a new country". About this he inquired on all hands.

The American trip made on him a great impression, which coloured all his future work.

Meanwhile he had been helping Fawcett, who was Professor, and Henry Sidgwick, to establish political economy as a serious study in the University of Cambridge. Two of his earliest pupils, H. S. Foxwell and, later on, my father, John Neville Keynes, who took the Moral Sciences Tripos in 1875, joined these three as lecturers on political economy in the University.

In 1876 Alfred Marshall became engaged to Miss Mary Paley, a great-granddaughter of the famous Archdeacon. Miss Paley was a former pupil of his and was a lecturer in Economics at Newnham. His first book, *Economics of Industry*, published in 1879, was written in collaboration with her; indeed it had been, at the start, her book and not his, having been undertaken by her at the request of a group of Cambridge University Extension lecturers. They were married in 1877. During forty-seven years of married life his dependence upon her devotion was complete. Her life was given to him and to his work with a degree of unselfishness and understanding that makes it difficult for friends and old pupils to think of them separately or to withhold from her shining gifts of character a big share in what his intellect accomplished.

Marriage, by involving the loss of his Fellowship, meant leaving Cambridge for a time, and Marshall went to Bristol as the first Principal of University College, and as Professor of Political Economy. Soon after his marriage his health and nerves began to break down, chiefly as a result of stone in the kidney. He went with his wife to Italy for nearly a year and came back to Bristol in 1882 with his health much restored; but he remained for the rest of his life somewhat hypochondriacal and inclined to consider himself on the verge of invalidism. In fact, his constitution was extremely tough and he remained in harness as a writer up to a very advanced age. But his nervous equilibrium was easily upset by unusual exertion or excitement or by controversy and difference of opinion; his power of continuous concentration on difficult mental work was inferior to his wishes; and he became dependent on a routine of life adapted to his whims and fancies. In truth he was haunted by a feeling that his physical strength and power of continuous concentration were inferior to the fields of work which he saw stretching ahead, and to the actual constructions he had conceived but not yet given to the world. By 1877, when he was thirty-five years of age, he had worked out within him the foundations of little less than a new science, of great consequence to mankind; and a collapse of health and strength during the five years following, when he should have been giving all this to the world, partly broke his courage, though not his determination.

On the premature death of Arnold Toynbee in 1883, Jowett invited Marshall to take his place as Fellow of Balliol and Lecturer in Political Economy to the selected candidates for the Indian Civil Service.

Marshall's Oxford career was brief but successful. He attracted able pupils, and his public lectures were attended by larger and more enthusiastic classes than at any other period of his life. He encountered with credit, on different occasions, Henry George and Hyndman in public debate, and was taking a prominent position in the University. In November 1884, however, Fawcett died, and in January 1885 Marshall returned to Cambridge as Professor of Political Economy.

Marshall's serious study of economic theory began in 1867; his characteristic doctrines were far developed by 1875; and by 1883 they were taking their final form. Nevertheless no part of his work was given to the world at large in adequate shape until 1890 (*Principles of Economics*), and that part of the subject, at which he had worked earliest and which was most complete by 1875, was not treated in a published book until nearly fifty years later, in 1923 (*Money, Credit and Commerce*). Meanwhile he had not kept his ideas to himself, but had shared them without reserve in lecture and in talk with friends and pupils. They leaked out to wider circles in privately printed pamphlets and through the writings of his pupils, and were extracted in cross-examination by Royal Commissions. Inevitably when the books themselves appeared, they lacked the novelty and path-breaking powers which would have been acclaimed in them a generation earlier, and those economists all over the world who know Marshall only by his published work may find it difficult to understand the extraordinary position claimed for him by his English contemporaries and successors. It is proper, therefore, that I should make an attempt to set forth the reasons or the excuses for the unhappy delay in their publication.

Marshall, as already pointed out above, arrived very early at the point of view that the bare bones of economic theory are not worth much in themselves and do not carry one far in the direction of useful, practical conclusions. The whole point lies in applying them to the interpretation of current economic life. Diagrams and pure theory by themselves might do more harm than good, by increasing the confusion between the objects and methods of the mathematical sciences and those of the social sciences, and would give what he regarded as just the wrong emphasis. In publishing his intellectual exercises without facing the grind of discovering their points of contact with the real world, he would be following and giving bad example. On the other hand, the relevant facts were extremely hard to come by—much harder than now.

The other valid reason was a personal one. At the critical moment of his life his health was impaired. After health was restored, the preparation of lectures and the time he devoted to his pupils made big interruptions in the writing of books. He was too meticulous in his search for accuracy, and also for conciseness of expression, to be a ready writer. He was particularly unready in the business of fitting pieces into a big whole and of continually rewriting them in the light of their reactions on and from the other pieces. He was always trying to write big books, yet lacked the power of rapid execution and continuous concentration (such as J. S. Mill had) and that of continuous artistic sensibility to the whole (such as Adam Smith had) which are necessary for the complete success of a Treatise.

Marshall was conscious of the great superiority of his powers over those of his surviving contemporaries. In his inaugural lecture of 1885 he said: "Twelve years ago England possessed perhaps the ablest set of economists that there have ever been in a country at one time. But one after another there have been taken from us Mill, Cairnes, Bagehot, Cliffe Leslie, Jevons, Newmarch and Fawcett." There was no one left who could claim at that date to approach Marshall in stature. To his own pupils, who were to carry on the Economics of the future, Marshall was ready to devote time and strength. But he was too little willing to cast his half-baked bread on the waters, to trust in the efficacy of the cooperation of many minds, and to let the big world draw from him what sustenance it could.

Moreover, did not Marshall, by keeping his wisdom at home until he could produce it fully clothed, mistake, perhaps, the true nature of his own special gift? "Economics", he said, "is not a body of concrete truth, but an engine for the discovery of concrete truth." This engine, as we employ it today, is largely Marshall's creation. He put it in the hands of his pupils long before he offered it to the world. The building of this engine was the essential achievement of Marshall's peculiar genius. Yet he hankered greatly after the "concrete truth" which he had disclaimed and for the discovery of which he was not specially qualified. I have very early memories, almost before I knew what economics meant, of the sad complaints of my father, who had been able to observe as pupil and as colleague the progress of Marshall's thought almost from the beginning, of Marshall's obstinate refusal to understand where his special strength and weakness really lay, and of how his unrealizable ambitions stood in the way of his giving to the world the true treasures of his mind and genius. Economics all over the world might have progressed much faster and Marshall's authority and influence would have been far greater, if his temperament had been a little different.

Two other characteristics must be mentioned. First, Marshall was too much afraid of being wrong, too thin-skinned towards criticism, too easily upset by controversy even on matters of minor importance. An extreme sensitiveness deprived him of magnanimity towards the critic or the adversary. This fear of being open to correction by speaking too soon aggravated other tendencies. Yet after all there is no harm in being sometimes wrong—especially if one is promptly found out. Nevertheless this quality was but the defect of the high standard he never relaxed—which touched his pupils with awe—of scientific accuracy and truth.

Second, Marshall was too anxious to do good. He had an inclination to undervalue those intellectual parts of the subject which were not *directly* connected with human well-being or the condition of the working classes or the like, although *indirectly* they might be of the utmost importance, and to feel that when he was pursuing them he was not occupying himself with the highest. It came out of the conflict, already remarked, between an intellect, which was hard, dry, critical, as unsentimental as you could find, with emotions and, generally unspoken, aspirations of quite a different type. When his intellect chased diagrams and foreign trade and money, there was an evangelical moralizer of an imp somewhere inside him, that was so ill-advised as to disapprove. Near the end of his life, when the intellect grew dimmer and the preaching imp could rise nearer to the surface to protest against its lifelong servitude, he once said: "If I had to live my life over again I should have devoted it to psychology. Economics has too little to do with ideals. If I said much about them I should not be read by businessmen." But these notions had always been with him. This was the defect of that other great quality of his, which always touched his pupils—his immense disinterestedness and public spirit.

At any rate, in 1877 Marshall turned aside to help his wife with the *Economics of Industry* (published in 1879), designed as a manual for Cambridge University Extension lecturers, which as it progressed became more and more his work. In later years Marshall grew very unfriendly to the little book. After the publication of the *Principles* he suppressed it and replaced it in 1892 with an almost wholly different book under the same title which was mainly an abridgement of the *Principles* and "an attempt to adapt it to the needs of junior students". Marshall's feelings were due, I think, to the fact that his theory of value, which was here first published to the world, was necessarily treated in a brief and imperfect manner, yet remained for eleven years all that the outside world had to judge from. His controversies in the *Quarterly Journal of Economics* in 1887 and 1888 with American economists who had read the little book accentuated this feeling. He also revolted later on from the conception of economics as a subject capable of being treated in a light and simple manner for elementary students by half-instructed extension lecturers aided by half-serious books. "This volume", he wrote in 1910 to a Japanese translator of the 1879 book, "was begun in the hope that it might be possible to combine simplicity with scientific accuracy. But though a simple book can be written on selected topics, the central doctrines of economics are not simple and cannot be made so."

Yet these sentiments do a real injustice to the book. It won high praise from competent judges and was, during the whole of its life, much the best little textbook available. If we are to have an elementary textbook at all, this one was probably, in relation to its contemporaries and predecessors, the best thing of the kind ever done.

After this volume was out of the way, Marshall's health was at its worst. When in 1881 he went abroad to recuperate, his mind did not return to money or to foreign trade, but was concentrated on the central theories which appeared in the *Principles*. The next nine years were spent on the preparation of this book which was published in July 1890.

By 1890 Marshall's fame stood high, and the *Principles of Economics, Volume 1*, was delivered into an expectant world. Its success was immediate and complete. The book was the subject of leading articles and full-dress reviews throughout the Press. The journalists could not distinguish the precise contributions and innovations which it contributed to science; but they discerned with remarkable quickness that it ushered in a new age of economic thought. The new political economy had arrived, and the old political economy, the dismal science, "which treated the individual man as a purely selfish and acquisitive animal, and the State as a mere conglomeration of such animals," had passed away. "It will serve", said the *Daily Chronicle*, "to restore the shaken credit of political economy, and will probably become for the the present generation what Mill's *Principles* was for the last." "It has made almost all other accounts of the science antiquated or obsolete," said the *Manchester Guardian*. "It is not premature to predict that Professor Marshall's treatise will form a landmark in the development of political economy, and that its influence on the direction and temper of economic inquiries will be wholly good." These are samples from a general chorus.

The way in which Marshall's *Principles of Economics* is written is more unusual than the casual reader will notice. It is elaborately unsensational and under-emphatic. Its rhetoric is of the simplest, most unadorned order. It flows in a steady, lucid stream, with few passages which stop or perplex the intelligent reader, even though he know but little economics. Claims to novelty or to originality on the part of the author himself are altogether absent. Passages imputing error to others are rare; and it is explained that earlier writers of repute must be held to have *meant* what is right and reasonable, whatever they may have said. The connexity and continuity of the economic elements, as signified in Marshall's two mottoes, "*Natura non facit saltum*" and "The many in the one, the one in the many," are the chief grounds of difficulty. But, subject to this, the chief impression which the book makes on the minds of uninitiated readers—particularly on those who do not get beyond Book 4—is apt to be, that they are perusing a clear, apt and humane exposition of fairly obvious matters.

By this stylistic achievement Marshall attained some of his objects. The book reached the general public. It increased the public esteem of economics. The minimum of controversy was provoked. The average reviewer liked the author's attitude to his subject-matter, to his predecessors, and to his readers, and delighted Marshall by calling attention to the proper stress laid by him on the ethical element and to the much required humanizing which the dismal science received at his hands; and, at the same time, could remain happily insensible to the book's intellectual stature. As time has gone on, moreover, the intellectual qualities of the book have permeated English economic thought, without noise or disturbance, in a degree which can easily be overlooked.

The method has, on the other hand, serious disadvantages. The lack of emphasis and of strong light and shade, the sedulous rubbing away of rough edges and salients and projections, until what is most novel can appear as trite, allows the reader to pass too easily through. Like a duck leaving water, he can escape from this douche of ideas with scarce a wetting. The difficulties are concealed; the most ticklish problems are solved in foot-notes; a pregnant and original judgment is dressed up as a platitude. The author furnishes his ideas with no labels of salesmanship and few hooks for them to hang by in the wardrobe of the mind. A student can read the *Principles*, be fascinated by its pervading charm, think that he comprehends it, and, yet, a week later, know but little about it. How often has it not happened even to those who have been brought up on the *Principles*, lighting upon what seems a new problem or a new solution, to go back to it and to find, after all, that the problem and a better solution have been always there, yet quite escaping notice! It needs much study and independent thought on the reader's own part, before he can know the half of what is contained in the concealed crevices of that rounded glove of knowledge, which is Marshall's *Principles of Economics*.

The Marshalls returned in 1855 to the Cambridge of the early years after the reforms, which finally removed restrictions upon the marriage of Fellows. They built for themselves a small house, called Balliol Croft, on St. John's College land in the Madingley Road. Here Alfred Marshall lived for nearly forty years.

He did not much care to go to other people's houses, and was at his best fitting his guests comfortably into a narrow space, calling out staff directions to his wife, in unembarrassed, half-embarrassed mood, with laughing, high-pitched voice and habitual jokes and phrases. He had great conversational powers on all manner of matters; his cheerfulness and gaiety were unbroken; and, in the presence of his bright eyes and smiling talk and unaffected absurdity, no one could feel dull.

In earlier days, particularly between 1885 and 1900, he was fond of asking workingmen's leaders to spend a weekend with him. Sometimes these visits would be fitted in with meetings of the Social Discussion Society, which the visitor would address. In this way he came to know most of the leading cooperators and trade unionists of the past generation. In truth he sympathized with the Labour Movement and with socialism (just as J. S. Mill had) in every way, except intellectually.

From 1885 to 1890 he was mainly occupied, as we have seen, with the *Principles*. These five years were the most active and productive of his life.

He gave two lectures a week in a general course, and one lecture a week on special theoretical difficulties, but he lectured, as a rule, in only two terms out of three, making about forty-five lectures in the year.

It was not Marshall's practice to write out his lectures. "He rarely used notes", Mrs Marshall writes, "except for lectures on economic history. He sometimes made a few notes before he went to lecture, and thought over them on his way to the class. He said that the reason why he had so many pupils who thought for themselves was that he never cared to present the subject in an orderly and systematic form or to give information. What he cared to do in lectures was to make the students *think with him*. He gave questions once a week on a part of the subject which he had not lectured over, and then answered the questions in class. He took immense pains in looking over the answers, and used red ink on them freely." I think that the informality of his lectures may have increased as time went on. Certainly in 1906, when I attended them, it was impossible to bring away coherent notes. But the above was always his general method.

After the publication of the *Principles* in 1890, his first task was to prepare the abridgement, entitled *Economics of Industry,* which appeared early in 1892. He also spent much time on the successive revisions of the *Principles*, the most important changes being introduced in the third edition, published in 1895, and the fifth edition in 1907. It is doubtful whether the degree of improvement effected corresponded to the labour involved. These revisions were a great obstacle to his getting on with what was originally intended to be Volume 2 of the *Principles.*

The main interruption, however, came from his membership of the

Royal Commission on Labour, 1891–4. He welcomed greatly this opportunity of getting into close touch with the raw material of his subject, and he played a big part in the drafting of the Final Report. The parts dealing with trade unions, minimum wage, and irregularity of employment were especially his work.

During his twenty-three years as Professor, he took part in three important movements: the foundation of the British Economic Association (now the Royal Economic Society), the women's degrees controversy at Cambridge, and the establishment of the Cambridge Economics Tripos.

In a formal sense Marshall was founder of the Cambridge School of Economics. Far more so was he its founder in those informal relations with many generations of pupils, which played so great a part in his life's work and in determining the course of their lives' work.

To his colleagues Marshall might sometimes seem tiresome and obstinate; to the outside world he might appear pontifical or unpractical; but to his pupils he was and remained a true sage and master, beyond criticism, one who was their father in the spirit and who gave them such inspiration and comfort as they drew from no other source. Those eccentricities and individual ways, which might stand between him and the world, became, for them, part of what they loved.

It is difficult to describe on paper the effect he produced or his way of doing it. The pupil would come away with an extraordinary feeling that he was embarked on the most interesting and important voyage in the world. He would walk back along the Madingley Road, labouring under more books, which had been taken from the shelves for him as the interview went on, than he could well carry, convinced that here was a subject worthy of his life's study. Marshall's double nature, coming out informally and spontaneously, filled the pupil seated by him with a double illumination. The young man was presented with a standard of intellectual integrity, and with it a disinterestedness of purpose, which satisfied him intellectually and morally at the same time. The subject itself had seemed to grow under the hands of master and pupil, as they had talked. There were endless possibilities, not out of reach.

It must not be supposed that Marshall was undiscriminating towards his pupils. He was highly critical and even sharp-tongued. He managed to be encouraging, whilst at the same time very much the reverse of flattering. Pupils, in after life, would send him their books with much trepidation as to what he would say or think.

Marshall retired from the Chair of Political Economy at Cambridge in 1908, aged sixty-six. He belonged to the period of small salaries and no pensions. Nevertheless he had managed out of his professorial stipend (of £700, including his Fellowship), which he never augmented either by examining or by journalism, to maintain at his own expense a small lending library for undergraduates, to found a triennial Essay Prize of the value of £60 for the encouragement of original research, and privately to pay stipends of £100 a year to one, or sometimes two, young lecturers for whom the University made no provision and who could not have remained otherwise on the teaching staff of the School of Economics. At the same time, with the aid of receipts from the sales of his books, he had saved just sufficient to make retirement financially possible. As it turned out, the receipts from his books became, after the publication of *Industry and Trade*, so considerable that, at the end of his life, he was better off than he had ever been; and he used to say, when Macmillan's annual cheque arrived, that he hardly knew what to do with the money. He had left his economic library to the University of Cambridge, and most of his estate and any future receipts from his copyrights are also to fall ultimately to the University for the encouragement of the study of economics.

Freed from the labour of lecturing and from the responsibility for pupils, he was now able to spend what time and strength were left him in a final effort to gather in the harvest of his prime. Eighteen years had passed since the publication of the *Principles*, and masses of material had accumulated for consolidation and compression into books. He had frequently changed his plans about the scope and content of his later volumes, and the amount of material to be handled exceeded his powers of coordination.

During this period the interruptions to the main matter in hand were inconsiderable. At last, in 1919, *Industry and Trade* appeared, a great effort of will and determination on the part of one who had long passed the age when most men rest from their labours.

It is altogether a different sort of book from the *Principles*. The most part of it is descriptive. A full third is historical and summarizes the results of his long labours in that field. The coordination of the parts into a single volume is rather artificial. The difficulties of such coordination, which had beset him for so many years, are not really overcome. The book is not so much a structural unity, as an opportunity for bringing together a number of partly related matters about which Marshall had something of value to say to the world.

Industry and Trade was a remarkable success with the public.

His powers of concentration and of memory were now beginning to fail somewhat rapidly. More and more he had to live for the book alone and to save for that every scrap of his strength. Talk with visitors tired him too much and interfered too seriously with his power of work. More and more Mrs Marshall had to keep them away from him, and he lived alone with her, struggling with time. He would rest much, listening to his favourite melodies on the auto-piano, which was a great solace to him during the last ten years of his life, or hearing Mrs Marshall read over again a familiar novel.

In August 1922, soon after his eightieth birthday, *Money, Credit and Commerce* was finished, and it was published in the following year, 1923. The scope of the volume differed from his design, in that it did not include "a study of the influences on the conditions of man's life and work which are exerted by the resources available for employment". But he managed to bring within the covers of a book his chief contributions to the theories of money and of foreign trade.

One day in his eighty-second year he said that he was going to look at Plato's *Republic*, for he would like to try and write about the kind of republic that Plato would wish for, had he lived now. But though, as of old, he would sit and write, no advance was possible.

In these last days, with deep-set and shining eyes, wisps of white hair, and black cap on his head, he bore, more than ever, the aspect of a sage or prophet. At length his strength ebbed from him. But he would wake each morning, forgetful of his condition and thinking to begin his day's work as usual. On 13 July 1924, a fortnight before his eighty-second birthday, he passed away into rest.

John Maynard Keynes

II
ALFRED MARSHALL

Marshall's greatest single contribution to the theory of value consisted in his classification of value problems in accordance with the element of time-value in the market, in the short period, and in the long period. In the case of the market we are dealing with a *stock* of goods already in existence, which are the fruits of past production, their costs having been already incurred.

In the short period we are dealing with a *flow* of output from a substantially fixed *stock* of instruments of production: the short period being defined in terms of "operational time", as any period of time too short to enable the stock of specialized plant, machinery and skill to be altered appreciably as a result of changes in the earnings of these factors.

In the long period we are dealing with a *flow* of output from a *flow* of all the factors of production which cooperate in producing that output: the long period being defined for purposes of the real world as any period long enough to enable the level of earnings of the specialized factors to influence appreciably their supply. There is, however, another sense in which Marshall uses the term "the long period", which is as a hypothetical position of full long-period equilibrium such as would be attained, *ceteris paribus*, if a given set of long-period forces remained constant for a long enough time for all the factors concerned to become fully adjusted to these conditions.

The influence of demand on the one hand and of prime and overhead costs on the other upon value differs fundamentally according to which of these time periods is under consideration. By his device of the representative firm he was able to draw a long-period supply curve, each point on which represented the full long-period marginal cost of production of the corresponding output, this marginal cost in turn being the average cost of production per unit of output (including a normal profit) of the firm which was representative in the sense (*inter alia*) that its size, internal and external economies, and so on were directly related to the size of the output in question. But Marshall's "long period", even in the full sense of the term, was only a "partial equilibrium", and very different from the stationary state. He conceived economic development as an evolutionary process, and never thought of economic forces as working to an achieved equilibrium. Thus his long period was set against a background of historical change—it was a tool of economic analysis rather than a picture of what actually happens in the real world.

An essential part in Marshall's time analysis is played by his doctrine of quasi-rent, which he defined as the excess of any of the total receipts from an instrument of production made by man, say a machine, over the prime costs, including wear and tear, of working that machine.

Amongst other important concepts which economics owes (in whole or in part) to Marshall may be mentioned: consumer's surplus; elasticity of demand and its mathematical expression as $\frac{\delta x}{x} \div -\frac{\delta y}{y}$; the significance for value theory and for economic policy of the distinction between increasing and decreasing returns; the role of internal and external economies; the notion of substitution at the margin; the limitations on the doctrine of maximum satisfaction; the distinction between average and marginal revenue in the case of monopoly and imperfect competition; and the discovery, to quote Keynes, "of a whole Copernican system by which all the elements of the economic universe are kept in their place by mutual counterpoise and interaction".

Finally, Marshall stands out amongst other economists for his consistent employment, in the handling of specific economic problems, of the method of partial equilibrium whereby a given set of economic forces is considered in isolation, all other repercussions and possible disturbing forces being impounded in *ceteris paribus*.

It is very necessary, however, for the reader of *The Principles of Economics* to bear in mind always that by design, though not in the result, it was intended to be Volume 1 of a systematic treatise extending to four or five volumes. It was only the foundations that he laid in this volume, while the greater part of the superstructure was never completed.

Claude William Guillebaud

SOURCES

Essay I

John Maynard Keynes, "Alfred Marshall," *Economic Journal*, 34 (1924). Abridged.

Essay II

Claude William Guillebaud, "Alfred Marshall", in *Handwörterbuch der Sozialwissenschaften*, Vol. 7 (ed. Gustav Fischer, J. C. B. Mohr, Vandenhoeck and Ruprecht, Stuttgart, Tübingen and Göttingen, 1961).

Signature

Marshall Library of Economics, Cambridge.

Portrait

Marshall Library of Economics, Cambridge.

BIBLIOGRAPHY

F. W. Taussig, "Alfred Marshall", *Quarterly Journal of Economics*, 39 (1924–5).

A. C. Pigou, *Memorials of Alfred Marshall* (London, 1925)

W. R. Scott, "Alfred Marshall, 1842–1924", in *British Academy, London,* "*Proceedings*", II (1925).

T. Parsons, "Wants and Activities in Marshall", *Quarterly Journal of Economics*, 4 (1931–2).

J. A. Schumpeter, "Alfred Marshall", *American Economic Review*, 31 (1941), reprinted in J. A. Schumpeter, *Ten Great Economists: From Marx to Keynes* (New York, 1951; London, 1952).

G. J. Stigler, *Production and Distribution Theories: 1870 to 1945* (New York, 1941), Chapter 4.

J. Viner, "Marshall's Economics in Relation to the Man and to His Times", *American Economic Review*, 31 (1941).

D. H. MacGregor, "Marshall and His Book", *Economica*, 9 (1942).

A. C. Pigou, *Alfred Marshall and Current Thought* (London, 1953).

B. Corry, "Alfred Marshall", in *International Encyclopedia of the Social Sciences*, Vol. 10 (New York, 1968).

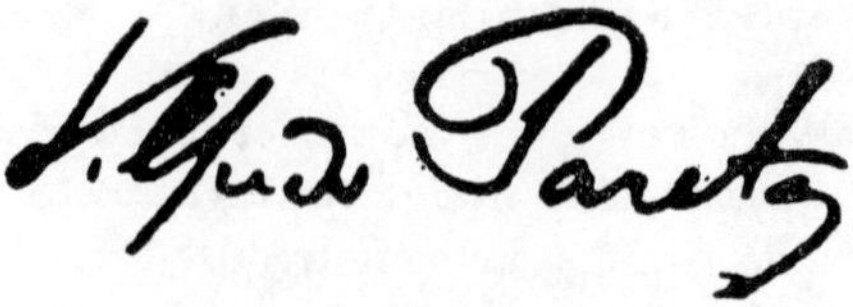

VILFREDO PARETO

1848–1923

Indépendant et égocentrique jusqu'à l'anarchie, ne souffrant pas la plus petite ombre de contrainte extérieure, de quelque coté qu'elle provienne, et spécialement de la part des puissants.

T. GIACALONE-MONACO

Paretos unstillbarer Hunger nach Wirklichkeit und sein kompromißloser Mut, das als wahr Erkannte, auch wenn es unbequem erscheint, ohne Rücksicht auf sich oder andere auszusprechen, lassen ihn so als unvergeßliches Vorbild einer aufrechten Forscherpersönlichkeit vor unserem geistigen Auge Gestalt gewinnen.

G. EISERMANN

. . . he always points beyond himself.

J. A. SCHUMPETER

Die Originalität von Pareto beruhte gerade darin, die Konzeption von Edgeworth sozusagen umzustülpen und ihre Technik als taugliches Instrument für den eleganten und strikten Ausdruck der lange in ihm herangereiften neuen Theorie der Wahlakte zu erkennen, aus der er "alles Erforderliche für die Gleichgewichtstheorie ohne Rückgriff auf die Ophelemität" ableiten konnte.

G. EISERMANN

In diesem Wunsch, Geschichte und Mathematik zusammenzufügen, erkennt man auf die Dauer alle bedeutenden Bahnbrecher auf dem Gebiete der Nationalökonomie.

JOHAN ÅKERMAN

I
VILFREDO PARETO

Vilfredo Pareto was born in Paris on 15 July 1848, of a French mother and of a father (exiled at the time) who belonged to a patrician Genoese family.[1]

Pareto's father was a highly cultured man, interested in all exercises of the mind. There is no direct information about the influence exerted by Raffaele Pareto over his son, Vilfredo.

We know little more than the name of Pareto's mother. Born in 1816 in Toulon (Nièvre, not the Mediterranean sea port), Marie Méteníer was the daughter of "*un vigneron*" (wine-grower). Three children—two daughters and a son—were born of the marriage between Raffaele Pareto and Marie Méteníer. My researches show that the mother was not a Protestant as some people told. There was no church wedding and the young Vilfredo was not baptized.

He came to Italy in his earliest years—it is not known exactly when: probably in 1853.

Destined, like his father, to become an engineer, he studied at the Polytechnic of Turin. In 1869 he submitted his thesis on the fundamental principles of the equilibrium of solids.

In a letter to A. Antonucci, he gives the following valuable indications on what he thought at the time. At the age of sixteen, he says, he had read Bossuet, whom he had disliked intensely, whereas Bastiat, on the contrary, fully satisfied his feelings of individual independence, which were completely opposed to those of his surroundings. "Whence I may say", he concludes, "that my views were not acquired but were the consequence of my character which was such from birth." At the age of twenty, he read Buckle who reminded him of the physical sciences and seemed to him the *non plus ultra*. His ideal at the time was based on liberal economics—"an almost perfect science". The sovereignty of the people was axiomatic for him, liberty a panacea, militarism and religion the scourges of mankind, the Cobden league "the most sublime thing in humanity".

[1] Vilfredo Pareto's family originates from the place known as della Fontana Buona near Chiavari (Riviera di Levante). It acceded to the nobility on 22 January 1729, in the person of Giovanni Lorenzo. The family arms are a black eagle on a green background. One of Giovanni Lorenzo's grandsons was the Marquis Giovanni Benedetto Pareto (1768–1831) who was, on 18 May 1811, according to a decree of Napoleon I, dated at Rambouillet, created *baron de l'Empire*. He had three sons by his marriage to Aurelia Spinola: Raffaele, the youngest, born at Genoa on 28 July 1812, was Vilfredo's father.

After a period as engineer with the Roman Railways from 1870 to 1873, Pareto settled in Tuscany and ended up in Florence as Director General of the *Ferriere Italiene* whose plants were at San Giovanni Val d'Arno. He retired in 1890.

His profession obliged him to make trips to England, Scotland and Germany, but he gained little scientific advantage from these journeys because he did not speak German and, although he could read English perfectly, he spoke it badly.

This phase of his life lasted for about twenty years. Between the end of 1889 and the spring of 1893 there were important changes in his life. In December 1889, after his mother's death, he married Alessandra ("Dina") Bakounine, aged 29. Whether her father was related to the famous revolutionary Prince Bakounine is unknown.

There were no children of this marriage, and this is not surprising, considering the ideas he frequently expounded to Pantaleoni on this subject. Leaving no possible doubts about his thinking, he invited him to take inspiration from the "divine Malthus", and to be the progenitor of science rather than of children. Dina was an educated woman; she spoke German and translated an article by her husband into English.

Pareto wrote of this marriage: "I do not thirst for money. On the contrary, I have performed acts in my life, including marriage, without regard for fortune, which very reasonable people would perhaps have regarded as open to objection."

The second event worthy of note is the beginning (on 1 October 1890) of his correspondence with Professor Maffeo Pantaleoni, at that time Director of the Commercial College of Bari (later, Professor at Naples and Rome Universities, as well as, for a short time, at Geneva). He also made the acquaintance of the French professor, Léon Walras, who was teaching at Lausanne, and whom he was to succeed in the scholastic year of 1892–3. But let us first of all deal with his Florentine period.

In his leisure moments and especially during his sleepless nights at the time, engineer Pareto accumulated a prodigious volume of the most varied knowledge in the fields of economics, sociology and history.

Three men exerted a considerable influence over him as far as his literary, culture is concerned; the philologist, Domenico Comparetti, the Aristophanes specialist, Augusto Franchetti, and Arturo Linaker, philosopher and philologist. At this time, Pareto was also influenced by Comte, Darwin, Bain and Spencer; later, however, he more or less denied this influence.

In particular his knowledge of Greco-Roman antiquity deepened[2]

[2] It is sufficient to look through his works to see the incalculable number of ancient writers he quotes: in the *Cours* (§ 246), in just a few pages, he mentions Tacitus, Stobeus, Aristophanes, Juvenal, Plato, Aristotle, Plutarch, Eubulus,

thanks to his complete mastery of the two languages concerned. He had a veritable passion for Greek, and his disciple Pierre Boven told me one day that taking up a text of Aristotle in the original, he reeled off the French translation.

In his *Sociologia* (§ 158) Pareto speaks of the Greek language with enthusiasm: "The many forms of the verb, and the precision of the part they play in syntax, constitutes an admirable whole." It is amusing to compare Pareto with Edgeworth, who went as far as to quote the Greek poets in the midst of his mathematical developments. Pareto took very little interest in other forms of art; for him, the sum of musical achievement was to be found in Offenbach's operettas; anything else was merely a noise.

But at this period, he was less interested in science than in action; he was, in the sense of the word current at the time, an intransigent liberal, particularly in the economic field.

He was not, however, very successful in his action. He stood twice, but vainly (1880 and 1882), for the legislative elections. In November 1882, he was beaten in the Pistoia-Prato constituency. In 1891, lectures he wanted to hold at Milan were interrupted by the police. He then published the text in the *Revue des Deux Mondes* in Paris.

His attitude on doctrinal matters was very clear. As a liberal, he would have none of "socialism", of state intervention, particularly if it is in favour of the bourgeoisie. And on this point he wrote with especial vigour. Speaking in a monograph about a workman in Romagna with an annual income of 586 lire, he calculated that a tenth of this wretched sum goes to the protectionist Government. He called for "A little more justice, a little less armament."

In the *Giornale degli Economisti*, December 1892, he had pointed out that the owners of the Italian ricefields were banding together in order to obtain protection from the Government and that, when "their workers ask for a little protection, in reply they are shot at. . . . The hour for expiation will come in the end for the governing classes. Slowly but surely, the socialist tide is mounting on the European continent." All this because free-trade was not practised, and Pareto proceeded to show at this time in a number of publications, as he was to do at Lausanne, the evils engendered by protectionism, which was ruining the country, hand in glove with militarism. Liberalism, on the contrary, remains the "intangible, frank, straight, sound doctrine, and the liberals gain nothing by choosing as their ground political manoeuvering." As for him, he adopts the slogan of the Cobden Club: "Free trade, peace, good will among nations".

Hesiod, Polybius, Pliny, Petronious, the *Digest*, Herodotus, Strabo, Ovid, and others, merely in discussion of the question of obstacles in the development of the population.

Although, shortly before becoming professor at Lausanne, in 1890, Pareto began to publish some works on mathematical economics, they were slight in scope and until the end of his Florentine period, or almost, Vilfredo Pareto, who was then over forty, contributed nothing to science. His immense erudition remained under a bushel. He had perhaps not spoiled his life, but nothing suggested that he was to do anything notable in the course of it. Such late flowerings of talent are extremely rare.

In Tuscany, Pareto was far from being an absolutely outstanding engineer. In politics not only had he no success, but he did not give the impression of being a very redoubtable adversary of the Government. He was an idealist, highly intelligent, of indomitable energy and profoundly honest, who was revolted (rather naively) at seeing the world so little in accordance with his ideal.

In 1890, Pareto discovered a small, but most important work, the *Principis d'economia pura*, by Maffeo Pantaleoni (1857–1924). Pantaleoni was to be the greatest Italian economist of his time, after Pareto himself, and they formed a lasting friendship, despite the differences of opinion which sometimes separated them. Pantaleoni's little book had a decisive importance in Pareto's scientific orientation. He has told how, thanks to it, he was able to grasp the value of works concerning pure economics, which put him on the track of mathematical economy, as elaborated by Léon Walras, and revealed to him the concept of general economic equilibrium. It is not an exaggeration to state that the idea of general equilibrium formed Pareto's scientific philosophy, and that the whole of his work, particularly his *Sociologia*, is based on this idea; only too often, however, this is not realized. Whatever the reason, it was from 1892 onwards, namely from the end of his stay in Tuscany, that he began his output of scientific work on pure economy—the sphere where his worth has now been accepted for many years.

It was about 1890 that Pareto learned of the work of Léon Walras (1837–1910), who had held the chair of economics from 1870 at the Academy (later University) of Lausanne.

Pareto succeeded Walras[3] (at a salary of 4000 francs, later 5000, "*e basta per tutta la vita*").[4] He delivered his inaugural lecture on 12 May 1893.

From this moment on, we must distinguish between two things in Pareto: 1. the man who, as formerly, fought for an ideal; and 2. the scholar who then emerged and whose work was steadily to take shape.

Until about the turn of the century, Pareto hardly changed his views, and in particular he continued to attack the Italian Government violently. We need not deal here with his works, but we would like to draw attention

[3] Gradually Walras gave up teaching in view of the state of his health.

[4] Letter to Pantaleoni, 16 January 1897. Fortunately, it was not exactly so.

to some other points concerning Pareto's personality on which his correspondence with Pantaleoni, among others, throws a very interesting light.

In the first place, there is material on Pareto's conception of friendship. He always remained very true to his friends, even when he was not in agreement with them (for example, during the Dreyfus affair when he was opposed to the anti-semitism of his friend Placci) and he even rendered the greatest services to the Italian Socialists fleeing their country after the disorders in Milan in 1898. Besides, Pareto always distinguished between the doctrines which he combated and the men professing them.

We would now like to draw attention to another aspect of Paretos' mentality, his irony. It is sparkling, and this has even been bad for his scientific work, for only too often—as when he indulges in polemics—he adopts a tone that is not generally found in scientific books.

In *Systèmes socialistes*, he observes that reformers now wish to crystallize society. If this had been so in former times, "we would not have had the works of Rousseau, Morelli, Comte—which would perhaps have been no great loss"—but neither would we have had those of Galileo, Newton and so on. An economist having had the misfortune to write that "price is a concrete manifestation of value", Pareto observed: "With this admirable phraseology, it may be said that the cat is the concrete manifestation of felinity", and so on.

In the years around 1900, great changes were to take place in Pareto's life and in his attitude to social problems.

In 1898, on the death of his uncle Domenico, Pareto had come into a rich legacy. In fact, says Pantaleoni, he became a millionaire (in gold francs). According to my information, he was at that time more than a millionaire.[5] This was one of the reasons that prompted him to leave the canton of Vaud[6] and to settle in Céligny, a small enclave of the canton of Geneva

[5] A figure of seventeen million lire has been mentioned as his fortune in 1923: it is not known if this is correct: it seems very high. Pareto's solicitor was *maître* César Drouin, of Geneva, whose records might yield information on this and other aspects of Pareto's life.

He invested most of the money in England and in other foreign shares. The First World War and the subsequent devaluations brought him severe losses. During the war, a large part of his assets having been requisitioned by the English government, he complained bitterly to his London bankers, but met with a very unenthusiastic reception. We shall see him later fighting to the bitter end to defend his fortunes against the ravages of the Socialists.

[6] The Constitution of Vaud of 1885 had instituted progressive taxation, with steep progressivity for personal fortune. As Pareto's wealth had increased considerably in 1898 as a result of the legacy from his uncle, it may be supposed that he considered the rate excessive and decided to settle in the canton of Geneva. "I wish to be neither robber nor robbed. I realize that this is not possible but at least I am looking for a place where one is robbed in modest proportions."

inside the canton of Vaud on the banks of the Lake of Geneva 40 kilometres from Lausanne and 20 from Geneva.

At Céligny he bought, in 1900, a villa that he called the "Angora" because of his predilection for the cats of that race.

Yet another major change took place in his private life, a short time after he had settled at Céligny. In November 1901, Pareto had to go to Paris, and at the same time his wife had to spend some time in Russia. The Marchioness Pareto, née Bakounine, did indeed leave for Russia, with thirty pieces of luggage, but she went in the company of a person of very low social standing: her chef.

Pareto immediately filed a suit for separation from Dina with the Florentine Tribunal.

The woman who was to become his second wife (he married practically on his death-bed) was Jeanne Régis ("Jane"), a Parisian girl; she was thirty-one years younger than Pareto.[7]

Of importance for us is the change that overcame Pareto as regards his attitude to social problems. He wished to be a scholar and nothing else. Now, at the same time, he became more and more a "reactionary", but in a very special sense. He thought that the degenerate bourgeoisie would be overthrown, but he saw no objection to that. The very idea amused him.

On two points, however, he varied fairly little: 1. Formerly a pacifist and a humanitarian, he was never in the future to praise war, and above all not war among European powers. 2. Formerly an out-and-out free-trader, he was now to recognize that, for sociological reasons, a certain degree of industrial protection could indirectly develop the riches of a country. However, he maintained, protection had always a direct effect. It destroyed wealth and, on the whole, the theories of classical economics appeared truer to him than the other theories.

The decisive and fairly abrupt swing lies elsewhere. In very general terms, from now on he lost his interest in action. Besides, his state of health became less and less satisfactory.

Pareto became more and more a religious, without showing himself anti-religious. He did not defend any ideal. Pareto tried to explain the change of attitude by the fact that from now on he wanted to "exclude feeling". There is almost always some truth in this as regards his theories, but he sets them out in a very strange manner for a scientist.

[7] What part did Jane Régis play in Pareto's life? It is difficult to give a definite opinion. Goethe was very happy with his Christiane Vulpius; Jane Régis, as far as her origin and education were concerned, was certainly not Christiane's inferior. The opinion of those who have known Jane are not unrestrictedly favourable.

To my mind, Pareto's explanation of his *revirement* is not entirely satisfactory, and we must seek an answer elsewhere. Could it be the result of old age? To be sure, he is not the only example of a man who turns conservative as he grows old. That is almost the rule. And then—at least I imagine so—the fact of having acquired a large fortune was not exactly likely to slow down this evolution. But what appears to me much more significant is that one finds in his earlier writings the seeds of this thought which was subsequently to take a quite different turn. Thus, I attach the greatest importance to this sentence, taken from his letter of 17 February 1892 to Pantaleoni: "When the radicals come to power, I will probably be in the opposition."

From all this we can, I think, deduce one of Pareto's psychological characteristics (apparently right up to his end)—the horror of what the Italians call *prepotenza*, a word which is difficult to translate. He refused to bow to the strong, not so much perhaps because they oppress the underdog, but above all because they are the strongest and because he, Pareto, is determined not to sit back passively, not to bend under that he regards as tyranny. He never sang the praises of any kind of power, not even Fascism.

We may therefore say that, in spite of everything, there is a certain continuity in Pareto's tendencies which can be explained by his temperament. Giacalone Monaco's judgment seems to me excellent: "Independent and egocentric to the point of anarchy, suffering not the slightest shadow of outward constraint from whatever direction it came, and above all from the powerful."

Once installed at Céligny, Pareto gradually gave up teaching at the University (in 1916, he gave his last series of lectures on sociology).

He also forwent travelling; and his trips to Italy became extremely rare. However, in 1906—and for the only time in his life—he did the University of Bologna the honour of delivering some courses in sociology, the only time that he ever lectured as Professor on Italian soil.

It was at Céligny that he drafted his last two great works: the *Manuale d'Economia Politica* and his *Trattato di Sociologia Generale*. Of all his other minor publications, we need only cite the *Mythe vertuiste* where he joins issue with the "Dominicans of virtue" and their efforts to hunt down "immoral writings". This little book published in French,[8] then in an expanded Italian edition, is interesting because, among other things, at the end, he strays from his subject in the strict sense and sets forth some of

[8] He had then already published in French his two first books: *Cours d'économie politique* (1896–7) and *Les systèmes socialistes* (1901–2).

his basic sociological theses on the role of feelings in society. It is a very clear and concentrated summary of the long and sometimes confused chapters of the *Sociologia*. He formulates this idea which is very true, although paradoxical for the unsuspecting reader who is accustomed to see in Pareto the greatest sceptic as regards all religions, all beliefs and all convictions: "Nothing is more practical than the ideal!" for it is this that impels men to action.

If Pareto thus gradually withdrew from the world, a generation of very young economists in his country grew up who were to look up to him as their inspiration, to the great chagrin of the University which reacted vigorously. The process, incidentally, was slow, but this generation is now dead.

It does not seem that Pareto did much to facilitate relations with the University authorities, especially the Italians, owing to his imperious character and his unwillingness to suffer the slightest contradiction.

Several disciples have confirmed to me that this was one of his weaknesses, and it did not disappear with age. Quite the reverse. Those who called on him were urged to observe the greatest prudence: "Above all, do not contradict", said Pantaleoni to F. Vinci before his pilgrimage to Céligny. The other fault of character was of the same order. Pareto was very accessible to flattery.

The University organized for him (as it had done for L. Walras in 1909) a Jubilee ceremony which took place in the middle of the War in the presence of German, French and Italian scholars on 6 July 1917. 11 November 1918 marked the end of the First World War. Pareto was seventy years old, and he still had a little less than five years to live.

Of this period, Pantaleoni has written that the Master's mission was accomplished. If he did not outlive himself, a certain weariness was noticeable in him, marked by repetitiveness, by a decline in his verve and in the liveliness with which he expressed himself—in place of the old torrential and sparkling originality. "He no longer surpassed himself, even if his productions were better than those of his contemporaries."

Among these last works we may note above all his Postscript to a collection of articles, entitled *Fatti e Teorie*, in which he studies the extent to which his forecasts, particularly as regards the war, have been borne out or not, and why Germany ended by losing the war. He also published a collection of four articles that originally appeared in the *Rivista di Milano*, forming a small book called *Transformazione della Democrazia*. He again, as in his younger days, wrote numerous articles, especially in the *Resto del Carlino*. It is said that having, as is certain, lost large sums as a result of the war, he tried to increase his earnings. Old people often suffer from the fear of being left without means.

He died on 19 August 1923 as a result of a heart attack. He had lived for some weeks beyond his seventy-fifth birthday.

Let us now say a few words of his outward appearance and of the milieu in which he lived after 1900.

What struck people at the Villa Angora was that the inside was old-fashioned, lacking in taste and without any personal touch. In the garden there were numerous animals but the Angora cats were rarely given permission to leave a sort of verandah which smelled badly. Everything about the Master himself was of the greatest simplicity. His desk, for example, consisted of a simple table of ordinary wood. In the room where he worked and in the library next to it a curious disorder seemed to reign. There were even volumes lying on the floor. But, it seems, he found his way about very well and knew where to put his hand on any of his books. He wrote on their parchment back the title of those that he had had bound. As far as I know, he did not annotate them. In his copy of *Capital*, now in my possession, there are sidelinings in red ink but all the annotation is by me. However, he placed little strips of paper in them by the way of bookmarks.

The same simplicity was visible in the Master's dress. He was always wrapped in one or more overcoats and mufflers, and on his head he usually had a cap or a hat. His spectacles had only a simple steel frame. His suit looked more like a sack than anything else. He wore half boots without any fastener. They were kept on by means of lateral rubber bands and were of a type which I think no longer exists. I have his watch. It is of steel. If he dressed more than modestly, the cooking and cellar were both abundant and select at the Villa Angora.

He had a fairly fine figure. His beard and his hair were "salt and pepper". Two things were notable about him. First of all his extremely elegant hands—slightly waxen, slim, delicately-shaped, with protruding blue veins and very long joints. Next, his gaze. His eyes were piercing, searching, ardent. But, contrary to what one might think, their expression was in no way sarcastic, even though they were sparkling and ironical. I would not go so far as to say that Pareto looked fundamentally indulgent. But, it is certain that any suspicion of basic malice was absent from this open face that breathed intellectual honesty. In this respect, then, he differed greatly from Voltaire to whom he has sometimes been compared, for the French thinker had an essentially sarcastic expression.

Vilfredo Pareto is a great, though somewhat strange figure in the history of human thought.

On the whole, his personality strikes one as attractive. His few defects are common to many. He always wanted to be right and would not suffer any contradiction. His qualities deserve the highest esteem. These are above all uprightness, straightforwardness, attachment to his friends, as is magnificently exemplified in his correspondence with Pantaleoni and with Emilia Peruzzi. In the last years of that correspondence he expresses again all his gratitude for the help he has experienced in his early years by the Peruzzi family.

The man's culture was outstanding. It was in the first place mathematical and classical, but his reading was extremely wide, and his quotations, when from other fields, are very much to the point, as I can testify as regards my own subject—that of Moslem scholars.

It is important to stress the quite predominant influence exercised on him by Léon Walras. To be sure, in his personal work on mathematical economics, Pareto made considerable efforts to escape from that influence. As against this, in his *Sociology* he comes back in certain ways to concepts close to those of Walras. Admittedly, other thinkers have influenced Pareto too, but none of them decisively.

As to his work, even if one is not willing to admit with the orthodox Paretians, including myself, that it bears the stamp of genius, one must bring out its exceptional importance:

1. In pure economics, he extended the scope of mathematical economics far beyond Walras—with the help of new methods.

2. In applied economics, he was a great forerunner of modern econometrics. Before anyone else, he recommended the application of interpolating statistical data for the discovery of empirical laws. Above all, he himself discovered the curve of income distribution. The explanation of this matter has not yet been worked out satisfactorily, but the facts are there, and I do not think that anyone has since discovered anything so important or so curious.

3. His criticism of socialism is, at least in its essentials, one of the most complete and most profound ever made, and it is carried out according to entirely new principles.

4. His sociology is similar in its scope. It is an astonishing attempt to understand what society really is, behind the veil of "derivations" in which men take such pleasure.

However, it must be admitted that his work, and particularly his *Sociologia generale* suffers from serious defects of form. It is set out in the most disorderly way, and sometimes the tone (I do not say the substance) of the reasoning is most unusual for a scientific study.

Nevertheless, the man and his work deserve the respect and admiration of economists and sociologists.

Georges-Henri Bousquet

II
THE WORK OF VILFREDO PARETO

Pareto's mathematical skill appears first of all in the *Cours*, which contains the equation of the curve of incomes, which is, among all researches of inductive economics on the basis of statistics, the most elegant, if not indeed the most fecund.

This equation is $N = Ax^m$, where N represents the number of persons who have an income higher than x, while A and m are two constants, the first of which measures the amount of the total wealth, and the second, its distribution. The parameter m is almost a constant and in this invariability from country to country and from epoch to epoch, which later researches have confirmed, approximately, is the deep significance of Pareto's discovery. The equation is not a mere statistical interpolation, but an instrument which allows us to penetrate deeply into the mechanism of the distribution of wealth.

Even more than in statistics, however, Pareto's mathematical skill shows its vigour in the construction of the general theory of economic equilibrium which is contained in the *Manuale* and still more in the French translation (*Manuel d'économie politique*), in which the mathematical appendix has been completely reworked.

Here is its fundamental concept.

Let us suppose that a certain number of independent parameters q_1, q_2, ..., q_n represent the configuration of a certain system, and that a certain function R (q_1, q_2, ..., q_n) has the following property: q_r being a generic variable, if to a positive increase Δq_r there corresponds for R a positive increase ΔR, the system moves in the direction in which all the q_r are positive; if, on the other hand, the increase ΔR corresponding to Δq_r is negative, the system moves in the direction in which all the q_r are negative; and, finally, if the increase ΔR corresponding to Δq_r is zero, the system does not move at all.

The configuration of equilibrium will be obtained, then, by writing the system of equations

$$\frac{\partial R}{\partial q_1}=0, \frac{\partial R}{\partial q_2}=0, \ldots, \frac{\partial R}{\partial q_n}=0.$$

A function R which has this property is called an *index function*.

These ideas are extremely general. They apply equally well to mechanical systems and to economic systems.

They have a still more general range. The form of the theories does not change, even if the meaning of the function R is changed; the essential is that it be an index of the direction in which it is anticipated that the system will move. If an index function of altruism could be found, substituting it for R, we should have the mathematical theory of altruism.

The simplest case is that of a single producer, the index function representing then the net profit of the production. By calling this profit F and the quantity sold q, F is a function of q and represents an index function in the sense indicated above. The configuration of equilibrium is then determined by the equation

$$\frac{dF}{dq}=0$$

which indicates that the producer aims at the maximum gain in money.

The treatment of the case of a single consumer is equally simple, *if it is admitted that one can measure pleasure.* The quantity which represents such a measure in function of consumption is then the index function of the system.

The function which measures pleasure was called *ophelimity* and from the study of it pure economics was born with the works of Gossen, Jevons, Walras, Marshall, Edgeworth, Pantaleoni, and Fisher. The quantities that measure what at the beginning was called *final degree of utility, scarcity*, were nothing but the partial derivatives of ophelimity. The determination of the position of economic equilibrium in the problems of exchange had been reduced, by the authors whom we have cited and by Pareto in the *Cours*, to the search for the relative maxima of the function of ophelimity.

For every individual the tastes of the others with whom he contracts are obstacles. If the quantity of goods must be divided among several persons, the fact that the quantity is fixed is decidedly an obstacle; if the good to be divided is produced, the fact that it can be obtained only by using other goods still constitutes an obstacle; likewise the fact that the good is not available in the place and at the time it is needed constitutes another obstacle. In general the meaning of obstacles is that economic goods are limited; that if violence and fraud, theft and donation are excluded, a thing cannot be had except by giving in exchange for it one of equal value *pro tempore*; that every product is the result of a certain combination of the factors of production utilizing whatever technology is known *pro tempore*; that the legal order and the economic organization fetter individual actions; and so on.

Exclusive of the introductory and complementary parts, the *Manuale* consists essentially of three chapters; in the first, a synthetic study is made of tastes, that is, the forces which impel to action; in the second, of the obstacles, that is, the constraints which are opposed to the tastes; in the third, are studied the configurations of equilibrium which arise from the contrast of those forces and of these constraints.

And what about production and exchange, consumption and distribution? There does not exist in real life a distinction in things corresponding to this distinction of words. There does not exist a problem of production, as distinct from a problem of distribution and vice versa, but all economic problems are included in the general conditions of equilibrium.

Classical economics rested and still rests in the main on the assumption —implicit, even if not always explicit—that economic equilibrium represents a typical configuration around which the real configuration oscillates now in one direction and now in another; or, in short, that equilibrium is *an idea*, in the Platonic sense, of which reality may offer the more or less deformed image. This concept, which forms the substratum of the antithesis between normal value and current value and was set forth in *The Wealth of Nations* by Adam Smith, inspired the greater part of the economic literature of the eighteenth century, and constitutes even today the fundamental theme of contemporary theoretical investigations. The *Manuale* does not go beyond it, but Pareto noted even then the theoretical deficiency of the doctrine of equilibrium, in so far as the dynamic aspect is the essential, not the contingent of economic reality, and this latter is not polarized around an ideal configuration, but moves incessantly in an eternal change, under the action of external and internal forces, which bind the present to the past, the future to the present. The external forces—the only ones that are explicitly considered in the *Manuale*—represent applied forces, the tastes and obstacles in Pareto's model.

It is at this point that the crux of Pareto's system becomes apparent. The internal forces of the economic system are not susceptible of a theoretical representation as simple, elegant, and universal as is the case for the applied forces. They are not only, as for the material macroscopic systems, forces of conservation, by which—to express it elegantly—the dead city dominates *through inertia* the living city; they are also directive forces or forces of impulsion, through which the living city *forms or attempts to form* the city of the future. The internal forces, therefore, are history, they are even ethics and politics, something powerful, but vague and indistinct, which is not susceptible of mathematical representation; an expression of the freedom of the will, which does not allow itself to be enclosed in the meshes of a mechanical representation, and, because it is mechanical, determinist.

Pareto succeeds in his purpose, basing his theory on the fact that the movement of economic phenomena cannot be separated from that of political and social phenomena. Economic dynamics merges into politics, or, to use Pareto's term, into sociology.

Luigi Amoroso

SOURCES

Essay I

Georges Henri Bousquet, "Vilfredo Pareto (1848–1923), biographical notes on the occasion of the publication of his letters to Pantaleoni", *Banca Nazionale del Lavoro, Quarterly Review*, 1961. Abridged. Supplemented by some passages from G. H. Bousquet, *Pareto (1848–1923), Le savant et l'homme* (Payot & Cie S.A., Lausanne, 1960).

Essay II

Luigi Amoroso, "Vilfredo Pareto" in *Enciclopedia Italiana*, 26 (Rome, 1935), reprinted in *Econometrica*, (1938). Abridged.

Signature

University Library, Lausanne.

Portrait

Photograph, 1909, in possession of Luigi Amoroso.

BIBLIOGRAPHY

Ch. Gide, "Le jublié Vilfredo Pareto", *Revue d'économie politique*, 31 (1917).

A. Loria, "Vilfredo Pareto", *Economic Journal*, 33 (1923).

M. Pantaleoni, "Vilfredo Pareto", *Economic Journal*, 33 (1923).

A. Cappa, *Vilfredo Pareto* (Turin, 1924).

L. Amoroso *et al.*, "Vilfredo Pareto", *Giornale degli economisti*, 64 (1924).

G. Rocca and V. P. Spinedi, "Bibliografia di Vilfredo Pareto", *Giornale degli economisti e rivista di statistica* (1924).

E. Schams, "Vilfredo Pareto", *Zeitschrift für Volkswirtschaft und Sozialpolitik*, N.F. 3 (1924).

"In memoria di Vilfredo Pareto", *Giornale degli economisti e rivista di statistica*, series 4, 64 (1924).

G. H. Bousquet, *Introduction aux systèmes socialistes de Pareto* (Paris, 1925).

G. H. Bousquet, *Précis de sociologie d'après Pareto* (Paris, 1925).

G. H. Bousquet, *Introduction à l'étude du Manuel de V. Pareto* (Paris, 1927).

R. Michels, *Bedeutende Männer: Charakterologische Studien* (Leipzig, 1927).

G. H. Bousquet, *Vilfredo Pareto: sa vie et son oeuvre* (Paris, 1928).

A. de Pietri-Tonelli, *Vilfredo Pareto* (Rome, 1935).

F. Borkenau, *Pareto* (London, 1936).

G. Pirou, *Les théories de l'équilibre économique*: *Walras et Pareto,* 3rd ed. (Paris, 1946).

W. Hirsch, *Vilfredo Pareto* (Zürich and Brussels, 1948).

O. Weinberger, "Vilfredo Pareto und seine Bedeutung für die Gegenwart", *Schweizerische Zeitschrift für Volkswirtschaft und Statistik,* 84 (1948).

"Nell' anniversario della nascita du Vilfredo Pareto: 15 luglio 1848–19 agosto 1923", *Giornale degli economisti e rivista di statistica,* No. 7, new series (1948).

G. H. Bousquet, "Pareto sociologue", *Revue d'économie politique,* 59 (1949).

G. Demaria, "L'œuvre économique de Vilfredo Pareto" *Revue d'économie politique,* 59 (1949).

E. Fossati, "Pareto dans son et notre temps", *Revue d'économie politique,* 59 (1949).

B. Nogaro, "Vilfredo Pareto", *Revue d'économie politique,* 59 (1949).

J. A. Schumpeter, "Vilfredo Pareto", *Quarterly Journal of Economics*", 63 (1949), reprinted in J. A. Schumpeter *Ten Great Economists: From Marx to Keynes,* (New York, 1951, London, 1952).

G. H. Bousquet, "Vilfredo Pareto, La sua famiglia, la sua infanzia, e la sua giovinezza", *Giornale degli economisti,* 15 (1956).

R. Aron, *Les grandes doctrines de sociologie historique,* Vol. 2: *Emile Durkheim, Vilfredo Pareto, Max Weber* (Paris, 1961).

J. R. Hicks, "Pareto Revealed", *Economica,* 28 (1961).

E. Schneider, "Neue Pareto-Literatur", *Weltwirtschaftliches Archiv,* 88 (1962).

G. H. Bousquet, "Pareto et ses systèmes socialistes", Institut de Science Economique Appliquée, *Cahiers Série* (1963), BA No. 2 (appendix).

N. Bobbio, "Introduzione", in *V. Pareto, Traffatio di sociologia generale,* 2nd ed. (Milan, 1964).

G. Busino, *Introduction à une histoire de la sociologie de Pareto,* (Geneva, 1966).

G. Perrin, *Sociologie de Pareto* (Paris, 1966).

M. Allais, "Vilfredo Pareto, Contributions to Economics", in *International Encyclopedia of the Social Sciences,* Vol. 11 (New York, 1968).

T. Parsons, "Vilfredo Pareto, Contributions to Sociology", in *International Encyclopedia of the Social Sciences,* Vol. 11 (New York, 1968).

JOHAN GUSTAV KNUT WICKSELL

1851–1926

Wicksell had always been extremely inefficient in practical affairs. Although an expert on taxation law, he could not complete his own income tax declaration.

T. GÅRDLUND

Two circumstances contributed to the tardy materialization of his academic career, his relatively late introduction to economics in about 1880 from graduate study of mathematics (which latter he pursued until 1885 when he went abroad for five years to study economics at the universities of England, France, Germany, and Austria), and his early reputation for social and religious unorthodoxy. The latter made his appointment a hotly contested issue and a decided victory for academic freedom.

C. G. UHR

He makes a clear distinction between pure and applied economics and also between political economy, sociology and economic history. In the theories of population, of capital, of money and of economic cycles, as well as in mathematical and statistical methodology, many economists now follow in his footsteps.

J. ÅKERMAN

I
WICKSELL'S LIFE AND WORK

Johan Gustav Knut Wicksell was born on 20 December 1851 and died on 3 May 1926. Internationally, he is now numbered among the great economists who were at work around the turn of the century. His influence, for a long time rather limited, has in recent years been growing noticeably, and even makes itself felt on the frontiers of economic theory. For Sweden, Wicksell's life-work has a special importance. For Wicksell was not only an ingenious scholar, but also a radical political thinker and untiring social reformer of great calibre. Through his contributions to political and cultural debates, he has decisively influenced the development of political ideas in Sweden, and has thereby also played a considerable part in the remarkable remoulding of Swedish society that took place in the last quarter of the nineteenth century and the first quarter of this.

Knut Wicksell was a Stockholmer. He said that it was music for him to walk along the streets of Stockholm when, on reaching his retirement, he had the opportunity of living once more in the neighbourhood of the capital. His father, who was descended from a farming family, was a provisions dealer. After five years at the Maria Elementary School, and four at Stockholm Secondary School, Knut Wicksell passed the *mogenhetsexamen* (school-leaving examination) in 1869, and in the autumn went to Uppsala, to study, first of all, mathematics, in which he had already particularly interested at school. He had also learnt Latin and Greek at school, however, and he passed the *fil.-cand.* (BA) examination at the beginning of 1872, after only five semesters of study. After this, it was not until 1885 that he was ready for his *fil.-lic.* (MA) examination, in which his subjects were mechanics, mathematics, and physics. In the meantime, however, Wicksel had gone through the experiences that brought him over into the social sciences.[1]

Wicksell's first appearance as a social reformer was as discussion leader at a temperance meeting in a mission hall in Uppsala on 19 February 1880. The address was repeated afterwards before a more academic audience, and was printed and published by the author, under the title "A few words on the most important cause of social misery and its remedy, with special reference to drunkenness". In it, Wicksell, in tactful but determined words, gave expression to the opinion that drunkenness was associated with poverty, and poverty was caused by overpopulation, so that it should be a holy duty for all married people to limit the size of the family to two or three children.

The address was a *succès de scandale*. Several thousand copies of the pamphlet were quickly sold, and gave rise to a heated discussion in the newspapers, and a whole series of counterblasts.

Wicksell's experiences during these years were of decisive significance for his future as a scholar and social reformer. It was his opponents' charge that he expressed himself on economic matters without having the necessary knowledge that led him to study economics seriously.

[1] Coming from a religious home, he seems to have gone through a religious crisis, about which he never spoke, however, even with those closest to him. After inner struggles, from the beginning of 1880 he supported the cause of the neo-Malthusians, for which he soon became notorious throughout the country. In his commemorative article on Wicksell, Sommarin points out that it was the translation into Swedish in 1878 of the work of the English doctor George Drysdale that awakened Wicksell's interest in population problems, from which he was led deeper and deeper into social and economic studies.

Sommarin has also rightly noted "that the controversy carried him even more deeply and broadly into the central problems of economics, and forced him from the outset to direct his critical vigilance towards the arguments of his opponents and towards the solidity of his own". One can also find confirmation of this in Wicksell's later, purely scientific, writings, where the positive presentation is nearly always built upon a penetrating examination of other writers' arguments.

Wicksell may also have found that shock tactics, such as those he involuntarily produced on his appearance as a social reformer, did not hinder the propagation of new ideas, for afterwards it became characteristic of him almost always to shock his opponents, achieving this deliberately by a skilful use of the weapons of irony and satire.

In the autumn of 1884 Wicksell left Uppsala, and after he had finished studying mathematics and natural science for the *licentiatexamen* (MA) (September 1885), he devoted himself entirely to the social sciences. At that time economics did not figure very prominently at the universities. In Uppsala, the lawyer and politician C. G. Hammarskjöld was Professor of Political Economy and Fiscal Law, but during his term of office as a Cabinet Minister the duties of the professorship were discharged, as far as economics was concerned, by David Davidson, who was three years younger than Wicksell, and had been appointed Docent (Assistant Professor) in Political Economy in 1879. (He became a full professor in 1890.) In Lund there was a chair in Administrative Law and Political Economy, which since 1862 had been held by Count G. A. K. Hamilton. Academic activity in the subject was limited, and Wicksell decided to transfer his economic studies abroad. On his list of qualifications he himself stated: "During the years 1885–6 and 1887–90, partly by my own resources, and partly as Lorén Scholar, I resided in England, France, Germany, and Austria for the purpose of studying political economy. During this time I attended lectures by Professors Leroy-Beaulieu and Desmoulins in Paris, Knapp and Brentano in Strasbourg, Wagner in Berlin, and Menger and Singer in Vienna. Where the opportunity arose, I also took part in seminar discussions."

The second period of resident study abroad was probably financed mainly by the Lorén Foundation, which later also generously supported the publication of Wicksell's three chief works in German, and the working out of his *Lectures*. At this time Wicksell had no support from any Swedish university, and his own meagre resources he probably used up during his first study trip.

The foreign economists mentioned above by Wicksell himself are not among those who influenced his thinking most, however. His teachers were first and foremost the classical English economists, especially Malthus,

John Stuart Mill and Ricardo; during his years of study abroad, he was also much impressed by the newer streams of thought in economics represented by the names Walras, Jevons, Menger, and Böhm-Bawerk.

When Wicksell appeared as an economic theorist before an international audience for the first time, it was with the article "Kapitalzins und Arbeitslohn" ("Interest and Wages") in *Conrads Jahrbücher,* December 1892, in which he completed Böhm-Bawerk's reasoning. The next year his first main economic work *Über Wert, Kapital und Rente nach den neueren nationalökonomischen Theorien* ("On Value, Capital and Rent in Recent Economic Theory") was published by Fischer at Jena. This work, of about one hundred and sixty pages in all, in which Wicksell tries to achieve, partly by applying mathematical methods, a synthesis of the Austrian theories of capital and marginal utility and Walras's equilibrium system, on the whole got a rather cool reception, especially from the representatives of the German historical school, who ranged themselves against Wicksell's mathematical method of presentation. Later, however, a remarkable reappraisal of this work took place. As George Stigler in particular pointed out in his well-known history of doctrine, Wicksell, through this book, became one of the founders of the marginal productivity theory.

By the compactness of its composition and the stringency of its reasoning, this book, with its moderate scope, is outstanding even from the technical viewpoint as Wicksell's most thorough scientific performance. As an academic pioneer he undoubtedly achieved more in *Geldzins und Güterpreise* ("Interest and Prices"), but this later work is written more in the style of an essay, and does not have the same precision and clarity as the earlier.

To posterity it seems extraordinary that Wicksell did not use this remarkable treatise as a doctoral dissertation. In fact, he did make an application to this effect, but it was rejected. In order to understand this, one should remember that in Sweden at that time the subject of political economy belonged to the law faculty, and that Wicksell had passed no law exams. Only after a special dispensation could the *licentiatxeamen* in political economy be taken in the philosophy faculty. Requests for such dispensation were sometimes granted, but by no means invariably, and from the faculty's protocols it appears that opinions there were often divided as to whether one should assist in such a *confusio facultatum.* Wicksell, however, got a dispensation to complete his *licentiatexamen* by submitting to a supplementary examination in political economy with public finance. In May 1895 the 43-year-old scholar was examined by the Professor, three years his junior, with whom he then hardly stood on so friendly a footing as in later years. Davidson had not, of course, in the earlier debate on neo-Malthusianism, shown any great sympathy with Wicksell's viewpoint. The examination seems to have gone off well, however, if one can judge by the grading (the highest). Wicksell was now able to defend his doctoral thesis, and as his doctoral dissertation he used a smaller paper (seventy-five pages) that he had written in the meantime: *Zur Lehre von der Steuerincidenz* ("the Theory of the Incidence of Taxation"). The theoretical apparatus that he had presented in *Value, Capital and Rent* was applied here to the problem of tax incidence. The disputation took place in Uppsala on 29 May 1895.

This was by no means the end of Wicksell's difficulties, however. The intention was, of course to get a docentur (assistant professorship) with the disputation, but an application for this, submitted to the philosophy faculty, was there recommended for rejection by 10 votes to 6, and was not approved by the Chancellor either. In the opinion of the majority, a docentur in political economy should be located in the faculty to which the subject belonged—the law faculty; moreover, Wicksell had no training in the humanities, and was also unsuited to teaching as he showed in his propaganda on the population question. After that, Wicksell turned to the law faculty, but since he had no law examination he there encountered an even more powerful opposition. Davidson supported him, to be sure, but with such reluctance on matters of principle that he really gave Wicksell no support at all. After this reverse, only one way stood open if Wicksell wished to carry out his intention of pursuing an academic career. Now 45 years old, and already an internationally esteemed economist, he was compelled to begin a systematic study of law. His energy was, however, equal to that too, and on 8 April 1899, he passed the *Juris utriusque kandidatexamen* (LlB) with honours in half the subjects. After that, he was immediately appointed Docent in Political Economy and Fiscal Law at Uppsala University.

On the whole, Wicksell's intellectual activity and creative power seem to have stood at their peak during the 1890s. It was during that period that he made his pioneering contributions as an economist. During the following twenty-five years too he was certainly a prolific writer, and his writings did in many respects enrich economic science.

After *Value, Capital and Rent* he turned to taxation problems and published in 1896 the sizeable volume *Finanztheoretische Untersuchungen nebst Darstellung und Kritik des Steuerwesens Schwedens* ("Investigations in Public Finance with a Critical Survey of the Swedish Tax System") which included the doctoral thesis as the first section. In a second section, "Concerning a New Principle of Equitable Taxation", Wicksell dealt with the theory of public finance, and on it he based a new interpretation of the "benefit principle": parliamentary decisions in taxation matters should, in principle, be unanimous, so as to give every group of citizens the possibility of ensuring (through their elected representatives) that their tax payments do not become greater than their benefits of the corresponding governmental activity. This treatise stimulated the present writer to produce a doctoral dissertation upon the principles of justice in taxation, but otherwise it does not seem to have attracted a great deal of attention, although its ideas are valuable from a theoretical viewpoint. In the third, and longest, section of the book (approximately 185 pages) Wicksell gave a critical survey of the development of the Swedish tax system during the last two centuries.

On the completion of this great work, Wicksell immediately set about studying monetary theory. In autumn 1896 we find him in Berlin. Now, for the first time, he had got a state grant of 1000 crowns from a fund for publishing learned works, and could pursue his researches for the next projected work: *Geldzins und Güterpreise* ("Interest and Prices"). In studying the problem of bimetallism, which at the time was particularly topical, Wicksell had come to the conclusion that the quantity theory was lacking, but that there was no other acceptable theory of the value of money, so that economics here showed a suspicious gap. It was now Wicksell's ambition to fill this gap, and the result of two years of persevering mental effort—the book was ready for publication at the beginning of 1898—was his famous theory that the relationship of the money rate of interest to the natural or real rate of interest on capital was of decisive importance for changes in the price level and in the value of money. In propounding this theory, which afterwards proved to have considerably greater scope than Wicksell himself supposed, and which gave rise to a new treatment of the entire dynamic problem in economics, Wicksell had made his most brilliant contribution to the science.

Beside this activity on high scholarly plane, Wicksell carried on extensive journalistic activity throughout the 1890s as the correspondent of several Swedish, Norwegian and Finnish newspapers, wrote a series of booklets of a more popular kind, especially on taxation questions, and continued to give lectures on social and political matters. This seems to have happened partly for financial reasons, for Wicksell had no paid position at this time, and the grants that he obtained from the Lorén Fund during the 1890s were probably devoted to the publication of his scientific works. At the same time, he now had a family to support. In 1889, when he was staying in Paris as Lorén Scholar, he had married the talented Norwegian Anna Bugge (1862–1928), who was later to take up a leading position in the movement for the emancipation of women, and their two sons were born at the beginning of the 1890s. The mystery is how Wicksell, during this period of his life, could find time for so much, for, as has already been mentioned, it was during the 1890s, when he lived under such poverty-stricken conditions and was besieged by troubles and adversities of various kinds, that Wicksell wrote his most important scientific papers.

The situation seemed to brighten at the beginning of 1900, when Hamilton's chair in administrative law and political economy at the Faculty of Law in Lund was divided up through the creation of a separate chair in political economy and fiscal law. Wicksell, then newly appointed Docent at Uppsala, gave notice of his intention of applying for the new professorship. His rivals were Gustav Cassel, Johan Lembke and Gustaf Steffen. The last two soon withdrew their applications, and Cassel eventually did so too, but not until after a fierce struggle had taken place between him and Wicksell.

Cassel, who was fifteen years younger than Wicksell, and had only been studying economics for three or four years, had not at this time written any of the works for which he later became so famous.

There is no doubt that Wicksell would have made a better showing as a teacher if he had had a larger faculty, as is now the case at the universities. Wicksell would then have been able to concentrate upon guiding the senior students and encouraging the junior ones in the discipline. Those who had the advantage of having their theses reviewed by him can testify to the interested effort he expended upon such a task. It seems that both he and the students would have derived benefit from having more lectures.

During the period at Lund, Wicksell devoted much time to the preparation of his *Föreläsningar i nationalekonomi* ("Lectures on Political Economy") which were published in many revised editions and were also translated into German (1913–22). During these years he was also a frequent contributor to *Ekonomisk Tidskrift*, which Davidson had founded in 1899, and afterwards edited single-handed for forty years, in spite of endless troubles.

Wicksell's participation in public debates increased rather than diminished after he became a professor. On at least two occasions his utterances were of such a kind that they were regarded as a nationwide scandal.

When, at the end of 1916, Wicksell was emeritus, he and his wife moved to Mörby in Stocksund, a garden suburb of Stockholm. A testimonial gift from friends and admirers had made it possible for them to build a small villa there, and there he was able to spend his last decade, the most peaceful and most carefree of his life.

The advent if retirement did not diminish Wicksell's intellectual activity. Right up to his death, which came suddenly after a chill, he was intensively occupied with his writing, which now consisted mostly of shorter works, articles for newspaper and journals, and also of officially commissioned inquiries. Through frequent visits to Stockholm he maintained contact with friends and colleagues. Among the latter he now stood out as the acknowledged and revered master. Wicksell was the focal point of the Economic Club which was formed for the exchange of views between economists in the Stockholm area.

Wicksell also frequently took part in public discussions, especially in the Economic Association. He was now no longer considered a danger to society, but the respected doyen of the Stockholm economists, whose individualistic contributions to the debate were always worth hearing. That the differences of opinion between Wicksell and society had to some extent been settled did not, however, mean that Wicksell had eventually conformed to the popular view. All through his life he maintained, with remarkable consistency, the view which he had formed during the 1880s concerning the population problem and other social and religious questions. Nor did he cease propagating them.

He remained a rebel to the end. The greater part of his activity as a writer during these ten years can be characterized as a running criticism of current economic policy. Wicksell was not a rabid economic radical, nor was he an adherent of "capitalistic bolshevism", to use Davidson's apt expression. Wicksell recommended only such interference with existing property rights as was well thought out, with due caution, with the object of bringing about more equal shares—for example, some taxation of inheritance. He determinedly opposed the unsystematic shifts in the distribution of property which resulted from deterioration in the value of money. Here, too, he tolerated no compromise.

Knut Wicksell's contributions, both as a practical and as a theoretical economist, are so extensive and penetrating that an account of them would carry me far beyond the bounds of this commemorative article. Only a few concluding remarks concerning his view of society and his more important contributions to economic theory will be added here.

Wicksell's political position can best be characterized as liberal, with a generous dash of social-radicalism. The demand for liberty, equality, and fraternity awoke deep echoes in him. He set himself up as the advocate of freedom of speech and of religion, as well as of political and economic equality between classes and between the sexes, which we in Sweden have come to associate with the "eighties".

In the economic field Wicksell was, in principle, a supporter of free competition, to be applied within each individual country as well as between countries. But he strongly emphasized that certain fundamental conditions must be fulfilled in order that free competition should bring about a favourable result. He maintained too that freely reached agreements between the parties were often better than unrestrained competition, and also that State intervention would be fully justified in some cases. The latter should, however, "occur with the greatest circumspection, having regard, *inter alia*, to the likely consequences, both direct and indirect, since an ill-judged regulation of economic affairs must always be expected to lead to worse results than no regulation at all, and regulation by voluntary agreements is as a rule to be preferred to compulsion."

The original points in Wicksell's economic programme lay in the restrictions he proposed to place upon the *laissez-faire* system:

1. *The population problem* was for him primary. Through birth control voluntarily applied in marriage, and supported by official policy, the population in each country should be kept at what Wicksell called the "optimum" size, which was where the national product per head attained its maximum. The number of favourable results that Wicksell hoped to attain simply by a rational solution of the population problem is amazing. Material well-being would be considerably increased, and prostitution and other unsatisfactory sexual relationships would almost disappear. In addition to this, peaceful cooperation between peoples would be facilitated, for Wicksell—who was a staunch pacifist and opposed military expenditure on principle—considered that it was ultimately the pressure of growing population that occasioned envy and mistrust between peoples, and imperialistic tendencies in certain states. Sometimes he seems vaguely to have considered a stationary population as an ideal, or at all events as a normal phenomenon in the *long* run. If the population ceased growing, welfare would increase inasmuch as the tempo of capital formation could be reduced, and a greater part of the national income would be devoted to the satisfaction of immediate needs.

2. In order that wealth should be distributed as evenly as possible, steps should be taken to eliminate the existing class-differentiation in society. In Wicksell's opinion, the most important step would be a radical *educational reform* to make possible increased general education for the masses and further higher education for all those who had the ability and need for it. It is interesting to note that Wicksell's educational programme—common primary schools, and free education (even at the higher stages), combined with *board*—coincides almost exactly with what is now being carried through almost forty years later.

3. The next step was a levelling out of property distribution by a *high inheritance-tax* or a change in the law of inheritance. Wicksell always maintained that the Government's share in inherited property should be considered as capital, and not squandered on current expenditure. In popular lectures he sometimes stimulated his audience with the idea that the capital which the Government obtains in this way should be shared out amongst the members of society, so that once in his life every citizen—upon attaining the age of 25 years, say—might draw his share of society's inheritance. This small capital sum he could then use to furnish a house or start a business, but he would have the moral obligation to leave behind at least an equally large capital sum at his death. With this important

exception, and the further limitation inherent in it, that certain unearned profits (such as those derived from the trade cycle and from appreciation of property values) should also be taxed, Wicksell respected the right to private property, and considered that it should be protected from the assaults of excessive taxation. In his opinion, the taxation of the various classes of society should, as a matter of principle, be kept within the bounds of what they would voluntarily undertake. In order to protect the rights of the minority, he went so far as to propose that they should have the right of veto on tax decisions in Parliament. On this point he thought that taxes should be voted at the same time as the corresponding expenditure, and in this way a compromise solution could in principle always be reached.

If the structure of society could be changed, in these three ways, everyone would be tolerably equally situated at the start, so that greater faith could then be placed in the principle of free competition.

4. Wicksell also fully appreciated, however, the importance of *free combination*, both in the productive and the distributive trades, as well as in the relationships on the labour market. Wicksell looked upon the trade-union movement with great sympathy, but maintained that the real significance of trade unions lay in the self-realization they entailed for the working class. They had increased the workers' self-consciousness and sense of dignity and responsibility. Through their activities they had also achieved an improvement in working conditions, but on the wage front he thought that their importance was over-rated, for he considered that wages were determined by competition between firms according to the marginal productivity theory, and that trade unions could not do much about it. He was, therefore, a zealous advocate of peace on the labour front, of mutual understanding, and amicable relationships between workers and employers. The struggle for further increases in the economic standards of the working class should be fought out on another battlefield, namely, the political front.

5. To the extent that the course of economic development tends towards monopoly and cartelization in various branches of industry, *nationalization* or some other similar form of State control should be considered. The object of this should be to make possible a price policy that is more favourable to the consumers. Price fixing in public companies which served the consumer should be based, in principle, on marginal costs, even if this entails the recovery of part of the fixed costs, by taxation. When the marginal costs are negligible, then the public should enjoy the goods or services *gratis*, as is the case, for instance, with roads and streets. It was, therefore, the possibility of achieving such technical gains and improved price policies, rather than the possibility of bringing about a more equal economic distribution, that would justify measures of nationalization in any particular

case, for according to Wicksell one could not hope for any important increase in wages themselves once the socialist state had been established. He thought that even there marginal productivity was the simplest and fairest norm for wage fixing.

6. As regards the Government's economic policy in other matters, Wicksell strongly emphasized that the *monetary policy* should be directed towards the maintenance of a constant value of money. He was one of the first to advocate the freeing of the currency from gold. If, in the face of this, exchange rates were to be kept fixed, it would be necessary for the central banks of the various countries to collaborate. After the fluctuations of the First World War, however, Wicksell became a supporter of free monetary standards (with variable exchange rates) in Sweden. He also asserted that a monetary policy aiming at price-stabilization would entail a levelling out of cyclical fluctuations. On the other hand, no expression can be found in his writings of the view that fiscal policy should also be used to this end, although such a conclusion follows logically from his own theories.

The theoretical part of his *Lectures on Political Economy*, which we will now consider, is certainly kept in so easily comprehensible a form that Wicksell's immediate pupils, the law students would have been able to read it with profit, yet it maintains a high level of scholarship, and, as has been rightly remarked, really has more the character of a "textbook for professors". Wicksell has here fused the theories that he developed in earlier writings into a unified system of extraordinary logical consistency. The essentials of the system are (1) the determination of stationary equilibrium, (2) the comparison of various stationary equilibria (comparative statics), and (3) the introduction of dynamic theory in the proper sense.

In determining the *stationary equilibrium*, Wicksell proceeded as follows. He first explained price formation in the market for goods, assuming incomes and quantities of goods to be given. Equilibrium prices were characterized by the fact that they would be proportional to the marginal utilities of the various goods for all individuals. In this price situation, therefore, no individual can increase his total utility by buying more of one good and less of another. The next task was to explain incomes and the quantities of goods. To this end, prices and technical knowledge were assumed to be given, and so were the amounts of the various sorts of productive factors. How much of each good to produce, and how to share the proceeds between the different factors, is then determined according to the marginal productivity principle. Equilibrium requires that productive factors be employed where they make the greatest contribution at the ruling prices. Later, when money and credit are introduced into the system, two further equilibrium conditions can be stated: the money rate of interest must coincide with the rate of interest on capital determined by marginal productivity, and the general price level must stand in a certain relationship (itself determined by a multitude of factors) to the actual volume of money.

Wicksell's theories have been completed by later scholars, but hardly superseded. I should especially like to draw attention to the fact that the full significance of Wicksell's definition of the character of stationary equilibrium has not been widely enough realized. As a rule, it can be supposed that a disturbance in any particular market will entail some shift in total demand and total supply, which will give rise to a new general equilibrium or to a dynamic process, before the tendency to return to the original market situation has had time to come into effect. From this the important conclusion may be drawn that stationary equilibrium should generally be considered—except in certain special cases—to be unstable.

In *comparative statics* too, where comparisons are made between different stationary equilibria varying in different respects, Wicksell interested himself above all in the treatment of capital problems. He showed that an increase in capital, other things being equal, would, after a point, involve a fall in the capitalists' relative share of the national product, and later of their absolute share too. In the same way, an increased quantity of capital involves a shift in the structure of real capital, inasmuch as the lower rate of interest increases the profitability of the longer investments, and thus modifies somewhat the change in distribution mentioned above. "In the peculiarity of capital that, when it grows, it grows, so to say, more in height than in breadth, there consequently lies a counterweight to the tendency of such growth to raise wages and rents." By this analysis, capital theory was carried far beyond the point reached by Böhm-Bawerk.

It should not be concealed, however, that Wicksell ran into difficulties when he tried to apply this *static* theory (as I conceive of it) to a *dynamic* process. When, for example, as above, the question was raised how an increase of capital influences the economy, the answer was really based on a comparison between alternative stationary equilibria, deviating from each other with regard to the amount of capital. Such a comparison does not imply, however, that a corresponding capital increase in any given society would involve precisely these effects. For, in the latter case, saving, and the capital accumulation associated with it, would set in motion a dynamic process, which may, certainly, be thought eventually to end up in a stationary position, but need not lead to the same result that one would expect from a static analysis. To elucidate the effects in this case is a much more involved problem, which can only be treated by dynamic methods. Wicksell did not always observe this distinction. But the relation between dynamic and comparative statics is still one of the questions that await definitive solution in economic theory.

In spite of this sometimes unsatisfactory application of static methods to dynamic problems, it turned out that Wicksell made his greatest contribution precisely by paving the way for *dynamic theory* in the proper sense. This he did by demonstrating that the discrepancy between the real rate of interest on capital and the money rate, so long as it persisted, gave rise to a cumulative process which, amongst other things, included a continually shifting price level.

With this theory, Wicksell did not only increase our understanding of the mechanism of price movements, he also demonstrated a fruitful method of attacking dynamic problems. Indeed, in pursuing his monetary theory further one is led into more general dynamic theory. He thus made a contribution to science which is of more than historical interest, for it is still a living force and an incentive to further research. The full significance of Wicksell's achievement as an economist can therefore not yet be appreciated.

The brief account of Knut Wicksell's life and work that has been given above can only give a very incomplete impression of his remarkable personality. He was a man of great calibre, combining qualities usually considered incompatible.

Wicksell was both a scholar and a social reformer, the latter on an ideological plane in his capacity as lecturer, debater, and writer of polemical pamphlets on social and political topics. One would think that it would be rather an abrupt switch for him to leave his hyper-theoretical work at the writing table to sally forth and deliver a propagandist speech to a demonstration rally, or to appear on the platform at a socialist youth meeting. But Wicksell was as absorbed in the one task as he was in the other. His time and energy sufficed both for the furthering of science and for participation in the work of removing the anomalies existing in society. And in his case it is clear that the one sphere of activity had a fruitful influence upon the other. As has already been pointed out, it was Wicksell's interest in social affairs that drove him over into economics. For him, therefore, scientific work was not an interesting game of theoretical trickery—although he certainly derived intellectual satisfaction from it — but was justified as a means of furthering our knowledge of the possibilities of increasing general well-being. Wicksell thereby obtained a firm grasp of the essential problems of economic theory, and because he always kept the welfare of the public in mind, his mode of presentation was more lively than is usually the case in scholarly investigations. In the other sphere, his social pronouncements gained in striking power, because they were founded on logical argument.

As a scientist Wicksell made great use of his mathematical gifts and training. In his days, mathematical economics was not as fashionable as it is now, and, like Marshall, Wicksell practically apologized for occasionally taking the liberty of expressing his economic theories in mathematical form. Nowadays, the pioneering work that he did in this field is considered especially to his credit. But Wicksell was not only a theoretician with mathematical inclinations, he also possessed literary gifts, which does not seem to be so very common among the many mathematical economists of today. That he wrote verse and drama during his student days, some of which was published, is perhaps, not so unusual, even for an economist. But all his literary work is marked by a finesse which makes his style easily accessible and affords the reader pleasure. It is also worth noting that Wicksell enjoyed refreshing himself in the evening by reading, in the original, the Latin and Greek authors that he had studied in his youth. The experts consider, however, that Wicksell was not much of a success as a historian, on the few occasions when he tackled problems in that field. He seems to have been conscious of his limitations in this respect himself. The combination of theoretical insight and historical vision is more noticeable in Wicksell's colleague Davidson, who was also decidedly superior to Wicksell in legal training.

Among Wicksell's scholarly attributes also belongs the fact that he was both a pioneer and a follower-up. He especially admired the English classics—he seems to have felt a particular spiritual affinity to John Stuart Mill and his liberal ideas—and considered that a thorough-going study of them should be part of every economist's training. In the exposition of his own theories he often refers to them, and on the whole he nearly always established a connection with earlier authors in the field. Indeed he does so to such an extent that the reader cannot always be sure how significant Wicksell's own contributions are.

Linked with this self-effacing attitude towards science is another of Wicksell's characteristics, namely, his personal modesty. He was completely free of vanity, and it is a matter for discussion whether he even had any real personal ambition. Against this may be contrasted the general impression of him in his public capacities. Wicksell became known throughout the country as a dangerous fighter for radical ideas, whose methods were certainly not marked by any great sensibility for the feelings of others.

We have now come to another noticeable characteristic of Wicksell: his strong sympathy for liberal ideas. He was an opponent of every form of oppression, and to him the demand for truth and justice was absolute. He tolerated no compromise, and it was for this reason that he so often felt himself compelled to act in an apparently impertinent manner. That Wicksell's persistent public activity may be interpreted in this way, and not as the outcome of a desire for self-assertion, becomes more plausible when it is remembered that Wicksell had a basically religious attitude towards life. The crisis that he went through in his youth—diary entries make it likely that it occurred in 1874—resulted in his replacing Christianity, as preached by the Church, by other ethical principles, which he embraced with the same intensity. Even his later ruthless struggle against those aspects of the teaching of the Church which, in his opinion, conflicted with historical reality—a struggle which made him so notorious as an enemy of religion—can be considered as a manifestation of his own religion. What was often taken by the public to be light-hearted mockery was actually the expression of his striving to further the search for truth.

This may also explain another apparent contradiction in Knut Wicksell. As a scholar he was always receptive to new ideas. His own solutions of economic problems were always put forward as hypotheses, which he was prepared to abandon or modify as soon as he got to know of something better. Consequently, he was anything but doctrinaire in this field, even though he demanded good positive reasons for changing his standpoint. In strong contrast to this was his unshakable adherence to what have been here called his ethical principles. The obstinacy with which he refused to make the slightest concession in this field often placed him and his family in an awkward situation. It has already been recounted above how, as a supporter of parliamentary government, and therefore on principle an opponent of the monarchy, he could not bring himself to place the word 'humbly' before his name in addressing the King, even though his livelihood was at stake. When the University of Lund decided to send a wreath to the funeral of Oscar II, Wicksell's dissension aroused unpleasant observations in the University Senate. As an opponent of the Church, he arranged for his children to be excused from religious instruction at school, which was, perhaps, not so remarkable, although it would attract attention. A more marked deviation from bourgeois conventions had occurred earlier, when, at his marriage, he refused to submit to a Church ceremony. Since there were no civil marriages at that time, the couple had no choice but to substitute a ceremony of their own arranging. For the bride and her family in particular, this sacrifice for the sake of principle must have been rather trying.[2]

[2] T. Gårdlund remarks on Wicksell's opposition to the rites of the Church: "Since adopting rationalism as his faith, Knut Wicksell had consistently refused the senseless and insidious rites of bourgeois society: academic formalities, the marriage ceremony, the christening and confirmation of his children. He would surely have hoped to avoid too the final earthly ceremony which is so steeped in Christian dogma. It is probably safe to assume that his wife, as so often before, insisted on the conventional procedure, objecting that too much importance should not be attached to a mere matter of form. However that may be, it was this view that triumphed. The funeral followed the usual pattern 'with strict regard to ritual', according to the wish, so one newspaper stated, of the deceased and his family."

Finally, it may be pointed out that although Wicksell espoused a materialistic and utilitarian philosophy—in this respect he was true to the "eighties" —he was not much concerned about material advantages of his own. He lived for ideas. The fact that even for a life of this kind there are material prerequisites certainly occasioned him trouble, but it never occurred to him to depart from his chosen course. In spite of the fact that he met with opposition from academic quarters the whole time instead of with encouragement, and although it was not until he was 50 years old that he succeeded in obtaining a meagre academic livelihood, he pursued his scholarly course with resolute consistency, and thereby laid the foundations of economics as an independent academic discipline in Sweden. At the same time, he continued, inflexibly and undauntedly, to play the still more trying role of social reformer outside the political parties. By these contributions, which were made possible by an unusual combination of brilliant intellect and strong character, he has richly earned the admiration and gratitude of later generations.

Erik Lindahl

SOURCES

Essay I

Erik Lindahl, "Introduction: Wicksell's Life and Work", in *Knut Wicksell, Selected Papers on Economic Theory* (Allen and Unwin, London, 1958). Abridged.

Signature

Kungliga Biblioteket, Stockholm.

Portrait

Photograph (Kungliga Biblioteket, Stockholm).

BIBLIOGRAPHY

B. Ohlin, "Knut Wicksell", *Economic Journal*, 36 (1926).

O. Weinberger, "Knut Wicksell", *Weltwirtschaftliches Archiv*, 24 (1926).

E. Sommarin, "Das Lebenswerk von Knut Wicksell", *Zeitschrift für Nationalökonomie*, 2 (1931–2).

E. Sommarin, *Studenter och arpetare* (Lund, 1947).

C. G. Uhr, "Knut Wicksell—A Centennial Evaluation", *American Economic Review*, 61 (1951).

T. Gårdlund, *The Life of Knut Wicksell* (Stockholm, 1956).

C. G. Uhr, *Economic Doctrines of Knut Wicksell* (Berkeley and Los Angeles, 1960).

T. Gårdlund, "Knut Wicksell", in *International Encyclopedia of the Social Sciences,* Vol. 16 (New York, 1968).

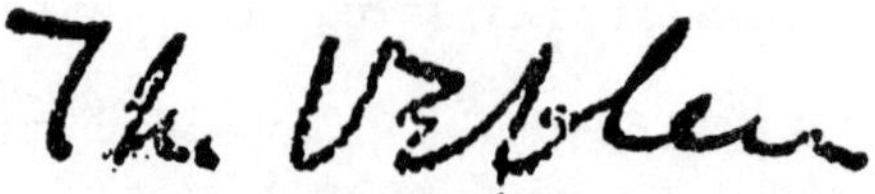

THORSTEIN BUNDE VEBLEN

1857–1929

Veblen had the strength of mind to resist assimilation, and the urge to inquire how conventions arise and spread. He was an original, whom the discipline of life in a land of "regular fellows" could not standardize.

Veblen was intrigued by what seemed to him the naive preconceptions entertained by the masters of political economy from Dr Quesnay to Dr Marshall. In particular their notions of human nature seemed to him curious.

W. C. MITCHELL

As to the merits of his work, opinions differ more widely and more fervently than on any other writer of equal prominence. He is rated among the great economists of history, or as no economist at all; as a great original pioneer or as critic and satirist without constructive talent or achievement. And he was, one might almost say, all of these things; from different standpoints and by different criteria, each of which it is possible to understand and even to appreciate.

Was Veblen an economist? He was not a mere economist, certainly. A philosopher first, and then a student of human cultures, he was always interested in these things for their own sakes as well as in their relation to purely economic facts. Was he a scientist? He was not, perhaps, by the criterion of John Stuart Mill, who held that it was only by virtue of competition and competitive equilibria that economists can be scientists at all. But that criterion can no longer be said to be orthodox.

J. M. CLARK

The development of the industrial arts . . . is the key to modern economic history. And since this process takes place autonomously it follows that the chief theoretical problem for Veblen is to analyse its impact on the economic process.

P. M. SWEEZY

It is apparent that the broad contours of his economic thought have stood the test of time successfully.

A glance around the world of today strongly suggests that Thorstein Veblen . . . belongs in many important ways more to the future than to the past.

A. G. GRUCHY

I
LIFE OF THORSTEIN VEBLEN

No study of Veblen's sociology would be intelligible without some account of his personality and career. This is true, no doubt, of every active worker in those sciences which touch personal and social activities. But it has a special application to the case of one of the great thinkers of our age whose thought, as exhibited in his writings, is so powerfully penetrated by the distinctive personal experience of his American environment. Veblen's thinking, for reasons which will be intelligible when we study it, never received much attention outside a small intellectual circle, even in his own country, and in England he is almost unknown among students of the social sciences, with the exception of a small company acquainted with his *The Theory of the Leisure Class* which they are apt to regard more as satire than as science, because they are unfamiliar with the American situation in its modern evolution.

The first point of significance in Veblen's life history is a certain independence and aloofness of attitude towards the American people and their institutions, due to his foreign origin. Born in 1857 of Norwegian stock, farmer immigrants into Wisconsin, Veblen spent his first seventeen years in a self-sufficient farmstead, which in its home life and its work preserved the character of rural Norway. The language and cultural interests remained those of Scandinavia, and they had practically no social intercourse with their English-speaking neighbours. Though English was taught and spoken in the public schools, it was ignored outside in the home, the Church and the playtime. Thorstein was the sixth child of a family of twelve. His father was a stubborn, taciturn, thoughtful but slow-witted man, his mother endowed with remarkable qualities of character. "It was from her that Thorstein got his personality and brains."

His father, deciding that Thorstein was suited for the Lutheran ministry, dispatched him at the age of seventeen to Carleton College Academy. Here he was plunged into a line of study taken over from the New England colleges, in which religion and moral philosophy were mingled with a study of the classics and a tincture of mathematics with a little botany and zoology, but no serious attempts at scientific teaching in the modern sense. "The moral philosophy" taught, "that the desire to possess, to appropriate, lies among the native and implanted principles of the soul," and that, "Man has not only the right of life and liberty, but also to *property*, or the possession and enjoyment of whatever he may, by his own industry or good fortune, or the gift of others, have honestly acquired."

Veblen, always a realist in the basis of his thinking, naturally discovered a sharp contrast between the "natural rights" theories of his philosophical and economic textbooks and the hard facts of the social-economic life with which he was familiar. But this was only one factor in his intellectual awakening. His mind spread itself profusely among the liberal philosophers and social thinkers available in the library, most of them outside the limits of the lecture room. Kant, Spencer, Mill, Hume, Voltaire, Huxley appealed to different strains of interest in him, and he began a study of Old Norse and its literature, together with the modern languages which his fine memory enabled him to absorb with ease as by-products of his more serious studies.

His public oration on graduation day did not, however, indicate a sociological career. Its subject was "Mill's examination of Hamilton's philosophy of the conditioned". His earliest post as a teacher was neither in philosophy nor economics, but in mathematics. For a year he taught in a Norwegian college in Madison, Wisconsin. When this college failed, Thorstein with a brother found his way to Johns Hopkins in Baltimore where philosophy at first continued to be his chief study. Failing to obtain a scholarship that would provide him with a living, he then turned to Yale, again with the purpose of studying philosophy. Continually hampered by financial difficulties, he managed to struggle through for two and a half years to his degree in 1884, with a dissertation upon "Ethical grounds of a doctrine of retribution".

Failing to obtain any acceptable teaching post, he returned to the farm settlement of his family and loafed and read for the next few years, writing a few articles which remained unpublished, and talking over economic and political problems with his father. This was the time when the growing grievances of the farmers evoked the Farmers' Alliance, while Henry George made his popular appeal for the single tax, and anarchism raised its head in the bombing at Chicago. Economic issues were forcing their way into a wider public attention, and liberal economists, Richard Ely and J. B. Clark at their head, were grouping themselves in the American Economic Association, with what was regarded by the older school as a "socialistic" tendency.

Veblen, in his bucolic retirement took no part in these movements, though following them with keen interest. With characteristic recklessness he married in 1888 the bright educated daughter of an Iowa farmer whom he had known as a Carleton fellow-student. After further failure to get a college teaching post, he registered as a student at Cornell in 1891, passing from history and law into the economics department then in charge of Professor J. L. Laughlin. Spencer's *Plea for Liberty* was then stirring controversy in American intellectual circles, and Veblen opened his distinctively sociological writings with an elaborate discussion of this essay, entitled *Some Neglected Points in the Theory of Socialism*. Obtaining a fellowship at Cornell, Veblen with his wife settled down there for a year during which the published several economic articles, discussing the wage-fund doctrine, Böhm-Bawerk and *The Overproduction Fallacy*. The next year, 1892, he followed Professor Laughlin to Chicago as a lecturer in economics and had his first experience of a great industrial centre. His age was now forty-five and he was at the beginning of his economic career as writer and teacher.

It was not until 1899 that his first book *The Theory of the Leisure Class, an Economic Study in the Evolution of Institutions* saw the light of day, marking the distinctive line of his sociology. Its popularity among radicals was chiefly due to its satirical commentary upon the upper classes, rather than to its scientific exposition of the facts of the American situation.

In 1900 he was promoted to the rank of assistant professor. This year began an era of sensational exposures of "high finance and corrupt politics" in which, however, Veblen took no personal part. He was more deeply concerned with two books which absorbed his attention, Ward's *Pure Sociology* and Sombart's *Der Moderne Capitalismus* in which he saw the beginnings of a genuinely scientific spirit applied to social changes, and a recognition of the vital distinction between industry and business. Having now more money at his disposal, Veblen made several visits to Europe.

At Stanford University in California he stayed for three years, teaching economics to small classes of undergraduates who were not easily attuned to his methods and manners. His knowledge was encyclopaedic but his attempts to impart it were singularly ineffective, partly from the disorderly method of his talk, partly from sheer physical defects. Even his ironic humour faded in his classes, and his brilliance of analysis failed to shine in this academic environment.

When the First World War broke out, Veblen was travelling in Norway where he obtained a recognition as a great man which he found very pleasing.

When America came into the War, Colonel House was instructed to prepare a memorandum upon the terms of a possible peace settlement, and Veblen was invited to take part in its preparation. His chief contribution *An Outline of a Policy for the Control of the Economic Penetration of Backward Countries and of Foreign Investments* indicates how far his mind was working in advance of the practical statesmanship of his time. His work was given no prominence in the report of the House Inquiry for reasons intelligible enough when its far-reaching implications are realized.

In June 1918 Veblen was appointed one of the editors of *The Dial* and moved to New York. A series of his articles was published in book form early in 1919 under the title *The Vested Interests and the State of the Industrial Arts*. The support of influential liberals in the *New Republic*, the *Nation* and other radical journals hoisted Veblen on to a pinnacle of temporary fame as the prophet of his time. Veblenists and Veblen Clubs acquired a vogue. But it is difficult in America for fame to dispense with some of those personal factors in which Veblen was so deficient. He could not "orate", he would not even talk to order or to expectation. As Dorfman says of him, "His protective mechanism of silence had become his master." Nor can it be supposed that articles imputed to him in *The Dial*, representing bolshevism as a menace to the vested interests, would help his reputation in any quarter but the negligible communists.

The "Red Terror" which swept over America in 1919–20, in which socialists, pacifists, internationalists, communists were subjected to all sorts of legal and illegal violence, drove such argumentation as that of Veblen into almost complete neglect. The gallant attempt to associate him with the establishment of the "New School for Social Research" which was "to seek an unbiased understanding of the existing order" and in which a number of Veblen's friends and admirers took part was of little lasting service to him. For his inability to hold the students attracted by his reputation soon became apparent. His position became precarious, and after the changes in the structure of the "New School" in 1922, he was driven to seek a new teaching post.

An attempt to organize technicians into an alliance for the furtherance of their control of industry failed to win the necessary support, and the brief notoriety of a movement of technology a few years later was subjected to such severe criticism in liberal as well as conservative quarters as to damage the practical reputation of the Veblenist position. The title of Veblen's last book, *Absentee Ownership*, denotes the strong persistence of his distinctive contribution to the brand of economic determinism assumed thirty years before. But by 1927 his failing health drove him back to Palo Alto to pass his last years in weakness and in poverty, relieved only by the contributions of one or two well-to-do friends. His death occurred in August 1929 in his seventy-third year. Had he lived to see the great depression which began in the next year, his grim humour might have felt a certain satisfaction in the débâcle of that finance which he held responsible for all modern economic maladies.

John Atkinson Hobson

II
SOURCE AND IMPACT OF VEBLEN

That Veblen's work continues to be a source of considerable controversy is indicative of its vitality. Some men effectively catch the drift of development and have a vision of things to come. Such men become active forces in that very development and their names become landmarks and turning points. Time alone is the final judge of a candidate's right to inclusion in this select list. For Veblen, time has rendered its verdict.

Veblen's story is complicated by his historical setting, his personality, and his style of writing. In Veblen, we have at least two men. There is the economist and there is the artist—a most unusual combination. Generally the two do not mix. In the history of Anglo-American economics the only other case that comes to mind is that of David Hume.

Let me take up Veblen the artist, first. Veblen is a person interested in writing and communication. He loves to tease, to exaggerate, to present fantastic and poetic images, to utilize symbolism and allegory and to mobilize folklore. He will even use archaic words and phrases to fit the mood of an archaic economic and social order. As he unfolds various aspects of Western civilization, he is a throwback to the saga tellers of his Norwegian forebears and the writers of epic poems with their tales of intermingled tragedy and comedy. The anthropologist and archaeologist in him, fed by his northern pride and heritage, provided him with an almost inexhaustible arsenal of examples, illustrations, and "models".

As he spins tales, so he spins webs that entrap the reader into the recognition of the seriousness of phenomena that he may have taken for granted. Veblen merely picked his Don Quixotes from the realm of economics. Behind the humour and the dead-pan, there is often a stark tale that is reminiscent of the privileged court jester. Veblen's shafts respect no class or group. There are no exceptions, not even himself. With his artistic temperament went the peccadilloes that are conventionally associated with it.

Having been reared in one culture and having matured in another, Veblen had a heightened instinct of curiosity. That curiosity received in the course of his academic training in the seventies and the eighties the benefit of the discipline and inspiration that seminal minds and provocative teachers give to promising youth, thereby enabling them to go beyond and transform the established positions—to lift them to a higher plane, as it were. For Veblen was indeed fortunate.

At sturdy Carleton College, he studied under the profound philosophic economist, John Bates Clark, who was developing on the one hand his comprehensive marginalist economics, beginning with his own version of marginal utility, and on the other hand formulating his creed of Christian socialism. Clark soon saw the promise of Veblen and encouraged him to go on to graduate work at Johns Hopkins with philosophy as his major and economics as his minor.

His stay at Johns Hopkins was brief but rewarding. He had the advantage of studying logic with Charles S. Peirce, the founder of pragmatism. He was impressed with the lectures of George S. Morris, the teacher of John Dewey, and one of the advance guard of the trained Hegelians from the German universities. There was on the social staff at Johns Hopkins his contemporary, Richard T. Ely, the *enfant terrible* of economics, who was already impressed with Veblen. Veblen established lifelong friendships with fellow students, for example that future noted American historian, James Franklin Jameson.

Veblen then went to Yale, where he had the benefit of the William Graham Sumner of the *Folkways* and the gruff philosopher, Noah Porter, who was making a last stand on behalf of the traditional common-sense philosophy against the onrush of Spencerian evolution and the Kantian and Hegelian idealist systems.

Thus at the very beginning of his career, Veblen stood in the thick of the battle of conflicting philosophic systems. But fortunately for us he left philosophy in the nineties for economics, although he never lost his original interest.

As an economist, his relation to his times is doubly significant, for he played a dual role. He was a theorist and catalyst of reform. He came upon the scene between two ages of social and intellectual ferment. Just as in the realm of affairs, so in the realm of knowledge there are great tides. Periods of reform and reconstruction rise to great crests; then come troughs marked by consolidation of gains, conservatism, and sometimes reaction. The last great crest of the seventies and eighties was marked by the triumph of the doctrine of evolution in science and a world-wide movement of political and social reform. In economics it was epitomized by the wave of interest in the German historical school. In its native land, this movement had sought to broaden economic analysis beyond the narrow foundation of the older classical school of economics and to that end it had attempted to develop such powerful instruments of research as statistics and history including comparative economic development. It also sought to give greater scope to the ethical nature of man than the dominant vulgarizers of the classical economics would permit.

In the realm of policy it sought to meet the wave of discontent and the the threat of socialism by a variety of reformist devices. These included the appeal to the churches to take an active part in solving such critical social questions as the relation between employers and employees, the appeal to government for easing the restrictions on trade-unions, and the support of national social security legislation such as workmen's compensation, old age and sickness insurance. It included also a concern with the problems of conserving natural resources and regulating "natural monopolies". On the one side, the movement seemed to provide the beginning of a richer synthesis for expanding knowledge and on the other side a basis for policies that would check the damage of excessive individualism without embracing the socialism of Marx.

To the younger generation of reforming American economists, encouraged by such eminent elders as General Francis A. Walker and Carroll D. Wright, this German historical movement, flanked as it was by a similar movement in Great Britain, seemed to offer the promise of adaptation to the needs of the developing American economy. As such it provided a basis for the "new economics". This included the revised classical tradition, which embraced the doctrine of marginal utility. In accordance with their Anglo-American heritage, the exponents thought that economic reform could be achieved largely by voluntary organizations and by state and local units more than by the national authority. "Planning" was city planning and "regulation" was largely that of railroads and other "natural monopolies" by state commissions.

After the turn of the century came stabilization, security, and consolidation, frowning on innovation and the depreciation of further reforms. The turning away from "social inventions" had its counterpart in the lack of enthusiasm for any kind of innovation in economic analysis. Thus, for example, the original leader of the movement of mathematical economics, Simon Newcomb, voiced doubts on the usefulness of further work in this area and he expressed the hope that economists would turn their energies to educating the public in the simpler "abstractions", as he called them, of the Ricardian economics of an earlier age. Economics had only just begun to have autonomy as an important area in its own right rather than as a limited, narrow topic in the course on moral philosophy. In such heated political struggles as that over "free silver" there was not a little feeling that moderation in matters of policy was essential to protect the infant profession. Narrow practical and intellectual ends became dominant, or so it seemed.

Of the older generation of leaders of the movement for reconstruction, some went into administrative work, others specialized in less controversial subjects such as public finance, and still others devoted themselves to the more abstract problems of the rationale of a static state. But even these protected themselves against the charge of lack of immediate practical reference by claiming that their analysis tested the validity of the existing economic system's right to survival. Social innovation was considered outside the realm of science.

But just because liberal reform found hard sledding in America, there appeared to be a greater need for a basic revaluation and reorientation. For this the special qualities and abilities of Veblen seemed particularly valuable. He was well equipped to survive intellectually in an age where basic thinking appeared to be at a discount. He just escaped being an immigrant. In effect, he was an "outsider" and therefore not easily engulfed in the passing mood. He had a special feeling for languages and old-world, particularly northern, sagas and cultures. His extraordinary linguistic equipment opened to him developments and literature in a variety of areas and lands. His cosmopolitan scholar's pervasive sense of history, along with his knowledge of anthropology, psychology, and the biological sciences, gave him perspective. Having received his doctorate in philosophy, he had special equipment for theoretical discussion and the relation of economics to other fields of knowledge. He had the comprehensive reach of the student of culture, the precision so essential for systematic thinking, and that rugged consistency, courage, and independence that refuses to bend to the expediencies of changing winds and fashions.

It is these qualities that distinguished him from the outset. With his strong sense for the fundamental, he fixed attention on central economic institutions of his time—and indeed of our own time; for example, the corporation and the technological process. Veblen implicitly recognized that the corporation is a mighty instrument for organizing production and promoting efficiency. But he regarded it as something much more than a mere embodiment of external mechanical forces. Rather it was a complex organism that lent itself to manipulation by passions and spirits that ran counter to the objective of its function in the economy. More fundamental still, it gave play to the intrigues and rivalry of inner groups whose habit of thinking in terms of money as an abstract aim overlay their functions in the institution. This habit at times ran counter, also, to the needs of the community, when it bred a reduction of output and employment to maintain solvency or increase profits. As the corporate form gains increasing sway over the economic life of the community, the consequences, if left uncontrolled, become all the more serious.

Veblen's view of technology, like his view of the corporation, was intimately related to his conception of human nature. Man to Veblen was a natural force acting upon all other forces of nature. Man was distinguishable by his special characteristics of imagination, playfulness, economic effort, and tasteful production. To a large extent, science and the machine are embodiments of these attributes. But there is an aspect of machine technology which leads to purely reflexive and habitual activity and sometimes machine technology has been abused to produce ugly things. This explains Veblen's simultaneous emphasis and admiration of technology as well as occasional concern over its effects. The techniques and institutions that man creates have a way of turning around, creating a life all their own and threatening to become his masters and gods. Veblen saw constantly re-enacted in history a dramatic saga between man's material interests and the institutions he creates to give them expression.

Veblen's views of technology, human nature and corporations, money and economy, do not add up to a closed structure of thought in the typical nineteenth-century sense. Such systems began with an overwhelming major premise and ineluctably drove, fall the chips where they may, towards a grand, simplified, logical conclusion; for example, a David Ricardo with his stationary state, an Auguste Comte with his positive religion, a Karl Marx with a classless society, and a Herbert Spencer with his idealized order of free contract where even a policeman would not be needed. Veblen is less doctrinaire, and less dogmatic. Where the authors of the great closed systems seek to dominate and organize, Veblen suggests, tempts, pleads, and even hypnotizes. In his method he is more evolutionary, more sensitive to psychological forces, more aware of the relations between the social sciences, and more cognizant of surprising changes in the configuration of forces. He combines forces and elements often thought of as disparate or irrelevant to each other. This is the reason why he occasionally surprised and even shocked his reader or fellow economist. His approach makes him at home with the spirit of the twentieth century and projects his influence forward.

Although bereft of the attractions of the great system-makers and the magic of the great programmatic reformers, his influence has been wide, pervasive, and enduring. Vital and original minds were drawn towards him from the beginning.

Certainly no economist of his and our day has commanded the respect of so many leaders in so many other disciplines: in literature and the fine arts, philosophy, psychology, sociology, political science, anthropology, history and even the biological and physical sciences.

Veblen is a "philosophical radical" in an American and twentieth-century setting. Unlike his British counterparts, he was free from Benthamite psychology, was not a system-builder, and was without a positive political programme. Yet his indirect influence upon men active in public affairs was very considerable, particularly following the great depression when many of our economic institutions became subject to criticism and revision. Veblen had made it abundantly clear that "prosperity" of business enterprises was not necessarily coincidental with the welfare of the community at large. During this period, some of Veblen's ideas, available for decades, fell at last on fertile soil and took root. His regret might have been that so many of them in application led to a further aggrandizement of the State. So while it may be impossible to point to a single piece of legislation that he would have proposed, there can be no doubt that men who had never read his books came unconsciously under the influence of his thought. No one can say exactly when or how Veblen's ideas, once widely regarded as radical and violently rejected by most of one generation, gradually became a part of our accepted common stock of ideas. We do know, however, that historically such a slow and pervasive infiltration is characteristic of the impact of an intellectual forerunner.

How did he do it? Here is a man who was often inchoate, obscure, tangential, unintelligible, and one-sided. He made his generous share of mistakes. Ultimately, his value lies in his role as an emancipator of the human mind. He tears down the walls of the institutions, prejudices, and fond illusions that imprison the human spirit. He sharpened the use of reason and presented it as a tool to those who would penetrate to the secrets of society. He transcended the function of the economist, but he also fulfilled it. He became a landmark in the cumulative growth of the science and the development of Western culture.

Joseph Dorfman

SOURCES

Essay I

John Atkinson Hobson, *Veblen* (Chapman and Hall, London, 1936). Biographical extracts.

Essay II

Joseph Dorfman, "Veblen centenary round table, source and impact of Veblen", *American Economic Review*, 48 (1958). Abridged.

Signature

From a letter in the possession of Joseph Dorfman.

Portrait

Photograph (The Viking Press Inc., New York).

BIBLIOGRAPHY

J. M. Clark, "Thorstein Veblen", *American Economic Review*, 19 (1929).

W. C. Mitchell, "Thorstein Veblen", *Economic Journal*, 39 (1929).

R. V. Teggart, *Thorstein Veblen* (Berkeley, 1932).

E. S. Bates, "Thorstein Veblen: A biography", *Scribner's Magazine*, (December 1933).

J. Dorfman, *Thorstein Veblen and His America*, 34 (New York, 2nd ed., 1961).

A. Johnson, "Thorstein Bunde Veblen", in *Encyclopaedia of the Social Sciences*, Vol. 15 (New York, 1935).

F. Veblen, "Thorstein Veblen, reminiscences of his brother Orson", *Social Forces*, 10 (1935).

M. Lerner, "Thorstein Veblen", in *Dictionary of American Biography*, Vol. 19 (1936).

W. C. Mitchell, "Thorstein Veblen", in *The Backward Art of Spending Money, and Other Essays* (New York, 1937).

R. L. Duffus, *The Innocents at Cedro: A Memoir of Thorstein Veblen and Others* (New York, 1944).

S. M. Daugert, *The Philosophy of Thorstein Veblen* (New York, 1950).

M. Lerner, *The Portable Veblen* (New York, 1953), preface.

D. Riesman, *Thorstein Veblen: A Critical Interpretation* (New York, 1953).

B. Rosenberg, *The Values of Veblen, A Critical Appraisal* (Washington, 1956).

A. K. Davis, "Thorstein Veblen Reconsidered", *Science and Society*, 21 (1957).

"Thorstein Bunde Veblen, 1857–1957", *Monthly Review*, 9 (1957).

D. F. Dowd (ed.), *Thorstein Veblen: A Critical Reappraisal* (Ithaca NY, 1958).

P. M. Sweezy, J. Dorfman, A. G. Gruchy, "Veblen centenary round table", *American Economic Review*, 48 (1958).

J. Dorfman, C. E. Ayres, *et al.*, *Institutional Economics, Veblen, Commons, and Mitchell Reconsidered: A Series of Lectures* (Berkeley, 1963).

A. K. Davis, "Thorstein Veblen", in *International Encyclopedia of the Social Sciences*, Vol. 16 (New York, 1968).

MAX WEBER

1864–1920

Es ist eher eine Scheu in ihm gewesen, daß die eigene nie einzuschläfernde Kritik und Schärfe des Verstandes sein Auge trüben könnte, die Überlegenheit eines andern im Sinne größerer Erfahrung oder schlichter Tatkraft oder kluger Bewältigung des Alltags nicht genug zu respektieren. Aber freilich, typisch ist auch, wie diese hintergründige Scheu und Bescheidenheit keinerlei Bremse bildete bei der direkten Begegnung im tätigen Moment. . . . Und doch ist auch da alsbald wieder die Zucht der Reserve, der Distanz, des Respekts vor der Freiheit und Selbständigkeit des andern. E. BAUMGARTEN

Max Weber is a figure intellectually as monumental as Marx. K. E. BOULDING

Webers Weltauffassung basiert auf der Überzeugung von der Unmöglichkeit, objektiv, rational und einzelwissenschaftlich ein Urteil über den Wert einer Sache, Theorie oder Verhaltensweise zu fällen; vielmehr muß das Individuum autonom zwischen Alternativen wählen. P. HONIGSHEIM

Ist denn aber für den Gelehrten im Bereich der Kulturwissenschaften das Auseinanderhalten von Denken und Werten, Erkennen und Wollen—dieser beiden ineinander verflochtenen geistigen Funktionen überhaupt möglich? Das wird von vielen Seiten bestritten, und Weber selbst weiß, daß es schwer ist, und daß er damit ein logisch-ethisches Ideal für den empirischen Forscher und Lehrer aufstellt, dessen voller Verwirklichung die Einheit der kontemplativen und aktiven Persönlichkeit widerstrebt. MARIANNE WEBER

Seine Forscherleistungen liegen vor in den gewaltigen Werken. Inhaltliche Neuentdeckungen sind verbunden mit dem hellsten methodischen Bewußtsein wie bei Galilei. Max Weber hat, wie jener in den Naturwissenschaften, in den Geisteswissenschaften den hier ganz andersartigen endgültigen Schritt getan zur reinen Wissenschaft, nicht nur in den längst gekannten philologischen und anderen Vorarbeiten, sondern in der Sache selbst.

Die Wirkung seines Werkes hat erst begonnen, vor allem in Amerika, aber auch in England, Frankreich und in Deutschland. Er hat die Soziologie aus dem allgemeinen Gerede und den billigen Selbstverständlichkeiten und spekulativen Torheiten zur Forschung erhoben und durfte wohl unwillig sagen: Das meiste, was unter dem Namen Soziologie geht, ist Schwindel. K. JASPERS

[*Weber*] *taught the reading world to appreciate the importance of* quantitative rationality *as a phase of modern social mind. This must stand as one of the great intellectual achievements of the age.* F. H. KNIGHT

I
CAREER AND PERSONAL ORIENTATION

Max Weber was born in 1864. His father, who came from a family of textile manufacturers in western Germany, was a well-to-do lawyer and National-liberal parliamentarian in the Germany of Bismarck; his mother was a woman of culture and piety whose humanitarian and religious interests were not shared by her husband. Weber spent most of the first twenty-nine years of his life in his parents' house, which was a meeting place for both prominent liberal politicians and celebrated professors from the University of Berlin. After completing school in 1882, he attended the University of Heidelberg, where he was enrolled as a law student. A year later, at the age of nineteen, he went to Strasbourg to serve his year of military training. After two more years at the universities of Berlin and Göttingen, he took his examination in law in 1886, while continuing his studies at Berlin.

His independent academic work began in the fields of law and legal history. In his doctoral dissertation, entitled "A contribution to the history of medieval business organizations" (1889), he examined the various legal principles according to which the cost, risk or profit of an enterprise were to be borne jointly by several individuals. After completing this dissertation Weber started the in-service training required for the German bench or bar. During this training (and also as a reserve officer on temporary duty), he became acquainted at first hand with the social and political problems of agrarian society in the provices east of the Elbe River. At the same time he began a study of legal institutions, which was formally to qualify him as an instructor in law at the University of Berlin. This second work was his "Roman agrarian history and its significance for public and private law" (1891). By examining the methods of land surveying in Roman society, the different terms used to designate the resulting land units, and the extant writings on agriculture by Roman authors, Weber analysed the social, political and economic developments of Roman society.

While completing this study, he prepared himself for his duties as a *Privatdozent* in Roman, German and commercial law at the University of Berlin. He also undertook an extensive investigation of rural labour in the German provinces east of the Elbe, which led to the publication of a 900-page volume in 1892, and he investigated the stock exchange. As full-time lecturer, consultant to government agencies, and researcher he carried an enormous burden. He was no doubt referring to this period when he wrote some years later of his "need to feel crushed under the load of work". In 1893 he married Marianne Schnitger and at last left the house of his parents. In the fall of 1894 he became full professor of economics at Freiburg University, where in 1895 he delivered his inaugural lecture on "The national state and economic policy". In 1896 he accepted a position at the University of Heidelberg.

In the fall of 1897, when he was 33, Wever fell ill and was forced to reduce and finally to suspend his regular academic work. For four years he suffered from an acute state of exhaustion and anxiety. Even small diversions proved too taxing at times, and this apparently vigorous man would sit for hours at the window, staring into space. Travel eventually proved to be one of the activities he could enjoy, and for major parts of this period he lived in Italy, especially in Rome. After almost four years he seemed to recover gradually and resumed his habit of omnivorous reading. Some of it was concerned with the history, organization and economic activities of medieval monasteries. The literature on this subject apparently provided one starting point for his subsequent studies of the relation between religious beliefs and economic activity.

In the years of his recovery, from about 1901 on, Weber returned to his scholarly work despite many temporary set-backs. In 1903 he accepted a position as associate editor of the *Archiv für Sozialwissenschaft und Sozialpolitik* ("Archives for Social Science and Social Welfare") and through this position renewed his contacts with the academic world. There were negotiations for a renewed offer of a professorship at Heidelberg, but in the end Weber felt unable to take the position. In 1904 he accepted an invitation to visit the United States and participate in the Congress of Arts and Sciences held in connection with the World's Fair at St Louis. In the same year the first results of his resumed scholarly activity were published: an essay on methodology, a discussion of agrarian policies in eastern Germany, and *The Protestant Ethic and the Spirit of Capitalism*. Despite his inability to resume regular academic duties, the University of Heidelberg, in co-operation with the Ministry of Education, made a generous financial arrangement with him, but in 1907 a private inheritance enabled him to terminate this burdensome, part-time association and to live as a private scholar. For the remainder of his life he engaged in intense and wide-ranging scientific activity which was disrupted only during the First World War when he served for a time as director of the army hospitals in Heidelberg. In 1918 he became a consultant to the German Armistice Commission in Versailles and to a commission charged with the drafting of the Weimar Constitution. In the summer of that year he also taught at the University of Vienna and in 1919 he accepted an offer from the University of Munich. In June, 1920, he died of pneumonia at the age of fifty-six.

This bare outline of Weber's career is relevant to an understanding of his scholarly work if we inquire into the extraordinary tensions that characterized his life and that would have incapacitated a lesser man. An attack of meningitis at the age of four, the stimulating environment of his family, and a predilection for books made him withdraw from his contemporaries early in life and resist the routine schooling offered by his teachers. Repelled by both the Victorian complacency of his father and the strong personal piety of his mother, he developed into a precocious student who wrote historical essays at the age of thirteen, adopted systematic study habits a year or so later, and created for himself a world of the mind in which he tested his rapidly growing intellectual strength in the assimilation and critical appraisal of historical and philosophical writings. But when he went to the University of Heidelberg at the age of eighteen, he quickly adopted the way of life of a German fraternity with its duelling, drinking bouts, and coarsely romantic conviviality. Without neglecting his studies, he turned from a slender, withdrawn adolescent into a large, pompously virile young man—so pompous and so virile that his mother could not hide her repugnance.

This ambivalence between withdrawal and forceful participation also was apparent in Weber's deliberations concerning his future career. Towards the end of his studies he felt increasingly oppressed by his financial dependence on his father, and he prepared for an academic career primarily in the hope of gaining his independence more quickly. But other feelings were expressed in his statement: "I am quite clear that I would never leave the life of practical experience since I know now that I could achieve something in this line, which is by no means certain in the case of an academic career."

Thus, shortly before his first academic appointment, he applied for a legal position with the municipal government of Bremen because of his "extraordinary longing for a practical job". Though he had made a reputation as a scholar by the age of twenty-seven and at twenty-nine had the definite prospect of a brilliant academic career, he wrote at that time: "I am not really a scholar after all; scientific activity is for me primarily an occupation for the leisure hours. . . . The feeling of being active in a practical way is entirely indispensable for me, and I hope that the pedagogic side of the teaching profession will satisfy this craving."

Weber chose an academic career but he held a regular academic position for only five years (1893–7). At thirty-three his severe psychopathological condition forced him to abandon his duties despite determined efforts to continue on a part-time basis. After his partial recovery in 1901 Weber made occasional attempts to return to academic life. But his wife's description of the psychological turmoil to which he deliberately subjected himself, when towards the end of his life he accepted a professorship at the University of Munich, is not only pathetic evidence of Weber's willpower but also a clear indication of his lifelong disability despite his impressive scholarly output.

The craving for practical activity and the inability to cope with the duties of an academic career was only one of the many paradoxes which marked Weber's life. Though he was a dedicated German nationalist, he considered for a time the possibility of emigration. In 1903, while negotiations with the University of Heidelberg were in progress, he went on six separate trips abroad. This indicates not only how difficult it was for Weber formally to terminate his academic career but also how such trips provided an escape from the country he loved. Unable to submit to academic routine, he nevertheless developed a rigorous ethic for the teaching profession and an unusual pedagogic intensity in his occasional relations with students. Committed as few others were to the exclusion of political value judgments from academic teaching, he nevertheless endowed his lectures with such passion that they bespoke a partisanship for impartiality. Though he was extraordinarily sensitive in his relations with others, his outlook on life was concerned with the pursuit of power. Unable to engage in the practical activity which he craved and unfit to serve in the German Army during World War I, he nevertheless thought of himself as a man predestined for political life and the military virtues. In his intellectual concern with the problem of power, Weber was detached and profoundly unconventional, yet he adhered throughout his life to many of the conventional beliefs of his class in imperial Germany. And his preoccupation with the struggle for power among nations went hand in hand with a rigorously puritanical ethic in his own personal affairs.

Many of these contradictions were reflected in Weber's style of writing. Not only long, involved sentences but qualifying phrases and digressions served him as a safeguard against the simple declarative sentence. This was not so much the mannerism of the German scholar as the necessary device of a man of tremendous learning, for whom every generalization was a precarious victory over the infinite complexity of facts. Yet this master of the qualified phrase and the dependent clause also was capable of writing or speaking in a terse and decisive manner and could say of himself that "heaven in its wrath" had endowed him with the "gift of a certain bluntness which was difficult to suppress." The same contradiction appears in Weber's political participation. The positions he took in his political writings were bold and unequivocal. His essays contain, among other things, a very realistic assessment of the role of the politician. But when it came to Weber's own political participation this decisiveness did not carry over. In 1918 he had an opportunity to be nominated for election to the National Assembly, but he refused to make any effort in his own behalf and consequently lost the nomination. A year later his wife suggested to him that the nation would yet call upon him, and he answered: "Yes, I have the feeling as if life has still withheld something from me." This suggestion and reply, together with Weber's actions, can mean only that he would not become active politically unless he were called upon to play the role of the great leader and statesman. In short, he continuously engaged in the simultaneous effort to be a man of science with the strenuous vigour more common in a man of action, and to be a man of action with all the ethical rigour and personal detachment more common in a man of science.

In this effort one may see a reflection of tendencies in German society at large. If Tocqueville could say that as a born aristocrat and lover of freedom he was able to look calmly upon the decline of his class and to see clearly the danger to freedom in the rising tide of democracy, Weber might have said that as a "lone wolf" born into a liberal, middle-class family in late nineteenth-century Germany he saw both the decline of liberalism in an emerging power-state and the threat to the individual in the bureaucratization of modern society. As a witness of Bismarck's unification of Germany and the virtual elimination of the liberal, middle-class movements from positions of political influence, Weber became convinced that great goals could be achieved only by power politics. For the rest of his life he set a premium upon examining political life without illusions, looking at it as a struggle between individuals and groups with conflicting beliefs and interests, always decided in the end by the reservoir power available to the winning side and by its greater ability to use that power effectively. Possibly this view was encouraged by the vicarious power-orientation that Bismarck had imparted to German liberalism. But it was also strongly sustained by Weber's own passionate quest for action and for proving his strength and his convictions in daily life.

German liberalism contained a strong belief in the importance of the individual. That belief had found its consummate expression in the German classical literature of the late eighteenth century, and the concern with humanistic learning and cultivation of the personality had remained a characteristic of the educated middle class. The political defeat of this class, especially in 1848 and in the Bismarck *Reich*, gave still greater importance to these cultural preoccupations.

Thus, the power-orientation of the educated blended with the humanistic orientation of the powerful, with the result that human relations were endowed with an emotional appreciation of personal values; personal choices, with the rigidity of ultimate moral decisions; and political issues, with a mixture of "brutality and romance".

Weber reflected this climate of opinion. As his wife tells it in her biography, he showed throughout his life an extraordinary appreciation for the problems other people faced and for the shades of mood and meaning that characterized their outlook on life. Men as divergent as the revolutionary poet Ernst Toller and the liberal monarchist Friedrich Naumann sought his counsel and guidance. Upon festive as well as tragic occasions, in his circle of friends and relatives Weber would express understanding and emotional warmth in his effort to discover the larger meaning in the life of each person. In his period of military training as well as on his many travels abroad, he showed a great facility in communicating with people in many walks of life, speaking in terms each could understand and spicing his conversations with a human touch and a fund of anecdotes. Yet for the greater part of his life this same man was incapacitated from active participation in his chosen career, too withdrawn to express his personal feelings to others, as he himself stated time and again, and painfully difficult through his uncompromising insistence upon rigid moral and intellectual standards, ostensibly applied to himself alone but inevitably a tacit accusation against all who did not live up to them. There is more than a little suggestion in Weber's life that his humanity found expression primarily in personal contacts outside his professional and political preoccupations, while the application of his rigid standards in the context of academic and political life helped exclude him from the active participation he consciously sought.

Whatever its psychological significance, the duality of his humanistic values and his orientation towards power was of major significance for Weber as a sociologist and a social historian. This perspective was the common property of German liberalism. It had found perhaps its consummate expression in Theodor Mommsen's *Roman History*, which had stripped the humanistic halo from the ancient world and combined a realistic history of group conflict with a celebration of Caesar as the personal embodiment of statesmanship and reason. But whereas Mommsen did not hesitate to use the language of nineteenth-century party struggles for his interpretation of Roman history, Weber gradually developed the same perspective into an image of society and a set of sociological categories, which he used in his world-wide comparative studies of religion and political organization.

I want to add a word concerning the moral dimensions of this scholarly work. Weber was preoccupied throughout his career with the development of rationalism in Western civilization. His lifetime study of this development revealed not only the complexity of its antecedents, but the precariousness of its achievements. He left no doubt that his profound personal commitment to the cause of reason and freedom had guided his choice of subject matter; and his research left no doubt that reason and freedom in the Western world were in jeopardy. Weber was a contemporary of Freud, whose lifework consisted in safeguarding man's reason after comprehending in full measure the depth of man's irrationality. Similarly, Weber sought to safeguard the great legacy of the Enlightenment after fully exploring the historical preconditions of that legacy. This exploration created in him a tragic consciousness of peril. When asked for the purpose of his scholarly research, Weber answered: "I want to see how much I can stand."

From this vantage point his frequently crude German nationalism may appear, not only as an acceptance of the conventional opinions of his day, but also as an acceptance of Germany's historic mission in defending Western civilization against the Russian menace. Yet Weber also combined this nationalism with a fundamental commitment to the study of non-European culture whose basic assumptions made sense and had value in their own terms.

One of Weber's most remarkable achievements was that he identified himself fully with the issues of German society but that he transcended their limitations by seeing them as incidents in a world-wide perspective. This combination of commitment and detachment was yet another aspect of the personal and intellectual tensions that marred his life and made it creative.

Reinhard Bendix

II
MAX WEBER AND THE CAPITALIST SPIRIT

Max Weber was a good deal more liberal than either Schmoller or Sombart, and his appeal was to reason and society. While he too sought evidence for his generalizations in historic materials, he did not by any means imitate his predecessors. Schmoller, for example, was something of a traditionalist and a staunch supporter of the German monarchy; Weber detested the Kaiser. Sombart spoke of history and nation as though these concepts were autochthonous forces; Weber preferred human rationality. The historicists suggested that society was an organism anterior as well as superior to the individual; Weber and the liberals viewed society in terms of autonomous individuals conditioned by social forces. History to the conservative was something transcendental; to their opponents it was but a stream of events which could be comprehended through the application of reason. Thus, though Weber's intellectual antecedents may be found in the camp of the historicists, he rejected the idea of the uniqueness of history and refused to believe that it exhibited it any way the sort of undefined transcendentalism so characteristic of Sombart. Weber has come to be as intellectually important as Marx, exhibiting a similar quality of rebellion against received theory. Unquestionably, he was an important source of many ideas which highlighted obscure regions in social science. Economics, however, he tended to put to one side, preferring rather a broader and more general range of problems.

A powerful personality, who exerted a profound and lasting influence on students and other scholars as well, Weber managed, at least among sociologists, to create a kind of school. Although he wrote many works which impinged on the subject matter of economics, he was not really an economist in the analytical sense. His main interest was economic sociology, through which he could view characteristic institutions. While he developed an institutional framework for economic action, he seldom inquired into what an economist would consider to be the really substantive issues. In his analysis of capitalism, for example, there is not much that one can find on business cycles. Whatever theory he used he took from the Austrians. He was essentially a polyhistor, a universal scholar who wanted to observe human beings through the science of sociology. The immediately practical did not concern him: he could easily pursue an idea that was quite distant from the pragmatic needs of the day. Consequently, he did not hesitate to investigate urbanism, music, art history, world religions, economic motivations, and other recondite matters. Although he was a nationalist

Arthur Cecil Pigou (1877–1959)

Joseph Alois Schumpeter (1883–1950)

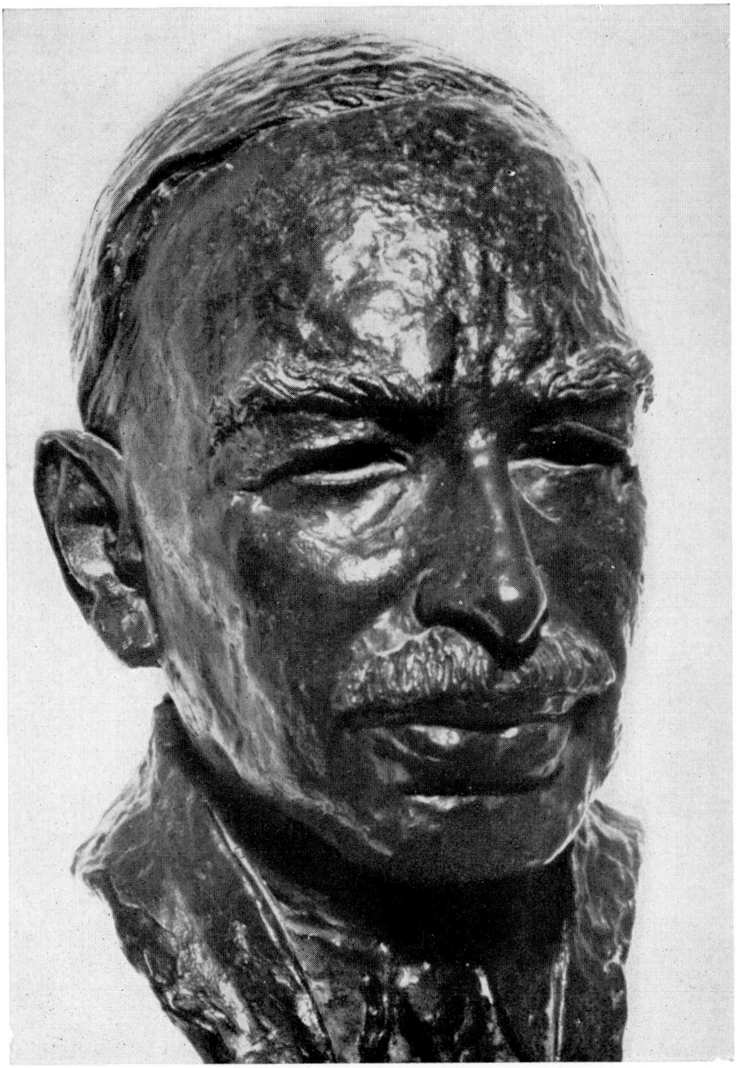

John Maynard Keynes (1883–1946)

Loss of National Income in the Great Depression in Germany

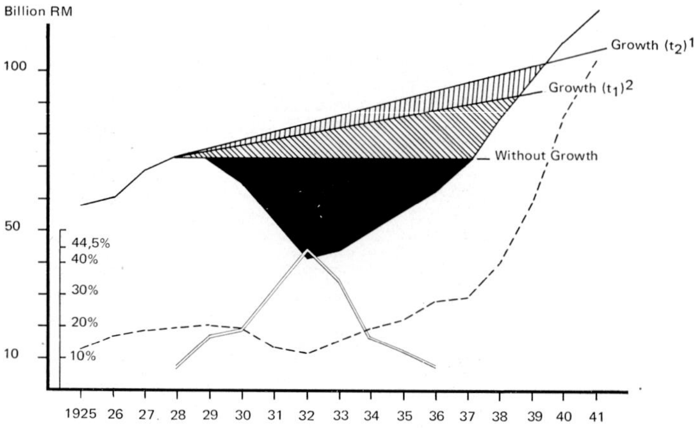

1) $t_2 = 69{,}745 + 2{,}655\ x$

2) $t_1 = 70{,}227 + 2{,}173\ x$

—— National Income

═══ Unemployment Rate

- - - Public Expenditures

Development of National Income in the Post-War-Period in Germany

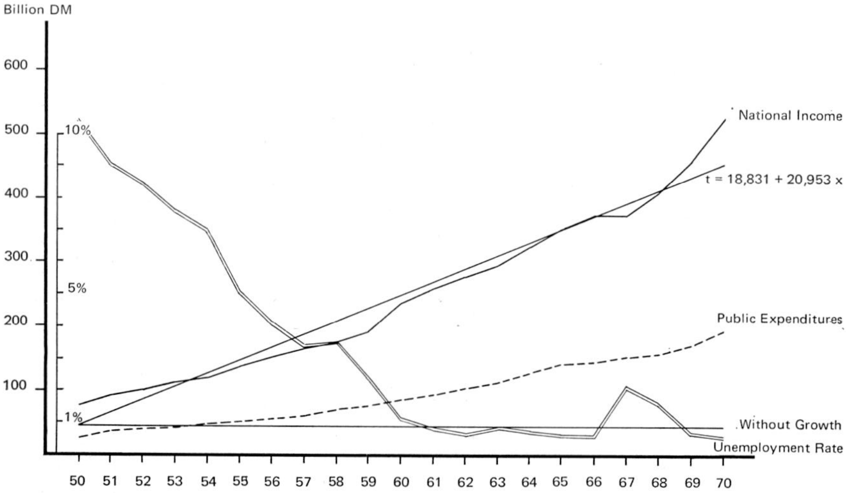

Figure 1

Government Functions (Public Expenditures) Germany 1872 – 1969

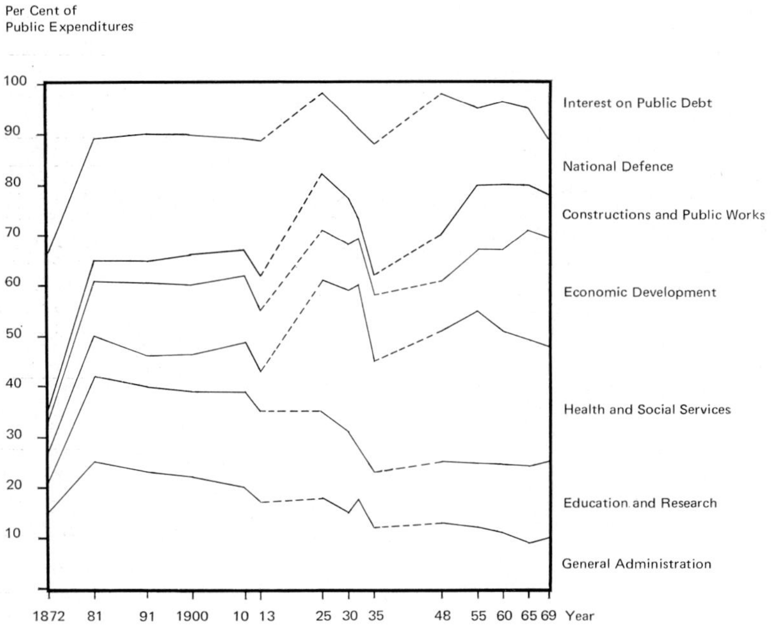

Figure 2

A System of Integrated Economic and Fiscal Policy

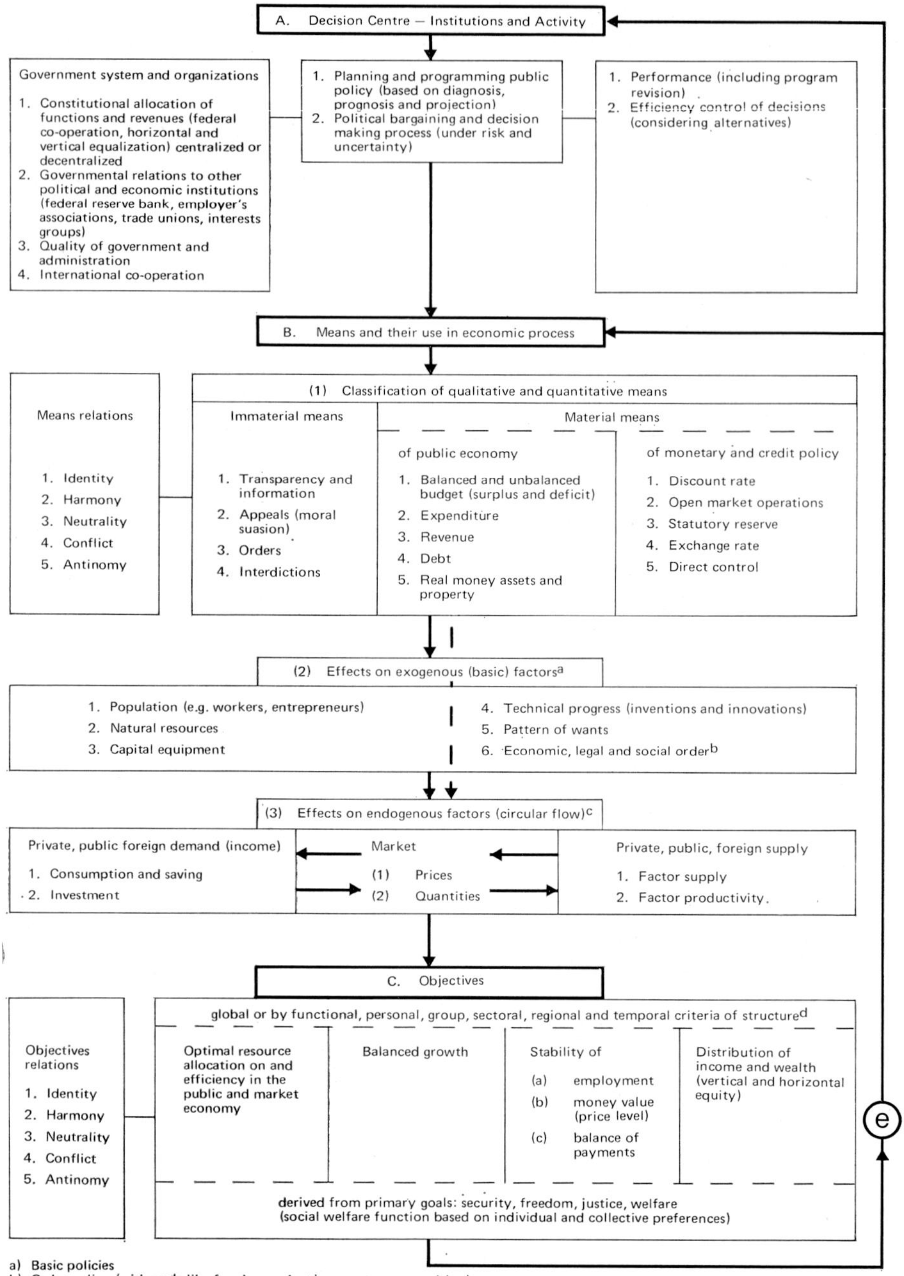

a) Basic policies
b) Order policy (with goals like freedom, private property, competition)
c) Process policy in short, middle, and long term
d) Comprehensive structure policy (concerning all objectives)
e) Reversal of the means-objective dichotomy. The question of how a change of the goal-variable does affect means, institutions, and activity is becoming a very important one for modern economic and fiscal policy.

Figure 3

Growth of Public Expenditures and Taxes, Germany 1821 — 1969

Shares of Net National Product
(and Growth of Per Capita Income)

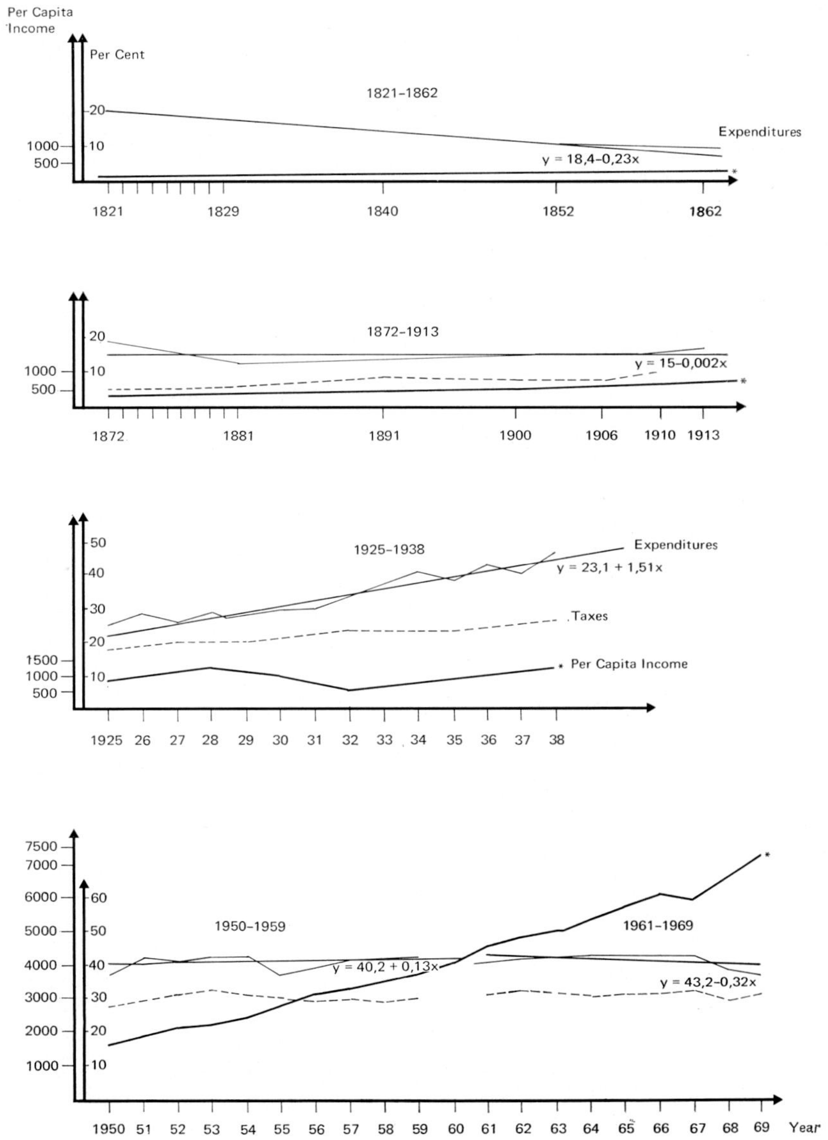

Figure 4

and a sometime believer in the notion of the *Herrenvolk*, he oddly enough stressed the importance of individual freedom, rejecting racism as a completely false ideology.

Weber's approach to historical problems was a good deal more careful than Sombart's. Concerned as he was with methodological questions, he began with a demolition of the preconceptions of the earlier historical economists, particularly Roscher and Knies, and this essay, together with his other methodological writings, exerted a lasting influence on the social sciences. In it Weber began his intellectual struggle against the banalities of a purely naturalistic approach as well as against the idealistic assertion that scientific work was not possible in the social sciences. His aim was to develop a rigorous conceptual structure that would order factual data more sensibly than was hitherto possible. Consequently, it was necessary to shed the heritage of the historical economists who were fusing in their work a curiously perverted Marxism with the romantic, idealistic view of "spirit" and thus smuggling into the study of society an intuitive but irrational methodology. Weber's purpose rather was to establish law, calculability, and rationality as the basis of social science. In no other way would it be possible to establish causality and provide a satisfactory explanation of human behaviour.

This led Weber to his "ideal type", one of the most famous tools in modern social science. Explanation, he said, was not merely a matter of description, but encompassed also interpretation of one's findings, so that the meaning of a culture might be comprehended more fully. This was his "interpretive sociology". He accepted fully the concept of *Verstehen*, but he gave it a meaning somewhat at variance with the one employed by his predecessors. Whereas they had talked in terms of genetic categories, understanding for Weber had to be grounded in certain theoretical structures which might be used to establish the necessary causal relationships. Knowledge, he said, was always abstract. This was true even of empirical data, for the only facts one really knew were those of immediate concern to the inquirer. Consequently, social phenomena were described against a particular conceptual backdrop, the construction of which was prior to the attempt to generalize. Four types of action, said Weber, encompassed the whole gamut of social actions: first, the type that fused numerous means to attain one's ends—*zweckrational;* second, that which was rational in means but nonrational in ends—*wertrational;* third, that which was guided primarily by emotional sentiments—*affektual;* and fourth, that which was based on habit and established patterns—*traditional.* This four-fold structure was directly related to Weber's ideal type concept and provided the basis for a description of society as a whole.

In this way, argued Weber, the social scientist created an abstraction, albeit for his own convenience, but one which nevertheless revealed the essential features of the situation he had before him. To grasp how this ideal type methodology functioned it appeared essential to understand the meaning that the individual or actor himself gave to social action. The ideal type was admittedly an artificial construct, but it contained elements of reality which became logical concepts when used as analytical tools. Illustrations were "economic man" or "feudalism". It described historical data in a comparative way: in fact, many ideal types would be constructed out of the materials of history that would enable one to comprehend much more easily the regularities of social and economic phenomena. It was a limiting concept, said Weber, to which the real situation was compared in order to extract certain significant components. In studying capitalism, for example, it was important to find out why it had failed to crop up in societies other than those of the west. The ideal type thus became a way of exploring the unique aspects of an historical situation. In so far as it succeeded, it was related in some ways to Sombart's notion of "system". Although Weber could not escape the idea of understanding so popular in his day, he did give it a rationalistic twist. His constructions—society and community—did not exhibit the transcendentalism that was characteristic of Sombart and most of German social science at the time. Rather they were used to explain the behaviour of the individual, and neither materialistic nor idealistic elements were allowed to predominate: both were viewed as particular types in a total milieu.

Much of Weber's investigative technique reflected the Marxian method, although he did quarrel frequently with the philosophy of historical materialism. Yet as Gerth and Mills remark, Weber's work in large part was an attempt to round out Marxian materialism with a political and military materialism. While Marx thought that he had discovered the keys to social reality in the relationships that were revealed through the mode of production, Weber concentrated on the control of weapons and political administration, for he was interested mainly in the numerous ways in which the material instrumentalities of political power were established. Marx's alienation from the means of production was matched by Weber's bureaucratization of political and social life. While in Marx political and economic powers were intimately related, Weber kept these realms quite distinct. He insisted that religious and political ideas exhibited a force of their own to which man was answerable. Ideas were no mere superstructure, they could generate conflict and tension just as readily as material self-interest. In short, Weber agreed with Marx that the State was the locus of political power. They differed only on the nature of the approaches. Ideology and material interests also were intertwined through the technique of "rationalization", a process that could be extended even to "proletarian" systems, as we have come to know in the history of the Soviet Union. As Stuart Hughes has said, both had essentially a radical analysis of society.

For Weber, capitalism was the epitome of rationality. To Marx, on the other hand, this would have been an intolerable concept simply because the forces of production were bound and restricted by existing social relationships. Weber insisted that the class struggle was not really central, being due merely to differences in property holdings and the varying success of participants in the market place. Socialism, said Weber, would merely extend the bureaucratization of economic life, something that he abhorred. While bureaucracy itself was rationalistic, the process enforced a deadly routine on its participants and depersonalized them. Alienation became a universal phenomenon that affected everyone.

Although none of this necessarily ruled out analytical economic theory, in Weber's hands an attitude of indifference seems to have been cultivated. In the main he accepted the findings of others, passing on to what appeared to him to be more critical matters. One of these was the relation of religious ideas to economic organization. A good part of his work in this area was incorporated in his *Economy and Society* in which he sought to outline the institutional framework of economic activity as well as the way in which this framework could be altered. The latter implied, of course, that the "natural order" of the classicists was to be discarded. The existence of deep tensions in society made it doubtful that stability could be maintained. Yet Weber insisted that the economic system was one in which participants based their decisions on a rational comparison of utilities and costs. This process, he said, was integral to the spirit of capitalism, stemming mainly from a favourable psychological attitude. A rational state and impartial legal system were also elements of the same economy.

Whatever economic analysis entered into Weber's presentation centred on money and its uses. He also expressed an interest in the structure of markets and the relation of economic units to them. Obviously, money was very important in this milieu, for it made possible an extension of exchange relationships and helped the development of indirect exchange. Moreover, it not only heightened the acquisitive orientation implicit in capitalist behaviour, but also made planning possible by facilitating the comparison of transactions. Since the existence of limited resources required allocation, behaviour patterns developed which employed choice as a major factor. Nevertheless, self-interest did not necessarily bring about a social benefit, as in Adam Smith's "unseen hand of Providence". In fact, Weber recognized the existence of strain between individual and social objectives, which he described, somewhat ponderously, as tension between formal and substantive rationality. Attainment of the latter—the social aims—might be defined as the way in which an economy could be operated to meet the needs of a population and still conform to some agreed upon ethical norm. Formal rationality, or the way in which the economy carried through individual acts of exchange, depended on capital accounting and a continuous extension of the market. Weber did not think that socialism was an effective solution to the problem: here he accepted the Mises' argument, but he did acknowledge that market equilibria were not sufficiently stable to prevent the development of alternative solutions. Still, the market theory of orthodox economics appeared to him to be the only rational answer—an answer which clashed harshly with his recognition of "approbation", whereby individuals were closed off from access to certain sectors of the economy. Monopoly was a case in point. Although Weber sought to escape the difficulty by relating appropriation to rights rather than things, it was quite evident that he was simply uninterested in the abstractions which formal economic analysis had to offer.

Weber's long discussion of labour-management relations yielded little in the way of fresh insights. He recognized that in large-scale production the worker had to be separated from the means of production and that centralized control based on private property rights was essential to its effective functioning. Yet with the growth of large organizations and a widening of the market, the economy tended to become increasingly more rigid, he said. Even the workers began to think in terms of a "property right" to a job, thereby adding to the rigidity of the system. According to Weber, the "formal rationality", the pattern of transactions, had to function in a context of laissez-faire. This implied private ownership, alienation of workers from tools, profit maximization, calculability, enforcement of contracts, and a rational money system. However, much of Weber's discussion of economic problems was fragmentary, albeit quite suggestive, as in his section on economic motivation. But to an economist it contained little that was original, particularly after one had met up with Veblen or Marx. Centring one's attention on market relationships and expressing a concern with the problem of calculation through the money economy can lead to some useful observations, but Weber evidently was not overly interested in these possibilities. He focused his sights rather on questions which were in the main sociological and noneconomic.

In his *Protestant Ethic and the Spirit of Capitalism*, however, Weber made a major contribution to the theory of capitalism's origins. In it he stressed the independent functioning of ideas as a significant basis for economic growth. Capitalism, he argued, required for its effective functioning a personality to whom spiritual and material ascetism were values in themselves. This he found in the Calvinist who sought to prove his worth as one of the chosen by making the success of an enterprise the prime objective. The Calvinist's theology dictated unremitting toil; he was not permitted the pleasurable ways of life. Gains could be reinvested only in business and from this ascetic behaviour there stemmed capital accumulation. Rationality, unceasing labour, precise accounting to reveal what was happening at any given point in time, and peaceful trade were the only things that complied with such an ethos. Weber also illustrated the effect of religion on economics in an essay on the Protestant sects in the United States, in which he observed that acceptance of one's business status was closely related to church membership. Sect membership, he said, was a certificate of moral qualification and business rectitude. Exclusion from a sect for a moral offence often meant a loss of economic position, while association with religion meant success in entrepreneurial endeavours. By stressing external factors in this way Weber was saying that the economy could be explained not through internal elements alone: it was necessary to incorporate significant exogenous forces into the theoretical structure as well. Weber was not trying to say that Protestantism had caused capitalism: he was merely seeking to determine the extent to which religious forces exerted an influence on economic development. The rationalistic form of capitalism known to the West had not manifested itself in India or China, and this, Weber felt, was because only in Europe had certain spiritual drives and material concerns coincided at a given point in history to create the economy with which we are familiar. Weber's point was that, in the case of occidental capitalism, religion helped form an effective instrument for the creation of wealth. Yet the more he became embittered with German politics, the more he realized how much material interest weighed in the success of an idea. He was beginning to approach the Marxist view in spite of himself.

Certain aspects of capitalism could be visualized more clearly, said Weber, if a distinction were made between different "types". In political capitalism, profit stemmed from war and conquest. Adventure, the drive for colonial power, and booty were outstanding characteristics of this form. Pariah capitalism embodied the actions of certain marginal economic groups, such as the Jews or Parsees. Imperialist capitalism accompanied political expansionism, as in the case of the British Empire. Fiscal capitalism, typical of some older societies, was based usually on tax farming, as in ancient Rome and the Ancien Régime in France. The significant form today, however, was industrial capitalism, in which emphasis was placed on factory production utilizing free labour (already alienated from the tools of production) and which was based upon a considerable investment in fixed capital. In this form, particularly, all the elements were neatly balanced via double-entry books of account.

Contemporary capitalism, said Weber, was actually a highly rational form. It was rather the religious elements and the unceasing drive to work that appeared irrational. Yet the system's very rationality enforced a compelling routine that often spelled a loss of freedom for the mass of men. Freedom was available only to the wealthy who could purchase escape from toil, and, warned Weber, a growing impersonality and routinization threatened mankind. Men of genuine culture had become fewer and were displaced by experts and devotees of organization. In this description Weber was able to link the notions of charisma and the growing bureaucratic organization of society. The general processes of rationalization made a bureaucratic structure inevitable, and this indubitably represented a threat to genuine personal freedom—as we have come to know in the modern organization man. Such a bleak prospect might be overcome, said Weber, by the charismatic personality who exhibited extraordinary qualities of leadership and authority in terms of the *specific* person. Out of the charismatic situation might come a new institution and thus a way out of the bureaucratic condition that threatened to engulf industrial man.

With this theory Weber denied that population growth or the infusion of precious metal from the New World were sufficient conditions for the rise of capitalism. His was essentially a theory of the psychological factors underlying the growth of capitalism. While geographic factors, military needs, and the demand for luxury goods were contributing elements, the main drive stemmed from the particular ethos about which he wrote. Although it resembled Sombart's theory, Weber rejected the idea that the Jews were the carriers of capitalism. They did not, commented Weber, invent bills of exchange, shares of stock, or the corporation. They were a "guest" folk standing outside political society and entirely without influence. The modern creator of capitalism was a Christian who did not fear innovation and who was willing to cast tradition aside. The spiritual quality, the necessary ethos, said Weber, was to be found in Calvinism—a theology that told the businessman that he was essentially an administrator for what God had given him. Capitalism became a "calling" and rational work the fulfilment of a God-given assignment. Thus, the pursuit of profit could be maintained without fear or guilt: the capitalist conscience was clear. The Calvinist entrepreneur "gave to his employees as the wages of their ascetic devotion to the calling and of cooperation in his ruthless exploitation of them through capitalism the prospect of eternal salvation". It would be many decades before this ethic would be stripped of its religious garb.

What merit was there in this thesis? Calvin had had some broad views of business practice which he had absorbed from the commercial thinking of the north Italian cities. He had always been close to business and businessmen and had often been consulted by merchants whose souls were troubled by their practices. After all, Luther had not altered the medieval view with regard to commerce. But the basic historical problem still remains. Did this new creed sustain the independent action of business and lead men to the new ways of the Kingdom of Heaven on earth, or did the enterprising middle class simply reach to the new theology to justify whatever it was doing? Weber's own views evidently came from some Puritan forebears: it was not too difficult for him to base bourgeois virtue on Calvinist theology. But the early Puritans had displayed few of the ascetic attributes which Weber said were essential. The Dutch Calvinists, English Puritans, and French Huguenots had not required religion as a spur. Nor had freebooting, fat monopolies, song, wine, and games been unknown to them. What was really common to their ethos had been a rejection of absolutism, an intransigent individualism, and a stubborn protest against the over-reaching authority of the new national state.

Neither Weber nor his chief opponent Lujo Brentano, who stressed political thought as the catalyst, had a complete explanation for capitalism's success. Surely the requirements of the State for an ever-increasing production were as significant as religious drives, if perhaps not more so. Even output for larger national armies and the hungry demands of royalty for luxuries to give their courtesans, something to which Sombart called attention, may have had some effect. Capitalism may have been, as he said, the "child of illegitimate love". Miriam Beard has suggested that Weber's and Sombart's ideas might be fused so that the old Calvinists might be considered "the ideal purveyors of cannon for the King's fleets and silk stockings for his mistresses". She continued: "It is possible, and at any rate it would be a pity to exclude altogether what is the only hilarious theory in the entire depressing range of the 'dismal science' of economics."

Be that as it may, Weber's excessive emphasis on the quality of rationality agreed at few points with the evidence. His approach seemed a limited one for grasping the nature of political or economic experience. Capitalism's rationality is deceptive: on this point Veblen's analysis of business ritual and the patent lack of genuine functionalism was much more relevant. Furthermore, the thesis of religious influence was a strained one. The commercial centres in southern Germany and Florence in the fifteenth century had been just as capitalistic as Geneva, yet they had been Catholic! It is even possible to prove that Catholicism was capitalism's driving force, as was attempted, in fact, by D. H. Robertson. Nor can one dismiss so easily as Weber does the impact of the age of discovery and the tremendous influx of gold and silver from America. Traces of capitalist enterprise existed prior to the religious changes he spoke of. And there were secular influences on capitalism which he seems to have overlooked, as for example, in the writings of businessmen on money and prices. Nor were the English Puritans precisely the kind of Calvinists that Weber believed them to be.

The individualism of late Puritanism would have been anathema to the Geneva Synod. And, as for the British, the Protestant ethic hardly would have encompassed aristocrat, leveller, merchant, and artisan. The capitalist spirit was a much more complex affair than Weber was willing to concede.

Ben Baruch Seligman

SOURCES

Essay I

Reinhard Bendix, *Max Weber, An Intellectual Portrait* (Doubleday & Co. Inc., New York, 1960), chapter I, "Career and personal orientation".

Essay II

Ben Baruch Seligman, *Main Currents in Modern Economics* (The Free Press of Glencoe, New York, 1962), chapter I (iv), "Max Weber and the capitalist spirit".

Signature

University Library, Heidelberg.

Portrait

Photograph (Bildarchiv zur Geschichte der Universität Heidelberg im Kurpfälzischen Museum).

BIBLIOGRAPHY

M. Weber, *Max Weber, Ein Lebensbild*, 2nd ed. (Heidelberg, 1950).

K. Jaspers, *Max Weber, Rede bei der von der Heidelberger Studentenschaft am 17. Juli 1920 veranstalteten Trauerfeier* (Tübingen, 1921).

M. Weber, *The Theory of Social and Economic Organization,* 2nd ed., (New York, 1940), preface by T. Parsons.

M. Weber, *Essays in Sociology* (New York, 1947 and 1950), introduction by H. H. Gerth and C. W. Mills.

H. H. Gerth and H. J. Gerth, "Bibliography on Max Weber", *Social Research*, 16 (1949).

K. Jaspers, *Max Weber, Deutsches Wesen im politischen Denken, im Forschen und Philosophieren* (Oldenburg/O., 1932), reprinted as *Max Weber, Politiker, Forscher, Philosoph* (Munich, 1958).

W. Mommsen, *Max Weber und die deutsche Politik 1890–1920* (Tübingen, 1959).

S. M. Miller, *Max Weber* (New York, 1963).

E. Baumgarten, *Max Weber—Werk und Person* (Tübingen, 1964).

"Max Weber, 1864–1964", *Sociological Quarterly*, 5 (1964).

P. F. Lazarsfeld and A. R. Oberschall, "Max Weber and Empirical Social Research", *American Sociological Review*, 30 (1965).

R. Bendix, "Max Weber", in *International Encyclopedia of the Social Sciences*, Vol. 16 (New York, 1968).

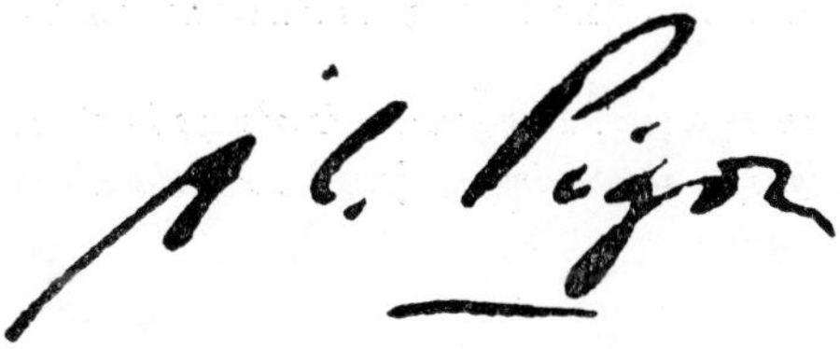

ARTHUR CECIL PIGOU

1877–1959

He was not one of those who enjoy giving their latest thoughts a trial run in oral delivery. THE TIMES

A good platform speaker, his characteristically British appearance made an excellent impression on audiences who gave him their confidence, despite the fact that this rugged physique was often untidily clothed. B. B. SELIGMAN

It is rare for relations between teacher and pupil to be so close as they were between Marshall and Pigou, or for a professor to teach so faithfully, thoroughly and persistently the doctrines of his predecessor. C. CLARK

Intellectually he derived from Sidgwick almost as much as from Marshall. This is a clue to his incompatibility with Keynes, who viewed Sidgwick in a very dim light. H. DALTON

The complicated analyses which economists endeavour to carry through are not mere gymnastics. They are instruments for the bettering of human life. The misery and squalor that surround us, the injurious luxury of some wealthy families, the terrible uncertainty overshadowing many families of the poor—these are evils too plain to be ignored. By the knowledge that our science seeks it is possible that they may be restrained. Out of the Darkness light! To search for it is the task, to find it perhaps the prize, which the "dismal science of political economy" offers to those who face its discipline. A. C. PIGOU

Despite the vast efforts of government agencies and bureaux in the last twenty years, Pigou's Economics of Welfare *remains the classic discussion of the definition of real national income.* P. A. SAMUELSON

Pigou is consistently an explorer. His interest is always in the margins or frontiers where, by dint of painstaking analysis, new knowledge is to be had.

A. A. YOUNG

I
A. C. PIGOU

Arthur Cecil Pigou was born at Ryde on 18 November 1877. Like his father, C. G. S. Pigou of the 15th Regiment, he was educated at Harrow. In 1896 he joined King's College, Cambridge, as a History Scholar. He obtained a First Class in the History Tripos in 1899 and in part II of the Moral Science Tripos in 1900 (the Economics Tripos came into being only in 1903). At Cambridge, he won the Chancellor's Medal for English Verse and the Cobden, Burney and Adam Smith Prizes. Being a debater with considerable rhetorical flourish, he was elected as President of the Cambridge University Union.

Pigou was deeply interested in poetry and moral philosophy. He submitted a thesis for a Fellowship at King's College on "Robert Browning as a Religious Teacher". When this did not succeed (fortunately for economics) he was advised by Alfred Marshall to write on "The Variations in the Prices of Tinned Meat in the Nineteenth Century". Pigou was elected as a life-time Fellow of King's College in 1902. Even as a student, Pigou had been considerably influenced by the personality of Alfred Marshall. Pigou was convinced that the chief value of economics was a handmaid to ethics, not an end in itself but a means to a further end; an instrument by the perfecting of which it might be possible to better the conditions of human life. In a memorial lecture on Marshall delivered in Cambridge on 24 October 1924, Pigou commented approvingly upon the vivid sense of the paradox of poverty and the strong stream of human sympathy that lay at the back of Marshall's intellectual work. Pigou agreed with Marshall that the contribution of economists is not to devise detailed practical expedients, but to provide an organization of thought and of method that would enable practical expedients to be devised successfully.

The sense of bondship that existed between Marshall and Pigou was characterized by mutual admiration and respect. Before he became Professor in 1908, Pigou published a book on *Protective and Preferential Import Duties.* Another work published by him during his pre-professorial period was on *The Principles and Methods of Industrial Peace.* Marshall must have given considerable thought to the question of a successor to himself in the chair of political economy, which at that time, undoubtedly, was the highest distinction that an economist could hope for. There is no wonder that Marshall had deep appreciation of Pigou's abilities to give unstinted devotion to the pursuit of economics and in the manner that he wished economics should be served. Marshall retired two years earlier than the scheduled date in order to give young Pigou a chance. The election of Pigou in 1908 to the leading post in the world of economics at the young age of thirty-one, caused considerable embarrassment amongst elder colleagues. While no one doubted Pigou's brilliance and abilities the question was whether the claims of men senior to him in age should have been overlooked.

In his inaugural address given at Cambridge on 30 October 1908 entitled "Economic Science in Relation to Practice", Pigou states how the cause of his first interest in economic science was not a reason, but the personal inspiration of the master, whose successor and whose pupil it was his high privilege to be. "It will be my earnest endeavour to carry on and to develop in this University the work that he has begun and to pass forward to others what I have learnt from him." Pigou stated that social enthusiasm was the beginning of philosophy.

Tall, gaunt and athletic, "handsome as a Viking", with a propensity to be untidy in dress, with an intensive dislike of administrative routine, with a nature unusually shy (a life-long celibate, he was reputed to be strictly aloof from the company of women), with deep interests in poetry, ethics and moral philosophy, with an unusual capacity for abstract thought (for he had "a passion that left the ground to lose itself in the sky"), with amazing powers of long concentration (amongst his colleagues the belief was that Pigou could always be relied upon to solve any problem of high theory), with an intense dislike of small talk, academic shop and gossip, with a great passion for the mountains of the Alps and the hills of Cumberland (a great mountain-climber as well as a mental climber), with an affectionate disposition towards students with whom he mixed in terms of equality, with a magnanimous grand soul which could unruffled take in any amount of bitter or drastic criticism of his views, with a penchant for precision in words and in thought, with a temperament and attitude which preferred to influence the world through the printed page rather than the spoken word—Pigou, whom Dalton termed the inhabitant of the temple of truth fixed in Cambridge, must undoubtedly have been a great spiritual and intellectual influence at Cambridge. Pigou's lecture manners have been described by Hugh Dalton as follows: "An attractive presence; complete clarity; great precision of thought and definition; a little, but not too much, geometry and algebra on the blackboard; an occasional joke to illustrate some proposition; never a note." Similar are the impressions of Harrod. "Pigou made a notable impression as Professor. Tall, athletic, lucid and unadorned in his lecture manner, yet going very effectively to the heart of the subject, he created great confidence. What appealed above all were his simplicity and utter lack of affectation or of pomposity."

Pigou held the Professorship till 1943 when he was succeeded by Professor Dennis Robertson. Thereafter he was Emeritus. He was a member of the (Cunliffe) Committee on the Currency and Foreign Exchange (1918–19), the Royal Commission on the Income Tax (1919–20), and the (Chamberlain) Committee on the Currency and Bank of England Note Issues (1924–5). He was an honorary president of the International Economic Association.

Pigou's life work encompasses the whole range of economic science. He was a great tool maker as well as a tool user. He conducted several piecemeal studies of a host of particular issues. Besides he also presented synthetic approaches to several aggregative problems. He opened up whole new branches of subject-matter. At the same time most of what he thought had an intimate significance upon economic well-being. The six great classics which he wrote have become part of the permanent stock of economic knowledge.

The Economics of Welfare is considered by many as the greatest work of Pigou. It was the first full-bodied treatise on the science of economic policy. The leading classical volumes on economics devoted only a small portion of their work to a discussion of the practical implications of the pure theory of the economic mechanism. This portion consisted largely of an examination of the various aspects in which the system of laissez faire required modifications. Sidgwick in his *Principles* devoted more attention to these problems than was the vogue of the day; he brought to the forefront the problem of divergences between private and social interests. Besides, he accepted the principle of diminishing marginal utility of income. Sidgwick's work opened up a vast possibility of analysis. Marshall, however, sought to free the science of well-being from dependence upon the ethics of utilitarianism. He wanted to evolve an apparatus which could quantify the various issues of economic well-being. Being deeply troubled by the welfare implications of the principles of resource allocation developed in the classical writings, he levelled three main objections against the system of economic freedom: (1) Under conditions of increasing returns, aggregate satisfactions might be increased by an appropriate system of taxes and subsidies; (2) The economic situation might be capable of multiple positions of equilibrium; (3) The marginal utility of income was not independent of the size of an individual's income and hence would tend to differ as between the rich and the poor.

Marshall developed the concept of consumers' and producers' surpluses and substituted the maximization of net consumers' and producers' surplus as the goal of community action in place of the quasi-physical criteria of aggregate or *per capita* income. Marshall suggested that many courses of action in economics would affect different individuals in similar proportion; hence, within limits, differences in aggregate money measures of satisfactions would indicate the relative superiority of different courses of action. Marshall could not, however, develop a full-fledged theory of the economics of welfare. This was left for Pigou who combined the contributions of Sidgwick and Marshall and evolved a comprehensive framework of the science of welfare. In this process, Pigou, however, did not follow Marshall very closely. He reintroduced the criteria of national and *per capita* income as indicators of welfare. Besides, he preferred to accept market prices as indicators of the relative utilities of different commodities. He went some steps further than Marshall in working out a case for equitable distribution of incomes on the ground of the law of diminishing marginal utility of real incomes. Pigou's framework of welfare analysis was largely from the angle of producers as pivotal agents in the process of resource allocation. Pigou, here, sought to build a general equilibrium approach towards economic welfare. The powerful tools he evolved in this connection—marginal private net product and marginal social net product—have now become commonplace in economic textbooks. These concepts are also today used in matters concerning economic development.

Recent years have witnessed high-powered discussions regarding the foundations of welfare economics. The approach of these writings has tended to be somewhat different from that of Pigou. It is from the consumers' end that the different problems are being looked at. Issues concerning interpersonal comparisons of utility have come again to the forefront. Pigou returned to this issue in 1951 ("The State of Welfare Economics", *AER*, 1954 and *Alfred Marshall and Current Thought*, 1964). Here Pigou took the position that interpersonal comparisons of utility have to be made. To deny the possibility of such comparisons would be to wreck not merely welfare economics but the whole apparatus of practical thought. Pigou noted how Marshall's utility theory, emphasizing as it does the importance of the money measure as an indicator of relative strengths, had operational significance. Yet Pigou noted how in matters in which different groups could be affected in different proportions, some criterion of comparison other than money has to be sought. This in fact is the basic unsolved question in welfare economics. It is difficult to establish from within economics a criterion by which equivalence scales in respect of the marginal utilities of different income groups can be derived. The Marshall-Pigou apparatus in essence remains unimpaired if the alternatives affect different groups in equal proportions. To the extent that they do not do so, some system of equivalence is necessary. It is here that welfare economics seeks guidance from elsewhere.

Various policy measures could be formulated under varying assumptions regarding equivalence scales. Yet it is true that in many economic policy issues discussions regarding distribution can be free from discussions regarding production. In building an adequate theory of welfare, one must remember that the amount of actual or potential compensation is itself governed by our assumptions regarding equivalence ratios. Hence money income cannot itself be a criterion in this respect. One can broadly visualize three sets of choices in regard to economic policy: (1) Choices in policy in which the different courses of action affect different individuals similarly; (2) Choices in which different individuals are affected dissimilarly, yet it is possible to arrive at some measure of agreement regarding equivalence ratios; and (3) Policy issues in which different measures affect different groups in dissimilar proportion and it is not possible to arrive at any common measure of agreement in regard to equivalence ratios. It is obvious that many economic policy issues would fall under the category of (1) and (2). Thus, provided one can disaggregate the effects of different policies, there is considerable scope yet for the traditional welfare economics of Marshall and Pigou.

Pigou's position in regard to short-period aggregative economics can be described as follows:

1. Unlike previous classical writers, Pigou does not accept the existence of automatic factors in the short period to bring about full employment. Pigou, thus, recognizes the possibility of unemployment in the short period. However, the unemployment which he considers is specially due to cyclical reasons. From the analytical point of view, Pigou was among the earliest of modern economists to recognize the implications of rigid money wage rates. He accepted variations in money wage rates as active short-period adjustment factors only for the nineteenth century. In this respect, Pigou made an advance upon the approach of Marshall, who tended to ignore the possibility of unemployment in the short period. If money wage rates are actually rigid, then fluctuations in investment demand would be reflected in fluctuations in employment. Pigou believed that during the classical period unemployment was insignificant if we take both booms and depressions together. Pigou argued that to the extent the trade unions were intransigent, some unemployment would emerge. Given the investment demand schedule, downward flexibility in money wage rates would imply higher volumes of employment in investment as well as in consumption.

2. There was one qualification: that the interest rate should be flexible downwards. To the extent that interest rates were inflexible downwards, money wage flexibility would not lead to increases in employment and income. However, an alternative route was visualized by him in this connection. Other conditions being equal, the lower the level of money wage rates, the lower the level of prices. The lower the level of prices, the larger the real value of liquid balances. The larger the real value of liquid balances, the larger the demand for consumption. The above mechanism, known as the "Pigou Effect", theoretically points out a way towards equilibrium at higher levels of employment. In this respect, the full implications of the Pigou effect have been reaped in the writings of Patinkin who re-worked monetary theory by introducing the real balance factor at each stage.

3. Pigou did not agree with the relatively neutral role assigned to monetary policy in classical economics. Pigou's analysis extends the cash balances approach to its logical conclusions. Pigou accepted the possibility of money being hoarded—that is, neither being spent on consumer goods nor on investment goods. As a result, the income velocity of money would be reduced. Hence with given money wage rates, employment and money income would fall.

4. Pigou accepted the position that under certain conditions, decisions to save might lead to reduced incomes—assuming that the level of wage rates is constant. In this connection, he took into account the effects of the scale of activity upon the volume of savings. In Pigou's neoclassical framework, savings would not only be a function of the rate of interest but also of the volume of income. Another factor which he emphasized was the distribution of income between wage earners and non-wage earners. The broad conclusion is that if we accept the scale of activity as well as the distribution of income between non-wage earners and wage earners as variables in the short period, higher levels of investment demand would entail a lower level of interest than would be the case otherwise. Thus it might be noted that the classical position undergoes a change, or rather, an improvement.

5. In later writings, Pigou noted how the effects of reduction in money wage rates would be similar to a downward shift in the liquidity preference schedule. Pigou preferred, however, to operate in terms of the income velocity of money. On the surface, it is possible to reach similar conclusions either through the Pigouvian or through the Keynesian route.

6. Whereas Pigou visualized the possibility of short-period unemployment, he ruled out the imminence of secular stagnation or the day of doom. This was largely because of the strength of the real balance effect in the long-run adjustment process of the economy.

It would, however, be unfair to Pigou to assume his post-*General Theory* writings reflected in essence the acceptance of the Keynesian approach. Apart from the question of money wage rates, there are vital differences between the two writers particularly in respect of the understanding of the mechanism. A brief idea of those differences will be given.

A fall in money wage rates in Pigou leads to an increase in employment and real income: with an increase in real income there is a downward shift of the savings schedule: this leads to a reduction in the rate of interest: a reduction in the rate of interest entails a decrease in the income velocity of money: a decrease in the income velocity of money implies a reduction in aggregate money incomes or in other words a downward shift of the money demand schedule for labour. A fall in money wage rates in Keynes leads to a reduction in money incomes: this entails a downward shift of the liquidity preference schedule: this implies a reduction in the rate of interest: a reduction in the rate of interest leads to an increase in the amount of investment: an increase in the amount of investment leads to an increase in employment and real income via the multiplier.

What are the distinctive features of the Keynesian theory? First, Keynes introduced the possibility of perfect elasticity in the demand for money at a lower interest rate. The rate of interest becomes insensitive to variations in the quantity of money after a particular stage. Second, Keynes at some stages in his argument argues that the investment demand schedule is interest-inelastic. Third, Keynes denies the direct influence of shifts in savings and investment schedules upon the rate of interest. An upward shift in the investment schedule leads to a rise in the rate of interest but because incomes have risen. A downward shift in the savings schedule leads to a reduction in the rate of interest again because incomes have fallen. Thus Keynes not merely denies the unimportance of the relationship between interest and consumption but also assumes that the savings and investment schedules determine only the level of incomes and not the rate of interest. Fourth, Keynes devises what he calls purely monetary theory of the rate of interest. The choice for a money holder is that between holding money or purchasing a bond. The decision to save is not brought in the picture at all; what is important is the decision to hoard or not to hoard.

In his post-*General Theory* writings Pigou modifies neoclassical theory to take into account changes in income as a factor affecting the savings schedule. But the rate of interest in this version equilibrates at the margin the decision to consume, the decision to hold money and the decision to save (and invest). Pigou assumes that changes in real income have a negligible inpact upon the income velocity of money.

Pigou accepted the assumption of diminishing marginal utility of income and hence made out a strong case for a more equitable distribution of income. Pigou believed in strict regulation of monopolies though he was among the earliest of economists to point out the superiority of monopolies from the welfare point of view in the case of certain indivisible investments. In *The Economics of Welfare* he worked out a systematic case for State intervention with a view to increasing the efficiency of resource allocation. As Colin Clark points out, Pigou carries the Marshallian position on increasing returns to its logical extreme. Under conditions of increasing returns, State intervention, and sometimes nationalization, may be necessary to obtain the best possible allocation of resources. In essence, Pigou accepted the need of the market mechanism and the pricing system. He suggested various taxes and subsidies with a view to making the allocation of resources as optimal as possible. It was Pigou who developed the idea of divergences between private returns and social returns. Pigou's value presuppositions were very close to those of Marshall, though Pigou does not appear to have emphasized the efficiency aspects of an increasing degree of State intervention as much as Marshall did. Pigou again appears to have under-emphasized the practical limitations of many of his propositions.

In fairness to Pigou, it must be said that he never allowed differences in values to come in the way of the economic analysis of various problems.

As already noted, in the monetary-fiscal area Pigou had moved miles away from the position held by the classical economists. He believed in an active monetary policy which tended to counteract the effects of changes in "liquidity preference". Pigou accepted the need of public works during periods when economic activity was very low. Although he emphasized the possibility of compensating adjustments under conditions in which money wage rates are flexible, he realized that in the short period money wage rates would tend to be rigid, and hence, other forms of action were necessary. Pigou had great faith in the beneficial influence of improvement in knowledge and in the degree of mobility. In the reforms he put forth for tax changes, he tended to emphasize the importance of saving. Even in *The Economics of Welfare*, he held the view that the public had a propensity to undervalue the future as compared to the present. He believed that some institutional discrimination in favour of saving would be a healthy step.

One might also note here that, disregarding the assumption of flexible money wage rates as impractical, Pigou's position in regard to the possible line of attack on the problem of unemployment was very similar to that of Keynes. Pigou, however, did not believe in continued State intervention as a permanent necessity in the light of the possibility of secular stagnation. Pigou did not believe in the imminence of secular stagnation.

The modern Welfare State must remember Pigou with great gratitude; for it was Pigou who first postulated the theoretical possibility of an economic system working with the objective of maximization of economic welfare. Again it was Pigou who worked out in detail the *forms* in which State intervention would have to be undertaken, granted the above objective. Pigou also examined in detail the working of various State institutions—the relationship between labour and capital, effects of monopoly on resource allocation, the effects of various forms of unemployment insurance, the effects of different types of taxes upon resource allocation etc.

Among many economists, the common impression is that whereas Pigou was undoubtedly one of the great economists of all times, Keynes was greater and obtained the richer prizes in the world of achievement. There are considerable similarities in the lives of both Pigou and Keynes. Both were amongst Marshall's dearest students and were immensely influenced in the formative period of their lives by his personality and teachings. Both of them had brilliant academic careers. Both spent a good proportion of their earlier lives in teaching and interpreting Marshall's ideas. Both excelled in the art of impassioned oratory. Both had widespread interests in mathematics, ethics, philosophy and poetry. Both were deeply immersed in the analysis of the problems of the day. Both their minds responded quickly to the challenges of the economic problems of the day. The period of Pigou encompassed two world wars, one major boom, and one world-shattering depression. It also witnessed a major practical movement towards the Welfare State and saw the emergence of the idea of economic planning. Pigou was always at work on the economic problems of the day and poured forth continuously pamphlets and tomes. The beginning of the century finds him examining the question of relevance of protection to Britain and the pros and cons of Imperial Preference. During the First World War, Pigou examined the problem of mobilization of resources for war. Thereafter, the post-war depression found Pigou absorbed in the analysis of unemployment. During the twenties Pigou concentrated on the problems of industrial fluctuations; in this connection he raised fundamental questions in regard to monetary and banking policies. The events of the great slump brought forth from him a full-bodied treatise on unemployment. Keynes's *General Theory* challenged orthodox economics and subjected Pigou particularly to much damaging criticism. Pigou took up the gauntlet and replied through a parallel framework in "Employment and Equilibrium", in which he made Keynes's theory a special case. Pigou was equal to Keynes in the matter of quick mental responses to economic problems. Nor were there deep divergences in the social philosophies of Pigou and Keynes. Pigou made out a systematic case for State intervention in order to improve economic betterment. He was also in favour of appropriate monetary and banking policies as well as fiscal action during periods of unemployment and deflation. He was a strong proponent of the movement towards a more equitable distribution of wealth and incomes.

But then, why did not Pigou's personality evoke as much response as Keynes's did? Pigou certainly had a complete understanding of the interrelationships of the economic system. Yet Pigou was not as directly interested in economic policy as Keynes was. Moreover, Pigou preferred to deal with ideas rather than men. Like Art, his personality lay in concealing it. He shied from the concrete world of money and the capital markets. He preferred to approach the concrete world through the route of abstract thought. Moreover, Pigou had a mind which visualized an encyclopaedic range of analytical possibilities. Whereas Keynes searched for a general theory of reality Pigou did not believe in the reality of a general theory. Again, Pigou eschewed all forms of ornamentation in writing. He refused to amuse himself (or others) by finding faults in the writings of fellow economists. He just ignored their deficiencies. As he grew older, he became half ashamed of even impassioned writing. His method of writing tended to be as precise as humanly possible. He never allowed himself the luxury of exciting *obiter dicta*. There are hardly any digressions in his writings. Unlike Marshall, Pigou did not believe in the smoke screen of economics made easy. Yet at each stage he devoted meticulous pains to presenting his ideas in a form intelligible to the layman.

Pigou represents the supreme triumph of the human spirit over human frailty. While young he set himself the mission of a single-minded pursuit of truth. Throughout his life, he never deviated from this purpose. Within himself he symbolized the best and the highest in the human personality. He was more Lamp than Man; and more Glow than Lamp. Though the man is dead and the lamp snuffed out, the glow continues to throw light forever.

Palahalli Ramaiya Brahmananda

SOURCES

Essay

Palahalli Ramaiya Brahmananda, "A. C. Pigou (1877–1959)", *Indian Economic Journal,* 6 (1958–9). Abridged.

Signature

A. C. Cooper, London.

Portrait

Painting by Edmund H. Nelson (A. C. Cooper, London).

BIBLIOGRAPHY

G. Champernowne, "Arthur Cecil Pigou, 1877–1959", *Journal of the Royal Statistical Society Series A*, 122 (1959), pp. 263–5.

H. G. Johnson, "Arthur Cecil Pigou, 1877–1959", *Canadian Journal of Economics and Political Science*, 26 (1960).

J. Sultmarsh and P. Wilkinson, *Arthur Cecil Pigou, 1877–1959* (Cambridge, 1960).

E. A. G. Robinson, "Arthur Cecil Pigou", *International Encyclopaedia of the Social Sciences*, Vol. 2 (New York, 1968).

JOSEPH ALOIS SCHUMPETER

1883–1950

Every scholar, as he grows in years, experience, and judiciousness, faces two insidious enemies which in the end usually take over: disillusioned scepticism and loss of enthusiasm. Schumpeter held these at bay.

He was quite the opposite of those celebrated scholars who rarely make an error and who instill in their best students an inferiority complex. Schumpeter's very imperfections gave hope and drive to his students. P. A. SAMUELSON

Schumpeter himself studied the personalities of his biographical subjects in order to discover what he called their "ideological bias". While he recognized and insisted that "vision" was essential, as a prescientific stage, to any advancement of knowledge, he hoped that scientific research could eliminate the element of bias and reveal the element of objective truth. In this, I think, he was unfair not only to others but especially to himself.

Walras provided the foundations for his [Schumpeter's] edifice, but Marx suggested to him the method of building on that foundation a structure that reflected his own vision. A. SMITHIES

No amount of mathematical technicality, however refined, can ever replace intuition, this inexplicable function which takes place in the brain of a great intellect who at the same time understands mathematics and economic theory in a more orthodox sense and who has lived long enough (or, more correctly, intensely enough) to accumulate human experience and a sense of facts. This intuition is an art, the art of realistic model building, the art of making realistic abstractions, the art in which such men as Ricardo and Schumpeter excelled. This intellectual activity is and will always be the vital part of our science and the true criterion of an econometrician. R. FRISCH

I
JOSEPH ALOIS SCHUMPETER

Joseph A. Schumpeter was one of the great economists of all time. His claim to that rare title—remember Keynes's famous dictum that "good economists are the rarest of birds"—rests as much on the fact that he was much more than an economist as on his achievements in the economic field itself. He himself used to say that an economist who is not also a mathematician, a statistician, and most of all a historian is not properly qualified for his profession. He was all these and more besides: he had an encyclopaedic knowledge not only of the history of economic doctrines, which was one of his special fields, but also of the history of economic facts and institutions and of general political and social history. He had not received professional training in mathematics, and the manipulation of numbers and of algebra did not come to him easily; but he acquired a great mathematical knowledge and could follow and effectively expound what even among mathematical economists is regarded as complicated mathematical analysis. He was not an expert statistical technician, but he had a profound understanding of the logic and limitations of statistical inference and kept abreast of new methods and of statistical source materials. All his life he was deeply interested in the theory of social relations and social philosophy and made important contributions to sociology and to social and political philosophy.

In some of these fields he had his superiors. There are in economics more refined and versatile mathematical theorists, there are more resourceful statisticians, and economic historians who know more about certain periods and certain subjects than he did. But as a master of all branches of economics and as a universal scholar, Schumpeter held a unique position among contemporary economists.

Schumpeter was not only a great scholar and original thinker, but he was also a strong, colourful, and exceedingly complex personality. A quite unusual capacity for understanding the minds and views of others, a strong touch of irony, which, at times, seemed to verge on cynicism, and a wonderful sense of humour were combined with deep moral convictions, absolute devotion to his friends, and intense likes and aversions. But his dislike of certain kinds of people was controlled by his kindheartedness and generosity. He was especially considerate to his students, and those who confided in him and sought his advice could always be sure of getting his help and counsel. Indeed, he spent a disproportionate amount of time, tutoring and helping students—those of limited as well as of superior ability.

He was an effective and dramatic speaker, a master of the spoken as well as of the written word, and his lectures and addresses were always stimulating, had usually some new idea and striking formulation, and were never stale or dull. No wonder that he was a tremendously inspiring teacher.

Schumpeter died from a cerebral haemorrhage in his sleep on 8 January 1950, one month before his sixty-seventh birthday.

Jozsi (pronounced Yoshi), as he was called at home and by his friends, was born in Triesch in the Austrian province of Moravia (now Czechoslovakia) on 8 February 1883, the only child of the cloth manufacturer (*Tuchfabrikant*) Alois Schumpeter and his wife Johanna. Little is known of the ancestry of Schumpeter's parents; but so much is certain: that he was the product of a typically Austrian mixture of several of the many nationalities that lived in the Austro-Hungarian monarchy.

Jozsi lost his father when he was four years of age, and the widow married at Kalksburg, near Vienna, on 9 September 1893, Sigismund von Kéler, Feldmarshalleutenant in the Austro-Hungarian army, a descendant of a German-Hungarian family. On 3 July 1906, her second marriage ended in divorce, but up to that time von Kéler had a considerable influence on Jozsi's education. The family lived in Vienna, and from 1893 to 1901 Schumpeter went as a day student to the Theresianum, the *Mittelschule* (approximately equivalent to the American high school plus the first two years of college) which was favoured by the Austrian aristocracy. Already he gave evidence of his fine intellect and was graduated with high honours in 1901. At the Theresianum he received a thorough classical education including Latin and Greek. The milieu at the Theresianum in conjunction with what must have been a highly cultured atmosphere in the home of his mother left a permanent imprint upon his personality. It was there that he acquired the agreeable, sometimes quaintly overpolite old-world manner, which, together with his natural charm, friendliness, and vitality, produced the man Schumpeter as we knew him.

In 1901, Schumpeter registered as a student in the Faculty of Law at the University of Vienna, and in 1906 the degree of *Doctor utriusque juris* (doctor of law—literally: doctor of each of the two laws, namely of Roman law and canon law) was conferred upon him. In Vienna, as in most continental universities, economics was (and still is) taught in the Faculty of Law, and for the law degree, courses and a comprehensive examination in economics and political science were (and still are) required. Schumpeter took his economics much more seriously than the average law student, but in passing it may be mentioned that he did not neglect his law. In fact, he practised it for a short time during 1907–8 before the International Mixed Court of Egypt in Cairo. He liked and was impressed by the historical approach to the study of law. He came, however, to the conclusion that the close connection between the study of law and economics as practised in the continental European universities was a great mistake.

At the beginning of the century Vienna was a great centre of economic learning. Menger had, however, withdrawn from active work in the University (including his celebrated seminar) before Schumpeter's time, although he did not resign his chair until 1903 when v. Wieser became his successor. Thus Schumpeter was not a student of Menger.

His first serious work in economics seems to have been done in what we would now call a statistical research seminar conducted by the eminent economic historian and statistican, K. Th. v. Inama-Sternegg, in conjunction with Franz v. Juraschek.

Other seminars he attended were those of F. v. Wieser and of E. v. Philippovich where he seems to have reported on the beginnings of his *Dogmengeschichte*. When Böhm-Bawerk resigned as Minister of Finance in 1904, he returned to academic life as a professor in the University of Vienna, and conducted in 1905 and 1906 a famous seminar, in which Schumpeter was an active participant. Other prominent members were Ludwig v. Mises and Felix Somary, his lifelong friend. It was made lively and at times stormy by the participation of a group of young Marxists who later became theoretical and political leaders in the Austrian and German Social Democratic parties. There was Otto Bauer, the brilliant theorist, dialectician, and intellectual leader of the Austrian socialists after 1918, who seems to have been mainly responsible for Schumpeter's appointment as Minister of Finance of the Austrian Republic in 1919. There was Rudolf Hilferding, the author of the famous book *Das Finanzkapital* and twice Minister of Finance of the German Republic. Another member was Emil Lederer, later Professor in Heidelberg and Berlin, who in 1934 became Alvin Johnson's main collaborator in the foundation of the Graduate Faculty at the New School for Social Research in New York. Schumpeter and Lederer were friends throughout the latter's life, and he seems to have been on good terms with Hilferding.

Schumpeter's profound knowledge of Marxian theory and his intimate familiarity with the Continental socialist movement as well as with the psychology of the socialist leaders, which lent colour and freshness to a long series of articles culminating in his book, *Capitalism, Socialism and Democracy* (see especially Part V, "A Historical Sketch of Socialist Parties"), originated in those seminar meetings.

A member of that seminar told the author of the present essay that in the heated debates between Böhm-Bawerk and the Marxists, Schumpeter attracted general attention through his cool, scientific detachment. The seemingly playful manner in which he took part in the discussion, an attitude which was strongly pronounced in his early writings (especially in his first book, *Wesen und Hauptinhalt der theoretischen Nationalökonomie*) and which never left him entirely, was evidently mistaken by many for a lack of seriousness or an artificial mannerism. Böhm-Bawerk, however, with whom Schumpeter had close personal connections, at once recognized his talents, and was instrumental in securing Schumpeter's *Habilitation* (granting the *venia legendi*, the right to lecture) in the University of Vienna in 1909 and his appointment to the chair of political economy in the University of Czernowitz in the same year. It must be mentioned, however, that the greatest Austrian economist of his generation never was offered a chair in his *Alma Mater Vindobonensis*, although there were many opportunites before he finally left his native country in 1925.

After graduation in 1906, Schumpeter went to England for a stay of several months, mainly in London, but with occasional visits to Cambridge and Oxford, where he paid his respects to Marshall and Edgeworth. In 1907, he married Miss Gladys Ricarde Seaver, daughter of a high dignitary of the Church of England, and in the same year the Schumpeters went to Egypt. In the autumn of 1909 he started his work as Professor in Czernowitz, the capital of Bukowina, the easternmost province of Austria, which was after 1918 included in Rumania, in 1939 annexed by Russia, in 1941 retransferred to Rumania, and is now a part of Russia.

The two years in Czernowitz seem to have been very happy ones, and the university, where the academic careers of many young Austrian scholars started, was by no means without inellectual stimulation.

In 1911, Schumpeter was called to the University of Graz, the capital of the Austrian province of Styria. He was appointed by Imperial Rescript (*Zufolge Allerhöchster Entschliessung*) against the vote of the faculty which had proposed some local nonentity. He was the youngest full professor in the faculty and, being the only economist in the University and having been put in charge of economic instruction at the *Technische Hochschule* as well, he had at first a very heavy teaching schedule ranging over the whole field of economics, including public finance.

In the stuffy provincial atmosphere of Graz, which had none of the oriental lures of Czernowitz, he never felt happy and at home. The academic year 1913–14 Schumpeter spent in New York at Columbia University, as Austrian exchange professor. He gave a course in theory, one in social classes, and a seminar. In March 1914, he received the honorary degree of Litt.D, from Columbia and returned to Austria just before the outbreak of the war. He left Graz late in 1918, but remained a member of the faculty until 1921.

Schumpeter's scientific output during the years between his graduation from the University in 1906 and the end of the First World War was stupendous.

In 1906 appeared his first major article "Uber die mathematische Methode der theoretischen Ökonomie"; in 1908, when he was barely twenty-five years old, he published his first great book, *Wesen und Hauptinhalt der theoretischen Nationalökonomie;* and in 1912 his celebrated *Theorie der wirtschaftlichen Entwicklung*. These two volumes immediately established his pre-eminence in the field of economic theory. "He never was a beginner" (Spiethoff in his beautiful obituary of Schumpeter in *Kyklos*, 1950). When he was thirty, he wrote a history of his science: *Epochen der Dogmen- und Methodengeschichte* is a profound and mature piece of work which, however, only the expert can fully appreciate.

A sort of supplement to his *Dogmengeschichte* is the booklet, which discusses the past and future of the social sciences. Having grown out of a lecture in Czernowitz in 1911, this essay is shorter and uses less heavy scholarly equipment than the *Dogmengeschichte*. It deals with economics and sociology in their relation to philosophy and history, but contains also interesting remarks on technical economic questions which foreshadow later developments. On page 125, for example, Schumpeter calls for empirical, "especially statistical", studies with a view to determining the shape of "demand curves". In addition to these books, every year there flowed from his pen a stream of important articles, some of them of considerable length, as well as innumerable book reviews.

His business cycle theory was first fully expounded in the *Theory of Economic Development*, but the article on economic crises in 1910 already gave an outline of what was to come, and in the preface to the *Theory of Economic Development* Schumpeter stated that he had conceived the fundamental ideas as early as 1905. His famous theory of interest was clearly sketched in his first book, although fully developed in the second. The first book also contains interesting thoughts on the theory of saving, which recurred later in the book on *Business Cycles*. "Saving is not a function of income." He holds that people quickly get used to higher income and do not really save more when their income rises.

Schumpeter's basic sociological views, too, which were first published in 1927 in a lengthy paper and were later elaborated in his *Capitalism, Socialism and Democracy*, seem to have crystallized at an early date. In a prefatory note to his 1927 article, he states that "the fundamental idea originated in 1910 and was first propounded in a series of popular lectures on 'State and Society' in Czernowitz during the winter 1910–11". Similarly, many of his views on socialism, with which the Anglo-American public became first acquainted through his widely read book on socialism in 1942, found clear expression as early as 1918 in the brochure *Die Krise des Steuerstaats*, in 1919 in his brilliant essay *Zur Soziologie der Imperialismen*, and in two exceedingly interesting and sparkling articles on socialism in England and in Austria.

Apart from the specific content, Schumpeter's very first publications display several features which are characteristic of all his work. There is, first, the great liking for the mathematical method in economics. It remained undiminished throughout his life, but it did not imply a neglect or underestimation of the importance of historical knowledge and research for the study of economics. On the contrary, he used to say that in case he had to give up either his historical or mathematical training, he would abandon the latter rather than the former.

His enthusiasm for the mathematical method was in contrast to the small use he made of it. In that respect, he was the exact opposite of Marshall: while Marshall had a mathematical bent of mind and mathematical training, and while his theoretical achievements would have been impossible without the use of mathematics, "he never gave full credit to the faithful ally" (mathematics) and "hid the tool that had done the work". Schumpeter did not have an essentially mathematical mind but he extolled the use of mathematics, and his enthusiasm stimulated scores of students to utilize and to perfect mathematical methods of analysis in economics. But more important is that his earliest writings reveal two qualities which were so characteristic of the man and the scholar: his ideas and style of expression are highly original and supremely independent of his scientific environment.

By the time he left the university, he had read and studied a vast amount of economic literature, classical and modern, especially in English. He was greatly impressed by, and highly admired, the work of Walras, the younger.

Schumpeter is usually regarded as a member of the Austrian school. The fact is, however, that as a man and as a scholar he was from the beginning a citizen of the world. He never liked to identify himself with any nationality, group, or school. What he said of Menger holds of Schumpeter himself: "He was nobody's pupil." This complete intellectual independence is already apparent in his earliest writings.

Schumpeter undoubtedly was influenced by Böhm-Bawerk's capital theory, and used the concept of roundabout methods of production in his theory of economic development. But he gave it a special dynamic slant and his interest theory is entirely different from the Böhm-Bawerkian.

The great intellectual independence of environmental influences, the absolute refusal to be swayed by current fashions in science and politics, the complete freedom of mind, all this (paradoxically combined with a quite unusual capacity of understanding other people's views—witness his biographical essays) was strikingly characteristic. People who did not know Schumpeter well frequently thought that this was nothing more than a passion to contradict, to take the opposite view, often intensified by an almost perverse pleasure in being unpopular and standing alone. It is true, he enjoyed *épater les bourgeois* and especially *épater les épateurs des bourgeois* (so he managed to shock and antagonize Philistines on the right and on the left at the same time), and he was quite capable occasionally of defending for argument's sake a position in which he did not believe. *L'art pour l'art* in discussions was by no means foreign to him. But he did not really relish being in a minority all the time. His independence was not a pose. One could truly say of him what Nietzsche said about Schopenhauer: "*Seht ihn nur an—Niemandem war er untertan.*"

Most of Schumpeter's life was wholly devoted to thinking, teaching and writing, although he was never merely a bookish sort of person. He always took a lively interest in public and world affairs, felt intensely about, and never hesitated to express emphatic opinions on, current political issues. But it was only during the brief period from the end of the First World War to 1924 that he was actively engaged first in political life and then in business.

During the war he made no secret of his pacifist, pro-Western (especially pro-British) and anti-German attitude. In the pamphlet on the crisis of the tax state, instead of adopting the official phraseology and speaking of "the heroic fight for freedom and survival" or something like that, he referred to the war as that "bloody madness' which was "devastating Europe".

After the armistice the German socialist government set up a socialization commission in Berlin with the purpose of studying and preparing for the nationalization of industries. The head of the commission was Karl Kautsky, and Hilferding and Lederer, Schumpeter's acquaintances from university days, were prominent members. He received a call to join the commission, and spent two or three months late in 1918 and early in 1919 in Berlin. The work seems to have consisted in holding something like seminar discussions on the subject of socialization and other economic problems.

Schumpeter's membership in the *Sozialisierungskommission* has often been taken as proof of his socialist convictions. This is incorrect. The *Sozialisierungskommission* was not entirely composed of socialists.

Schumpeter's attitude was revealed by his answer to the question, put to him by a young economist, of how he, who had extolled the role of the entrepreneur and the efficiency of the private enterprise system, could be connected with the socialization commission: "If somebody wants to commit suicide, it is a good thing if a doctor is present."

On 16 February 1919, the first republican parliament was elected in Austria. The strictly Marxist socialists (official title: Social Democrats) emerged as the largest party and a coalition government of the socialists and the so-called Christian Social party (a Catholic conservative party) was formed with Dr Karl Renner, a right-wing socialist, as head. Neither of the two political parties was eager to take responsibility for the almost insoluble and politically unrewarding task of grappling with Austria's finances. So they agreed to let a nonpolitical expert try his hand at that hopeless and unpopular job. Otto Bauer, who was Secretary for Foreign Affairs in the Renner Government, proposed Schumpeter for the position of *Staatssekretär für Finanzen*.

Schumpeter could not be called a successful Finance Minister by any conventional standard, but it is more than doubtful whether anybody could have been successful during that turbulent period. Politically and economically the situation was indeed chaotic.

No wonder that in such a milieu it was impossible to avoid inflation. The financial difficulties were tremendously complicated by the problems arising out of the dissolution of the Austro-Hungarian Empire. The new Austria was saddled with a disproportionate share of the debt of the old state, and had to take over a much larger number of the civil servants (and army officers) of the old Empire than were needed.

Apart from the insurmountable difficulties of his task, Schumpeter seems to have run into personal friction and suspicion right from the beginning. Many conservatives distrusted him, because they suspected him of being a socialist or, at least, of being too friendly with the socialists, having been "discovered" by Otto Bauer, the leader of the radical wing of the socialists. This was especially true of the powerful, highly competent and efficient, but somewhat unimaginative, permanent officials at the Treasury who were deeply distrustful of the outsider—a colourful young man, a brilliant theorist and eloquent speaker who had, however, never gone through the bureaucratic mill, but had been thrust upon them by the new rulers.

Moreover, he soon had really serious trouble with his socialist colleagues, and that caused his eventual downfall. Disagreements with the socialists were unavoidable, because his views and financial policies were essentially conservative and irreconcilable with the radical financial and economic policies advocated by the socialist party. It has been often said that Schumpeter, at the time he became Minister of Finance, favoured nationalization and radical financial policies. The record of his writings and his actions as a member of the government completely refute this contention.

The pamphlet *Die Krise des Steuerstaats*, mentioned above, contained an outline of the financial and economic policy that the author favoured for the postwar period.

According to the author, there are two ways of solving the fiscal problem. The first is to let inflation take its course and so wipe out the war debt. The second is to eliminate the war debt by a capital levy. "I confess that at one time I favoured the second method and I still believe that it is, in principle, the correct one. If I have become doubtful about its success, the reasons have nothing to do with the economics of the matter. But only a strong government with the broadest political basis, which impresses the people with real strength and with the personal prestige of its members, could dare to tackle the task of overcoming all obstacles, especially of preventing the capital levy from falling upon too small a segment of the economy, crushing it under its weight. Real political and financial ability is needed by the man who is to undertake that task—and in addition he needs a strong will and brilliant eloquence, which the people trust." When Schumpeter entered the government a year or so later, he thought he was that man; he tried and failed. He tried although he realized that "the fiscal policy up to now has made it nearly impossible to adopt the correct solution of the problem".

On the question as to whether it was more advisable to rely on planning and governmental guidance than on the market mechanism and free enterprise for the transition from war to peace production, his answer was equally emphatic. The best thing the government could do was to refrain from interfering and to "release the tremendous reserves of energy which in Austria are wasted by the incessant battle against the shackles by which foolish legislation, administration, and politics restrain every economic move, and which deflect the entrepreneur from his organizational, technical, and commercial tasks, leaving him as the only way to success the back stairs to political and administrative bureaux." He favoured free enterprise, also, in the field of foreign trade. "Every good bank has more credit abroad than the government." And a free system "will provide imports quickly and cheaply, if the bureaucracy does not hinder it by putting a mountain of paper and red tape between us and the needed raw materials."

As Secretary of Finance Schumpeter never had a real chance to carry out his plan. As he had said himself, only a strong and united government could have done that. But the government was neither strong nor united. True, the socialists liked the idea of a capital levy, but they wanted it for the purpose of furthering the nationalization of industry by procuring for the State shares in industrial property. This was entirely incompatible with his ideas.

On the other hand, it soon must have become clear to Schumpeter that even under the most favourable circumstances a capital levy alone could not have restored financial stability and prevented further inflation; for elimination of the war debt, which he wished to achieve by means of the capital levy, would have been insufficient for the restoration of monetary equilibrium. He realized that the foremost requirement for financial and economic reconstruction was a foreign loan. On this assumption he based the grand financial plan which he worked out during the summer of 1919.

After his resignation inflation continued at an accelerated rate. It reached its peak and was stopped in 1922, but not before the Western powers had agreed to grant Austria a large international stabilization loan which was launched and administered under the supervision of the League of Nations.

It is not known exactly what led to his sudden resignation. But it was clear that his relations with the socialists had become very strained. Passive resistance of the powerful bureaucracy certainly contributed to his downfall.

The socialists found it difficult for a variety of reasons to carry out their programme of nationalization and were glad to find a scapegoat on whom they could blame their failure to keep their election promises to nationalize basic industries.

There is no evidence that Schumpeter took his misfortune in statesmanship as a great tragedy.

Attacks on Schumpeter by the socialist press and in Parliament were rude and bitter, and he was rather brusquely forced to resign. The treatment he received from the socialists must have been galling at the time, especially for a man like Schumpeter, who was extremely sensitive to any kind of vulgarity; but later he did not show any resentment. For example, his two articles *Der Sozialismus in England und bei uns* in 1924 contain a good-natured, occasionally slightly ironical but at the same time sympathetic, criticism of the strategy and tactics of the Continental and especially the Austrian Socialist party, against the background of the British socialist movement. There is, however, not trace of annoyance or vindictiveness. This was typical of the man.

About two years after he left the Government, Schumpeter became President of the Biedermann Bank, a small but old and highly respected private banking house. The bank did not long survive the stabilization crisis. It went bankrupt in 1924, and since it was one of the first banks to fail and many people lost money—during the following years Austrians had to get used to bank failures, in fact hardly a single bank escaped that fate—the collapse of the Biedermann Bank came as a great shock and put its president in a difficult position.

He decided to return to academic life and accepted an invitation to be a guest professor in Japan. But when soon after he received an invitation from the Prussian Ministry of Education to a chair at the University of Bonn, which had become vacant by the retirement of Heinrich Dietzel, the eminent liberal economist, he went there instead. In his later years he never forgot that it had been a Japanese and a German university that offered him the opportunity to resume the quiet life of a scholar.

Before he left Vienna, he married a charming and beautiful Viennese girl, Annie Reisinger, of humble origin, to whose schooling he had contributed for several years. This marriage was entirely happy, but very brief.

His wife died in 1926 in childbirth in Bonn. Her death and that of his mother (also in 1926), to whom he had been greatly devoted, came as a terrible shock, and after that time a streak of resignation and pessimism was unmistakable in his character.

Schumpeter's last twenty-five years were devoted entirely to scholarship and teaching. It was his second period of enormous productivity and also a period of tremendous academic success as measured by influence on students and recognition by the economic profession at large. He was one of the founders of the Econometric Society and its president from 1937 to 1941. In 1948 he became president of the American Economic Association, and when in 1949 plans were laid for the founding of an International Economic Association, there was unanimous agreement that he was to be the first president of the new society.

The move to Bonn constituted a complete break with his past life in more than one respect. As a typical member of the old Austrian (pre-1914) society, Schumpeter had never been a friend and admirer of Germany. In spite of that he soon felt at home in the scholarly and cultured atmosphere of the old university town on the Rhine. He formed a new set of lasting and intimate friendships. That does not mean that he forgot is old friends. But he never visited his native country again.

The change from Bonn to Harvard was less abrupt. He taught in Harvard during the academic year 1927–8, and again during the autumn term of 1930. But after he resigned from Bonn and went to Harvard permanently in 1932, he never revisited Germany although he spent the next three summers (until 1935) in Europe.

The chair Schumpeter held in Bonn was that of public finance. Economic theory and business cycles were taught by Arthur Spiethoff. But the course in public finance gave him plenty of opportunity to discuss theory. There was also the famous Schumpeter seminar which was concerned largely with theory, including the theory of money and especially, as befitted a German university, with epistemology. In respect to the last subject, Schumpeter saw his main function, I am sure, in debunking the application of particular philosophical systems to economics (which was so popular in Germany) and in disabusing his students of the philosophic preconceptions with which many were heavily overloaded. During the few years in Bonn, Schumpeter exerted a strong and lasting influence on German economics through his teaching as well as his writing. The revival of economic theory in Germany was due to a large extent to the fact that he put his full prestige behind it. The many dissertations, articles, and books that dealt with his theories provide documentary proof of that contention.

While at Bonn, Schumpeter published a thoroughly revised edition of his *Theory of Economic Development* and an incredibly large number of very important articles of which only a few can be mentioned. In 1926 appeared a long and searching appraisal of the work of Schmoller, whose so-called "realistic" approach to economics was compared with the work of American institutionalists and especially with that of W. C. Mitchell. In 1927 appeared three brilliant articles on the work of Wicksell, Cassel and Sombart as well as a long and penetrating essay of thirty large pages on the state of economic theory in Germany and Austria in the four-volume book, *Die Wirtschaftstheorie der Gegenwart*. In the same year he published an essay of almost book length on the theory of social classes. In addition to all that, he found time for many book reviews and a large number of articles on current economic questions, especially problems of public finance. Most of these articles appeared in *Der deutsche Volkswirt* (1926–32) with whose editor, Gustav Stolper (member of the German Reichstag and formerly editor of *Der österreichische Volkswirt*), Schumpeter was connected by the bonds of a lifelong close friendship.

In 1931, after a term in Harvard, Schumpeter returned to Germany by way of the Pacific and the Far East. He spent several months lecturing in Japan. His teaching and writing had a profound influence on Japanese economists among whom he has many devoted disciples. Most of his books are translated into Japanese; he was mourned there at the time of his death and even the daily newspapers published full-length obituaries.

The outward course of his life during the eighteen years at Harvard (1932–50) is quickly traced. Apart from three brief summer vacations in Western Europe, a short lecture trip to Mexico (winter, 1948) and another one to neighbouring Montreal, he did not leave the country.

These were years of most intense work. He always had a most ambitious writing programme and as time went on he tried more and more to economize his time. All his life he kept a short diary in which each day would get a high or low mark according to whether he thought he had accomplished much or little. But despite a feeling of increasing pressure to gather the harvest of a fertile mind and a full life's learning, reading, observing, and reflecting, he never refused to take time out for conversations with students and colleagues on their problems, reading their manuscripts, writing letters of recommendation, and the like.

The first years at Harvard he lived with F. W. Taussig. In 1937 he married Elizabeth Boody, a descendant of an old New England family and an economist in her own right. As time went on, he leaned more and more on her devotion and wise counsel in all practical matters. Without her loving and understanding care, he could not have achieved as much as he did.

During the years of the gathering storm and of the Second World War, Schumpeter found himself again in the minority because of his political views and convictions. While during the First World War he had been pro-British and anti-German (of course only in a political sense), during the Second World War he gave the impression of being pro-German. Needless to say he had no sympathies with the Nazi regime. He knew and said repeatedly, that if he had remained in Germany he would have been one of the first candidates for the concentration camp. But most of his friends thought that he underestimated the dangers, the aggressive power and intentions of Hitlerism. He felt that Germany had genuine grievances, that she had been treated badly after the First World War, and that excessive nationalism was the unfortunate reaction thereto. But he hoped that if she were left alone she would eventually calm down. War was for him such a terrible calamity that to avoid it almost no price seemed too high. And he foresaw clearly the rise of communism in the wake of the war and all it meant for Western civilization. At any rate he reacted strongly against anti-German (as distinguished from anti-Nazi) propaganda and policies. Thus the war years must have been among the most sombre and depressing of his life. Out of sympathy with the policies of his adopted country and out of touch with many of his friends, Schumpeter buried himself in his scientific work, unhappily watching the decline of much that he considered valuable in the Western world.

The scholarly achievements of his Harvard years are most impressive indeed. There is first the great two-volume work *Business Cycles* (1939), which is better described by its subtitle, "A Theoretical, Historical, and Statistical Analysis of the Capitalist Process". It is a monument to theoretical acumen, truly encyclopaedic erudition, painstaking scholarship, and perseverance. The main ideas, which are those of his *Theory of Economic Development*, as well as the general scope of the work, are well known and need not be indicated here. But what is not generally known, and perhaps sounds improbable, is that, apart from some clerical assistance, he wrote the book single-handed. The fact is that, although he was a very sociable man and appreciated the necessity and usefulness of scientific teamwork, Schumpeter was always a lone wolf in his scientific work. Everything he published he wrote out in longhand, and for a long time, having no secretary, he had even to write his letters in his own hand.

But he always had the rare and priceless talent—Böhm-Bawerk called it a "gift of God", adding that it could be a dangerous gift—of easy and quick expression. He could read and absorb new ideas and facts with amazing speed, and he never found it difficult in writing or speaking to find the right word or phrase from a tremendous vocabulary in both German and English. In fact, he used the English language with a verve and pungency that few could equal. However, in the short-run the reception of the business cycle book was disappointing. The reasons are not hard to understand. The book is not well arranged and is not easy to read. It is written in a heavy and often involved style with no concessions to the reader or to current fads. It appeared at the beginning of the war at a time when the wave of Keynesianism and depresson economics was at its very height. But apart from these unfavourable external circumstances, it is the kind of book which takes considerable time to exert its full influence.

The next book, *Capitalism, Socialism and Democracy*, was (for a serious book, not a textbook) a great popular success. It has appeared in several editions, and was translated into at least five foreign languages. It was written within a year or two and the author regarded it as nothing more than a *parergon*.

During the last years Schumpeter had been working on a great history of economic analysis.[1]

Apart from these books, he wrote many articles, among them the historical and biographical masterpieces on Taussig, Marshall, Keynes, Fisher, Pareto, and Mitchell (in that order).[2]

During all his Harvard years (excepting two sabbatical terms which he spent working in his home in Taconic), Schumpeter carried a full teaching load, and, especially during the earlier part of the period, organized and attended all sorts of special discussion groups and seminars.

Schumpeter was the most cooperative and considerate colleague anyone could imagine. He was always ready to offer his help, to serve on a committee, or to substitute for an indisposed colleague in a lecture or seminar, and was most reluctant and apologetic in asking for similar favours. His standards concerning the dignity and social status of university professors and scholars were of the highest order, and he often complained that, in most American universities and in American society at large, scholars did not enjoy the social status they ought to have and were overburdened with administrative duties. He nevertheless did his full part, along with the youngest instructors, in performing menial chores, such as foreign language examinations. He never behaved like a prima donna, although he was often regarded as one, especially by outsiders.

Schumpeter kept working to the very end which came with merciful suddenness without serious illness or pain, though not without premonitions. He attended the annual meeting of the American Economic Association in New York from 26 to 30 December 1949, where he faithfully took part in all the meetings of the executive committee and performed with his usual verve and brilliance. There he presented his last paper, entitled

[1] Published in 1954 as *History of Economic Analysis*, edited by Elizabeth Schumpeter.

[2] These essays, together with earlier ones on Walras, Menger, Böhm-Bawerk and the essay on Marx from Part I of *Capitalism, Socialism and Democracy* were published in 1954 as *Ten Great Economists: From Marx to Keynes*.

"The March into Socialism". Characteristically he spoke from notes and not from a prepared paper. He returned, very tired, to Taconic and started to write out this paper for the Proceedings and to put the finishing touches to a series of six lectures which he was to give in the University of Chicago under the title *American Institutions and Economic Progress*. During the night of 7–8 January he passed away peacefully in his sleep.

The time for a complete and detailed appraisal of Schumpeter's scientific achievements and of his place in the history of economics has not yet arrived. Full appreciation of a work of such magnitude and complexity requires greater time distance for proper perspective, especially inasmuch as his last great book, the *History of Economic Analysis*, which promises to be in itself a major event in the history of economic thought, is not yet available. The following remarks are therefore nothing more than a preliminary sketch.

Schumpeter's own work is much more difficult to describe, and his place in modern economics not easy to define. There are several reasons for this. It is true that Schumpeter, like Böhm-Bawerk and most great social scientists (Edgeworth might perhaps be regarded as an exception), had a broad overall picture of the socio-economic process, a "vision" as Schumpeter used to call it which, like the plot in a good drama, gives unity to his work. His "grand design", the contours of which can already be discerned in his first book (*Wesen und Hauptinhalt*, 1908), found its full expression in his *Theory of Economic Development* (1912) and was lavishly, sometimes laboriously worked out, illustrated, and tested in his *Business Cycles* and further elaborated in his *Capitalism, Socialism and Democracy*. It is much more complex than that of Böhm-Bawerk and other neoclassical economists.

In the first place, while Böhm-Bawerk's model (also that of Walras but not that of Marshall) is essentially static, Schumpeter's model is dynamic in nature. It is not dynamic in the sense of modern sequence analysis; it is not "micro-dynamics", "micro" being here used not in the sense of dealing with the behaviour of the smallest economic units (household and firm) as contrasted with aggregate quantities (national income, consumption, investment). In this latter sense, Schumpeter is a "micro-theorist", at least as far as his methodological credo is concerned. He was always suspicious of aggregates and averages—"beware of averages", he said in his very first paper—and he often urged that economic analysis should be based on the theory of household and firm. But in his "theoretical practice", he was, it seems to me, as other economists who hold similar views, unable to avoid the use of aggregates and averages. "Micro" is here used in the sense of being concerned with minor, unimportant fluctuations. Schumpeter's theory was not micro-dynamics as exemplified by modern post-Keynesian multiplier-acceleration models, and the like. He was quite familiar with those models. He highly appreciated the mathematical ingenuity which goes into their construction, discussed them in considerable detail in his classes, and was willing to make limited use of them for the explanation of minor oscillations around the great waves of economic development, but he felt that they are just as incapable of explaining the great economic rhythm as the ripples caused by high winds on the surface of the sea are incapable of influencing the great rhythm of the tide.

Schumpeter's dynamic mechanism is driven by more powerful forces than the vagaries of the propensity to consume and the acceleration principle. The nature of these forces (technological and organizational innovations, entrepreneurial activity, and the credit mechanism which enables the dynamic innovator to draw productive resources from the static "circular flow" economy) are too well known to make detailed discussion necessary.

In the preface to the Japanese edition of his *Theory of Economic Development* he says: ". . . When in my beginnings I studied the Walrasian conception and the Walrasian technique . . . I discovered not only that it is rigorously static in character . . . but also that it is applicable only to a stationary process. These two things must not be confused. A static theory . . . can be useful in the investigation of any kind of reality, however disequilibrated it may be. A stationary process, however, is a process which *actually* does not change of its own initiative, but merely reproduces constant rates of real income as it flows along in time. If it changes at all, it does so under the influence of events which are external to itself, such as natural catastrophes, wars, and so on. Walras would have admitted this. He would have said (and as a matter of fact, he did say it to me the only time I had the opportunity to converse with him) that . . . economic life is essentially passive and merely adapts itself to the natural and social influences which may be acting on it, so that the theory of a stationary process constitutes really the whole of theoretical economics. . . . I felt very strongly that this was wrong, and that there was a source of energy within the economic system which would of itself disrupt . . . equilibrium. If this is so, then there must be a purely economic theory of economic change which does not merely rely on external factors. . . . It is such a theory that I have tried to build and I believe . . . that it contributes something to the understanding . . . of the capitalist world and explains a number of phenomena . . . more satisfactorily than . . . either the Walrasian or Marshallian apparatus."

I have strong doubts that the sharp distinction between disequilibrating forces working from within the economic system and those operating on the economic system from the outside contributes anything to the understanding of economic development. But the concrete mechanism of economic change, as described and analysed by Schumpeter, undoubtedly constitutes a great advance over traditional neoclassical economics.

In these respects he felt himself to be, and actually was, closer to Marx than to Walras, Böhm-Bawerk and, even more, than to Keynes. Indeed, all his life he was attracted by the grandeur of the Marxian system, although he was by no means an uncritical admirer of Marx, and, in recent years, he scornfully disapproved of what he derisively referred to as "the Keynesianization of Marx", that is of the attempts at interpreting Marx in terms of the Keynesian system; this he regarded as a complete emasculation of the Marxian system. There are two other characteristics of Schumpeter's system which seem to put him closer to Marx than to Walras, Böhm-Bawerk, and Marshall. These are, first, the important role assigned to social relationships and to the institutional framework (as against "purely economic" factors) and second, the historical slant and intent of his theory.

These differences between Schumpeter on the one hand and Böhm-Bawerk and other "pure" economists on the other are, however, only a matter of degree. He had no sympathy whatever for the vague, almost metaphysical "collectivism" of which there is so much in Marxist writings. By this I mean "the special and exclusive outlook upon the whole of social life" claimed by the Marxists—an outlook which postulates social forces that operate on and influence individual behaviour and are somehow independent of the totality of individual actions. Schumpeter always adhered to what he called "methodological individualism"—the principle that social phenomena and forces must be defined and interpreted in terms of interrelations and interactions, often of great complexity, between individuals and their subjective motivations.

According to Schumpeter, Böhm-Bawerk's theory—and here again Böhm-Bawerk stands for modern theoretical economics—is not "unsocial", but the "sociological framework" is only "lightly indicated". It should be observed that Böhm-Bawerk sharply distinguishes between the individual household economy (Robinson Crusoe economy), the competitive price economy, and the centrally planned (socialist) economy. It is true, however, that Böhm-Bawerk and other marginalists are largely concerned with analysing economic relationships which hold wherever men apply scarce resources to unlimited wants, irrespective of the particular social organization of society. Schumpeter did not deny that there are such all-embracing regularities, but he was of the opinion that they are of more limited validity than traditional economic theories assume. In that sense his theory is more "social", that is, it differentiates more according to the social framework than that of Böhm-Bawerk and other modern theorists.

The difference comes to a head in connection with the problem of interest, capital accumulation, and the business cycle. In the *Theory of Economic*

Development and in his famous controversy with Böhm-Bawerk on the rate of interest, Schumpeter argued that the rate of interest is institutionally and dynamically determined. There would be no interest either in a stationary or semi-stationary price economy nor in a centrally planned (socialist or single household) economy (whether stationary or progressive), while according to Böhm-Bawerk, the rate of interest is a basic economic category, independent of the concrete social and institutional arrangements. In this particular respect most economists, including many modern socialists, would side with Böhm-Bawerk, holding that as a calculating or accounting category (though not as a distributive share) the rate of interest has a place also in the socialist economy.

It should not be overlooked that Schumpeter's contribution to interest theory is not confined to the somewhat questionable proposition that in a stationary state the rate of interest would be zero. He might well have admitted that there must be a positive rate of interest in a stationary state, but insisted that the interest rates which we find in practice are raised above the stationary level by the dynamic forces described in his theory.

The controversy concerning the rate of interest is, however, only one facet of the whole problem. The differences between Schumpeter's scheme of things and that of Böhm-Bawerk (and Böhm-Bawerk here stands again for a large part of neoclassical economics) goes deeper; it concerns the whole conception of the process of capital accumulation and economic progress. Let me briefly indicate the difference.

According to Böhm-Bawerk and most other modern economists (including especially F. H. Knight) the process of capital accumulation is essentially, or at least potentially, smooth and continuous. People save and savings are invested. Thus the capital stock grows and output increases. In addition, the production function changes, new methods and processes are invented all the time, and output increases for that reason too. These writers recognize, of course, that the process of economic development through capital accumulation and advances in technological knowledge is often interrupted. The business cycle and the recurrence of economic depressions are not ignored. But these phenomena are regarded as inessential deviations, due to monetary disturbances and the like—disturbances that could be avoided or at least reduced to insignificant proportions by appropriate policies.

Schumpeter would not deny that some progress can be realized in a smooth and orderly fashion by continuous accumulation of capital and gradual improvement of technology. But he thinks it could not amount to much. The really big changes which shape the course of economic development are not made, cannot be made, gradually and continuously; they must be forced upon the stationary, circular flow economy in intermittent pushes. The business cycle (at least the major cycle), which for many other theorists is the result either of monetary surface phenomena (avoidable aberrations of monetary policy (Mises, Hayek) or of lags and frictions (Hawtrey) or of the vagaries of multiplier and acceleration principle and the like, becomes in Schumpeter's theory an integral part of the process of economic development in the capitalist system. The complicated mechanism which produces this result and its constituent parts, the path-breaking role of the innovator-entrepreneur and of the host of imitators who follow suit, the function of productive credit inflation and forced saving succeeded by autodeflation and all the rest, is well known. Capitalism for Schumpeter becomes, thus, a narrower concept than for Böhm-Bawerk and most neoclassical economists. It is not synonymous with an individualistic price economy and still less with an economy which uses capital on a large scale; it is a very special type of price economy, namely, that one which is so organized that the indicated rhythmic mechanism can operate. "... Capitalism is defined by three features . . .: private ownership of the physical means of production; private profits and private responsibility for losses; and the creation of means of payments—bank notes and deposits—by private banks. The first two features suffice to define private enterprise. But no concept of capitalism can be satisfactory without including the set of typically capitalist phenomena covered by the third."

The complicated interaction of social and economic forces reappears again, on a higher level as it were, in the theory of the socio-political disintegration of capitalism as fully elaborated in his *Capitalism, Socialism and Democracy*, although clearly foreshadowed in earlier writings. Schumpeter finds that economically speaking the capitalist system has served the human race very well indeed. It has raised the volume of output and standard of living tremendously. Glaring inequalities of income could easily be removed without serious impairment of the productivity of the economic machine. He saw no economic reason why capitalism should not continue to function with equal success in the future. But, at the same time, he was convinced that capitalism was doomed, because by its very success it is bound to destroy its own supporting and protecting social structures. This piece of social dynamics is not widely accepted, nor does it seem to be a necessary consequence of the rest of Schumpeter's theoretical structure. But it throws into high relief the great complexity and the close interrelations of economic and social forces that are so characteristic of Schumpeter's work.

It was said above that Schumpeter's theory is more historical than that of Böhm-Bawerk and of most other modern economists. Schumpeter was always deeply interested in historical problems and a strong supporter of the historical method of understanding social and economic phenomena. He had historical feeling and perspective, and a tremendous historical knowledge. Many of his writings had a historical slant. His *Wesen und*

Hauptinhalt (1908) and *Theory of Economic Development* (1912) are, however, entirely unhistorical, although the theory expounded in the latter book is the basis of later historical interpretations. Schumpeter was, however, not a "historicist" in the sense in which Hegel and Marx were, that is to say, he did not enunciate sweeping historical laws, although he evidently played with the idea of predetermined historical evolution, and was much intrigued by Marx's historical construction. But his devotion to exact methods and rigid scientific discipline did not permit him to go far in the direction of historico-philosophical speculation. He found much truth in the "materialistic interpretation" of history. Economic factors go a long way to explain the course of history, but not all the way: an acceptable "philosophy of history" must "leave adequate room for the quality of leading personnel and in the special case at hand [he was speaking of Bolshevist Russia] for the quality of the leading individual," namely, Stalin.

This is, then, in bare outline Schumpeter's socio-economic world picture, an exceedingly complex structure indeed. The basic ideas were conceived at a very early time, but much of his work throughout his life was spent in elaborating details, making adjustments here and there, and testing his theory against the facts of history; but unlike Böhm-Bawerk he did not defend his theory in extensive polemics. Moreover (again unlike Böhm-Bawerk, whose self-denial and moderation in that respect he had praised so highly), Schumpeter permitted himself the luxury of spending much effort in fields and on subjects that were not at all, or only loosely, connected with his main work. In fact, there is no branch of economics in which he was not deeply interested and well versed, and few to which he has not made important contributions.

Static theory was covered by his first book and by many articles, especially in his earlier period. To the theory of money he made an important contribution in his celebrated paper "Das Sozialprodukt und die Rechenpfennige" (1917) and elsewhere. In its dynamic aspects the theory of money, credit and banking is, of course, an integral part of his theory of economic development and as such found extensive treatment in numerous writings. There are two long chapters on "Money, Credit, and Business Cycles" in the *History of Economic Analysis*. There are, furthermore, his sociological studies, mainly in the essays on the theory of social classes (1927) and imperialism (1919) and in his *Capitalism, Socialism and Democracy* (1942), which are, it is true, closely connected with his basic model, but go far beyond it in several directions. And above all, there are his biographical essays and his extensive studies in the history of economic thought culminating in the posthumous *History of Economic Analysis*. Once more, unlike Böhm-Bawerk, he deals not only with those aspects of the work of other economists and of other theoretical systems which have a direct or indirect bearing on his own structure, but tries to understand them, men as well as theories, in their totality.

The wide range and complexity of Schumpeter's scientific work reflects accurately the universality and complexity of his mind. He begins the preface of his first book with the quotation "*Alles verstehen, heisst alles verzeihen*"—"*Tout comprendre c'est tout pardonner.*" This adage is indeed a clue to his mind. He understood every theory, every standpoint, every method, and found in each something true and useful, realizing clearly, at the same time, their defects and limitations. He was extremely openminded, saw all sides of every question without being eclectic, that is to say, without trying to reconcile the irreconcilable, or merely to assemble unconnected and uncoordinated theorems and facts.

Let me illustrate by a few examples. He was deeply interested in pure static theory and was a real connoisseur of mathematical refinements in that area, a "theoretical *gourmet*" as he himself put it. He was, nevertheless, fully aware of the limitations, or what he thought were the limitations, of static theory and was very critical of what he regarded as uncritical applications, for example, those typically made of the theory of monopoly and monopolistic competition in the area of welfare economics. He was enraptured by the econometric method, but again became quite impatient with certain econometric analyses of the trade cycle. He had a very high opinion of the productive power of capitalism and an ingrained dislike for socialism. At the same time, he was not blind to what he thought were the cultural drawbacks of capitalism and went out of his way to prove that socialism could work and was compatible with democracy.

The complexity, diversity, and universality of Schumpeter's mind is the key to a proper understanding of the man and his work. It explains a certain lack of systematic arrangement and neatness in his writings which became more pronounced in later years and is especially evident in his book on *Business Cycles*, where he tried to deal with the capitalist process in all its complexity. The great wealth of ideas which constantly streamed through his mind, and his acute awareness of all sides of every question, and of the limitations of each standpoint and method, made it very hard for him to present his views on any subject neatly and systematically. He was not always able fully to integrate his ideas, and he easily gave the impression of being undecided about important issues or even contradictory. He was fully aware of these shortcomings in his presentations and envied those writers who, because they held simpler views, were not troubled by such difficulties.

His somewhat involved literary style which can be perhaps best described as "baroque" gives adequate expression to the complex structure of his mind. It is characterized by long sentences, numerous qualifying phrases, qualifications of qualifications, casuistic distinctions of meanings. These qualities of his style are especially pronounced, as one would expect, in his German writings, because the German language offers more freedom for complicated constructions.

I have often asked myself the question and have heard it raised by others, why there are no Schumpeterians in the sense in which there are Keynesians, or even Böhm-Bawerkians and Marshallians, not to mention Marxians. Schumpeter had many ardent admirers and scores of devoted students. Wherever he taught he attracted the cream of the student body, and literally hundreds of economists in all lands have been profoundly influenced by his teaching and writing. But there is no Schumpeter school.

It would be tempting to explain this in terms of external circumstances: Schumpeter was born in a less fortunate part of the world than Keynes, a comparison with whom is especially instructive because he (1883–1946) was Schumpeter's exact contemporary. Schumpeter's real fatherland, the Austro-Hungarian monarchy, disintegrated while he was still in the beginning of his scientific career. The new Austria did not offer him an opportunity for academic success; in Germany he arrived on the eve of a horrible revolution, which did not leave him enough time to take root; and seven or eight of the eighteen years in the quiet haven of Harvard were largely lost, as far as the formation of a school was concerned, through the emotional and intellectual disturbances incident to war and preparations for war. This may sound plausible. But I do not think it is the real explanation. Whatever the influences of the course of his life on his external success as well as his character and personality—and they must have been considerable—the basic, internal structure of Schumpeter's mind and work offers a better explanation for the fact that he did not found a school.

Schumpeter's universality and open-mindedness and the complexity of his system made the crystallization of a Schumpeter school difficult. *Tout comprendre c'est tout pardonner* is not a powerful rallying cry. What he said of Marshall—that "unlike Mill, he would never have said that some problem or other was settled for all time to come and there was nothing about it that called for further explanation either by himself or another writer"—holds fully of Schumpeter himself. "I wish never to say anything definitive; if I have a function it is to open doors not to close them"—he said in the informal farewell address to his students in Bonn. He was, thus, prevented by a self-imposed injunction from constructing a neat simplified version of his theory as Keynes did. The construction of such a simplified system is evidently necessary for the formation of a compact group of disciples. But above all, unlike Marshall and Keynes, Schumpeter was constitutionally unable "to give his readers exactly what they craved—a message which was both high-minded and comforting—and at the same time to answer to the call of his conscience". He did not and could not, like Marshall, "cheerfully sympathize, from a warm heart, with the ideals of socialism, and patronizingly talk down to socialists from a cool head". With him it was rather the other way round; he disliked intensely the ideals of the socialists but found much truth in their teaching. Again, he was unlike Marshall and Keynes in that it *was* "primarily intellectual curiosity" that "brought [Schumpeter] into the economist's camp. He was [*not*] driven to it from ethical speculations by a generous impulse to help in the great task of alleviating the misery and degradation . . . among the . . . poor."

To summarize: the main reason why no Schumpeter school developed is that Schumpeter was neither a reformer nor an enthusiastic partisan of capitalism, socialism, planning, or any other "ism"; he was a scholar and an intellectual. It is hardly a compliment to economics as a science, but it seems to me to be a fact that non-scientific factors play such an important role in the formation of economic schools. In the purely scientific sphere Schumpeter's open-mindedness and universality, the lack of fighting spirit for any particular approach, the fact that he found something useful and acceptable in almost every theory and method helped to prevent development of a Schumpeter school.

Schumpeter himself was conscious of all this. In his farewell address to his students in Bonn he said: "I have never tried to bring about a Schumpeter school. There is none and it ought not to exist. . . . Economics is not a philosophy but a science. Hence there should be no 'schools' in our field. . . . Many people feel irritated by this attitude. For in Germany alone there are half a dozen economists who regard themselves as heads of such 'schools' as fighters for absolute light against absolute darkness. But there is no use combating that sort of thing. One should not fight what life is going to eliminate anyway. Unlike politics and business, immediate success should not matter in science. . . . I for my part accept the judgment of future generations."

This was his philosophy in these respects. But he would have been less human than he was, if his feelings had been as austere and resigned as his philosophy. In fact, he was far from unreceptive to external success and popularity; and, although he rarely showed it, he often suffered from lack of response and appreciation. He was a good laugher and could enjoy exuberantly a stimulating conversation, a good story, a brilliant joke, but he was fundamentally not a happy man. And at the bottom of his unhappiness and resignation was, I believe, the cleavage between his high and austere ideals on the one hand and his human feelings and impulses on the other. Again, he was aware of this, and he envied those who—like the utilitarians and Victorians, like Marshall and Keynes—are not plagued by an unbridgeable gulf between their ideals and their emotions, who manage "at the same time to answer the call of their conscience" and to be "comforting" to themselves and to others.

Gottfried Haberler

SOURCES

Essay

Gottfried Haberler, "Joseph Alois Schumpeter (1883–1950)", *Quarterly Journal of Economics*, 64 (1950). Abridged.

Signature

Österreichische Nationalbibliothek, Vienna.

Portrait

Photograph in possession of Gottfried Haberler, Harvard.

BIBLIOGRAPHY

A. Spiethoff, "Joseph Alois Schumpeter in memoriam", *Kyklos*, 3 (1949).

W. Leontief, "Joseph Alois Schumpeter (1883–1950)", *Econometrica*, 18 (1950).

E. Schneider, "Joseph Alois Schumpeter in memoriam", *Weltwirtschaftliches Archiv*, 64 (1950).

E. B. Schumpeter, "Bibliography of the writings of Joseph A. Schumpeter", *Quarterly Journal of Economics*, 64 (1950).

A. Smithies, "Memorial, Joseph Alois Schumpeter, 1883–1950", *American Economic Review*, 40 (1950), reprinted in S. E. Harris *et al.* (ed.), "Schumpeter: social scientist" (see below).

D. McC. Wright, "Schumpeter and Keynes", *Weltwirtschaftliches Archiv*, 65 (1950).

R. Frisch, "Some Personal Reminiscences on a Great Man", *Econometrica*, 19 (1951).

O. Morgenstern, "Joseph Alois Schumpeter, 1883–1950", *Economic Journal*, 61 (1951).

W. Weber, "Joseph Alois Schumpeter", *Zeitschrift für Nationalökonomie*, 13 (1951).

S. E. Harris, G. Haberler, *et al.* (ed.), "Schumpeter: social scientist", *Review of Economics and Statistics*, 33 (1951).

M. Kessler, "The Synthetic Vision of Joseph Schumpeter", *Review of Politics*, 23 (1961).

W. F. Stolper, "Joseph A. Schumpeter", in *International Encyclopedia of the Social Sciences*, Vol. 14 (New York, 1968).

E. Schneider, *Joseph A. Schumpeter, Leben und Werk eines großen Sozialökonomen* (Tübingen, 1970).

JOHN MAYNARD KEYNES

1883–1946

A puritan in soul and bodily habit, he yet was fond of sumptuous things, of old books, social breakfasts, de luxe *travel and petits chevaux: and fond above all of being in the swim.* C. R. FAY

He was ready to take infinite trouble to make things clear to the obtuse; he was patient even with the pomposity and pretentiousness of which undergraduates, no less than bank chairmen, are sometimes capable. G. WANSBROUGH

His tastes were catholic, and he had the gift of achieving a knowledge of many subjects to a level that made him the respected confidant of those that professed it. With philosophers, mathematicians, historians, bibliophiles, with the critics and exponents of modern painting and of the ballet, just as truly as with economists, financiers, civil servants and politicians, he could speak on a ground of equality of knowledge and understanding. And because of this, what one man saw in Maynard Keynes was likely to be something different from what another might see. E. A. G. ROBINSON

What he did was not chiefly to discover new truths, but to bring into the centre of the picture and illuminate with strong light aspects of economic analysis whose vital significance for practice had not been seen before . . . he was not interested in any merely formal mathematical construction, intellectually satisfactory but practically sterile. His constructions were designed to stand in close relation to facts susceptible of statistical measurement; to help forecasts and guide policies; to be lighthouses, not hermits' cells. A. C. PIGOU

To put the matter quite bluntly, I believe that the future historian of economic thought will regard the assistance rendered by Keynes on the road of progress as far more important than that of his revered master, Alfred Marshall. He seems, to my judgment, to stand rather in the same class as Adam Smith and Ricardo. In logical penetration he was much superior to Adam Smith, in lucidity of writing to Ricardo. R. F. HARROD

I
JOHN MAYNARD KEYNES

The year 1925 divides broadly the years of reconstruction from the subsequent phases both of European economic history and of Keynes's personal life. And I think the year 1925 was significant in Maynard Keynes's own life in another very important sense. On 4 August 1925, he married Lydia Lopokova, brought up in the Imperial Ballet School at St Petersburg, great dancer and great personality—as remarkable in her world as Maynard in his. No ordinary woman could have provided as she did the perfect partner to Maynard. Lydia, herself a great authority, assured in her judgment in those arts in which her knowledge and experience were supreme, never attempted to rival Maynard in those other arts that were completely his. And it was under Lydia's hand that the passionate missionary of the twenties gradually mellowed and grew first into the scholar and creative thinker of the thirties and then into the philosopher and statesman of the forties.

If Maynard Keynes had died in 1925 it would have been difficult for those who knew intimately the power and originality of his mind to have convinced those who had not known him of the full measure of Keynes's ability. In the twenties, we who were his pupils of the younger generation in Cambridge thought of him, indeed I suspect that he thought of himself, primarily as one who had in unusual degree the capacity to apply to the economic problems of the day the corpus of economic thinking which he had inherited from Marshall. Above all, we thought of him as the perfect example of the thesis that in economics what can be thought clearly can be said clearly. In the twenties, it is true, he had made minor improvements to Cassel's now unfashionable purchasing-power-parity theory of exchange. But his exposition of the factors determining the value of money owed obvious debts to Marshall and to Irving Fisher.

It is difficult to say precisely where in time begins the development that was ultimately to give Keynes high claims to be included among those who have made the most original contributions to economic thought. I think it is most convenient, though not necessarily most accurate, to begin from 1925, when the problems of unemployment began to succeed to the problems of financial reconstruction for priority both in practical urgency and in Keynes's attention.

More important from the point of view of the development of Keynes's analytical thinking, the beginning of 1926 saw the publication of D. H. Robertson's *Banking Policy and Price Level,* at which he had been working during 1925. That book was the first to bring two things that were fundamental to all the subsequent work on monetary and employment theory: first, the essential distinction between the act of saving and the act of investment; second, the essential interconnections between what hitherto we had regarded as monetary phenomena—variations in the velocity of circulation, or in the desire to hold money, or in the real value of the current income stream—and the process of saving.

Apart from Dennis Robertson, it was probably Wicksell who exercised most influence on these early stages of Keynes's thought. Keynes was mainly instrumental in securing the translation of *Geldzins und Güterpreise* into English and its publication by the Royal Economic Society. In the *Treatise* he makes considerable use of Wicksell's ideas, and if he later abandoned them, it was with a consciousness of having advanced with their aid. But apart from Wicksell his debts to writers outside the English language were inconsiderable. He read German indeed, but not with great facility, and he said on one occasion that he had never comprehended through the medium of German an idea that was new to him.

While there is little doubt that 1925 had seen the first planting of the seeds of certain new ideas in Keynes's mind, it was some time before they germinated and bore fruit. The years 1926–8 are in retrospect, and measured by Keynes's own standards, relatively barren of academic output, though certainly not of activity or thought. From 1927 onwards, however, Keynes was already working at the *Treatise on Money*, which appeared in 1930, and the ideas which he printed there were progressively developing. Each year from 1926 onwards he gave a short course of eight lectures, usually in the Michaelmas Term, on the theory of money, and year by year the form and content of his ideas developed. But as late as 1927–8 the theoretical structure was, so far as I can discover, of an essentially "velocity of circulation" design, though with important improvements of his own. Much of the final version of the *Treatise on Money* is still comparatively little changed from this earlier pattern.

It so happened that the publication of the *Treatise* coincided in time with a remarkable younger generation in Cambridge. R. F. Kahn had just been made a Fellow of King's; J. E. Meade was spending a year in Trinity before returning to Oxford; they with P. Sraffa, C. H. P. Gifford, A. F. W. Plumptre, Joan Robinson and several others of us formed a "circus" which met weekly for the discussion of the *Treatise*, and R. F. Kahn retailed to Keynes the results of our deliberations. We managed quickly to seize on the formal importance of some of the implied assumptions regarding employment and output levels and within a few weeks Keynes had not only seen the force of our criticisms, as well as those of a number of others both inside and outside Cambridge, but was dashing ahead of us in redeploying his ideas in terms of a variable level of employment.

At no moment in his life, I think, did Keynes's greatness of character appear more strongly than at this time. He had just completed what he might reasonably have regarded as his *magnum opus*. There are few authors who would not have been sorely tempted to take up a position and to use their authority and reputation to maintain it until dislodged by sheer weight of opposition. Keynes never even appeared to hesitate. He was off with the rest of us in pursuit of truth with as enthusiastic a zest as if he were demolishing the work of his worst enemy.

In the years following the publication of the *Treatise* Keynes continued his practice of giving eight lectures annually. Each year he gave us the development of his ideas to date. And these lectures became something wholly unlike anything else that I have ever known in Cambridge lectures. Apart from the third-year undergraduates, to whom officially the course was addressed, there were to be found there the whole body of research students, at least half the members of the Faculty, a visiting Professor or two from America, Australia or where you will, and on occasion a few spies from London, Oxford or elsewhere. Gradually year by year the essential features of the *General Theory* emerged. Thus, when it was finally published in 1936, Cambridge at least knew fairly well what to expect.

To the world outside, however, the *General Theory of Employment, Interest and Money* came as a shock. Keynes had meant to shock. An ordinary book, wooing with sweet reason, would not have fulfilled his purpose. The ideas that happened to be congenial might have been accepted, the others discarded according to taste. Keynes was firmly convinced, as he said in his preface, that "if orthodox economics is at fault, the error is to be found not in the superstructure, which has been erected with great care for logical consistency, but in a lack of clearness and of generality in the premises." He had, as he saw it, to force his fellow economists to decide whether *in toto* they were for or *in toto* against. For if he was right in his analysis, the basic assumptions of the automatism of the economic system were at fault. Because he believed it necessary that economists should face these issues, he deliberately heightened differences and emphasized controversy.

This involved saying things that hurt about men that he had admired—including in their number Alfred Marshall. It involved also that subsequent discussion was conducted very much in the atmosphere of the revivalist meeting: "Brother, are you saved?" I am not sure that this may not have been because Keynes himself had found it a severe moral struggle to let go of his old liberal faith in the ultimate automatism of the economic system. But now that the Moody and Sankey of those days has come near to being orthodoxy, some of us can look back and smile at the odd and ever-changing divisions between the sheep and the goats. The first to be saved seemed to include not only the pure of heart, but a large admixture of the empty of head. The sinners were not only those who preferred to remain in darkness, but many whose intellectual honesty forbade them to commit themselves to the support of conclusions so radically opposed to all that they had learned and taught without a very thorough process of sifting, and many others also who felt that the *General Theory* contained exaggerations or misrepresentations which might discredit what they still believed to be true and important in their own and others' past thinking.

To the outside world the development of the theories of money and employment by and around Keynes appeared necessarily as a spasmodic and episodic process, though rumours of the developing ideas, passed on by travelling research students, had made known that the *Treatise* was not Keynes's final word. To those in Cambridge the whole process seemed much more continuous, and both the *Treatise* and the *General Theory* appeared much more as instantaneous photographs of an athlete in action than as carefully posed studio pictures with every limb perfectly set. Already, before the war, Keynes was himself moving ahead again, as in his contribution to the Irving Fisher *Festschrift* (*The Lessons of Monetary Experience*), and was finding himself prepared to accept certain developments or modifications of his ideas propounded by writers in England, America and elsewhere. It would be a disaster, and wholly alien to Keynes's own concept of the academic pursuit of truth, if the effect first of the interruption of the war and then of Keynes's own death were to be to establish for the first time a fixed and immutable creed that it is wrong to criticize or change or develop. I can conceive no memorial to Keynes's teaching that he would more passionately have assailed.

The charge of inconsistency has been levelled against Keynes at frequent intervals from 1920 onwards. A careful study will, I believe, show him to have been remarkably consistent in his strategic objectives, but extraordinarily fertile in tactical proposals for achieving them. Like a resourceful tactician, he would probe, try to find the enemy's weak points; if repulsed he would quickly fall back and regroup and put in another attack elsewhere. But in the end his victory was complete. Full employment of resources has become the national objective; some would say it has obscured other objectives. Ordered flexibility of exchange rates has become the agreed world system.

Keynes was consistent also, possibly over-consistent, in another sense. He began life as a liberal. He belonged by birth, upbringing and natural abilities to the class for which the *carrière ouverte* is the natural aim. He was not a stagnant liberal; he sought to prevent liberalism becoming a backward-looking and uncritical worship of laissez-faire; he did not in any narrow sense regard the criterion of the market-place as final and decisive, and in an essay in 1932 in *The Political Quarterly* he argued for the economically unsound as the ultimate and distant ideal, to be reached through the economically sound. But he belonged to the world of reason. He was possessed of an inherent distaste for isms and shibboleths and emotionally reached views. He was never anti-socialist, but he was anti-doctrinaire. I do not think that a fashionable school of historians who believe that a glimpse of a man's pass-book can explain the whole of his character will have an easy task with Keynes. He had made himself rich, it is true, in a liberal world; but he had nothing to fear in socialism; he would have been a perfectly loyal, happy and financially care-free Governor of the Bank and the Fund, or whatever might come his way, in a socialist world or in any other. His objectives were included in their objectives. His political liberalism was seldom obtruded in later life. I do not know (and I doubt if anyone knows) what his final views would have been upon the present moves towards nationalization. Neither, I suspect, wholly unfavourable nor wholly favourable. Yet it was natural to him, in trying to make a framework within which the world economic system might develop, to think of it in the essentially liberal terms of markets and prices and discounts and borrowing rates. And when the *General Theory* was interpreted as an argument for closing national economic systems, or his pupils expressed scepticism whether interest rates could ever provide a wholly perfect and effective working link between the volume of saving and the volume of investment in full employment, Keynes's fundamental belief in the liberal economy was apt to find itself in conflict with his passionate care for his objectives. He never, I believe, satisfactorily resolved that conflict for himself, and he has left it as a conflict for our generation.

From his undergraduate days Keynes had been a collector of books, and in his later years possessed a very fine library, which he left to King's. It came to represent a more or less complete collection of the early editions of authors particularly important in the history of thought. The philosophers predominated, but it included also a remarkable collection of the work and papers of Isaac Newton.

He had a small but interesting collection of modern paintings, particularly of the French School, and for very long his close friendship with Roger Fry, Duncan Grant, Clive and Vanessa Bell and others meant that he was in close touch with the leaders of English criticism and painting. His rooms in King's had been decorated for him by Duncan Grant and Vanessa Bell.

His interest in the ballet went back to the early years in London just after the first war. His more intimate touch with it began after he first got to know Lydia Lopokova, and developed during the following years, and with and through her he played a large part in the growth of ballet in England.

All these inevitably made calls upon Keynes's time. They represented, in fact, his hobbies, together with his farming plans at Tilton and on the College estates in Lincolnshire, and, I suspect, his operations on the stock and commodity markets. How far did they interrupt more serious work? I think, very little. For Keynes had, as I have said earlier, a marked incapacity for doing nothing, for wasting time, as most of us waste it, with worthless books and worthless thoughts.

Professor Schumpeter, in a charming and penetrating study of Keynes, has suggested that he permitted his later work to suffer unduly from haste and interruption, and that, instead of castigating Marshall for his slowness, Keynes ought to have learned from him. That is, I believe, to misunderstand Keynes's capacity for work. He was always a very rapid worker who thought quickly, and did his best work quickly. I myself would argue that all his best work was done very rapidly, at white heat, and that the work which, whether in literary form or in logic and lucidity of presentation, was below his best very often represented overmuch work and a process of mental development between the beginning and the end, as did both the *Treatise* and the *General Theory*. True, in such cases he might at the end have rewritten completely. But even to one of Keynes's rapidity that would have been a long, as well as a tedious, task. The development of ideas in the field of monetary theory was exceedingly rapid in the 1930s. Would it have been better to postpone each of those books by a year or eighteen months in order to rewrite? Was it not better, in the words that he himself wrote of Marshall, "to be willing to cast his half-baked bread on the waters, to trust to the efficacy of the cooperation of many minds, and to let the big world draw from him what sustenance it could"?

Nor do I feel certain that Keynes's speed of work was excessive. When I first started to do research and was finding a beginner's difficulty in getting my ideas on paper, Keynes urged me to follow his own rule of life—to try every day to write three pages. He did not always keep to this rule of life, but he was persuaded (and surely he was right) that mental constipation was best cured by regular writing.

That Keynes compressed much into his life is undeniable. It is undeniable also that he suffered much from interruptions, though I doubt whether his opportunities for continuous work were inferior to those of the ordinary university teacher. He gave himself unstintingly to his friends and, whatever the load upon him, was always welcoming and apparently unhurried. All of us relied upon him, consulted him, and made no major decision in our lives without him. He loved to entertain, loved good conversation, to meet people and to argue with them. Would it have been better if he had been different, more of a hermit, more of an academic, and less a man of many worlds? I think not. For Keynes surely brought to economics, as did Ricardo, the critical wisdom of one who saw it in its relations and applications to the work-a-day world. Certainly to his younger pupils that was Keynes's compelling strength. And, if we think back, we realize that for a generation it is Keynes who has first been asking the questions that we have all been trying to answer—that almost throughout the period current economic controversy has turned on whether Keynes was right or Keynes was wrong. At different times and at different places conviction, or sometimes, I suspect, even fashion, has dictated that a majority should be his critics or his supporters. But economics has been about Keynes. In a sense we have all been parasitic upon him. And that is the true measure of his dominance.

When war broke out in 1939 Keynes was a sick man. None of us imagined it possible that he should play a part in this war comparable to the part that he had played in 1914–18. Nevertheless, within a few weeks of the outbreak of war he had developed ideas of the scale of the British war potential and of the methods of war finance which were later to form the basis of the whole operation of the British war economy. The study of the problems of war potential he published in the *Economic Journal* of December 1939. His proposals for financing the war were published in the form of a pamphlet *How to Pay for the War*, which had very wide currency. Some of us were already in government service, and Keynes's ideas were known to us. When *How to Pay for the War* was published we quickly convinced our seniors that it was right to set up a small section in the Cabinet Office to improve our national income estimates. Within a few weeks James Meade and Richard Stone were at work, and the first fruits of Keynes's original idea and of their labours were available in time to influence the budget of 1941.

But by then Keynes, in defiance of all expectations, was already himself at work in the Treasury. He had this time no specific responsibilities. He was there to help the Chancellor, and in practice to share some of the heavier burdens with the Second Secretaries, on whom fall the main responsibilities for the ordinary day-to-day business of the Treasury. In the earlier years he was much concerned with the problems of internal finance, and there can be little doubt that the budget speeches of 1941 and 1942 were considerably influenced by Keynes. But increasingly Keynes became concerned with post-war problems. The broader problems of internal war finance had by 1942 in the main been reduced to order. In the British system the general economic planning of the war was by then conducted almost exclusively in terms of the real resources, in manpower allocations, in raw materials allocations, in shipping allocations, in building allocations, and the like; the needs of civil consumption were taken into account at that stage, and the problems of war finance increasingly became, as Keynes had argued that they should, those of seeing that taxation and savings mopped up as much as possible of the redundant purchasing power, and that inflation was thus kept within as narrow bounds as possible. Keynes's own preoccupations increasingly became those of foreseeing and planning the problems of the transition from war to peace, whenever that might come.

In the course of 1940, moreover, the transition of Keynes from outside critic, outspoken, fearless and therefore disreputable, to inside adviser and maker of policy, respectable and acceptable, had been advanced an important stage by his election to the Court of the Bank of England.

Meanwhile it was inevitable that Keynes, with the double advantage of great inside knowledge of our financial problems and freedom from routine responsibilities, should be used in some degree as a kind of financial ambassador. He went to Washington as early as May 1941 to discuss Lend-Lease and other financial problems confronting the two countries. But his period of almost continuous service in this capacity began in 1943, and was primarily, but by no means exclusively, concerned with the great problems of financial and economic reconstruction upon which he had been working for some time past.

Keynes's greatest endeavours in this field, his contributions to Bretton Woods, to the Land-Lease settlements and to the American Loan are still, and will long remain, in the zone of controversy.

With the Bretton Woods Bill finally passed, Keynes began to think of rest. For the previous three years the man whom before the war we had begun to think of as a lifelong invalid had carried an almost insupportable burden. Lydia had accompanied him on all his journeys; he and she treasured an official letter from the Admiralty assuring them that they had incurred their Lordships' displeasure by insisting on her travelling on a transport in war-time. She guarded him, cared for his health as best she might, and shared with him the joys and sorrows. But no care could protect him from the inevitable strains that these missions had involved, or from his own impulsive energies.

There remained, however, one further step in relation to Bretton Woods—a step which he and most of us had regarded as a formality—the Inaugural Meetings of the Fund and the Bank on both of which Keynes had been made Britain's Governor. But the Savannah Conference did not in practice turn out like that. There were unexpected last-moment differences, and the British position was made more difficult by the slow progress of the US Loan in its journey through Congress; final approval came only after Keynes's death. Because he had gone in no expectation of the differences of opinion that emerged, Keynes found it the most exhausting conference that he had attended.

He arrived home from Savannah very tired, and went to Tilton to rest. On Sunday 21 April 1946, Easter Day, he had a sharp heart attack. He died within a couple of hours of the onset.

For some years before 1946 both Keynes himself and his friends had known the possibility, even the likelihood, that if he continued to work as he was working the end would come one day just as it did. Despite this knowledge he carried on. This was his contribution to the war and to the future of his country.

His death left a gap everywhere. In the Treasury, where, despite his amorphous position, he carried a massive share of the total responsibilities for the country's financial welfare. In the world of academic economics, where for so many years he called the tune to which the rest of us had danced. In his College and University, where his learning and his leadership alike were irreplaceable. In the world of ballet and the arts, where his sustaining energies had kept so much alive that might so easily have died. Not least, in his own family. But perhaps some day we may learn to say that it was right that he, like others whom the gods love, should die young. At sixty-two he was in the plenitude of his powers. That brilliant mind was still at its best—rapier sharp, leaping always with intuitive rapidity far ahead of the rest of us. The memory that will remain is of that mind at its perfection.

In the six years from the outbreak of war to its end Maynard Keynes had subtly changed. At its outbreak he was still fundamentally the academic and the philosopher, with truth and right as his objectives. He was still the critic, trying to persuade, and content if sometimes the process of persuasion involved an element of over-emphasis on the component that was undervalued by others. The war brought him into a position of responsibility where action followed close upon advice, and advice needed therefore to be measured. And as his ambassadorial journeys took him to place after place and problem after problem, he came insensibly to think of issues more, as does the civil servant, in terms of what was practicable; of what could or could not be secured in a given international set-up. His love for the verities never deserted him, but he was readier than the young Cassandra had been to believe that a desired destination could be reached by speeding slowly.

As a civil servant he had God-given weapons—a voice and a pen. No account of Maynard Keynes would be complete without a reference to that voice. To many is given the gift of dissuasion: every word they utter seals the fate of the object they so passionately desire. To Maynard Keynes was given a voice that could persuade. One who was by force of circumstances for the moment his opponent said to me after a meeting dominated by Keynes: "The worst of it is that Keynes's voice can persuade me of anything, however wrong-headed I believe it to be." That beautiful, musical, resonant voice, allied to an unparalleled power of lucid exposition and to a range of vocabulary and a joy in words comparable only to that of Winston Churchill in his generation, made him a pleasure to listen to, whether you agreed or disagreed, whether you knew all about what he was talking about, or nothing about it. He never bored. He never exhausted. He was never trite.

And allied to the voice, the pen. To the jaded civil servant, wearied by a perpetual surfeit of the clichés that conveyed, by a process of automatic writing, the tired thoughts of tired men to the tired eyes of more tired men, those occasional official papers that Keynes wrote were champagne—a sparkle of ideas set out in words which fizzed into one's memory. Many of them were entirely of the moment. Some will, I fear, never be able to see the light of day. But others should surely, after due interval, be published. May we hope that the Treasury wil give thought to such a kindly act of piety?

To the arts of persuasion Keynes added, as a civil servant no less than as an academic, his divine intolerance of nonsense. To his immediate colleagues, and to those who agreed with him, this intolerance was wholly delightful. To those in other departments his facility in argument and in demolishing their carefully reasoned cases was often disturbing—the more so as they often felt that it was not the case but the arguing of it that was at fault. But if the case was good, reason would quickly prevail. Keynes would often laughingly say that he possessed the shortest memory in the world. And I believe there was truth in this—he had a wonderful memory for arguments, but no memory for their authors. If next day you returned to the same problem, you were as likely to find him parading your arguments of yesterday—if they were good arguments—as his own. And those of us who knew him learned to retreat when worsted today and to re-engage tomorrow.

And to these others he added the greatest gift of the civil servant, the power to inspire devotion. The missions which he led were all happy parties. They involved, as I have said, almost unbelievable pressure of sustained effort, not only for Keynes himself, but also for all who were engaged either in responsible or routine work. All drove themselves, partly because Keynes was driving himself, but at least as much because he filled them with his own sense of urgency. He was utterly informal, almost without sense of hierarchy, approachable by everyone who had a problem on which to brief him, or a difficulty in his own particular negotiations, extraordinarily quick to see the point at issue and to fasten on to the problems that were worrying you, extraordinarily rapid in judgment and decision.

I can with difficulty think of others who were nearly Keynes's equal in a fastidious forensic ability; of others who approached him in the power to clothe perfect clarity of thought in a perfect choice of words; of others, again, who shared his mastery of technical and administrative necessities; of yet others who had grasped the fundamental economic problems of our age, if not so well, yet not very markedly less well. But no other man in our age has combined all these rare qualities so remarkably in one person. It was because he was all these things and more that Maynard Keynes was utterly unique.

Eduard Austin Gessage Robinson

II
PERSONALITY OF JOHN MAYNARD KEYNES

Considering the range of Keynes's brilliant talents, he may well be ranked as the outstanding man of genius in England in the first half of the twentieth century. While writers like George Bernard Shaw and H. G. Wells had greater popular appeal and influence, their thinking often showed a lack of orderly development and rested on less certain philosophical foundations. Keynes's arguments were always based on rigidly defined first principles, and so he made a deeper impression on the best brains of his time.

The basis of his thinking was a highly developed gift of rational deduc-duction. He was a proficient, although not professional, mathematician and his work on probability was on the borderline of mathematics and philosophy. With his extraordinary power of systematization, he could see at a glance the implications of developing a theory in one branch of a subject for the subject as a whole. This systematizing gift particularly stood out in his later work on economics.

With a natural capacity for abstract thought, however, he combined a penetrating sense of realism. In his mind's eye he was always aware in minute detail—more distinctly that with any economist of his time—of the expected consequences of a general economic tendency on the actual course of the economy. While always going to great pains to give his theories the greatest possible degree of general validity, he did not fall into the error of deriving them from postulates which are so abstract as to lose touch with reality. He had an excellent appreciation of the quantitative weight of various possible economic causes, which was why his economic studies were so fruitful. He was an experienced statistician and prepared the way for the development of "global" statistics, which are in such widespread use today.

These gifts of a strictly scientific kind were matched by noble literary qualities. Keynes had a wonderful lucidity at his command. He also had the art of persuasion, and he rarely failed to win an audience. He used his deep-set sense of humour to enliven—often with amusing jokes—his explanation of the driest economic themes. Perhaps his most remarkable characteristic was his striking speed of thought, which very often sealed the fate of his opponent in an argument.

A strain of the artistic in his nature recommended him to writers and to painters as a kindred spirit. That he was successful in acquiring with comparatively small means a valuable art collection might be taken to denote good judgment in artistic matters. This, however, has at times been called in question and it may be that he actually relied on the advice of friends.

He was a good son to his parents, who survived him, and a true and loving friend. His sympathies went out to men of the most diverse sorts and kinds, the wayward as well as the reliable, the humble as well as the exalted.

Failings also figure in his portrait. In his younger days especially, he was reckoned to be arrogant. Accustomed as he was to being on familiar terms with men of outstanding gifts, he could be inconsiderate when faced with clumsiness, pomposity or narrow-mindedness. For a time he subscribed, at least in part, to the theory that it was only the chosen few, only men of highly developed intellect and sensibility, who mattered. In his riper years his sympathies considerably broadened, although the superior manner of his youth was never wholly lost, remaining as a barrier with certain types of people. As a young man, too, he was not readily susceptible to female influence.

Throughout his life he was continually being blamed for inconsistency. It is not easy to decide how widely this was justified. Close students of his writings have detected a remarkable consistency in the course of a long development. The accusation may have been due partly to his great speed of thought, enabling him to alter his interpretation of current events very rapidly at each new state of affairs. Moreover, a contributory factor may have been the fact that many who attacked him had not rightly understood his ideas from the start. For all that, it is perfectly true that he was always following new events or theories which might give him cause to change his point of view and that he even gloried in his readiness to change. When taking up a new position he would make no effort to conceal it, and he was at no pains, like so many public figures, to find means of reconciling what he said today with what he had said yesterday, as long as changing circumstances gave him grounds for taking up a new position. But he could occasionally forget some previous utterances and take others severely to task for saying today exactly what he had himself pronounced not long before.

He thought all methods fair in argument and never hesitated to expose his adversaries to ridicule—unless they were his pupils or essentially his juniors. By ordinary standards he was extremely caustic in controversy and thereby made many enemies.

In the ordinary flow of talk he was addicted to exaggeration. He was apt to magnify a trifling error into a monstrous absurdity. This sometimes gave the impression that he lacked a sense of responsibility and power of judgment; but, in fact, these errors, if they may be so called, hardly went beyond the requisites of dialectic; on the other hand, in practical matters Keynes was the soul of wise discretion and allowed the weight of his opponent's arguments to have full justice.

One might claim that in the sphere of intellectual matters he was somewhat egocentric. One can do full justice to the great importance of his contribution to the theory of economics, and yet be of the opinion that he wilfully extolled its novelty at the expense of the established doctrine, and that this propensity of his was harmful to the uniform development and the repute of economic science. In this respect, Keynes found himself in diametric opposition to his teacher, Alfred Marshall, who perhaps went too far in the opposite direction, in that he gave economics the appearance of a logical and undisturbed development and brought together obviously divergent theories into a synoptic scheme. Perhaps it was a similar tendency that lured Keynes into over-confidence in his ability to win the world to his opinions and to bring it to appreciate the ideas lying locked up in his teaching.

Roy Forbes Harrod

III
LORD KEYNES AND THE GENERAL THEORY

I have always considered it a priceless advantage to have been born as an economist prior to 1936 and to have received a thorough grounding in classical economics. It is quite impossible for modern students to realize the full effect of what has been advisably called "The Keynesian Revolution" upon those of us brought up in the orthodox tradition. What beginners today often regard as trite and obvious was to us puzzling, novel and heretical.

To have been born as an economist before 1936 was a boon—yes. But not to have been born too long before!

"Bliss was it in that dawn to be alive,
But to be young was very heaven!"

The *General Theory* caught most economists under the age of 35 with the unexpected virulence of a disease first attacking and decimating an isolated tribe of South Sea islanders. Economists beyond 50 turned out to be quite immune to the ailment. With time, most economists in between began to run the fever, often without knowing or admitting their condition.

I must confess that my own first reaction to the *General Theory* was not at all like that of Keats on first looking into Chapman's Homer. No silent watcher, I, upon a peak in Darien. My rebellion against its pretensions would have been complete except for an uneasy realization that I did not at all understand what it was about. And I think I am giving away no secrets when I solemnly aver—upon the basis of vivid personal recollection—that no one else in Cambridge, Massachusetts, really knew what it was about for some twelve to eighteen months after its publication. Indeed, until the appearance of the mathematical models of Meade, Lange, Hicks, and Harrod there is reason to belive that Keynes himself did not truly understand his own analysis.

Fashion always plays an important role in economic science; new concepts become the *mode* and then are *passé*. A cynic might even be tempted to speculate as to whether academic discussion is itself equilibrating: whether assertion, reply, and rejoinder do not represent an oscillating divergent series, in which—to quote Frank Knight's characterization of sociology—"bad talk drives out good."

In this case, gradually and against heavy resistance, the realization grew that the new analysis of *effective demand* associated with the *General Theory* was not to prove such a passing fad, that here indeed was part of "the wave of the future". This impression was confirmed by the rapidity with which English economists, other than those at Cambridge, took up the new Gospel: e.g., Harrod, Meade, and others at Oxford; and still more surprisingly, the young blades at the London School like Kaldor, Lerner, and Hicks, who threw off their Hayekian garments and joined in the swim.

In this country it was pretty much the same story. Obviously, exactly the same words cannot be used to describe the analysis of income determination of, say, Lange, Hart, Harris, Ellis, Hansen, Bissell, Haberler, Slichter, J. M. Clark, or myself. And yet the Keynesian taint is unmistakably there upon every one of us. (I hasten to add—as who does not?—that I am not myself a Keynesian, although some of my best friends are.)

Instead of burning out like a fad, today ten years after its birth the *General Theory* is still gaining adherents and appears to be in business to stay. Many economists who are most vehement in criticism of the specific

Keynesian policies—which must always be carefully distinguished from the scientific analysis associated with his name—will never again be the same after passing through his hands.

It has been wisely said that only in terms of a modern theory of effective demand can one understand and defend the so-called "classical" theory of unemployment. It is perhaps not without additional significance in appraising the long-run prospects of the Keynesian theories that no individual who has once embraced the modern analysis has—as far as I am aware—later returned to the older theories. And in universities where graduate students are exposed to the old and new income analysis, I am told that it is often only too clear which way the wind blows.

Finally, and perhaps most important from the long-run standpoint, the Keynesian analysis has begun to filter down into the elementary textbooks; and as everybody knows once an idea gets into these, however bad it may be, it becomes practically immortal.

Thus far, I have been discussing the new doctrines without regard to their content or merits, as if they were a religion and nothing else. True, we find a Gospel, Scriptures, a Prophet, Disciples, Apostles, Epigoni, and even a Duality; and if there is no Apostolic Succession, there is at least an Apostolic Benediction. But by now the joke has worn thin, and is in any case irrelevant.

The modern saving-investment theory of income determination did not directly displace the old latent belief in Say's Law of Markets (according to which only "frictions" could give rise to unemployment and overproduction). Events of the years following 1929 destroyed the previous economic synthesis. The economists' belief in the orthodox synthesis was not overthrown, but had simply atrophied: it was not as though one's soul had faced a showdown as to the existence of the Deity and that faith was unthroned, or even that one had awakened in the morning to find that belief had flown away in the night; rather it was realized with a sense of belated recognition that one no longer had faith, that one had been living without faith for a long time, and that what after all was the difference?

The nature of the world did not suddenly change one black October day in 1929 so that a new theory became mandatory. Even in their day, the older theories were incomplete and inadequate: in 1815, in 1844, 1893, and 1920. I venture to believe that the eighteenth and nineteenth centuries take on a new aspect when looked back upon from the modern perspective; that a new dimension has been added to the rereading of the mercantilists, Thornton, Malthus, Ricardo, Tooke, David Wells, Marshall, and Wicksell.

Of course, the great depression of the thirties was not the first to reveal the untenability of the classical synthesis. The classical philosophy always had its ups and downs along with the great swings of business activity.

Each time it had come back. But now for the first time, it was confronted by a competing system—a well-reasoned body of thought containing among other things as many equations as unknowns. In short, like itself, a synthesis; and one which could swallow the classical system as a special case.

A new *system*, that is what requires emphasis. Classical economics could withstand isolated criticism. Theorists can always resist facts; for facts are hard to establish and are always changing anyway, and *ceteris paribus* can be made to absorb a good deal of punishment. Inevitably, at the earliest opportunity, the mind slips back into the old grooves of thought since analysis is utterly impossible without a frame of reference, a way of thinking about things, or in short a theory.

Herein lies the secret of the *General Theory*. It is a badly written book, poorly organized; any layman who, beguiled by the author's previous reputation, bought the book was cheated of his 5 shillings. It is not well suited for classroom use. It is arrogant, bad-tempered, polemical, and not overly generous in its acknowledgments. It abounds in mares' nests and confusions: involuntary unemployment, wage units, the equality of savings and investment, the timing of the multiplier, interactions of marginal efficiency upon the rate of interest, forced savings, own rates of interest, and many others. In it the Keynesian system stands out indistinctly, as if the author were hardly aware of its existence or cognisant of its properties; and certainly he is at his worst when expounding its relations to its predecessors. Flashes of insight and intuition intersperse tedious algebra. An awkward definition suddenly gives way to an unforgettable cadenza. When it finally is mastered, we find its analysis to be obvious and at the same time new. In short, it is a work of genius.

It is not unlikely that future historians of economic thought will conclude that the very obscurity and polemical character of the *General Theory* ultimately served to maximize its long-run influence. Possibly such an analyst will place it in the first rank of theoretical classics along with the work of Smith, Cournot, and Walras. Certainly, these four books together encompass most of what is vital in the field of economic theory; and only the first is by any standards easy reading or even accessible to the intelligent layman.

In any case, it bears repeating that the *General Theory* is an obscure book so that would-be anti-Keynesians must assume their position largely on credit unless they are willing to put in a great deal of work and run the risk of seduction in the process. The *General Theory* resembles the random notes over a period of years of a gifted man who in his youth gained the whip hand over his publishers by virtue of the acclaim and fortune resulting from the sucess of his *Economic Consequences of the Peace*.

Like Joyce's *Finnegans Wake*, the *General Theory* is much in need of a companion volume providing a "skeleton key" and guide to its contents: warning the young and innocent away from Book I (especially the difficult Chapter 3) and on to Books III, IV, and VI. Certainly in its present state, the book does not get itself read from one year to another even by the sympathetic teacher and scholar.

Too much regret should not be attached to the fact that all hope must now be abandoned of an improved second edition, since it is the first edition which would in any case have assumed the stature of a classic. We may still paste into our copies of the *General Theory* certain subsequent Keynesian additions, most particularly, the famous chapter in *How to Pay for the War* which first outlined the modern theory of the inflationary process.

This last item helps to dispose of the fallacious belief that Keynesian economics is good "depression economics" and only that. Actually, the Keynesian system is indispensable to an understanding of conditions of overeffective demand and secular exhilaration; so much so that one anti-Keynesian has argued in print that *only* in times of a great war boom do such concepts as the marginal propensity to consume have validity. Perhaps, therefore, it would be more nearly correct to aver the reverse: that certain economists are Keynesian fellow-travellers only in boom times, falling off the bandwagon in depression.

If space permitted, it would be instructive to contrast the analysis of inflation during the Napoleonic and First World War periods with that of the recent War and correlate this with Keynes's influence. Thus, the "inflationary gap" concept, recently so popular, seems to have been first used around the spring of 1941 in a speech by the British Chancellor of the Exchequer, a speech thought to have been the product of Keynes himself.

No author can complete a survey of Keynesian economics without indulging in that favourite indoor guessing game: Wherein lies the essential contribution of the *General Theory* and its distinguishing characteristic from the classical writings? Some consider its novelty to lie in the treatment of the *demand for money*, in its liquidity-preference emphasis. Others single out the treatment of *expectations*.

I cannot agree. According to recent trends of thought, the interest rate is less important than Keynes himself believed; therefore, *liquidity preference* (which itself explains part of the lack of importance of the interest rate, but only part) cannot be of such crucial significance. As for expectations, the *General Theory* is brilliant in calling attention to their importance and in suggesting many of the central features of uncertainty and speculation. It paves the way for a theory of expectations, but it hardly provides one.

I myself believe the broad significance of the *General Theory* to be in the fact that it provides a relatively realistic complete system for analysing the level of effective demand and its fluctuations. More narrowly, I conceive the heart of its contribution to be in that subset of its equations which relate to the propensity to consume and to saving in relation to offsets-to-saving. In addition to linking saving explicitly to income, there is an equally important denial of the implicit "classical" axiom that motivated investment is *indefinitely expansible or contractable*, so that whatever people *try* to save will always be fully invested. It is not important whether we deny this by reason of expectations, interest-rate rigidity, investment inelasticity with respect to overall price changes and the interest rate, capital or investment satiation, secular factors of a technological and political nature, or what have you. But it is vital for business-cycle analysis that we do assume definite amounts of investment which are highly variable over time in response to a myriad of exogenous and endogenous factors, *and which are not automatically equilibrated to full-employment saving levels by any internal efficacious economic process.*

With respect to the level of total purchasing power and employment, Keynes denies that there is an "invisible hand" channelling the self-centred action of each individual to the social optimum. This is the sum and substance of his heresy. Again and again through his writings there is to be found the figure of speech that what is needed are certain "rules of the road" and governmental actions, which will benefit everybody but which nobody by himself is motivated to establish or follow. Left to themselves during depression, people will try to save and only end up lowering society's level of capital formation and saving; during an inflation, apparent self-interest leads everyone to action which only aggravates the malignant upward spiral.

Such a philosophy is profoundly capitalistic in its nature. Its policies are offered "as the only practical means of avoiding the destruction of existing economic forms in their entirety and as the condition of the successful functioning of individual initiative".

From a perusal of Keynes's writing, I can find no evidence that words like these resemble the opportunistic lip-service paid in much recent social legislation to individual freedom and private enterprise. The following quotations show how far from a radical was this urbane and cosmopolitan provincial English liberal:

"How can I accept [the communistic] doctrine which sets up as its bible, above and beyond criticism, an obsolete economic textbook which I know to be not only scientifically erroneous but without interest or application for the modern world? How can I adopt a creed which, preferring the mud to the fish, exalts the boorish proletariat above the bourgeois and intelligentsia who, with all their faults, are the quality of life and surely carry the seeds of all human advancement? Even if we need a religion, how can we find it in the turbid rubbish of the Red bookshops? It is hard for an educated, decent, intelligent son of Western Europe to find his ideals here, unless he has first suffered some strange and horrid process of conversion which has changed all his values. . . .

So, now that the deeds are done and there is no going back, I should like to give Russia her chance; to help and not to hinder. For how much rather, even after allowing for everything, if I were a Russian, would I contribute my quota of activity to Soviet Russia than to Tsarist Russia."

Nothing that I can find in Keynes's later writings shows any significant changes in his underlying philosophy. As a result of the great depression, he becomes increasingly impatient with what he regards as the stupidity of businessmen who do not realize how much their views toward reform harm their own true long-run interests. But that is all.

With respect to international cooperation and autonomy of national policies, Keynes did undergo some changes in belief. The depression accentuated his post-World-War-I pessimism concerning the advisability of England or any other country's leaving itself to the mercy of the international gold standard. But in the last half-dozen years, he began to pin his hopes on intelligent, concerted, multilateral cooperation, with, however, the important proviso that each nation should rarely be forced to adjust her economy by *deflationary* means.

Paul Anthony Samuelson

SOURCES

Essay I

Eduard Austin Gessage Robinson, "John Maynard Keynes (1883–1946)", *Economic Journal*, 62 (1947). Abridged.

Essay II

Roy Forbes Harrod, "John Maynard Keynes", in *Handwörterbuch der Sozialwissenschaften*, 5 (1956). Passage on Keynes's personality.

Essay III

Paul Anthony Samuelson, "Lord Keynes and the General Theory", *Econometrica*, 14 (1946). Abridged.

Signature

National Mutual Life Insurance Company, London.

Portrait

Photograph by Edward Leigh, Cambridge, of a bust by Benno Elkan, 1947.

BIBLIOGRAPHY

J. A. Schumpeter, "John Maynard Keynes", *American Economic Review*, 36 (1946).

P. M. Sweezy, "John Maynard Keynes", *Science and Society*, ii (1946), reprinted in *The New Economics*, ed. S. E. Harris (London 1947).

L. R. Klein, *The Keynesian Revolution* (London and New York, 1947).

A. C. Pigou, *John Maynard Keynes, Baron Keynes of Tilton, 1883–1946* (London and New York, 1947).

J. M. Keynes, *Two Memoirs* (London 1949), part 2: *My Early Beliefs*.

Council of King's College, *John Maynard Keynes, 1883–1946, Fellow and Bursar, A Memoir Prepared by Direction of the Council of King's College* (Cambridge, 1949).

P. S. Frankland, "The Life of John Maynard Keynes", *Cambridge Review*, 73 (1951).

R. F. Harrod, *The Life of John Maynard Keynes*, 2nd ed. (London and New York, 1963).

L. R. Klein, "The Life of John Maynard Keynes", *Journal of Political Economy*, 59 (1951).

M. J. Bonn, "John Maynard Keynes, (1883–1946)", *Schmollers Jahrbuch*, 72 (1952).

A. H. Hansen, *A Guide to Keynes* (New York, 1953).

S. E. Harris, *John Maynard Keynes, Economist and Policy Maker* (London and New York, 1955).

R. Lekachman (ed.), *Keynes' General Theory: Reports of Three Decades* (New York, 1964).

R. F. Harrod, "John Maynard Keynes, contributions to economics", in *International Encyclopedia of the Social Sciences*, Vol. 8 (New York, 1968).

D. V. Lindley, "John Maynard Keynes, contributions to statistics", in *International Encyclopedia of the Social Sciences*, Vol 8 (New York, 1968).

R. Lekachman, *The Age of Keynes* (New York, 1968).

Political Economy Today and in the Future

I
THE SKILLS OF THE ECONOMIST

The skill of the economist depends on his ability to abstract a system from the complex social and physical world around him. The basis of the economist's system is the notion of a commodity. The economist sees the world not as men and things, but as commodities, and it is precisely in this abstraction that his peculiar skill resides. A commodity is anything *scarce*, that is; in order to get more of it a quantity of some other commodity must be relinquished.

Scarcity is most obviously manifested in the institution of exchange where one commodity is given up and another acquired by one party and the first commodity is acquired and the second given up by the other party. Exchange, however, is not the only manifestation of scarcity. There are economic systems, like that of Robinson Crusoe, in which there is no exchange in the literal sense of the word. Nevertheless, there is scarcity in the sense that Crusoe's resources of time and energy are limited and therefore the various commodities acquire a value in substitution—what economists generally call *alternative cost*. Thus, if Crusoe wishes to build a house he must do without the things he might have acquired, or might have enjoyed, with the time spent in building the house. In this sense his house might be *worth* so many fish, or so many coconuts, or so many hours of dreaming in the sun which he had to give up in order to build it. From his point of view this alternative cost is a form of exchange, almost as if he had bought the house from someone else with fish or coconuts.

Similarly it is not difficult to see that all production is essentially a form of transformation of commodities akin to exchange. The miller exchanges flour for wheat by grinding it. The milkman exchanges milk-in-the-dairy for another commodity, milk-in-the-house, by transporting it from the dairy to the doorstep. It is not too much to claim that the phenomenon of exchange is at the heart of the economist's abstraction and the ability to recognize and analyse exchange constitutes the core of his skill.

An economic system, then, is a system of commodities which are exchanged (i.e. re-shuffled by their owners), produced (transformed from other commodities) and consumed (destroyed). If this process is to be continuous there must be a constant stream of some original commodity or commodities (factors of production) which then undergo the processes of transformation, exchange, and eventual consumption. The system can be regarded from various points of view along the scale from static to dynamic. A purely static snapshot of such a system would reveal various commodities in the possession of various organizations and owners. For each owner or organization a physical balance sheet can be made up listing the various commodities (assets) which he (or it) possesses or controls. Even at this stage the existence of a financial system as well as a system of physical commodities is apparent—debts, money, and securities as well as iron, steel, wheat and houses. These financial assets have the interesting property that they generally appear in at least two balance sheets—in one as a positive item and in another as a negative item. Thus a debt is a positive item in the balance of the creditor and a negative item in the balance sheet of the debtor. Debts and other financial instruments are, however, commodities in the sense that they are exchangeable for other things.

Even in taking a static snapshot of the system it is possible to observe a phenomenon akin to *pricing*. The various heterogeneous physical balance sheets can be reduced to homogeneous financial balance sheets by the process of *valuation*—which in essence means expressing each asset (positive or negative) in terms of some common denominator or *numeraire* by multiplying it by a *valuation coefficient*. Thus suppose, what is usual though not necessary, that the numeraire is money—let us say dollars. Suppose then that the valuation coefficient of wheat is $2.00 per bushel. Any quantity of wheat in bushels can then be expressed as a dollar value by multiplying it by the appropriate coefficient of valuation. Fifty bushels of wheat would thus appear as $100. When all the items of a physical balance sheet are similarly reduced to a single numeraire (dollars), the total can be summed (both positive and negative items) and the sum is the *net worth* of the individual or organization concerned.

We now let the system begin to move. A complex system of events is observed. Some assets are consumed, as food is eaten, clothes wear out, fuel is burned, houses decay. Some assets are being exchanged among various owners or organizations in the process of buying and selling. Some assets are being produced, partly by the consumption of other assets, partly by the use of labour, land, and equipment. The use of these things, incidentally, is not the same thing as their consumption. In a given time period we can observe a universe of dynamic economic quantities: we observe amounts of commodity consumed, produced, transformed, exchanged, and the ratios of transformation (prices and costs) at which exchange and production transformations take place.

In the very simple model known as the stationary state or stationary equilibrium (Schumpeter's "Circular Flow"), all the balance sheet quantities continually reproduce themselves, like the trees of the forest, so that, even though there is constant change the whole system remains unchanged. Every time a commodity is consumed an equivalent amount is produced;

every time a loan is paid back a new one is incurred. Both the human population and the population of all commodities and assets are in stationary equilibrium, with constant age distributions, births equal to deaths, and so on. This state of affairs is never found in reality though it has been approximated in some stationary societies.

In our society especially, the economic scene is continually changing. Populations of men and of things are constantly changing—usually growing, but some may be declining even in a generally advancing society as they are displaced by superior forms. Old processes and old commodities are constantly being displaced by new processes and new commodities. These changes frequently come in waves—one growth curve flattening off and then another coming along to accelerate the pace of change once more. The succession of growth curves gives the impression of cycles around the statistical trend. In addition to these apparent cycles there may be true cycles superimposed on the growth curves by certain dynamic instabilities of the system resulting, for instance, in a downward dip of the growth curves at the end of a growth period instead of a mere flattening off.

Such a system is immensely complex, and, if it is to be analysed, various analytical devices and tricks must be used to reduce the intolerably complex mass even of this abstract system to manageable dimensions. In spite of the dynamic nature of the general system the most powerful tool which has been employed to date is still the idea of an *equilibrium* position of the various variables. This is a notion which can be employed usefully in varying degrees of looseness. It is an absolutely indispensable part of the toolbag of the economist and one which he can often contribute usefully to other sciences which are occasionally apt to get lost in the trackless exfoliations of purely dynamic systems.

The familiar equilibrium of demand and supply is the classical example of this method and it should not be despised even in a day of difference equations and linear programming. The equilibrium value of any economic variable, say the price of wheat, is that point at which there are no net forces making for change. If we may go beyond the strictly abstract world of commodities and recognize that they are in fact created, consumed, and exchanged by human beings, we may then say that, when an economic quantity is in equilbrium, no one who has the power to change it has the will and no one who has the will has the power.

Thus, in the competitive equilibrium of supply and demand, the price is such that the "market is cleared"—that is, the quantity offered for sale and the quantity offered for purchase are equal. Sellers would like a higher price, but, if one seller raises his price above the others he will sell nothing; if all sellers raise their prices together there will be excess supply—that is, the quantity offered will exceed the quantity demanded and some sellers will be left unsatisfied and, in a competitive market, will respond by lowering their price. Similarly buyers would like a lower price but do not have the power to lower it for a like reason. Even if they all lower their price together there will be unsatisfied buyers who will have both the power and the will to raise it again.

The equilibrium of demand and supply for a particular commodity can easily be generalized mathematically to the whole universe of commodities and we get the *general equilibrium systems* of Walras and Pareto. The ability to work with systems of general equilibrium is perhaps one of the most important skills of the economist—a skill which he shares with many other scientists, but in which he has perhaps a certain comparative advantage.

A general equilibrium system is one in which relationships exist among the variables so that only one, or a limited number, of sets of values of the variables is possible which satisfy *all* the relationships. The relationships are so defined that a failure to satisfy any one of them is either impossible (where the relationship is a formal identity) or results in changes in one or more variables through the behaviour of some person or other agency capable of affecting the variables. The latter type of relationship may be called a *behaviour equation* because, if it is not satisfied, behaviour ensues in the direction of an attempt to satisfy it. In a general system, with many equations and many unknowns, behaviour which is directed towards satisfying one behaviour equation is likely to result in upsetting certain other behaviour relationships with secondary, tertiary, and even further levels of behaviour resulting. Nevertheless, if the system is stable, a divergence from the position of general equilibrium (at which all the behaviour equations are satisfied), must result in overall behaviour which will eventually restore the equilibrium.

General equilibrium systems are of course met with in most, if not in all, sciences. The equations of motion of a solar system are one example; ecosystems in biology are another important example. The general principles of all such systems are essentially similar. A number of essential variables are selected. All possible identities relating these variables are formulated. Suppose there are m of these. Then n—m behaviour equations relating the various identities are postulated. These behaviour identities must be based on some empirically founded postulate regarding the behaviour of the prime elements of the system. Such a system is called a *model.* It is clear that the building of models is not a purely mechanical process but requires skill of a high order—not merely mathematical skill but a sensitivity to the relative importance of different factors and a critical, almost an artistic, faculty in the selection of behaviour equations which are reasonable, tentative hypotheses in explaining the behaviour of actual economies.

It is not enough, however, merely to set up a model with n equations and n unknowns. It is necessary to explore the *properties*, especially the dynamic properties of the model if it is to have any validity as an instrument of analysis or of prediction. Unfortunately, the more complex the model the more difficult it is to study its properties.

Three rather separate skills have been developed by economists to deal with this problem. The most general of these skills might be described as the method of plausible topology. We generally do not know the exact form of the behaviour functions of our models. Nevertheless, we do know something about the general topological characteristics of these functions—i.e. their general shapes—even without extensive empirical investigation. Many of these topological assumptions can be derived from purely logical, or *reductio ad absurdum*, arguments. The famous law of diminishing returns is a good example. This, in any of its various forms, is an expression of the general topology of production or transformation functions of all kinds. In the case of the application of variable to fixed factors, the law can be demonstrated from the *reductio ad absurdum* argument that, if it were not true, we could grow all the world's food in a single flowerpot. Even in the somewhat more controversial form of eventually diminishing returns to scale, with all factors variable, certain *a priori* reasonings (e.g. the impossibility of making scale models of any organizational structure) are the foundations of the principle.

In certain other cases the topological assumptions about the nature of behaviour functions are based on very broad general knowledge of human nature derived from introspection and non-quantitative observation. This is not to be despised as a source of valid knowledge, even in this day of econometrics and survey research. It is, after all, the kind of practical knowledge on which we depend in the conduct of our daily lives and in the innumerable small predictions in regard to human behaviour on which all human interaction is based. When I stretch out my hand to an acquaintance I am in effect predicting that he will do the same and I am usually justified! The assumptions about the shape of demand and supply curves are, in large part, of the above nature. They are assumptions which have been abundantly confirmed in more quantitative, empirical research and even the exceptions to the general rules, in the shape of positively sloped demand curves for inferior goods, or backward sloping supply curves for individual labour, are very well understood and can easily be derived from equally plausible assumptions about the nature of preference functions. The assumed topology of the consumption function (relating consumption to income) in the Keynesian system is likewise an example of the method of plausible topology. It is not necessary to conduct elaborate empirical research to establish its validity as a first approximation regardless of how important second approximations, involving other variables, may turn out to be in the matter of economic forecasting.

The usefulness of graphical methods in economics is closely related to this method of plausible topology. The analysis of two or three variables graphs can express general assumptions about the topology of functions more simply than algebraic expressions. When it comes to the generalization of the analysis to more than three dimensions, graphic analysis tends to break down, whereas algebraic analysis does not, even though the weaknesses of conventional algebra persist. It may well be that the generalized topological analysis which mathematicians are now developing may turn out to be an important analytical tool for the economist.

The more variables a model contains the more difficult the task of exploring its properties. One of the most important skills of the economist, therefore, is that of *simplification of the model.* Two important methods of simplification have been developed by economists. One is the method of partial equilibrium analysis, generally associated with the name of Alfred Marshall and the other is the method of aggregation, associated with the name of John Maynard Keynes.

The partial equilibrium method consists essentially in the exploration of cross-sections in two or three dimensions of the n-dimensional model. This is the real meaning of the *ceteris paribus* (other things being equal) assumption. We can illustrate again from the equilibrium of demand and supply. In the complete model we recognize that the quantity depends on many variables besides the price of the commodity concerned—for instance, on incomes and their distribution (which in turn depend on the quantities of other commodities and their prices), on prices of substitute or complementary commodities, on selling costs, or even on the weather or the political news. The quantity supplied similarly depends on a host of variables. Nevertheless, in order to explore the most significant properties of the general model, we assume all variables constant except the price and quantity of the particular commodity, and draw the familiar intersecting demand and supply curves to determine the equilibrium price. What we have done here is to cut the general n-dimensional figure with a plane in the price-quantity dimensions, going through the points in the other dimensions which correspond to the variables assumed constant. Having explored the properties of the model in this plane, we can now assume a change in one of the other variables, and in effect draw another plane across the model. Thus, by degrees, we explore its whole topology. We see therefore that the method of partial equilibrium is in no sense contradictory to the method of general equilibrium—it is, in fact, a method, and a highly successful method within limits, for exploring the properties of the general equilibrium models.

Only if it is taken as an end in itself does it contradict the principles of general equilibrium.

Writers like Marshall and Wicksteed are skilled in the method of particular equilibrium but from them the student can often get a better notion of the properties of general equilibrium systems that he can by studying Walras's formal mathematical expositions of general equilibrium or even the empirical model-builders like Leontief or Lawrence Klein. By the time Wicksteed, for instance, has finished explaining how money contributed to a Chinese famine relief fund in England actually relieves famine in China, there is hardly a corner of the world that we have not explored. By then the student should have a fair idea of the immense ramifications of a general equilibrium model.

The second method for the simplification of general equilibrium models is the method of aggregation. This consists in adding and otherwise combining large masses of variables and treating the resultant aggregate as if it were a single homogeneous variable capable of entering into behaviour equations which express in some measure the behaviour of the whole aggregates in relation to one another. Thus if the particular equilibrium method consists essentially of *slicing* the n-dimensional model, the method of aggregation consists in *squashing* it—in compressing great complex chunks of n-space into a single line through the construction of indices of aggregates.

Instead of working with a thousand different quantities of output of a thousand different commodities, we make an index of output as a whole and use this as a single dimension in our model. This is the economics of the bludgeon rather than of the scalpel. Nevertheless it has an important place in the understanding of the gross dimensions and properties of the system. Furthermore it enables us to understand the mass phenomena of the system—such as mass unemployment, inflation or deflation—much better than the more refined methods of partial equilibrium analysis. It should be observed that the method of aggregation is not confined to economics. We resort to it constantly in other sciences and in daily life, whenever it is necessary to reduce a complex multi-dimensional mass of data to some unitary measure. When a professor grades a class, for instance, he is bludgeoning a complex mass of personality and achievement data into a simple (and misleading) linear scale of grades. Psychologists use the method constantly in the construction of tests, and even in the physical and biological sciences there is probably more aggregation of essentially heterogeneous data than is generally recognized. In economics, however, the problems, the successes, and the failures of the method of aggregation show up with remarkable clarity. It is here perhaps the economist has a peculiar contribution to make.

The most striking example of both the success and the intrinsic difficulties of the method of aggregation is to be found in the simple Keynesian models. It is hardly too much to say that the understanding of the Keynesian model constitutes the difference between an almost total failure to comprehend the phenomena of mass unemployment and a reasonable understanding of its essential nature. It is a remarkable tribute to the power of the method that a model so crude and so full of faults should at the same time be so powerful in producing what might be called rough comprehension—and rough comprehension is infinitely better than no comprehension at all!

There are two areas I have not yet mentioned in which the economist can claim some special skill. The first is the theory of maximization, or more generally, the theory of rational behaviour. The second is the theory of difference equations, or of dynamic processes.

In the course of his pursuit of the laws which govern the universe of commodities, it has proved to be impossible for the economist to insulate himself altogether from the world of human and organizational behaviour. Consequently the economist has developed an elaborate theory of *economic behaviour*, based on the simple assumption that the individual maximizes something, something which is a function of the set of variables which are relevant to the individual's economic position and some of which are under his control. This theory is known as the *marginal analysis*. In the case of the firm the maximand is generally assumed to be some measure of financial profits. In the case of the household an abstract preference-quantity known as *utility* is supposed to be maximized, though, as I hope to show, the assumption of profit maximization in the case of the firm is a highly special case, valid only under certain conditions. Even in the case of the firm it must generally be assumed that "utility" is maximized.

This theory of behaviour is far removed from those based on stimulus and response patterns in psychology or on crisis and adjustment patterns in sociology. The economist is not much of an economic man when it comes to borrowing from other sciences. Generally speaking, if, in the pursuit of the world of commodities he stumbles into the world of men, he prefers to make up his own psychology on the spot rather than borrow from the psychologists. The psychologists, not unnaturally, are somewhat critical of this insular behaviour. Nevertheless, once it is understood that the economist's interest is not human behaviour but the behaviour of commodities then his development of something as psychologically peculiar as the marginal analysis takes on more meaning. The core of the economist's interest is not human behaviour as such but the *behaviour functions* which relate his economic quantities, his prices, and his quantities of commodity produced, consumed, or exchanged. The marginal analysis has retained the interest of the economist because it seems to yield as a *conclusion* the assumptions about behaviour functions which are the *postulates* of economic analysis proper.

Any other behaviour theory would be just as acceptable to the economist which yielded the same conclusions and helped answer the following type of question: "Do higher prices mean smaller purchases?", "Do higher wages mean smaller output?" The marginal analysis has provided what seemed to be a reasonable answer to these questions, or at least a rationale for obtaining those answers, and its long-continued popularity with the economists is undoubtedly related to the failure of substitute theories of behaviour to provide any answers at all. It is possible, as I shall indicate later, that we are on the verge of developing better and more relevant theories of behaviour. The economist will not give up the marginal analysis, however, until something emerges which is clearly of more use to him for his special purposes.

In spite of all the space given to it in the textbooks of economics the marginal analysis appears to be more of a front porch than an integral part of the edifice of economics. It is a large and imposing porch trimmed with fine arches and handsome diagrams but it could be torn down and a different structure erected without seriously affecting the main building.

If the marginal analysis is a front porch, process analysis is perhaps the back porch—something which has been developed by economists but which clearly leads into other fields and other uses. If we know exactly how tomorrow is related to today we can obviously proceed to an indefinite series of tomorrows. Tuesday can be derived from Monday, and now having got Tuesday we can derive Wednesday, and from Wednesday, Thursday, and so on to the Day of Judgment. The astronomers got there with this game long before the economist and one wonders how possible it will be to find stable relationships of this sort (i.e. difference equations) in the social sciences. It is certainly worth trying, and the predictive power of economics, like that of any other science, depends on its ability to find stable difference equations within its universe of variables. However, skill in the analysis of these dynamic processes is not peculiar to the economist. It is something he must share with many other sciences.

Perhaps the best way to test the skill of the economist is to put him in the position of Economic Adviser to the Philosopher King (or President!). If he has any skill at all it will soon be revealed. One needs, of course, a proper humility. There are a great many questions on which the economic adviser cannot presume to give advice, even fundamental questions regarding the most desirable structure of the economic system, or relatively trivial questions about a tariff on buttons. Also there are a great many economic questions which are bound up with matters of peace and war, with the retention of power and the satisfaction of political obligations, with social justice and the racial or cultural stratifications of society, in which the economist has no special competence.

When, however, it comes to the question of what to do about a depression or an inflation, whether price control can applied without rationing, what sort of public finance leads to inflation, and even on some of the more obvious conditions of economic development, the economist has something to say by virtue of his peculiar skills even if only to give a sense of direction. And if one compares the kind of answers and understanding which the economist is able to give to the question, for instance, of how we avoid or get out of a depression, with the kind of professional answers that the political scientist might give when asked what policies decrease the possibility of war, or the answers a sociologist might give to the question of what policies promote happy families or good race relations, the economist may at least be pardoned a touch of the disagreeable pride that comes from odious comparison.

Kenneth Ewart Boulding

From: Kenneth E. Boulding, *The Skills of the Economist* (Cleveland: Howard Allen Inc., 1958), parts.

II
FROM PUBLIC FINANCE TO PUBLIC ECONOMICS

A. Introductory Remarks. Every historical period makes its own impression on science, however much each branch may attempt to isolate itself, either institutionally or intellectually, and withdraw into a shell of self-confidence or even complacency. In the same way every intellectual revelation, for example, in the form of economic ideas and theories, be they true or false, influences and even shapes the historical period in which it is made. Today we may observe that the time-lag of these reciprocal and interdependent effects is becoming shorter.

Thus the theory of an unbalanced State budget, as a way of controlling the business cycle, took thirty years, a whole generation, before it was accepted in practice as part of fiscal policy, and then only half-heartedly and with reservations. On the other hand cost-benefit analysis as an aid to measuring efficiency barely needed a decade to work its way from the fringe towards, but not yet into, the centre of government activity and decision-making—a remarkable success in a budget system whose structure is somewhat fossilized.

But quite independently of this "endless give and take" (J. A. Schumpeter) between theory and reality, a decisive factor for every branch of science which sees itself as an *ars inveniendi*, as Francis Bacon considered it, is that it can always summon up enough energy and spirit to ask new and fundamental questions in order to query and, where necessary, discard its own foundations, methods and findings. Every form of science receives its strongest impulse in this way, for doubt, wherever it may appear, together with intellectual curiosity, is and always will be a powerful driving force in scientific progress whereas any kind of orthodox thinking may signify the death of a science.

Yet it is all too easy to overlook the fact that many things acclaimed as new discoveries are not new at all and not necessarily better or more "progressive" than what went before, especially in this day and age, when it seems to have been forgotten that scientific results or ideas should be related to historical experience and observed fact.

B. The Evolution of the Private and Public Sector. At the present time we are in the midst of a historical upheaval concerning the real object of national economy—i.e. the market and public economy and the environmental which affects these two. There have been such fundamental changes in technical, economic, political, and social development since the two world wars that economic activity on both market and government levels has acquired a new significance merely because of its scale. This can be said to be unprecedented in any other peacetime period in history, as the evidence shows.

If we consider only the *volume* of private *and* Government activity in Germany between 1950 and 1970, the total economic output, expressed in terms of the gross national product, increased *sevenfold* in these two decades. Our nominal income grew annually by about 9 per cent—an increase unknown even during the nineteenth century when the foundations of industry were laid. This extraordinary rise in the prosperity of broad sections of society has led Galbraith to speak of an affluent society. However critical one may be of his theories some of which are exaggerated and others one-sided, it seems true to say that much (but not all) of the evidence suggests that we are now just at the outset of a time in which prosperity and wealth are widely distributed.

A second epoch-making event beside inflation was the great depression of the thirties. This crisis, together with an exceptional economic growth in the postwar years (accompanied by sustained full and over-employment in many countries) and the absence of (classic) trade cycles, has fundamentally influenced the *substance* of market and public economy (Figure 1).

No one could have foreseen a generation ago the rate at which the whole structure of supply and demand would change, largely because of technical progress. Firms are constantly adding new or better commodities to their production programmes and it is no longer only consumer goods that rapidly grow obsolete; the same also applies to an increasing degree to more durable goods and to capital equipment. Hard manual labour is dying out while qualified manpower is in great demand. At the same time leisure is becoming a much sought-after commodity and the way it is spent in turn affects consumer demand. It is amazing how *smoothly* the market system integrates in this expansion process the manpower released by technical progress.

We may observe a similar picture in the field of *public* goods and services. *What* government undertakes is changing to a great extent and apparently at a swifter rate than *the manner* in which it is done. Now at a generally high standard of living the *fundamental functions* of modern government appear in a new light. The related principles and doctrines of capitalism, socialism and communism seem no longer sufficient to explain and interpret the reality, quite apart from the fact that they are unsuited to serve as any kind of standard or normative guide.

Completely new public wants are emerging, often caused by or complementing private consumption whereas traditional ones are decreasing in importance even if this process tends to be slow. As a result the whole structure of government investment, consumption and transfer payments is changing considerably. The same applies to our system of meeting and distributing the cost of these public activities by means of taxation and loans.

Indeed, in Germany certain traditional government tasks as well as social and economic services have taken on a fundamentally new form and essence which, from a secular point of view, no one could ever have foreseen. As urbanization spreads, the production and consumption of both private and public commodities affect other goods that are (still) *free*, such as air, water and the countryside. The damage to our surroundings occurs quite independently of the economic and social system and has reached such a degree that the protection of our environment is becoming a vital question for everyone. A further example is the demand for better educational facilities for all and for more expensive research.

This far-reaching transformation is closely linked with a process of democratization and decentralization which is still going on in most spheres of life. In fact, we know amazingly little about how much the pluralistic element in our society actually contributes or costs (including time) in either the public or the private sector. In the middle of the twentieth century government activity has acquired further new features; *external* influences also play an important part. For example, the world-wide tension and conflict sparked off by the different social and economic systems in the East and the West sometimes reach such a pitch that armament production in the widest sense (including space programmes) and government-financed research are given high priority. On the other hand, world trade, as a result of international division of labour, is growing rapidly. At the same time, the developing countries press for economic and social emancipation supported by various forms of international aid.

Figure 2 indicates these structural changes in public expenditure during the last century.

Finally the relative importance of public and market goods has also altered crucially. Thus the state's share of the national income or product has leapt in just over two generations from a tenth, which corresponds approximately to the familiar "tithe" of the past, to nearly 40 per cent. For some this is a danger signal—to F. A. v. Hayek, for example, it signifies the beginning of the road to serfdom. But on the other hand public goods have played only a constant or decreasing part in the national product since the Second World War, which means that Adolph Wagner's law of growing state activity is being undermined (see Figure 4).

C. Political Economy in a Period of Historical Upheaval. It is not difficult to see how these evolutionary changes in economic and social reality are bound to give strong impetus to a branch of science whose subject and model is public and market economy—their functions, mechanism, and institutions as well as their instruments and objectives. Both fundamental fields of modern political economy have been influenced: (1) *normative* economics, which asks what form market and government economy *should* take, (2) *positive* economics which attempts to recognize, describe and explain what form our economy really takes, why it is so today, its structure in the past and its likely development in the future. The latter function has been more strongly emphasized in recent times. But even political economy understood as a science of *decision-making* or as an art seeking the means and experiences which can help to shape reality systematically and finding a possible (an optimum or a second-best) solution, is also included in this whole process of re-examining former knowledge and findings and acquiring new ones. Here we are dealing with the problem of recognizing and classifying the economic and social factors in the light of decision-theory under uncertainty and risk.

We may begin with the theory of the market or barter economy. In the field of microeconomics the market and price theory, as developed by Cournot and Marshall, has been considerably extended and refined, but it has obviously encountered obstacles which restrict its value as an aid to interpreting the facts. Even dynamic approaches are unlikely to overcome this deadlock if no way is found to rethink the whole subject of microeconomics on the basis of decision theory. Here game theory (Neumann–Morgenstern) and the concepts of linear and non-linear programming are being used to give new insights in the fields of oligopoly or bilateral monopoly.

The Walras and Pareto system, long the theoretical foundation of political economy, which tries to *explain* the micro- and macroeconomic equilibrium and the efficient allocation of our scarce resources no longer suffices to grasp and (above all) mould the complex reality. One-sided or narrow theories cannot predict the way Robinson Crusoe should act in a world of uncertainty and risk, where various information is offered and where dependences change. Side by side with the self-centred and powerless consumer and producer new behaviour patterns are emerging which may help to explain and change concrete phenomena more easily. Strategic considerations and group behaviour are now being included in economic theory. This also may lead to a change in the characteristics of competition which has always been and still is the driving force in a free market economy; it all leads, too, to a modified concept of welfare as a yardstick in judging economic and social benefit or gain.

As far as macroeconomics is concerned, I should like to draw attention to Kenneth Boulding's preceding essay.

Figure 3 is intended to give a systematic review of the economic effects in a circular flow analysis and also of the theory of political decision-making. Figure 3 is meant, too, as a guide to the reader to find the location of modern problems in economic science.

The concept combines the neoclassical *market* theory with post-Keynesian *income* theory. Both approaches throw light on the process and interdependence of market and public economy. These insights are important in the successful control of a rational economic and social policy. In all countries political economy has played a significant role in solving the problem of underemployment in the Keynesian era and in getting rid of or at least limiting business cycles in the *classical* sense.[1]

I

First of all let us take a look at the decision centre. Instead of speculative political theories and formalized budgeting rules, theoretical and empirical investigations are now being made (1) of the process by which the political mind or will develops and (2) of all the forces which *really* influence the planning, management and control of political decisions in our pluralistic society, both inside and outside of the parties, parliament, government and administration. We are still a long way from attaining a complete theory of (optimum) organizations but modern *decision theory* may help to reform

[1] The failure of control by means of economic policy during the Great Depression led to a loss of at least 263 thousand million Reichsmark in Germany alone. Details from H. C. Recktenwald, second edition, *Finanz politik* (Tübingen 1972).

efficiently the political and administrative organization. The elements of the framework of government are the organization of the state, and the structure of society and the systems of political choice (voting). Should political decisions be made centrally, and, if not, how in a federal state are functions and revenue to be decentralized and coordinated by means of financial equalization on both a horizontal and vertical level? Federal cooperation between the regional authorities in large-scale joint projects and in economic councils plays, for instance, a significant role in Germany. Similar problems crop up in the equally new international institutions (EEC). Here the coordination of national financial policies as well as currency and trade sovereignty give rise to special problems.

Since political initiative now lies in the hands of the executive, the efficiency of the government machine depends mainly on its quality and organization. Yet we know very little about the relation of the scope and function of an institution to the political programme. Thus the general demand for an administrative *management* body has not been met because the government programme, as far as it is reflected in the budget, is still forced to conform to a budgetary system which is unsuited to planning and efficient performance as it is divided by ministries instead of by functions.

This means that planning projects tend to perish in a budget which in typical administrative manner is extrapolated from year to year. Rigid departmental particularism is largely responsible for preventing rational, coordinated action.

Obviously the purely mechanical processes are being strikingly improved with the help of computers but, nevertheless, budget, capital assets and liabilities still remain to a great extent separated parts. If the budget, together with the market system, is to be an instrument to order and regulate *activities* in the modern industrial and welfare state, then it must be capable of setting down the government's short- and medium-term plans, decisions and actions in concrete figures. This budget will help (1) parliament and government in formulating and resolving decisions, (2) the administrative agencies to execute efficiently the programmes, and (3) the electorate to be well informed of the situation. Performance and control must be adapted to the political programme and not vice versa as has been usual for decades in many countries. The same holds, of course, for budgeting technique and patterns and for budgeting law, neither of which should ever be considered as ends in themselves but merely as an instrument of politics.

The American system of planning, programming and budgeting (PPBS) is a first attempt to put these ideas into practice; yet here too, any satisfactory integration of the budget programmes as well as the link between the three basic functions of budgeting are also lacking. The development of new procedures which take the classical public goods (such as defence or police protection) and distribution into account while, at the same time, creating a sensible form of coordination via social indicators remains one of the most important tasks of modern public economics.

As far as political decision-making is concerned, voting systems (such as plurality voting) have been developed which, although still unsatisfactory, are supposed to reveal people's preferences for public goods, in order to maximize the total benefits (more or less according to the Pareto optimum) or the number of votes. These electoral systems can make allowance for strategic considerations, for example by providing protection for a minority. As they are based on *individual* preferences an analogy can be made, of course in a limited sense, to the way a market works.

2

Values and standards which derive from ethics or philosophy, as well as moral axioms or ethical rules, are difficult to transform into *tangible* or quantified *objectives*. Where moral norms are evident in a social group, tradition and ideology may often determine the ranking of the aims. In the literature, final concepts are often defined as welfare or social benefit functions. In most cases they are "empty shells" (Musgrave) and their interpretation ranges from the abstract rule to a Utopian correlation of social situations right down to the very foundations of political decision-making.

A suitable formulation of the objective is therefore of great significance in practical politics. It should also clarify the other aims and reveal the contrasts in order that the fundamental form of interaction of conflict, neutrality and harmony may easily be recognized. Further help will be given if the aims of the government programme are expressed in concrtete terms.

Let us now take a closer look at those main objectives which can be expressed in concrete terms. As far as the optimum allocation of the nation's productive resources and the efficient supply of public services are concerned, both aims are closely linked. Economic theory has developed a comprehensive system (Samuelson, Musgrave) to explain efficiency in market *and* public economy in a normative way. On the basis of calculating individual benefits, private and public goods are evaluated and compared. The opportunity costs involved in the utilization of public services are integrated into the system thus considering the receipt and expenditure of the budget. Unfortunately, however, its feasibility in the control of the social balance (Galbraith) is much limited.

Positive public economic theory also attempts to reveal the mechanism which leads to growth in government activity, of course within the framework of economic and political development, to help to ensure social balance in the future. Adolph Wagner's brilliant evaluation in his theory of growing government activity is no longer an adequate tool to make any kind of long-term prognosis or even to explain the past. Thus, however the government's share in the national product is measured, it has sunk in Germany in the twenty years since revaluation although all determining factors mentioned by Wagner (population growth, urbanization and industrialization, combined with technical progress) were fully at work.

Obviously anxiety about a stable currency and the conflicting aims involved in a liberal order and a fair income distribution decisively limit the development of government activity (Recktenwald).

Recently political economy has developed another concept which is supposed to help in finding the best possible way of allocating the nation's scarce resources in a mixed economy. It should also help in planning public services. *Cost-benefit analysis* has already proved its practical worth in some cases. Its method is to maximize the present value of all benefits, with costs subtracted, taking into account special constraints, risk, and uncertainty, and, more recently, the effects on income distribution. The decision-making refers as far as possible to market values and includes political and administrative (technical) evaluations of intangibles. The coordination of the various projects in a consistent programme is very difficult to achieve, so sub-optimal solutions have to be accepted at present.

In addition to these new methods new criteria are being sought in modern welfare economics for defining and evaluating public goods. As our modern society gradually becomes more and more urbanized, interdependent and complex, the range of the externalities which come from both public *and* private activity and inactivity is increasing so that the dividing line between public and private goods is becoming fluid. Thus technical progress, a rising standard of living and wide distribution of wealth make it necessary to revise the frontier between both types of goods and to rethink their financing.

In the same connection, the theory of *taxation* and the principle of *fees* for public services are also being reconsidered. The principle of paying fees now appears as a way of making obvious the immediate relation between individual advantage and the costs of public services (mostly borne by society) and to strengthen personal responsibility and social sense. Any amount of personal participation, however small it is, must help to clarify the *distribution* of costs and benefits of the public services. Even the theoretical basis of (fair) taxation, that is the ability-to-pay and the benefit principles, is now being questioned and the private excess burden of direct taxes is much criticized. Value-added taxes and the idea of an expenditures tax are becoming increasingly significant.

The theory of state debt has also been changing for the last generation. Under the influence of Keynes's ideas, the scope of public debt was the subject of open controversy, but in the course of the last decade, two problems have come to the fore: (1) The classical question of whether the present generation or the future should bear the "burden" of public debts. Analysis of this problem is now being dealt with in more detail considering both the costs and the benefits of collective goods; in short, the *temporal incidence* of the state debt is of most interest today. (2) On the fringe of money and credit theory two questions arise: (a) How any change in the public debt might influence the central aims of economic policy, and furthermore (b) how to optimize the financing and holding of the public debt (portfolio selection).

3

Even the (so unfortunately named) *fiscal theory* and *fiscal policy* are in the midst of a period of swift change. Their subject is the stabilization of short-term effects in the market economy to avoid inflation and deflation, to ensure full employment and to achieve a stable balance of payments. The tools of modern micro- and macroeconomics are being successfully applied here: sequence and circular flow analysis, the use of multiplier and accelerator, expectations and delays.

The results of fiscal theory concerning employment and the business cycle have both directly and indirectly influenced—through teams of scientific consultants—the economic policy of nearly all the industrial nations of Europe in recent years. And in future no wise politician will be able to dispense with any of these implements of fiscal policy.

Of course, even in this "revolution", set in motion by Keynes, we may find some overbidding and exaggeration. Many results will undoubtedly land on the "muck heap of the history of dogma", as Karl Marx put it, simply because the economic situation today is completely different from that of the thirties or even the fifties. Underemployment à la Keynes has very little in common with the unemployment caused by technological progress in an expanding economy. And since 1945 business cycles in a classical sense are indeed unknown. In a market economy where technical progress determines our material wealth and ensures that the proportion of completely new commodities in the total supply is growing extremely rapidly, the current adjustments encounter new and serious problems in market and budget mechanism. New and better goods, new services, new methods and techniques are the motor which drives the market economy forward. It tends to break up traditional market forms. All this demands adjustment on the part of the community and a different attitude of the state to the market economy and vice versa.

Indeed fiscal policy has taken a new turn in the last few years. Research is now being done on the relationship which exists between public economy and the development of productive resources, in short, on the economic basis of a market economy. Research is taking place on two main levels: first, the extension of the narrow growth theories à la Domar and Harrod where state activity is only formally considered, and second the further advance of the development theories proper as outlined by Marx, Wagner, Schumpeter and Rostow.

The fruitless results of the limited growth theories—either of the neo-classical or the post-Keynes variety—are as evident as their methodological weakness and inadequate assumptions. The combination of the short-term (trade cycle) with the long-term (growth) view gives rise to a medium-term analysis as a new basis of modern budget planning. A fiscal policy which is *neutral* to the business cycle along a warranted growth path should help to avoid a perverse conflict situation characterized by a coincidence of inflation and stagnation. The controlling devices (including monetary policy) are in the process of being greatly improved and adapted to the complex and differentiated mechanism in the highly developed industrial nations.

4

Recently, *social stability* of a nation based on social justice has come more and more to the fore as a central aim in political programmes since even the less inspired governments have learnt to provide for full employment and thus, at the same time, for *social security*. The relative prosperity of much of society as the result of continuous economic expansion has not led to a diminution of the age-old desire of mankind for social justice. On the contrary, in a society which just seems to be taking up the idea of enlightenment in all spheres, political stability definitely depends on a tolerable distribution of income and wealth. It is based (1) on whether distribution *and* performance are justly dealt with by the market and (2) on the political objective of successful redistribution by means of the budget. As yet very little research has gone into the conflict between the three kinds of justice.

Here the structure theory begins to intervene. It does not only limit itself to distributing income and wealth on a vertical and horizontal level by global transfer payments but asks who bears the costs and receives the benefits of public goods. The measure which supplies neutral criteria to structure this aim is sixfold—functional, personal, sociological, sectional, regional and temporal. There is no problem in formulating welfare functions which correspond with these six structural forms, and the same may be said of the other aims.

It is astonishing how little we really know of the actual burden or support distributed to individuals, single groups or regions, although it is some people's daily job to judge or decide whether political measures should be condemned or fostered in the name of social justice.

To investigate satisfactorily the mechanism by which tax burdens and allowances and benefits from public goods are distributed is the core of the theory of income and expenditure incidence. It is extraordinarily difficult indeed to follow up and measure the actual *shifting* of tax load and benefits in the whole market and budget process.[2] Microeconomic and macroeconomic incidences pose almost insoluble problems. It does not mean, however, that we are released from our duty of discovering at least the *formal distribution* of tax incidence and approximately the group that gets allowances or privileges.

The more successfully we can lay bare the links in this network and shed light on the problem of tax load and tax relief, the more rationally we shall be able to formulate and put into practice a redistributive financial policy and the more fair this policy will become.

Finally there is a third, equally significant, question which is linked to this: how can income and wealth best be distributed without endangering incentives and productivity. Here, too, there is a wide field of activity for theory and research.

5

In the light of this outline of development it is possible to see more clearly the lasting value, the limitations and the deficiencies of all earlier knowlege in the field of public finance. For example the following could be mentioned: the features of a public enterprise economy in mercantilism; the treatment of public economy as an outside element in the market system and its logical allocation to consumption which was economically of no interest to some classical writers, such as Jean-Baptiste Say. Then the apparently modern interpretation of government activity as being the production of nonmaterial goods (services) by Friedrich List and Adolph Wagner should be mentioned, and also the emphasis on the character of collective economy in contrast to market economy by Albert Schäffle and his successors.

Emil Sax with his "ingenious narrowness" (Erwin v. Beckerath) confined public economy to the subject of (individual and collective) benefits (subjective value theory), while Knut Wicksell and Erik Lindahl made a magnificent attempt to supply *one* combined political and economic model in order to show the allocation of various resources on the market and public sectors. Lastly I should name Arthur C. Pigou's one-sided interpreta-

[2] Details from H. C. Recktenwald, *Tax Incidence and Income Redistribution* (Wayne State University Press) Detroit, 1971.

tion of taxation, and also his far-sighted view of *social* benefits and costs.

In our time the special feature of political economy is the strong element of formalization and mathematization. Both have led to the development of new procedures and techniques but they have also given rise to fruitful discussions about suitable methods in research and theory. Yet the danger of undermining the substance of economics and taking refuge in pure technicalities is easily overlooked. Indeed, both sharp and patient observation of reality and dense historical experience—the one-sided postulates of Gustav von Schmoller—seem to be an important countervailing power against undue generalization of pure deduction from unproved or untested and changing hypotheses and against the simple-mindedness of the systematists. And it seems to open a way to a renaissance of the Continental version of Political Economy, the (improved) *Wirtschaftliche Staatswissenschaften.*

D. Future Prospects. If my judgment is correct, political economy will be called upon, more than anything else, to help bridge the gulf between individual and collective decisions on efficiently meeting our human needs. Hopefully this means that the tension which exists between public and market economy can be relaxed without endangering personal initiative and personal freedom. This could contribute to the relaxation and eventual elimination of the ideological convulsion which conceals itself behind the worn-out catchwords "capitalism" and "socialism". The whole identity or legitimacy of political economy lies in its main objective: to direct and apply market and budget mechanisms wisely as being the theoretical and practical tools of allocating resources in modern industrial nations of the West. These two forms of organization determine the meaningful incorporation and efficient utilization of the resources of a nation and regulate the distribution of goods so that economic and social balance can be ensured with a tolerable degree of fluctuation and a steady rate of economic growth. As soon as we recognize what can be expected of these two concepts in the economic circulation and what functions they are able to fulfil successfully, we shall be able to utilize and allocate our scarce resources fairly.

As we have already seen much has become fluid because traditional and modern branches of political economy are being thoroughly re-examined with the aid of new techniques and methods.

In the last few years much research has been done within the framework of fiscal policy on the question of how government revenue, expenditure and debt may affect the scope, composition and growth of the national product in both the short and the long run. Other investigations have been made into the problem of how fiscal and monetary means can best be utilized as part of practical economic policy. On the other hand, relatively little time has been spent on the same problem *in reverse*. In my opinion it will be necessary to abandon this "one-way street" and the (now customary) dichotomy between means and ends (see Figure 3), in future, when warranted growth is going on, so that the following questions can be examined: how the organization of public finance and particularly the structure and volume of revenue and expenditure are affected by a protracted expansion in prosperity, a noticeable depreciation in the value of money or a significant redistribution of income and wealth; and how these factors affect the process of political bargaining and influence those forces, motives, and criteria which mould the final public and private decisions.

The question, for example, of budgetary changes *caused* by growth rather than those *necessary to* economic growth is part of such a feedback investigation.

It is clear that in a prosperous society with comparatively widespread material well-being, functions and structure of public and market economy are bound to change, including an out-of-date regional and departmental system of administration and the whole infrastructure. *Improved* cost-benefit analysis as the foundation of a workable budget programme is speeding up this process and it provides us with technical, economic or political efficiency and equity indicators. The wise application of decision theory in the field of public economy is proving especially productive. A key to further economic progress is an efficient infrastructure, an important link between public and market economy.

Even the hierarchy of established values and normative standards—often fruits of cultural tradition and ideology—begins to crumble if the material welfare of society shows signs of permanent improvement and if the individual is for the first time in a position to share intellectual and cultural advantages, whether he does so actively or receptively and passively.

And even more than this—in a scientific age in which speculation is of less importance than formerly, while special emphasis is laid on rational thinking (in models and schemes of circulation), it is necessary to seek a harmonious relationship with historical and empirical experience in order to avoid all partiality and to understand and shape accordingly our rapidly changing environment. Most modern analysts and political economists realize the unity of theory (mathematics) and reality (history), and possess a feeling for history and may see it in perspective. They also share Max Weber's most valuable personal experience "that the true worth or dignity of any norm is only discovered when it has been put into practice". It helps to prevent ourselves from developing the myopia of the specialists or the narrow-mindedness of the systematists.

CHRONOLOGY

YEAR	BORN	DIED	IMPORTANT WORKS
1694	Quesnay		
1711	Hume		
1723	Smith		
1727	Turgot		
1739/40			*Treatise on Human Nature* (Hume)
1741/42			*Essays Moral and Political* (Hume)
1752			*Political Discourses* (Hume)
1758			*Tableau économique, Maximes générales du gouvernement économique d'un royaume agricole* (Quesnay)
1759			*Theory of Moral Sentiments* (Smith)
1766	Malthus		
1767	Say		
1769			*Mémoire sur les prêts d'argent* (Turgot)
1769/70			*Réflexions sur la formation et la distribution des richesses* (Turgot)
1772	Ricardo		
1774		Quesnay	
1776		Hume	*Wealth of Nations* (Smith)
1781		Turgot	
1783	Thünen		
1789	List		
1790		Smith	
1798			*An Essay on the Principle of Population* (Malthus)
1801	Cournot		
1803			*Traité d'économie politique* (Say)
1806	J. St. Mill		
1810	Gossen		*The High Price of Bullion* (Ricardo)
1815			*Catéchisme d'économie politique* (Say)
1816			*Proposals for an Economical and Secure Currency* (Ricardo)
1817			*On the Principles of Political Economy and Taxation* (Ricardo)
1818	Marx		
1820			*Principles of Political Economy* (Malthus)
1823		Ricardo	
1826			*Der isolierte Staat*, part 1 (Thünen)
1827			*Definitions in Political Economy* (Malthus)
1828/29			*Cours complet d'économie politique pratique* (Say)
1832		Say	
1834	Walras	Malthus	
1838	Schmoller		*Recherches sur les principes mathématiques de la théorie des richesses* (Cournot)

YEAR	BORN	DIED	IMPORTANT WORKS
1841			*Das nationale System der politischen Ökonomie* (List)
1842	Marshall		
1843			*A System of Logic* (Mill)
1846		List	
1848	Pareto		*Principles of Political Economy* (Mill) *Das kommunistiche Manifest* (Marx)
1850		Thünen	*Der isolierte Staat*, part 2, section 1 (Thünen)
1851	Wicksell		
1853/54			*Entwicklung der Gesetze des menschlicher Verkehrs und der daraus fließenden Regeln für menschliches Handeln* (Gossen)
1857	Veblen		
1858		Gossen	
1859			*Zur Kritik der politischen Ökonomie* (Marx)
1863			*Principes de la théorie des richesses* (Cournot) *Der isolierte Staat*, part 2, section 2 and part 3 (Thünen)
1864	Weber		
1867			*Das Kapital*, book 1 (Marx)
1873		J. St. Mill	
1874			*Éléments d'économie pure*, till 1877, 2 vols. (Walras)
1877	Pigou	Cournot	
1879			*The Economics of Industry* (Marshall)
1881			*Mathematische Theorie der Preisbildung wirtschaftlicher Güter* (Walras)
1883	Keynes, Schumpeter	Marx	*Zur Methodologie der Sozialwissenschaften* (Schmoller) *Théorie mathématique de la richesse sociale* (Walras)
1885			*Das Kapital*, book 2 (Marx)
1886			*Théorie de la monnaie* (Walras)
1890			*Principle of Economics* (Marshall)
1894			*Das Kapital*, book 3 (Marx)
1896			*Finanztheoretische Untersuchungen* (Wicksell)
1896/97			*Cours d'économie politique* (Pareto)
1898			*Über einige Grundfragen der Sozialpolitik und Volkswirtschaftslehre* (Schmoller) *Geldzins und Güterpreise* (Wicksell)
1899			*The Theory of the Leisure Class* (Veblen)
1900			*Grundriß der allgemeinen Volkswirtschaftslehre*, Vol. 1 (Schmoller)
1902/3			*Les systèmes socialistes* (Pareto)
1904			*Grundriß der allgemeinen Volkswirtschaftslehre*, Vol. 2 (Schmoller) *The Theory of Business Enterprise* (Veblen) *Objektivität sozialwissenschaftlicher und sozialpolitischer Erkenntnisse* (Weber)

YEAR	BORN	DIED	IMPORTANT WORKS
1906			*Manuale di economia politica* (Pareto)
1908			*Wesen und Hauptinhalt der theoretischen Nationalökonomie* (Schumpeter)
1910		Walras	
1912			*Wealth and Welfare* (Pigou) *Theorie der wirtschaftlichen Entwicklung* (Schumpeter)
1913			Business Cycles (Mitchell) 1913–22: *Vorlesungen über Nationalökonomie* (Wicksell)
1917		Schmoller	
1920		Weber	*The Economics of Welfare* (Pigou)
1922			*Wirtschaft und Gesellschaft, Gesammelte Aufsätze zur Wissenschaftslehre* (Weber)
1923		Pareto	*A Tract on Monetary Reform* (Keynes) *Money, Credit and Commerce* (Marshall) *Absentee Ownership and Business Enterprise in Recent Times* (Veblen)
1924		Marshall	*Gesammelte Aufsätze zur Soziologie und Sozialpolitik* (Weber)
1926		Wicksell	
1928			*A Study in Public Finance* (Pigou)
1929		Veblen	
1930			*A Treatise on Money* (Keynes)
1936			*General Theory* (Keynes)
1937			*Socialism versus Capitalism* (Pigou)
1939			*Business Cycles* (Schumpeter)
1942			*Capitalism, Socialism and Democracy* (Schumpeter)
1946		Keynes	
1950		Schumpeter	
1954			*History of Economic Analysis* (Schumpeter)
1959		Pigou	

SELECTED LITERATURE

Economics: Introductory and General Textbooks

K. E. Boulding, *Economics as a Science* (New York, 1970.)

P. A. Samuelson, *Economics. An Introductory Analysis* (New York and Tokyo, 1970).

R. G. Lipsey and P. O. Steiner, *Economics* (New York, 1969).

K. E. Boulding, *Economic Analysis*, Vol. 2 (New York, 1966).

Economic Policy

W. W. Heller, *New Dimensions of Political Economy* (Cambridge, Mass., 1966).

J. Tinbergen, *Economic Policy: Principles and Design* (Amsterdam, 1967).

Lord Robbins, *Politics and Economics. Papers in Political Economy* (London and New York, 1963).

Public Economics (Public Finance)

R. A. Musgrave, *The Theory of Public Finance* (New York, Toronto and London, 1959).

C. S. Shoup, *Public Finance* (Chicago, 1969).

A. R. Prest, *Public Finance in Theory and Practice* (London, 1967).

L. Johansen, *Public Economics* (Amsterdam, 1965).

J. M. Buchanan, *The Public Finances* (Homewood, Ill., 1970).

H. C. Recktenwald, *Tax Incidence and Income Redistribution* (Detroit, 1971).

History of Political Economy

J. A. Schumpeter, *History of Economic Analysis* (New York, 1955).

J. R. Hicks, *A Theory of Economic History* (Oxford, 1969).

R. L. Heilbroner, *The Great Economists. Their Lives and their Conceptions of the World* (London, 1955).

J. J. Spengler and W. R. Allen, *Essays in Economic Thought: Aristotle to Marshall* (Chicago, 1962).

B. B. Seligman, *Main Currents in Modern Economics. Economic Thought Since 1870* (New York, 1963).

National Economies: Systematic Introduction

K. W. Roskamp, *Die amerikanische Wirtschaft* (Stuttgart, 1973). (English edition, 1974).

H. C. Recktenwald, *Die deutsche Volkswirtschaft* (Stuttgart, 1973). (English edition, 1974).

INDEX OF NAMES